A

LIST

OF ALL THE

OFFICERS

OF THE

ARMY AND ROYAL MARINES

ON

FULL AND HALF-PAY:

WITH AN INDEX

War Office, 13th March, 1815.

The Naval & Military Press Ltd

published in association with

FIREPOWER
The Royal Artillery Museum
Woolwich

Published by
The Naval & Military Press Ltd
Unit 10 Ridgewood Industrial Park,
Uckfield, East Sussex,
TN22 5QE England
Tel: +44 (0) 1825 749494
Fax: +44 (0) 1825 765701
www.naval-military-press.com

in association with

FIREPOWER
The Royal Artillery Museum, Woolwich
www.firepower.org.uk

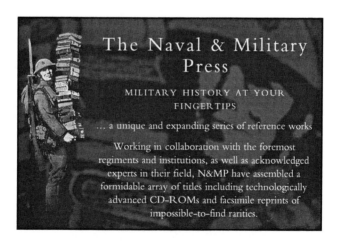

*In reprinting in facsimile from the original, any imperfections are inevitably reproduced
and the quality may fall short of modern type and cartographic standards.*

Printed and bound by Antony Rowe Ltd, Eastbourne

War-Office, 13th *March,* 1815.

A

LIST

OF ALL THE

OFFICERS

OF THE

ARMY AND ROYAL MARINES

ON

FULL AND HALF-PAY:

WITH

AN INDEX.

———————

Officers distinguished by the undermentioned Marks have received
Honorary Crosses, Medals, &c.

Cross.

Crosses with Clasps.

Medal.

Medals with Clasps.

Those having * prefixed to their Names have temporary rank only.

N. B. Commanding Officers of Regiments are requested to point out, from time to time, any Errors or Omissions which may be discovered in the Army List, especially in regard to the Honorary Distinctions granted to particular Corps, or individual Officers.—All communications on the subject to be addressed to the Secretary at War, marking the words *" Army List "* at the corner of the letter.

CONTENTS.

CONTENTS.

COMMANDER IN CHIEF OF ALL HIS MAJESTY'S FORCES,

FIELD-MARSHAL

HIS ROYAL HIGHNESS

FREDERICK, *Duke of* YORK, *K. G. & G. C. B.*

FIELD-MARSHALS.

	General.	Lt. Gen.	M. Gen.	Colonel.
His Royal Highness Fred. *Duke of* York, *K. G. & G. C. B.*	10Feb. 95	12Apr.93	27Oct. 84	20Nov.82	1Nov.80
His Royal Highness Edward, *Duke of* Kent, *K. G. & G. C. B.*	5Sept.05	10May 99	12Jan. 96	2Oct. 93	30May 86
▆▚▆ Arthur, *Duke of* Wellington, *K.G. & G. C. B.*	21June 13	{ in Spain & Portugal, 31July, 1811 }	25Apr. 08	29Apr. 02	3May 96
His Royal Highness Er. *Duke of* Cumberland, *K. G. & G. C. B.*	26Nov.	25Sept.03	18May 98		
His Royal Highness A.F. *Duke of* Cambridge, *K. G. & G. C. B*	do.	do.	24Aug.		

A   GENERALS.

GENERALS.

		Lt. Gen.	M. Gen.	Colonel.
C.Mar.of Drogheda,K.St.P.	12Oct. 93	29Aug. 77	30Aug.70	19Feb. 62
Hon. Alexander Maitland	do.	do.	25May 72	do.
Hon. Henry St. John	26Jan. 97	28Sept. 87	19Feb. 79	11Jan. 76
Sir George Osborn, Bt.	do.	do.	do.	7Aug. 77
Hon. William Gordon	1Jan. 98	12Oct. 93	19Oct. 81	29do.
Robert Prescott	do.	do.	do.	do.
William, Earl Harcourt	do.	do.	20Nov. 82	do.
Henry, E. of Carhampton	do.	do.	do.	do.
Thomas Bland	1Jan.1801	3May 96	do	19Feb. 79
Felix Buckley	do.	do.	do.	do.
10 George Garth	do.	do.	do.	do.
Richard Grenville	do.	do.	do.	do.
John, Earl of Suffolk	29Apr. 02	26Jan. 97	28Sept. 87	17Nov.80
Hon. Chapple Norton	do.	do.	do.	do.
Sir David Dundas, G.C.B.	do.	do.	28Apr. 90	14Feb. 81
Sir R.Abercromby,G.C.B.	do.	do.	do.	15do.
James Coates	do.	do.	do.	16May
Sir Alured Clarke, G.C.B.	do.	do.	do.	do.
Samuel Hulse	25Sept. 03	1Jan. 98	12Oct. 93	20Nov. 82
Albemarle, Earl of Lindsey	do.	do.	do.	do.
20 Sir J. Steuart Denham, Bt.	do.	do.	do.	do.
Thomas Carleton	do.	do.	do.	do.
Cavendish Lister	do.	do.	do.	do.
Charles Leigh	do.	do.	do.	do.
Alex. Earl of Balcarres	do.	do.	do.	do.
Sir Cornelius Cuyler, Bt.	do.	do.	do.	do.
Charles, E. of Harrington	do.	do.	do.	do.
Nisbett Balfour	do.	do.	do.	do.
Edmund Stevens	do.	do.	do.	do.
Fra. Earl of Moira, K.G.	do.	do.	do.	do.
30 Edmund Fanning	25Apr. 08	26June 99	do.	25Dec.
Henry Johnson	do.	do.	20Dec.	28Feb. 83
John Watson Tad. Watson	do.	do.	do.	22Aug.
Lowther, Lord Muncaster	do.	do.	do.	do.
Francis Edward Gwyn	do.	do.	do.	19Oct. 87
Robert Morse	do.	do.	do.	6June 88
Tho. Sloughter Stanwix	do.	do.	do.	9Apr. 89
His Highness Wm. F. D. of Gloucester, K.G.&G.C.B.	do.	13Nov.	26Feb. 95	21Feb. 94
Robert Donkin	25Oct. 09	1Jan. 01	3Oct. 94	18Nov.90
40 James Balfour	do.	do.	do.	do.

Sir

		Lt. Gen.	*M. Gen.*	*Colonel.*
Sir James Duff, *Kt.*	25Oct. 09	1Jan. 01	3Oct. 94	18Nov. 90
Henry, *Earl of* Mulgrave	do.	do.	do.	do.
Grice Blakeney	do.	do.	do.	do.
Sir Paul.Æmil.Irving, *Bt.*	1Jan. 12	do.	do.	do.
George Harris	do.	do.	do.	do.
Richard Vyse	do.	do.	do.	do.
Wm. *Earl* Cathcart, *K.T.*	do.	do.	do.	do.
Banastre Tarleton	do.	do.	do.	do.
Sir Hew Dalrymple, *Bt.*	do.	do.	do.	do.
Gordon Forbes	do.	do.	do.	do.
50 John Floyd	do.	do.	do.	do.
Oliver de Lancey	do.	do.	do.	do.
Anthony Farrington	do.	29Apr. 02	26Feb. 95	16Mar. 91
James Stuart	do.	do.	do.	8Aug. 92
John Whyte	do.	do.	do.	12Oct. 93
Andrew John Drummond	do.	do.	do.	do.
John W.*E. of* Bridgewater	do.	do.	do.	do.
Ellis Walker	do.	do.	do.	do.
William Maxwell	do.	do.	do.	do.
Geo.*E. of* Pembroke,*K.G.*	do.	do.	do.	do.
60 John,*E.of* Chatham, *K.G.*	do.	do.	do.	do.
Alexander Campbell	do.	do.	do.	do.
William Morshead	do.	do.	do.	do.
Francis Dundas	do.	do.	do.	do.
Alexander Ross	do.	do.	do.	do.
Hon. Francis Needham	do.	do.	do.	20Dec.
Henry Pigot	do.	do.	do.	do.
George Bernard	4June 13	25Sept. 03	3May 96	28do.
Sir G.Nugent,*Bt.&G.C.B.*	do.	do.	do.	do.
John Barclay	do.	do.	do.	1Mar. 94
70 William Macarmick	do.	do.	do.	do.
Sir Robert Stuart, *Bt.*	do.	do.	do.	do.
Sir Wm. Keppel, *G.C.B.*	do.	do.	do.	do.
J.*Ld.*Hutchinson, *G.C.B.*	do.	do.	do.	do.
John Hamilton	do.	do.	do.	do.
Alexander L-- Hay	do.	do.	do.	do.
James Stewart	do.	do.	do.	do.
Sir Charles Hastings, *Bt.*	do.	do.	do.	do.
Robert Manners	do.	do.	do.	do.
William Loftus	do.	do.	do.	do.
80 Oliver Nicolls	do.	do.	do.	do.
Alexander Mercer	do.	do.	do.	do.
Sir George Hewett, *Bt.*	do.	do.	do.	do.
Philip Martin	4June 14	1Jan. 05	1Jan. 98	30May
Sir E.Coote,*G.C.B.&K.C.*	do.	do.	do.	24Jan. 95
Ch.*D.of* Richmond, *K.G.*	do.	do.	do.	28do.
John Adolphus Harris	do.	do.	do.	26Feb.
William John Arabin	do.	do.	do.	do.
George Don	do.	do.	do.	do.
90 *Sir* J. F. Cradock, *G.C.B.*	do.	do.	do.	do.

Lord

		Lt. Gen.	*M. Gen.*	*Colonel.*
Lord Charles Fitzroy	4June 14	1Jan. 05	1Jan. 98	26Feb. 95
Napier Christie Burton	do.	do.	do	do.
Richard Rich Wilford	do.	do.	do.	do.
Edward Morrison	do.	do.	do.	do.
Sir Charles Asgill, *Bt.*	do.	do.	do.	do.
Thomas Garth	do	do.	do.	do.
Vaughan Lloyd	do.	do.	do.	6Mar.
James, *Earl of* Rosslyn	do.	do.	do.	20May
Andrew Cowell	do.	30Oct.	18June	21Aug.
100Joseph Dusseaux	do.	do.	do.	do.
Colin Mackenzie	do.	do.	do.	do.
John Dickson	do.	do.	do.	do.
John Money	do.	do.	do.	do.
Thomas Murray	do.	do.	do.	do.
Sir G. Beckwith, *G.C.B.*	do.	do.	do.	do.
Thomas Roberts	do.	do.	do.	do.
G.J.*Earl* Ludlow,*G.C.B.*	do.	do.	do.	do.
Rich.*Earl of* Cavan,*K.C.*	do.	do.	do.	do.
⊚*Sir* D Baird,*Bt.GCB.&KC.*	do.	do.	do.	do.
110*Hon.* Frederick St. John	do.	do.	do.	do.
Lord Cha.Hen.Somerset	do.	do.	do.	do.
John Despard	do.	do.	do.	do.
William Wemyss	do.	do.	do.	do.
⊚*His Royal Highness* WilliamFrederick Henry *the Hereditary Prince of* Orange, *G. C. B.*	25July	8July 14	13Dec. 13	17Oct. 11

LIEU.

LIEUTENANT-GENERALS.

			Major Gen.		Colonel.	
William Souter Johnstone	1Jan.	1801	3Oct.	1794	18Nov.	1790
Charles Tarrant	25Sept.	03	3May	96	1Mar.	94
Henry Read	1Jan.	05	1Jan.	98	26Feb.	95
Archibald Robertson	30Oct.		18June		21Aug.	
Hon. Henry Astley Bennett	do.		do.		do.	
Hon. Robert Taylor	25Apr.	08	1Jan.	1801	3May	96
George Milner	do.		do.		do.	
George, Marquis of Huntly	do.		do.		do.	
Hon. Edward Finch	do.		do.		do.	
10Isaac Gascoyne	do.		29Apr.	02	do.	
Hon. Sir Bry.T.Henniker, Bt.	do.		do.		do.	
David Douglas Wemyss	do.		do.		do.	
Hon. John Leslie	do.		do.		do.	
Henry Wynyard	do.		do.		do.	
William Thornton	do.		do.		do.	
⊚Sir John Stuart, G.C.B.&K.C.						
Count of Maida	do.		do.		do.	
Duncan Campbell	do.		do.		do.	
Thomas Grosvenor	do.		do.		do.	
John Calcraft	do.		do.		do.	
20⊚John, LordNiddery, G.C.B.	do.		do.		do.	
Charles Barton	do.		do.		do.	
James, Lord Forbes	do.		do.		do.	
⊚HenryE. of Uxbridge, G.C.B.	do.		do.		do.	
Sir J.Doyle, Bt.G.C.B.&K.C.	do.		do.		do.	
Sir Robert Brownrigg, G.C.B,	do.		do.		do.	
William Knollis	do.		do.		do.	
Hon. Edmund Phipps	do.		do.		do.	
William Cartwright	do.		do.		15Sept.	
Ferdinand, Baron Hompesch	do.		do.		8Oct.	
*His Serene Highness						
30Wm. D. of Brunswick Oels	1July	09				
George Elliot	25Oct.		25Sept.	03	26Jan.	97
Baldwin Leighton	do.		do.		do.	
John Coffin	do.		do.		do.	
Richard Armstrong	do.		do.		do.	
John Murray	do.		do.		do.	
Sir Charles Green, Bt.	do.		do.		do.	
William St. Leger	do.		do.		do.	
Richard Northey Hopkins	do.		do.		do.	
Thomas Hartcup	do.		do.		do.	
40Patrick Sinclair	25July	10	do.		do.	

George

		Major Gen.		Colonel.	
George Fead	25July 1810	25Sept. 1803		26Jan.	1797
Sir Thomas Blomefield, Bt.	do.	do.		do.	
Gother Mann	do.	do.		do.	
John Pratt	do.	do.		do.	
Forbes Champagné	do.	do.		do.	
Josiah Champagné	do.	do.		do.	
Sir Harry Calvert, G. C. B.	do.	do.		do.	
George Cockburn	do.	do.		do.	
Edward Dunne	do.	do.		do.	
50James Drummond	do.	do.		do.	
William Dowdeswell	do.	do.		do.	
Alexander Mackenzie	do.	do.		do.	
George Moncrieffe	do.	do.		do.	
Thomas Meyrick	do.	do.		do.	
⊠Thomas,Ld.Lynedock,G.C.B	do.	do.		do.	
Charles Craufurd	do.	do.		do.	
George Henry Vansittart	do.	do.		do.	
Hon. Charles Fitzroy	do.	do.		do.	
Francis Hugonin	do.	do.		do.	
60Fred. Baron Drechsel	4June	11	14Aug.	04	
Cha.Baron Linsingen, K.C.B.	do.	18do.			
George Rochfort	do.	1Jan.	05	1Jan.	98
John Spens	do.	do.		do.	
William Scott	do.	do.		do.	
Robert Tipping	do.	do.		do.	
Archibald Campbell	do.	do.		do.	
Alexander Trotter	do.	do.		do.	
Francis Fuller	do.	do.		do.	
Sir James Affleck, Bt.	do.	do.		do.	
70George Vaughan Hart	do.	do.		do.	
John Robinson	do.	do.		do.	
George Warde	do.	do.		do.	
R.Hon.Tho.Maitland, G.C.B.	do.	do.		do.	
Richard Bright	do.	do.		do.	
James Campbell	do.	do.		do.	
Sir Hildebrand Oakes, Bt.	do.	do.		do.	
Sir George Prevost, Bt.	do.	do.		do.	
William Waller	do.	do.		do.	
Mervyn Archdall	do.	do.		do.	
80◉SirJ.C.Sherbrooke, G.C.B.	do.	do.		do.	
Sir Gord.Drummond, K.C.B.	do.	do.		do.	
James Wharton	do.	do.		do.	
◉Sir William Payne, Bt.	do.	do.		do.	
Hon. Edward Bligh	do.	do.		do.	
William, Earl Craven	do.	do.		do.	
◉Lord Wm. Bentinck, G.C.B.	do.	do.		do.	
Edmund, Earl of Cork	do.	do.		do.	
Hon. Henry George Grey	do.	do.		do.	
◉Hon.SirEdwardPaget, G.C.B.	do.	do.		do.	
90◉ Sir Brent Spencer, G.C.B.	do.	do.		do.	

Stapleton,

			Major Gen.		Colonel.
☉S. Ld Combermere, G.C.B.	1Jan.	1812	30Oct.	1805	1Jan. 1800
Samuel Dalrymple	do.		do.		do.
William Johnstone	do.		do.		do.
⊠Rowland, Lord Hill,G.C.B.	do.		do.		do.
Hon. William Stapleton	do.		do.		do.
Denzil Onslow	do.		do.		do.
Sir John Murray, Bt.	do.		do.		do.
William Twiss	do.		do.		do.
Hon. Charles Hope	do.		do.		do.
100Sir George Pigot, Bt.	do.		do.		do.
Frederick Maitland	do.		do.		do.
John Levison Gower	do.		do.		do.
Martin Hunter	do.		do.		do.
Rd. E. of Donoughmore	do.		do.		do.
H.SirJ.Abercromby,K.C.B.	do.		do.		do.
⊠Wm. Carr, LordBeresford, G.C.B.	do.		25Apr.	08	do.
John Evelegh	4June	13	do.		do.
☉-Geo. E.ofDalhousie,G.C.B.	do.		do.		do.
Thomas Baker	do.		do.		do.
110George Porter	do.		do.		do.
Sir James Erskine, Bt.	do.		do.		do.
Henry Williams	do.		do.		do.
Francis, Earl Conyngham	do.		do.		do.
Hon. Sir Alex.Hope, G.C.B.	do.		do.		do.
John Fraser	do.		do.		do.
Peter Heron	do.		do.		do.
Robert Lawson	do.		do.		do.
Thomas Peter	do.		do.		do.
Hon. Montague Mathew	do.		do.		do.
120John Ramsay	do.		do.		do.
Sir John D. Broughton, Bt.	do.		do.		do.
William Dyott	do.		do.		do.
☉Sir R. C. Ferguson, K.C.B.	do.		do.		do.
Andrew Gammell	do.		do.		do.
Robert Macfarlane	do.		do.		do.
☉SirSam. Auchmuty,G.C.B.	do.		do.		do.
John Gustavus Crosbie	do.		do.		do.
Edward Stack	do.		do.		1Jan. 01
Hon. John Brodrick	do.		do.		do.
130☉Sir Henry Warde,K.C.B.	do.		do.		do.
James Durham	do.		do.		do.
Hon. David Leslie	do.		do.		do.
⊠-Sir James Leith, G. C. B.	do.		do.		do.
John Manners Kerr	do.		do.		do.
Thomas Scott	do.		do.		do.
William Robertson	do.		do.		do.
Matthew Baillie	do.		do.		do.
Sir Hilgrove Turner, Kt.	do.		do.		do.
☉Christopher Chowne	do.		do.		do.
140William Simson	do.		do.		do.

Hon.

		Major Gen.	Colonel.
Hon. W. Mord. Maitland	4June 1813	25Apr. 1808	1Jan. 1801
William Munro	do.	do.	do.
James Campbell	do.	do.	do.
☒—Sir Thomas Picton, G. C. B.	do.	do.	do.
John Gordon Cuming	do.	do.	do.
Hon. John Crewe	do.	do.	do.
☒—Hon. Sir G.L. Cole, G. C.B.	do.	do.	do.
Sir Gonville Bromhead, Bt.	do.	do.	do.
Quin John Freeman	do.	do.	do.
150George, Earl of Granard	do.	do.	do.
Stafford Lightburne	do.	do.	do.
John Henry Loft	do.	do.	do.
Francis Moore	do.	do.	do.
Robert, Visc. Lorton	do.	do.	do.
SirW.HenryClinton,G.C.B.	do.	do.	do.
Edward Stephens	do.	do.	2Apr.
☒Hon.SirW.Stewart,G.C.B.	do.	do.	do.
Francis Thomas Hammond	4June 14	25Oct. 09	29Apr. 02
◉—Sir John Hamilton, Bt.	do.	do.	do.
160Robert Dudley Blake	do.	do.	do.
Robert Douglas	do.	do.	do.
Hon. Robert Meade	do.	do.	do.
◉Sir Wm. Houstoun, K.C.B.	do.	do.	do.
John Prince	do.	do.	do.
George Michell	do.	do.	do.
Sir Thomas Hislop, Bt.	do.	do.	do.
John Macleod	do.	do.	do.
Walter Cliffe	do.	do.	do.
William Wynyard	do.	do.	do.
170Alexander Wood	do.	do.	do.
Alexander Dirom	do.	do.	do.
Anthony Lewis Layard	do.	do.	do.
Thomas, Earl of Elgin	do.	do.	do.
David Hunter	do.	do.	do.
John, Earl of Breadalbane	do.	do.	do.
◉—John Slade	do.	do.	do.
William Spencer	do.	do.	do.
Samuel Graham	do.	do.	do.
James Montgomerie	do.	do.	do.
180◉Fred. Augustus Wetherall	do.	do.	do.
William Wright	do.	do.	do.
John Daniel Arabin	do.	do.	do.
William Buchanan	do.	do.	do.
◉William Murray	do.	do.	do.
Hon. Sir W. Lumley,K.C.B.	do.	do.	do.
Robert Brereton	do.	do.	do.
◉J. Timms Hervey Elwes	do.	do.	do.
Moore Disney	do.	do.	do.
John M'Kenzie	do.	do.	do.
190Alexander Graham Stirling	do.	do.	do.

John

		Major Gen.	*Colonel.*
William Thomas	4June 1814	25Oct. 1809	29Apr. 1802
John Michel	do.	do.	do.
Frederick, *Baron* Decken	do.	25July 10	28July 03
John Ramsey	do.	do.	13Sept.
Christopher Darby	do.	do.	25do.
William Wilkinson	do.	do.	do.
Henry Tucker Montresor	do.	do.	do.
Sir Albert Gledstanes, *Kt.*	do.	do.	do.
Charles Stevenson	do.	do.	do.
200John Hodgson	do.	do.	do.
Richard Thomas Nelson	do.	do.	do.
◎*Sir* W. P. Acland, *K. C. B.*	do.	do.	do.
Nicholas Nepean	do.	do.	do.
James Taylor	do.	do.	do.
◎*Sir* Miles Nightingall, *K.C.B*	do.	do.	do.
James Hay	do.	do.	do.
William Cockell	do.	do.	do.
Leonard Shafto Orde	do.	do.	do.
Richard Bingham	do.	do.	do.
210John Lee	do.	do.	do.
◎-*Sir* H. Clinton, *G. C. B.*	do.	do.	do.
John Sontag	do.	do.	do.
James Robertson	do.	do.	do.
E. Wm. Leyb. Popham	do.	do.	do.
James Dunlop	do.	do.	do.
Fitzroy Grafton Maclean	do.	do.	do.
Walter Ker	do.	do.	do.
◎*Sir* Alex. Campbell, *Bart.*	do.	do.	do.
◎-*Sir* H. F. Campbell, *K. C. B.*	do.	do.	do.
220William Burnett	do.	do.	do.
☒-Cha. Wm. *Lord* Stewart, *G. C. B.*	do.	do.	do.

MAJOR-GENERALS.

		Colonel.	
George Morgan	28 Apr. 90	16 May 81	Late of 2 Foot Gds.
James Hugonin	do.	do.	Late of 4 Dragoons
William Fawcett	3 Oct. 94	18 Nov. 90	Governor of Limerick
Wm. Maddox Richardson	3 May 96	1 Mar. 94	Gov. of N. Yarmouth
Jeffery Amherst	1 Jan. 98	26 Jan. 95	Gov. of Upnor Castle
William Gooddy Strutt	18 June	21 Aug.	Governor of Quebec
Stephen Poyntz	1 Jan. 1801	3 May 96	Late of 1 Life Gds.
Hay Ferrier	29 Apr. 02	do.	Lt. G. of Dunbarton
Lawrence Bradshaw	25 July 10	25 Sept. 03	Late of 1 Life Gds.
10 Aug. *Baron* Veltheim	do.	17 Apr. 04	The King's Ger. Leg.
Thomas Trotter	do.	20 July	Royal Artillery
John Smith	do.	do.	do.
William Cuppage	do.	do.	do.
Thomas Seward	do.	do.	do.
Francis Laye	do.	do.	do.
Bayly Willington	do.	do.	do.
Peter Du Plat	do.	18 Sept.	The King's Ger. Leg.
Augustus Hontsedt	do.	15 Dec.	do.
◎-Victor, *Baron* Alten	do.	19 do.	do.
20 ◎-S. *Baron* Low, *K.C.B.*	do.	20 do.	do.
Adolphus, *Baron* Barsse	do.	21 do.	do.
✗C. *Baron* Alten, *K. C. B.*	do.	22 do.	do.
John Croker	do.	1 Jan. 05	
Lewis Bayley Wallis	do.	do.	
◎ John Hope	do.	do.	From 60 F.
George Meyricke	do.	do.	
Sir Mont. Burgoyne, *Bt.*	do.	do.	
◎ *Sir* A. Cameron, *K. C. B.*	do.	do.	79 F.
Andrew, *Lord* Blayney	do.	do.	From 89 F.
30 *Hon.* Stephen Mahon	do.	do.	From 7 Dr. Gds.
John Sullivan Wood	do.	do.	8 Dr.
Daniel O'Meara	do.	do.	
Fran. *Baron* Rottenburg	do.	do.	Roll's Regt.
✗ *Hn. Sir* C. Colville, *K.C.B.*	do.	do.	
Fred. Charles White	do.	do.	From 1 F. G.
Gore Browne	do.	do.	Lt. Gov. of Plymouth
Lewis Lindenthal, *K. C.*	do.	do.	From 97 F.
Roger Coghlan	do.	do.	
✗ *Sir* Henry Fane, *K. C. B.*	do.	do.	4 Dr. Gds.
40 Robert Bolton	do.	do.	13 Dr.

◎ Robert

		Colonel.	
⊚Robert Cheney	25July 10	1Jan.1805	From 1 F. G.
⊚ Sir Geo. Anson, K.C.B.	do.	do.	23 Dr.
⊚SirK.A.Howard, K.C.B.	do.	do.	FromColst.F.G.LGov.
Thomas Nepean	4June 11	1Mar.	R. Eng. [of Portsm.
Thomas R— Charleton	do.	28June	Royal Artillery
Hen. de Hinüber,K.C.B.	do.	9July	The King's Ger. Leg.
Sir Charles Shipley, Kt.	do.	13do.	Royal Engineers
Sir Henry Bell, K. C. B.	do.	15Aug.	Royal Marines
Thomas Strickland	do.	do.	do.
50Hon. Thomas Mahon	do.	30Oct.	9 Dr.
Sir J. Shaw Maxwell, Bt.	do.	do.	
⊚William Thomas Dilkes	do.	do.	From 3 F. G.
Henry Rudyerd	do.	do.	Royal Inval.Engineers
⊚ SirJohnOswald, K.C.B.	do.	do.	1 Greek Lt. Inf. Regt.
James M— Hadden	do.	do.	Royal Artillery
William Doyle	do.	do.	From 62 F.
John Hatton	do.	do.	From 66 F.
Pinson Bonham	do.	do.	From 69 F.
John Burnet	do.	do.	
60✕ SirW.Anson, K.C.B.	do.	do.	From 1 F. G.
John Bouchier	do.	do.	Late R. Irish Artillery
George William Ramsay	do.	do.	60 F.
⊚ Sir E. Howorth, K.C.B.	do.	29Dec.	Royal Artillery
John Dorrien	do.	19Jan. 06	R. Regt. of HorseGds.
Thomas Desbrisay	do.	1June	Royal Artillery
Charles Terrot	do.	do.	do.
William Fyers	do.	1July	Royal Engineers
George Glasgow	do.	24do.	Royal Artillery
Robert Winter	do.	24Sept.	Royal Marines
70William Bentham	do.	13Jan. 07	Royal Artillery
Edward Stehelin	do.	1Feb. 08	do.
John Augustus Schalch	do.	do.	do.
Henry Hutton	do.	do.	do.
Thomas Barrow	do.	25Apr.	From 5 W. In. Regt.
John Simon Farley	do.	do.	From 68 F.
John Wood	do.	do.	
Sir Tho. Saumarez, Kt.	do.	do.	
Horace Churchill	do.	do.	Corps of Art. Drivers
John Jenkinson	do.	do.	
80Theophilus Lewis	do.	do.	Royal Marines
Thomas Dunbar	do.	do.	From 3 West India R.
Francis Delaval	do.	do.	
Richard Williams	do.	do.	Royal Marines
Campbell Callendar	do.	do.	From 88 F.
Lawrence Desborough	do.	do.	Royal Marines
John Mackelcan	do.	do.	Royal Engineers
John Thomas Layard	do.	do.	From 54 F.
John Skinner	do.	do.	From 16 F.
James Meredith	do.	do.	Royal Marines
90Robert Hill Farmar	do.	do.	do.

Watkin

		Colonel.	
Watkin Tench	4 Jun. 1811	25 Apr. 08	Royal Marines
⊚John Strat. Saunders	do.	do.	From 61 F.
Lachlan Maclean	do	do.	Q. M G. West Indies
George Wilson	do.	do.	Royal Invalid Artillery
Samuel Rimmington	do.	do.	do.
David Ballingall	do.	do.	Royal Marines
David Shank	do.	do.	Canadian Fenc. Inf.
Æneas Shaw	do.	do.	
George Dyer	do.	do.	Royal Marines
100 John James Barlow	do.	do.	
Christopher Jeaffreson	do.	do.	
William Minet	do.	do.	From 80 F.
W. Marm. Peacocke	do.	do.	From Coldstream F.G.
Sir W. Cockburn, Bt.	do.	do.	
John Pare	do.	do.	
Waldegr. Pelham Clay	do.	do.	
Sir Charles Wale, K.C.B.	do.	do.	From 66 F.
John Le Couteur	do.	do.	
Trevor Hull	do.	do.	From 62 F.
110 ⊚–James Kemmis	do.	do.	40 F.
⊚–Robert Burne	do.	do.	Fm. 36 F. G. of Carlisle
⊚ Sir J.O. Vandeleur, KCB	do.	do.	19 Dr.
Charles Pye	do.	do.	From 3 Dr.
Sir Wm. Aylett, Kt.	do.	do.	
John Rigby Fletcher	do.	do.	From 6 Dr.
Robert Browne	do.	do.	12 Dr.
Hugh Mackay Gordon	do.	do.	York Chasseurs
Alexander John Goldie	do.	do.	6 D. G.
Robert Ballard Long	do.	do.	15 Dr.
120 ⊚–Sir R.H. Sheaffe, Bt.	do.	do.	From 49 F.
John Hughes	do.	do.	
Alexander Duff	do.	do.	
George Airey	do.	do.	Fm. 8 F. Q.M.G. in Irel.
⊚Rufane Shaw Donkin	do.	do.	Q. M. G. Medit.
⊚–Hon. Edward Stopford	do.	do.	From 3 F. G.
George Cooke	do.	do.	From 1 F. G.
Tho. Joseph Backhouse	do.	do.	From 47 F.
John Wilson	do.	do.	4 Ceylon Regt.
⊚William Eden	do.	do.	84 F.
130 Fra. Gerard, Visc. Lake	do.	do.	60 F.
⊚–Sir G.T. Walker, K.C.B.	do.	do.	Meuron's Regt.
Richard Stovin	do.	do.	17 F.
Kenneth Mackenzie	do.	do.	
Sir Jo. Dalrymple, Bt.	do.	da.	From 3 F. G.
Francis John Wilder	do.	do.	From 35 F.
⊚Hon. George de Grey	do.	do.	1 Dr.
⊚Samuel Hawker	do.	do.	14 Dr.
William Raymond	1 Jan. 12	25 Aug.	13 R. Vet. Batt.
Terence O'Loghlin	do.	1 Sept.	1 Life Gds.
140 Flower M— Sproule	do.	16 Dec.	Royal Artillery

⋈ΞSir

Name		Colonel.	
Sir Geo.Murray,G.C.B.	1Jan.1812	9Mar. 09	60F.Lt.G.ofEdin.Cas.
Sir Ja. Kempt, K.C. B.	do.	do.	60F.Lt.G.FortWilliam
William Borthwick	do.	30Apr.	Royal Artillery
Charles N— Cookson	do.	20June	do.
William Johnston	do.	24do.	Royal Engineers
John Burton	do.	4Sept.	Royal Artillery
*J. H. C. de Bernewitz	do.	24do.	Of late Brunswick Inf.
*W.deDornberg,*K.C.B.*	do.	25do.	Brunswick Cav.
Harry Chester	do.	25Oct.	From Coldstr. F. G.
150 Evan Lloyd	do.	do.	17 Dr.
Matthew Sharpe	do.	do.	
John Lindsey	do.	do.	
D. L. T. Widdrington	do.	do.	
Richard Blunt	do.	do.	From 3 F.
Henry Bayly	do.	do.	From Coldstr. F. G.
Francis Slater Rebow	do.	do.	1 Life Guards
George Stracey Smyth	do.	do.	
William Guard	do.	do.	From 45 F.
Hon. Sir E. M. Pakenham, G. C. B.	do.	do.	6 West India Regt.
160 *Sir* Tho. Rich. Dyer, *Bt.*	do.	do.	From R. YorkRangers
*Sir*R.R.Gillespie,*KC.B.*	do.	do.	25 Dr.
Henry Conran	do.	do.	1 F.
Joseph Baird	do.	do.	83 F.
Sir W.H.Pringle,*K.C.B.*	do.	do.	R. Newfound. Fenc.
James Hare	do.	do.	22 Dr.
Oliver Thomas Jones	do.	do.	From 18 Dr.
Philip K— Skinner	do.	do.	56 F.
William Kersteman	4June 13	28May 10	Roy.InvalidEngineers
Gerrard Gosselin	do.	25July	
170 William Alexander	do.	do.	
*Sir*F. P.Robinson,*K.C.B*	do.	do.	
Charles Campbell	do.	do.	
Arthur Robert Dillon	do.	do.	
Duncan Darroch	do.	do.	From 36 F.
John Grey	do.	do.	
Francis Stewart	do.	do.	From 1 Ceylon Regt.
John Murray	do.	do.	From 96 F.
Arthur Aylmer	do.	do.	
John Mackenzie	do.	do.	
180 *Sir*E.Barnes,*K.C.B.*	do.	do.	From 46 F.
Edmund Reilly Cope	do.	do.	
Phineas Riall	do.	do.	69 F.
William Brooke	do.	do.	From 5 D. G.
*H.Sir*WPonsonby,*KCB*	do.	do.	5 Dr. Gds.
Thomas Molyneux	do.	do.	
Geo. And. Armstrong	do.	do.	
Augustus Fitzgerald	do.	do.	
Benjamin Forbes	do.	do.	From 80 F.
Haviland Smith	do.	do.	From 27 F.
190 William Peachey	do.	do.	

William

		Colonel.	
◎ William Inglis	4Jun.1813	25July 10	From 57 F.
John Vincent	do.	do.	From 49 F.
George Lewis	do.	do.	Royal Invalid Artillery
Robert Lethbridge	do.	do.	
Henry Proctor	do.	do.	41 F. [M. Gen.
John Brown	do.	do.	Roy. StaffCorpsDp.Q.
Joseph Walker	do.	do.	Late Roy. Irish Art.
William Hutchinson	do.	do.	From 48 F.
Daniel Seddon	do.	do.	
200George Robert Ainslie	do.	do.	25 F.
◎ Sir J. Byng, K.C.B.	do.	do.	From 3 F. G.
◎ Sir T. Brisbane, K.C.B.	do.	do.	
Richard O'Donovan	do.	do.	6 Dr.
Charles Neville	do.	do.	Royal Invalid Artillery
◉ Hon. Tho. W. Fermor	do.	do.	From 3 F. G.
John Hall	do.	do.	
Alexander Halkett	do.	do.	From 104 F.
Hugh Swayne	do.	do.	Late Royal Irish Art.
Hon. William Fitzroy	do.	do.	
210Sir William Keir, Kt.	do.	do.	
✕ Sir D. Pack, K.C.B.	do.	do.	From 71 F.
Charles Griffiths	do.	do.	11 F.
◎ SirGran.T.Calcraft, Kt.	do.	do.	3 D. G.
◎ Ld. REHSomerset,KCB	do.	do.	4 Dr.
Hon. Arthur Annesley	do.	do.	
Boyle Travers	do.	do.	From 56 F.
Edward Scott	do.	do.	Late of 96 F.
William M'Caskill	do.	do.	
John Crowgey	do.	do.	From 70 F.
220Frederick Wm. Buller	do.	do.	From Cold. F. G.
✕ Sir T. Bradford, K.C.B.	do.	do.	From 82 F.
John Granby Clay	do.	do.	
William Lockhart	do.	do.	30 F.
Alex. Cosby Jackson	do.	do.	66 F.
Gage John Hall	do.	do.	From 7 W. I. Regt.
Hon. Wm. Blaquiere	do.	do.	
Henry Green Barry	do.	do.	From 15 F.
Thomas Browne	do.	do.	69 F.
◎ Louis de Watteville	do.	do.	Watteville's Regt.
230◎Sir J.Lambert,K.C.B.	do.	do.	From 1 F. G.
Sir J.W.Gordon,K.C.B.	do.	do.	R. Af.CorpsQ.M.Gen.
Michael Head	do.	do.	13 Dr.
◎ Joseph Fuller	do.	do.	From Cold. F. G.
◎ Sir Man.Power, K.C.B.	do.	do.	From 32 F.
Adam Gordon	do.	do.	From 67 F.
Thomas GageMontresor	do.	do.	22 Dr.
Mat.Chit. DarbyGriffith	do.	do.	From 1 F. G.
◎ Ralph Darling	do.	do.	From 51F. D.A. Gen.
George Horsford	do.	do.	From 18 F.
240Randolph Marriott	do.	do.	From 24 F.

Lachlan

		Colonel.	
Lachlan Macquarie	4Jun.1813	25July 10	73 F.
⊚Sir Sam. Gibbs, K.C.B.	do.	do.	From 59 F.
Herbert Taylor	do.	do.	From Coldst. F. Gds.
Sir R. Tho. Wilson, Kt.	do.	do.	From 22 Dr. [in Irel.
⊚M. Ld. Aylmer, K.C.B.	do.	do.	Fm.Cold. F.G. Adj.G.
*Digby Hamilton	12Aug.	5Nov. 03	R.Wagg. Train Wagg.
SirCharlesHolloway,Kt.	4June 14	1May 11	R. Eng. [Mas.Gen.
John Humfrey	do.	do.	do.
Sir Charles Imhoff, Kt.	do.	4June	
250Gabriel Gordon	do.	do.	
Archibald Steuart	do.	do.	From 1 F.
⊚Alexander Adams	do.	do.	78 F.
Hon. Godf. Bosville	do.	do.	From 1 F. G.
Thomas Norton Powlett	do.	do.	
SirEdw.Ger. Butler, Kt.	do.	do.	87 F.
Samuel Need	do.	do.	24 Dr.
Edward Webber	do.	do.	
Michael Edward Jacob	do.	do.	
Thomas L'Estrange	do.	do.	
260SirT.BrookePechell, Bt.	do.	do.	
William Latham	do.	do.	From 7 D. G.
David Dewar	do.	do.	
Charles Craven	do.	do.	
Joseph Foveaux	do.	do.	
George Kinnaird Dana	do.	do.	
James Moore	do.	do.	40 F. [in N. Am.
Edward Baynes	do.	do.	Gleng.L.I.Fen.Adj.G.
⊚James Stirling	do.	do.	From 42 F.
Robert Young	do.	do.	From 8 F.
270SirH.M.M.Vavasour,Bt	do.	do.	
Edward Vicars	do.	do.	From 21 Dr.
James Miller	do.	do.	Royal Inv. Art.
William Dacres	do.	do.	
Henry Raleigh Knight	do.	do.	
Robert Douglass	do.	do.	Fm. 55F. Adj.G.W. I.
✕Sam. Venables Hinde	do.	do.	From 32 F.
Tho. Norton Wyndham	do.	do.	From 1 Dr.
Berkenhead Glegg	do.	do.	
Hon. James Ramsay	do.	do.	
280Lewis Mosheim	do.	do.	For. Depotat Lymingt.
Francis Streicher	do.	do.	York Light Inf. Vol.
Charles Auriol	do.	do.	
⊚-Sir Colq. Grant, K.C.B.	do.	do.	15 Dr.
⊚-James Lyon	do.	do.	97 F.
William Gifford	do.	do.	From 43 F.
James Orde	do.	do.	From 99 F.
• J. Baron de Sonnenberg	do.	do.	Roll's Regiment
CharlesBulkeleyEgerton	do.	do.	
⊚SirT.S.Beckwith,K.CB.	do.	do.	95F. Q.Mas.G.in Can.
290⊚HenryJohnCumming	do.	1Jan.1812	11 Dr.

Charles

		Colonel.	
Charles Irvine	4Jun.1814	1Jan.1812	
Charles Phillips	do.	do.	44 F.
Henry Bruce	do.	do.	31 F.
Tho. Birch Reynardson	do.	do.	
John, *Lord* Proby	do.	do.	From 1 F. G.
Sir Wm. Nicholson,*Bt.*	do.	do.	From 72 F.
Peregrine Maitland	do.	do.	From 1 F. G.
Hon. Edward Capel	do.	do.	do.
Sir Wm. Sheridan, *Bt.*	do.	do.	From Coldstr. F. G.
300Thomas Carey	do.	do.	From 3 F. G.
Godfrey Basil Mundy	do.	do.	From 2 F.
◎-William Grant	do.	do.	From 82 F.
George Johnstone	do.	do.	From 93 F.
W. T. *Visc.* Molesworth	do.	do.	1 Ceylon Regiment
✕*Hon. Sir* R. W. O'Callaghan, *K. C. B.*	do.	do.	From 39 F.
◎*Sir* J. Keane, *K. C. B.*	do.	do.	From 60 F.
Wm. Henry Beckwith	do.	do.	
Lord George Beresford	do.	do.	From 2 D. G.
Robert Campbell	do.	do.	
310Robert Balfour	do.	do.	From 2 Dr.
Dugald Campbell	do.	do.	From 3 W. I. Regt.
Robert Alex. Dalzell	do.	do.	From 60 F.
James Cuming	do.	do.	47 F.
Rich. Aug. Seymour	do.	do.	
Henry Eustace	do.	do.	Late Eng. in Ireland
◎-*Sir* C. Halkett, *K. C. B.*	do.	do.	The Kg's Ger. Legion
◎*Sir*H.E.Bunbury, *K.C.B.*	do.	do.	FromR.Newf.Fen.Inf.
Sir Hudson Lowe, *Kt.*	do.	do.	R. Corsican Rangers
Frederick Adam	do.	20Feb.	From 21 F.
320◎*Sir*RHVivian,*K.C.B.*	do.	do.	From 7 Dr.
◎*Sir* H. Torrens, *K.C.B.*	do.	do.	From 8 F. G.
Benjamin Bloomfield	do.	do.	Royal Artillery
George Cookson	do.	17Mar.	do.

COLONELS.

COLONELS.

His Royal Highness *The Prince Regent, K. G.*	19Nov.	1782	10 Dr.
John Yorke	12Mar.	83	Deputy Lieut. of the Tower
John Drouly	18Nov.	90	Captain of Cowes Castle
Thomas Nesbitt	1Mar.	94	Half-pay Unattached Officers
A. *Count* Walsh de Serrant	1Oct.		Late Irish Brigade
Hon. Henry Dillon	do.		do.
Count Daniel O'Connel	do.		do.
Richard Brooke	21Aug.	95	Late of 3 Dr. Gds.
Alexander Mair	do.		6R.V.Bn.Dep.Gov.of Ft.Geo.
10Cha. *Visc.* Walsh de Serrant	3Mar.	96	Late Irish Brigade
John Elford	26Jan.	97	Lieut. Gov. of St. John's
Charles Handfield	do.		C. Gen. of Stores, &c. in Irel.
David Cunynghame	do.		Half-pay 82 F.
Jos. Fred. Walsh Desbarres	1Jan.	98	Late of 60 F.
Edward Madden	do.		—— 15 F.
John Carnegie	do.		—— 11 Dr.
William Stewart	1Jan.	1800	—— 89 F.
Hon. John Vaughan	do.		Half-pay Loyal Sheffield Regt.
John Thomas Maddison	do.		—— Royal Kelso Regt.
20Barth. *Count* O'Mahony	1Jan.	01	Late of Irish Brigade
John Taubman	do.		Half-pay 110 F.
Edward Dillon	do.		Of late Dillon's Regt.
Thomas Brownrigg	29Apr.	02	Late of 3 F.
Charles M'Murdo	do.		—— 31 F.
Henry Mord. Clavering	do.		Half-pay 98 F.
William Dickson	25Sept.	03	Lieut. Gov. of Cork
John Fletcher	21Dec.		Half-pay Royal Marines
Henry Anderson	do.		Late of Royal Marines
Sir John Burke, Bt.	22May	04	98 F.
30John O'Toole	1Jan.	05	Half-pay late Irish Brigade
Robert Uniacke	do.		—— 104 F.
William Charles Madan	do.		—— Indep. Comp.
James Phillips Lloyd	do.		Late of 10 F.
Sir Fred.John Falkiner,Bt.	28Feb.		100 F.
Henry Aug. Visc. Dillon	20Aug.	06	101 F.
John Magrath	25Apr.	08	Half-pay Unattached Officers
Wm. Tooke Harwood	do.		—— 19 Dr.
Francis William Grant	25Oct.	09	—— 2 Argyll. Fenc. Inf.
William Say	25July	10	—— 99 F.
40Robert Campbell	do.		—— Pr. of Wales's Fenc.

C

Hugh

Hugh Baillie	25July	1810	Half-pay Surry Rangers
James Butler	do.		Lieut. Gov. R. Mil. Col.
Hon. William John Gore	do.		Half-pay 9 F.
Hamps. Prevost Thomas	do.		—— Roy. Waggon Train
John R— Broadhead	do.		—— 121 F.
Charles Browne	4June	11	—— 96 F.
John Dick Burnaby	1Jan.	12	Late of 1 F. G.
Thomas Mellor	do.		Half-pay Cambrian Rangers
Pierre L'Ardy	do.		Late of Meuron's Regt.
50ⓞ *Sir* John Elley, *K.C.B.*	7Mar.	13	R. Regt. Horse Gds.
Lewis Grant	4June		70 F.
Hon. Fulk Grev. Howard	do.		Half-pay 9 Gar. Bn.
Lord Frederick Bentinck	do.		1 F. G.
Isaac Pattison Tinling	do.		1 F. G.
Claus, *Baron* Decken	do.		Foreign Vet. Batt.
William Douglas	do.		98 F.
Arthur Brooke	do.		44 F.
Peter Carey	do.		84 F.
Thomas William Kerr	do.		2 Ceylon Regiment
60Frederick Hardyman	do.		17 F.
Philip Riou	do.		Royal Artillery
John F— S— Smith	do.		do.
William Mudge	do.		do.
Henry Shrapnell	do.		do.
Henry Sheehy Keating	do.		Bourbon Regiment
John M'Nair	do.		90 F.
Lemuel Warren	do.		27 F.
Patrick M'Kenzie	do.		81 F.
William Nedham	do.		1 Garrison Bn.
70ⓞ Alexander Wallace	do.		88 F.
Hastings Fraser	do.		86 F.
ⓞRobert, *Lord* Blantyre	do.		Half-pay late 8 Garr. Bn.
☒James Campbell	do.		94 F.
Sebright Mawby	do.		53 F.
Edward Codd	do.		60 F.
Robert Sewell	do.		89 F.
ⓞCha. Amedee Harcourt	do.		Half-pay 40 F.
George Hill	do.		3 F. Gds.
Samuel Swinton	do.		75 F. [Wight
80John M— Mainwaring	do.		Half pay 26 F. Com. Isle of
☒Charles Philip Belson	do.		28 F.
ⓞ*Sir*W.Aug.Prevost, *K.C.B.*	do.		67 F.
ⓞ*Hon.* John Meade	do.		Half-pay 45 F.
George Pownell Adams	do.		25 Dr.
William Rodewald	do.		Late of the King's Ger. Leg.
Edward Drummond	do.		—— 86 F.
*Sir*J.PringleDalrymple, *Bt.*	do.		Of late R. Regt. of Malta
ⓞ William Kelly	do.		24 F.
John Macleod	do.		78 F.
90George Crump	do.		Half-pay Ogle's late Levy
			Henry

Henry Elliot	4June 1813	96 F.
Robert Kelso	do.	22 F.
Overington Blunden	do.	12 Dr.
John Nugent Smyth	do.	55 F.
John Lamont	do.	Half-pay 92 F.
William Fuller	do.	1 D. G.
William Armstrong	do.	Half-pay late 2 Garr. Bn.
✕⊏*Sir* W.H.deLancey,*K.C.B*	do.	Dy.Qua. Mast.Gen.N.Britain
✕⊏*Sir* Benj.D'Urban, *K.C.B.*	do.	2 West India Regt.
100John Locke	do.	84 F.
✕F.*B.*deArentssehildt,*KCB*	do.	The King's German Legion
⊙Christ. *Baron* Ompteda	do.	do.
George Wulff	do.	Royal Artillery
⊙John Taylor	do.	88 F.
Robert D'Arcy	do.	Royal Engineers
George Bridges	do.	do.
Samuel T— Dickens	do.	do.
George William Dixon	do.	Royal Artillery
Wiltshire Wilson	do.	do.
110Thomas Reynell	do.	71 F.
✕-*Sir* G.Rid.Bingham,*K.C.B*	do.	53 F.
Thomas Bligh St. George	do.	Insp. F. Off. of Mil. in Canada
John Murray	do.	do.
✕⊏*Hon.Sir*C.J.Greville *KCB*	do.	38 F.
Loftus William Otway	do.	Half-pay 26 F.
William Nicolay	do.	Royal Staff Corps
Edward Kerrison	do.	7 Dr.
Alex. Mark K. Hamilton	do.	5 West India Regiment
⊙Hamlet Wade	do.	95 F.
120Julius Stirke	do.	12 F.
Lionel Smith	do.	65 F.
Sir George Leith, *Bt.*	do.	Half-pay 42 F.
Robert Barton	do.	60 F.
Thomas Austen	do.	do.
William Paterson	do.	21 F.
Richard Hamilton	do.	Royal Artillery
Charles du Plat	do.	The King's German Legion
⊙George Allen Madden	do.	Late of 12 Dr.
⊙John Guise	do.	3 F. G.
130John Miller	do.	Royal Marines
Charles William Doyle	do.	87 F.
⊙James Bathurst	do.	Half-pay Argyllshire Fen.
Paul Anderson	do.	60 F. Dep. Adj. Gen. in Malta
⊙Hugh Henry Mitchell	do.	51 F.
John Dalrymple	do.	22 F.
Brooke Young	do.	Royal Artillery,
✕-*Sir*H.Framingham,*K.C.B*	do.	do. [H.R.H.thePr.Reg.
Lord James Murray	do.	H.-p.lateManxFen.Aidede C.
✕⊏*Sir*And.F.Barnard,*K.C.B.*	do.	95 F. Aide de C. H.R.H. Pr.R.
140Alleyne Hampden Pye	4June 14	Hp.10W.I.R.D.Q.M.G.Jam.

John

John Graham	4June 1814	Cape Regiment
John Shaw -	do.	Half-pay 15 Gar. Bn.
Richard Pigot	do.	21 Dr.
Sir John Wardlaw, Bt.	do.	64 F.
ⓞJames Watson	do.	14 F.
John Sheldrake	do.	Royal Artillery
George Ramsay	do.	do.
ⓞJohn Lemoine	do.	do.
Spencer C— Parry	do.	do.
150John Rowley	do.	R. Eng.Dep.Insp.G. of Fortif.
Augustus de Butts	do.	Royal Engineers
Martin Campbell Cole	do.	Royal Marines
Robert Evans	do.	Royal Artillery
Christopher Myers	do.	100 F. D. Q. M. G. in Canada
William Pollock	do.	101 F.
Launcelot Holland	do.	Half-pay 134 F.
Richard Bourke	do.	——— Lowenstein's late Levy
Richard Harry Foley	do.	Royal Marines
Hon. Patrick Stewart	do.	19 F.
160Hon. J— T— F— Deane	do.	38 F.
George William Phipps	do.	R. M. Acad. at Woolwich
Hon. Basil Cochrane	do.	36 F.
William Miller	do.	Royal Artillery
ⓞHon. Henry Brand	do.	Coldstream F. Gds.
ⓒ-James Stevenson Barnes	do.	1 F.
James Graves	do.	18 F.
Joseph Gubbins	do.	Insp. F. Off. of Mil. in No. Sc.
William George Harris	do.	73 F.
Sir Howard Douglas, Bt.	do.	H. p. York Rang. R. Mil. Col.
170✕Sir Wm. Robe, K.C.B.	do.	Royal Artillery
George D— Robertson	do.	Sicilian Regt.
ⓞ John Nugent	do.	Half-pay 38 F.
William Chabot	do.	——— 50 F.
William Binks	do.	Royal Marines
Richard Bidlake	do.	Late of Royal Marines
Patrick Ross	do.	Half-pay 8 Gn. Bn.
' Henry Benedict Dolphin	do.	6 West India Regiment
David Walker	do.	58 F.
James Forster	do.	Half-pay Anc. Irish Fen. Inf.
180Theophilus Pritzler	do.	22 Dr.
John Goulston Price Tucker	do.	41 F.
Charles Turner	do.	Royal W. India Rangers
✕–Sir H. Walton Ellis, K.C.B.	do.	23 F.
Montagu Burrows	do.	14 F.
ⓞHon. Arthur Percy Upton	do.	1 F. G. [Hos. to the Forces
*Archibald Christie	do.	Of late 12 R.V.B.Com.Gen. of
✕–Sir John Cameron,K.C.B.	do.	9 F.
· Samuel Huskisson	do.	67 F.
· James Inglis Hamilton	do.	2 Dr.
190George Salmon	do.	Royal Artillery

Henry

Henry Monckton	4 June 1814	72 F.
Charles, *Visc.* Petersham	do.	Half-pay 3 West India Regt.
William Fenwick	do.	Royal Engineers
⊚Francis Hepburn	do.	3 F. G.
John Maister	do.	34 F.
Hon. George Murray	do.	2 Life Guards
Henry Askew	do.	1 F. G.
Henry Darling	do.	Half-pay late 8 Gar. Bn.
William Stewart	do.	8 West India Regt.
200 William Henry Rainsford	do.	19 F.
Hon. William Stuart	do.	1 F. G.
⊚Jasper Nicolls	do.	14 F. Q. M. Gen. in E. Ind.
Charles Morice	do.	69 F. [in Irel.
. Samuel Browne	do.	York Lt. Inf. Vol. D. Q.M.G.
Dennis Herbert	do.	In. F. Off. of Mil. in No. Sco.
Henry C— Darling	do.	Nova Scotia Fencibles
⊚George Cuyler	do.	11 F.
⊚John Ross	do.	66 F. Dy. Adj. Gen. in Irel.
⊚-*Hon.* Henry King	do.	5 F.
210 ⊚ *Hon.* A. Abercromby	do.	Coldstream Foot Guards
William Thornton	do.	85 F.
✖✚ *H.Sir* R. LeP. Trench, *KCB*	do.	74 F.
Robert Wright	do.	Royal Artillery
Joseph Maclean	do.	do.
John Harris	do.	do. [H. the P. R.
Sir Geo. Adam Wood, *Kt.*	do.	R. Art. Aide de Camp to H. R.
. Richard Dickinson	do.	Royal Artillery
⊚Wm. Edgell Wyatt	do.	Late of 23 F.
Henry Tolley	do.	16 F.
220 ⊚John M'Donald	do.	Half-pay 1 Gar. Bn.
⊚ *Sir* Charles Pratt, *K.C.B.*	do.	5 F.
Nathaniel Blackwell	do.	62 F.
David Stewart	do.	Half-pay 96 F.
Hon. John B— O'Neill	do.	19 Dr.
Alex. M'Gregor Murray	do.	4 Ceylon Regiment
Hon. G. A. C. Stapylton	do.	Half-pay 45 F.
Anthony Salvin	do.	Insp. Field Offi. Rec. District
Anthony Walsh	do.	do.
Le *Chev.* de Nacquard	do.	Royal Foreign Artillery
230 John Robertson	do.	Insp. Field Offi. Rec. District
Jonas Fitzherbert	do.	99 F.
⊚-William Johnston	do.	68 F.
Francis Newberry	do.	24 Dr.
⊚Patrick Doherty	do.	13 Dr.
Richard Buckby	do.	58 F.
Robert Stewart	do.	Late Royal Irish Artillery
⊚Lewis Davies	do.	Half-pay 36 F.
Alexander Armstrong	do.	Late Royal Irish Artillery
Sampson Freeth	do.	Half-pay 15 F.
240 John Buckland	do.	53 F.

Thomas

Thomas Mac Mahon	4June 1814	53 F.
Joseph Lambrecht	do.	Royal Marines
ⓢJohn Cameron	do.	92 F.
Victor Fischer	do.	De Watteville's Regiment
Francis Sherlock	do.	4 D. G.
Daniel Francis Blommart	do.	62 F.
Benjamin Wynne Ottley	do.	91 F.
Joseph Muter	do.	6 Dr.
ⓢEdward Copson	do.	5 F.
250✘Sir E. Blakeney, K.C.B.	do.	7 F.
James Charles Dalbiac	do.	4 Dr.
Alexander Bryce	do.	Royal Engineers
Francis Burke	do.	H. p. late Lowenstein's Levy
John Pine Coffin	do.	Dep.Qua. Mast.Gen.Mediter.
✘Sir John Maclean, K.C.B.	do.	27 F.
George B— Fisher	do.	Royal Artillery
James Home	do.	Late of Royal Marines
✘Sir R. D. Jackson, K.C.B.	do.	Coldstream F. Guards
ⓢ-Sir Neil Campbell, Kt.	do.	54 F.
260John, Earl of Portarlington	do.	23 Dr.
George Molle	do.	46 F.
Thomas Hawker	do.	20 Dr. [the Pr. Regent
George Quentin	do.	10Dr.Aide deCamp to H.R.H.
James Campbell	do.	Royal Marines
ⓢ Sir Wm. Douglas, K.C.B.	do.	91 F.
Augustus Röttiger	do.	The King's German Legion
✘=Sir ColinCampbell, K.C.B.	do.	Colds.F. Gds.As.Qua.M.Gen.
Paulette W— Colebrooke	do.	Royal Artillery
George Mackie	do.	60 F.
270ⓢSir John Wilson, Kt.	do.	Royal York Rangers
ⓢRobert Travers	do.	10 F.
S. Ford Whittingham	do.	Portuguese service—Aide de Camp to H.R.H. the Pr. Regt.
✘Sir John Colborne, K.C.B.	do.	52 F. do.
✘Sir Arch.Campbell,K.C.B.	do.	Portuguese service do.
Thomas M'Mahon	do.	17 F. do.
ⓢ-Alex. George Woodford	do.	Coldstream Ft. Gds. do.
ⓢ Hon. F— C— Ponsonby	do.	12 Dr. do.
Charles Palmer	do.	Half-pay 23 Dr. do.
✘Sir T. Arbuthnot, K.C.B.	do.	57 F. do.
280 ⓢ Sir HFBouverie, KCB.	do.	Coldstream F. G. extra do.
ⓢ F— B— Hervey	do.	14 Dr. do. .do.
Hon. A— B— Craven	do.	H. p. Independ. do. .do.
Frederick, Baron Eben	do.	Roll's Regt. do. do.
John, Lord Burghersh	do.	Half-pay 63 F. do. do.

[1815]

LIEUTENANT-COLONELS.

Sir Andrew Cathcart, Bt.	15 Aug.	1781	Half-pay 73 F.
Richard Temple	19 Feb.	83	——— 87 F.
Thomas Wollocombe	do.		——— Unattached Officers
Hon. S. Digby Strangways	22 Aug.		——— 76 F.
Joseph Buckeridge	19 Dec.	86	Late Indep. Comp.
Arthur Browne	12 Oct.	93	Lieut. Gov. of Kinsale
George Vaughan	1 Mar.	94	Late R. Inv. Gov. of Fishguard
Francis Downman	do.		Royal Invalid Artillery
Evelyn Anderson	do.		Half pay 85 F.
10 Francis, Earl of Guildford	do.		Captain of Deal Castle
Charles Martin	do.		Late Roy. Invalids [of Galway
Peter Daly	do.		Of late 4 Royal Vet. Bn. Gov.
Harry Ditmas	do.		Late Royal Invalids
Wentworth Serle	19 May		Half-pay 106 F.
Henry Haldane	13 Apr.	95	Royal Invalid Engineers
Mungo Paumier	1 Sept.		Half-pay 108 F.
John Drinkwater	do.		Late Commissary of Accompts
Edward Hill	16 do.		Late of Royal Marines
George Duke	30 Dec.		Half-pay 65 F.
20 Francis Erskine	2 Jan.	96	——— 99 F.
Redmond Browne	3 May		——— 5 Dr.
James O'Hara	do.		Clanalpine Fen. Inf.
Francis Cunynghame	23 Nov.		Lieut. Gov. of Hull
Ninian Imrie	1 Jan.	98	Half-pay 122 F.
Francis O'Dogherty	do.		——— Royal Marines
Robert Anderson	do.		Late of Royal Marines
James Wemyss	do.		Half-pay Unattached Officers
Malcolm M'Neil	do.		Retired Invalids
William Morris	do.		do.
30 Hugh Dawes	do.		Late of Royal Marines
Molesworth Phillips	do.		Half-pay Royal Marines
Francis Seymour	do.		——— 87 F.
Thomas Frederick	do.		——— 84 F.
James Nicholson	do.		——— Royal Marines
Daniel Paterson	do.		Ret. Inval. Lt. Gov. Quebec
Frederick Hill Flight	do.		Half-pay Royal Marines
Sir James Bontein, Kt.	1 Jan.	1800	——— Royal Kelso Regt.
Robert Sachev. Newton	do.		——— Macdonald's Rec. Cor.
Wm. Cha. Visc. Clermont	do.		——— Unattached Officers
40 Wm. E. of Lonsdale, K.G.	do.		——— 84 F.

Hon.

Hon. George Carnegie	1Jan.	1800	Half-pay 110 F.
Tho. Partridge Tharpe	do.		—— 134 F.
Hon. Robert Clive	do.		—— 110 F.
Philip Walsh	do.		—— Irish Brigade
David Barry	do.		—— do.
Henry Zouch	do.		Retired Invalids
James Francis Bland	do.		Half-pay 107 F.
John Charles Tuffnell	do.		—— Unattached Officers
George Vigoureux	do.		Of late 2 R. V. Bn. Lt. Gov.
50Charles Newton	do.		Half-pay 134 F. [Scilly Isl.
William Booth	do.		Royal Invalid Engineers
David Gordon	do.		Late Royal Invalids
Frederick de Chambault	do.		Half-pay 109 F.
John Rutherford	25Dec.		—— Royal Staff Corps
Hon. L. H. Hutchinson	1Jan.	01	—— 112 F.
George Henry Mason	do.		—— 102 F.
Alexander Colston	do.		—— 102 F.
John Grey	do.		—— York Fen. Inf.
Hon. John Creighton	do.		Governor of Hurst Castle
60Tho. Cha. Le Foreister	25Apr.		Late of Chasseurs Britanniques
Alexander Loraine	25June		Dep. Gov. South Sea Castle
William Bray	29Apr.	02	Half-pay 7 West India Regt.
Wm. Osborne Hamilton	do.		8 Royal Veteran Bn.
Gustavus R— Matthews	do.		Half-pay Unattached Officers
John Alex. Castleman	do.		—— 9 F.
John Grant	do.		—— Unattached Officers
Thomas Inglis	do.		—— 126 F.
John West	25Dec.		Of late 3 Royal Veteran Bn.
John Wilbar Cook	do.		Retired Invalids
70*Hon.* William Grey	31Mar.	03	Of late 7 R.V.B.L.G. of Chester
Robert Walker	25Sept.		Ret. Inv. Lt. Gov. of Sheerness
Charles Augustus West	5May	04	Of late 1 R.V.B.L.Gv.Lang.F.
Hon. William Collyear	1Jan.	05	Half-pay 28 Dr.
*Morris Robinson	30May		Ass. Bas.Mas.Gen.at Gibraltar
Henry Powlett	25Nov.	06	11 R.Vet.B.Cap.of Carisb.Cas.
Henry Le Blanc	5Feb.	07	Of late 5 R.V.B.Maj.of Chel.H.
John Farquharson	3Mar.	08	Lt. Gov. of Carlisle
*Peregrine Fra. Thorne	8Apr.		Mil. Aud. Gen. of Acc.Ceylon
◎—William Fenwick	15Dec.		Lt. Gov. of Pendennis Castle
80*Hugh Colvill	12Jan.	09	Hibernian School
Henry Loftus	16do.		Coldstream F. Guards
Robert Moncrieff	15Feb.		Royal Marines
James Cassell	do.		Late of Royal Marines
John Macintosh	do.		Royal Marines
Lewis Charles Meares	do.		do.
William Cox	do.		Serv. with the Portuguese Army
Robert Ellice	16Mar.		6 Dr.
◎Lewis, *Baron* Bussche	29do.		The King's German Legion
◎—John Buchan	30do.		4 West India Regiment
90Edward W— Pritchard	30Apr.		Royal Artillery

Thomas

Thomas Francklin	1 May 1809	Royal Artillery
Norman M'Leod	4do.	1 F.
M — Charles O'Connell	do.	73 F.
John White	12do.	80 F.
James P— Murray	25do.	Half-pay late 5 Garrison Bn.
James Viney	20June	Royal Artillery
Robert Pilkington	24do.	Royal Engineers
Henry Evatt	do.	do.
⊚John Bromhead	26do.	77 F.
100Cosmo Gordon	20July	Half-pay late 16 Garr. Bn.
George Elliot Vinicombe	25do.	Royal Marines
Montagu J— Wynyard	28do.	Half-pay late 2 Garr. Bn.
☒Hugh Gough	29do.	87 F.
Richard W— Unett	4Sept.	Royal Invalid Artillery
James Macdonell	7do.	Coldstream F. Guards
Lorenzo Moore	14do.	35 F.
*Ernst de Schrader	26do.	Brunswick Cavalry
John Potter Hamilton	25Oct.	3 F. Gds.
Bohun Shore	do.	4 Dr.
110Alexander Sharpe	do.	Half-pay late 16 Garr. Batt.
Colin Dundas Graham	do.	L.ScotchB. FortMaj.of Edinb.
Philip Vaumorel	do.	30 F.
Cavendish Sturt	do.	39 F.
Ralph Hamilton	do.	Half-pay Limerick Fenc. In.
Francis Dunne	do.	7 D. G.
Thomas Marlay	do.	Half-pay 1 F. G.
Duncan J— Cameron	do.	Of late 1 Royal Veteran Batt.
Hon. H. G. P.Townshend	26do.	1 F. G.
⊚John Gardiner	29do.	6 F. [in Nova Scotia
120Andrew Pilkington	2Nov.	H.p. 2 CeylonRegt.D.A.Gen.
⊚George Middlemore	do.	—— late 12 Garr. Bn.
⊚John H— Dunkin	15do.	77 F.
☒←Sir Wm.Williams,K.C.B.	do.	13 F.
James Lomax	16do.	60 F.
John M'Combe	do.	Royal Corsican Rangers
Charles Waller	17do.	Royal Artillery
Joseph W— Morrison	30do.	89 F.
James Maitland	do.	32 F.
⊚Charles de Belleville	7Dec.	Foreign Vet. Bn.
130James W— Sleigh	14do.	11 Dr.
Clement Martin Edwards	do.	3 Ceylon Regiment
Alexander Nesbitt	21do.	Dep. Q.M.G. in theMauritius
⊚William Gabriel Davy	28do.	Half-pay late 7 Garr. Bn.
☒Sir H.H.Bradford,K.C.B.	do.	1 F. Gds.
Charles Maxwell	29do.	Royal African Corps
⊚Charles Ashworth	18Jan. 10	Serv.withthePortugueseArmy
Robert Beevor	22do.	Royal Artillery
⊚Archibald Campbell	8Mar.	6 F.
Mark Napier	29do.	90 F.
140Archibald Campbell	do	84 F.

D   Humphrey

Humphrey Bland	3May 1810	47 F.
ⓢCharles de Jonquieres	7do.	The King's German Legion
John Wardlaw	10do.	76 F.
Wm. Augustus Johnson	17do.	Half-pay 3 Ceylon Regt.
Samuel Ferrior	22June	1 Life Guards
Donald M'Bean	1July	89 F.
Jonathan Yates	19do.	49 F.
William Armstrong	25do.	Nova Scotia Fenc. Inf.
James Kearney	do.	2 Dr. G.
150Edward James O'Brien	do.	Half-pay P. C. of Wales's F. I.
John Cooke	do.	———— late 28 Dr.
Thomas Foster	do.	———— York Hussars
Charles de Vogelsang	do.	Roll's Regiment
James Dunsmore	do.	Half-pay 10 Gar. Bn.
John Drigue Morgan	do.	———— 5 F. Insp. Field Off.
Horace St. Paul	do.	———— 5 F.
John Le Mesurier	do.	———— 17 F.
Ralph Gore	do.	———— late York Fuzileers
Alexander Stewart	do.	———— 4 F.
160Hon. D. G. Halyburton	do.	———— Corsican Rangers
Hon. John Ramsay	do.	———— ClanalpineFen.Inf.
Samuel Dales	do.	———— Macdonald'sRec.C.
ⓢJohn Frederick Brown	do.	56 F.
J. Alexander Farquharson	do.	25 F.
George Robertson	do.	Canadian Fenc. Inf.
Robert Owen	do.	H.p.5G.Bn.A.Q.M.G.in Irel.
ⓢCharles Hill	do.	50 F.
ⓢAmos Godsill Norcott	do.	95 F.
George Evans	do.	2 West India Regt.
170ⓢ—Charles Bruce	do.	39 F.
Nutall Green	do.	Half-pay 35 F.
ⓢ—John Foster Fitz Gerald	do.	60 F.
Charles Hicks	do.	24 F.
James Shortall	do.	Late Royal Irish Artillery
Richard Legge	do.	do.
Robert Crawford	do.	73 F.
ⓢAlexander M'Leod	do.	59 F.
ⓢMark Joseph Dufaure	do.	Of late ChasseursBritanniques
David Rattray	do.	63 F.
180William Carden	do.	17 Dr.
Charles Tudor	do.	Half-pay Royal Waggon Train
ⓢJames Erskine	do.	48 F.
ⓢ—Arthur Benjamin Clifton	do.	1 Dr.
William Marlay	do.	3 W. I. Reg. A. Q. M. Gen.
Ernest Missett	do.	Half-pay late 8 Gar. Bn.
Hilaire Urbain de Lafitte	do.	
ⓢ—John, Baron Bulow	1Aug.	The King's German Legion
ⓢWilliam Stewart	16do.	3 F.
ⓢWilliam C— Eustace	23do.	Half-payoflateChass.Britann.
190ⓢ Cha.M.LordGreenock	30do.	Assist. Q. M. General

Frederick

Frederick Griffiths	27Sept. 1810	Royal Artillery
◎ Rudolphus Bodecker	22Oct.	The King's German Legion
William de Ulmenstein	23do.	do.
Neil M'Kellar	6Dec.	1 F.
Alexander Mackenzie	20do.	York Light Inf. Vols.
◎William Gwyn	27do.	Insp. Field Off. Rec. District
Francis William Cashell	3Jan. 11	10 F.
John Castle	10do.	6 West India Regt.
Philip Philpot	24do.	24 Dr.
200Frederick de Schlutter	25do.	Late of the King's Germ. Leg.
David Martin	26do.	do.
◎ Sir Alex. Leith, K.C.B.	7Feb.	31 F.
✕–Francis Brooke	14do.	4 F.
Nathaniel Burslem	1Mar.	14 F.
◎Hon. Edward Acheson	6do.	Coldstream Foot Guards
◎John Ross	do.	95 F.
Peter Renaud	7do.	Of late Dillon's Regt.
Francisco Rivarola	do.	Sicilian Regt.
Sir John Brown, Kt.	14do.	1 Greek Light Inf.
210Benjamin Ansley	28do.	Half-pay Roy. Corsican Rang.
✕–H.SirRL.Dundas, K.C.B.	11Apr.	Royal Staff Corps
William Henry Ford	1May	Royal Engineers
Frederick Wm. Mulcaster	do.	do.
William Gravatt	do.	Royal Invalid Engineers
George Gauntlett	2do.	62 F.
Lord Robert Manners	do.	10 Dr.
◎Hon. Hugh Arbuthnot	9do.	Half-pay 52 F.
✕SirRob.Arbuthnot, K.C.B	22do.	Coldstream Foot Guards
Charles M'Carthy	30do.	Royal African Corps
220◎Guy G. C. L'Estrange	do.	26 F.
◎William Collis Spring	do.	57 F.
◎Thomas Pearson	do.	Insp. F. O. of Mil. in Canada
◎–Robert Nixon	do.	28 F.
◎–Dugald Little Gilmour	do.	95 F.
✕SirCharles Sutton,K.C.B.	do.	Half-pay 23 F.
◎William Woodgate	do.	60 F. [N. Brit.
◎Sir G—H—B—Way, Kt.	do.	Half-pay 22 F. Dep. Adj. Gen.
✕Sir James Douglas, K.C.B.	do.	Serv. with the Portug. Army
◎–John Waters	do.	do.
230◎ William Macbean	do.	do.
William Parker Carrol	do.	do.
✕Sir Hen. Harding, K.C.B.	do.	1 F. Gds.
Philip Keating Roche	do.	Serv. with the Portug. Army
◎ Sir George Elder, Kt.	do.	do.
C— C— Patrickson	do.	43 F.
John Campbell	4June	Half-pay 68 F.
Henry Shadforth	do.	——— Queen's Rangers
◎Alexander Hamilton	do.	30 F.
Michael White Lee	do.	Half-pay 96 F.
240John French	do.	——— 121 F.

Robert

Robert Lucas	4June 1811	Half-pay York Rangers
Arthur Lloyd	do.	98 F.
John M— Hamerton	do.	44 F.
Alexander Chaplin	do.	2 Ceylon Regiment
John Pringle	do.	Half-pay late 31 Dr.
Alexander Light	do.	25 F.
David Campbell	do.	9 F.
George Augustus Tonyn	do.	31 F.
◎-Henry Thornton	do.	40 F.
250 Andrew Davidson	do.	15 F.
◎Thomas Chamberlin	do.	24 F.
◎-John Hicks	do.	32 F.
Frederick Muller	do.	1 F.
Fletcher Barclay	do.	56 F.
Parry Jones Parry	do.	Half-pay late 6 Garr. Bn.
David Ximines	do.	62 F.
William Spearman	do.	2 D. G.
Thomas Weston	do.	Half-pay late 14 Garr. Bn.
Daniel Colquhoun	do.	———— 7 Garr. Bn.
260 Samuel Taylor Popham	do.	24F. Dy.Q.M.Gen. West Ind.
William Brydges Neynoe	do.	27 F.
Thomas Carnie	do.	6 F.
John Ross	do.	28 F.
James Kyrle Money	do.	H. p. Armstrong's Recr.Corps
Peter Thomas Roberton	do.	8 F.
Samuel G— Higgins	do.	3 F. Gds.
Augustus Meade	do.	91 F.
Richard Payne	do.	H.p.Hompesch's M. Riflemen
John Stafford	do.	63 F.
· 270 Colin James Milnes	do.	65 F.
Willoughby Cotton	12do.	3 F. Gds.
Jacob Brunt	13do.	83 F.
St. George French	do.	6 Dr. G.
Charles Nicol	do.	66 F.
William Tuyll	do.	25 Dr.
✖C Sir G.H.F.Berkeley, KCB	do.	35F. Dy. Adj. Gen. in Holland
◎John Mervin Nooth	20do.	7 F.
◎Patrick Lindesay	do.	39 F. [Lew. Islands
Sackville Berkeley	do.	16 F. Dep. Adj. Gen. Wind.&
280 ◎Charles Napier	27do.	Half-pay 50 F.
Luke Allen	11July	8 W. I. Regt.
Clement Wm. Whitby	do.	1 W. I. Regt.
John Lyons Nixon	do.	4 W. I. Regt.
◎ Sir Jer. Dickson, K.C.B.	1Aug.	Ass. Qua. Mast. Gen.
Augustus Warburton	do.	41 F.
◎ Lord Charles S—Manners	do.	3 Dr. [Col. Troops, Ceyl.
Frederick Hankey	15do.	2 Ceylon Reg. D. Ins. Gen. of
◎Walter Symes	27do.	69 F.
Sir J. M. Doyle, K.C.B.	26Sept.	Insp. of Mil. in Guernsey
290 ◎Richard Butler	30do.	89 F. Dy. Adj. Gen. at Java
		Octavius

Octavius Carey	30Sept. 1811	10 F.
✗–*Sir* Tho. Noel Hill, *K.C.B*	3Oct.	1 F. Gds.
John Campbell	do.	Serving with the Portug. Army
◎ Michael M'Creagh	do.	do.
◎ George Holmes	10do.	3 Dr. G.
Nigel Kingscote	17do.	56 F.
Charles Wade Thornton	4Nov.	Late of the Royal Artillery
◎ Richard Harvey Cooke	7do.	1 F. Gds.
Henry Frederick Cooke	do.	12 F.
300 Henry Milling	21do.	81 F.
◎ Henry King	31Dec.	82 F.
Foster Coulson	1Jan.	12 Late Royal Irish Artillery
Peter Kettlewell	do.	do.
Richard Uniacke	do.	do.
Robert Thornhill	do.	Royal Artillery
George Irving	do.	Late Royal Irish Artillery
◎ William Smith	do.	Half-pay 50 F.
Hon. Thomas Mullens	do.	44 F.
H. R. Featherstonhaugh	do.	Half-pay 46 F.
310 John Ashley Sturt	do.	80 F.
John Watling	do.	39 F.
Philip Nicoll	do.	17 F.
Francis Weller	do.	13 F.
Charles Maxwell	do.	67 F.
Henry Cox	do.	69 F.
Molyneux Marston	do.	48 F.
Garret Fitzsimmons	do.	17 F.
J— Henry Fitz Simon	do.	65 F.
John James	do.	Late of Royal Marines
320 Robert Smyth	do.	18 F. [H.R.H.thePr.Regent
George, *Visc.* Forbes	do.	Meuron's Regt. Aide de C. to
Francis H— Doyle	do.	Half-pay 54 F.
William Belford	do.	——— late 5 Garrison Bn.
Henry Yonge	do.	53 F.
William Gray	do.	1 F.
Henry Bird	do.	5 F.
Henry Westenra	do.	8 Dr.
Thomas Williamson	do.	Half-pay 85 F.
E. Cornwallis Moncrieffe	do.	Of late 4 R. Vet. Bn.
330 Harris W— Hailes	do.	Canadian Fen. Inf.
John Boland	do.	Half-pay 36 F.
Edward Darley	do.	62 F.
Ralph James	do.	Half-pay 5 Dr.
David Leckey	do.	45 F.
Phelep, *Baron* de Capol	do.	Roll's Regiment
Anthony Mohr	do.	do.
Henry Nixon	do.	44 F.
William Haly	do.	Nova Scotia Fen. Inf.
◎ John R— Ward	do.	Half-pay 36 F.
340 Henry Williams	do.	——— late 2 Garrison Bn.

Francis

Francis Plunkett	1Jan. 1812	3 F.
Charles Best	do.	The King's German Legion
V— W— Hompesch	do.	25 F.
⊚John Mansel	do.	53 F.
Christopher Hamilton	do.	Insp.Fld.Off.of Mil. in Canada
John Daniel	do.	99 F.
Hugh Henry	do.	5 West India Regiment
⊚Wm. Williams Blake	do.	20 Dr.
⊚–Edward Miles	do.	38 F.
350Hercules Renny	do.	Insp.F.O.of Mil.in NovaScotia
George Teesdale	do.	1 Dr. G.
George Macgregor	do.	59 F.
John Otto Beyer	do.	10 F.
Francis M— Miller	do.	87 F.
Robert Henry	do.	21 F.
John Shedden	do.	Half-pay 114 F.
⊚–Hugh Halkett	do.	The King's German Legion
⊚Adolphus, *Baron* Beck	do.	do.
William Marlton	do.	60 F.
360Francis Frye Brown	do.	6 West India Regiment
Waldegrave Tane	do.	Late of Royal Marines
John Boscawen Savage	do.	Half-pay Royal Marines
⊚George Harding	do.	44 F.
⊚W. H. Knight Erskine	do.	Half-pay Bradshaw's Levy
Christopher Bird	do.	Half-pay 99 F.
George James Reeves	do.	27 F.
Thomas Timins	do.	Royal Marines
⊚Robert Travers	do.	22 Dr.
Simon Hart	do.	37 F.
370Hugh Holland	do.	Late of Royal Marines
⊚–Sir R. Macara, K.C.B.	do.	42 F.
⊚SirR.ChambreHill, Kt.	do.	Royal Regt. of Horse Guards
Robert Evat Acklom	do.	1 D. G.
Mathew Mahon	do.	Royal York Rangers
Hon. Henry Murray	2do.	18 Dr.
⊚*Hon.* Lincoln Stanhope	do.	17 Dr.
John M— Everard	23do.	34 F.
Henry Austen	25do.	59 F.
Wilbraham Tol. Edwards	do.	Bourbon Regiment
380John Hamilton	30do.	Coldstream F. Guards
Lucius F— Adams	31do.	do.
John Grey	6Feb.	5 F.
⊚Edward Gibbs	do.	52 F.
⊚Russell Manners	do.	74 F.
Francis Battersby	do.	Glengarry Lt. Infantry Fen.
*Hon.Sir*A.Gordon, K.C.B	do.	3 F. Gds.
⊚George Thomas Napier	do.	3 F. Gds.
Reginald James	20do.	37 F.
Henry F— Mellish	do.	Sicilian Regiment
390Delancy Barclay	28do.	1 F. Gds.

Henry

Henry Willoughby Rooke	28 Feb. 1812	3 F. Gds.
Thomas Geils	5 Mar.	do.
George Wyndham	13 do.	20 Dr.
William Dixon	17 do.	Royal Artillery
Raymond Pelly	23 Apr.	16 Dr.
S— R— Chapman	26 do.	Royal Engineers
✕⊏*Sir*Hen. Wm. Carr, *K.C.B.*	27 do.	83 F.
◎ *Sir* Charles Broke, *K.C.B.*	do.	Ass. Quar. Mas. General
◎ John Philip Hunt	do.	Insp. Field Off. of Rec. District
400 John Rudd	do.	77 F.
◎ *Hon.* Her. R. Pakenham	do.	Coldstream Foot Guards
◎ Charles Rowan	do.	52 F.
Mathew Shawe	do.	59 F.
◎ Alexander Cameron	do.	95 F.
✕⊏*Ld*.F.J.H.Somerset,*K.C.B*	do.	1 F. Gds.
✕*Sir* James Wilson, *K.C.B.*	do.	Half-pay 48 F.
◎ Alexander Tulloh	do.	Royal Artillery
◼✕⊏*Sir*Alex.J—Dixon,*KCB*	do.	do.
◎-*Sir* John May, *K. C. B.*	do.	do.
410 Harcourt Holcombe	do.	do.
◎ John F— Burgoyne	do.	Royal Engineers
◎ John T— Jones	do.	do.
Philip Hughes	14 May	do.
Thomas Burke	20 do.	Of late Dillon's Regiment
Rodolphe de May	21 do.	Watteville's Regiment
Alexander Lawrence	28 do.	2 Garrison Battalion
✕*F.A.de Hertsberg,*K.C.B.*	do.	Of late Brunswick Inf.
Edward Stables	4 June	1 F. Gds.
◎ John Bacon Harrison	19 do.	50 F.
420 ◎ Charles Cother	do.	71 F.
Edward Currie	do.	90 F. [Canada
John Harvey	25 do.	103 F. Dep. Adjut. Gen. in
William Carr Royall	23 July	61 F.
William Evans	13 Aug.	41 F. [the East Indies
E. J. M‘Gregor Murray	do.	8 Dr.Dep.Quar.Mas.Gen. in
✕-Julius Hartman, *K.C.B.*	17 do.	The King's German Legion
◎ Frederick Newman	do.	11 F.
◎ David Williamson	do.	4 F.
◎-Thomas Dalmer	do.	23 F.
430 ◎ Gustavus Brown	do.	60 F.
◎-John Piper	do.	4 F.
◎-Colin Campbell	do.	1 F.
◎ Leonard Greenwell	do.	45 F.
◎ *Sir*GeorgeScovell, *K.C.B.*	do.	H.p.late Staff Corps of Cavalry
✕*Sir*WilliamGomm,*K.C.B.*	do.	Coldstream Foot Guards
R.C.St.John, *Lord*Clinton	20 do.	Half-pay late 8 Garr. Bn.
James Dawson West	27 do.	1 F. Gds.
Sir Ulysses Burgh, *K.C.B.*	5 Sept.	do.
Effingham Lindsay	17 do.	22 F. D. Adj. G. Isle of France
440 James Williamson		Royal Military Asylum

✕*Sir*

Name	Date	Regiment
⚔*Sir* Fra.D'Oyly, *K.C.B.*	23Sept. 1812	1 F. Gds.
Charles de Saluberry	24do.	Sup. Corps Volt. in Canada
Edward Walker	1Oct.	Half-pay 18 F.
◉-Robert Henry Dick	8do.	42 F.
John Clitherow	do.	3 F. Gds.
John Johnson	25do.	86 F.Dep. Adj.Gen. East Ind.
Charles Morland	29do.	9 Dr.
Richard Church	19Nov.	*Of late* 2 Greek Lt. Infantry
John, *Earl* Waldegrave	26do.	54 F.
450◉-Neill Douglas	3Dec.	79 F.
James Johnstone Cochrane	10do.	3 F. Gds.
◉Thomas Downman	17do.	Royal Artillery
John Hanbury	20do.	1 F. Gds.
*Sir*Rich.Williams, *K.C.B.*	21Jan. 13	Royal Marines
Leslie Grove Jones	do.	1 F. Gds.
Francis Rey	23do.	Royal Artillery
◉A— W— Young	25do.	3 West India Reg.
Archibald Maclaine	do.	7 West India Reg.
Wm. Gordon M'Gregor	4Feb.	9 F.
460◉James Hay	18do.	16 Dr.
John Austin	25do.	Half-pay
Alexander Maclean	1Apr.	2 West India Reg.
William Wood	8do.	85 F.
Henry Packe	do.	1 F. Gds.
Charles, *Baron* Maydell	26do.	The King's German Legion
William Warre	13May	23Dr.D.Q.M.G.Capeof G.H.
Robert Oswald	18do.	1 Greek Lt. Inf.
Charles Ashe A'Court	19do.	1 GreekLt.Inf.A.G. in Sicily
Charles George D'Aguilar	20do.	1 Greek Lt. Inf.
470Henry D'Oyly	27do.	1 F. Gds.
Charles William Pasley	do.	Royal Engineers
◉G— J— Robarts	2June	Half-pay 9 Dr.
◉-*Hon.* James Stewart	3do.	3 F. Gds.
William Henley Raikes	do.	Coldstream F. Gds.
George Grogan	4do.	Dublin Garrison
Jacob Glyn Cuyler	do.	Cape Regt.
*Sir*JamesMalcolm,*K.C.B.*	do.	Royal Marines
Thomas Athorpe	do.	Royal Regt. Horse Gds.
Walter Nathaniel Leitch	do.	72 F.
480◉Thomas Emes	do.	5 F.
John Napper	do.	83 F.
Frederick de Wissell	do.	3 Line, King's G. Leg.
John Bennet	do.	32 F.
William, *Baron* Linsingen	do.	The King's German Legion
John de Schroeder	do.	do.
George Edward Roby	do.	Royal Marines
John Wardell	do.	66 F.
◉Richard Diggens	do.	11 Dr.
Thomas George Fitzgerald	do.	H.p.l.8G.Bn.A.Q.M.G.inIre.
490George O'Malley	do.	101 F.

Richard

Richard Lee	4June 1813	Royal Marines
Robert Mowbray	do.	Sicilian Regiment
Charles Plenderleath	do.	Half-pay 49 F.
Abraham Schummelketel	do.	Royal Corsican Rangers
Robert Dale	do.	93 F.
Nicholas Ramsay	do.	Half-pay late 5 Garrison Bn.
Peter D'Arcy	do.	——— late 7 Garrison Bn.
Edward Gregory	do.	44 F.
Alexander Milne	do.	Half-pay 15 F.
500⊚John Gillies	do.	40 F.
John Macdonald	do.	64 F.
Henry Lee	do.	Royal Marines
Robert M'Cleverty	do.	do.
Charles Turner	do.	Half-pay 135 F.
Wm. F— W— B— Loftus	do.	——— 38 F.
Francis Skelly Tidy	do.	14 F.
Edward O'Hara	do.	York Light Infantry Vol.
Thomas Bates	do.	21 Dr.
Edward O'Rourke	do.	Royal West India Rangers
510George Burrell	do.	90 F.
James Ogilvie	do.	8 F.
Aug. *Baron* Linsingen	do.	The King's German Legion
Meuron Bayard	do.	Meuron's Regiment
Isaac Blake Clarke	do.	2 Dr.
James Farrer	do.	81 F.
Robert Ross	do.	4 D. G.
James Lewis Higgins	do.	6 D. G.
⊚James F— De Burgh	do.	2 F.
Peter Warren Lambert	do.	9 F.
520Thomas B— Aylmer	do.	do.
Thomas Wright	do.	90 F.
Henry de Lutterman	do.	Late of the King's Germ. Leg.
William Kinloch	do.	67 F.
L— Augustus Northey	do.	Assist. Qua. Mast. Gen.
James M'Dermott	do.	Royal Military College
Henry James Riddell	do.	Ass. Qua. Mast. Gen.
Robert Skeene	do.	Cavalry Depôt at Maidstone
Benjamin K— Lavicourt	do.	Royal West India Rangers
George Taylor	do.	Insp. F. O. of Mil. in Canada
530R— George Elrington	do.	47 F.
Andrew Geils	do.	73 F.
Christopher Maxwell	do.	30 F.
Price Robbins	do.	69 F.
⊚H. C. E. Vernon Graham	do.	Insp. F. O. in Nova Scotia
⊚Serjentson Prescott	do.	5 D. Gds.
John Ready	10do.	Half-pay late 1 Garr. Bn.
Redmond Hervey Morres	do.	9 Dr.
Simon George Newport	do.	do.
*Thomas Armstrong	19do.	Late of Coldstream Foot Gds.
540⊚Charles A— Vigoureux	21do.	30 F.

E

❎Bryan

⊠Bryan O'Toole	21June 1813	Half-pay
⊚Frederick Hartwig	do.	The King's German Legion
⊚–Daniel Dodgin	do.	66 F.
⊚–*Alexis Du Hautoy	do.	Of late Chass. Britanniques.
⊚Sir Jas.Arch.Hope,K.C.B.	do.	3 F. Gds.
⊚ Sir AugustusFraser,K.C.B.	do.	Royal Artillery
⊚–David Roberts	do.	51 F.
⊚–Henry Worsley	do.	34 F.
⊚R— J— Harvey	do.	Serving with the Port. Army
550⊚ Sir HewD.Ross,K.C.B	do.	Royal Artillery
⊠D. St. Leger Hill	do.	Half-pay
⊚Geo. Marq. of Tweeddale	do.	100 F.
⊚ John P— Hawkins	do.	68 F.
⊠Sir E. K. Williams, K.C.B.	do.	Half-pay
Nathaniel Cameron	24do.	79 F.
Henry Sullivan	1July	56 F.
⊚John George Woodford	do.	1 F. Gds.
⊚Howard Elphinstone	21do.	Royal Engineers
Elias Durnford	do.	do.
560George Whitmore	do.	do.
Frederick Thackeray	do.	do.
HenryAndersonMorshead	do.	do.
John F— Birch	do.	do.
John Handfield	do.	do.
Robert M'Douall	29do.	Glengarry Fenc.
Henry John	9Aug.	60 F.
William Augustus Keate	do.	3 F. Gds.
Charles Fox Canning	19do.	do.
Charles Steevens	26do.	20 F.
570Robert H— Burton	do.	13 Royal Veteran Bn.
Henry Gomm	do.	6 F.
⊚Donald M'Neil	do.	91 F.
⊚–William Grove White	do.	48 F.
Francis B— Campbell	do.	58 F.
⊚ Richard Armstrong	do.	Serving with the Port. Army
Andrew Brown	do.	79 F.
Hugh Maurice Scott	do.	6 F.
⊚Robert Waller	do.	Perm. Ass. Qua. Mast.Gen.
⊚ Maxwell Grant	do.	Half-pay 42 F.
580⊠Frederick Stovin	do.	28 F.
⊚Charles Tryon	do.	88 F.
⊚Sir Guy Campbell, Bart.	do.	6 F.
Gustavus Nicholls	1Sept.	Royal Engineers.
John Herries	16do.	102 F.
⊚Richard G— Hare	do.	12 F.
⊚Arnold Gerber	21do.	The King's German Legion
Sir Charles F—Smith, Kt.	do.	Royal Engineers
⊚–J. Humph. Edw. Hill	do.	23 F.
⊚Alexander Thompson	do.	74 F.
590⊚Charles Ellicombe	do.	Royal Engineers

Henry

Henry Goldfinch	21 Sept. 1813	Royal Engineers
◎-James Webber Smith	do.	Royal Artillery
Wm. Keith Elphinstone	30do.	33 F.
John Tucker	do.	29 F.
William Mein	7Oct.	52 F.
Lewis Meyer	10do.	The King's German Legion
James C— Smyth	20do.	Royal Engineers
Thomas Dorville	21do.	1 F. Gds.
John William Mallett	6Nov.	Half-pay 56 F.
600 Andrew Coghlan	11do.	York Chasseurs
Donald Macpherson	18do.	10 Royal Veteran Bn.
◎William Cross	22do.	36 F.
◎Samuel Rice	do.	51 F.
◎ Richard Buckner	do.	Royal Artillery
◎-Wm. Fra. Patr. Napier	do.	43 F.
John Oke	do.	61 F.
◎Martin Lindsay	25do.	78 F.
Archibald Macdonald	do.	1 Garrison Battalion
Fred. William Trench	do.	Half-pay
610 Wm. Chester Master	9Dec.	3 F. Gds.
George Fead	13do.	1 F. Gds.
Nicholas Eustace	16do.	12 F.
Leighton C— Dalrymple	do.	15 Dr.
Charles Gold	17do.	Royal Artillery
Douglas Mercer	20do.	3 F. Gds.
Charles Dashwood	25do.	do.
Charles Thomas	do.	1 F. Gds.
Francis Sutton	do.	Coldstream F. Guards
Francis M— Milman	do.	do.
620 Alexander, *Lord* Saltoun	do.	1 F. Gds.
John Reeve	do.	do.
Thomas Gore	do.	Coldstream F. Guards
Jacob Tonson	26do.	84 F.
Donald M'Neill	do.	Serving with the Port. Army
Wm. Alexander Gordon	do.	50 F.
Stephen Goodman	do.	Half-pay 48 F.
Frederick W— Hoysted	do.	59 F.
Thomas Kenah	27do.	58 F. Dep. Adj. Gen. Sicily
Clement Hill	30do.	Royal Regt. Horse Gds.
630 Alexander M'Donald	2Jan.　14	Royal Artillery
John Haverfield	7do.	Assist. Q. Master General
Henry Daubeny	20do.	84 F.
Henry Wyndham	do.	Coldstream F. Guards
Augustus de Wissell	26do.	1 Hussars K. G. L.
Henry Roberts	27do.	34 F.
✕Joseph Carncross	14Feb.	Royal Artillery
Archibald Campbell	17do.	46 F.
George Macdonnell	24do.	Insp.F.Off.of Mil. in Canada
◎-John Galiffe	3Mar.	60 F.
640 Charles Edward Conyers	do.	82 F.

E 2　　　　　　　　　　　　　　　◎William

Name	Date	Regiment
◎William Cowell	3Mar. 1814	42 F.
James Mitchell	do.	92 F.
◎William Beatty	do.	64 F.
◎Joseph Fred. Desbarres	do.	87 F.
◎–Robert Gardiner	do.	Royal Artillery
William Lewin Herford	do.	Half-pay 23 F.
William Miller	do.	1 F. Gds.
George Ramsden	10do.	do.
Francis Home	15do.	3 F. Gds.
650Samuel Lambert	16do.	1 F. Gds.
George Muttlebury	17do.	69 F.
Alexander Hog	do.	55 F.
Hon. James Stanhope	do.	1 F. Gds.
Rich. Henry Marsac	do.	do.
John Fremantle	21do.	Coldstream F. Guards
John Midgley	7Apr.	H.-p. Y.Fuz.Com.atTilb. Fort
◎William Balfour	12do.	Late of 40 F.
◎–John Dyer	do.	Royal Artillery
◎John William Beatty	do.	7 F.
660Duncan Cameron	do.	79 F.
Lord George Wm.Russell	do.	102 F.
George Aug. Henderson	do.	2 F.
George Jenkinson	do.	Royal Artillery
◎–John Bell	do.	
Samuel Benj. Auchmuty	do.	7 F.
Edward Wynyard	28do.	1 F. Gds.
◎James Fergusson	16May	3 F.
George Landman	do.	Royal Engineers
Henry Roberts	19do.	3 F.
670Colquhoun Grant	do.	11 F.
John Chetham	do.	Half-pay 61 F.
Thomas W— Brotherton	do.	14 Dr.
◎–Thomas Lightfoot	do.	Half-pay 45 F.
Adolph. John Dalrymple	1June	60 F.
James Henry Reynett	do.	52F.Dy.Q.M G.No.of Germ.
Thomas Aird	2do.	Half-pay R. Waggon Train
Thomas Barrow	do.	Coldstream F. Guards
R— *Earl of* Athlone	4do.	Half-pay 95 F.
William Smelt	do.	103 F.
680Charles Newhouse	do.	Royal Invalid Artillery
Charles Thompson	do.	27 F.
Roger Parke	do.	39 F.
William Lambton	do.	33 F.
◎Rob. Barclay Macpherson	do.	88 F.
Thomas Pate Hankin	do.	2 Dr.
J— Maillard Clifton	do.	1 West India Regt.
Charles Holland Hastings	do.	Insp. Field Offi. Rec. District
Thomas Stephen Sorell	do.	Half-pay Bradshaw's 2d Levy
Edmund Coghlan	do.	Insp. Field Offi. Rec. District
690Geo. Hamilton Gordon	do.	71 F.

Sir

Sir Cha. W. Burdett, *Bt.*	4 June 1814	56 F.
Shapland Boyse	do.	13 Dr.
Rowland Heathcote	do.	R. Newfoundland Fenc.
J— Carrington Smith	do.	Half-pay 19 F.
James Spawforth	do.	——— 96 F.
James Grant	do.	60 F.
⊚George Wilkins	do.	95 F.
Richard Thomas Fuller	do.	Half-pay 41 F.
William Henry Boys	do.	Royal Marines
700 Henry Reddish Furzer	do.	Late of Royal Marines
Thomas Davey	do.	Half-pay Royal Marines
Thomas Abernethie	do.	Royal Marines
John Hart	do.	Insp. Field Offi. Rec. District
Thomas Deane	do.	1 F.
Hector Munro	do.	Half-pay late 1 Garrison Bn.
Philip Hay	do.	18 Dr.
John Slessor	do.	35 F.
Hans Allen	do.	Late Royal Irish Artillery
James Irving	do.	do.
710 John Johnston Dunkin	do.	Half-pay 18 F.
John Carr	do.	10 F.
Lewis Prevost	do.	Royal Foreign Artillery
Charles Massey Baker	do.	14 Dr.
Patrick M'Neight	do.	Half-pay 22 F.
Jacob Ormsby	do.	——— 63 F.
John Handasyde	do.	——— Steele's late Rec. Corps
William Geddes	do.	83 F.
William Battely	do.	60 F.
Richard Graham	do.	Late of Royal Marines
720 Francis Lynn	do.	——— do.
James West	do.	Royal Artillery
Robert Frederick	do.	55 F.
Jacob Jordan	do.	60 F.
Randall Gossip	do.	Half-pay 11 Garr. Bn.
Walter Tremenheere	do.	——— Royal Marines
James Wemyss	do.	Late of Royal Marines
Richard Timpson	do.	do.
Richard Armstrong	do.	76 F.
Charles de Menard	do.	Royal Foreign Artillery
730 Harry Percival Lewis	do.	Royal Marines
John Maule	do.	104 F.
Robert Coote	do.	Half-pay 32 F.
David Williams	do.	Depôt Isle of Wight
Adam Ormsby	do.	49 F.
Andrew Creagh	do.	93 F.
Edward Vincent Eyre	do.	Half-pay Unattached Officers
Edward Gillman	do.	81 F.
Francis Heaton Thomas	do.	16 F.
John Clark	do.	Royal Marines
740 Charles Stanser	do.	do.

George

George Dunsmuire	4June 1814	Royal Marines
William Minto	do.	Royal Marine Artillery
John Long	do.	Royal Marines
Henry Aldborough Head	do.	7 D. G.
Thomas Walker	do.	8 West India Regiment
Cæsar Colclough Armett	do.	35 F.
Francis Gomer	do.	Foreign Depôt
Peter Nicolson	do.	27 F.
James Chisholm	do.	Royal African Corps
750 Helier Touzel	do.	Insp. of Militia in Jersey
Swan Hill	do.	1 F.
George Granby Hely	do.	11 F.
Horton Coote Brisco	do.	Bourbon Regt.
*Charles A— Quist	do.	Royal Artillery Drivers
Alexander Fraser	do.	76 F.
Charles Philip de Bosset	do.	Roll's Regiment
John Blaney	do.	Half-pay late R. Regt. of Malta
Henry Brückmann	do.	The King's German Legion
Norris William Bailey	do.	30 F.
760 Geo. Alexander Gordon	do.	73 F.
William M'Carthy	do.	97 F.
Ferd. *Baron* Ompteda	do.	The King's German Legion
Edmund Lascelles	do.	66 F.
Oswald Werge	do.	17 Dr.
Benjamin Preedy	do.	90 F.
John Edwards	do.	80 F.
Francis Eddins	do.	4 West India Regiment
Robert Johns	do.	Half-pay late 1 Garrison Bn.
Fiennes S— Miller	do.	6 Dr.
770 William Shaw	do.	22 F.
Thomas Fraser	do.	1 F.
Alexander Watson	do.	Royal Artillery
Arthur Jones	do.	71 F.
Henry Charles Dickens	do.	34 F.
James Allan	do.	94 F.
Henry King	do.	3 F.
Edward Worsley	do.	Royal Artillery
Nicholas Alexander Mein	do.	43 F.
*Franz de Fragstein	do.	Of late Brunswick Inf.
780 Robert Ellis	do.	25 Dr.
*Wilhelm von Weisin	do.	Brunswick Cav.
*Carl von Tempsky	do.	do.
◎A. C. W. Crookshank	do.	Half-pay 38 F.
Francis P. G. de Preval	do.	Of late Foreign Engineers
John Campbell	do.	——— Royal Irish Artillery
Kane Bunbury	do.	7 D. Gds.
Richard Fitz Gerald	do.	2 Life Guards
John Thomas Prentice	do.	Cape Regiment
Palms Westropp	do.	Royal Marines
790 ——— de Villicy	do.	Royal Foreign Artillery

William

William J— Tucker	4June 1814	Late Royal Irish Artillery
Arthur Wilkinson	do.	13 F.
John Fowell Goodridge	do.	62 F.
Philip Dorville	do.	1 Dr.
Maine S— Walrond	do.	H. p. 60 F. Fort Maj. at Dom.
⊚Henry Pynn	do.	Serving with the Port. Army
⊚Edward Hawkshaw	do.	Half-pay
George Morris	do.	3 F.
Robert B— M'Gregor	do.	88 F.
800James M'Nab	do.	19 F.
Robert Nixon	do.	1 F.
Arthur Johnston	do.	Royal Corsican Rangers
Archibald Money	do.	11 Dr.
*Meyrick Shawe	9do.	Late of 76 F.
P— T— Ryves	16dc.	Assist. Qua. Mast. Gen.
Ch.delaHoussayeBouverie	14July	60 F. [in Holland
Robert Torrens	do.	1 West IndiaReg.D.Q.M.G.
William Henry Milnes	25do.	1 F. Gds.
Daniel M'Kinnon	do.	Coldstream F. Guards
810Henry Edmund Joddrell	do.	1 F. Gds.
Henry Stables	do.	do.
Hon. John Walpole	do.	Coldstream F. Guards
Henry Dawkins	do.	do.
Goodwin Colquitt	do.	1 F. Gds.
Edward Bowater	do.	3 F. Gds.
Charles West	do.	do.
⊚Henry Watson	28do.	Serving with the Port. Army
⊚David Forbes	do.	78 F.
⊚Joseph Wells	4Aug.	43 F.
820John Ewart	15Sept.	York Chasseurs
William Jervoise	22do.	57 F.
George Edward Raitt	25do.	2 F. D. Q. Ma. Gen. at Malta
A— Dodsw. Faunce	29do.	4 F.
⊚Timothy Jones	do.	do.
George Brown	do.	85 F.
Henry Debbeig	do.	44 F.
John A— Johnson	do.	do.
Robert Renny	do.	21 F.
Richard Gubbins	do.	85 F.
830Cornelius Mann	30do.	Royal Engineers
John S— Williamson	13Oct.	Royal Artillery
Thomas Fenn Addison	do.	100 F.
Robert Moodie	27do.	104 F.
Francis Cockburn	do.	New Brunswick Fencibles
William Wauchope	8Dec.	Half-pay 48 F.
John Aitchison	15do.	3 F. Guards [Jamaica
Thomas Steele	29do.	Coldst.F.Gds.Dy.Adj.Gen.in
Thomas Roberts	31do.	Roll's Regt.

MAJORS.

[1815]

40

M A J O R S.

Name	Date		Notes
Hugh Lord	30May	1778	Late Royal Invalids
John Vignoles	17Nov.	80	Half-pay 76 F.
William Chester	do.		—— Ld. Strath. late Corps
William Shairp	12June	82	Late of Royal Marines
Brereton Poynton	do.		Half-pay 22 F.
Francis Lindsay	do.		Late of Royal Marines
Perkins Magra	19Feb.	83	Half-pay 88 F.
Alexander Duffe	19Mar.		—— 99 F.
Robert Hamilton	do.		—— Indep. Comp.
10Patrick Jacob	do.		—— 95 F.
Walter Scott	do.		—— 26 F.
Hon. J— Stuart Wortley	23Apr.		Of late 92 F.
Rob.E.of Buckinghamshire	15Aug.		Late of 18 Dr.
Robert Clayton	27July	85	Half-pay 82 F.
George Duff	30Sept.	89	—— Lucas's Corps
Benjamin Weir	18Nov.	90	Late of Royal Marines
George Lind	5July	93	Half-pay 97 F.
Samuel Biggs	1Mar.	94	Late of Royal Marines
Charles Stewart	do.		—— do.
20William Bowater	do.		Half-pay Royal Marines
James Sholto Douglas	do.		—— 25 F.
William Adlam	do.		—— Royal Marines
William Ramsay	do.		—— do.
Peter Desbrisay	do.		Late of Royal Marines
Charles Berkeley Money	do.		do.
Ashton Shuttleworth	do.		Royal Invalid Artillery
Charles St. Ours	do.		Half-pay 132 F.
Edward Charlton	do.		—— 111 F.
James Murray Grant	do.		—— 3 F. G.
30George Aubrey	do.		—— Unattached Officers
Sam. Beaulieu Johnstone	11Oct.		Late of York Fuzileers
Edward Blewitt	30do.		Half-pay 112 F.
John Wilks	6May	95	Royal Invalid Artillery
Charles Leigh	20do.		Late Royal Invalids
Edward Dawes Payne	1Sept.		Half-pay 29 Dr.
John Grant	9do.		Late Royal Invalids
Henry Vinnell	11Nov.		Provincial Half-pay
William West	3May	96	Late of 9 Royal Veteran Bn.
P— D— Fellowes	26Jan.	97	Of late 3 Royal Veteran Bn.
40William H— Horndon	1Jan.	98	Late of Royal Artillery

John

John Gordon	15 Aug. 1798	Half-pay 8 West India Regt.
James Weir	6 Dec. 99	Late of Royal Marines
Edward Wood	1 Jan. 1800	Royal Invalid Artillery
David Reid Parker	21 do.	Half-pay Nugent's Levy
Thomas Brown	29 Jan. 02	—— 9 F.
George Ball	29 Apr.	Late of Royal Marines
Arthur Ball	do.	do.
David Douglas	do.	Late Scotch Brigade
Alexander Scott	do.	do.
50 John Cameron	do.	do.
James Urquhart	do.	do.
James Douglas	do.	Of late 7 Royal Veteran Bn.
Thomas Huxley	do.	Half-pay 8 West India Regt.
Edward Letherland	do.	—— 22 Dr.
Alexander Taylor	do.	Late Royal Eng. in Irel.
Robert Brown	25 Dec.	Of late 3 Royal Veteran Bn.
Robert M'Crea	do.	—— 5 do.
James Rose	do.	Late Royal Invalids
Henry Bowen	do.	do.
60 Hugh Maxwell	9 July 03	Late of 48 F.
George Stephens	25 Sept.	Late Royal Invalids
Henry King	8 Oct.	Half-pay 128 F.
Tho. Berkeley Campbell	13 May 04	11 Royal Vet. Batt.
Simon Fraser	14 Sept.	Of Late 1 Royal Veteran Bn.
P— Joseph Donzel	23 do.	Late of Meuron's Regt.
Thomas Fortye	24 Oct.	6 Royal Veteran Bn.
Martin E— Alves	8 Dec.	Dep. Gov. of St. Maws
Philip Stewart	1 Jan. 05	Of late 9 Royal Veteran Bn.
William White	do.	—— 2 do.
70 John Clarke	do.	—— 11 do.
E— J— R— Green	4 Mar. 07	10 F.
Alexander Rose	10 Dec.	9 Royal Veteran Bn.
◎ Charles Thalman	18 Jan. 08	Foreign Vet. Bn.
James Erroll Gordon	25 Apr.	Late of Royal Marines
John Williams	do.	Half-pay Royal Marines
Thomas Guilford	do.	Late of Royal Marines
David Wilson	do.	do.
John Lodington	do.	Half-pay Royal Marines
William Collis	do.	Of late 12 Royal Veteran Bn.
80 Peter Grant	23 June	Late of 92 F.
*H— Clermont	15 Sept.	7 West India Regiment
David de Bachellé	17 Aug. 09	Late of the King's Germ. L.
James Jonathan Fraser	4 Jan. 10	Of late 7 R.V.B. T. M. of Gib.
Edward Shearman	11 do.	26 F.
Frederick Jones	15 Feb.	26 F.
Thomas Watkin Forster	22 do.	24 F.
Nathan Wilson	do.	17 Dr.
Robert Shelton	1 Mar.	57 F.
Samuel Hall	8 do.	89 F.
90 John Huskisson	do.	4 Ceylon Regiment

F

Thomas

Thomas Phipps Howard	15Mar. 1810	23 Dr.
Thomas Brereton	do.	Royal West India Rangers
William Henry Wilby	do.	90 F.
Nathaniel Warren	1Apr.	65 F.
A— S— King	3May	99 F.
H— Richardson	17do.	Half-pay 32 F.
Alexander James Ross	31do.	21 F.
Robert Macleroth	28June	63 F.
Paul Hunt	25July	Half-pay Royal Marines
100Henry Evelegh	do.	Royal Artillery
Archibald Maclachlan	do.	69 F.
William Parke	do.	66 F.
Anthony Rumpler	do.	60 F.
Richard S— Brough	do.	Royal Artillery
Charles C— Bingham	do.	do.
Benjamin Dickinson	do.	Royal Marines
George Wolfe	do.	Late of Royal Marines
William Barry	do.	Royal Marines
David Byron Davies	do.	100 F.
110Andrew Bredon	do.	Royal Artillery
Robert William Mills	do.	9 F.
William Markh. Combe	do.	Royal Marines
Stephen George Adye	do.	Royal Artillery
Richard O'Farrell Friend	do.	41 F.
Alexander Clerk	do.	49 F.
John Chapman	2Aug.	3 D. G.
William Cheyne	9do.	47 F.
William Claud. Campbell	16do.	3 F.
Peter Deshon	do.	85 F.
120Hon. Henry Percy	do.	14 Dr.
Edward Nicolls	28do.	Royal Marines
Hugh Hamilton	20Sept.	96 F.
George Soest	do.	The King's German Legion
⊚Charles Aly	9Oct.	do.
John Dunn	25do.	88 F.
Alexander Ligertwood	do.	60F.D.Q.M.Gen. NovaScotia
Frederick Reh	26do.	The King's German Legion
Edward Parkinson	27do.	33 F.
Richard B— Handcock	1Nov.	13 F.
130Frederick Ashworth	22do.	58 F.
John Ross	do.	2 West India Regiment
Miller Clifford	29do.	89 F.
Richard Ashton	3Dec.	Late of 12 F.
James Stewart Lynch	6do.	1 F.
Richard Kelly	do.	4 Ceylon Regiment
G. Ralph Payne Jarvis	20do.	Half-pay 36 F.
Robert Brice Fearon	do.	31 F.
John Romer Meadows	27do.	15 F.
William Ogilvie	do.	4 Dr. G.
140Thomas Reade	3Jan.	11	27 F.

Alexander

Alexander Andrews	17Jan. 1811	60 F.
Richard Covell	24do.	24 Dr.
Henry Odell	do.	25 Dr.
Frederick de Lutterman	25do.	The King's German Legion
ⓢHans, *Baron* Bussche	26do.	do.
Frederick de Robertson	27do.	do.
J— S— Hawkshaw	7Feb.	Half-pay 31 F.
Thomas Trustey Trickey	do.	10 F.
Alex. Wolf M'Donell	7Mar.	25 F.
150Valentine Winter	do.	Watteville's Infantry
Donald Mackay	do.	3 Ceylon Regiment
*——— Combremont	do.	Of late ChasseursBritanniques
Robert Torrens	12Apr.	Royal Marines
William Munro	2May	Late Royal Regt. of Malta
Hon. Frederick Howard	9do.	10 Dr.
ⓢPhilip, *Baron* Gruben	30do.	The King's German Legion
George Krauchenberg	do.	do.
Hon. Henry E— Butler	do.	2 Garrison Bn.
Thomas Hunter Blair	do.	91 F.
160Henry Balneavis	do.	27 F.
Robert Foy	4June	Half-pay Royal Marines
Vincent Edward Eyre	do.	Late Horse Grenadier Gds.
William Richardson	do.	Of late 5 Royal Veteran Bn.
Paul Crebbin	do.	Royal Marines
James Cullen	do.	22 F.
Richard Robarts	do.	62 F.
Frederick Tompkins	do.	58 F.
James Power	do.	Royal Artillery
Hector Hall	do.	22 F.
170Nathaniel Foy	do.	Royal Artillery
Arthur H— Gordon	do.	5 D. Gds.
Hugh Massey	do.	1 F.
Thomas Mitchell	do.	Royal Marines
Francis Williams	do.	do.
Anthony Stransham	do.	do.
Martin Horlock	do.	do.
Sam. Madden Middleton	do.	do.
Michael Arnett	do.	do.
Henry Graham	do.	1 D. Gds.
180William Morrison	do.	Royal Marines
Henry Phillott	do.	Royal Artillery
Peter Fyers	do.	do.
Hon. William Gardner	do.	do.
William Scott	do.	do.
Charles Baynes	do.	do.
ⓢJames Hawker	do.	do.
Frederick Walker	do.	do.
Humphrey Owen	do.	do.
George Desbrisay	do.	do.
190Turtliffe Boger	do.	do.

William

William Fraser	4June 1811	18 F.
James Price -	do.	58 F.
Hugh Mole	do.	75 F.
John Hardy	do.	2 Garrison Battalion
Evan M'Pherson	do.	79 F.
Benjamin W. M'Gibbon	do.	Late of Royal Marines
Albert Steiger	do.	Roll's Infantry
George Mortimer	do.	Royal Marines
John Fraser	do.	36 F.
200Clark Caldwell	do.	8 Royal Veteran Battalion
Alexander Macpherson	do.	Insp. F. O. Rec. District
William Gordon	do.	2 Dr. Gds.
Abraham J— Clason	do.	do.
John Fox	do.	Half-pay 36 F.
Samuel Williams	do.	Royal Marines
William M— Leake	do.	Royal Artillery
Percy Drummond	do.	do.
William Massey	do.	7 West India Regt.
Francis Maule	do.	Half-pay Skerrett's Regt.
210Thomas Ralph Congreve	do.	70 F.
Charles Poitiers	do.	7 West India Regt.
Peter Ryves Hawker	do.	30 F.
Patrick Burke	do.	Half-pay 96 F.
Charles Mackenzie	do.	60 F.
James Allen	do.	Half-pay 23 Dr.
John Massey Stacpoole	do.	45 F.
Thomas Buck	6do.	8 F.
Burgess Camac	11do.	Half-pay Bradshaw's Levy
Richard Trench	13do.	89 F.
220Jeffery Piercy	do.	53 F.
Charles Macalister	do.	35 F.
John Whetham	do.	40 F.
Henry Wm. Davenport	do.	87 F.
Tho. Dundas Campbell	do.	50 F.
Peter Hodge	20do.	29 F.
Thomas Shadforth	do.	57 F.
Thomas Wooldridge	do.	Half-pay 91 F.
ⓞGilbert Cimitiere	do.	48 F.
ⓞGeo. Leigh Goldie	do.	66 F.
230Robert Grant	27do.	56 F.
Gustavus Rochfort	10July	102 F.
Joshua Gledstanes	11do.	3 West India Regt.
Philip le Geyte	do.	Half-pay 63 F.
Mark Butcher	do.	27 F.
Wm. Henry Forssteen	18do.	12 F.
Hugh Stacpoole	do.	45 F.
George O'Halloran	1Aug.	4 F.
Hamilton Archdall	29do.	Half-pay 50 F.
William Thorne	30Sept.	25 Dr.
240William Robison	3Oct.	24 F.

William

William Ingleby	24 Oct. 1811		53 F.
George Tod	31 do.		29 F.
Dawson Kelly	do.		73 F.
Allan Kelly	do.		54 F.
Duncan Macpherson	7 Nov.		78 F.
Peter Waterhouse	21 do.		81 F.
James M'Vean	14 Dec.		78 F.
James Hugonin	19 do.		4 Dr.
Sir John M. Tylden, Kt.	do.		43 F.
250 ⊚ Robert Bull	31 do.		Royal Artillery
John William O'Donoghue	do.		47 F.
Joseph W— Tobin	1 Jan.	12	Royal Artillery
Henry Grove	do.		Half-pay Cape Regt.
Richard Chetham	do.		——— 47 F.
Francis Power	do.		Royal Artillery
Francis Polhill	do.		12 F.
Fletcher Wilkie	do.		38 F.
Thomas Gerrard	do.		23 Dr.
Joseph Twigg	do.		5 West India Regt.
260 Charles Hames	do.		32 F.
Joseph Vallack	do.		Royal Marines
Thomas Younghusband	do.		7 D. G.
Edward Cheney	do.		2 Dr.
Richard Henry Tolson	do.		Half-pay 36 F.
Henry Broome	do.		22 Dr.
William Sandys Elrington	do.		11 F.
John Campbell	do.		46 F.
James Stewart	do.		46 F.
John Buckworth	do.		64 F.
270 William O'Brien	do.		58 F.
Henry Standish	do.		39 F.
Robert Innes Thornton	do.		21 Dr.
Philip Ray	do.		Half-pay 3 F. Gds.
James Fynmore	do.		——— Royal Marines
Alexander Gordon	do.		93 F.
Henry B— B— Adams	do.		96 F.
William Vandeleur	do.		16 F.
Charles Scott	do.		10 F.
Hugh Fraser	do.		Royal Artillery
280 J— W— Aldred	do.		60 F.
James Vivion	do.		Royal Artillery
Robert Pym	do.		do.
William R— Carey	do.		do.
Henry Cumming	do.		81 F.
Alexander Mackay	do.		93 F.
Henry Marsh	do.		Royal Artillery
Thomas H— Dawes	2 do.		22 Dr.
Joseph Hanna	do.		56 F.
James Conolly	do.		Half-pay 26 F.
290 Mathew Read	do.		4 West India Regt.

Charles

Charles Bayley	2Jan. 1812	1 Garrison Bn.
Godfrey Starck	do.	Royal York Rangers
Carlo Joseph Doyle	23do.	2 Garrison Bn.
Alexander Barry	25do.	Half-pay Bradshaw's Levy
⊚Martin Leggatt	30do.	36 F.
Edward Warner	do.	Half-pay 26 F.
James T— Robertson	do.	6 F.
Thomas Evans	6Feb.	8 F.
⊚John Duffy	do.	43 F.
300⊚George Miles Milne	do.	10 R. Veteran Battalion
George Macleod	do.	Royal Engineers
Peter William de Haren	20do.	Canadian Fenc. Inf.
Geo. Fred. Waldo. Fluker	do.	Bourbon Regt.
Thomas Forest Fisher	do.	6 D. Gds.
Andrew Tilt	do.	37 F.
Frederick, *Baron* Gruben	25do.	The King's German Legion
⊚John Camac	1Mar.	1 Life Gds.
Geo. Edw. Pratt Barlow	26do.	34 F.
Robert Anstruther	16Apr.	Half-pay 42 F.
310Richard Llewellwyn	23do.	28 F.
⊚–George Langlands	27do.	13 Royal Vet. Bn.
⊚John Thomas Leahy	do.	Half-pay 23 F.
Charles M'Gregor	30do.	70 F.
⊚–William Cardon Seton	do.	88 F.
Donald Gregorson	do.	91 F.
Henry Adolphus Proctor	do.	82 F.
Charles Purvis	7May	1 Dr.
John Nicolls	do.	98 F.
Edward Hodge	do.	7 Dr.
320George Gore	do.	9 Dr.
John Henry Belli	do.	16 Dr.
Hon. Henry B— Lygon	do.	16 Dr.
⊚George King	14do.	7 F.
Charles de Villatte	21do.	Watteville's Regt.
Arch. John Maclean	28do.	73 F.
⊚Frederick de Ziegesar	do.	The King's German Legion
*Frederick de Dornberg	do.	Of late Brunswick Inf.
Henry de la Douespe	10June	69 F.
C— I— Barrow	11do.	69 F.
330Donald M'Donald	do.	19 F.
Nicholas Hamilton	18do.	Insp. F. O. Rec. District
George Hewett	do.	22 F.
Herman Stapleton	19do.	Half-pay 50 F.
Robert Charles Lang	25do.	81 F.
John Chapman	9July	Half-pay 63 F.
John Owen	20do.	61 F.
⊚Robert Macdonald	17Aug.	Royal Artillery
Thomas Evans	do.	38 F.
⊚–Robert Lawson	do.	Royal Artillery
340William Beresford	do.	Half-pay 31 F.

Joseph

Joseph Hawtyn	17Aug. 1812	23 F.
John Crowder	do.	7 F.
◎-Richard Bishop	do.	5 F.
Ja. Milford Sutherland	10Sept.	91 F.
◎James Hughes	24do.	18 Dr.
Benjamin Graves	do.	72 F.
John Maxwell	8Oct.	15 F.
John A— Whitaker	do.	21 F.
John Baskeville Glegg	do.	49 F.
350Foster Lech. Coore	do.	3 West India Regt.
Augustus Friedericks	14do.	The King's German Legion
Richard Bayley	15do.	12 F.
Philip Bainbrigge	do.	Perm. Ass. Q. M. Gen.
Gebhardus Timæus	20do.	The King's German Legion
William Hedderwick	22do.	24 F.
*Henry, Prince Reuss	23do.	The King's German Legion
John Mac Niel	29do.	18 F.
Patrick Savage	do.	24 Dr.
◎Edward Griffith	5Nov.	15 Dr.
360William Carroll	do.	69 F. Insp. of Col. Troops in the Islands of Bourbon, Mauritius, and Java
George Arthur	do.	7 West India Regt.
Matthew G— Blake	12do.	Cape Reg. D.A.G.C. of G. H.
Donald Macdonald	26do.	92 F.
James Dennis	28do.	49 F.
William Holcroft	do.	Royal Artillery
James F— Fulton	do.	Canadian Fenc. Inf.
John Williams	do.	49 F.
Thomas Kennedy	3Dec.	Half-pay 96 F.
James Paul Bridger	10do.	12 Dr.
370Thomas Hutchins	do.	3 Dr.
Michael Coast	31do.	31 F.
William Phipps	7Jan. 13	Half-pay 92 F.
Neil Cockburn	25do.	8 West India Regt.
Samuel Moffatt	28do.	1 Ceylon Regt.
John Moore	4Feb.	15 F.
Alexander Ogilvie	do.	46 F.
Courtland Schuyler	11do.	84 F.
Jonathan Brown	16do.	75 F.
George Coulon	17do.	The King's German Legion
380George Müller	18do.	do.
◎George Home Murray	do.	16 Dr. [Gen. Ceylon
William Willermin	do.	2 Ceylon Regt. D. Qr. Mr.
John Prior	25do.	Serv. with the Portug. Army
Werner, Baron Bussche	1Mar.	The King's German Legion
Ernest Otto Tripp	1Apr.	60 F.
Edward Fleming	do.	2 West India Regt.
George Druitt	4do.	58 F.
William Thornhill	8do.	7 Dr.
John Jordan	22do.	27 F.Dep.Adj.Gen.Ionian Isl.
390William Fawcett	do.	14 F.

Thomas

Thomas Drake	22Apr. 1813	95 F. Dep.Q.M.G. Ionian Isls.
Robert Cockburne	13May	84 F.
◎Robert Christopher Packe	do.	Royal Regt. Horse Guards
Murdoch Hugh Maclaine	20do.	77 F.
P— A— Lautour	do.	23 Dr.
Joseph Phillott	27do.	25 F.
George Tito Brice	do.	3 D. G.
George Watts	do.	do.
William Wemyss	do.	93 F.
400 Robert Lisle	4June	19 Dr.
James Poole	do.	2 Dr.
George Davidson	do.	42 F.
James Powell	do.	103 F.
Samuel Reynell	do.	Invalid Bn. of Roy. Artillery
William Payne	do.	Royal Artillery
George Forster	do.	do.
John Caddy	do.	do.
Alexander Campbell	do.	do.
H— M— Farrington	do.	do.
410 George Skyring	do.	do.
C— H— Fitzmayer	do.	do.
Joseph Brome	do.	do.
Charles Younghusband	do.	do.
George Crawford	do.	do.
Maxwell Close	do.	Half-pay late 1 Garrison Bn.
Amande de Courten	do.	Watteville's Regt.
Matthew Ryon	do.	30 F.
George Elrington	do.	3 West India Regt.
J— Lewis Watson	do.	69 F.
420 Thomas Hunter	do.	104 F.
James Mylne	do.	24 Dr.
A— Douglas	do.	93 F.
Goodwin Purcell	do.	32 F.
William Henry Taynton	do.	60 F.
William Loftie	do.	6 West India Regt.
James Winnett	do.	68 F.
George Lawrence	do.	13 Dr.
John Staunton	do.	13 F.
George Lewis	do.	Royal Marines
430 Robert P— Boys	do.	do.
George John Sale	do.	17 Dr.
Henry Skelton	do.	19 Dr.
John Giles	do.	53 F.
George Prescott Wingrove	do.	Royal Marines
Thomas Shepherd	do.	do.
Hon. Edward Mullens	do.	Half-pay 28 F.
William Irwin	do.	5 Dr. G.
Eyre Smith	do.	62 F.
J— B— Hirtz	do.	Of late Dillon's Regt.
440 Elias Lawrence	do.	Royal Marines

John

John Reed	4June 1813	4 West India Regt.
William Johnstone	do.	Half-pay Royal Marines
Francis Smith	do.	Royal Artillery
Henry Shum	do.	6 Dr. G.
Charles Eagan	do.	Royal Artillery
Fountain Elwin	do.	44 F.
John Bartleman	do.	Royal Marines
William Onslow	do.	4 Dr.
Henry Hickman	do.	Royal Artillery
450 Joseph Mignan May	do.	Royal Marines
George Evatt	do.	55 F.
Hon. Charles Murray	do.	Royal Regt. Horse Guards
John Campbell	do.	11 F.
George Saville Burdett	do.	1 West India Regt.
Wm. Mansfield Morrison	do.	7 Dr. G.
Thomas J— Forbes	do.	Royal Artillery
Wm. Hart Lapsley	do.	39 F.
Thomas Hole	do.	25 Dr.
Richard Annesley	do.	Royal West India Rangers
460 John Howard	do.	97 F.
Henry de la Harpe	do.	3 Ceylon Regt.
John M— Close	do.	Royal Artillery
Lionel C— Hooke	do.	2 Ceylon Regt.
William Ormsby Gore	do.	1 Dr. G.
Henry Ryhiner	do. -	Roll's Regt.
Joseph Cookson	do.	80 F.
Charles Haynes	do.	47 F.
James Peat	do.	25 F.
William Fitz Gerald	do.	82 F.
470 Nathaniel Benjafield	do.	67 F.
Mark A— Bozon	do.	Half-pay 15 F.
Walter M'Gibbon	do.	57 F.
Wheeler Sparrow	do.	27 F.
Hon. Gerard de Courcy	do.	70 F.
Hugh Cameron	do.	73 F.
Henry White	do.	24 F.
Edward Carlyon	do.	66 F.
James Mundy	5do.	8 F.
George Germ. Cochrane	10do.	37 F.
480 Frederick Heriot	do.	Canadian Voltigeurs
Aug. *Baron* Reitzenstein	13do.	The King's German Legion
John Hare	17do.	27 F.
Alexander Thistlethwayte	do.	90 F.
C. E. de May Duzisdorff	do.	Meuron's Regt.
Hon. Sir Cha. Gordon, *Kt.*	19do.	Of late 2d Greek Regt.
⊚ George Marlay	21do.	14 F.
George Baring	do.	The King's German Legion
Jonathan Leach	do.	95 F.
⊚ Robert Anwyll	do.	4 F.
490 ⊚ Partick Campbell	do.	52 F.

G   ⊚ William

[1815]
MAJORS.

⊚ William Perceval	21June 1813	95 F.
Peter Brown	do.	23 F.
⊚-Samuel Mitchell	do.	95 F.
⊚ Archibald Ross	do.	91 F.
⊚ John Schoedde	do.	60 F.
William Moore	do.	74 F.
✖ James Miller	do.	74 F.
⊚ Samuel Hext	do.	83 F.
Thomas Wemyss	do.	50 F.
500 ⊚-Augustus Heise	do.	The King's German Legion
George Couper	do.	92 F.
✖-Alexander Anderson	do.	Half-pay
Thomas F— Wade	do.	42 F.
Thomas Weare	do.	35 F.
Charles, Baron During	do.	The King's German Legion
Henry Barrington	24do.	3 Dr.
Boyle O— Loane	1 July	1 Ceylon Regiment
George Raitt	do.	72 F.
Abraham Freer	do.	25 F.
510 Gabriel Burer	do.	37 F.
George Nixon	15do.	3 Ceylon Regiment
Thomas Burke	22do.	4 F.
Rich. Bingham Newland	5 Aug.	20 Dr.
T— B— Bamford	12do.	6 West India Regiment
William Martin	13do.	8 Dr.
Abraham Brunt	19do.	83 F.
Allan M'Lachlan	26do.	75 F.
John Burrowes	do.	57 F.
⊚ Arthur Rowley Heyland	do.	40 F.
520 Richard Egerton	do.	34 F.
⊚-William Campbell	do.	36 F.
⊚ James Bogle	do.	94 F.
⊚ John B— Walmsley	do.	82 F.
Robert B— Gabriel	do.	2 Dr. G.
⊚ Henry Thomas	do.	27 F.
⊚ Thomas Bell	do.	48 F.
O— G— Fehrzen	do.	53 F.
Lewis Rumann	do.	97 F.
William Chalmers	do.	52 F.
530 Francis Dalmer	do.	23 F.
Alexander Todd	do.	Royal Staff Corps
⊚-John Macdonald	do.	Half-pay
William Chuden	28do.	The King's German Legion
Samuel Sankey	2 Sept.	9 F.
Leslie Walker	do.	71 F.
John Mervin Cutcliffe	do.	23 Dr.
Matthew Scott	21do.	2 F.
William Morrison	do.	Royal Artillery
⊚ Cha. Stewart Campbell	do.	26 F.
540 Thomas Ferrars	do.	9 F.

⊚ John

ⓞJohn Williamson	21Sept. 1813	4 F.
ⓞRobert Campbell	do.	52 F.
Hector Cameron	do.	9 F.
Thomas Willshire	do.	38 F.
ⓞGeorge H— Henderson	do.	Royal Engineers
ⓞJohn Murray	do.	20 F.
James Taylor	do.	48 F.
William Power	do.	Royal Artillery
ⓞJohn Parker	do.	do.
550ⓞGeorge Halford	do.	59 F.
ⓞ–Kenneth Snodgrass	do.	Half-pay
Robert M'Donald	do.	1 F.
David Jolly	23do.	8 West India Regt.
Joseph Creighton	do.	59 F.
John T— Horsley	24do.	59 F.
Byse Molesworth	29do.	47 F.
Ernest, *Baron* During	30do.	The King's German Legion
Adam Peebles	7Oct.	9 F.
Meriz de Muller	10do.	The King's German Legion
560Patrick Campbell	14do.	Royal Artillery
ⓞHenry Oglander	do.	Half-pay late 1 Gar. Bn.
Charles Irvine	21do.	6 Dr. G.
Samuel South	do.	20 F.
George Sackville Fraser	do.	Cape Regt.
William S— Forbes	6Nov.	56 F.
Charles Mill	10do.	27 F.
John Alexander Mein	11do.	74 F.
Henry Fitz Gerald	do.	60 F.
William Linsingen	do.	The King's German Legion
570John Joseph Maling	do.	Royal African Corps
Charles Duke	do.	York Chasseurs
Daniel Marston	18do.	86 F.
William Vincent	do.	82 F.
George D'Arcey	22do.	39 F.
George Clarke	do.	5 F.
ⓞCharles Cameron	do.	3 F.
ⓞBayntun Stone	do.	58 F.
ⓞWilliam Balvaird	do.	95 F.
Thomas Samuel Nicolls	do.	31 F.
580ⓞWilliam N— Ramsay	do.	Royal Artillery
James Roupell Colleton	do.	Royal Staff Corps
ⓞSempronius Stretton	do.	40 F.
Denis O'Kelly	do.	11 F.
Chath. Hor. Churchill	do.	1 F. Gds.
Joseph D'Arcy	25do.	Royal Artillery
Duncan Mac Gregor	do.	78 F.
Ralph Ouseley	do.	Serving with the Portug. Army
ⓞVictor de Arentsschildt	do.	The King's German Legion
ⓞ–John Rolt	do.	Serving with the Portug. Army
590Peter Johnston	1Dec.	14 F.

William

William Read	9Dec. 1813	Perm. Ass. Qua. Mast. Gen.
Hon. W— E— Cochrane	16do.	15 Dr.
C— L— L— Forster	19do.	Half-pay 6 West India Regt.
John Martin	do.	100 F.
William Robinson	do.	8 F.
George Augustus Eliot	do.	103 F.
J— H— Holland	do.	69 F.
Richard Vyse Fawcett	do.	100 F.
William Baird	25do.	86 F.
600⊚George David Wilson	26do.	4 F.
John Easting Kipping	do.	4 F.
John Gomersall	do.	58 F.
Patrick Dowdall	do.	31 F.
⊚Joseph Marke	do.	57 F.
Peter Adamson	do.	Half-pay
James Jenkin	do.	84 F.
Thomas Napier	do.	Half-pay late Chass. Britann.
Henry Montgomery	do.	50 F.
Robert Henry Sale	30do.	12 F.
610H— Blois Lynch	1Jan. 14	Half-pay York Rangers
⊚Thomas Laing	6do.	94 F.
*Charles Turner	do.	Half-pay R. Waggon Train
John Keightley	13do.	14 F.
Donald Campbell	do.	79 F.
Robert Melville Browne	do.	Half-pay
James Payler	do.	Half-pay
George Dean	do.	Half-pay
Charles M— St. Paul	do.	Half-pay
John Carter	20do.	84 F.
620Henry Bristow	do.	11 F.
William Aly	26do.	2 Hussars, King's Ger. Leg.
William Gosset	2Feb.	Royal Engineers
John Fogerty	3do.	101 F.
James Stopford	10do.	60 F.
John Mackenzie	17do.	46 F.
⊚Duncan Campbell	3Mar.	39 F.
James Poole Oates	do.	88 F.
Sackville Taylor	do.	6 F.
J— Cully	do.	5 F.
630William Greene	do.	61 F.
George Westcott	do.	77 F.
William Russell	do.	20 F.
⊚George Miller	do.	95 F.
Charles Beckwith	do.	95 F.
Benjamin Rowe	do.	50 F.
William Rowan	do.	52 F.
James Campbell	do.	45 F.
James Lepper	do.	24 F.
Nathaniel Thorn	do.	3 F.
640Andrew Hamilton	do.	4 West India Regiment

William

William Henry Sewell	3 Mar. 1814	60 F.
Thomas Rynd	10do.	100 F.
Tobias Kirkwood	do.	New Brunswick Fencibles
George Lionel Dawson	do.	Half-pay 1 Dr. Gds.
Sir George Hoste, *Kt.*	17do.	Royal Engineers
Michael Chamberlain	do.	Half-pay
Edward Michell	do.	Royal Artillery
William Cochrane	do.	103 F.
Hugh Percy Davison	19do.	67 F.
650 Charles Pratt	24do.	Half-pay 96 F.
George Spottiswoode	31do.	71 F.
Anthony Boden	3 Apr.	3 Line, King's German Leg.
James Fullerton	7do.	95 F.
◎George Beane	12do.	Royal Artillery
Robert Dalzell	do.	43 F.
James Walsh	do.	91 F.
James Walker	do.	42 F.
James Lee	do.	Half-pay 92 F.
Henry Hooper	do.	87 F.
660 Alex. Maxwell Bennett	do.	5 F.
John Marcus Clements	do.	18 Dr.
George Teale	do.	11 F.
William Wingfield	do.	36 F.
Loftus Gray	do.	95 F.
John Mac Alester	do.	13 Dr.
Edward Pares Sparrow	do.	Half-pay 61 F.
Thomas Potter Milles	do.	14 Dr.
Edward Purdon	do.	60 F.
John Campbell	do.	42 F.
670 ◎William Greene	do.	Royal Artillery
◎-Robert M— Cairnes	do.	do.
William Campbell	do.	23 F.
Charles Campbell	do.	94 F.
William Dunbar	do.	66 F.
Francis Gualey	do.	11 F.
Hamlet Obins	do.	20 F.
William Cator	do.	Royal Artillery
Edmund L'Estrange	do.	71 F.
Mathew Forster	do.	38 F.
680 George Tovey	do.	20 F.
Gilbert Elliot	do.	83 F.
John Dorset Bringhurst	do.	1 Dr. Gds.
William Lindsay Darling	14do.	Half-pay late 2 Gar. Bn.
Thomas Bunbury	do.	Glengarry Fencibles
Hon. H— Cecil Lowther	do.	10 Dr.
Sir Eman. Felix Agar, *Kt.*	20do.	2 Life Guards
Andrew Long	21do.	Staff Corps
Henry Tarleton	do.	60 F.
Charles de Petersdorff	6 May	8 Line, King's German Leg.
690 James Horton	18do.	Half-pay 61 F.

Andrew

Andrew Hartley	19May 1814	Half-pay 61 F.
James Laing	do.	do.
Hector M'Laine	do.	57 F.
⊙John O'Flaherty	do.	Half-pay 45 F.
Henry D— Loftus	do.	9 F.
Peter Warburton	26do.	97 F.
Henry Godwin	do.	5 West India Regt.
Tho. Tray. Ful. El. Drake	do.	52 F.
Joseph Skerrett	1June	76 F.
700 Patrick Anderson	do.	19 Dr.
Richard Carroll	2do.	Serv. with the Portug. Army
Charles Ramus Forrest	do.	34 F.
George Darley	do.	Royal Waggon Train
Edward Anth. Angelo	do.	21 F.
T— W— Hewitt	do.	Serv. with the Portug. Army
Thomas St. Clair	do.	do.
George William Paty	do.	do.
William Lewis Herries	do.	Ass. Qr. Mast. Gen.
⊙-George Henry Zulke	do.	Serv. with the Portug. Army
710 Joshua W— Green	do.	do.
James Boucheir	4do.	11 Dr.
Hon. F. Leicester Stanhope	do.	17 Dr.
Thomas Rogers	do.	Royal Artillery
J— Coutquelvin	do.	Royal Foreign Artillery
Thomas Gamble	do.	Royal Artillery
Alexander Munro	do.	do.
James P— Cockburn	do.	do.
John Bradish	do.	2 Ceylon Regt.
Philip Delatre	do.	1 Ceylon Regt.
720 William Davis	do.	7 D. Gds.
John Dalrymple	do.	80 F.
William Derenzy	do.	41 F.
William Bernard	do.	70 F.
Richard Jones	do.	55 F.
Adam Ormsby	do.	5 D. Gds.
David Supple	do.	17 Dr.
Robert Horsley	do.	11 Dr.
Edward Fawconer	do.	93 F.
Thomas Manners	do.	49 F.
730 Robert Durie	do.	24 Dr.
Joseph Gordon	do.	22 Dr.
Alexander Alexander	do.	3 Ceylon Regt.
John Campbell	do.	55 F.
William Hull	do.	62 F.
Donald Mac Neill	do.	Cape Regt.
Hamilton Bagwell	do.	88 F.
Lewis de Mangou	do.	60 F.
Weston Hames	do.	2 Dr. Gds.
William Collins	do.	Royal Marines
740 Robert Maunsell	do.	Half-pay 39 F.

George

George S— Thwaites	4 June 1814	48 F.
Philip de Mauriage	do.	60 F.
Wm. Hen. Milson Bayley	do.	Royal Marines
Samuel Claperton	do.	do.
Alexander Watson	do.	do.
Thomas John Sterling	do.	do.
John Burn	do.	Late of Royal Marines
Arthur H — Ball	do.	Royal Marines
Archibald M'Auley	do.	44 F.
750 Henry Lindsay	do.	69 F.
John Cruice	do.	44 F.
Jeffrey O'Connell	do.	18 F.
William Sall	do.	Half-pay 47 F.
Martin Corry	do.	47 F.
Mark Robinson Glaze	do.	Royal Marines
Robert Percival	do.	18 F.
Samuel Bircham	do.	30 F.
Samuel Colberg	do.	58 F.
Basil Fisher	do.	63 F.
760 J— C— L— Carter	do.	44 F.
Wm. Prescott Meacham	do.	28 F.
William Irving	do.	28 F.
Frederick P— Noble	do.	67 F.
Robert Hilliard	do.	Half-pay 45 F.
John Whetstone	do.	53 F.
Elias Pipon	do.	Royal Newfoundland Fenc.
Thomas Smoke	do.	24 Dr.
J— Murray	do.	73 F.
Charles Baldwin	do.	58 F.
770 J— William Rogers	do.	77 F.
Lord Robert Kerr	do.	Half-pay late 6 Garr. Bat.
Robert Marcus Shearman	do.	86 F.
William R— Lawrence	do.	72 F.
James Grant	do.	18 Dr.
John Scott Lindesay	do.	Half-pay Irish Brigade
Christopher Noble	do.	———— Royal Marines
George Bunce	do.	24 Dr.
Henry Cox	do.	Royal Marines
Edward Carter Hornby	do.	do.
780 Henry Rennells	do.	60 F.
Francis Wemyss	do.	Royal Marines
George Jones	do.	do.
Joseph Beausire	do.	Royal Foreign Artillery
Rodolphe de Bersey	do.	Watteville's Regt.
Andrew Kinsman	do.	Royal Marines
William Riddell	do.	62 F.
Francis Clarke	do.	Royal Foreign Artillery
Nathan Hamilton English	do.	Royal Marines
John Hore Graham	do.	do.
790 William Sladden	do.	do.

©Richard

©Richard Bunce	4June 1814	Royal Marines
James Butler Fletcher	do.	do.
Nicholas Brutton	do.	8 Dr.
William Morris	do.	Royal Newfoundland Fenc.
Richard Rochfort	do.	Army Depôt
Edward Powell	do.	10 F.
Lewis A— de Noe	do.	Army Depôt
John M'Mahon	do.	60 F.
Daniel O'Donoghue	do.	Half-pay late 1 Garr. Bn.
800Thomas Ware	do.	90 F.
Alexander M'Donald	do.	76 F.
Philip Durnford	do.	Royal Artillery
John Sinclair	do.	do.
William Lloyd	do.	do.
Blaney Walsh	do.	do.
Robert H— Birch	do.	do.
James Armstrong	do.	do.
Richard Dyas	do.	do.
Edward Willmott	do.	do.
810George W— Unett	do.	do.
Philip J— Hughes	do.	do.
James Maclachlan	do.	do.
William J— Lloyd	do.	do.
James Adams	do.	do.
Henry Vernon	do.	36 F.
Thomas Adair	do.	Royal Marines
Joseph Jerrard	do.	Half-pay late 6 Garr. Bn.
Robert Terry	do.	25 F.
George Brock	do.	27 F.
820John Phillips	do.	Half-pay Royal Marines
William Williams	do.	86 F.
William Roberts	do.	Royal Artillery
John Fead	do.	do.
Thomas Amory	do.	Half-pay late 5 Garr. Bn.
Eyre Coote	do.	14 F.
Milchior, *Baron* Decken	do.	6 Line King's German Legion
George Chuden	do.	4 do. do.
Frederick Breymann	do.	2 do. do.
John Joseph Seelinger	do.	38 F.
830Charles Pringle	do.	7 Line King's German Legion
Robert Murray	do.	30 F.
George Jervis	do.	Army Depôt
Edward Geils	do.	19 Dr.
John Thomas Whelan	do.	Royal Newfoundland Fenc.
Nich. Philip de Brem	do.	Of late Chass. Britanniques
David Scott	do.	67 F.
Arthur Morris	do.	2 Garr. Bn.
Thomas Paterson	do.	Royal Artillery
Adam Wall	do.	do.
840William Cleeve	do.	do.

John

John Jameson	4 June 1814	64 F.
Thomas Jackson	do.	30 F.
John Bridge	do.	Half-pay 63 F.
George Baile	do.	Royal Marines
John Jackson	do.	do.
James William Wilson	do.	39 F.
Charles D— Shekelton	do.	Half-pay 54 F.
John Campbell	do.	16 F.
Nicholas Muller	do.	Roll's Infantry
850 Frederick Crofton	do.	York Lt. Infantry Vols.
Frederick Franchesson	do.	do.
Charles Meredith	do.	Royal Marines
Abraham Creighton	do.	55 F.
David Gregory	do.	Half-pay late 1 Garr. Bn.
Baptist J— Barton	do.	do.
Samuel Maxwell	do.	92 F.
Roger P— Symons	do.	Half-pay Royal Marines
M. S. O'Callag. Caulfield	do.	——— 32 F.
Brook Lawrence	do.	13 Dr.
860 Adam Muir	do.	41 F.
John Ridley	do.	Royal Marines
Ambrose Lane	do.	44 F.
Richard Weston	do.	1 West India Regt.
Leonard Gibbons	do.	60 F.
Charles Stisted	do.	3 Dr.
George Russell Deare	do.	8 Dr.
Thomas Read	do.	Half-pay late 5 Garr. Bn.
Nathaniel W— Oliver	do.	Royal Artillery
William Owen	do.	67 F.
870 Charles Reynolds	do.	5 West India Regt.
J— C— Eddington	do.	6 do.
William Holland	do.	90 F.
Henry Capadoce	do.	56 F.
Richard Young	do.	1 Garr. Bn.
George Wright	do.	Royal Engineers
William Thwaites	do.	51 F.
Edward Lenn	do.	3 Ceylon Regt.
Benjamin Sullivan	do.	Half-pay
Denis Kingdon	do.	80 F.
880 Richard Hart	do.	2 Garr. Bn.
John Charles Smith	do.	Sicilian Regt.
Charles Robinson	do.	72 F.
Charles Souter	do.	Half-pay 5 F.
John Parry	do.	Royal Marines
James T— Cowper	do.	Royal Artillery
Adolphus Bosewell	do.	2 Lt. Inf. King's Germ. Leg.
Robert Hart	do.	Royal Marines
William Gough	do.	68 F.
Robert Hawthorne	do.	Late of 4 Garr. Bn.
890 Thomas Hare	do.	98 F.

H   Henry

Henry Croasdaile	4June 1814	98 F.
Samson Carter -	do.	Half-pay late 1 Garr. Bn.
William Milne	do.	98 F.
Thomas Bayley	do.	3 Ceylon Regt.
Nathaniel Bean	do.	17 F.
James Moultrie	do.	Half-pay late 1 Garr. Bn.
John Jessop	do.	44 F.
Wheeler Coultman	do.	53 F.
George de Muller	do.	Late 1 Huss. Kg's Germ.Leg.
900Henry Kuhlmann	do.	Artillery King's Germ. Leg.
George Bristow	do.	34 F.
George Humphrey	do.	12 F.
John Thomas Keyt	do.	51 F.
Nicholas Turner	do.	Royal Artillery Drivers
Edmund Power	do.	7 Dr. G.
Charles H— Godby	do.	Royal Artillery
James St. Clair	do.	do.
Richard J— J— Lacy	do.	do.
John A— Clement	do.	do.
910◎-Robert Douglas	do.	do.
John Hassard	do.	Royal Engineers
Edward P— Wilgress	do.	Royal Artillery
Lewin de Harling	do.	6 Line King's German Leg.
John W— Audain	do.	16 F.
Francis Hawker	do.	96 F.
◎Stewart Maxwell	do.	Royal Artillery
Dugald Campbell	do.	do.
William George Elliott	do.	do.
Frederick Campbell	do.	do.
920George Turner	do.	do.
William Bailie	do.	25 F.
William Waldon Brome	do.	10 F.
William Boyce	do.	2 Life Gds.
James Butler	do.	62 F.
John Wynne	do.	63 F.
William Burke Nicolls	do.	72 F.
Patrick Cruice	do.	31 F.
John M'Niel	do.	7 West India Regt.
Thomas Charles Green	do.	24 F.
930Valentine Joseph Quin	do.	21 F.
John Austin	do.	25 F.
John Field Oldham	do.	2 Garr. Bn.
James Sullivan	do.	83 F.
Benjamin Lutyens	do.	11 Dr.
Wade Rothwell	do.	Half-pay late 6 Garr. Bn.
Alexander Stewart	do.	31 F.
Thomas Conolly	do.	15 F.
William Langworthy	do.	Half-pay 24 F.
Jacob Watson	do.	14 F.
940Garnet Wolseley	do.	25 F.

Oliver

Oliver Mills	4June 1814	45 F.
William Wright Swain	do.	36 F.
Henry Ross Lewen	do.	32 F.
Daniel Roberts	do.	5 West India Regt.
F— B— Eliot	do.	Half-pay 26 F.
J— A— Gibson	do.	Of late 4 Garr. Bn.
Robert K— Abbey	do.	72 F.
Augustus Berensbach	do.	Engineers King's Germ. Leg.
John Weeks	do.	7 West India Regt.
950 George Marlay	do.	1 F.
Henry Hardy	do.	19 F.
Stuart Home Douglas	do.	21 F.
Henry Nooth	do.	14 F.
Alexander Stewart	do.	1 F.
Murdock M'Laine	do.	Late of 42 F.
James M'Haffie	do.	21 F.
John Gordon	do.	1 F.
John Blossett	do.	5 West India Regt.
Edward Michael Bird	do.	1 F.
960 Henry Boone Hall	do.	101 F.
John Edward Courtenay	do.	Nova Scotia Fenc.
William Moore	do.	27 F.
William Grierson	do.	15 F.
Ludovick Stewart	do.	24 F.
Hamilton Newton	do.	1 Garr. Bn.
Lawrence Oakes	do.	89 F.
John Pollock	do.	62 F.
Joseph Dacre Lacey	do.	Half-pay late 2 Garr. Bn.
Robert Elder	do.	31 F.
970 George Barrow	do.	15 F.
Charles Hughes	do.	24 F.
Andrew Wood	do.	90 F.
John Berger	do.	1 Life Gds.
Thomas Hutchings	do.	65 F.
Tho. Chaloner Martelli	do.	72 F.
William Conolly	do.	18 F.
Donald Mac Lean	do.	1 F.
George Juxon	do.	25 F.
James Thompson	do.	Royal Marines
980 Thomas Henry Morrice	do.	do.
Heneage Wm. Creswell	do.	do.
John Cameron	do.	Half-pay late 2 Garr. Bn.
Adolphus Munstal	do.	25 F.
Alex. Baron Moncrieff	do.	13 F.
William H— Toole	do.	32 F.
Charles Johnstone	do.	71 F.
William Taylor	do.	38 F.
Gideon Gorrequer	do.	18 F.
Allan Cameron	do.	83 F.
990 William Dammers	do.	3 Line King's Germ. Leg.

H 2   Kuckuck

—— Kuckuck	4June 1814	3 Line King's German Leg.
John Gualey	do.	56 F.
Paulus Æmilius Irving	do.	62 F.
Alexander Daniel	do.	Half-pay 63 F.
Thomas Somerfield	do.	83 F.
Henry Meyer	do.	4 Line King's German Leg.
Joseph Maclean	do.	3 West India Regt.
James Cassidy	do.	1 do.
John L— Gallie	do.	38 F.
1000 Albert D'Alton	do.	90 F.
Dominique Rossi	do.	Royal Corsican Rangers
Joseph Berbie	do.	Roll's Infantry
Richard F— Cleaveland	do.	Royal Artillery
William T— Skinner	do.	do.
James Vallance	do.	73 F.
Skene Keith	do.	62 F.
Alexander J— Callender	do.	91 F.
John Blackmore	do.	8 F.
Nicholas Fuchs	do.	Meuron's Infantry
1010 Thomas Shaw	do.	Half-pay late 6 Garr. Bn.
George Dods	do.	1 F.
Thomas Craig	do.	24 F.
J— Clifton Andrews	do.	53 F.
George Jackman Rogers	do.	18 F.
Charles Vigny	do.	60 F.
George L— Spinluff	do.	1 Garr. Bn.
George Noleken	do.	83 F.
William Richardson	do.	Half-pay late 5 Garr. Bn.
William Hutcheon	do.	25 F.
1020 James Ward	do.	4 F.
Peter Wallace	do.	Royal Artillery
George Lene	do.	4 Line King's German Leg.
Ernest, *Baron* Linsingen	do.	3 Hussars do.
Augustus Sympher	do.	Artillery do.
John Hilton	do.	25 Dr.
B— R— Lynch	do.	30 F.
Robert Vernon	do.	2 Dr.
William Hill	do.	6 West India Regt.
William Power	do.	7 Dr. Gds.
1030 Rob. Bartholomew Lynch	do.	Royal Marines
Daniel Falla	do.	57 F.
Thomas Molloy	do.	27 F.
Henry Bishop	do.	64 F.
Richard Edwards	do.	62 F.
Charles E— Radclyffe	do.	1 Dr.
Richard Jones	do.	Royal Artillery
Charles Cranston Dixon	do.	90 F.
Michael de Wendt	do.	60 F.
John S— Jackson	do.	72 F.
1040 John Malone	do.	98 F.

Edward

Edward Watkin	4 June 1814	65 F.
George Mackay	do.	Half-pay Kelso Regt.
Lorenzo Nunn	do.	89 F.
Octavius Temple	do.	14 F.
Edward Dudreneux	do.	81 F.
Thomas Howard	do.	70 F.
John E— Jones	do.	Royal Artillery
William H. C. Benezette	do.	do.
⊚-Thomas A— Brandreth	do.	do.
1050 Alexander Gillespie	do.	Royal Marines
George Williamson	do.	90 F.
⊚ Fielding Browne	do.	40 F.
Eyre Evans Kenny	do.	80 F.
P— B— Foley	do.	9 F.
Thomas Reignolds	do.	2 Dr.
Persse O'Keefe Boulger	do.	93 F.
Richard Maxwell	do.	Half-pay late 6 Garr. Bn.
George Ross	do.	6 West India Regt.
W— W— Higgins	16 do.	21 Dr.
1060 Robert Brownrigg	do.	52 F. D. Adj. G. in Ceylon
John By	23 do.	Royal Enginers
Norman Pringle	do.	21 F.
W— B— Tylden	do.	Royal Engineers
Thomas W— Taylor	7 July	10 Dr. Dep. Q. M. G. Java
John Guthrie	do.	33 F.
Augustine Fitzgerald	14 do.	49 F.
⊚ Charles Jackson	28 do.	2 Life Guards
Hon. Fred. Cathcart	do.	2 Dr.
Horatio George Broke	do.	58 F.
1070 Colin Campbell Mackay	11 Aug.	78 F.
William Haverfield	do.	43 F.
L— Arguimbeau	do.	1 F.
Wm. Brewse Kersteman	18 do.	10 F.
Michael Childers	28 do.	11 Dr.
George Warb. White	2 Sept.	Half-pay late 6 Garr. Bn.
John Michell	29 do.	Royal Artillery
William C— Ball	do.	85 F.
Joseph Paterson	do.	York Chasseurs
Henry George Smith	do.	95 F.
1080 Thomas Blanshard	do.	Royal Engineers
Thomas Falls	do.	20 F.
Charles M— Graham	13 Oct.	71 F.
D— Macdougall	20 do.	85 F.
George Tryon	27 do.	99 F.
Richard Leonard	do.	104 F.
Henry Rea	do.	Royal Marines
Lewis Carmichael	do.	Royal Artillery
Harry Bulteel Harris	do.	Half-pay 86 F.
John Ciravegnac	do.	Sicilian Regt.
1090 John Robyns	do.	Royal Marines

Felix

Felix Calvert	27Oct.	1814	Of late Dillon's Regt.
W— P— de Bathe	do.		85 F.
John Allen	1Dec.		10 F.
Matthew Stewart	8do.		Royal York Rangers
J— F— Brigges	do.		Half-pay 28 F.
Thomas Fane	do.		Meuron's Regt.
William Staveley	15do.		Royal Staff Corps
Edward Barwick	12Jan.	15	37 F.

Aides-de-Camp to His Royal Highness the Prince Regent.

George Quentin	8Feb.1811	Col.	4June 1814	10 Dr.
Charles Palmer	do.	—	do.	H.-pay 23 Dr.
George, Visc. Forbes	do.	Lt. Col.	1Jan. 12	Meuron's Reg.
Thomas M'Mahon	7Feb. 12	Col.	4June 14	17 F.
✗Sir T. Arbuthnot, K.C.B.	do.	—	do.	57 F.
Lord James Murray	4June 13	—	4June 13	Hp. ManxFen.
✗Sir A.F.Barnard,K.C.B.	do.	—	do.	95 F.
✗Sir Geo.AdamWood, Kt.	4June 14	—	4June 14	Royal Artillery
S— Ford Whittingham	do.	—	do.	Portug. Service
✗SirJohnColborne,K.C.B.	do.	—	do.	52 F.
✗Sir A.Campbell, K.C.B.	do.	—	do.	Portug. Service
◎-Alex. George Woodford	do.	—	do.	Coldst. F. G.
◎ Hon. F. C. Ponsonby	do.	—	do.	12 Dr.

Extra Aides-de-Camp.

◎ Sir H.F.Bouverie, KCB.	4Jun.1814	Col.	4June 1814	Coldst. F. G.
◎ F— B— Hervey	do.	—	do.	14 Dr.
Hon. H— A— B— Craven	do.	—	do.	H.p.Independ.
Frederick, Baron Eben	do.	—	do.	Roll's Regt.
John, Lord Burghersh	do.	—	do.	Half-pay 63 F.

GENERAL

GENERAL

AND

FIELD OFFICERS

Having Local Rank.

GENERALS.

Wm. *Earl* Cathcart, *K. T.*	13Nov. 1805	Continent
✕-T.*Lord* Lynedock, *G.C.B.*	7Dec. 13	Holland & adjacent Countries

LIEUTENANT-GENERALS.

*Sir*J.Doyle, *Bt. G.C.B.&K.C.*	14Mar. 1805		Guernsey
Hon. Henry George Grey	20July	06	Cape of Good Hope
*R.Hon.*T.Maitland,*G.C.B.*	31do.		Ceylon
Sir George Prevost, *Bt.*	Jan.	08	Nova Scotia
◎*Sir* J.Stuart, *G.C.B. & K.C.* *Count of Maida*	11Feb.		Mediter. (Gibraltar excepted)
-✕Wm. Carr *Ld.*Beresford, *G.C.B.*	16Feb.	09	Portugal
◎*Sir* J.C.Sherbrooke, *G.C.B.*	12Apr.		do.
◎*Sir* William Payne, *Bt.*	do.		do.
◎*Hon. Sir*Edw.Paget,*G.C.B.*	do.		do.
10◎*Ld.*Wm.Bentinck,*GCB.*	17Aug.		do.
◎ St.*Ld.*Combermere,*GCB.*	31do.		Spain and Portugal
✕Row. *Lord* Hill, *G. C. B.*	do.		do.
Forbes Champagné	18Mar.	10	East Indies
*Hon.Sir*JAbercromby,*K.C.B.*	19do.		Bombay
◎*Sir*Sam.Auchmuty, *G.C.B.*	do.		Madras
Sir Hildebrand Oakes, *Bt.*	30Apr.		Malta
◎ *Sir* Brent Spencer, *G.C.B.*	5May		Spain and Portugal
◎*Ld.* Wm. Bentinck, *G.C.B.*	1Mar.	1	{ Mediter. (Malta,Gozo, and { Gibraltar excepted)
Frederick Maitland	do.		do.
20✕-*Sir* James Leith, *G.C.B.*	6Sept.		Spain and Portugal

✕C*Sir*

LIEUTENANT-GENERALS.

✖☾*Sir* Thomas Picton, *G.C.B.*	6Sept.	1811	Spain and Portugal
✖☾*Hon. Sir* Galbraith Lowrey Cole, *G.C. B.*	do.		do.
◎Christopher Chowne	11Nov.		do.
◎*Sir* Alex. Campbell, *Bt.*	9Mar.	12	Isles of France and Bourbon
25*Sir* Thomas Hislop, *Bt.*	28do.		Bombay
◎–G. E. *of* Dalhousie, *G.C.B*	3Sept.		Spain and Portugal
✖*Hon.Sir*W.Stewart,*G.C.B.*	do.		do.
Sir W. H. Clinton, *G. C.B*	22Dec.		do.
Count Walmoden, *K. C. B.*	21Jan.	13	Continent of Europe
30James Campbell	26do.		Ionian Islands
◎–*Sir*HenryClinton, *G.C.B.*	8Apr.		Spain and Portugal
✖–Charles William, *Lord* Stewart, *G. C. B.*	do.		Continent of Europe
Kenneth Macpherson	4June		East Indies
George Russell	do.		do.
35*Sir* Ewen Baillie, *Bt.*	do.		do.
John Macdonald	do.		do.
William Palmer	do.		do.
James Dunn	do.		do.
James Dickson	do.		do.
40John Pater	do.		do.
George Roberts	do.		do.
Urban Vigors	do.		do.
Archibald Brown	do.		do.
Robert Croker	do.		do.
45Samuel Watson	do.		do.
George Hardyman	do.		do.
Francis Torrens	do.		do.
Cary Lalande	do.		do.
James Kerr	do.		do.
50Richard Gore	do.		do.
Sir Thomas Hislop, *Bt.*	16Dec.		do.
David Campbell	4June	14	do.
John Wiseman	do.		do.
John Orr	do.		do.
55John Richardson	do.		do.
Henry Oakes	do.		do.
Elisha Trapaud	do.		do.
Daniel M'Niele	do.		do.
Thomas Marshall	do.		do.
60Charles Reynolds	do.		do.
William Kinsey	do.		do.
Thomas Bowser	do.		do.
Hugh Stafford	do.		do.
James Morris	do.		do.
65Peregrine Powell	do.		do.
Robert Phillips	do.		do.
✖☰*Sir*GeorgeMurray,*G.C.B.*	19Dec.		North America

MAJOR-

MAJOR-GENERALS.

Sir H. A. Mont. Cosby, *Kt.*	20Dec.	1793	East Indies
Charles Morgan	do.		do.
Thomas Bridges	26Feb.	95	do.
William Jones	do.		do.
5 William Popham	do.		do.
Robert Stuart	3May	96	do.
Thomas Geils	do.		do.
Gabriel Johnston	do.		do.
George Deare	do.		do.
10 James Nicol	do.		do.
George Conyngham	do.		do.
John Peché	1Jan.	98	do.
Thomas Trent	do.		do.
Robert Nicholson	do.		do.
15 Richard Tolson	do.		do.
Vere Warner Hussey	do.		do.
David Smith	18June		do.
Richard Jones	1Jan.	1801	do.
Wm. Nevil Cameron	do.		do.
20 Daniel Burr	1Jan.	05	do.
Robert Blair	25July	10	do.
Alexander Kyd	do.		do.
John Macintyre	4June	11	do.
Henry de Castro	do.		do.
25 Bennet Marley	do.		do.
Thomas Hawkshaw	do.		do.
Dyson Marshall	do.		do.
Daniel Coningham	do.		do.
John Garstin	do.		do.
30 Samuel Bradshaw	do.		do.
ⓖGeorge Wood	do.		do.
John Haynes	do.		do.
Robert Mackay	do.		do.
Hector Maclean	do.		do.
35 Andrew Anderson	do.		do.
Charles Boye	do.		do.
☒*Hon. Sir* E. M. Pakenham, *G. C. B.*	26Oct.		Spain and Portugal
☒*Sir* James Kempt, *K.C.B.*	4Nov.		do.
ⓖWilliam Borthwick	do.		do.
ⓖJ. H. C. de Bernewitz	23do.		do.
Gabriel Doveton	1Jan.	12	East Indies
Thomas Dallas	do.		do.
Alexander Cuppage	do.		do.
Aldwell Taylor	do.		do.
45 John Chalmers	do.		do.

I

John

MAJOR-GENERALS.

Alexander Dyce	1 Jan. 1812	East Indies
Keith Macalister	do.	do.
Hon. Arthur Sentleger	do.	do.
Charles Corner	do.	do.
50 John J— Durand	do.	do.
*—— Gneiseau	21 Jan. 13	Continent of Europe
Nicholas Carnegie	4 June	East Indies
John Horsford	do.	do.
John Gordon	do.	do.
55 Thomas Saunders Bateman	do.	do.
Robert Bell	do.	do.
Tredway Clarke	do.	do.
William H— Blachford	do.	do.
Malcolm Grant	do.	do.
60 John Bailie	do.	do.
William Williamson	do.	do.
John Cuppage	do.	do.
Ross Lang	do.	do.
Henry White	do.	do.
65 Gabriel Martindell	do.	do.
James M'Gregor	do.	do.
Charles Rumley	do.	do.
George S— Brown	do.	do.
Walter D— Fawcett	do.	do.
70 ◎—James Lyon	16 July	Continent of Europe
Alexander Beatson	1 Aug.	Island of St. Helena
Thomas Brown	4 June 14	East Indies
George Prole	do.	do.
Archibald Ferguson	do.	do.
75 Charles Stuart	do.	do.
John Williams	do.	do.
James Innes	do.	do.
Colin Macaulay	do.	do.
Richard Cook	do.	do.
80 George Holmes	do.	do.
William M'Cullock	do.	do.
St. George Ashe	do.	do.
David Ouchterlony	do.	do.
Henry F— Calcraft	do.	do.
85 Edward S— Broughton	do.	do.
Francis Aiskill	do.	do.
John Eales	do.	do.

BRIGADIER.

BRIGADIER.

HenryMordauntClavering 25Apr. 1807 | South America

COLONELS.

Arthur Owen	15June	1782	East Indies
John, *Duke of* Athol	24Apr.	90	Isle of Man
Sir Mark Wood, *Bt.*	16Feb.	95	East Indies
William Duncan	3May	96	do.
5 Roger Elliott Roberts	1Jan.	98	do.
Patrick Hay	do.		do.
Henry Malcolm	do.		do.
Archer A— Langley	do.		do.
Count Bentinck de Rhone	9Oct.	99	Continent of Europe
10 Arthur Disney	25July	1810	East Indies
Henry P— Lawrence	do.		do.
John Dighton	4June	13	do.
Robert Haldane	do.		do.
Thomas Munro	do.		do.
15 William Toone	do.		do.
Thomas Hawkins	do.		do.
Francis Rutledge	do.		do.
John Crow	do.		do.
Lambert Loveday	do.		do.
20 Lewis Thomas	do.		do.
Richard Mabert	do.		do.
Thomas Hardwicke	do.		do.
Thomas T— Bassett	do.		do.
William Macleod	do.		do.
25 Edward O'Reilly	do.		do.
Henry Webber	do.		do.
George Bowness	do.		do.
Jeremiah Simons	do.		do.
Samuel William Ogg	do.		do.
30 Robert Gregory	do.		do.
John Doveton	do.		do.
Philip D'Auvergne	do.		do.
Sir John Malcolm	do.		do.
John H— Symons	do.		do.
35 Nathaniel Forbes	do.		do.
Augustus Floyer	do.		do.
Richard Frith	do.		do.
James George Graham	do.		do.
George Martin	do.		do.
40 Samuel Wilson	do.		do.

I 2

Andrew

COLONELS.

Andrew Macally	4 June 1813	East Indies
Henry Grace	do.	do.
John Arnold	do.	do.
Charles Crawford	do.	do. [of Elba
45 ◉–*Sir* Neil Campbell, *Kt.*	30 Apr. 14	Continent of Europe & Island
John W— Morris	4 June	East Indies
William Atkins	do.	do.
Thomas Hayes	do.	do.
William East	do.	do.
50 Robert Hunt	do.	do.
Robert Fletcher	do.	do.
Thomas Marriott	do.	do.
Thomas Wilson	do.	do.
Richard Doveton	do.	do.
55 Patrick Walker	do.	do.
John Skelton	do.	do.
George Hanb. Pine	do.	do.
James George Scott	do.	do.
William Bedell	do.	do.
60 Alexander Hynde	do.	do.
Hamilton Hall	do.	do.
James Tetley	do.	do.
Letteles Burral	do.	do.
George Dick	do.	do.
65 Robert Munro	do.	do.
John Griffith	do.	do.
J— Cunningham	do.	do.
Mark Wilks	do.	do.
Thomas Shuldam	do.	do.
70 James Leith	do.	do.
Patrick Bruce	do.	do.
Strickland Kingston	do.	do.
Charles Trotter	do.	do.
James Plumer	do.	do.
75 Robert Barclay	do.	do.
George Fleming	do.	do.
James Urquhart	do.	do.
Frederick Pierce	do.	do.
William H— Hewett	do.	do.

LIEUTENANT-

LIEUTENANT-COLONELS.

Charles Maitland	1 Mar. 1794	East Indies
George Saxon	3 May 96	do.
John West	9 Nov.	Jersey
Robert Baillie	1 Jan. 98	East Indies
5 Richard Scott	do.	do.
James Meredith Vibert	do.	do.
William Denby	do.	do.
Robert Ogle	do.	do.
James Pearson	do.	do.
10 Thomas Welsh	do.	do.
Jabez Mackenzie	do.	do.
Patrick Douglas	do.	do.
Thomas Edwards	do.	do.
Lodovick Grant	do.	do.
15 William Flint	do.	do.
William Rattray	do.	do.
George Waight	do.	do.
Cromwell Massey	do.	do.
Thomas Hallcott	do.	do.
20 James Campbell	do.	do.
Joseph Little	do.	do.
Lewis Grant	do.	do.
Sir John Kenneway	do.	do.
Joseph Burnett	do.	do.
25 Edward Gibbings	1 Jan. 1800	do.
Robert Cameron	do.	do.
Francis William Bellis	do.	do.
George W— Mignan	do.	do.
William Home	do.	do.
30 John Macdonald	do.	do.
Jacob Tomson	do.	do.
Richard Howley	29 Apr. 02	do.
Andrew Glass	do.	do.
George Bridges	8 Dec.	Ceylon
35 ◎ Colin Mackenzie	25 Oct. 09	East Indies
George Neale	4 June 11	do.
Helier Touzel	15 Aug.	Jersey
Thomas Davey	19 Dec.	New South Wales
Francis A— Daniel	1 Jan. 12	East Indies
40 William H— D— Knox	do.	do.

William

LIEUTENANT-COLONELS.

William Henry Cooper	1Jan.	1812	East Indies
Hugh Rose	4June	13	do.
William Lewis	do.		do.
Charles Mouatt	do.		do.
45John Colebrooke	do.		do.
John Crosdell	do.		do.
Richard Willoughby	do.		do.
John Nuthall	do.		do.
Montague Cosby	do.		do.
50Samuel Dalrymple	do.		do.
William Brooks	do.		do.
George Raban	do.		do.
Anthony Adams	do.		do.
William Nicholl	do.		do.
55⊚Peter Grant	do.		do.
William Cuppage	do.		do.
Henry, *Prince* Reuss	30Dec.		Continent of Europe
Ernest Otto Tripp	27Jan.	14	do.
Charles Philip de Bossett	14Apr.		do.
60Albert Steiger	19May		do.
Daniel V— Kerins	4June		East Indies
James Parlby	do.		do.
David Lumsden	do.		do.
Paris Bradshaw	do.		do.
65F— Wilford	do.		do.
Robert Morrell	do.		do.
Bartlett Kellie	do.		do.
Donald Macleod	do.		do.
Joseph O'Halloran	do.		do.
70Robert Francis	do.		do.
D— V— Kerin	do.		do.
John Ainslie	do.		do.
George Macmorine	do.		do.
Charles Mm. Lamborne	do.		do.
75Thomas Fetherstone	do.		do.
Wm. George Maxwell	do.		do.
Atty Hennessy	do.		do.
William Rankin	do.		do.
John Leslie	do.		do.
80William Franklin	do.		do.
Elliott Voyle	do.		do.
Martin Fitz-Gerald	do.		do.
Goddard Richards	do.		do.
Martin White	do.		do.
85Frederick Trench	do.		do.
Benjamin Stewart	do.		do.
Thomas Penson	do.		do.
John J— Bird	do.		do.
Thomas Robinson	do.		do.
90Philip H— Keay	do.		do.

John

LIEUTENANT-COLONELS.

John Johnson	4 June 1814	East Indies
John Nath. Smith	do.	do.
Thomas M — Weguelin	do.	do.
James Russell	do.	do.
95 Udney Yule	do.	do.
John P— Keasberry	do.	do.
Charles Farran	do.	do.
Edward Boardman	do.	do.
Alexander Mackintosh	do.	do.
100 Frederick R. Muller	do.	do.
Wm. Henry Vaughan	do.	do.
Francis Thompson	do.	do.
Charles Mandeville	do.	do.
N— Cumberledge	do.	do.
105 Arthur Frith	do.	do.
George Wahab	do.	do.
Alexander Grant	do.	do.
Charles Lucas	do.	do.
David C— Kenny	do.	do.
110 Josiah Marshall	do.	do.
Robert Webb	do.	do.
John Taynton	do.	do.
Robert Barclay	do.	do.
John Payton	do.	do.
115 George Custance	do.	do.
Richard Podmore	do.	do.
William Cowper	do.	do.
Robert Houston	do.	do.
William Mealy	do.	do.
120 J— D— Sherwood	do.	do.
Frederick W— Gifford	do.	do.
Arthur Molesworth	do.	do.

MAJORS.

M A J O R S.

Thomas Gamble	18 Nov. 1780	America
Henry Bowen	26 Sept. 1796	Scilly Islands
Anthony Gordon	2 Mar. 97	Alderney
James Davidson	25 Apr. 1808	East Indies
5 Richard Hodgson	do.	do.
William S— Pryor	do.	do.
John Leathart	do.	do.
Richard Hay	do.	do.
John Y— Bradford	do.	do.
10 Arnold King	do.	do.
David Sloane	do.	do.
John Drummond	do.	do.
Robert Blackhall	do.	do.
Peter Littlejohn	25 July 10	do.
15 John Maclean Stewart	do.	do.
Mathew Macnamara	do.	do.
Lawrence B— Morris	do.	do.
George Fuller	do.	do.
George Mason	do.	do.
20 Robert Spottiswoode	do.	do.
Francis Drummond	do.	do.
Alexander Macleod	do.	do.
Edward William Butler	do.	do.
Gregory Hickman	do.	do.
25 ⊚Dennis H— Dalton	do.	do.
Gervaise Pennington	do.	do.
Archibald Campbell	do.	do.
Henry Jacques	do.	do.
Malcolm Macleod	do.	do.
30 Achison Maxwell	do.	do.
James Mouatt	do.	do.
Robert Stevenson	do.	do.
David Robertson	do.	do.
Jeremiah M— Johnson	do.	do.
35 John Meller	do.	do.
Sir Thomas Ramsay, Bt.	do.	do.
Robert Hetzler	do.	do.
Clement Brown	do.	do.
Horatio Greene	do.	do.
40 Albert N— Mathews	do.	do.

William

MAJORS.

William Hopper	25July 1810	East Indies
Thomas Anburey	do.	do.
Thomas Wood	do.	do.
Charles Millingchamp	1Jan. 12	do.
45William Smith	do.	do.
Adam Brown	do.	do.
John Lloyd Jones	do.	do.
David Fowlis	do.	do.
R— Fotheringham	do.	do.
50John Fortune	do.	do.
Edward Bagshaw	do.	do.
Thomas Stewart	do.	do.
Augustus Andrews	do.	do.
William Burke	4June 13	do.
55James Limond	do.	do.
Hugh O'Donnell	do.	do.
Patrick George Blair	do.	do.
⊚John Noble	do.	do.
James D— Brown	do.	do.
60Anthony Weldon	do.	do.
Robert Bentley	do.	do.
William Dickson	do.	do.
Archibald Watson	do.	do.
Henry Roome	do.	do.
65William Dick	do.	do.
John Wissett	do.	do.
Thomas Fiott de Haveland	do.	do.
Henry Rudland	do.	do.
John Cotgrave	do.	do.
70John Fotheringham	do.	do.
Anthony Monin	4June 14	do.
Brackley Kennett	do.	do.
John S— Jerdan	do.	do.
James M'Clintock	do.	do.
75Robert Taylor	do.	do.
Charles M'Leod	do.	do.
Henry Yarde	do.	do.
Mark West	do.	do.
John Nixon	do.	do.
80James Nicol	do.	do.
John Weston	do.	do.
George B— Bellassis	do.	do.
James Lighton	do.	do.
John C— Franke	do.	do.
85Watson Hunter	do.	do
George H— Fagan	do.	do.
Charles G— Butter	do.	do.
John P— Dunbar	do.	do.
Henry Mason	do.	do.
90William G— Waugh	do.	do.

K   Sydenham

MAJORS.

Sydenham Smith	4 June 1814	East Indies
R— E— Langford	do.	do.
Anselm Jones	do.	do.
E— F— Edwards	do.	do.
95 William G— Pearse	do.	do.
Charles S— Bond	do.	do.
Valentine Blacker	do.	do.
Samuel Noble	do.	do.
Charles Sealy	do.	do.
100 James Ahmuty	do.	do.
Francis Walker	do.	do.
Charles Marriott	do.	do.
Horace Durand	do.	do.
T— H— S— Conway	do.	do.
105 Hugh Griffiths	do.	do.
Andrew Aitchison	do.	do.
Major H— Court	do.	do.
Robert J— Latter	do.	do.
John Petre Keble	do.	do.
110 Robert Patton	do.	do.
Thomas Whitehead	do.	do.
William H— Perkins	do.	do.
William H— Richards	do.	do.
Jos. James Alldin	do.	do.
115 Henry Carter	do.	do.
William Lamb	do.	do.
Dun. Macpherson	do.	do.
George M— Popham	do.	do.
Edward P— Wilson	do.	do.
120 Robert Macpherson	do.	do.
William Innes	do.	do.
William P— Price	do.	do.
Hastings Dare	do.	do.
James Scott	do.	do.
125 John Lindsay	do.	do.
William Agnew	do.	do.
Edward Roughsedge	do.	do.
Michael Keating	do.	do.
William Hamilton	do.	do.
130 William Joseph Mathews	do.	do.
J— A— P— M'Gregor	do.	do.
Charles Porteous	do.	do.
Colin Campbell	do.	do.
Henry Manley	do.	do.
135 Alexander Campbell	do.	do.
Joseph Hair	do.	do.
Robert Pitman	do.	do.
M— W— Browne	do.	do.
William Richards	do.	do.
140 Henry Stark	do.	do.

William

MAJORS.

William Mitchell	4 June 1814	East Indies
Gilbert Waugh	do.	do.
Charles Addison	do.	do.
Charles R— Lester	do.	do.
145 William Clapham	do.	do.
Thomas Webster	do.	do.
John Moodie	do.	do.
William C— Oliver	do.	do.
Charles Pasley	do.	do.
150 Edward Edwards	do.	do.
Jos. T— Johnson	do.	do.
John C— Stokoe	do.	do.
Thomas H— Smith	do.	do.
Charles Saltwell	do.	do.
155 Skeffington Lutwidge	do.	do.
James Macbean	do.	do.
George L— Lambert	do.	do.
Sutherland M'Dowall	do.	do.
Charles H— Powell	do.	do.
160 John Dymock	do.	do.
⊚ Patrick V— Agnew	do.	do.
E— M— G— Showers	do.	do.
Charles Hopkinson	do.	do.
George J— Goreham	do.	do.
165 Samuel Cleaveland	do.	do.
Mungo Campbell	do.	do.
Henry W— Sealy	do.	do.
Christopher Hodgson	do.	do.
William Thomas	do.	do.
170 George F— Harriott	do.	do.
William J— Eldridge	do.	do.
William Woodhouse	do.	do.
John Woulfe	do.	do.
Stephen Nation	do.	do.
175 John Lindsay	do.	do.
S— Sinclair Hay	do.	do.
Henry H— Pepper	do.	do.
John Gibbs	do.	do.
William Gilbert	do.	do.
180 George Hare	do.	do.
William Midwinter	do:	do.
Brook B— Parlby	dc.	do.
James Henry Brooke	do.	do.
John Owen	do.	do.
185 Thomas D— Broughton	do.	do.
Henry Faithfull	do.	do.
John Gillespie	21 July	do.
Ernest de Schmiedern	20 Sept.	Continent of Europe

K 2   STAFF

STAFF

AND

MISCELLANEOUS APPOINTMENTS

Held by Commission.

ADJUTANT GENERAL TO THE FORCES.

Lieutenant General Sir Harry Calvert, *G. C. B.*, 14 *F.*

Deputy Adju- } ☺*M. Gen.* Ralph Darling, 51 *F.*
tant General }

QUARTER-MASTER GENERAL TO THE FORCES.

M. Gen. Sir James Willoughby Gordon, *K. C. B. Royal African Corps,*

Dep. Quarter } *M. Gen. J.* Brown, *Royal Staff Corps*
Master Gen. }

Assist. do. ☒ { *Lt. Col.* W— Marlay, 3 *West India Regt.*
{ *Capt. Sir* Nicholas Trant, *Kt. Royal Staff Corps.*
{ *Col. Sir* Colin Campbell, *K. C. B. Coldstream F. Gds.*
{ *Lt. Col.* John Haverfield

PERMANENT ASSISTANT QUARTER-MASTERS GENERAL

(Not holding *Regimental* Commissions.)

Lieut. Col.☺ { *Sir J—* Dickson, *K.C.B.* 1Aug.1811|
{ Chas.M—*Lord*Greenock28July1814|30Aug.1810
{ L— Augustus Northey   do.   4June1813

Major - ☺ { Henry James Riddell   4Jan.1810|Lt.Col. 4June1813
{ Peter Thomas Ryves   17May |Lt.Col. 16June1814
{ *Sir* Charles Broke,*K.C.B.*7Feb.1811|Lt.Col. 27Apr.1812
{ Philip Bainbrigge   15Oct.1812|
{ William Read   9Dec.1813|
{ Wm. Lewis Herries   28July1814| 2June1814
☺ { Robert Waller   10Nov. |Lt.Col.26Aug.1813

Waggon

Waggon Master General   *M. Gen.* Digby Hamilton
Insp. of Mil. at Jersey -   *Lt. Col.* Helier Touzel
Do. at Guernsey   -   ☒*Lt. Col. Sir* John M— Doyle,*K.C.B.*
Provost-Marshal General   John Hicks, 21 Sept. 1796
Drum-Major General -
Surgeon to the Savoy - Tho. Becket, 28 Sept. 1809 = 8 July 1795
Provost Marshal to the } Thomas Bass, 25 Feb. 1798
   Foot Guards - - - }

NORTH BRITAIN.

Dep. Adjutant General ◎*Lt.Col.Sir* G.H.B. Way, *Kt.* h.p. 22 *F.*
Dep. QuarterMasterGen. ☒*Col.Sir* W. Howe de Lancey, *K.C.B.*
Deputy Judge Advocate Gilbert Hutcheson

IRELAND.

Adjutant General - ◎*M. Gen.* Mat. *Lord* Aylmer, *K.C.B.*
Deputy do. - - - ◎*Col.* John Ross, 66 *F.*
Quarter-Master General *M. Gen.* George Airey, 8 *F.*
Deputy do. - - - - *Col.* Sam. Brown, *York Lt. Inf. Vol.*
Dep. Barrack Master Gen. *Lt. Gen.* Quin John Freeman
Provost Marshal - - - *Lieut.* Robert Speedy
Commandant of Hiber- } *Lt. Col.* Hugh Colvill
   nian School - - }

DEPOTS.

ISLE OF WIGHT.

Commandant   *Col.* John M—Mainwaring, h.p. 26 F.

Captains not holding *Regimental* Commissions			
George Jervis	19 Nov. 1803	Major	4 June 1814
David Williams	17 Dec.	Lt.Col.	4 June 1814
John Young	3 Jan. 1811	7 June 1805	
Lewis A— Denoe	24 Dec. 1812	Major	4 June 1814
Richard Rochfort	8 Apr. 1813	Major	4 June 1814

Chief Paymaster Henry Knyvett   25 Oct. 1802
Deputy Paym. John Cockburn   7 May 1803

Adjutant - - Thomas Baylis   5 Dec. 1805 | Captain 5 Dec. 1805

HARWICH.

Paymaster - William Henry Souper 10 June 1813
Adjutant - -
Assist. Surgeon J— F— Frank   23 Dec. 1813

MAID-

MAIDSTONE.

Major - - -	Robert Skeene	17Dec.1807	Lt.Col.25Mar.1813
Captain - -	Charles Wayth	25Nov.1811	
Adjutant - -	Thomas Wilkinson	22Dec.1814	Lieut. 22Dec.1814
Quarter-Master	Thomas Agar	5Oct.1809	Lieut. 25Mar.1813
Vet. Surgeon	Edward Henry Steed	15Mar.1798	

HILSEA.

Captain - -	Henry Eyre	30Aug.1810	19Feb. 1806
Adjutant - -	H.Baron,of late1R.V.B.	22Dec.1803	Lieut. 28Feb.1805

TILBURY FORT.

Commandant	John Midgley	25May1813	Lt.Col. 7Apr.1814

YORK HOSPITAL.

Comm. Gen.	Lt.Col.A.Christie,oflate12R.V.B.		*Col. 4June1814
Captain - -	A—Dalgetty	15Oct.1812	
Adjutant -	J.Watson,of late5R.V.B.11Aug.1814		Lieut. 26Sept.1811
Quarter-Master	Thomas Adey	1Dec.1814	

CHELSEA HOSPITAL.

		Per. Ann.		
		£.	s.	d.
Governor - - - - -	Gen. Sir David Dundas, G. C. B.	500	0	0
Lieut. Governor - - -	Gen. Samuel Hulse	400	0	0
Major - - - - - -	Lt. Col. Henry Le Blanc	300	0	0
Adjutant - - - - -	Capt. George Acklom	100	0	0
Physician - - - - -	Benjamin Moseley	365	0	0
Surgeon - - - - -	Thomas Keate	1000	0	0
Apothecary - - - -	Richard Robert Graham	50	0	0

ROYAL

Per Ann.

ROYAL MILITARY COLLEGE.

		£.	s.	d.
Governor - - - -	*I.Gen.Hon.Sir*A.Hope,*G.C.B.*	1500	0	0
Lieut. Governor - -	*Colonel* James Butler	1098	0	0
Chaplain, Librarian, &c.	*Rev.* William Wheeler	300	0	0
Secretary - - - -	*Capt.* John Garvock, 12 F.	300	0	0
Treasurer - - - -	George Samuel Collyer	300	0	0
Paymaster - - - -	*Capt.* Charles Stone	300	0	0
Surgeon - - - -	Ninian Bruce	274	10	0
Assistant Surgeon - -	John Pickering	187	5	0
Quarter-Master - - -	Alexander Calder	183	0	0

Senior Department.

Inspector Gen. of Instructions and Commandant }	*Colonel Sir* H. Douglas, *Bt.*	549	0	0

Junior Department.

Major - - - - -	*Lt. Col.* James M'Dermott -	352	5	6
Captains of Companies of Gentlemen Cadets {	Charles Wright	274	10	0
	David Erskine	274	10	0
	John Otto	274	10	0
	*Thomas Abraham	274	10	0

ROYAL MILITARY ASYLUM.

Commandant - - -	*Lt. Col.* James Williamson	365	0	0
Secretary and Adjutant -	*Capt.* John Lugard	182	10	0
Quarter-Master & Steward	Joseph Hill	180	0	0
Surgeon - - - -	Peter Macgregor	273	15	0

RECRUITING DISTRICTS.

Paymaster - {	Thomas Money	25 Dec. 1797
	Wm. Geo. Daniel Tyssen	do.
	A— P— Skeene	do.
	William Rawstorn Russell	do.
	F— Bowes	16 Apr. 1801
	John Flynn	17 Nov. 1802
	William H— Phillips	26 Apr. 1803
	James Fisher	23 July
	James Innes	25 Dec.

Paymaster

Staff and Miscellaneous Appointments
held by Commission.

Paymasters -	{ Sir W.Vachel, *Kt.* (*Irel.*) 27 July 1804	
	H— E— M'Neill (*do.*) 20 Mar. 1806	
	H— J— Reynett (*do.*) 23 Aug.	
	William Jones 9 Aug. 1809	
	James N— Frood (*Irel.*) 12 Jan. 1810	
	Francis Wemyss (*do.*) 25 May 1811	
	John Hall 2 Oct. 1812	

Adjutants with the rank of Lieutenant	George Moss 21 May 1796	
	William Deans 25 Dec.	
	James Roy 4 Apr. 97	
	Thomas Shields (*Irel.*) 28 July 1803	3 Aug. 1801
	Peter M'Craw 7 Jan. 1804	
	Thomas Hill (*Ireland*) 8 Jan. 1805	
	George Gregory 25 Feb. 1806	
	John Gourlay 31 Oct. 1808	3 Oct. 1805
	Thomas Hassell (*Irel.*) 11 July 1809	26 Dec. 1795
	John Maguire (*do.*) 4 Aug.	9 Oct. 1806
	James Ross 9 Sept.	
	C— T— Gladwin (*Irel.*) 28 do.	
	James Brewer 24 Jan. 1811	31 Jan. 1807
	Valentine Munbee 28 Feb.	
	R— F— Raynes 22 Aug.	
	Richard Fletcher 4 Mar. 1813	7 Mar. 1811
	Thomas Agar 25 do.	
	Henry Bertles 3 June	
	William A— Blakeney 11 Nov.	

DETACHMENTS.

Paymaster - Thomas Le Breton 2 Oct. 1813

SICILY.

Commander of the Forces	Ⓜ *Lt.Gen.* Ld.Wm. Bentinck, *G.C.B.*
Adjutant General - - -	*Lt.Col.* Cha.Ashe A'Court, 1 Gk.Lt.I.
Deputy do. - - - - -	*Lt. Col.* Thomas Kenah, 58 F.
Quarter-Master General -	
Deputy do. - - - - -	*Colonel* John Pine Coffin
Fort Adjut. of Messina -	Peter Gordon
Town Adjut. of do. - -	James Worsley

IONIAN

IONIAN ISLANDS.

Deputy Adjutant General   *Major* John Jordan, 27 F.
Deputy Quarter-Mast. Gen. *Major* Thomas Drake, 95 F.

GIBRALTAR.

Assist. Barrack Master Gen. *Lt. Col.* Morris Robinson
Barrack Masters - - - { William Goddard
                              { Richard Hockings

MALTA.

Deputy Adjutant General   *Colonel* Paul Anderson, 60 F.
Dep. Quarter-Master Gen.   *Lt. Col.* George Edward Raitt, 2 F.
Assistant Barrack Masters { John Booth
                              { Philip Montanaro

WEST INDIES.

Commander of the Forces   *Lt.Gen. Sir* James Leith, *G. C. B.*
Adjutant General - - - *M. Gen.* Robert Douglass
Deputy do. - - - - - *Lt. Col.* S— Berkeley, 16 F.
Quarter-Master General - *M. Gen.* Lachlan M'Lean
Deputy do. - - - - - *Lt. Col.* S— T— Popham, 24 F.
Deputy Judge Advocate - Matthew Coulthurst

JAMAICA.

Commander of the Forces   *Lt. Gen.* Francis Fuller
Deputy Adjutant General   *Lt. Col.* Thomas Steele, Coldst. Gds.
Dep. Quarter-Master Gen. *Colonel* Allan Hampden Pye

BAHAMAS.

Barrack Master - - - James Taitt

L

NORTH AMERICA.

Commander of the Forces   *Lt. Gen. Sir* George Prevost, *Bt.*
Adjutant General - - -   *M. Gen.* Baynes, Glengarry Lt. In. F.
Quarter-Master General   ☉ *M.Gen.Sir* T.S.Beckwith, *K.C.B.* 95F.

CANADA.

Deputy Adjutant General   *Lt. Col.* John Harvey, 103 F.
Dep. Quarter-Master Gen.   *Colonel* Myers, 100 F.
Dep. Barrack Master Gen.   Philip Van Cortlandt

INSPECTING FIELD OFFICERS OF MILITIA

(Not holding *Regimental* Commissions.)

	Thomas Bligh St.George	22Dec.1808	Col.	4June1813
	John Murray	18July1811	Col.	4June1813
Lieut. Col. ☉	Thomas Pearson	28Feb.1812	30May 1811	
	George Taylor	4June1813		
	Christopher Hamilton	17Feb.1814	1Jan. 1812	
	George Macdonnell	24do.		

NOVA SCOTIA.

Deputy Adjutant General   *Lt. Col.* Andrew Pilkington
Dep. Quarter-Master Gen.   *Major* Ligertwood, 60 F.
Dep. Barrack Master Gen.   George Francis Lynn
Barrack Master - - -   Samuel F— Monk
Dep. Judge Advocate - -   Edw. Brab. Brenton

INSPECTING FIELD OFFICERS OF MILITIA

(Not holding *Regimental* Commissions.)

	Dennis Herbert	28Jan.1808	Col.	4June1814
Lieut. Colonel	Joseph Gubbins	16Nov.1809	Col.	4June1814
	Hercules Renny	1Jan.1812		
☉	H. C. E.Vernon Graham	4June1813		

NEW BRUNSWICK.

Ass. Dep. Barr. Mast. Gen.   Andrew Rainsford

ST. JOHN'S, NEWFOUNDLAND.

Barrack Master -   ▪ Charles Andrews

CAPE

CAPE OF GOOD HOPE.

Commander of the Forces	*Gen. Lord* Charles Henry Somerset
Deputy Adjutant General	*Major* Matthew G. Blake, *Cape Reg.*
Dep. Quarter-Master Gen.	*Lt. Col.* William Warre, 23 *Dr.*
Dep. Barrack Master Gen.	George Hamson Denniss

SPAIN AND PORTUGAL.

(Not holding *Regimental* Commissions.)

Lieut. Colonel	✖	*Sir* A. Campbell, *K.C.B.*	16Feb.1809	Col.	4June1814
		William Cox	do.		
	◎	Charles Ashworth	18Jan.1810		
	✖	*Sir* J. Douglas, *K.C.B.*	16Feb.1809	Lt.Col.	30May1811
	◎-	John Waters	do.	———	do.
	◎	William M'Bean	do.	———	do.
		John Campbell	do.	———	3Oct.
		William Parker Carrol	13Apr.	———	30May
		Philip Keating Roche	do.	———	do.
	◎	*Sir* George Elder, *Kt.*	do.	———	do.
	◎	Michael M'Creagh	27do.	———	3Oct.
	◎	Henry Pynn	15Nov.	Lt.Col.	4June1814
	◎	Henry Watson	18Jan.1810	Lt.Col.	28July1814
Major	◎	S— Ford Whittingham	12Mar.	Col.	4June1814
		Richard Armstrong	30May1811	Lt.Col.	26Aug.1813
		Donald M'Niell	25July	Lt.Col.	26Dec.1813
	◎	Robert John Harvey	do.	Lt.Col.	21June1813
		John Prior	25Feb.1813		
		Ralph Ouseley	25Nov.		
	◎-	John Rolt	do.		
		Richard Carroll	2June1814		
		T— W— Hewitt	do.		
		Thomas St. Clair	do.		
		G— W— Paty	do.		
	◎-	George H— Zulke	do.		
		Joshua W— Green	do.		

NORTH OF GERMANY.

Dep. Quarter Master Gen.   *Lt. Col.* J— H— Reynett, 52 F.

HOLLAND.

Commander of the Forces { *Gen. His Royal Highness* Wm. Fred. Henry, *the Hereditary Prince of* Orange, *G. C. B.*
Deputy Adjutant General   *L.Col. Sir* G.H.F.Berkeley,*KCB*.35 F.
Dep.Quarter-MasterGen.   *Lt.Col.* Robert Torrens, 1 W. I. Regt.

EAST INDIES.

Commander in Chief -   *Gen.* Francis, *Earl of* Moira, K.G.
Adjutant General - -   *Col.* Thomas M‘Mahon, 17 F.
Deputy do. - - - -   *Lt.Col.* John Johnson, 86 F.
Quarter-Master General *Col.* Jasper Nicholls, 14 F.
Deputy do. - - - -   *Lt.Col.* E. J. M‘Gregor Murray, 8 *Dr.*
Comm.of Must.atMadras   Richard Yeldham
Dep. Comm. of Musters   William Macleod

ISLE OF FRANCE.

Commander of the Forces *Lt. Gen. Sir* Alexander Campbell, *Bt.*
Deputy AdjutantGeneral   *Lt.Col.* Effingham Lindsay, 22 F.
Dep.Quarter-MasterGen.   *Lt. Col.* Alex. Nesbitt
Insp. of Colonial Troops in Bourbon, Mauritius, and Java - - - - } *Major* William Carroll, 69 F.
Military Auditor in Mauritius - - - - - } *Lieut.* G. F. Dick, 1 *Ceylon Regt.*

CEYLON.

Commander of the Forces *Lt.Gen. Sir* Robert Brownrigg,*G.C.B.*
Deputy Adjutant General   *Major* Robert Brownrigg, 52 F.
Dep.Quarter-MasterGen.   *Major* Wm. Willermin, 2 *Ceylon R.*
Dep. Inspector Gen. of Colonial Troops - - } *Lt. Col.* Frederick Hankey
AuditorGen.of Accompts *Lt. Col.* Pereg. Fra. **Thorne**

COMMISSARIAT DEPARTMENT.

COMMISSARY IN CHIEF.

(Ireland and the East Indies alone excepted.)

John Charles Herries   1October 1811

PRINCIPAL DEPUTY COMMISSARY GENERAL.

Leonard Becher Morse   5January 1809

COMMISSARIES GENERAL.

William Henry Robinson 1May1805
SirGeorgeBurgman,*Kt.* 27Nov.
Gabriel Wood   8July1806
Joseph Bullock   1Mar.1807
James Drummond   25Aug.1808
John Murray   2Nov.
Sir R. H. Kennedy, *Kt.*   3do.
John Bisset   31July1811
Sir Cha. Dalrymple, *Kt.* 29Jan.1812
James Pipon   10Dec.1814
Augustus Granet   25do.
Thomas Dunmore   do.

DEPUTY COMMISSARIES GENERAL.

Leonard Becher Morse 25Apr.1793
Isaac Low   25May 97
John Butler Butler   19July 99
Wm. Jesser Coope   2Aug.1801
John Freeman   3do.
Charles Wright   24Dec.1802
Gilbert Young   1Mar.1805
Alexander Fernandes   21do.
Edward Couche   12Aug.1806
Lawrence Donavan   19Sept.
Richard Manby   13Oct.
Francis Daniell   2Feb.1807

James Dickens   17Mar.1807
Peter Turquand   20do.
Thomas Wethered   21do.
James Toole   19Apr.1808
Henry Cocksedge   13July
Charles Lutyens   26June1809
John Vaux   2Sept.
John Drake   2Apr.1810
I— Humphreys   do.
George Miles   8Sept.
William Thomson   5Oct.
Charles Aylmer   21Jan.1811
Robert Hill   11July
Richard John Anderson 16Aug.
William Dowler   do.
Thomas Dumaresq   18Dec.
William Gauntlett   18Mar.1812
Augustus Schmidchen   27July
William Grieve   3Feb.1813
Charles Pratt   do.
Jos. Hollingworth Adams 4May
Daniel Allan   13June
George Damerum   23do.
T— P— Luscombe   13July
Alexander Wm. Young 28Sept.
Joseph F— Verbeke   15Nov.
William Jackson   10Dec.
John M'Kenzie   18Mar.1814
  Frederick

Frederick Drennan	23Apr.1814	P— D— Arentz	25May1813
Alexander Murray	1July	William Heydinger	do.
Isaac W— Clarke	3Aug.	Augustus Kuper	28Nov.
Edward Pine Coffin	4do.	Edward Cooke Robinson	26Jan.1813
William Lukin	2Sept.	William Mackay	23Feb.
Fred. *Baron* de Diemar	25Dec.	George Ainslie	29Mar.
A— Majoribanks	do.	William Swainson	do.
William Poppleton	do.	Thomas Bennett	11May
John F— Hagenau	do.	James Coffin	do.
Christopher Rodwell	do.	William Booth	27Aug.
Edward Dillon	do.	James Woodhouse	1Oct.
Richard Edwards	do.	Jacob Samuel Eschauzier	do.
John Glynn	do.	AlphonsoFrancisMatthey	9Nov.
Samuel Hopkins	do.	Robert Gilmour	10Jan.1814
Buchan Fraser Telfer	do.	Ralph Rogerson	31Mar.
William Wemyss	do.	William Hewetson	do.
C— W— Sidney	do.	James B— Franklin	do.
		John Cobbe	2May

ASSIST. COMMISSARIES GENERAL.

		John Spurrier	1July
Const. John Palmer	4Feb.1806	James Laidley	do.
David Elliott	25Sept.	J— S— Dobree	do.
William Brown	29do.	Thomas Price	do.
Frederick Corbin	1Feb.1807	George Crookshank	3Aug.
Joseph H— Vaux	18Mar.	Thomas Osborne	do.
Edward Dance	23do.	Christopher Pecco	26do.
William Lamont	24do.	George Moore	25Sept.
Byham Redhead	7Sept.	John Lawrence	1Nov.
Stewart Abernethy	21Nov.	John Coffin	do.
John M'Clellan	16Jan.1808	G— W— Wilgress	do.
Alexander Somerville	15Feb.	Richard Stonier Gomm	do.
G— C— Turney	31Aug.	M— Rossiter	do.
George White	24Feb.1810	William Cumming	25Dec,
Per. Bourdieu	do.	W— H— Snelling	do.
William Beech	do.	Donald Macleod	do.
Benj. T— Gaskin	do.	John Lane	do.
Richard Barney	do.	George Head	do.
David Carruthers	do.	P— R— Wybault	do.
C— I— Forbes	do.		
G. S. N. HodgesNugent	10Aug.1811	DEPUTY ASSISTANT COMMISSARIES GENERAL.	
William Filder	do.		
Tupper Carey	do.	John Finlay	23May1810
John Forbes	do.	Charles Bonomi	7Aug.
Fra. William Haden	do.	William Telfair	19Nov.
Alexander Strachan	do.	Edward Wood	20do.
Peter C— L— de St. Remy	do.	James Buhot	do.
John W— Wilkinson	do.	John Bruce	do.
Charles Purcell	do.	Patrick Davidson	do.
William Lane	29Apr.1812	Thomas White	do.
John Beckwith	do.	A— Fraser	do.
Thomas Forth Winter	do.	John Lewis	do.

Robert

Robert Duport	20Nov.1810	Patrick Calder	2Jan.1813
William Shakespear	do.	Charles Ragueneau	do.
Joshua Brook	22do.	George Lefebvre	9do.
David Gardiner	4Feb.1811	Alex. Young Spearman	12do.
W— H— Priestley	5July	John Rendall	21do.
Walter Porteous	27do.	Charles Hopkins	do.
William Miller	5Aug.	John Cleaveland Green	27do.
Thomas Clarke	10do.	George Yeoland	3Feb.
William Auther	do.	G— T— W— B— Boyes	do.
Thomas Lefevre	do.	J— J— Schmitter	do.
Henry Lasius	do.	W— Armstrong	do:
William Laidley	do.	T— L— Skelton	do.
John Laurie	do.	W— C— Richardson	do.
George Manville	16do.	Fra. Leon. Chiaranda	do.
Benjamin Watson	29do.	William Duke	do.
Adolphus Vieth	13Dec.	Henry Curll	do.
John Laidley	11Jan.1812	William Green	16Mar.
William Jennings	2Mar.	Robert Cotes	22do.
William Hayward	do.	William de Reden	15Apr.
John Wood	do.	William Barron	do.
J— P— Houston	10do.	William A—Thompson	11May
William Wetherman	12do.	Robert Reynolds	do.
William Furmidge	30do.	Thomas A— Stayner	do.
Robert Ward	29Apr.	William Smith Lukin	24do.
Edward Holland	do.	Charles Gunning	do.
Fra. William Major	do.	Thomas Lane	23June
John J. Augustus Boocock	do.	William Thomson	28do.
Francis Edward Knowles	5May	J— M— Simpson	13July
Lovell Pennell	23do.	Charles Blackader	29do.
P— Gould Hogan	25do.	John Damant	19Aug.
Vincent Vella	do.	William Stanton	4Sept.
R— F— Poussett	do.	Michael Bailey	do.
William Pemberton	do.	J— Woolrabe	do.
J— B— Knight	do.	John Finlay	do.
Henry Basnett	do.	John S— Jesse	16do.
William Winter	do.	George Ackroyd	do.
Henry Hendy	do.	Alexander Trotter	27Oct.
John Tench	do.	Thomas Tringham Smith	9Nov.
John K— Macbreedy	do.	Thomas Wharton Ramsay	25do.
Francis Hall	do.	John Davidson	do.
William Lithgow	24July	John Leggatt	do.
James Thomson	2Nov.	J— A— Toole	16Dec.
Robert Allsop	do.	Edward Stuart Baynes	do.
Samuel D— Fleming	do.	Edward Byndloss	31do.
William Henry Robinson	do.	Lionel Davis	4Jan.1814
Taunatt H— Thomson	8Dec.	William Bailey	10do.
Samuel Cumming	11do.	David Cairns	15do.
Thomas Hill	do.	Thomas Nugent	do.
Charles A— Clarke	15do.	George Hull	do.
Thomas Bissett	18do.	Affleck Moodie	do.

Ernest

Ernest Eyl	15Jan.1814		Charles Thornton	13July1814
John Appleton	do.		Alexander Macgregor	do.
Peter Davies	do.		Robert Lindsey	do.
William Downs	31do.		Henry Bourhill	3Aug.
John Lane, jun.	do.		Gilbert Dinwiddie	5Sept.
Robert Grindlay	11Feb.		William Plant	do.
Arthur Burrows	18do.		Samuel M'Douall	do.
George Swinney	23do.		Beverley Robinson	do.
John Phipps Hood	5Mar.		Charles Graham	do.
David Scott K. Maclaurin	7do.		John Irvine	9do.
George Withers	11do.		Francis Thomas Billings	do.
Thomas Wetherall	24do.		Henry C— Darling	12do.
William Ragland	31do.		John David Anderson	11Oct.
John William Prentice	do.		John David	do.
Samuel Beltz	do.		William Ross	3Nov.
Eber. F. Wm. Steinkopff	4Apr.		Oliver Goldsmith	17Dec.
William Broughton	15do.		William Low	do.
Woodbine Parish	30do.		Robert Lee	25do.
William W— Yeates	do.		John Freeborn	do.
Francis Robert Foote	do.		Louis Donatti	do.
James Thompson	2May		Alexander Grant	do.
Alexander Brander	do.		Allen Jackson Nightingale	do.
Thomas Howie	do.		Joseph Verfenstein	do.
William Braybrooke	do.		James Horne	do.
George Hayward	do.		George Stevens	do.
W. B. Moore	4do.		James Anderson	do.
Andrew Chalmers	do.		B— R— Curran	do.
William Bowman	do.		Henry Addington Bayley	do.
Henry Nibbs Browne	do.		Edward Pitman	do.
James Slade	do.		James Mason	do.
Thomas James Powell	do.		William Stevens	do.
Henry Le Mesurier	do.		John Edye	do.
George H— Monk	13do.		David Bowman	do.
W— J— Greig	do.		Thomas Scobell	do.
Thomas Arnold	do.		Daniel Hardy	do.
Thomas Ridout	do.		William Hall	do.
John Ashworth	31do.		J— George Eyl	do.
James Phillips	do.		Nathan Jackson	do.
Sir John Murray, Bt.	17June		John Banner Price	do.
John Jarvis	1July		Thomas Harvey	do.
James Bishop	do.		John Cooper	do.
James Hughes	8do.		Thomas Bell	do.
Bazil Bodan	do.		Robert Johnstone	do.
John Sarmon	12do.		Thomas Rae	do.
Thomas Sedgwick	do.		Samuel Petrie	do.
George Fisher	do.		Ernest A— Hoffay	do.
George Pierce	13do.		A— C— Harris	do.
Israel Armstrong	do.		Henry Bowers	do.
David Burnett	do.		Thomas Thornton	do.
John Lindsay	do.		John James Simpson	do.

Thomas

Thomas Bunnett	25Dec.1814	Henry Thynne	25Dec.1814
Augustus G— Faxardo	do.	Colin Miller	do.
George Young	do.	Thomas Hemington	do.
William Henry Louis	do.	James Wilson	do.
Charles Williams	do.	Francis Moseley Richardson	do.
Augustus Wathen	do.	Samuel Harrison	do.
Joseph Charlier	do.	Charles Tidmarsh	do.
John Jennings	do.	Charles S— Meredith	do.
Charles Hambly	do.	Alexander Macrae	7Jan.1815

Commissariat Department of Ireland.

COMMISSARY GENERAL.

Colonel Charles Handfield   2Jan.1798

DEPUTY COMMISSARY GENERAL.

Pau. Æm. Singer   25Mar.1803

ACTING COMMISSARY GENERAL.

William Webb

ASSISTANT COMMISSARIES.

James Goldrisk	25June1802
William Henderson	25Mar.1803
William Hannagan	do.
Thomas Gelston	25June
William Maturin	25Sept.
William Dillon	19Mar.1807
John Grant	
Conway Heatly	
Nich. Mallassez	

ACTING COMMISSARY.

Andrew Gallagher

MEDICAL DEPARTMENT.

DIRECTOR GENERAL.

John Weir   24February1810

PRINCIPAL INSPECTORS.

Charles Ker, *M. D.*   24February1810
William Franklin, *M. D.*   12July

INSPECTORS.

Robert Jackson, *M. D.*   28Apr.1795
LewisVersturme, *M.D.* 25Nov.
John Wright, *M. D.*   16Jan.1800
James Borland, *M. D.*   22Jan.1807
William Ferguson   18Feb.1813
James Robert Grant   14July1814
Francis Burrowes   25Oct.

Local Rank.

W.W.Fraser(*Gibraltar*)29Dec.1814

DEPUTY INSPECTORS.

William Hussey, *M. D.* 17Dec.1803
Abraham Bolton   1Nov.1804
William Somerville   25Mar.1805
John Warren   22Aug.
Robert Grieves, *M. D.* 18Sept.1806
JamesMuttlebury,*M.D.*23Aug.1807
W — A — Burke, *M.D.*   do.
Adair Blackwell   27Oct.1808
Edward Tegart   25May1809
Thomas Gunning   11July1811
John Robb   28May1812

John Gunning   17Sept.1812
Summers Higgins   12Nov.
Ebenezer Brown   25Dec.
Thomas Forbes   21Jan.1813
Donald M'Neil   do.
Thomas Thomson   do.
Edward Porteus   13May
James Macaulay   29July
George F— Albert   4Nov.
Andrew High   21Dec.
Stephen Woolriche   26May1814
John R— Hume   do.

Local Rank.

Benj. Bloomfield, *M.D.* 19Nov.1812

PHYSICIANS.

Edmond Somers, *M.D.* 18Mar.1795
Wm. Lempriere, *M.D.* 25June1805
Joseph Skey, *M.D.*   18July
Wm.H.Moseley, *M.D.* 28Nov.
Robert Calvert, *M.D.* 22Oct.1807
Thomas Hume, *M.D.* 16June1808
Jas. M'Dougall, *M.D.* 25Aug.

John

John M'Mullen, *M.D.*	19Oct.1808	George W— Cockell	29June1809
J. D. C. L'Affan, *M.D.*	13June1811	John Glasco	do.
Charles Farrell, *M.D.*	1Aug.	Ninian Bruce, *Mil. Coll.*	20July
John Erley, *M.D.*	3Sept.1812	Quinten M'Millan	do.
Thomas Walker, *M.D.*	18Feb.1813	James Strachan	do.
John Dwyer, *M.D.*	do.	John Pooler	17Aug.
AlexanderMenzies, *M.D.*	25do.	John Q— Short	do.
Edward Keating, *M.D.*	25Mar.	J— A— Bruff	do.
George Denecke, *M.D.*	17June	Cha. Mapother	do.
John Mackenzie, *M.D.*	15do.	WilliamWallace, *Rec. Dist.*	do.
William Robson, *M.D.*	30Sept.	William Storey	12Oct.
James Wright, *M.D.*	26May1814	John Walker	24Jan.1811
Edward O'Leary, *M.D.*	do.	Henry Grasset	31do.
		Andrew White	23May
		John Kidstone	4July
SURGEONS.		George Power	11do.
		Thomas Duncan	8Aug.
James Roy, *(Fort Geo. Inv.)*	1788	James Sharpe	26Sept.
Charles Griffiths	9Apr. 94	Jordan Roche	6Feb.1812
Dickens Buckle	30July	Alexander Boyle	19Mar.
John Shean	16Sept. 95	Edward O'Reilly	26do.
James William Dunkin	18July 96	John Howell	16Apr.
George Henckel	11Oct.	John Wasdell	28May
Alexander Lawrie	1Mar. 97	John Aug. Knipe	do.
William Richard Morell	4Sept. 99	William Hill	3Sept.
Francis Downing	4Apr.1800	Alexander Baxter	do.
Ely Crump	do.	John Cole	do.
Geo. Robertson Baillie	28Mar.1801	John Maling	do.
John Saumarez	15Oct.1802	William Stewart	10do.
John Cossins	27Aug.1803	William Harper	15Oct.
Thomas Kidd	do.	Christopher Widmer	5Nov.
Stephen Panting	25May1804	John V— Thompson	25Dec.
Joseph Thomas	2June	John White	do.
Nodes Dickenson	19July	William Henderson	14Jan.1813
Joseph Tholon	4June1807	Robert Hartle	28do.
David Brownrigg	18do.	Charles Groskopf	4Feb.
Jonathan Cotgrave	15Oct.	Henry Robertson	25do.
John Taylor	4Feb.1808	Jacob Bath	do.
Charles Jordan	3Mar.	John Leath	15Apr.
John Preston	10do.	Andrew Halliday	29do.
George E— Griffin	23June	Charles Tucker	13May
Wm. Henry Lys	14July	William H— Blicke	do.
Hen. G. Emery, *M.D.*	11Aug.	James Safe	20do.
Thomas Draper	1Sept.	Alexander Thom	29July
John Burnall	8June1809	Donald M'Leod	9Sept.
Robert Brown	do.	Colin Dakers	do.
Thomas Inglis	do.	William Caldwell	do.
John Rice	do.	Theodore Gordon	do.
William Adams	15do.	Henry Forcade	do.
Jacob Adolphus	29do.	John Murray	do.
William Gordon	do.		

M—N 2   Thomas

Thomas O'Maley	23Sept.1813	B— Nicholson	29Apr.1813
James Elliot	14Oct.	Romaine Amiel	3June
Henry Marshall	21Dec.	J— R— Savery	10do.
William Hackett	6Jan.1814	H— V— Haskins	17do.
Edward Dow	17Mar.	James Weir	9Sept.
Michael Mabey	12May	George Gregory	25Nov.
Samuel Cooper	26do.	Wm.Williams(*Gibraltar*)26do.	
Henry Dun	do.	John Ramsay	30Dec.
Cornelius Ryan	do.	William Twining	10Mar.1814
John Williams	do.	T— Soden	do.
William Randall	do.	R— C— Hall	do.
Frederick Loinsworth	7July	Thomas Rolston	5May
Robert Kerr	do.	Thomas M'Whirter	26do.
William Cowdery	28do.		
George Morse	25Oct.	PURVEYORS.	
John Clarke	do.		
William Wynn	do.	James White	23Nov.1796
		Richard Moss	13Nov.1800
Local Rank.		William Cathcart	25May1804
		Robert Stewart	22Aug.1805
W— C— Bach	29Apr.1813	William Usher	2June1814
R— H— Bolton	7Oct.		
P— White	do.	DEPUTY PURVEYORS.	
George Lardner	10do.		
		Thomas Cooke	25May1804
		Charles Clark	23Nov.
SURGEONS OF RECRUITING		Richard Pinckard	21Mar.1805
DISTRICTS.		Charles Bradford	12Sept.
		John Moore	5Dec.
J— H— Beaumont	26Sept.1795	Richard Cleave	29June1809
Robert Freer	6Apr.1803	David Parker Sheppard	28Sept.
Wm. Wallace (*Ireland*)	21Apr.1804	Henry J— Bonnin	do.
(*Forces*)	17Aug.1809	John White	11July1811
J—H—Radford(*Ireland*)	9Apr.1807	Jonathan Croft	16Apr.1812
Robert Waugh	15Oct.	George Winter	15Oct.
Francis Coull	4Feb.1808	Charles Soare	do.
James Brady	3Mar.	George Keys	25Mar.1813
Joseph Deakin (*Ireland*)	24Jan.1809	J— Browning	5Aug.
W. P. Drumgole (*do.*)	11May	J— Raymond	19do.
Christopher Codrington	30Nov.	Lachlan Macpherson	do.
John Simson	24Feb.1810	Henry Y— Everett	26May1814
Thomas Brown	17Nov.1814	John Moore	25Sept.
Forces	10Feb.1814	James Edghill	6Oct.

ASSISTANT SURGEONS.

		APOTHECARIES.	
Robert Harris	28Aug.1801		
Christopher Bette	5Apr.1810	Philip Hoffe	21Apr.1804
Edward Doughty	5Nov.1812	John Lewis	8Sept.1807
W— H— Booty	12do.	Edmund Starkie	8Oct.
William Sibbald	11Feb.1813	Samuel Leeson	17Mar.1808
James Dease	11Mar.	Richard Matthews	6Apr.1809
			John

John Brown	31Aug.1809	W— T— Gylby	15Apr.1813
Jonathan Courtney	do.	WilliamRobertBurrowes	13May
John Graham	do.	James Powell	8July
Sam. Barnwell Bruce	5Apr.1810	George Hume Reade	9Sept.
William Wheadon	18Oct.	Joseph Schembri	14Oct.
William Tiffin Iliff	31Oct.1811	Andrew Huggan	25Nov.
George Montgomery	do.	*Local Rank.*	
Richard Morris	3Sept.1812		
John Carter	11Mar.1813	J— Cooke	10Oct.1813

Medical Department of Ireland.

PHYSICIANS GENERAL.

C— W— Quin, *M. D.*
William Harvey, *M. D.*

SURGEON GENERAL.

P— Crampton

DIRECTOR GENERAL.

G— Renny, *M. D.*

DEPUTY INSPECTORS.

R— M— Peile
James Pitcairne
William Comins
H— Bigger, *M. D.*

SURGEONS.

Alexander Graydon
Edward Eagle, *M. D.*
Samuel Banks
Joseph Stringer
Henry Purdon
T— L— Whistler, *M. D.*
P— V— Crofton
James Rodgers
P— Ormsby
Tho. Brown, *Rec. Dist.* 10Feb.1814

DEPUTY PURVEYOR.

Hugh Power

APOTHECARIES.

Edward O'Brien
John Halloran

CHAPLAINS.

CHAPLAINS.

CHAPLAIN GENERAL.

Reverend Archdeacon John Owen   8Mar.1810

CHAPLAINS TO THE FORCES.

Rev. Samuel Briscall	25Dec.1809	
—— James Scott	do.	
—— Wm. Granger Cautley	do.	
—— John Hughes	do.	
—— Jos. Goodall Corsellis	do.	
—— John Heyward	21Feb.1810	
—— W— W— Dakins	16Mar.	
—— George Jenkins	5Apr.	
—— Samuel Hill	20Sept.	
—— M. A. Mackereth	25Dec.	
—— John Metcalfe	4Mar.1811	
—— Edw. Cockayne Frith	4May	
—— Horace Parker	10do.	
—— Samuel Leggatt	31July	
—— Charles Dayman	18Oct.	
—— George Winnock	11Nov.	
—— Robert Edw. Jones	29do.	
—— Matthew Arnold	23Jan.1812	
—— Thomas Ireland	28Mar.	
—— J. T. H. Le Mesurier	16Apr.	
—— John Cracroft	23May	
—— W. Cockayne Frith	25June	
—— Rowl.Grove Curtois	11Sept.	
—— Jos. Langley Mills	12Oct.	
—— Thomas Norris	14do.	
—— John Cha. Moore	23Dec.	
—— Rob. Wm. Tunney	13Mar.1813	
—— OrfeurWm.Kilvington	8Apr.	
—— Henry John Symons	12May	
—— J— Shortt Hewitt	10Aug.	
—— George Hunt	25do.	
—— Maurice James	25Nov.	
—— George Watson	1Apr.1814	
—— Geo.Griffin Stonestreet	4do.	

BARRACK

BARRACK DEPARTMENT.

INSPECTORS GENERAL.

Frederick E. B.	*London*
Macpherson C. *Capt.*	*Edinburgh*

ASSISTANT INSPECTORS GENERAL.

Archdall R.	*Plymouth*
Barberie O.	*Lewes*
Baddeley J. *Capt.*	*Colchester*
Grant J. M. *Major*	*York*
Brace Jas. *Major*	*Canterbury*
Nairne Wm. *Capt.*	*Edinburgh*
Mackenzie Geo.	*London*
Milbanke, J.P. *Capt.*	*Nottingham*
Torriano Geo. *Capt.*	*Portsmouth*
Hope J—	*London*
Teesdale H—	*Guernsey*

BARRACK MASTERS.

Adams Samuel	*Berryhead*
Alexander J.	*Dunbarton*
Austin John	*Scilly*
Bartlett T.	*Wareham*
Basleigh S. F.	*Barnstaple*
Bayntun, C. *Capt.*	*Brighton*
Beever J.	*Hull*
Berdmore Thomas	*Winchester*
Bowater W. *Major*	
Baybrooke W.	*Ramsgate*
Brown J.	*Hamilton*
Buchanan Arthur	*Fort William*
Buncombe J.	*Taunton*
Bygrave G. A.	*Parkhurst*
Caldwell J.	*Chelmsford*
Carrington W. H.	*Harwich*
Chaundy J. A. *Capt.*	*Nottingham*
Child W. G.	*Colchester*

Cleather George	*Dartmoor*
Clover J.	*Norwich*
Collier R.	*Glasgow*
Conolly W.	*Birmingham*
Cooke Robert	*Out Posts, I. of Wight*
Corben William	*Guernsey*
Covell J.	*Hythe*
Cowell J. C.	*Southampton*
Dewell T. *Lt.*	*Haslar & Fort Monckton*
Dickson, J. *Lt. G.*	*Sunderland*
Downe J. G.	*Bridport*
Downman F. *Lt. C.*	*Maidstone*
Du Pre J. W.	*Canterbury*
Durnford A. Wm.	*Hounslow*
Dusautoy Jas. *Lt.*	*Totness*
Forbes A. *Major*	*Stirling Castle*
Foster N. *Lt.*	*Battle*
Foulerton A.	*Aberdeen*
Galbreath J. *Capt.*	*York*
Gledstanes R.	*Plymouth, &c.*
Gray A.	*Chester*
Hamilton Charles	*Tower*
Hanmer William	*Alderney*
Hay John	*Dundee*
Hill Tho. *Capt.*	*Paignton*
Hobbs T. *Capt.*	*Coventry*
Hughes John	*Hyde Park*
Hulton Henry	*Isle of Man*
Hunt W.	*Dover Heights*
Hunter R. H.	*Margate and Westgate*
Johnston G.	*Croydon*
Jones J. T.	*Gosport (New)*
Kelly F. J.	*Romford*
King Joseph	*Deal (New)*
Kinsey J.	*Windsor (Cav.)*
Lambley Joseph	*Truro*
Laye George	*Braybourn Lees*
	Leake

Leake G. M.	*King Street*	Sandby W.	*Trowbridge*
Lefanu Henry	*Forton*	Scott George	*Sheerness*
Lefroy A. *Capt.*	*Arundel*	Sheers S. *Serj.*	*Kew*
Lempriere S	*Jersey*	Sheldon T. *Capt.*	*Hastings&Bopeep*
Little Geo. *Lieut.*	*Carlisle*	Sheppard W.	*Deal (Old)*
Logan David	*Greenlaw*	Sly Richard	*Romney*
——— George	*Berwick*	Stanley Henry	*Tilbury Fort*
Luke Samuel	*Shoreham*	Stewart Jas. *Ens.*	*Fort Augustus*
Lumley H.	*Bellericay*	Suckling W.	*Windsor (Inf.)*
M'Donald W.	*Bexhill Huts*	Tambs Thomas	*Hampton Court*
——— J.	*Edinb.Castle,&c.*	Tennent R.	*Ayr*
Mackenzie Allan	*Hilsea*	Thomas J.	*Portsmouth&Portsea*
Madden W. H.	*Horsham*	Thompson J.	*Eymouth*
Mahon G.	*Yarmouth I.of Wight*	Thornly Thomas	*Manchester*
Manford W.		Tonkin W. Hill	*Exeter*
Mann Robert	*Tynemouth*	Tooze Henry	*Dorchester*
Marshall R.	*Modbury*	Townsend J.	
Mason R. *Lieut.*	*Chichester*	Travers Joseph	*Yarmouth, Norfolk*
Mennie R.	*Sandown I. of Wight*	Tregent H. J. *Capt.*	*Liverpool*
Middlemas C.		Tudor James	*Bexhill (Old)*
Moore Chas. *Capt.*	*Bognor*	Utterton John	*Ipswich (New)*
Morrant W.	*Hurst Castle*	Vinter George *Capt.*	
Mouat J.	*Fort Charlotte*	WalkerPeter *Knightsbridge,Kensing-*	
Mowatt R. *Capt.*	*Eastbourne*		*ton and Savoy*
Oates M. *Capt.*	*Pendennis Cast.*	——— Samuel	*Maker Heights*
Page J.	*Maldon*	Warren Robert	*Norman Cross*
Palmer S.		Warrington J. P.	
Pierce James	*Languard Fort*	Wathen G. *Lieut.*	*Guildford*
Pittman Henry	*Dover*	Watts John	*Chatham&Upnor*
Ralston Gavin	*Piers Hill*	Wellwood A. M.	*Shorncliff*
Roberts John	*Dungeness*	Whistler W.	*Blatchington*
Rodber Thomas	*Weymouth and*	Wightman W.	*Portchester*
	Radipole	Williams W.	*Fort George*
Rollo John	*Perth*	Wilson B.	*Scarborough*
Roope George	*Rye&Winchelsea*	Winter J. William	*Northampton*
Roughhead J.		Wright Cha. *Capt.*	*Sheffield*

LIST OF OFFICERS

TO WHOM HIS MAJESTY HAS GRANTED

HONORARY CROSSES, MEDALS, &c.

In Commemoration of having been engaged in any of the following Actions, viz. Battles of Maida, 4th July, 1806 ; Roleia and Vimeira, 17th and 21st August, 1808 ; the several Occasions where the Cavalry had an opportunity of distinguishing themselves in the Campaign in Spain, under Sir John Moore, December, 1808, and January, 1809; the Battles of Corunna, 16th January, 1809 ; Talavera de la Reyna, 27th and 28th July, 1809 ; Busaco, 27th September, 1810 ; Fuentes de Onor, 5th May, 1811 ; Albuhera, 16th May, 1811 ; Salamanca, 21st July, 1812 ; Vittoria, 21st June, 1813 ; the Pyrenees, from 28th July to 2d August, 1813; the Nivelle, 10th November, 1813 ; and in the Assaults and Captures of the Island of Java, August and September, 1811 ; and of the Fortresses of Ciudad Rodrigo, January, 1812 ; Badajoz, March and April, 1812 ; and St. Sebastian, August and September, 1813.

N. B. *For the Regulations relative to the different Distinctions of Crosses, Medals, and Clasps to be worn by the Officer, vide General Order of His Royal Highness the Commander in Chief, published in the Gazette of 9th Oct. 1813.*

	No. of Distinctions received by each Officer.
Auchmuty, Lieut. General *Sir* Samuel, *G. C. B.* - -	1
Ackland, Lieut. General *Sir* Wroth Palmer, *K. C. B.* -	1
Alten, Major General Victor, *Baron* - - -	2
Alten, Major General Charles, *Baron, K. C. B.* - -	4
Anson, Major General *Sir* George, *K. C. B.* - -	3
Anson, Major General *Sir* William, *K. C. B.* - -	5
Aylmer, Major General *Lord, K. C. B.* - - -	3
Adams, Major General Alexander	1
Abercromby, Colonel *Hon.* Alexander, *Coldstream Guards* -	3
Arbuthnot, Colonel *Sir* Thomas, *K. C. B.* 57 *F.* - -	4
Ashworth, Lieut. Colonel Charles, *Portuguese Army* -	3
Acheson, Lieut. Colonel *Hon.* Edward, *Coldstream Guards*	1
Arbuthnot, Lieut. Colonel *Hon.* Hugh, *h. p.* 52 *F.* -	1
Arbuthnot, Lieut. Colonel *Sir* Robert, *K. C. B. Cold. Gds.*	4
Armstrong, Lieut. Colonel Richard, *Portuguese Army* -	3
Aly, Major Charles, *King's German Legion* - -	1
Anwyll, Major Robert, 4 *F.* - - - -	1
Anderson, Major Alexander, *Portuguese Service* - -	5
Agnew, Major Patrick V. *East Ind. Comp. Service* -	1
Annesley, Captain Marcus, 61 *F.* - - -	1

* M-N

Baird,

7

[1815]

Officers who have received Honorary Distinctions.

	No. of Distinctions received by each Officer.
Baird, General *Sir* David, *G. C. B.* - - - -	1
Bentinck, Lieut. General *Lord* William - - -	1
Beresford, Lieut. General *Lord, G. C. B.* - -	8
Burne, Major General Robert - - - -	2
Borthwick, Major General William, *Royal Artillery* -	1
Barnes, Major General *Sir* Edward, *K. C. B.* - -	3
Byng, Major General *Sir* John, *K. C. B.* - - -	3
Brisbane, Major General *Sir* Thomas, *K. C. B.* - -	3
Bradford, Major General *Sir* Thomas, *K. C. B.* - -	4
Beckwith, Major General *Sir* Sidney, *K. C. B.* - -	3
Bunbury, Major General *Sir* Henry Edward, *K. C. B.*- -	1
Blantyre, Colonel Robert, *Lord* - - - -	1
Belson, Colonel *Sir* Charles Philip, *K. C. B.* 28 *F.* -	5
Bingham, Colonel *Sir* George Ridout, *K. C. B.* 53 *F.* -	5
Bathurst, Colonel James, *late Mil. Sec. to the D. of Wellington*	3
Barnard, Colonel *Sir* Andrew, *K. C. B.* 95 *F.* - -	6
Brand, Colonel *Hon.* Henry, *Coldstream Gds.* - -	1
Barnes, Colonel James Stevenson, 1 *F.* - - -	2
Blakeney, Colonel *Sir* Edward, *K. C. B.* 7 *F.* - -	4
Bouverie, Colonel *Sir* Henry Fred. *K. C. B. Coldstream Gds.*	3
Bussche, Lieut. Colonel Lewis, *Baron, King's German Legion*	1
Buchan, Lieut. Colonel John, 4 *West India Regt.* - -	2
Bromhead, Lieut. Colonel John, 77 *F.* - - -	1
Bradford, Lieut. Colonel *Sir* Henry Hol. *K. C. B.* 1 *F. G.*	4
Brown, Lieut. Colonel John F. 56 *F.* - - -	1
Bruce, Lieut. Colonel Charles, 39 *F.* - - -	2
Bulow, Lieut. Colonel John, *Baron, King's German Legion* -	2
Bodecker, Lieut. Colonel Rudolphus, *do.* -	3
Brooke, Lieut. Colonel Francis, 4 *F.* - - -	5
Berkeley, Lieut. Colonel *Sir* Geo. Hen. Fred. *K. C. B.* 35 *F.*	6
Butler, Lieut. Colonel Richard, 89 *F.* - - -	1
Blake, Lieut. Colonel W. W. 20 *Dr.* - - -	1
Beck, Lieut. Colonel Adolphus, *Baron, King's German Legion*	1
Broke, Lt. Col. *Sir* Charles, *K. C. B. Assist. Qua. Mast. Gen.*	3
Burgoyne, Lieut. Colonel John F. *Royal Engineers* -	3
Brown, Lieut. Colonel Gustavus, 60 *F.* - - -	3
Buckner, Lieut. Colonel Richard, *Royal Artillery* - -	3
Beatty, Lieut. Colonel William, 64 *F.* - - -	1
Balfour, Lieut. Colonel William, *late of* 40 *F.* - -	1
Beatty, Lieut. Colonel J. W. 7 *F.* - - -	1
Bell, Lieut. Colonel John, *Assist. Qua. Mast. Gen.* -	2
Bussche, Major Hans, *Baron, King's German Legion*	1
Bull, Major Robert, *Royal Artillery* - - -	1
Bishop, Major Richard, 5 *F.* - - - -	2
Bogle, Major James, 94 *F.* - - - -	1
Bell, Major Thomas, 48 *F.* - - - -	3
Balvaird, Major William, 95 *F.* - - - -	1
Beane, Major George, *Royal Artillery* - - -	1

Bunce

[1815]

Officers who have received Honorary Distinctions.

Officer	No. of Distinctions received by each Officer.
Bunce, Major Richard, *Royal Marines*	1
Brandreth, Major Thomas A. *Royal Artillery*	2
Browne, Major Fielding, 40 *F.*	1
Combermere, Lieut. General *Lord*, G. C. B.	3
Chowne, Lieut. General Christopher	1
Cole, Lieut. General *Hon. Sir* Lowrey, G. C. B.	6
Clinton, Lieut. General *Sir* Henry, G. C. B.	2
Campbell, Lieut. General *Sir* Alexander, *Bt.*	1
Campbell, Lieut. General *Sir* Henry Frederick, K. C. B.	2
Cameron, Major General *Sir* Alan, K. C. B.	1
Colville, Major General *Hon. Sir* Charles, K. C. B.	4
Cheney, Major General Robert	1
Calcraft, Major General *Sir* Granby T.	1
Cumming, Major General Henry John	1
Campbell, Colonel James, 94 *F.*	4
Cameron, Colonel *Sir* John, K. C. B. 9 *F.*	5
Cuyler, Colonel George, 11 *F.*	1
Cameron, Colonel John, 92 *F.*	1
Copson, Colonel Edward, 5 *F.*	1
Campbell, Colonel *Sir* Neil, 54 *F.*	2
Campbell, Colonel *Sir* Colin, K. C. B. *Coldstream Gds.*	8
Colborne, Colonel *Sir* John, K. C. B. 52 *F.*	4
Campbell, Colonel *Sir* Archibald, K. C. B. *Portu. Army*	4
Campbell, Lieut. Colonel Archibald, 6 *F.*	1
Clifton, Lieut. Colonel A. B. 1 *Dr.*	2
Chamberlin, Lieut. Colonel Thomas, 24 *F.*	1
Cooke, Lieut. Colonel R. H. 1 *F. G.*	1
Caldwell, Lieut. Colonel Alexander, *Bengal Artillery*	1
Carr, Lieut. Colonel *Sir* Henry Wm. K. C. B. 83 *F.*	6
Cameron, Lieut. Colonel Alexander, 95 *F.*	3
Cother, Lieut. Colonel Charles, 71 *F.*	1
Campbell, Lieut. Colonel Colin, 1 *F.*	2
Campbell, Lieut. Colonel *Sir* Guy, *Bt.* 6 *F.*	1
Cross, Lieut. Colonel William, 36 *F.*	1
Carncross, Lieut. Colonel *Sir* Jos. K. C. B. *Royal Artillery*	4
Cowell, Lieut. Colonel William, 42 *F.*	1
Crookshank, Lieut. Colonel A. C. W. *h. p.* 38 *F.*	1
Cimetiere, Major Gilbert, 48 *F.*	1
Camac, Major John, 1 *L. Guards*	1
Campbell, Major Patrick, 52 *F.*	1
Campbell, Major William, 36 *F.*	2
Campbell, Major Charles S. 26 *F.*	1
Campbell, Major Robert, 52 *F.*	1
Cameron, Major Charles, 3 *F.*	1
Campbell, Major Duncan, 39 *F.*	1
Cairnes, Major Robert M. *Royal Artillery*	2
Dalhousie, Lieut. General *Earl of*, G. C. B.	2
Disney, Lieut. General Moore	1

* M—N 2

Dilkes,

Officers who have received Honorary Distinctions.

	No. of Distinctions received by each Officer.
Dilkes, Major General William Thomas - - -	1
Donkin, Major General Rufane Shaw - - -	1
De Grey, Major General *Hon.* George - - -	1
De Bernewitz, Major General, J. H. C. - - -	1
Darling, Major General Ralph - - -	1
De Lancey, Colonel *Sir* Wm. Howe, *K. C. B.* - -	6
D'Urban, Colonel *Sir* Benj. *K. C. B.* 2 *W. I. Regiment*	6
De Arentsschildt, Colonel, *Baron, K. C. B. King's G. Legion*	4
Doherty, Colonel Patrick, 13 *Lt. Dr.* - - -	1
Davies, Colonel Lewis, *h. p.* 36 *F.* - - -	1
Douglas, Colonel *Sir* William, *K. C. B.* 91 *F.* - -	3
Dunkin, Lieut. Colonel John H. 77 *F.* - - -	1
De Belleville, Lieut. Colonel Charles, *For. Vet. Battalion*	1
Davy, Lieutenant Colonel William Gabriel, *h. p.* -	1
De Jonquieres, Lieut. Colonel Charles, *King's Ger. Legion*	1
Dufaure, Lieut. Colonel M. J. *late Chasseurs Britanniques* -	1
Dundas, Lieut. Col. *Hon. Sir* Rob. Law. *K.C.B. Royal Staff Corps*	5
Douglas, Lieut. Colonel *Sir* James, *K. C. B. Portug. Army*	4
Dickson, Lieut. Colonel *Sir* Jeremiah, *K.C.B. Ass.Q.M.Gen.*	3
Doyle, Lieut. Colonel *Sir* J. M. *K. C. B. late Portuguese Army*	4
Dickson, Lieut. Colonel *Sir* Alex. *K. C. B. Royal Artillery*	8
De Hertzberg, Lieut. Colonel F.Aug. *K.C.B. late Brunswick Reg.*	4
Dalmer, Lieut. Colonel Thomas, 23 *F.* - - -	2
D'Oyly, Lieut. Colonel *Sir* Francis, *K. C. B.* 1 *Foot Gds.*	4
Dick, Lieut. Colonel R. H. 42 *F.* - - -	2
Douglas, Lieut. Colonel Neil, 79 *F.* - - -	2
Downman, Lieut. Colonel Thomas, *Royal Artillery* -	1
Diggens, Lieut. Colonel Richard, 11 *Light Dragoons* -	1
De Burgh, Lieut. Colonel J. F. 2 *F.* - - -	1
Dodgin, Lieut. Colonel Daniel, 66 *F.* - - -	2
Du Hautoy, Lieut. Colonel A. *late Chasseurs Britanniques* -	2
Desbarres, Lieut. Colonel J. F. 87 *F.* - - -	1
Dyer, Lieut. Colonel *Sir* John, *K. C. B. Royal Artillery*	2
Dewar, Lieut. Colonel James, *East India Comp. Bengal Inf.*	1
Duffy, Major John, 43 *F.* - - - -	1
De Ziegesar, Major Frederick, *King's German Legion*	1
De Arentsschildt, Major Victor, *King's German Artillery* -	1
Douglas, Major Robert, *Royal Artillery* - - -	2
Dalton, Major D. H. *East India Comp. Bengal Infantry* -	1
Eden, Major General William - - - -	1
Elley, Colonel *Sir* John, *K. C. B. Royal Horse Gds.* -	3
Ellis, Colonel *Sir* H. Walton, *K. C. B.* 23 *F.* -	5
Erskine, Lieut. Colonel James, 48 *F.* - - -	1
Eustace, Lieut. Colonel W. C. late *Chasseurs Britanniques*	1
Elder, Lieut. Colonel *Sir* George, *Portuguese Army* -	3
Erskine, Lieut. Colonel W. H. Knight, *h. p.* - -	1
Emes, Lieut. Colonel Thomas, 5 *F.* - - -	1
Elphinstone, Lieut. Colonel H. *Royal Engineers* - -	1

Ellicombe,

Officers who have received Honorary Distinctions.

	No. of Distinctions received by each Officer.
Ellicombe, Lieut. Colonel C. *Royal Engineers* - -	1
Ferguson, Lieut. General *Sir* Ron. Crau. *K. C. B.* -	1
Fane, Major General *Sir* Henry, *K. C. B.* - -	4
Fermor, Major General *Hon.* T. W. - - -	1
Fuller, Major General Joseph - - - -	1
Framingham, Colonel *Sir* Haylett, *K. C. B. Royal Artillery*	5
Fenwick, Lieut. Colonel William, *late of* 34 *F.* - -	2
Fitz Gerald, Lieut. Colonel John F. 60 *F.* - -	2
Fraser, Lieut. Colonel *Sir* Augustus, *K. C. B. Royal Art.*	3
Fergusson, Lieut. Colonel James, 3 *F.* - - -	1
Forbes, Lieut. Colonel David, 78 *F.* - - -	1
Guard, Major General William - - - -	1
Gillespie, Major General *Sir* Robert R. *K. C. B.* -	1
Gibbs, Major General *Sir* Samuel, *K. C. B.* - -	1
Grant, Major General *Sir* Colquhoun, *K. C. B.* - -	2
Grant, Major General William - - - -	2
Greville, Colonel *Hon. Sir* Chas. James, *K. C. B.* 38 *F.* -	6
Guise, Colonel John, 3 *F. G.* - - - -	3
Gough, Lieut. Colonel Hugh, 87 *F.* - - -	4
Gardiner, Lieut. Colonel John, 6 *F.* - - -	1
Greenock, Lieut. Colonel *Lord, A. Q. M. Gen.* - -	3
Gwyn, Lieut. Colonel William, *Inspecting Field Officer*	1
Gilmour, Lieut. Colonel D. L. 95 *F.* - - -	2
Gibbs, Lieut. Colonel Edward, 52 *F.* - - -	3
Greenwell, Lieut. Colonel Leonard, 45 *F.* - -	1
Gomm, Lieut. Colonel *Sir* William, *K. C. B.* Coldst. Gds.	4
Gillies, Lieut. Colonel John, 40 *F.* - - -	1
Grant, Lieut. Colonel Peter, *East India Comp. Bengal Inf.*	1
Graham, Lieut. Colonel H. C. E. Vernon, *Inspecting Field Officer in Nova Scotia* - -	1
Grant, Lieut. Colonel *Sir* Maxwell, *K. C. B. h. p.* 42 *F.*	3
Gerber, Lieut. Colonel A. *King's German Legion* - -	1
Galiffe, Lieut. Colonel John, 60 *F.* - - -	2
Gardiner, Lieut. Colonel *Sir* Robert, *K. C. B. Royal Art.*	2
Gruben, Major Philip, *Baron, King's German Legion* -	1
Goldie, Major George Leigh, 66 *F.* - - -	1
Griffith, Major Edwin, 15 *Lt. Dr.* - - -	1
Greene, Major William, *Royal Artillery* - - -	1
Griffiths, Major Hugh, *East India Comp. Service* - -	1
Gall, Captain George Herbert, *do.* - -	1
Gell, Captain Thomas, 29 *F.* - - - -	1
Hill, Lieut. General *Lord, G. C. B.* - - -	6
Hamilton, Lieut. General *Sir* John, *Bt.* - - -	2
Houstoun, Lieut. General *Sir* Wm. *K. C. B.* - -	1
Hope, Major General John - - - -	1
Howard, Major General, *Sir* Ken. Alex. *K. C. B.* -	1
Howorth, Major General *Sir* Edward, *K. C. B. Royal Artillery*	3
Hawker, Major General Samuel, - - -	1

Hinde,

Officers who have received Honorary Distinctions.

	No. of Distinctions received by each Officer.
Hinde, Major General Samuel Venables - - -	4
Halkett, Major General *Sir* Colin, *K. C. B.* - -	2
Harcourt, Colonel C. A. *h. p. late of* 40 *F.* - -	1
Hepburn, Colonel F. 3 *F. G.* - - - -	1
Hervey, Colonel F. B. 14 *Lt. Dr.* - - -	3
Hill, Lieut. Colonel Charles, 50 *F.* - - -	1
Hardinge, Lieut. Colonel *Sir* Henry, *K. C. B.* 1 *F. G.* -	7
Hamilton, Lieut. Colonel Alexander, 30 *F.* - -	1
Hicks, Lieut. Colonel John, 32 *F.* - - -	2
Hill, Lieut. Colonel *Sir* Tho. Noel, *K. C. B.* 1 *F. Gds.* -	5
Holmes, Lieut. Colonel George, 3 *Dr. Gds.* - -	1
Halkett, Lieut. Colonel Hugh, *King's German Legion* -	2
Harding, Lieut. Colonel George, 44 *F.* - - -	1
Hill, Lieut. Colonel *Sir* Robert, *Royal Horse Gds.* -	1
Hunt, Lieut. Colonel J. P. *Insp. Field Officer* - -	3
Harrison, Lieut. Colonel J. B. 50 *F.* - - -	1
Hartman, Lieut. Colonel Julius, *K. C. B. King's Ger. Art.*	5
Hay, Lieut. Colonel James, 16 *Light Dr.* - -	1
Hartwig, Lieut. Colonel F. *King's German Legion* -	1
Hope, Lieut. Colonel *Sir* Ja. Arch. *K. C. B.* 3 *F. Gds.* -	1
Harvey, Lieut. Colonel R. J. *Portuguese Army* - -	1
Hill, Lieut. Colonel D. St. Leger, *do.* - -	4
Hawkins, Lieut. Colonel John P. 68 *F.* - - -	3
Hare, Lieut. Colonel R. G. 12 *F.* - - -	1
Hill, Lieut. Colonel J. H. E. 23 *F.* - - -	2
Hawkshaw, Lieut. Colonel Edward, *h. p.* - .	1
Hawker, Major James, *Royal Artillery* - -	1
Hughes, Major James, 18 *Lt. Dr.* - - -	1
Hext, Major Samuel, 83 *F.* - - - -	1
Heise, Major Augustus, *King's German Legion* - -	2
Heyland, Major A. R. 40 *F.* - - - -	1
Henderson, Major George H. *Royal Engineers* - -	1
Halford, Major George, 59 *F.* - - - -	1
Jones, Major General Oliver Thomas - - -	1
Inglis, Major General Wm. - - - -	3
Johnston, Colonel William, 68 *F.* - - -	2
Jackson, Colonel *Sir* Rich. Downes, *K. C. B. Coldstream Gds.*	4
Jones, Lieut. Colonel John T. *Royal Engineers* - -	1
Jones, Lieut. Colonel Timothy, 4 *F.* - - -	1
Jackson, Major Charles, 2 *L. Gds.* - - -	1
Kemmis, Major General James - - - -	2
Kempt, Major General *Sir* James, *K.C.B.* - -	4
Keane, Major General *Sir* John, *K. C. B.* - -	3
Kelly, Colonel William, 24 *F.* - - -	3
King, Colonel *Hon.* Henry, 5 *F.* - - -	2
King, Lieut. Colonel Henry, 82 *F.* - - -	1
King, Major George, 7 *F.* - - - -	1
Lynedock, Lieut. General *Lord*, *G. C. B.* - -	4

Leith,

Officers who have received Honorary Distinctions.

	No. of Distinctions received by each Officer.
Leith, Lieut. General *Sir* James, *G. C. B.* - - -	5
Lumley, Lieut. General *Sir* William, *K. C. B.* - -	1
Low, Major General S. *Baron*, *K. C. B.* - - -	2
Long, Major General Richard B. - - - -	1
Lambert, Major General *Sir* John, *K. C. B.* - -	1
Lyon, Major General James - - - -	2
Lemoine, Colonel John, *Royal Artillery* - - -	1
Leith, Lieut. Colonel *Sir* Alexander, *K. C. B.* 31 *F.* -	3
L'Estrange, Lieut. Colonel, Guy G. C. 26 *F.* - -	1
Lindesay, Lieut. Colonel Patrick, 39 *F.* - - -	1
Lindsay, Lieut. Colonel Martin, 78 *F.* - - -	1
Lightfoot, Lieut. Colonel Thomas, *h. p.* 45 *F.* - -	2
Leggatt, Major Martin, 36 *F.* - - - -	1
Langlands, Major George, 13 *R. V. B.* - - -	2
Leahy, Major John Thomas, *h. p.* 23 *F.* - - -	1
Lawson, Major Robert, *Royal Artillery* - - -	2
Murray, Major General *Sir* George, *G. C. B.* - -	7
Meade, Colonel *Hon.* John - - - -	1
Madden, Colonel George Allen - - - -	1
Mitchell, Colonel Hugh Henry, 51 *F.* - - -	1
M'Donald, Colonel John, *half-pay* - - -	1
Maclean, Colonel *Sir* John, *K. C. B.* 27 *F.* - -	4
Middlemore, Lieut. Colonel George, *half-pay.* - -	1
Mackenzie, Lieut. Colonel Colin, *Madras Engineers* - -	1
M'Leod, Lieut. Colonel Alexander, 59 *F.* - - -	1
Macbean, Lieut. Colonel William, *Portuguese Army* - -	3
Manners, Lieut. Colonel *Lord* Charles, 3 *Dr.* - -	1
M'Creagh, Lieut. Colonel M. *Portuguese Army* - -	3
Mansel, Lieut. Colonel John, 53 *F.* - - -	1
Miles, Lieut. Colonel Edward, 38 *F.* - -	2
Macara', Lieut. Colonel *Sir* Robert, *K. C. B.* 42 *F.* - -	2
Manners, Lieut. Colonel Russell, 74 *F.* - -	3
May, Lieut. Colonel *Sir* John, *K. C. B. Royal Artillery* -	2
M'Neil, Lieut. Colonel Donald, 91 *F.* - - -	1
Macpherson, Lieut. Colonel R. B. 88 *F.* - -	1
Milne, Major George Miles, 10 *R. V. Bn.* - -	1
Macdonald, Major Robert, *Royal Artillery* - -	1
Murray, Major George Home, 16 *Lt. Dr.* - -	1
Marlay, Major George, 14 *F.* - - - -	1
Mitchell, Major Samuel, 95 *F.* - - -	2
Miller, Major James, 74 *F.* - - -	4
Macdonald, Major John, *Portug. Service* - -	2
Murray, Major John, 20 *F.* - - -	1
Marke, Major Joseph, 57 *F.* - - -	1
Miller, Major George, 95 *F.* - - -	1
Maxwell, Major Stewart, *Royal Artillery* - -	1
Michell, 1st Lieut. Charles C. *do.* - -	1
Niddery, Lieut. General *Lord*, *G. C. B.* - -	1

Nightingall.

[1815]

Officers who have received Honorary Distinctions.

	No. of Distinctions received by each Officer.
Nightingall, Lieut. General *Sir* Miles, *K. C. B.* - -	1
Nugent, Colonel John, *h. p.* 38 *F.* - - -	3
Nicolls, Colonel Jasper, 14 *F.* - - -	1
Norcott, Lieut. Colonel A. G. 95 *F.* - -	1
Nixon, Lieut. Colonel Robert, 28 *F.* - - -	2
Nooth, Lieut. Colonel J. M. 7 *F.* - - -	1
Napier, Lieut. Colonel Charles, *h. p.* 50 *F.* - -	1
Napier, Lieut. Colonel George T. 3 *F. G.* - -	1
Newman, Lieut. Colonel Frederick, 11 *F.* - - -	3
Napier, Lieut. Colonel W. F. P. 43 *F.* - - -	2
Noble, Major John, *Madras Horse Artillery* - -	1
Orange, General *the Hereditary Prince of* - - -	3
Oswald, Major General *Sir* John, *K. C. B.* - -	3
O'Callaghan, Major General *Hon. Sir* Robert, *K. C. B.* -	4
Ompteda, Colonel *Baron, King's German Legion* - -	1
O'Toole, Lieut. Colonel B. *Portuguese Army* - -	4
Oglander, Major Henry, *h. p.* - - - -	1
O'Flaherty, Major John, *h. p.* 45 *F.* - - -	1
Payne, Lieut. General *Sir* William, *Bt.* - - -	1
Paget, Lieut. General *Hon. Sir* Edward, *G. C. B.* -	1
Picton, Lieut. General *Sir* Thomas, *G. C. B.* - -	6
Pakenham, Major General *Hon. Sir* Edward, *G. C. B.* -	4
Pringle, Major General *Sir* Wm. Henry, *K. C. B.* - -	3
Ponsonby, Major General *Hon. Sir* William, *K. C. B.* -	2
Pack, Major General *Sir* Denis, *K. C. B.* - - -	8
Power, Major General *Sir* Manley, *K. C. B.* - -	3
Prevost, Colonel W. A. 67 *F.* - - - -	1
Pratt, Colonel *Sir* Charles, *K. C. B.* 5 *F.* - - -	3
Ponsonby, Colonel *Hon.* F. C. 12 *Lt. Dr.* - -	3
Pearson, Lieut. Colonel Thomas, *Inspecting Field Offic. in Canada*	1
Pakenham, Lieut. Colonel *Hon.* H. R. *Coldstream Gds.* -	3
Piper, Lieut. Colonel John, 4 *F.* - - - -	2
Prescott, Lieut. Colonel S. 5 *Dr. G.* - - -	1
Pynn, Lieut. Colonel *Sir* H. *Portuguese Army* - -	1
Packe, Major R. C. *Royal Horse Gds.* - - -	1
Perceval, Major William, 14 *F.* - - - -	3
Parker, Major John, *Royal Artillery* - - -	1
Robinson, Major General *Sir* Fred. Phil. *K. C. B.* - -	2
Robe, Colonel *Sir* William, *K. C. B. Royal Artillery*	4
Ross, Colonel John, 66 *F.* - - - -	1
Ross, Lieut. Colonel John, 95 *F.* - - -	1
Raban, Lieut. Colonel William, *East India Comp. European Bn.*	1
Rowan, Lieut. Colonel Charles, 52 *F.* - - -	3
Robarts, Lieut. Colonel G. J. *h. p.* 9 *L. Dr.* - -	1
Roberts, Lieut. Colonel David, 51 *F.* - - -	2
Ross Lieut. Colonel *Sir* Hew D. *K. C. B. Royal Artillery* -	3
Rice, Lieut. Colonel Samuel, 51 *F.* - - -	1
Ross, Major Archibald, 91 *F.* - - - -	1

Ramsay,

Officers who have received Honorary Distinctions.

	No. of Distinctions received by each Officer.
Ramsay, Major William N. *Royal Artillery* - -	2
Rolt, Major John, *Portuguese Service* - - -	1
Stuart, Lieut. General *Sir* John, *G. C. B.* - - -	1
Sherbrooke, Lieut. General *Sir* John, *G. C. B.* - -	1
Spencer, Lieut. General *Sir* Brent, *G. C. B.* - -	3
Stewart, Lieut. General *Hon.* Sir William, *G. C. B.* -	4
Slade, Lieut. General John - - - -	2
Stewart, Lieut. General *Lord, G. C. B.* - - -	5
Saunders, Major General J. S. - - - -	1
Stopford Major General *Hon.* Sir Edward, *K. C. B.* -	2
Smith, Major General Haviland - - - -	1
Somerset, Major General *Lord* Edward, *K. C. B.* - -	3
Stirling, Major General James - - - -	3
Stewart, Lieut. Colonel William, 3 *F.* - -	1
Spring, Lieut. Colonel W. C. 57 *F.* - - -	1
Sutton, Lieut. Colonel *Sir* Charles, *K. C. B. h. p.* 23 *F.* -	6
Symes, Lieut. Colonel Walter, 69 *F.* - - -	1
Smith, Lieut. Colonel William, *h. p.* 50 *F.* - -	1
Stanhope, Lieut. Colonel *Hon.* Lincoln, 17 *L. Dr.* -	1
Somerset, Lieut. Colonel *Lord* Fitzroy, 1 *F. G.* - -	6
Scovell, Lieut. Colonel *Sir* Geo. *K. C. B. late Staff Corps of Cav.*	3
Stewart, Lieut. Colonel *Hon.* James, 3 *F. G.* - -	2
Stovin, Lieut. Colonel *Sir* Fred. *K. C. B.* 28 *F.* - -	4
Smith, Lieut. Colonel J. Webber, *Royal Artillery* - -	2
Seton, Major William Carden, 88 *F.* - - -	2
Schoedde, Major John, 60 *F.* - - - -	1
Snodgrass, Major Kenneth, *Portuguese Service* - -	2
Stone, Major Bayntun, 58 *F.* - - - -	1
Stretton, Major Sempronius, 40 *F.* - - -	1
Torrens, Major General *Sir* Henry, *K. C. B.* - -	1
Taylor, Colonel John, 88 *F.* - - - -	1
Trench, Colonel *Hon.* Sir Robert Le Poer, *K. C. B.* 74 *F.* -	7
Travers, Colonel Robert, 10 *F.* - - - -	1
Thornton, Lieut. Colonel Henry, 40 *F.* - - -	2
Travers, Lieut. Colonel Robert, 22 *Dr.* - - -	1
Tulloh, Lieut. Colonel Alexander, *Royal Artillery* - -	3
Tweeddale, Lieut. Colonel *Marquess of*, 100 *F.* - -	1
Tryon, Lieut. Colonel Charles, 88 *F.* - - -	1
Thompson, Lieut. Colonel Alexander, 74 *F.* - -	1
Thalman, Major Charles, *Foreign Veteran Bn.* - -	1
Thomas, Major Henry, 27 *F.* - - - -	1
Uxbridge, Lieut General *Earl of, G. C. B.* - -	1
Vandeleur, Major General *Sir* John, *K. C. B.* - -	3
Vivian, Major General *Sir* Richard Hussey, *K. C. B.* -	1
Upton, Colonel *Hon.* Arthur P. 1 *F. G.* - - -	1
Vigoureux, Lieut. Colonel C. A. 30 *F.* - - -	1
Wellington, *Field Marshal Duke of, K. G. & G. C. B.* -	10
Warde, Lieut. General *Sir* Henry, *K. C. B.* - -	1

** M—N   Wetherall,

[1815]

Officers who have received Honorary Distinctions.

	No. of Distinctions received by each Officer.
Wetherall, Lieut. General F. A.	1
Walker, Major General *Sir* George Towns. *K. C. B.*	2
Watteville, Major General Louis	1
Wood, Major General George, *East India Service*	1
Wallace, Colonel Alexander, 88 *F.*	3
Wade, Colonel Hamlet, 95 *F.*	1
Watson, Colonel James, 14 *F.*	1
Wyatt, Colonel W. E. *late of* 23 *F.*	1
Wilson, Colonel *Sir* John, *Royal York Rangers*	1
Woodford, Colonel Alexander George, *Coldst. Gds.*	3
Williams, Lieut. Colonel *Sir* William, *K. C. B.* 13 *F.*	5
Woodgate, Lieut. Colonel William, 60 *F.*	1
Way, Lieut. Colonel *Sir* G. H. B. *h. p.* 22 *F.*	1
Waters, Lieut. Colonel John, *Portuguese Army*	2
Ward, Lieut. Colonel John R. *h. p.* 36 *F.*	1
Wilson, Lieut. Colonel *Sir* James, *K. C. B. h. p.* 48 *F.*	4
Williamson, Lieut. Colonel David, 4 *F.*	1
Worsley, Lieut. Colonel H. 34 *F.*	2
Williams, Lieut. Colonel *Sir* Edm. K. *K. C. B. Portuguese Army*	4
Woodford, Lieut. Colonel J. G. 1 *F. G.*	1
White, Lieut. Colonel W. G. 48 *F.*	2
Waller, Lieut. Colonel R. *Assistant Quarter Master General*	1
Wilkins, Lieut. Colonel George, 95 *F.*	1
Watson, Lieut. Colonel Henry, *Portuguese Army*	1
Wells, Lieut. Colonel Joseph, 43 *F.*	1
Walmsley, Major John B. 82 *F.*	1
Williamson, Major John, 4 *F.*	1
Wilson, Major George David, 4 *F.*	1
Western, Captain Charles, *Portuguese Service*	1
Young, Lieut. Colonel A. W. 3 *West India Regt.*	1
Yule, Lieut. Colonel Udney, *East India Comp. Bengal Infantry*	1
Zulke, Major George Henry, *Portuguese Service*	2

MILITARY

MILITARY OFFICERS

OF THE

MOST HONOURABLE ORDER OF THE BATH.

Knights Grand Crosses. (*G. C. B.*)

THE SOVEREIGN.
Field Marshal *his Royal Highness*
the *D. of* YORK, *K. G.* (*acting
as Grand Master*), 1 *F.G. & 60 F.*
Field Marshal *His Royal Highness*
the *Duke of* KENT, *K. G.* 1 *F.*
Field Marshal *His Royal Highness*
the *Duke of* CUMBERLAND, *K. G.*
15 *Dr.*
Field Marshal *His Royal Highness*
the *Duke of* CAMBRIDGE, *K. G.*
Coldstr. F. G. & King's Ger. Leg.
General *His Highness the Duke of*
GLOUCESTER, *K. G.* 3 *F. G.*
Abercromby, General *Sir* Rob. 75 *F.*
Auchmuty, Lieut. Gen. *Sir* S. 78 *F.*
Baird, Gen. *Sir* David, 24 *F.*
Beckwith, Gen. *Sir* G. 2 *W. I. R.*
Bentinck, Lt. Gen. *Ld.* W. Cavendish, 11 *Dr.*
Beresford, Lieut. Gen. *Ld.* W.Carr, 88 *F.*
Brownrigg, Lieut. Gen. *Sir* R. 9 *F.*
Calvert, Lt. Gen. *Sir* Harry, 14 *F.*
Clarke, Gen. *Sir* Alured, 7 *F.*
Clinton, Lt. Gen. *Sir* Henry, 60 *F.*
Clinton, Lt. Gen. *Sir* W. H. 55 *F.*
Cole, Lieut. Gen. *Hon. Sir* Galbraith Lowrey, 70 *F.*
Combermere, Lieut. Gen. *Lord* Stapleton, 20 *Dr.*

Coote, Gen. *Sir* Eyre, 34 *F.*
Cradock, Gen. *Sir* J. F. 43 *F.*
Dalhousie, Lieut. Gen. *E. of,* 26 *F.*
Doyle, Lieut. Gen. *Sir* J. *Bt.* 87 *F.*
Dundas, Gen. *Sir* D. 1 *U. G. & 95F.*
Hill, Lieut. Gen. *Lord,* 94 *F.*
Hope, Lt. Gen. *Hon. Sir* A. 47 *F.*
Hutchinson, Gen. *Lord,* 18 *F.*
Keppel, Gen. *Sir* W. 67 *F.*
Leith, Lieut. Gen. *Sir* J. 4 *W. I. R.*
Ludlow, Gen. *Earl,* 38 *F.*
Lynedock, Lieut. Gen. *Lord,* 90 *F.*
Maitland, Lieut. Gen. *Rt. Hon. Sir*
Thomas, 10 *F.*
Murray, Major Gen. *Sir* G. 60 *F.*
Niddery, Lieut. Gen. *Lord,* 92 *F.*
Nugent, Gen. *Sir* G. 6 *F.*
Orange, Gen. *His Royal Highness
the Hereditary Prince of*
Paget, Lieut. Gen. *Hon. Sir* E. 10 *F.*
Picton, Lieut. Gen. *Sir* T. 77 *F.*
St. Vincent, Gen. *E. of, Roy. Mar.*
Sherbrooke, Lt. Gen. *Sir* J. C. 33 *F.*
Spencer, Lieut. Gen. *Sir* B. 95 *F.*
Stewart, Lieut. Gen. *Lord,* 25 *Dr.*
Stewart, Lt. Gen. *Hon. Sir* W. 95 *F.*
Stuart, Lieut. Gen. *Sir* John, 20 *F.*
Uxbridge, Lieut. Gen. *E. of,* 7 *Dr.*
Wellington, Field Marshal *Duke of,*
K. G. Royal Horse Gds.

* * M—N 2   *Knights*

Knights Commanders. *(K. C. B.)*

Abercromby, Lieut. Gen. *Hon. Sir* J. 53 *F.*

Acland, Lieut. Gen. *Sir* W. P.

Anson, Major Gen. *Sir* G. 23 *Dr.*

Anson, Major Gen. *Sir* W.

Arbuthnot, Col. *Sir* T. 57 *F.*

Arbuthnot, Lieut. Col. *Sir* R. *Colds. F. G.*

Aylmer, Major Gen. *Lord*

Barnard, Col. *Sir* And. F. 95 *F.*

Barnes, Maj. Gen. *Sir* E. *from* 46 *F.*

Beckwith, Maj.Gen. *Sir* T. S. 95 *F.*

Bell, Maj. Gen. *Sir* Hen. *Roy. Mar.*

Belson, Col. *Sir* C. B. 28 *F.*

Berkeley, Lieut. Col. *Sir* G. H. F. 35 *F.*

Bickerton, Major Gen. *Sir* R. *Bt. Royal Marines*

Bingham, Col. *Sir* G. R. 53 *F.*

Blakeney, Col, *Sir* Edward, 7 *F.*

Bouverie, Col. *Sir* H. F. *Coldst.F.G.*

Bradford, Lt. Col. *Sir* H. F. 1 *F. G.*

Bradford, Major Gen. *Sir* T. *late of* 82 *F.*

Brisbane, Major Gen. *Sir* T.

Broke, Lt. Col. *Sir* C. *Assist. Qua. Mast. Gen.*

Bunbury, Major Gen. *Sir* Henry E. *Royal Newfoundland Fenc.*

Burgh, Lieut. Col. *Sir* U. 1 *F. G.*

Byng, Major Gen. *Sir* John

Cameron, Major Gen. *Sir* A. 79 *F.*

Cameron, Col. *Sir* John, 9 *F.*

Campbell, Col. *Sir* A. *Portug. Serv.*

Campbell, Col. *Sir* C. *Coldstr. F. G.*

Campbell, Lieut. Gen. *Sir* Henry F.

Carncross, Lieut. Col. *Sir* J. *R.Art.*

Carr, Lieut. Col. *Sir* H. W. 83 *F.*

Colborne, Col. *Sir* John, 52 *F.*

Colville, Major Gen. *Hon. Sir* C.

De Lancey, Col. *Sir* W. H. *Deputy Quarter Master General*

Dickson, Lt. Col. *Sir* A. J. *R.Art.*

Dickson, Lieut. Col. *Sir* J. *Assistant Quarter Master General*

Douglas, Lt. Col. *Sir* J. *Portug.Serv.*

Douglas, Col. *Sir* Wm. 91 *F.*

Doyle, Lieut. Col. *Sir* J. M. *Insp. of Militia in Guernsey*

D'Oyly, Lieut. Col. *Sir* Fra. 1 *F. G.*

Drummond, Lieut. Gen. *Sir* G. 97*F.*

Dundas, Lieut. Col. *Hon. Sir* R. L. *Royal Staff Corps*

D'Urban, Col. *Sir* B. 2 *W. I. R.*

Dyer, Lieut. Col. *Sir* John, *R. Art.*

Elley, Col. *Sir* J. *R.Reg. Horse Gds.*

Ellis, Col. *Sir* H. Walton, 23 *F.*

Fane, Major Gen. *Sir* H. 4 *Dr. Gds.*

Ferguson, Lieut. Gen. *Sir* R. Crauf.

Sicilian Regt.

Framingham, Col. *Sir* H. *Roy. Art.*

Fraser, Lieut. Col. *Sir* Aug. *do.*

Gardiner, Lt. Col. *Sir* R. *do.*

Gillespie, Maj. Gen. *Sir* R. R. 25*Dr.*

Gomm, Lt. Col. *Sir* W. *Coldst.F.G.*

Gordon, Lt. Col. *Hon. Sir* A. 3 *F.G.*

Gordon, Maj. Gen. *Sir* J. W. *Royal African Corps*

Grant, Major Gen. *Sir* Colq. 15 *Dr.*

Grant, Lt. Col. *Sir* Maxwell, 42 *F.*

Greville, Col. *Hon. Sir* C. J. 38 *F.*

Halkett, Maj. Gen. *Sir* Colin, 2 *Lt. Inf. King's German Legion*

Hardinge, Lieut. Col. *Sir* H. 1 *F.G.*

Hill, Lieut. Col. *Sir* T. N. 1 *F. G.*

Hope, Lt. Col. *Sir* J. A. 3 *F. G.*

Houstoun, Lt. Gen. *Sir* W. 2 *G. B.*

Howard, Major Gen. *Sir* K. A.

Howorth, Major Gen. *Sir* Edward

Jackson, Col. *Sir* R. D. *Coldstr.F.G.*

Keane, Major Gen. *Sir* J. *from* 60*F.*

Kempt, Major Gen. *Sir* J. 60 *F.*

Lambert, Major Gen. *Sir* John

Leith, Lieut. Gen. *Sir* A. 31 *F.*

Lumley, Lieut. Gen. *Hon. Sir* Wm. *Royal West India Rangers*

Macara, Lieut. Col. *Sir* R. 42 *F.*

Maclean, Col. *Sir* John, 27 *F.*

Malcolm, Lt. Col. *Sir* J. *Roy. Mar.*

May, Lieut. Col. *Sir* John, *Roy.Art.*

Nightingall, Lieut. Gen. *Sir* M. 69*F.*

O'Callaghan, Major Gen. *Hon. Sir* R. W. *late of* 39 *F.*

Oswald, Major Gen. *Sir* J. 1 *Greek Light Inf.*

Pack, Maj. Gen. *Sir* D. *late of* 71 *F.*

Ponsonby,

[1815]

Military Officers of the Order of the Bath.

Ponsonby, Major Gen. *Hon. Sir* W. 5 *Dr. G.*
Power, M. Gen. *Sir* M. *late of* 32 *F.*
Pratt, Col. *Sir* Charles, 5 *F.*
Pringle, Major Gen. *Sir* Wm. H. *Royal Newfoundland Fenc.*
Robe, Col. *Sir* Wm. *Royal Art.*
Robinson, Major Gen. *Sir* F. P. *late* 2 *Gar. Bn.*
Ross, Lieut. Col. *Sir* H. D. *Roy.Art.*
Scovell, Lieut. Col. *Sir* George, *late Staff Corps of Cavalry*
Somerset, Lt. Col. *Ld.* Fitz. 1 *F. G.*
Somerset, M. Gen. *Ld.* R. E. 4 *Dr.*
Stopford, Major Gen. *Hon. Sir* E.
Stovin, Lieut. Col. *Sir* F. 28 *F.*
Sutton, Lieut. Col. *Sir* Cha. 23 *F.*
Torrens, Major Gen. *Sir* Henry
Trench, Col. *Hon. Sir* R. Le Poer, 74 *F.*
Vandeleur, M. Gen. *Sir* J. O. 19 *Dr.*
Vivian, Major Gen. *Sir* R. H. *late of* 7 *Dr.*
Wale, Maj. Gen. *Sir* C. *late of* 66 *F.*
Walker, Major Gen. *Sir* G. T. *Meuron's Regt.*
Warde, Lieut. Gen. *Sir* H. 68 *F.*
Williams, Lt. Col. *Sir* E. K. 81 *F.*

Williams, Lt. Col. *Sir* R. *Roy.Mar.*
Williams, Lt. Col. *Sir* W. 13 *F.*
Wilson, Lt. Col. *Sir* James, 48 *F*

Honorary Knights Commanders.

Alten, M. Gen. C. *Baron*, 1 *Lt. Inf. King's German Legion*
Arentschildt, Col. Fr. *Baron* De, 3 *Huss. King's German Legion*
Dornberg, Maj. Gen. W. De, *Brunswick Inf.*
Hertsberg, Lieut. Col. F. A. De, *Brunswick Inf.*
Hinuber, Major Gen. H. De, 3 *Line King's German Legion*
Hartmann, Lt. Col. J. *Art. King's German Legion*
Linsingen, Lieut. Gen. C. *Baron*, 1 *Huss. King's German Legion*
Low, Major Gen. Siegesm. *Baron*, 4 *Line King's German Legion*
Nugent, Lieut. Gen. *Count*
Walmoden, Lt. Gen. *Count*, 1 *L.D. King's German Legion*

Rank.	Name.	Regiment.	Army.
		Rank in the	
Colonel -	Charles, E. of Harrington	5Dec.1792	Gen. 25Sept.1803
Lieut. Colonel and Colonel	Terence O'Loghlin	1Sept.1808	M.Gen. 1Jan.1812
Supernumer. Lieut. Colonel	Francis Slater Rebow	20Aug.1807	M.Gen. 1Jan.1812
Major and Lieut. Colonel	Samuel Ferrior	22June1810	
Major -	⊚John Camac	1Mar.1812	
Captain -	John Whale	13Nov.1809	
	Montague Lind	22June1810	
	Edward Kelly	2Aug.	13Sept.1805
	George Calcot Gough	17Sept.1812	
	Richard Lothian Dickson	23do.	
	John Berger	20May1813	Major 4June1814
	Hon. F. C. Stanhope	24June	18Aug.1808
	Edward Pellew	15Nov.	
Lieutenant -	George Randall	15Apr.1811	
	George James Sulivan	26Sept.	
	William Mayne	do.	
	John Brydges Leonard	22Sept.1812	2Mar.1809
	Benjamin Fox	23do.	
	Cha. Sawkins Williams	10Jan.1813	
	Edw. Trant Bontein	21Nov.	
	Henry Wyatt	22do.	
Cornet & Sub-Lieutenant	Francis Scrimes Pilcher	12Mar.1812	23Jan. 1812
	Thomas Eman	18Oct.	Adjutant
	R— Dean	1Jan.1813	
	Wm.StewartRichardson	23Feb.	
	Wilkins George Terry	1June1814	22Apr. 1813
	Samuel Cox	do.	
Adjutant - -	Thomas Eman	18Oct.1812	Cornet 18Oct.1812
Surgeon - -	M— L— Este	3Oct.1812	
Assistant Surg.	Richard Gough	22Sept.1812	
	John Haddy James	27Oct.	
Veterin. Surg.	Samuel Anth. Bloxham	17Jan.1805	
	Francis Dalton	20May1813	

Scarlet.—Facings blue.—Lace gold.

Agent, Messrs. Greenwood, Cox and Hammersley.

N. B. *The Officers who have no Date in the Column of Rank in the Army, take Rank in the Army by their Regimental Commissions.*

Rank.	Name.	Rank in the Regiment.	Army.
Colonel -	Wm. *Earl* Cathcart, *K.T.*	7Aug.1797 Gen.	1Jan.1812
Lieut. Colonel and Colonel	Charles Barton	14June1805 L.Gen.	25Apr.1808
Supernumer. Lieut. Colonel	William John Arabin	25June1788 Gen.	4June1814
Major and Lieut. Colonel	*Hon.* George Murray	20Aug.1807 Col.	4June1814
Major - -	*Sir* Eman. F. Agar, *Kt.*	28Apr.1814 20Apr.1814	
Captain -	⊚ Charles Jackson	13Apr.1807 Major	28July1814
	Hon. Edw. P— Lygon	15Feb.1808	
	Thomas Charretee	23Jan.1812 25Dec.1807	
	William Boyce	30Apr. Major	4June1814
	Richard Fitz Gerald	18May Lt.Col.	4June1814
	Hon. Hen. Edw. Irby	22Sept. 7Aug.1806	
	Ja. Park Miller Kenyon	23do.	
	William Moreton	30Jan.1814	
Lieutenant -	*Sir* John Cox, *Bt.*	25May1810 14Apr.1806	
	Richard Meares	23Sept.1812 10Mar.1808	
	William Elliott	27Nov.	
	Francis Upjohn	28Mar.1813 4Sept.1810	
	Samuel Waymouth	do.	
	Chum Barton	30Jan.1814	
	John Lowe	16June	
	Frederick Evelyn	23July	
Cornet & Sub-Lieutenant	Hugh William Barton	12Nov.1812	
	Abraham Kenyon	24June1813	
	Thomas Smith	14Aug. Lieut.	15Nov.1812
	Thomas Marten	22Nov.	
	Wallis Grieves	30Jan.1814	
	Henry Hamilt. Douglas	12Mar.	
	Alexander M'Innes	16June	
Adjutant - -	J— Clues	24June1813	
Surgeon -	James Moore	1Oct.1806	
*	Samuel Broughton	22Sept.1812	
Assistant Surg.	Thomas Drinkwater	22Sept.1812	
Veterin. Surg.	John Field	31Jan.1805	
	Jeremiah Field	24Apr.1813	

Scarlet.—Facings blue.—Lace gold.

Agent, Messrs. Greenwood, Cox and Hammersley.

Royal

Rank.	Name.	Rank in the Regiment.	Army.
Colonel ⊟✖	Arthur, *Duke of* Wellington, *K. G.*	1Jan.1813	Field Marshal 21June1813
Lieut. Col. ⊙̵	John Dorrien	25Dec.1799	M.Gen. 4June1811
	John Elley	6Mar.1806	Col. 7Mar.1813
	Sir R. Cham. Hill, *Kt.*	13May181?	1Jan. 1812
Major - ⊚	Thomas Athorpe	6Mar.1806	Lt.Col. 4June1813
	Robert Christ. Packe	13May1813	
Captain - -	John Thoyts	22Aug.1805	
	William Rob. Clayton	27Apr 1809	
	Clement Hill	4Apr.1811	Lt.Col. 30Dec.1813
	Wm. Tyrwhitt Drake	29Aug.	
	William Richardson	26Dec.	
	Geo. W. Vill. Villiers	17Sept.1812	
	John Taylor	30do.	
	Hon. Charles Murray	1Oct.	Major 4June1813
	John Jebb	13May1813	
	Henry Hanmer	18Nov.	
Lieutenant -	John Buck Riddlesden	4Apr.1811	
	Wm. Cunliffe Shawe	26Dec.	
	Edward Hill	17Sept.1812	
	Everard Wm. Bouverie	15Oct.	
	Charles Aug. Fitzroy	16do.	
	Henry Ellis Boates	28Jan.1813	
	Tathwell Bak. Tathwell	9Sept.	
	Simeon Hirst	10do.	Adjutant
	George Smith	18Nov.	
	Hon. Geo. John Watson	24Mar.1814	
	Lord Wm. Pitt Lennox	3Nov.	
Cornet - -	John Kirkby Picard	2Sept.1813	
	Ar. Bro. de Capel Brooke	30do.	19Aug.1813
	Lionel Edw. Heathcote	28Oct.	
	Philip Paulett Doyne	23Dec.	
	Lewis Clutterbuck	28Apr.1814	
	Gustavus Brander	9June	
	James Arnold	1Sept.	
	Robert James Harrison	3Nov.	
Adjutant - -	Simeon Hirst	16Oct.1812	Lieut. 10Sept.1813
Surgeon - -	David Slow	18July1805	23Aug.1799
Assistant Surg.	George Hickman	28Sept.1809	
	John Langford	5Mar.1812	18July 1811
Veterin. Surg.	James Seddall	23Dec.1797	
	John Seddall	10Oct.1812	

Blue.—Facings scarlet.—Lace gold.

Agent, Messrs. Greenwood, Cox and Hammersley.

Rank.	Name.	Regiment.	Rank in the Army.	
Colonel - -	*Sir* David Dundas, *K.B.*	27Jan.1813	Gen.	29Apr.1802
Lieut. Colonel	William Fuller	22Aug.1805	Col.	4June1813
Major - - {	George Teesdale	30May1805	Lt.Col.	1Jan.1812
	Robert Evatt Acklom	21Nov.	Lt.Col.	1Jan.1812
	Henry Graham	12June1799	Major	4June1811
	William Gore	17Dec.1802	Major	4June1813
	Michael Turner	4July1805		
	Richard Barrow	2Jan.1806		
Captain -	James Frank. Naylor	15May		
	William Elton	11May1809		
	John Dorset Bringhurst	24Oct.1811	Major	12Apr.1814
	John Paget Sweny	9Jan.1812		
	George Fairholme	20Feb.		
	Robert Wallace	20Oct.1814		
	James Leatham	12June1806		
	John Fisk	28July1808		
	Thomas Nutc. Quicke	4Aug.		
	Wm. Alex. Maxwell	15Aug.1811		
	William Stirling	19Mar.1812		
Lieutenant -	Ralph Babington	18June		
	Francis Brooke	31Dec.		
	Hon. W— S— Bernard	15July1813	16Aug.1810	
	Robert Toovey Hawley	30Sept.		
	Tho. Coventry Brander	30Mar.1814		
	Thomas Shelver	31do.	Adjutant	
	Edward Hamill	17Nov.		
	Wm. D'Arcey Irvine	11June1812		
	George Quicke	15Apr.1813		
	Jos. Edward Greaves	22do.		
Cornet - -	Tho. Falkiner Middleton	28Oct.		
	John Nembhard Hibbert	13Jan.1814		
	Hon. H— B— Bernard	15June		
	Wm. Warburton Huntley	16do.		
	*			
Paymaster -	John Webster	30July1807		
Adjutant - -	Thomas Shelver	28Feb.1812	Lieut.	31Mar.1814
Quarter-Master	James Scott	25Aug.1809		
Surgeon - -	John Going	17Dec.1801		
Assistant Surg. {	William M'Auley	16Aug.1810	8Feb. 1810	
	R— Pearson	13May1813		
Veterinary Surg.	William Clarkson	25May1805	21Dec.1803	

Scarlet.—*Facings blue.*—*Lace gold.*

Agent, Mr. Adair, Pall Mall Court.

2d

Rank.	Name.	Rank in the Regiment.	Rank in the Army.
Colonel - -	Charles Craufurd	18Sept.1807	Lt.Gen. 25July1810
Lieut. Colonel	James Kearney	16June1814	25July 1810
Major - -	William Spearman	5July1810	Lt.Col. 4June1811
	William Gordon	21July1814	4June1811
Captain -	Weston Hames	25June1803	Major 4June1814
	Robert B— Gabriel	9May1805	Major 26Aug.1813
	Henry Tower	30Oct.1806	
	John Lateward	29June1809	
	Peter Hunter	2Nov.	15June1809
	Henry Boyd Gamble	30do.	
	William Chamberlayne	9May1811	
	William Rogers	4Mar.1813	
Lieutenant -	John Hames	30July1806	
	F— Collins	30Nov.1809	Adjutant
	Harry Bradburne	18Oct.1810	
	Edward Dyer	16May1811	
	John Hunter	30do.	
	John Horton	10Dec.1812	
	Walter Raleigh Soulsby	4Mar.1813	
	George Page	4Aug.1814	
	Charles Kearney	8Sept.	
Cornet - -	Thomas Wood	25June1812	
	Edward Ruffo	19Nov.	23July 1815
	George Knox	10Dec.	
	Clayton Bayley	23Dec.1813	
	Fergus James Graham	27Jan.1814	
	Wm. Richards. Graham	10Feb.	
	Lawrence Pigou	17Nov.	
	*		
Paymaster -	George Watson	17Sept.1805	
Adjutant - -	F— Collins	25Mar.1808	Lieut. 30Nov.1809
Quarter-Master	—— Marsden	25Aug.1809	
Surgeon - -	John Abercrombie	17Mar.1814	19June1800
Assistant Surg.	Matt. B— Cowie	17Sept.1812	
	James Kane	29Apr.1813	
Veterinary Surg.	William Woodman	25Feb.1813	

Scarlet.—Facings black.—Lace silver.

Agent, Messrs. Greenwood, Cox and Hammersley.

Rank.	Name.	Rank in the Regiment.	Rank in the Army.
Colonel - -	Richard Vyse	2Apr.1804	Gen. 1Jan.1812
Lieut. Col.	SirGran.T.Calcraft,Kt. / George Holmes	25Dec.1800 / 10Oct.1811	M.Gen. 4June1813
Major - -	John Chapman / George Watts	26Mar.1812 / 27May1813	2Aug.1810
Captain -	George Tito Brice / William Tiede / George White / —— Evans / Edmund Richard Storey / Nathaniel Storey / George Maunsell / John Ferrier	17Dec.1803 / 2Nov.1809 / 16do. / 7Dec. / 21do. / 30May1811 / 18July / 17Oct.	Major 27May1813
Lieutenant -	Sentleger Hill / George Goate / John Walker Gray / Lawford Burne / Edward Homewood / John Grant / Beyrimhof de Daubrawa / John Leggett / George Towell / Alexis Pellichody / Alex. F— Macintosh / William Stuart	11Sept.1806 / 19Feb.1807 / 6Aug. / 11Aug.1808 / 30May1811 / 24July / 10Oct. / 30Apr.1812 / 13May / 28do. / 11June / 16July	22Aug.1805 / 3Sept.1801 / 15Sept.1808 / Adjutant / 27Jan. 1808
Cornet - -	T— B— Lane / Robert Mulhallen / Francis John Greene / Ja. Warring. LaGrange / John Addison	10Oct.1812 / 8do. / 27Jan.1814 / 10Mar. / 1Sept.	15July 1813
Paymaster -	John Arscott	23June1808	
Adjutant - -	George Towell	9Aug.1810	Lieut. 13May1814
Quarter-Master	John Martin	22Feb.1810	
Surgeon - -	William Marsden	24Aug.1797	
Assistant Surg.	John Coleman / Samuel Bell	31Aug.1797 / 11June1812	
Veterinary Surg.	Thomas Rose	5Jan.1809	

Scarlet.—Facings white.—Lace gold.

Agent, Messrs. Collyer, Park Place, St. James's.

4th

Rank.	Name.	Rank in the Regiment.	Army.
Colonel - -	☒Henry Fane	3 Aug. 1814	M.Gen. 25 July 1810
Lieut. Colonel	Francis Sherlock	16 Feb. 1809	Col. 4 June 1814
Major - -	Robert Ross	16 July 1807	Lt. Col. 4 June 1813
	William Ogilvie	27 Dec. 1810	
Captain -	John White	5 June 1805	
	H Le Grange Dougan	29 May 1806	
	Patrick Hamilton	28 Aug.	
	Thomas Boyd	27 Dec. 1810	
	Charles D— Sibthorpe	23 May 1811	
	John King	20 Aug. 1812	
	Mervyn Richardson	17 Sept.	
	Thomas Hutton	1 Dec. 1814	
Lieutenant	James Shaw	7 Sept. 1804	22 Oct. 1799
	Richard Falkiner	7 July 1808	
	Alderson Hodson	22 Aug. 1811	
	William Burn	23 do.	
	Frederick Horn	12 Dec.	
	William Woods	23 Jan. 1812	28 Dec. 1809
	James Rallet	1 Apr.	Adjutant
	Thomas Woodcock	2 do.	
	John Dexter	3 Sept.	6 Apr. 1809
	John Searanke	18 Feb. 1813	
	James B— Smith	26 Aug.	
	Hon. George Blaquiere	25 Nov.	5 Mar. 1812
	Frederick Polhill	24 Aug. 1814	
	Giles Rickaby	1 Dec.	
Cornet - -	Thomas Shuttleworth	29 July 1813	
	George Williamson	7 Apr. 1814	
	Richard Lawless	21 do.	
Paymaster -	Erasmus Goodwin	7 Mar. 1805	
Adjutant - -	James Rallet	18 July 1811	Lieut. 1 Apr. 1812
Quarter-Master	John Jolly	25 Aug. 1809	
Surgeon - -	Robert Pyper	3 Sept. 1812	30 Jan. 1800
Assistant Surg.	John Freer	16 Nov. 1809	
	Frederick Brown	25 June 1812	4 Jan. 1810
Veterinary Surg.	Andrew Kirwan	21 July 1798	

Scarlet.—Facings blue.—Lace silver.

Agent, Messrs. Hopkinson, No. 5, St. Alban's Street, Pall Mall.

5th

112 5th (or Princess Charlotte of Wales's) Regt. of Dragoon Guards.

Permitted to bear on their Colours and Appointments the Word " SALAMANCA," in Commemoration of the Battle of 21st July, 1812.

Colonel - -	Thomas Bland	18Nov.1790	Gen. 1Jan.1801
Lieut. Col. ◎–{	*Hon.* Robert Taylor	28Feb.1792	L.Gen. 25Apr.1808
	Hon. William Ponsonby	24Feb.1803	M.Gen. 4June1813
◎(	Serjentson Prescott	4June1813	
Major - - {	Arthur H— Gordon	8Apr.1813	4June1811
	William Irwin	4June	
	Adam Ormsby	25June1803	Major 4June1814
	Richard Drake Cane	20Dec.1810	
	William Walker	8Aug.1811	
Captain - {	Stephen Gordon	15Jan.1812	
	Henry Jackson Close	16do.	
	John Brunskill	20Aug.	
	Edward Houghton	22Apr.1813	
	George Bradshaw	17June	23Jan. 1812
	Edward Kellett	2Aug.1805	
	Fra. G— Bradshaw	30Apr.1807	5Dec. 1805
	Charles Walker	20Dec.1810	
	Joseph Jackson	7Mar.1811	Adjutant
	Wm. Nunn Richards	18Apr.	
Lieutenant {	George Miles	16May	
	Braithwaite Christie	3Oct.	
	Thomas Mathews	6Feb.1812	
	Edward Barrington	13do.	
	Ashton Johnson Byrom	22Sept.1814	25Feb. 1813
	Arthur Baker	3Nov.	7Oct. 1813
	James Spence	9Apr.1812	
	Daniel Stephens	23do.	
Cornet - - {	John Watson	20Aug.	
	Henry Higinbotham	13May1813	
	Aylmer Burke	7Oct.	
	William Locke	9June1814	
Paymaster -	James Brunker	26July1806	
Adjutant - -	Joseph Jackson	9Dec.1808	Lieut. 7Mar.1811
Quarter-Master ——	Cochrane	17June1813	
Surgeon - -	Henry Job	5Nov.1812	18Apr.1811
Assistant Surg. {	Thomas Charlton Speer	29Apr.1813	
	Isaac Ambrose	9Sept.	
Veterinary Surg.	John Brown Stanley	1June1798	

Scarlet.—Facings green.—Lace gold.

Agent, Messrs. Collyer, Park Place, St. James's.

Rank.	Name.	Rank in the Regiment.	Army.
Colonel - -	Hen. E. *of* Carhampton 23June1788	Gen.	1Jan.1798
Lieut. Colonel	{ Alexander John Goldie 12Sept.1799 { St. George French 13June1811	M.Gen.	4June1811
Major - -	{ James Lewis Higgins 24July1807 { Charles Irvine 21Oct.1813	Lt. Col.	4June1813
Captain -	(Henry Shum 12Sept.1805 | Thomas Forrest Fisher 2Apr.1807 | William Rutledge 7July | Francis Hartwell 31Mar.1808 | Patrick Heron Goldie 14Feb.1811 | Henry Archdall 19Apr. | Andrew Ferguson 13June (William Serle 20do.	Major 4June1813 Major 20Feb.1812 25Feb. 1808 28Nov.1806
Lieutenant -	(Sampson T— French 30June1804 | Robert M'Dowall 30Sept.1807 | William French 20Dec.1810 | John Jones 28Feb.1811 | John Goldie 19Apr. | *Hon.* Geo. Cathcart 1July | David Hay 31Oct. | John Stephenson 28Feb.1812 | John Caulfield 17Nov.1813 (Charles Philip Hodson 18do.	27May 1802 Adjutant 11Nov.1807 25May 1810 25May 1809 7Dec.1809
Cornet - -	(Thomas Raikes 28Feb.1811 | William C— Hamilton 10Oct. | Tho. Gardiner Marshall 20Feb.1812 | William Martin 16July | James Stewart 17Mar.1814 | William Miles Kington 7Apr. (Mark Blake 19May	
Paymaster -	David Hay 7Apr.1808	
Adjutant - -	Robert M'Dowall 19Sept.1805	Lieut. 30Sept.1807
Quarter-Master	Charles Short 25Aug.1809	
Surgeon - -	Warren Champion 9Sept.1813	
Assistant Surg.	{ Gilbert Austin 4Nov.1813 { Thomas Howell 19May1814	4July 1811
Veterinary Surg.	John Hayward 29Apr.1813	

Scarlet.—*Facings white.—Lace silver.*
English Agent, Messrs. Collyer, Park Place, St. James's.
Irish Agent, Messrs. Armit and Borough, Dublin.
P   7th

[1815]

114 7th (or Princess Royal's) Regt. of Drag. Guards.

Rank.	Name.	Rank in the Regiment.	Army.
Colonel - -	Richard Rich Wilford	20Nov.1813	Gen. 4June1814
Lieut. Colonel	Francis Dunne	16June1814	25Oct. 1809
Major - -	Henry Aldborough Head	2June1814	Lt. Col. 4June1814
	Kane Bunbury	24July	Lt. Col. 4June1814
Captain - -	Thomas Younghusband	3May1800	Major 1Jan.1812
	William Davis	25June1803	Major 4June1814
	Wm. Mansfield Morrison	2June1804	Major 4June1813
	Edmund Power	19July	Major 4June1814
	William Power	1Dec.	Major 4June1814
	Edw. Ralph C. Sheldon	20Aug.1807	6Aug.1807
	Henry Westropp	1Nov.1810	
	Ralph Smyth	21July1814	
Lieutenant	John Darke	23July1803	28Aug.1801
	John Scholey	14July1804	
	John Burton Phillipson	14Mar.1805	
	R— Hay	17Apr.1806	25June1803
	John Lovewell	7Dec.1809	
	Henry Crotty	28Mar.1811	
	Joshua Dunwoody	4July	Adjutant
	David Robb	2Jan.1812	16Oct. 1809
	James Bennett	2Dec.1813	
	James Fawsett	21July1814	
Cornet - -	John Graham	13Dec.1810	
	William Kelly	14Feb.1811	
	Henry Chivers Vince	18Mar.1813	
	Thomas Armstrong	17June	
	—— Blood	2Dec.	
	George Green Nicolls	11Aug.1814	
	George Henry Arnold	17Nov.	
Paymaster -	John Jennings	26Dec.1805	
Adjutant - -	Joshua Dunwoody	18May1809	Lieut. 4July1811
Quarter-Master	Hugh Langshaw	25Nov.1813	
Surgeon - -	Joseph Rose	30June1795	28Sept.1793
Assistant Surg.	John Lyster	14July1808	31Mar.1808
	John Williamson	28Oct.1813	22Apr. 1813
Veterinary Surg.	John Mellowes	6Nov.1801	

Scarlet.—Facings black.—Lace gold.

Agent, Mr. Bownas, Whitehall.

Rank.	Name.	Rank in the Regiment.	Army.
Colonel - -	Thomas Garth	7Jan.1801	Gen. 4June1814
Lieut. Col.	Hon. George de Grey	6June1799	M.Gen. 4June1811
	Arthur Benj. Clifton	22Nov.1810	25July 1810
Major - -	Philip Dorville	17Oct.1811	Lt.Col. 4June1814
	Charles Purvis	7May1812	
Captain -	Charles E— Radcliffe	1Dec.1804	Major 4June1814
	Henry Stisted	5Jan.1809	
	Alex. Kennedy Clark	13Dec.1810	
	Paul Phipps	25July1811	
	Nathaniel Eckersley	16Oct.	
	Ralph Heathcote	17do.	
	Frederick Watson	7May1812	
	Edward Cha. Windsor	18June	
Lieutenant -	Charles Foster	18Nov.1807	
	Henry Robert Carden	13Apr.1809	
	George Gunning	7Dec.	2Sept.1807
	Frederick Ross	27Sept.1810	20Sept.1810
	—— Cook	24Oct.	Adjutant
	Townshend Rich. Keily	25do.	
	Sigismund Trafford	25July1811	
	Frederick Cobbold	15Aug.	
	Lewis Gasquet	14Nov.	
	Samuel Windowe	21do.	
	Charles Bridges	20Feb.1812	
Cornet - -	—— Magniac	2Sept.1813	
	William Sturges	30Dec.	
	—— Stevenson	24Mar.1814	
	Hon. John Massey	31do.	
	Stephen Simpson	11May	3June1813
	Henry Pulleine	12do.	
Paymaster -	Michael Byrne	15Oct.1807	19Oct. 1804
Adjutant - -	—— Cook	1June1809	Lieut. 24Oct.1810
Quarter-Master	William Waddell	8July1813	
Surgeon - -	George Steed	17Jan.1811	
Assistant Surg.	Christo. Rich. Alderson	28Oct.1813	4Oct. 1810
	Thomas Prosser	9Dec.	29Aug.1811
Veterinary Surg.	William Ryding	2June1804	2May 1800

Scarlet.—Facings blue.—Lace gold.

Agent, Messrs. Greenwood, Cox and Hammersley.

[1815]

116   2d (or Royal North Brit.) Regt. of Dragoons.

Rank.	Name.	Regiment.	Rank in the Army.
Colonel - -	W. *Mar. of* Lothian, K.T. 27 Jan. 1813	Gen.	3 May 1796
Lieut. Colonel	James Inglis Hamilton 16 June 1807	Col.	4 June 1814
Major - -	Isaac Blake Clarke 16 June 1807	Lt. Col.	4 June 1813
	Thomas Pate Hankin 4 Apr. 1808	Lt. Col.	4 June 1814
Captain -	Edward Cheney 3 May 1800	Major	1 Jan. 1812
	James Poole 25 May 1803	Major	4 June 1813
	Robert Vernon 23 Nov. 1804	Major	4 June 1814
	Thomas Reignolds 25 Dec.	Major	4 June 1814
	George James 16 June 1807		
	Hon. Fred. Cathcart 11 Feb. 1808	Major	28 July 1814
	Lever Legge 13 June 1811		
	Henry Gee Barnard 29 Sept. 1814	15 July 1813	
Lieutenant	John Stobo 25 June 1803		
	William Walker 10 Apr. 1805		
	Henry M'Millan do.	Adjutant	
	David Ronald. Dickson 19 Dec.		
	John Mills 5 May 1808		
	Edward Payne 13 Oct.		
	Francis Stupart 14 Dec. 1809		
	G— H— Falconar 21 Nov. 1811		
	James Wemyss 15 Sept. 1814	19 Nov. 1812	
Cornet - -	——— Hodgson 11 July 1811		
	James Carruthers 22 Aug.		
	Charles James 21 May 1812		
	James Gape 29 Apr. 1813		
	Charles Wyndham 13 May		
	Jas. Reg. Tovin Graham 20 Jan. 1814		
	Edward Westby 12 May	17 Feb. 1814	
	*		
Paymaster -	William Dawson 13 Oct. 1814		
Adjutant - -	Henry M'Millan 1 Oct. 1802	Lieut.	10 Apr. 1805
Quarter-Master	John Lennox 3 June 1813		
Surgeon - -	Robert Daun, M. D. 4 Aug. 1814		
Assistant Surg.	Robert Buchannon 4 Aug. 1808		
	James Alexander 9 Jan. 1812		
Veterinary Surg.	John Trigg 17 Dec. 1807	23 Dec. 1797	

Scarlet.— Facings blue.—Lace gold.

Agent, Mr. Croasdaile, Silver Street, Golden Square.

3d

3d (or the King's own) Regiment of Dragoons. 117

Permitted to bear on their Colours and Appointments the Word " SALAMANCA," in Commemoration of the Battle of 21st July, 1812.

Rank.	Name.	Regiment.	Army.
		Rank in the	
Colonel - -	William Cartwright	18Nov.1807	Lt.Gen. 25Ap.1808
Lieut. Colonel	☉ *Lord* Charles Manners	2July1812	1Aug.1811
Major - -	{ Thomas Hutchins	10Dec.1812	
	{ Henry Barrington	24June1813	
Captain -	⌈ Rich. Staunton Sitwell	22Sept.1808	
	⎮ William Henry Cooper	5Apr.1809	
	⎮ Shallcross Jacson	27July	
	⎬ Charles Stisted	7Feb.1811	Major 4June1814
	⎮ Thomas C— Watson	25July	
	⎮ John Hunter	31Dec.1812	
	⎮ William Burn	28Jan.1813	
	⌊ Edward Page Turner	12Nov.1814	25Dec. 1812
Lieutenant -	⌈ John Bowater	10Oct.1810	
	⎮ Croston Johnson	14Mar.1811	
	⎮ William Manfull	31Oct.	
	⎮ George Lloyd Hodges	16Jan.1812	7Jan. 1808
	⎮ Jeremiah Ratcliffe -	11Mar.	
	⎮ David Gansell Jebb	12do.	
	⎬ Robert Webb	25do.	
	⎮ Delacy Evans	26do.	1Dec.1808
	⎮ Thomas Tatlock	7May	15Aug.1811
	⎮ B— Burnet	11June	
	⎮ George Watson	22Oct.	
	⎮ George Crabtree	29do.	Adjutant
	⌊ Mark Johnson	26Nov.	
Cornet - -	⌈ George Lloyd	30Dec.1813	23Oct. 1813
	⎬ William Semple	2Mar.1814	
	⎮ Cha.Wm.S.Dal.Holmes	21Apr.	
	⌊ Henry Hunter	9June	
Paymaster -	John Jones	23July1812	
Adjutant - -	George Crabtree	11Mar.1812	Lieut. 29Oct.1812
Quarter-Master	Richard Brunton	25Aug.1809	
Surgeon - -	Thomas French	25Aug.1808	9Oct. 1794
Assistant Surg. {	James Dawn	28Oct.1813	
	Thomas Backhouse	24Feb.1814	
Veterinary Surg.	John Blanchard	26Oct.1804	4May 1801

Scarlet.—Facings blue.—Lace gold.

Agent, Messrs. Greenwood, Cox and Hammersley.

4th

118 4th (or the Queen's own) Regiment of Dragoons.

Permitted to bear on their Colours and Appointments the Word " SALAMANCA," in Commemoration of the Battle of 21st July, 1812.

Rank.	Name.	Regiment.	Rank in the Army.
Colonel - -	Francis Hugonin	9Nov.1808	Lt.Gen. 25July1810
Lieut. Col. ☜ {	Lord R. E. H.Somerset	3Sept.1801	M.Gen. 4June1813
	James Charles Dalbiac	25Nov.1808	Col. 4June1814
Major - - {	James Hugonin	19Dec.1811	
	Bohun Shore	28Feb.1812	Lt.Col. 25Oct.1809
Captain - {	William Onslow	29Aug.1805	Major 4June1813
	Carlisle Spedding	17July1806	
	John Lewis Phillips	17Nov 1807	5Feb. 1806
	Charles Walton	11Feb.1808	
	James Holmes	28Apr.	
	William Henry Wright	19May	
	Hon. Dudley Carleton	10Oct.1811	
	William H— Fryer	26Dec.	
Lieutenant - {	George Chantry	17June1807	Adjutant
	Edward Wildman	29Oct.	14May 1807
	Norcliffe Norcliffe	28Apr.1808	
	Arthur Francis Gregory	19May	
	John Carleton	11Apr.1809	
	Hamond Alpe	12do.	
	William Tongue	2Oct.	
	William Fendall	3do.	
	*		
Cornet - - {	Michael Kirby	25June1812	
	Robert Burrowes	25Feb.1813	
	Harry Cazalet	27May	
	Henry Pratt	1July	
	John Charles Farmer	9Sept.	5Nov.1812
	Bicknell Coney	1Dec.	
	Robert Lawr. Townsend	2do.	
	George Hawkins	23do.	
Paymaster -	Hugh Patrickson	23Oct.1806	
Adjutant - -	George Chantry	23May1805	Lieut. 17June1807
Quarter-Master	Hugh Allan	14Sept.1809	
Surgeon - -	John F— Wylde	4June1812	12Feb. 1807
Assistant Surg. {	Thomas Hickson	12Jan.1809	
	John Barry	26May1814	
Veterinary Surg.	Thomas Bird	6Apr.1809	

Scarlet.—Facings green.—Lace silver.

Agent, Messrs. Hopkinson, No. 5, St. Alban's Street, Pall Mall.

Rank.	Name.	Rank in the Regiment.	Army.
Colonel -	Geo. E. *of* Pembroke,*K.G.* 15Dec.1797		Gen. 1Jan.1812
Lieut. Colonel {	Richard O'Donovan 2May1800		M.Gen. 4June1813
	Joseph Muter 4June1813		Col. 4June1814
Major - - {	Fiennes S— Miller 25May1809		Lt.Col. 4June1814
	Robert Ellice 25June1812		Lt.Col.16Mar.1809
Captain - {	Henry Madox 19Dec.1805		
	Wm. Frederick Browne 7May1807		2Apr. 1807
	Thomas Mackay 3Dec.		
	William Fred. Hadden 28Jan.1808		14Jan. 1808
	Edward Holbech 25May1809		
	Thomas Chapman 21Dec.		
	Hon. Sholto Douglas 23Aug.1810		24May 1810
	James Heywood 1Aug.1811		
Lieutenant - {	Theophilus Biddulph 22May1806		
	Augustus Saltern Willet 27Aug.1807		
	John Linton 25Jan.1809		
	Henry William Petre 26do.		
	Barth. Edward Barry 22Mar.1810		
	Alexander Hassard 23Apr.1812		
	Frederick Johnstone 18Feb.1813		
	Samuel Black 8July		
	Richard Down 31Mar.1814		
	John Mussen 23June		
Cornet - - {	Paul Ruffo 29Aug.1811		
	Michael Clusky 9Jan.1812		Adjutant
	Mansell Dames 6Feb.		
	John Ramsden 16Sept.1813		
	John Delancy Allingham 7Oct.		
	William Armstrong 23June1814		
	W— R— Ellis 25Aug.		
Paymaster -	William Armstrong 18Oct.1813		
Adjutant - -	Michael Clusky 9Jan.1812		Cornet 9Jan.1812
Quarter-Master	James Kerr 9Dec.1813		
Surgeon - -	John Bolton 14Sept.1791		
Assistant Surg. {	Wm. Henry Picketts 16Mar.1809		
	William Campbell 25Oct.1814		28Oct. 1813
Veterinary Surg.	Richard Vincent 25Nov.1797		

Scarlet.—Facings yellow.—Lace silver.

English Agent, Mr. Browell, Stable Yard, St. James's.
Irish Agent, Messrs. Atkinson, Dublin.

120 7th (or the Queen's own) Regt. of (Light) Dragoons.
(HUSSARS.)

Rank.	Name.	Regiment.	Rank in the Army.
Colonel -	⊙Henry, *E. of* Uxbridge	16May1801	Lt.Gen. 25Ap.1808
Lieut. Colonel	Edward Kerrison	4Apr.1805	Col. 4June1813
Major - -	{ Edward Hodge { William Thornhill	7May1812 8Apr.1813	
Captain -	{ Thomas Pipon William Verner Thomas Wm. Robbins Edward Keane Peter Augustus Heyliger Thomas Wildman James Hamlyn James John Fraser Charles Moray James D. Elphinstone	27Feb.1807 21July1808 25May1809 15June 2Aug.1810 18Feb.1813 8Apr. 17June 11Aug.1814 25Sept.	1Dec. 1806 9Mar.1809 23Dec. 1813
Lieutenant -	{ Arthur Myer John George Maddison Standish O'Grady William Shirley William Grenfell Robert Douglas Robert Uniacke John Robert Gordon Henry, *Lord* Paget John Daniel Edward James Peters John Harcourt Powell	24May1810 7May1812 6Aug. 7Jan.1813 11Mar. 17June 15July 15Sept. 21July1814 21Oct. 10Nov. 12do.	Adjutant 19Nov.1812. 30Mar.1813
Cornet - -	{ John Symmonds Breedon John Wildman Frederick Beatty Stephen Rice Frederick Towers	6May1813 3June 6Oct. 7do. 18Nov.	
Paymaster -	James Crooke Thomson	31Jan.1811	
Adjutant -	Arthur Myer	23Mar.1809	Lieut. 24May1810
Quarter-Master	John Greenwood	25Aug.1809	
Surgeon - -	David Irwin	22July1795	
Assistant Surg.	{ Robert Alex.Chermside James Moffitt	16Aug.1810 24Oct.1811	
Veterinary Surg.	Richard Dorville	13Dec.1810	

Blue.—Facings white.—Lace silver.

Agent, Messrs. Greenwood, Cox and Hammersley.

8th

8th (or the King's Royal Irish) Regiment of 121 (Light) Dragoons.

Rank.	Name.	Rank in the Regiment.	Army.
Colonel - -	John Floyd	13Sept.1804	Gen. 1Jan.1812
Lieut. Colonel	{ John Sullivan Wood	16June1803	M.Gen.25July1810
	Christopher Johnston	24Jan.1811	
	{ Henry Westenra	13Aug.1813	1Jan. 1812
Major - -	{ Ev. J. M'Gregor Murray	6June1811	Lt.Col. 13Aug.1812
	{ William Martin	13Aug.1813	
Captain -	⎧ George Russell Deare	25Feb.1804	Major 4June1814
	⎪ Nicholas Brutton	12July1806	Major 4June1814
	⎪ George Brown	26Mar.1807	26Feb. 1807
	⎪ William Locker	9July	
	⎪ George Warren Walker	5Apr.1809	
	⎨ John G— Baumgardt	10Jan.1810	
	⎪ John Williams	11do.	
	⎪ Thornhill Warrington	23Jan.1812	
	⎪ Edward Carter	8Apr.1813	9June1808
	⎪ Yarrell Johnson	9June	
	⎩ Samuel T— Edwards	13Aug.	
Lieutenant -	⎧ Tho. D— Burrowes	17June1805	
	⎪ Tho. Wm. Harrington	25Mar.1806	30June1804
	⎪ A.AhmutyVanCourtland	15Nov.	
	⎪ Thomas Patterson	1Feb.1807	
	⎪ Andrew Creagh	19Mar.	
	⎪ Thomas Pottinger	27Aug.	13July 1806
	⎪ Thomas Brett	8Oct.	
	⎪ JosephWickham Mayer	23Sept.1808	
	⎪ Thomas Morgell	24do.	
	⎪ J— K— Taylor	5Apr.1809	
	⎪ Henry Heyman	1July	
	⎨ Thomas Pratt Barlow	13Aug.1810	
	⎪ Thomas Ker	18Oct.	12July 1810
	⎪ Morton Slaney	10Jan.1811	24Aug.1807
	⎪ William Brett	23Jan.1812	
	⎪ J— D— Fearon	16May	
	⎪ Nathaniel Sneyd	17do.	
	⎪ Edw. Eilerker Williams	28Apr.1813	
	⎪ John Fraser	9June	21Mar.1811
	⎪ Henry Young	1July	
	⎪ George Bygrave	15Aug.	
	⎪ James M'Alpine	24Feb.1814	
	⎩ John Cranston Green	12Nov.	23June1814

Cornet

122   8th (or the King's Royal Irish) Regiment of
(Light) Dragoons.

Rank.	Name.	Rank in the Regiment.	Army.
Cornet - -	John Elliott	25 Aug. 1812	
	Hugh Cochrane	4 Feb. 1813	
	Donald Keith M'Donald	9 Apr.	
	Robert Selwood Hewett	28 do.	
	David Wedd. Mackenzie	29 June	
	A— J— Stammers	30 do.	Adjutant
	Conrad Edw. Rycroft	15 July	
	George Cox	14 Aug.	
	Charles Wetherall	15 do.	
	John Fleming Kelso	11 Nov.	
	Jaspar Farmar	30 Dec.	
	Henry Parker	27 Jan. 1814	

Rank	Name	Regiment	Army
Paymaster -	James Somerville Darby	7 May 1807	
Adjutant - -	A— J— Stammers	11 Nov. 1813	Cornet 30 June 1813
Quarter-Master	——— Masters	16 Apr. 1812	
Surgeon - -	James Smet	1 June 1809	
Assistant Surg.	George M— Callow	3 Mar. 1808	27 June 1805
	W— B— Carter	22 Feb. 1810	23 Mar. 1809
Veterinary Surg.	Wm. Shotter Rickwood	11 Mar. 1813	

Blue.—Facings scarlet.—Lace gold.

Agent, Messrs. Greenwood, Cox and Hammersley.

Rank.	Name.	Rank in the Regiment.	Army.
Colonel - -	James, *Earl of* Rosslyn	1 Aug.1801	Gen. 4June1814
Lieut. Colonel	*Hon.* Thomas Mahon	1Jan.1797	M.Gen. 4June1811
	Charles Morland	4Mar.1813	29Oct. 1812
	Simon George Newport	10June	
Major - -	Redm. Hervey Morres	24Jan.1811	Lt.Col. 10June1813
	George Gore	7May1812	
Captain -	Benjamin Handley	12May1808	
	James Delancey	19do.	25Feb. 1808
	Benjamin Keene	30June	3Oct. 1805
	John Godfrey Peters	22Dec.	
	James Hurt	27Dec.1810	25June1807
	Dennis Daly	10Oct.1811	13May 1807
	Francis Warren	5Nov.1812	
	Simeon Henry Stuart	12Nov.1814	1Aug.1811
Lieutenant	Henry Thomas Parker	25Sept.1806	
	Joseph Rolfe	9Oct.	14Sept.1804
	Robert Robertson	22Feb.1810	
	John B — Ker	4June1811	
	George Boss	5do.	
	Henry Webster	13do.	
	Thomas Stannus	4Sept.	1Oct. 1805
	H— J— Richardson	5do.	
	William Barras	19do.	
	John Minchin	4Feb.1812	
	John Wright	5do.	Adjutant
	Sir Charles Payne, *Bt.*	6do.	
	Lord George Lennox	18Aug.1814	14Jan. 1813
Cornet -	B— C— Browne	17June1813	
	John Gurdon	12May1814	
	Geo. Bos. W. Stackpoole	3June	
	Geo. Gordon Smith	29Dec.	
Paymaster -	Benjamin Chapman	27Aug.1803	
Adjutant - -	John Wright	4July1811	Lieut. 5Feb.1812
Quarter-Master	Thomas Hely	2Nov.1809	
Surgeon - -	James O'Connor	16Feb.1815	3Feb. 1803
Assistant Surg.	John M'Andrew	15Feb.1810	
	James Knox	25Aug.1814	12Nov.1812
Veterinary Surg.	——— Norton	2Oct.1814	

Blue.—Facings crimson.—Lace gold.

English **Agent, Messrs.** Greenwood, Cox and Hammersley.
Irish Agent,

[1815]

124   10th (or the Prince of Wales's own Royal) Regiment of (Light) Dragoons.

(HUSSARS.)

Colonel	{ *His Royal Highness*		
	{ *The Prince Regent, K. G.* 18July1796	19Nov.1782	
Lieut. Colonel	{ George Quentin 13Oct.1808	Col. 4June1814	
	{ *Lord* Robert Manners 12Nov.1814	2May1811	
Major - -	{ *Hon.* Frederick Howard 9May1811		
	{ *Hon.* H. Cecil Lowther 12Nov.1814	14Apr.1814	

	{ Samuel Bromley	26Aug.1813	
	{ Thomas W— Taylor	12Nov.1814	Major 7July1814
	{ H— C— Stapylton	do.	3Nov.1808
	{ John Grey	do.	6Apr.1809
Captain -	{ John Gurwood	do.	6Feb.1812
	{ Charles Wood	do.	17Sept.1812
	{ Valentine Jones	do.	11Mar.1813
	{ Henry Floyd	do.	2Dec.1813
	{ Arthur Shakespear	do.	27Jan.1814
	{ *Hon.* John Jones	do.	9June1814

	{ Charles Holbern	6Feb.1812	
	{ Francis Edw. Meynell	26Aug.1813	
	{ Robert Curtis	24Mar.1814	15Apr.1813
	{ John Whitehill Parsons	12Nov.	3Dec.1805
	{ William Slayter Smith	do.	17Nov.1808
	{ Henry John Burn	do.	11Oct.1810
	{ Robert Arnold	do.	13May1812
Lieutenant	{ Christ. J— Allingham	do.	30June1813
	{ William Cartwright	do.	6Jan.1814
	{ Samuel Hardman	15Dec.	9Dec.1813 Adjut.
	{ Geo. Orlando Gunning	26do.	8Apr.1813
	{ J— C— Wallington	27do.	
	{ E— Hodgson	28do.	
	{ William C— Hamilton	29do.	
	{ Anthony Bacon	9Feb.1815	11Mar.1813

Cornet - -	{ W— Paxton Jervis	11Jan.1815	
	{ William Lindsey	12do.	

Paymaster -	James Tallon	15Dec.1813	
Adjutant - -	Samuel Hardman	15Dec.1814	Lieut. 9Dec.1813
Quarter-Master	James Rogers	5July1810	
Surgeon - -	Charles Morrison	20June1811	
Assistant Surg.	{ W— R— Rogers	7Nov.1811	
	{ George Samuel Jenks	22Oct.1812	
Veterinary Surg.	Henry C— Sannerman	29Mar.1810	7Dec.1809

Blue.—Facings scarlet.—Lace silver.

Agent, Messrs. Greenwood, Cox and Hammersley.

11th

11th Regiment of (Light) Dragoons. 125

Permitted to bear on their Colours and Appointments a " SPHINX," with the word " EGYPT," in commemoration of the Campaign of 1801.

Rank.	Name.	Rank in the Regiment.	Army.
Colonel	◉*Ld.*Wm.Caven.Bentinck,*K.B.*	27Jan.1813	Lt.Gen. 4June1811
Lieut. Col.	◎ { Henry John Cumming	17Feb.1803	M.Gen. 4June1814
	James Wallace Sleigh	14Dec.1809	
Major -	◎ { Richard Diggens	14Aug.1806	Lt.Col. 4June1813
	Archibald Money	14Dec.1809	Lt.Col. 4June1814
Captain -	{ James Bouchier	20Jan.1803	Major 4June1814
	Robert Horsley	25June	Major 4June1814
	Benjamin Lutyens	4Aug.1804	Major 4June1814
	Michael Childers	14June1805	Major 25Aug.1814
	Cranstoun Geo. Ridout	2Mar.1809	
	James Alfred Schreiber	19Nov.1812	
	John Jenkins	22Dec.1814	
	Thomas Binney	26Jan.1815	
Lieutenant	{ George Sicker	20Feb.1805	Adjutant
	Frederick Wood	14June	
	William Smith	21Apr.1808	
	Richard Coles	29June1811	
	Benjamin Leigh Lye	30do.	
	Edward Phelips	3July	
	James Richard Rotton	9Jan.1812	
	James Moore	13Oct.1814	7Apr. 1813
	Robert Milligan	22Dec.	
Cornet - -	{ Thomas Hoskins	7Apr.1813	
	Barton Parker Browne	8do.	
	Timothy Grindred	3June	
	Humphrey Orme	5Aug.	
	George Schreiber	23Dec.	
	Henry R— Bullock	30do.	
	Philip Haughton James	29Dec.1814	
Paymaster -	Daniel Lutyens	19Oct.1804	
Adjutant - -	George Sicker	26Jan.1815	Lieut. 20Feb.1805
Quarter-Master	John Hall	29Sept.1814	
Surgeon - -	James O'Meally	11Mar.1813	11July 1811
Assistant Surg.	{ M'Conochie Tomlinson	8Nov.1810	
	Henry Steele	28Apr.1814	25June1812
Veterinary Surg.	George Gross	29July1813	

Blue.—Facings buff.—Lace silver.

Agent, Messrs. Collyer, Park Place, St. James's.

12th

126 12th (or the Prince of Wales's) Regiment of (Light) Dragoons.

Permitted to bear on their Colours and Appointments a " SPHINX," with the word " EGYPT," in commemoration of the Campaign of 1801.

		Rank in the	
Rank.	*Name.*	*Regiment.*	*Army.*
Colonel - -	ⓢ *Sir* William Payne, *Bt.*	12Jan.1815	Lt.Gen. 4June1811
Lieut. Col. ⓢ	{ Robert Browne	30Aug.1799	M.Gen. 4June1811
	{ *Hon.* F. C. Ponsonby	11June1811	Col. 4June1814
Major - -	{ Overington Blunden	30Aug.1799	Col. 4June1813
	{ James Paul Bridger	10Dec.1812	
Captain -	⎧ Samson Stawell	29Jan.1806	28Feb. 1805
	⎜ George F— Erskine	19May1808	
	⎜ Edwin W. T. Sandys	30Mar.1809	19Aug.1808
	⎨ Houston Wallace	10Jan.1811	11Jan. 1810
	⎜ Alexander Barton	17do.	
	⎜ Henry Andrews	9July1812	
	⎜ William Webb	27Aug.	
	⎩ William Cowper Coles	19Nov.	
Lieutenant	⎧ Richard Fulton	30May1805	
	⎜ William Heydon	13June	
	⎜ Joseph Philips	22June1809	8Dec. 1808
	⎜ James Chatterton	6June1811	
	⎜ John Vandeleur	10July	30May 1811
	⎨ William Hay	11do.	
	⎜ Ansalm Evans Taylor	1Aug.	27Apr. 1809
	⎜ Wm. H— Dowbiggen	31Dec.	8Aug.1811
	⎜ John Eddington	23Jan.1812	
	⎜ Albert Goldsmid	20Feb.	
	⎩ James Dur.Calderwood	12Mar.	
Cornet - -	⎧ —— Liddell	11Feb.1813	
	⎜ —— Griffiths	29July	Adjutant
	⎨ Thomas Reed	26Aug.	
	⎜ John Elliott Lockhart	28Apr.1814	
	⎜ St. George Ryder Barry	23June	
	⎩ Richard Bury Pallisar	12Nov.	2Nov.1813
Paymaster -	William Otway	14Feb.1811	
Adjutant - -	—— Griffiths	29July1813	Cornet 29July1813
Quarter-Master	Richard Sidley	10June1813	
Surgeon - ··	Benjamin Robinson	15Oct.1803	2Feb. 1795
Assistant Surg.	{ Patrick Egan	10Oct.1812	27Apr. 1809
	{ John G— Smith	28Oct.1813	11Mar.1813
Veterinary Surg.	James Castley	17Aug.1809	18June1807

Blue.—Facings yellow.—Lace silver.
Agent, Messrs. Greenwood, Cox and Hammersley.

13th

			Rank in the	
Rank.	*Name.*	*Regiment.*	*Army.*	

Rank.	Name	Regiment	Army
Colonel - -	*Hon.* Hen. George Grey	30Dec.1811	Lt.Gen. 4June1811
Lieut. Col. ⓒ	Robert Bolton	7June1797	M.Gen. 25July1810
	Patrick Doherty	4June1813	Col. 4June1814
Major - -	Shapland Boyse	4June1813	Lt.Col. 4June1814
	George Lawrence	24do.	4June1813
Captain -	Brook Lawrence	3Feb.1804	Major 4June1814
	Joseph Doherty	19Mar.1807	
	James Macalester	25June	Major 12Apr.1814
	Mansell Bowers	8Mar.1810	1Mar.1810
	James Gubbins	7Feb.1811	18May 1809
	Charles Gregorie	20June	4Aug.1808
	Samuel Holmes	10Sept.1812	
	James Lennox	17June1813	
Lieutenant	John Irving Moss	7Mar.1805	
	John Major	19Dec.	20Aug.1803
	James Considine	6Feb.1806	
	George Doherty	18Sept.	
	Frederick Geale	3Mar.1808	
	William D'Arcy	28Apr.	25July 1804
	John H— Drought	8Sept.	
	Charles Robert Bowers	18Oct.1810	
	Allan T— Maclean	11July1811	
	John Geale	25do.	
	Robert Nisbett	26Dec.	
	James Lawrence	26Aug.1813	Adjutant
	George Wombwell	12Nov.1814	4Nov.1812
Cornet - -	Henry Acton	6Jan.1814	
	John Wallace	10Feb.	
	J— Æ— Irving	24Mar.	
	John Horatius Maitland	28Apr.	
	Joseph Wakefield	26May	
Paymaster -	Alexander Strange	11Apr.1811	
Adjutant - -	James Lawrence	10Sept.1812	Lieut. 26Aug.1813
Quarter-Master	William Minchin	10Sept.1812	
Surgeon - -	Thomas Galbraith Logan	9Sept.1813	24Dec.1812
Assistant Surg.	Abraham Armstrong	18May1809	
	William Dillon	18Jan.1810	
Veterinary Surg.	John Constant	3Mar.1814	

Blue.—*Facings buff.*—*Lace gold.*

English Agent, Messrs. Greenwood, Cox and Hammersley.
Irish Agent,

14th

128 14th (or the Duchess of York's own) Regiment of (Light) Dragoons.

Permitted to bear on their Colours and Appointments the " PRUSSIAN EAGLE."

Colonel -	John Wm. E. *of* Bridgewater	1June1797	Gen. 1Jan.1812
Lieut. Col.	Samuel Hawker	12June1800	M.Gen. 4June1811
	F— B— Hervey	12July1810	Col. 4June1814
Major - -	Charles Massey Baker	30Jan.1812	Lt.Col. 4June1814
	Tho. Wm. Brotherton	26Mar.	Lt.Col. 19May1814
	Thomas Potter Milles	9July1807	Major 12Apr.1814
	John Babington	27Dec.1809	
	Daniel Capel	8Mar.1810	
	Hon. Henry Percy	21June	Major 16Aug.1810
Captain -	Francis Anderson	2Aug.	
	Joseph Dowson	6Dec.	
	John Townsend	6June1811	
	Lovell B— Badcock	12Dec.	
	William Wainman	13Feb.1812	
	Augustus Foster	18Mar.1813	
	Benjamin Shotten	20Mar.1806	
	William Jones	5Jan.1809	
	J— W— E— Brydges	15Feb.1810	
	Francis Fowke	6Dec.	
	Charles Ward	1Jan.1811	10May 1809
	Francis Hall	28Mar.	
	Archibald Douglas	23Jan.1812	26Dec.1810
	James Clavering	28Feb.	
	John Harvey Thursby	17Sept.	
Lieutenant	C. Gard. Humphreys	11Mar.1813	
	Francis William Taylor	25do.	
	James Bennett	21Oct.	
	James Blake	9Dec.	
	Charles M'Carthy	20Jan.1814	Adjutant
	George Hutchinson	29Sept.	14July 1814
	Hon. Charles Petre	3Nov.	
	Saint John Charlton	10do.	
	Charles Wyndham	12do.	5Nov.1812
	Thomas Molyneux	7Dec.	28Feb. 1812
	Stephen Simpson	8do.	
	Robert Carr Hammond	7Apr.1814	
	David Brown	14July	
Cornet -	William Wilton	18Aug.	
	Constant. Estwick Trent	7Dec.	
	Francis Onslow Trent	8do.	
Paymaster -	Samuel Rofe	3Sept.1812	
Adjutant - -	Charles M'Carthy	5May1814	Lieut. 20Jan.1814
Quarter-Master	Henry Smith	11Mar.1813	
Surgeon - -	Arthur Richardson	5Nov.1812	27July 1809
Assistant Surg.	Elijah Bush	24Oct.1811	
	Daniel Owen Davis	25Mar.1813	
Veterinary Surg.	——— Black	10Nov.1814	

Blue.—Facings orange.— Lace silver.

Agent, Messrs. Colyer, Park Place, St. James's.

15th

[1815]

15th (or the King's) Regt. of (Light) Dragoons. 129
(HUSSARS.)

Colonel {	*His Royal Highness* Ernest, *D. of* Cumberland, *K.G.*	28Mar.1801	F.Mar.26Nov.1813
Lieut. Col. ◎ ◎- {	Robert Ballard Long	12Dec.1805	M.Gen. 4June1811
	Colquhoun Grant	25Aug.1808	M.Gen. 4June1814
	Leighton C. Dalrymple	16Dec.1813	
Major - ◎ {	Edwin Griffith	5Nov.1812	
	Hon. W. E. Cochrane	16Dec.1813	
Captain - {	Joseph Thackwell	9Apr.1807	
	Skinner Hancox	11May1809	
	John Whiteford	24July1811	
	Philip Wodehouse	26Dec.	14June1811
	Fred. Charles Philips	16Apr.1812	
	Charles Carpenter	16July	
	Thomas Dundas	13Aug.	26Dec.1811
	William Booth	17Sept.	
	J— Buckley	6Oct.1813	
	John Penrice	7do.	
Lieutenant {	John Carr	21Dec.1809	3Oct. 1809
	Edward Barrett	28June1810	
	Ralph Mansfield	16Aug.	
	Isaac Sherwood	13Sept.	
	Hon. Rich. Pepper Arden	3Oct.1811	
	William Bellairs	7May1812	
	Henry Lane	3Sept.	
	William Byam	17do.	
	Edward Byam	29Apr.1813	
	George A. F. Dawkins	3June	
	Henry Dixon	25Aug.	
	John James Douglas	26do.	
	William Stewart	6Jan.1814	
	John N— Pennington	13do.	8Feb. 1810
	William Ramsay	24Feb.	18Mar.1813
	Henry Buckley	25Aug.	
Cornet - - {	Jacob William Hinde	5May1814	
	Joseph Griffith	4Aug.	Adjutant
Paymaster -	JamesCoppinCocksedge	27May1813	
Adjutant - -	Joseph Griffith	4Aug.1814	Cornet 4Aug.1814
Quarter-Master	Samuel Jenkins	5Oct.1809	
Surgeon - -	Thomas Cartan	9Sept.1813	
Assistant Surg. {	Samuel Jeyes	28Nov.1811	
	William Gibney	28Oct.1813	
Veterinary Surg.	Conrad Dalwig	29Apr.1813	

Blue.—Facings scarlet.—Lace silver.

English Agent, Messrs. Greenwood, Cox and Hammersley.
Irish Agent, Messrs. Armit and Borough, Dublin.

Rank.	Name.	Rank in the Regiment.	Army.
Colonel - -	Wm. *Earl* Harcourt	20Oct.1779	Gen. 1Jan.1798
Lieut. Colonel ⊚	{ *Sir* James Affleck, *Bt.*	25Mar.1795	Lt.Gen. 4June1811
	Raymond Pelly	23Apr.1812	
	James Hay	18Feb.1813	
Major - ⊚	{ *Hon.* Hen. Beauc. Lygon	7May1812	
	George Home Murray	18Feb.1813	
Captain -	{ John Henry Belli	29Jan.1807	Major 7May1812
	Clement Swetenham	11June	
	Richard Weyland	5Sept.1811	18July 1811
	William Persse	23Jan.1812	
	Harry Wrixon	30Apr.	1Mar.1812
	John Phillips Buchanan	28May	
	William Tomkinson	3June	12Mar.1812
	Charles King	18Feb.1813	
Lieutenant	{ J— Barra	4Oct.1808	Adjutant
	William Osten	17Nov.	
	John Grimes	1Nov.1810	
	Trevor Wheler	11July1811	
	Francis Swinfin	1Aug.	
	George Baker	15do.	
	Wm. Henry Snow	23Jan.1812	
	Richard Beauchamp	19Feb.	
	Nath. Day Crichton	20do.	
	Edward B— Lloyd	12Mar.	
	William Nepean	2Apr.	
	Jas. Arch. Richardson	12Nov.1814	1Apr. 1813
Cornet - -	{ William Beckwith	7Jan.1813	
	William Polhill	1July	
	George Nugent	7Oct.	
	Alexander Hay	11Nov.	
	James Baillie	28Apr.1814	
	William Hawkins Ball	27Oct.	
Paymaster -	George Neyland	10Sept.1812	
Adjutant - -	J— Barra	27Aug.1807	Lieut. 4Oct.1808
Quarter-Master	John Harrison	25Jan.1810	
Surgeon - -	Isaac Robinson	21Apr.1804	22Dec. 1803
Assistant Surg.	{ John Evans	22Aug.1811	
	John M'Gr. Mallock	16Apr.1812	
Veterinary Surg.	John Jons	25Nov.1813	

Blue.—Facings scarlet.—Lace silver.

Agent, Messrs. Collyer, Park Place, St. James's.

17th

| | | Rank in the | |
| | | Regiment. | Army. |

Rank.	Name.	Regiment.	Army.
Colonel - -	Oliver de Lancey	20May1795	Gen. 1Jan.1812
Lieut. Colonel ⊚ {	Evan Lloyd William Carden Hon. Lincoln Stanhope	11Feb.1799 24Jan.1811 2Jan.1812	M.Gen. 1Jan.1812 25July 1810
Major - - {	Oswald Werge Nathan Wilson	20Apr.1809 22Feb.1810	Lt.Col. 4June1814
Captain - - {	David Supple Jonathan Willington George John Sale William Moray Henry Walker Daniel M'Neale Hugh Percy Davison Hon. F. Leic. Stanhope John Atkins Tho.PerrouetThompson Joseph Smyth	25June1803 6Mar.1807 10Feb.1808 11do. 24Mar. 28Dec.1809 17Dec.1812 21Jan.1813 25Feb. 20Oct.1814 12Nov.	Major 4June1814 Major 4June1813 14Feb. 1807 26Nov.1807 Major 4June1814 30Nov.1809 7July 1814 5Nov.1812
Lieutenant {	Benjamin Adams John Brackenbury John D'Arcy Michael Ryan Joseph Budden Wm. Henry Robinson Charles Byrne Sale Fred. Wm. Hutchinson Robert Coulthard Francis Curtayne James Cockburn Robert Willington William Daniel Henry Bond Francis Haworth Benjamin Astley Tho. Ramsay Wharton George Daun Cortl.Geo. A—Skinner Isidore Blake William Hacket	19Sept.1805 28Apr.1808 29do. 2Feb.1809 16do. 30Mar. 25May 3Aug. 23Nov. 11Oct.1810 11Apr.1811 10Oct. 25do. 9Nov. 28Feb.1812 24June1813 1Sept. 8Oct. 11Nov. 17Mar.1814 8Dec.	22Dec. 1804 28Nov.1805 19Dec. 1802 10Sept.1803 1Mar.1811 19Dec. 1811 Adjut.

R 2

Cornet

Rank.	Name.	Rank in the Regiment.	Rank in the Army.
Cornet	——— Carew	1 Mar. 1811	1 Jan. 1811
	William Macfarlane	11 July	
	Richard Willington	1 Oct. 1812	
	John Tomlinson	7 Jan. 1813	
	Thomas Hurring	25 Feb.	14 May 1812
	William Gibson Peat	8 Apr.	
	Oliver de Lancey	3 June	
	William Potts	11 Nov.	
	George Clarke	17 Mar. 1814	
	James Patch	20 Oct.	
Paymaster	Robert Harman	26 May 1808	
Adjutant	William Hacket	8 Dec. 1814	Lieut. 19 Dec. 1811
Quarter-Master	Thomas Carson	19 Oct. 1809	
Surgeon	Alexander Young	26 Sept. 1812	25 May 1809
Assistant Surg. {	John Lorimer	4 June 1812	
	Eugene M'Swyny	3 Dec.	
Veterinary Surg.	Edward Coleman	17 Mar. 1804	

Blue.—Facings white.—Lace silver.

Agent, Messrs. Greenwood, Cox and Hammersley.

Colonel	Cha. *M. of* Drogheda, *K. St. P.*	3 Aug 1762	Gen. 12 Oct. 1793
	Lt. Col. Com.	7 Dec. 1759	
Lieut. Colonel	*Hon.* Henry Murray	2 Jan. 1812	
Major - ⊚	{ Philip Hay	2 Jan. 1812	Lt. Col. 4 June 1814
	{ James Hughes	24 Sept.	
Captain -	⌈ John Marcus Clements	20 Aug. 1807	Major 12 Apr. 1814
	│ Charles Milner	18 Jan. 1810	
	│ Arthur Kennedy	11 July 1811	
	│ Edward Burke	2 Jan. 1812	
	⟨ Richard Croker	9 July	
	│ Richard Ellis	24 Sept.	
	│ James Grant	17 Dec.	Major 4 June 1814
	│ George Luard	21 July 1813	
	│ Hugh Owen	22 do.	
	⌊ Jas. Rich. Lewis Lloyd	12 Nov. 1814	25 Aug. 1809
Lieutenant	⌈ Charles Hesse	4 May 1809	
	│ Christopher Blackett	11 do.	
	│ William Gibbs	8 Feb. 1810	
	│ —— M'Cartney	21 Feb. 1811	
	│ Thomas Dunkin	19 Sept.	
	│ James Henry Waldie	13 Feb. 1812	
	│ James Morris	22 Oct.	
	│ George Woodberry	10 Dec.	
	│ John Dolbel	22 Apr. 1813	
	⟨ *Hon.* Lio. C— Dawson	24 June	10 Nov. 1807
	│ Martin French	14 Oct.	29 Oct. 1812
	│ Thomas Prior	6 Jan. 1814	22 Aug. 1805
	│ Robert Coote	22 Feb.	
	│ Henry Duperier	23 do.	Adjutant
	│ John Thomas Machell	24 do.	
	│ Rich. Rich Wilford Brett	24 July	
	│ Donald M'Duffie	29 Sept.	10 Mar. 1814
	│ Horace Seymour	12 Nov.	29 Dec. 1812
	⌊ Henry Somerset	do.	30 Dec. 1812
Cornet - -	{ William Henry Rowlls	26 May 1814	
	{ Cha. Champion Moller	16 June	
Paymaster -	William Deane	13 Aug. 1802	
Adjutant - -	Henry Duperier	15 May 1813	Lieut. 23 Feb. 1814
Quarter-Master	Charles Tarleton	25 Aug. 1809	
Surgeon - -	William Chambers	25 Feb. 1804	9 July 1803
Assistant Surg.	{ Lucas Pulsford	14 Mar. 1811	17 May 1810
	{ John Quincey	5 Mar. 1812	
Veterinary Surg.	Daniel Pilcher	13 June 1811	

Blue.—Facings white.—Lace silver.

Agent, Messrs. Greenwood, Cox and Hammersley.

19th

Permitted to bear the " ELEPHANT," with the word " ASSAYE" superscribed, on their Colours and Appointments, in commemoration of the Battle of the 23d Sept. 1803.

			Rank in the	
Rank.	Name.	Regiment.	Army.	
Colonel - -	◎Sir Wm. Payne, Bt.	13July1814	Lt.Gen.	4June1811
Lt. Col. ◎	John OrmsbyVandeleur	16Apr.1807	M.Gen.	4June1811
	Hon. John B. O'Neill	29Mar.1810	Col.	4June1814
Major - -	Robert Lisle	17Mar.1814	4June1813	
	Patrick Anderson	1June		
Captain -	Henry Skelton	21Oct.1801	Major	4June1813
	Edward Geils	22Nov.1803	Major	4June1814
	Charles Abdy Chapman	7Jan.1808		
	Ld.ArthurJ.H.Somerset	12Sept.1811	26June1806	
	James Verner	10Dec.1812		
	William Browne	25Feb.1813	30May 1809	
	George Austin Moultrie	4Mar.		
	Colin Anderson	15Apr.		
	John Eustace	17Mar.1814		
	William Armstrong	4Aug.		
Lieutenant -	Henry Arthur Gladwin	1Oct.1805		
	Benjamin Burton	29Oct.1807		
	James Rathbone	18May1809	Adjutant	
	William Rhodes	12Mar.1812		
	John Lang	10Dec.		
	William F— Arnold	7Jan.1813		
	George Snoad	18Mar.		
	John Hammersley	15Apr.		
	William Veredit Horton	24Feb.1814		
	Lionel Goldsmid	17Mar.		
	William Long Wrey	25Aug.		
Cornet - -	Thomas Walker	28Jan.1813		
	Richard Earle Welby	17Mar.1814		
	William Dungan	4Aug.		
	George Maquay	25do.		
	Charles John Peshall	9Nov.		
	Henry Georges	10do.		
Paymaster -	Wm. Frederick Neville	23Nov.1809		
Adjutant - -	James Rathbone	30Apr.1807	Lieut.	18May1809
Quarter-Master	John Gloag	25Aug.1809		
Surgeon - -	John Murray	17July1805		
Assistant Surg.	Edward Pilkington	19Aug.1813	16May 1811	
	William Pardy	12May1814	4Mar.1813	
Veterinary Surg.	Lawrence Bird	29June1809		

Blue.—Facings Yellow.—Lace gold.

Agent, Messrs. Greenwood, Cox and Hammersley.

20th

Colonel	◎ Stap. *Ld.*Combermere,*K.B.*27Jan.1813	Lt.Gen. 1Jan.1812
Lieut. Colonel	{ Thomas Hawker 2Sept.1808	Col. 4June1814
	{ George Wyndham 10Dec.1812	13Mar.1812
Major -	◎ { Wm. Williams Blake 21Mar.1805	Lt.Col. 1Jan.1812
	{ Rich. Bingham Newland 5Aug.1813	
Captain -	⌈ Edward Molesworth 15Oct.1807	
		Edward Mortimer 28Jan.1808	
		George Foljambe 14Apr.	11Sept.1806
		Maximillian Joerres 22Sept.	
	⌡ Richard Du Cane 1Feb.1810	
	⌐ John Woodgate 11June1812	20Feb. 1812
		Edward Cormick 23Sept.1813	
		Walter Jacks 21Oct.	
		Benjamin Harding 12Nov.1814	25Jan. 1810
	⌊ Charles Synge do.	12Aug.1813
Lieutenant -	⌈ William Lea 24July1805	
		Thomas Harrison 14Aug.	
		Thomas Willson 4Feb.1808	
		Thomas Richardson 10Mar.	
		Henry Lecky 19Oct.	
		C. Fletcher Champion 17Nov.	15Dec. 1804
		James Edward Scott 22Dec.	17Nov.1808
		James Bridger 2Jan.1809	
		William Howsham 5do.	
		Beauchamp Harvey 21Dec.	
	⌡ Henry John Atkinson 24May1810	
		John Eaton 17Jan.1811	
		Robert Saunders 15Aug.	Adjutant
		Thomas Irwin 29Oct.1812	
		John Court 24Dec.	7Feb. 1811
		James Smith 21Oct.1813	
		Cha. Aug. du Ruvyne 23Dec.	6Feb. 1812
		John Edwards 30do.	
		Hon. William Massey 7Feb.1814	
		James M'Dermott 31Mar.	
	⌊ John James Pomeroy 25Aug.	
Cornet - -	⌐ Corbet D'Avenant 21Oct.1813	
	⌡ Joseph Kelly 17Feb.1814	
	⌡ Cha. Rob. Cureton 20Oct.	24Feb. 1814
	⌊ James Cook 27do.	
Paymaster -	John Atkinson 11Sept.1806	
Adjutant - -	Robert Saunders 14Dec.1809	Lieut. 15Aug.1811
Quarter-Master	William Edwards 30Nov.1809	
Surgeon - -	Thomas Short 7Oct.1813	
Assistant Surg.	{ Joseph W— Gullifer 19Dec.1811	
	{ Edward Magrath 21Jan.1813	
Veterinary Surg.	James S— Darley 28Apr.1808	

Blue.—Facings orange.—Lace gold.

Agent, Messrs. Collyer, Park Place, St. James's.

Rank.	Name.	Rank in the Regiment.	Army.
Colonel - -	Banastre Tarleton	29Apr.1802	Gen. 1Jan.1812
Lieut. Colonel	Richard Pigot	1May1806	Col. 4June1814
Major - -	{ Thomas Bates 13Apr.1807 { Westenra W—Higgins 16June1814		Lt. Col. 4June1813
Captain -	⎧ William Gleadowe 21Mar.1805 ⎪ James R— Crawford 13Apr.1807 ⎪ Abiathan Hawkes 21May ⎪ John Bertram Ord 9June1808 ⎪ Robert Innes Thornton 11May1809 ⎨ Alexander Lecky 27July ⎪ Thomas Jones 3May1810 ⎪ Anthony Alex. O'Reilly 21Jan.1813 ⎪ Abraham Jos. Cloete 28Oct. ⎪ William Underwood 28July1814 ⎩ Ld. Arthur W. M. Hill 12Nov.		31Jan. 1805 27Feb. 1807 Major 1Jan.1812 23Jan. 1812 5Nov.1812 25Aug.1813
Lieutenant	⎧ William J— Kent 5Oct.1804 ⎪ John Gibson Whitaker 31Oct.1805 ⎪ James Dunbar 26Dec. ⎪ William Williams 12Feb.1806 ⎪ Joseph Hare 15May ⎪ William Proctor 29Dec.1808 ⎪ Henry Elliott 1June1809 ⎪ James Alex. Fehrzen 2Aug.1810 ⎪ William Hake 1Nov. ⎪ Walter Newton 2do. ⎪ George Aitken 19Mar.1812 ⎨ Joseph Leeson 6Oct. ⎪ William Hooper Boys 7do. ⎪ Andrew Bond 8do. ⎪ Francis de Visme 18Mar.1813 ⎪ Colin Johnstone 1Apr. ⎪ Robert Whaley 22do. ⎪ James Heywood 27May ⎪ Henry Tomkinson 23Sept. ⎪ Charles William Hughes 21Oct. ⎪ James Buck 30Dec. ⎪ William Bull Stapleton 6Jan.1814 ⎩ And. Alex. M'Conchey 28July		20Nov.1801 Adjutant 7Sept.1804 19May 1808 31Dec. 1812 18Mar.1813 22July 1813 25Feb. 1813

Cornet

Rank.	Name.	Rank in the Regiment.	Army.
Cornet -	Samuel Carter	2Dec.1813	9Dec.1813
	James Wood	29do.	
	John Henry Loft	30do.	
	John S— Porter	7Apr.1814	
	Charles T— Bishop	14do.	
	—— Browne	16June	
	George Story	4Aug.	
Paymaster -	James Collier	22Aug.1805	
Adjutant - -	William Williams	16Mar.1805	Lieut. 12Feb.1806
Quarter-Master	Aug. Fred. Fortesquieu	5Mar.1812	
Surgeon - -	Richard Spencer	22May1806	9July 1803
Assistant Surg.	Thomas Price	13Nov.1806	
	Alexander Menzies	4Oct.1810	
Veterinary Surg.	John Schroeder	25June1812	

Blue.—Facings black.—Lace silver.

Agent, Messrs. Greenwood, Cox and Hammersley.

Rank.	Name.	Rank in the Regiment.	Army.
Colonel - -	Francis Edward Gwyn	9Mar.1794	Gen. 25Apr.1808
Lieut. Colonel	{ James Hare	22Aug.1805	M.Gen. 1Jan.1812
	Tho. Gage Montresor	2Jan.1812	M.Gen. 4June1813
	Theophilus Pritzler	4June1813	Col. 4June1814
	⊚ { Robert Travers	do.	1Jan. 1812
Major - -	{ Thomas H— Dawes	2Jan.1812	
	Henry Broome	4June1813	1Jan. 1812
Captain -	{ Joseph Gordon	25June1803	Major 4June1814
	Thomas Chadwick	17June1805	
	William Blundell	18do.	
	John Floyd Paterson	25Oct.	
	Charles Randall	14Feb.1811	
	James Adshed	21Nov.	
	Williamson Wood	2Jan.1812	
	Joseph Vernon	22do.	
	Richard Slegg	15Oct.	
	Charles Knatchbull	25do.	18Aug 1808
	Charles Dudley	4June1813	
Lieutenant -	{ B— J— Smith	15Feb.1805	
	George Keir	12Aug.1807	
	John Eden	14do.	
	Charles Middleton	25Feb.1810	28Apr. 1806
	John William Murray	1May	
	William Mills	7June	
	Alexander Moorhead	1Sept.1811	
	George John Moore	22Jan.1812	
	Matthew Smith	23do.	
	Sydney John Cotton	13Feb.	
	Richard Montague Oakes	20do.	2Jan. 1811
	William Bott	3Apr.	Adjutant
	Samuel Enderby	16do.	
	George Paton	1July	
	Pringle Taylor	2do.	
	William Hodgson	10Sept.	
	Sir John Gordon, Bt.	5Nov.	
	John Hyde Bromwich	11Apr.1813	
	James Boalth	6May	
	Daniel Carrol	3Sept.	
	Henry Fitz Clarence	12Nov.1814	15Aug.1811
	George Gill	8Dec.	

Cornet

Rank.	Name.	Rank in the Regiment.	Rank in the Army.
Cornet - -	John Rogers	2July1812	
	Francis Blundell	11Apr.1813	
	R— R— Montague	3Sept.	
	John Rolland	3Feb.1814	
	Tho. Barring. Tristram	21Apr.	
	John Bebb	23June	
	Henry Davis	4Aug.	
Paymaster -	Joseph Barrell	9Sept.1813	
Adjutant - -	William Bott	1Jan.1811	Lieut. 3Apr.1812
Quarter-Master	Thos. Willock Edwards	3Dec.1812	
Surgeon - -	Francis Edwards	9Mar.1794	
Assistant Surg.	Robert Greig	24Oct.1811	
	—— Reilly	1Nov.1813	
Veterinary Surg.	—— Stephenson	4Aug.1814	

Blue.—Facings white.—Lace gold.

Agent, Messrs. Collyer, Park Place, St. James's.

Permitted to bear on their Colours and Appointments a " SPHINX," with the word " EGYPT," in commemoration of the Campaign of 1801.

Rank.	Name.	Regiment.	Rank in the Army.
Colonel -	©̄ George Anson	3Aug.1814	M.Gen.25July1810
Lieut. Colonel	{ John, E. *of* Portarlington	6Apr.1809	Col. 4June1814
	{ Charles Palmer	12Nov.1814	Col. 4June1814
Major - -	{ John Mervin Cutcliffe	2Sept.1813	
	{ Peter Augustus Lautour	6Jan.1814	20May 1813
Captain -	⌠ Tho. Phipps Howard	25May1803	Major 15Mar.1810
		William Warre	7Aug.1806	Lt.Col. 13May1813
		Charles Webb Dance	9Apr.1807	
	⎨ Philip Zachariah Cox	15Mar.1810	
	⎨ John Martin	8Feb.1813	
		Andrew Hamilton	3June	26Dec. 1805
		Thomas Gerrard	1July	Major 1Jan.1812
	⌡ George Fred. Knipe	6Oct.1814	2July 1813
Lieutenant -	⌠ George Dodwell	25Apr.1805	
		A— Bolton	16Oct.1806	19Dec.1805
		Stephen Coxen	17Nov.1808	
		W— S— Easterby	30Mar.1809	
		—— Dodwell	17Aug.	
	⎨ Charles Tudor	14Mar.1810	26Oct. 1808
	⎨ John Banner	15do.	
		John Lewes	4Mar.1813	
		Cæsar Bacon	14Oct.	
		Samuel Hardman	9Dec.	Adjutant
		Barbazon Disney	15Sept.1814	5Aug.1813
	⌡ Robert Johnson	20Oct.	
Cornet - -	{ John Humph. Palmer	11Nov.1813	
	{ Geo. Wm. Blathwayt	25do.	
Paymaster -	Thomas Dillow	31Jan.1809	
Adjutant - -	Samuel Hardman	12Aug.1813	Lieut. 9Dec.1813
Quarter-Master	Joseph Crouchley	15Feb.1810	
Surgeon - -	Samuel L— Steele	20Apr.1809	12Nov.1803
Assistant Surg.	{ H— Cowen	4Aug.1808	
	{ Duncan Henderson	3Nov.1814	16Apr.1812
Veterinary Surg.	John Ship	3Apr.1806	

Blue.—Facings crimson.—Lace silver.

Agent, Messrs. Collyer, Park Place, St. James's.

Permitted to bear on their Colours and Appointments the " ELEPHANT," with the word " HINDOOSTAN" inscribed around it, in commemoration of the Actions at Alli-Ghur, 4th September, and Delhi, 9th September, 1803, and of their General Services in India.

Rank.	Name.	Rank in the Regiment.	Army.	
Colonel - -	William Loftus	14Aug.1802	Gen.	4June1813
Lieut. Colonel	Samuel Need	22June1809	M.Gen.	4June1814
	Philip Philpot	24Jan.1811		
	Francis Newberry	16June1814	Col.	4June1814
Major - - ⊚	Richard Covell	24Jan.1811		
	G— J— Robarts	12Nov.1814	Lt.Col.	2June1813
Captain -	James Mylne	7Aug.1801	Major	4June1813
	Robert Durie	25June1803	Major	4June1814
	Thomas Smoke	9July	Major	4June1814
	George Bunce	10do.	Major	4June1814
	Charles Deane	2Jan.1806		
	W— Hill Wallis	3do.		
	Vincent Beatty	4Apr.1807		
	John Kearney	21Feb.1811		
	John Tritton	22Jan.1812		
	Hon. Augustus Curzon	21Jan.1813	4Apr. 1811	
	George Fitz Clarence	12Nov.1814	2Aug.1811	
Lieutenant -	H.ClintonVanCourtland	1Nov.1803		
	Charlton Tucker	3Mar.1804	27Aug.1802	
	Michael White	14May1805		
	—— Macan	3Jan.1806		
	James Procter	1Mar.		
	Edward Picard	5June	4Apr. 1805	
	Charles Deane	6July		
	Joseph Mico Gibson	1Nov.1807		
	James Mylne	1Jan.1808		
	Thomas Valiant	25Mar.	21June1805	
	Henry Nisbett	16Feb.1809		
	A. St. Leger M'Mahon	1Sept.1810		
	Henry Llewellyn	1June1811	21June1809	
	Archibald Sharpin	23Jan.1812		
	James Richmond	1May		
	Charles Pellichoddy	1Feb.1813	Adjutant	
	William Hickman	3do.		
	Arthur Macartney	4do.		
	James Baratty	6May		
	Thomas Medwin	16Sept.		
	George Gar. Shaw	21Dec.		
	Charles Wardell	3Feb.1814		
	William Tho. Loftus	13Oct.	14Mar.1811	

Cornet

Rank.	Name.	Rank in the Regiment.	Army.
Cornet - - {	Samuel Ward Watson	7 Mar. 1811	
	William White	28 May 1812	
	John Tritton	14 Jan. 1813	
	Henry Sharpin	4 Feb.	
	Henry Dwyer	11 do.	
	Richard James Shaw	18 do.	2 Aug. 1802
	Thomas Alsop	6 May	
	Edw. Aug. Day Maxwell	16 Sept.	10 Oct. 1811
	I— G— Palling	21 Dec.	
Paymaster -	John Wardell	1 May 1805	
Adjutant - -	Charles Pellichoddy	1 Aug. 1808	Lieut. 1 Feb. 1813
Quarter-Master	—— Payne	16 Dec. 1813	
Surgeon - -	John Ruxton	13 Feb. 1806	27 June 1796
Assistant Surg. {	B— L— Sandham	1 Feb. 1812	12 Nov. 1807
	William Brown	2 Apr.	
Veterinary Surg.	William Anderson	9 Apr. 1807	

Blue.—Facings light grey.—Lace gold.

Agent, Messrs. Greenwood, Cox and Hammersley.

25th Regiment of (Light) Dragoons.

Permitted to bear the "ELEPHANT" and the word "LESWAREE" on their Colours and Appointments, in commemoration of the Battle of First November, 1803.

Rank.	*Name.*	Rank in the *Regiment.*	Rank in the *Army.*
Colonel	C. Wm. *Ld.* Stewart, *K.B.*	20Nov.1813	Lt.Gen. 4June1814
Lieut. Col.	George Pownell Adams	8Dec.1804	Col. 4June1813
	Robert Rollo Gillespie	5Jan.1809	M.Gen. 1Jan.1812
	William Tuyll	13Feb.1812	13June1811
Major - -	Robert Ellis	27Sept.1809	Lt.Col. 4June1814
	Henry Odell	24Jan.1811	
Captain -	John Hilton	20Nov.1804	Major 4June1814
	William Thorne	23June1807	Major 30Sept.1811
	Philip Henry Byrne	4Feb.1808	
	Thomas Hole	11do.	Major 4June1813
	North Dalrymple	22Feb.1810	8Feb. 1810
	H— Wyborn Slade	1Jan.1811	25Sept.1808
	Benjamin Scott	1Aug.	
	Samuel Newman	25Nov.	
	Thomas Shaw	1July1813	21Jan. 1813
	Hon. Geo. Fortescue	13Sept.	24Dec. 1812
	G— H— M— Greville	18Nov.	24Sept.1812
Lieutenant -	John Ralston	10July1806	
	Robert Nichols	12do.	
	Edward G— Taylor	16Oct.	30Jan. 1806
	Samuel Burton Jeffries	4Feb.1808	
	William Hilton	1Jan.1809	
	George Smith M'Kenzie	do.	
	Joseph Prager	1June	
	Abel Neale	1Jan.1810	Adjutant
	Charles Blakiston	22Feb.	13July 1808
	Charles Mackintosh	24Aug.	
	Benjamin Jones	25do.	
	Henry Lovelace	24May1811	
	William Keddey	1June	16Nov.1809
	Hirzel Le Marchant	9Nov.	
	Raymond Williams	25do.	25July 1811

Rank.	Name.	Rank in the Regiment.	Army.
Lieutenant -	⎧ John Perring ⎪ Henry Court Amiel ⎪ Matthew B— Taylor ⎨ Thomas Kingdon ⎪ William Murphy ⎪ Brotherton Brown ⎩ Warren Hast. Angelo	13Feb.1812 18July 19do. 10Sept. 8May1813 1Sept. 29Sept.1814	
Cornet - -	⎧ Robert Gordon Davidson ⎪ Aldwell Taylor ⎪ Ambrose D'Letang ⎨ A— Williams ⎪ James Gordon Brunton ⎪ Wm. Scheve Arney ⎩ Edward Henry Steed	1Apr.1810 19July1812 13Sept.1813 16do. 2Dec. 28July1814 29Sept.	
Paymaster -	Thomas Perry	18Feb.1813	
Adjutant - -	Abel Neale	31Dec.1807	Lieut. 1Jan.1810
Quarter-Master	John Houghton	14Dec.1809	
Surgeon - -	P— Paterson	15Apr.1804	12Mar.1796.
Assistant Surg. ⎰	Samuel Barry	25Feb.1813	
⎱	James Mouat	29Sept.1814	1Oct.1812
Veterinary Surg.	George Morri	7May1812	

Blue.—Facings light grey.—Lace silver.

Agent, Messrs. Greenwood, Cox and Hammersley.

1st Regiment of Foot Guards. 145

Permitted to inscribe on their Colours and Appointments the word " LINCELLES," in commemoration of the Action of 18th August, 1793; also the words " CORUNNA" and " BARROSA" for the Battles of 16th Jan. 1809, and the 5th March, 1811.

Rank.	Name.	Regiment.	Rank in the Army.
Colonel	{ *His Royal Highness* Frederick, *D. of* York, *K.G.* 5Sept.1805		F.Mar. 10Feb.1795
Lieut. Colonel	*Lord* Fred. Bentinck 25July1814	Col.	4June1813
First Major - ◎	*Hon.* Arth. Percy Upton 25July1814	Col.	4June1814
Second Major	Henry Askew 25July1814	Col.	4June1814
Third Major	*Hon.* William Stuart 25July1814	Col.	4June1814
	{ *Hon.* H.T.P.Townshend 26Oct.1809	Col.	4June1813
	Isaac Pattison Tinling 14Feb.1811		
◎	Richard Harvey Cooke 7Nov.		
	Edward Stables 4June1812		
	James Dawson West 27Aug.		
✖	Francis D'Oyly 23Sept.		
	John Hanbury 20Dec.		
	Leslie Grove Jones 21Jan.1813		
	Henry Packe 8Apr.		
	Henry D'Oyly 27May		
◎	John George Woodford 1July		
	Thomas Dorville 21Oct.		
	George Fead 13Dec.		
	Charles Thomas 25do.		
Captain and	Alexander, *Lord* Saltoun do.		
Lt. Colonel	John Reeve do.		
	William Miller 3Mar.1814		
	George Ramsden 10do.		
	Samuel Lambert 16do.		
	Richard Henry Marsac 17do.		
	Edward Wynyard 28Apr.		
	Hon. James Stanhope 25July		17Mar.1814
	Henry Edmund Joddrell do.		
	Henry Stables do.		
	Goodwin Colquitt do.		
	William Henry Milnes do.		
✖	Henry Hollis Bradford do.		28Dec. 1809
✖	Henry Harding do.		30May 1811
✖-	*Sir* Thomas Noel Hill, *Kt.* do.		3Oct. 1811
	Delancey Barclay do.		28Feb. 1812
✖	*Lord* Fitzroy J. H. Somerset do.		27Apr. 1812
	Ulysses Burgh do.		5Sept.1812

T   Lieutenant

| Rank. | Name. | Rank in the | |
		Regiment.	Army.
Lieutenant and Captain	Alexander Higginson	14Sept.1809	
	Robert Adair	26Oct.	
	Thomas Streatfield	23Nov.	
	J— H— Davies	7Dec.	4Feb. 1808
	Charles Allix	13Dec.1810	Adjutant
	Thomas Brooke	14Feb.1811	
	Turner Grant	20do.	
	Benjamin Charlewood	21do.	14June1810
	George P— Higginson	3Apr.	
	Lord James Hay	27June	8Feb. 1810
	Hugh Edward Hunter	8Aug.	Adjutant
	Edward Grose	26Sept.	
	James Gunthorpe	7Nov.	Adjutant
	Robert Thoroton	9Apr.1812	
	Cha. Rob. Mann. Molloy	4June	
	Tho. B. Bridges Barratt	30July	
	Chath. Hor. Churchill	27Aug.	Major 22Nov.1813
	Hon. Robert Clements	23Sept.	
	Lord Charles Fitzroy	do.	
	John Hely Hutchinson	19Nov.	
	James Lindsay	10Dec.	
	Robert Ellison	20do.	
	John Lloyd Dukenfield	20Jan.1813	
	Henry Vernon	21do.	
	Harry Weyland Powell	22do.	
	Newton Chambers	7Apr.	
	George Desbrowe	8do.	
	Sir Henry Lambert, Bt.	27May	
	Wm. Gordon Cameron	10June	
	Harry Brereton Trelawny	7July	
	Philip Clarke	8do.	
	Lonsdale Boldero	20Oct.	
	Hon. A.J.H.FitzG. deRos	21do.	
	Robert Wm. Phillimore	13Dec.	
	Lane Augustus Fox	do.	
	Hon. Orlando Bridgeman	8Jan.1814	
	Thomas Starke	9do.	
	Charles Parker Ellis	10do.	
	James Simpson	11do.	
	Aug. Fred. Visc. Bury	12do.	
	Edward Clive	13do.	
	Philip Joshua Perceval	10Mar.	
	William Fred. Johnstone	16do.	
	Francis Fownes Luttrell	17do.	
	Thomas Brown	22do.	

Lieutenant

| Rank. | Name. | Rank in the | |
		Regiment.	Army.
Lieutenant and Captain	Edward Pery Buckley 23Mar.1814 Francis Dawkins 28Apr. James Nixon 12May Charles F. R. Lascelles 9June William George Moore 30Sept. Samuel Wm. Burgess 20Oct.		14Apr. 1814
Ensign - -	Rees Howell Gronow 24Dec.1812 Robert Batty 14Jan.1813 John Home 19do. Richard Master 21do. Augustus Dashwood 22do. William Barton 4Feb. John Ord Honyman 4Mar. Hon.H.Sed.Ven.Vernon 8Apr. Edward Pardoe 29do. Courtney Chambers 10June James Butler 23do. Tho. Robert Swinburne 24do. Charles James Vyner 2Sept. Edward Burrard 23do. Fred. Dashwood Swann 20Oct. James Lord Hay 21do. John Grant 4Nov. John Pasley Dirom 18do. John Fra. Miller Erskine 1Dec. Fred. Thoroton Gould 2do. Robert Bruce 9do. Richard Fletcher 16do. Sackville Walter L. Fox 6Jan.1814 Samuel Long 10do. Hon.T.SeymourBathurst 11do. Hon. Ern. A. Edgcumbe 12do. George Fludyer 13do. Godfrey Thornton 20do. Francis Henry Needham 26do. William Fred. Tinling 27do. Algeron Greville 1Feb. George Thomson Jacob 3do. Donald Cameron 17do. Samuel Hurd 3Mar. Fletcher Norton 17do. Henry Lascelles 7Apr. George Mure 14do. George Allen 21do.	9May 1811 12Dec. 1811 17June1813 Lieut. 2Sept.1818 Lieut. 9Dec.1813	

T 2   Ensign

Rank.	Name.	Rank in the	
		Regiment.	Army.
Ensign	Thomas Elmsley Croft 28 Apr.1814 William Henry Barnard 9June T— C·— Askew 17Nov. Hon.S.S.Perc.Barrington 24do. Joseph St. John 25do. Daniel Tighe 26do.		7Sept.1814
Adjutant	James Gunthorpe 19Nov.1811 Charles Allix 13Dec.1813 Hugh Edward Hunter 11Mar.1814	Capt. 7Nov.1811 Capt. 13Dec.1810 Capt. 8Aug.1811	
QuarterMaster	George Hodder 25Dec.1802 George Darby 23July1803 Robert Colquhoun 25Nov.1812	21Aug.1806	
Surgeon Major	Thomas Nixon 9June1814		
Battalion Surg.	William Curtis 5Oct.1809 Samuel Wm. Watson 25Dec.1813 John Bacot 9June1814	21Aug.1806 14July 1809	
Assistant Surg.	Robert Gibson 8Dec.1804 John Harrison 29June1809 Andrew Armstrong 18July1811 William Lambert 9Jan.1812 John Gardner 25Dec.1813 Frederick Gilder 9June1814		
Solicitor	John Wilkinson 27June1811		

Facings blue.—Lace gold.

Agent, Messrs. Greenwood, Cox and Hammersley.

Coldstream

Permitted to inscribe on their Colours and Appointments the word " LINCELLES," in commemoration of the Action of 18th August, 1793; also the words, " TALAVERA" and " BARROSA," for the Battles of 27th and 28th July, 1809, and 5th March, 1811. The 1st Bn. also to bear a " SPHINX," with the word " EGYPT," for the Campaign of 1801.

Rank.	Name.	Rank in the Regiment.	Rank in the Army.
Colonel	{ His Royal Highness A.F. Duke of Cambridge, K.G.	5 Sept. 1805	F. Mar. 26 Nov. 1813
Lieut. Colonel	⦾ Hon. Henry Brand	25 July 1814	Col. 4 June 1814
First Major -	⊠ Rich. Downes Jackson	25 July 1814	Col. 4 June 1814
Second Major	⦾ Alex. George Woodford	25 July 1814	Col. 4 June 1814
Captain and Lieut. Col.	⦾ { Henry Fred. Bouverie	28 June 1810	Col. 4 June 1814
	James Macdonell	8 Aug. 1811	7 Sept. 1809
	John Hamilton	30 Jan. 1812	
	Lucius F— Adams	31 do.	
	Henry Loftus	23 July	16 Jan. 1809
	Wm. Henley Raikes	3 June 1813	
	Francis Sutton	25 Dec.	
	Francis Miles Milman	do.	
	Thomas Gore	do.	
	Thomas Barrow	2 June 1814	
	Daniel M'Kinnon	25 July	
	Hon. John Walpole	do.	
	Henry Dawkins	do.	
⦾	Hon. Alex. Abercromby	do.	Col. 4 June 1814
⊠	Colin Campbell	do.	Col. 4 June 1814
⦾	Hon. Edward Acheson	do.	6 Mar. 1811
⊠	Robert Arbuthnot	do.	22 May 1811
⦾	Hon. Herc. Rob. Pakenham	do.	27 Apr. 1812
⊠	William Gomm	do.	17 Aug. 1812
	Henry Wyndham	do.	20 Jan. 1814
Lieutenant and Captain	{ Thomas Steele	1 June 1809	
	George Bowles	1 Feb. 1810	
	Thomas Sowerby	27 June	
	Edward Lascelles	28 do.	Adjutant
	Patrick Sandilands	19 July	
	John Fremantle	2 Aug.	Lt. Col. 21 Mar. 1814

Lieutenant

Rank.	Name.	Regiment.	Rank in the Army.
Lieutenant and Captain	John Prince 29Oct.1810 James Vigors Harvey 17Jan.1811 Wm. Lovelace Walton 7Mar. Alexander Wedderburn 7Nov. Charles White 30Jan.1812 Thomas Bligh 13Feb. Charles Shawe 23Apr. Cha.Au.Fred.Bentinck 24Sept. John Talbot 26Nov. George Harvey Percival 25Mar.1813 Walter George Baynes 1June William Stothert 2do. John Stepney Cowell 9Sept. Edward Sumner 23do. John Lucie Blackman 11Jan.1814 William Grimstead 12do. Beaumont, *Lord* Hotham 13do. Windham Anstruther 17Mar. *Hon.* John Rous 4May Charles Shirley 5do. John Drummond 26do. *Hon.* Robert Moore 2June Charles Andrew Girardot 1Sept. Thomas Chaplin 6Oct.		Adjutant 24Sept.1812
Ensign	Edward Clifton 25Apr.1811 Henry Salwey 13June George Gould Morgan 4July Tho. Sling. Duncombe 17Oct. Francis Eyre 26Dec. *Hon.* James Forbes 13Feb.1812 Thomas Powys 30Apr. Henry Gooch 23July Augustus Cuyler 15Oct. Mark Beaufoy 12Nov. William Kortright 26do. Henry Armytage 27do. *Hon.* Wm. Rufus Rous 17Dec. H. John Wm. Bentinck 25Mar.1813 Francis Manby Shawe 6May Humphrey Mildmay 9Sept. Frederick Tho. Buller 30Dec. Henry Fred. Griffiths 25Jan.1814		9June1812 26Mar.1812

Ensign

| | | Rank in the | |
Rank.	Name.	Regiment.	Army.
Ensign -	James Fred. Buller	26Jan.1814	
	John Montagu	27do.	
	GeorgeRichard Buckley	17Feb.	
	James Hervey	15Mar.	
	Henry Vane	16do.	
	Francis James Douglas	17do.	
	Robert Bowen	24do.	
	Frederick Fitz Clarence	12May	
	Alexander Gordon	19do.	
	Hon. Walter Forbes	2June	
	Charles Short	13Oct.	
	William Serjeantson	17Nov.	
Adjutant -	Cha. Au. Fred. Bentinck	4June1812	Capt. 24Sept.181?
	Edward Lascelles	3Dec.	Capt. 28June1810
Quarter Master	Thomas Dwelly	15Oct.1812	
	Benjamin Selway	26Nov.	
Surgeon Major	John Treadw. Simpson	11Mar.1802	
Battalion Surg.	John Rose	26Nov.1812	
	William Whymper	25Dec.1813	
Assistant Surg.	Thomas Maynard	21Feb.1811	
	George Smith	17Dec.1812	
	Septimus Worrell	29Apr.1813	
	William Hunter	10Feb.1814	
Solicitor - -	John Wilkinson	24Feb.1814	

Facings blue.—Lace gold.

Agent, Messrs. Greenwood, Cox and Hammersley.

3d Regiment of Foot Guards.

Permitted to inscribe on their Colours and Appointments the word " LINCELLES," in commemoration of the Action of 18th August, 1793; also the words " TALAVERA" and " BARROSA" for the Battles of the 27th and 28th July, 1809, and 5th March, 1811. The 1st Bn. also to bear a " SPHINX," with the word " EGYPT," for the Campaign of 1801.

		Rank in the	
Rank.	Name.	Regiment.	Army.
Colonel {	His Highness W.F. Duke of Gloucester,K.G. 26May1806	Gen.	25Apr.1808
Lieut. Colonel	George Hill	25July1814	Col. 4June1813
First Major ◎	John Guise	25July1814	Col. 4June1813
Second Major ◎	Francis Hepburne	25July1814	Col. 4June1814
	Willoughby Cotton	12June1811	
	Thomas Fotheringham	28Feb.1812	1Jan. 1812
	Henry Willough. Rooke	do.	
	John Clitherow	8Oct.	
	Ja. Johnstone Cochrane	10Dec.	
	Thomas Geils	9Aug.1813	5Mar.1812
	William Aug. Keate	do.	
	William Chester Master	9Dec.	
Captain and Lieut. Colonel {	Douglas Mercer	20do.	
	Hon. Alexander Gordon	25do.	6Feb. 1812
	Charles Dashwood	do.	
	Francis Home	15Mar.1814	
	Charler Fox Canning	31do.	19Aug.1813
	Edward Bowater	25July	
	Charles West	do.	
	John Potter Hamilton	do.	25Oct. 1809
	Samuel G— Higgins	do.	4June1811
◎	George Thomas Napier	do.	6Feb. 1812
◎-	Hon. James Stewart	do.	3June1813
◎	James Archibald Hope	do.	21June1813
	John Aitchison	22Nov.1810	
	William Henry Scott	28Mar.1811	
	Hugh Seymour	do.	
	William Stothert	4Apr.	Adjutant
Lieutenant and Captain {	Charles Talbot	28May	
	William Drummond	24Oct.	
	Robert Bamford Hesketh	31do.	
	Henry Hawkins	12Dec.	
	R— H— Wigston	19do.	
	Hon. Ja. Berk. Rodney	5Mar.1812	

Lieutenant

Rank.	Name.	Rank in the	
		Regiment.	Army.

Rank.	Name.	Regiment.	Army.
Lieutenant and Captain	Charles John Barnet 16Apr.1812 Joseph Wm. Moorhouse 23do. Arnold Burrowes 8Oct. *Sir* Arch. J. Murray,*Bt.* 10Dec. Charles Hornby 26Aug.1813 Frederick Colville 9Dec. Charles Hall 20do. Alexander Fead 30do. Charles Sandes 10Jan.1814 John H— J— Stapleton 11do. Cha. O'Neil Prendergast 12do. Rich. Fra. G. Cumberland 13do. William Stockdale 17Mar. Edward Brydges Fairfield 24do. George Evelyn 31do. *Hon.* Hastings Forbes 5May John Elrington 19do. Hugh Ber. Montgomerie 9June Thomas Craufurd 1Sept. John Ashton 2do.		Adjutant
Ensign -	George Tuffnell 27June1811 Charles Lake 31Oct. *Hon.* Edward Stopford 7Nov. Barclay Drummond 5Mar.1812 William Grant 12do. George Douglas Standen 19do. Henry Paxton 7May David Baird 18June William James 4Mar.1813 William Fred. Hamilton 1Apr. Wm.Geo.Stepn.Cowell 15July Tho. Welby Northmore 5Aug. William Fred. Forster 26do. William Thomas Knollys 9Dec. Henry Colville 29do. Thomas Berry 30do. Digby Murray 5Jan.1814 Robert Henry Russell 6do.		10June1813

U

Ensign

		Rank in the	
Rank.	Name.	Regiment.	Army.

Rank.	Name.	Regiment.	Army.
Ensign	*Hon.* George Anson	8Jan.1814	
	Frederick Walpole Keppel	9do.	
	Randal Gossip	10do.	
	Thomas Wedgewood	11do.	
	Whitwell Butler	12do.	
	Andrew Coutts Cochrane	13do.	
	Jeffery Prendergast	2Feb.	
	—— Simpson	3do.	
	Hugh Seymour Bland	31Mar.	
	James Fortescue Rodd	7Apr.	
	Henry Montague	21do.	
	Hon. —— Westenra	4May	
	Philip James Yorke	5do.	
	Charles Douglas	19do.	
	Chidley Coote	9June	
Adjutant	William Stothert	25Aug.1809	Capt. 4Apr.1811
	Sir Arch. J. Murray, *Bt.*	19May1814	Capt. 10Dec.1812
Quarter Master	George Steel	26July1797	
	John Skuce	22Mar.1810	
Surgeon Major	Wm. Alexander Hay	12Jan.1796	
Battalion Surg.	Edward Salmon	25May1808	
	Samuel Good	25Dec.1813	
Assistant Surg.	Wm. Troward Gilder	25May1808	
	J— R— Warde	27Apr.1809	21Aug.1806
	Fran. Gashry Hanrott	10Dec.1812	
	Robert Tyndal	25Dec.1813	
Solicitor	Moses Hoper	25July1811	

Facings blue.—Lace gold.

Agent, Messrs. Greenwood, Cox and Hammersley.

1st

Permitted to bear on their Colours and Appointments a " SPHINX," with the word " EGYPT," in commemoration of the Campaign of 1801.

Rank.	Name.	Rank in the Regiment.	Rank in the Army.
Colonel -	His Royal Highness Edw. D. of Kent, K.G.	21 Aug. 1801	F. Mar. 5 Sept. 1805
Lieut. Colonel ⊙	Henry Conran	7 May 1807	M. Gen. 1 Jan. 1812
	James Stevenson Barnes	21 Apr. 1808	Col. 4 June 1814
	Norman Macleod	29 Mar. 1810	4 May 1809
	Neil M'Kellar	6 Dec.	
	Frederick Muller	2 Jan. 1812	4 June 1811
Major - ⊙	Thomas Deane	25 June 1808	Lt. Col. 4 June 1814
	Swan Hill	21 July	Lt. Col. 4 June 1814
	Thomas Fraser	8 June 1809	Lt. Col. 4 June 1814
	Robert Nixon	8 Feb. 1810	Lt. Col. 4 June 1814
	Colin Campbell	27 Sept.	Lt. Col. 17 Aug. 1812
	James Stuart Lynch -	6 Dec.	
	Valentine Chisholm	26 Aug. 1813	
	Alexander Stewart	1 Dec. 1814	4 June 1814
Captain -	John Gordon	24 Aug. 1804	Major 4 June 1814
	Edward Michael Bird	25 do.	Major 4 June 1814
	Donald Maclean	1 Sept.	Major 4 June 1814
	J— P— Gordon	14 Feb. 1805	
	Archibald Stoddart	7 Mar.	
	John Lee	14 do.	7 Mar. 1805
	Thomas Campbell	23 May	
	George Aug. Wetherall	27 Nov. 1806	13 May 1805
	John Selby Smyth	4 Dec.	31 July 1806
	James Rowan	12 Apr. 1807	
	John Wilson	7 May	1 Jan. 1807
	Saville Spear	21 July 1808	
	L— Arguimbau	9 Mar. 1809	Major 11 Aug. 1814
	Abraham Logan	25 Apr.	
	John Octavius Glover	6 July	
	William Gray	3 Aug.	Lt. Col. 1 Jan. 1812
	Robert Mullen	25 do.	
	Robert Macdonald	8 Feb. 1810	Major 21 Sept. 1813
	William Buckley	11 Oct.	

Captain

Rank.	Name.	Rank in the	
		Regiment.	Army.
Captain -	Hugh Massey	9May1811	Major 4June1811
	Bessel Harvey	20June	11Apr. 1811
	David Deuchar	12Dec.	
	William Gordon	16Jan.1812	
	George Marlay	14May	Major 4June1814
	Robert Dudgeon	30July	
	George Dods	24Sept.	Major 4June1814
	Currell Smith Hopkins	23Dec.	
	John M'Ra	28Jan.1813	23Dec.1812
	William L— Brereton	1July	
	Angus M'Lachlin	8do.	
	Henry Cowell	21do.	
	Thomas Mosse	22do.	
	James Cowell	19Aug.	
	Joseph Wetherall	25do.	
	William Hulme	26do.	
	Donald M'Queen	12Apr.1814	
	Ludovic Grant	13do.	
	Peter M'Gregor	14do.	
	George Gordon	26May	
	Menzies Fullerton	4Aug.	
	William Sutherland	18do.	
	Hugh Brodie	8Sept.	
	William Haswell	6Oct.	
	James Hamilton	1Dec.	
Lieutenant -	Patrick Grant	30Sept.1806	
	Richard Rothwell	2Oct.	
	Peter Grant	20do.	
	Lachlan M'Lean	29do.	
	George Galbraith	30do.	Adjutant
	Angus M'Donald	13Nov.	
	John Clyne	21May1807	
	Alexander Campbell	26Nov.	1Feb. 1807
	John T— Connell	5Jan.1808	1Jan. 1807
	William Billing	6do.	
	Richard Vaughan	8do.	
	Barry Fox	10do.	
	George Jackson	13do.	
	Richard O— Jenoway	14do.	
	Charles Hendrich	31Mar.	
	Leonard Henry Dubbin	26Aug.	
	Archibald Morrison	27Oct.	3Dec. 1806

Lieutenant

Rank.	Name.	Rank in the	
		Regiment.	Army.
Lieutenant	Arthur M'Clure	26Apr.1809	
	John Armstrong	27do.	
	John E— O'Neill	8June	21Apr. 1808
	William James Rea	22do.	30July 1807
	John Ingram	12July	18Oct. 1808
	William Wetherall	14do.	
	George Todd	15do.	
	Richard Vallancey	20do.	
	James Bland	25Aug.	
	John Magawley Balfour	26do.	
	John M'Killigan	30Nov.	
	John Tracey Holebrooke	11Jan.1810	
	Peter Mac Pherson	8Feb.	
	William Gordon	1Mar.	21Dec. 1809
	A— Macdonnell	5Apr.	
	William Clarke	21June	
	Charles Eyre	18Oct.	
	Thomas Bell	13Dec.	
	Alexander B— Higgins	20do.	21June1810
	John Cross	7Mar.1811	
	Norman Maclean	13do.	23Feb. 1809
	William M'Beath	14do.	
	Ebenezer Lorimer	21do.	
	Charles Thomas Grant	13June	2May 1811
	Richard Lamont	8Aug.	
	Nathan Ashurst	12Sept.	5Jan. 1805
	William Orrock	21Nov.	
	John M'Gregor	28do.	
	James Moloney	16Jan.1812	
	Ja. Hamilton Wardrop	23do.	
	Horace Suckling	28Feb.	
	Charles Campbell	2Apr.	
	James Conran	23July	
	William Campbell	30do.	
	G— C— Johnstone	8Oct.	
	Joseph Fowler	19Nov.	4July 1805
	Allan Robertson	24Dec.	
	Thomas Gordon	18Feb.1813	2July 1812
	Robert Bothamiey	6May	10July 1801
	Wm. Munro Mackenzie	3June	
	Thomas Stewart	5do.	
	Donald Macleod	29do.	
	William Mac Ewen	30do.	Adjutant

Lieutenant

Rank.	Name.	Rank in the Regiment.	Army.
	Allen Cameron	1July1813	26June1812 Adj.
	Thomas Miller	do.	
	Donald Fraser	3do.	
	John Stoyte	4do.	
	Joseph Jeffries	5do.	
	Edward Babington	.6do.	
	James Waller Hewett	7do.	
	Robert Horsman Scott	8do.	
	J— H— Thompson	22do.	
	T. B. M. Sutherland	12Aug.	4Nov.1811
	George Macartney	19do.	
	Thomas Weir	22do.	
	George Church	23do.	
	T— Paul Williamson	24do.	
	William Midgley	25do.	
	George Lane	26do.	
	Joseph Hoskins	22Sept.	
	Joseph Symes	23do.	
Lieutenant -	James Alstone	21Oct.	
	William Younge	4Nov.	
	Eleazer Jenkins	16Dec.	
	Edward Scott	6Jan.1814	16Oct. 1811
	William Sibbald	12Apr.	
	Theo. de St. Marguerite	13do.	
	James Vernon Fletcher	14do.	
	Duncan Cameron	21do.	
	Nathan Ashurst	28do.	
	John Muirson	24May	
	Willoughby Carter	25do.	
	Alexander Quarrier	26do.	
	William D— Barclay	4Aug.	
	James Mann	18do.	
	George Mathias	22Sept.	
	William Dobbs	29do.	
	John Fitzwilliam Miller	6Oct.	
	John Stewart	7do.	Adjutant
	Thomas Bayly	19do.	
	Hugh Gordon	30Nov.	
	James Oliphant Clunie	1Dec.	
	George Stewart	2do.	15Dec.1813
Ensign -	Joseph Ambrose Collins	19Sept.1813	
	John Clancy	20do.	
	W— Howe	22do.	
	Alexander Glen	21Oct.	

		Rank in the	
Rank.	Name.	Regiment.	Army.
	Charles Mudie	4Nov.1813	
	John Campbell	9Dec.	
	John Miller	16do.	
	Charles Black. Vignoles	13Jan.1814	10Nov.1794
	Joseph Crowther	17Feb.	
	Francis Crowther	22do.	
	Edward Crowther	23do.	
	Charles Bushe Clarke	24do.	
	John Dixon	10Mar.	
	Henry James Bichner	24do.	
	James Grant Kennedy	12Apr.	
	Edwin Mainwaring	13do.	
	J— D— Morris	14do.	
Ensign - -	Edward Holland	21do.	
	——— Clarke	24May	
	G— F— Munns	25do.	
	——— Hanbury	26do.	
	Charles Pieters	4Aug.	
	——— Eddington	18do.	
	Charles Lewis	22Sept.	9June1813
	Charles Graham	28do.	9June1814
	Thomas Stevens	29do.	
	Joseph M'Kay	6Oct.	
	Alexander Robertson	20do.	
	William Anderson	27do.	14July 1814
	H— J— Frederick	1Dec.	
	Rowland Savage	2do.	
Paymaster - 2	Charles Fortnum	5Jan.1805	
4	Alexander Gibson	11May1809	
3	Mark Lindus Daniel	4Mar.1813	
1	Benjamin Bovill	3June	
Adjutant -	George Galbraith	12Mar.1807	Lieut. 30Oct.1806
	William Mac Ewen	11Oct.1810	Lieut. 30June1813
	Allen Cameron	1July1813	Lieut. 26June1812
	John Stewart	29Sept.1814	Lieut. 7Oct.1814

Quarter

Rank.	Name.	Rank in the Regiment.	Army.
QuarterMaster	Samuel Petto	13Apr.1809	
	——— Day	20Aug.1811	
	Thomas Griffith	4Aug.1814	
	——— Francis	20Oct.	
Surgeon - -	James Davidson	19July1804	
	William Wilson	10Nov.1808	
	William Galliers	20Apr.1809	10Sept.1807
	William Roberts	19Nov.1812	29Oct. 1812
Assistant Surg.	James Ballingall	10July1806	
	John Johnson	20Oct.1808	7Apr. 1808
	James Macleod	22Aug.1811	
	David Griffiths	26Sept.	
	William Finnie	12Nov.1812	
	Alexander Sinclair	3Dec.	
	Thomas Bolton	9Dec.1813	5Mar.1812
	William Stoddart	14July1814	

Facings blue.—Lace gold.

Agent, Mr. Kirkland, No. 8, Bennett Street, St. James's.

2d

[1815]

2d (or the Queen's Royal) Regiment of Foot. 161

*Permitted to bear on their Colours and Appointments a " SPHINX," with the word " EGYPT,"
in commemoration of the Campaign of 1801.*

Rank.	Name.	Rank in the Regiment.	Army.
Colonel - -	James Coates	20Dec.1794	Gen. 29Apr.1802
Lieut. Colonel	Geo. Aug. Henderson	16June1814	12Apr. 1814
Major - -	George Edward Raitt	19Aug.1813	Lt.Col.25Sept.1814
	Matthew Scott	16June1814	21Sept.1813
Captain -	John Gordon	14Aug.1806	11Apr. 1805
	Ja. Florence de Burgh	25Dec.	Lt.Col. 4June1813
	Sir Freeman Barton, Kt.	29June1809	
	John Gordon	26Apr.1810	
	Charles Cox	7June	14Apr. 1808
	John Johnstone	1Aug.1811	
	Patrick Carney	6Aug.1812	
	John Williams	17June1813	
	Charles Borlase	1Sept.	
	John Morle	2do.	
	John Alexander Wilson	14July1814	
Lieutenant -	John Thomas Wood	11June1807	7May 1807
	William Clutterbuck	17Mar.1808	
	Andrew Hair	12May	
	George Williams	19June1809	
	Duncan M'Dougall	20do.	
	William Gordon	21do.	
	G— Pilkington	23do.	
	James E— Hudson	17Aug.	29May 1806
	John Rutledge Kell	31do.	
	Richard Berford	12Sept.	
	William Gray	13do.	
	William Goodall	21Dec.	
	George Nicholson	8Mar.1810	17Mar.1808
	John Ballan. Norman	26Apr.	
	John C— Glasson	25Apr.1811	
	J— Adams	22Aug.	
	William Hutton	6Oct.1812	
	Charles Grant	7do.	
	W— D— Collingwood	8do.	
	Charles Girdlestone	9June1813	
	——— Spencer	10do.	Adjutant
	Andrew Simpson	17do.	
	Isaac Barrington Perrin	15Sept.	
	Edward Mac Donnell	do.	
	G— W— Prosser	16do.	
	David Griffiths	28July1814	

X   Ensign

		Rank in the	
Rank.	Name.	Regiment.	Army.

Rank	Name	Regiment	Army
Ensign	Fred. William Frankland 7Oct.1812		22July 1812
	H. Whosewood Greenwood 8do.		
	Thomas Bernard 8Apr.1813		
	Percy Scott 10June		
	C. Routledge O'Donnell 9Sept.		
	Andrew Richmond 11Nov.		
	David Jenkins 25Dec.		
	George Newenham 29Sept.1814		

Rank	Name	Regiment	Army
Paymaster	William Cary Bowden	12May1808	
Adjutant	——— Spencer	25Mar.1811	Lieut. 10June1813
Quarter-Master	——— Jones	6May1802	
Surgeon	William Maxton	25June1801	
Assistant Surg	David Law	27May1813	
	Alexander John Ralph	29Sept.1814	31Mar.1814

Facings blue.— Lace silver.

Agent, Messrs. Greenwood, Cox and Hammersley.

Permitted to bear on their Colours and Appointments the word " DOURO," in commemoration of the passage of that river 12th May, 1809.

Rank.	Name.	Rank in the Regiment.	Rank in the Army.
Colonel - -	Charles Leigh	29Dec.1809	Gen. 25Sept.1803
Lieut. Col.	◎ { William Stewart	16Aug.1810	
	◎ { James Fergusson	16May1814	
Major - -	{ Henry Roberts	17Nov.1808	Lt.Col. 19May1814
	{ Henry King	17Aug.1809	Lt.Col. 4June1814
	{ George Morris	16Nov.	Lt.Col. 4June1814
	{ Wm. Claud. Campbell	16Aug.1810	
Captain -	◎ { Charles Cameron	1Dec.1804	Major 22Nov.1813
	{ Charles Parke	30Jan.1806	
	{ Henry Marlay	8July1807	
	{ Peter Campbell	2Nov.1809	
	{ Nathaniel Thorn	4Jan.1810	Major 3Mar.1814
	{ William Fowden	do.	
	{ Francis Plunkett	12July	Lt.Col. 1Jan.1812
	{ Michael Murphy	16Aug.	
	{ Cassius M— Clenchey	20June1811	
	{ Pierre Edward Fleming	4June1812	23Mar.1809
	{ Mathew Latham	13May1813	11Feb.1813
	{ H— Guy Colclough	26Aug.	
	{ William Nicholls	27Jan.1814	
	{ William Juxon	26May	
	{ Richard Houghton	7July	
	{ John M'Crohan	13Oct.	
	{ John Gardiner	24Nov.	
	{ William Light	25do.	
	{ Richard Hooper	8Dec.	
Lieutenant -	{ William Clifford	13Nov.1806	1Aug.1805
	{ John Shepherd	27do.	
	{ William Tetlow	5Apr.1807	
	{ Samuel Wright	13Aug.	
	{ Henry Gillman	18Dec.1808	
	{ Charles Jackson	29June1809	
	{ Ja. Campbell Fielding	3Aug.	
	{ John Sutherland	31do.	

Lieutenant

Rank.	Name.	Rank in the Regiment.	Army.
Lieutenant -	William Manders	2Nov.1809	
	David Skiell	26Dec.	
	William Penefather	17Jan.1810	
	William Alment	do.	
	Edward Blair	18do.	
	William Woods	31Jan.1811	
	Charles Walsh	19June	
	R— Meech	do.	
	M— C— Horner	29Apr.1812	Adjutant
	John West	24Sept.	
	John Home	26Nov.	
	John Simpson Hughes	25Feb.1813	
	William Mackay	5May	
	Francis Bernard Fielding	6do.	
	W— Farquharson	24June	
	Robert Fitz Gibbon	24Aug.	
	John Twigg	do.	
	George T— Benson	25do.	
	F— Murphy	26do.	
	Robert Blake	23Sept.	
	Thomas Henry Owen	21Oct.	
	Thomas Everndern	31Mar.1814	
	William Wrighte	26May	
	Robert Stirling	11Aug.	
	Archibald Innes	3Nov.	
Ensign -	Christopher Dexter	11June1812	
	William M'Minn	20Aug.	
	Tobias Laffey	17Sept.	
	John Tharpe Clarke	5Nov.	
	Thomas Barrett	15Apr.1813	
	William Caldwell	26Aug.	
	Henry Young	7Oct.	
	Ambrose Moore	14do.	
	John Miller	21do.	
	J— B— Kingsbury	25Dec.	
	Samuel Blythe	do.	
	Carden Williams	do.	

Ensign

Rank.	Name.	Rank in the Regiment.	Army.
Ensign - -	Richard Nelson	27 Jan. 1814	Adjutant
	R— de Courcy	14 July	
	John Lewis Corrigan	22 Nov.	
	William Spiller	23 do.	
	John Willock	24 do.	
Paymaster - 2	Thomas Henry Mann	23 July 1807	
1	William Boyd	18 Mar. 1813	
Adjutant -	M— C— Horner	25 Apr. 1810	Lieut. 29 Apr. 1812
	Richard Nelson	24 Nov. 1814	Ensign 27 Jan. 1814
QuarterMaster	William Herring	11 Feb. 1808	
	J— Roberts	28 Apr.	
Surgeon -	Thomas Anderson	25 Dec. 1802	4 Apr. 1800
	Robert Shekelton	9 Sept. 1813	
Assistant Surg.	Robert Ivory	23 Nov. 1809	
	Alexander Bremner	3 Sept. 1812	
	John Morrison	6 May 1813	

Facings buff.—Lace silver.

Agent, Messrs. Greenwood, Cox and Hammersley.

4th

166   4th (or the King's own) Regiment of Foot.

The 1st Battalion permitted to bear the word " CORUNNA," on their Colours and Appointments in commemoration of the Action of the 16th Jan. 1809.

			Rank in the	
Rank.	*Name.*	*Regiment.*	*Army.*	

Colonel	- John, *Earl of* Chatham, *K.G.* 5 Dec.1799	Gen.	1 Jan.1812

| Lieut. Col. | ✗ { Francis Brooke | 14 Feb.1811 | |
| | ⊚ { David Williamson | 22 July 1813 | 17 Aug.1812 |

Major	-	⊚— { John Piper	16 Aug.1810	L.Col. 17 Aug.1812
	⊚ { A— Dodsw. Faunce	14 Feb.1811	L.Col. 29 Sept.1814
	{ George O'Halloran	1 Aug.	
	{ Thomas Burke	22 July 1813	

Captain	-	⊚ { John Williamson	6 Aug.1804	Major 21 Sept.1813
	⊚	George David Wilson	7 do.	Major 26 Dec.1813
		John Easting Kipping	8 do.	Major 26 Dec.1813
	⊚	Timothy Jones	11 do.	L.Col. 29 Sept.1814
	⊚	Robert Anwyll	14 do.	Major 21 June 1813
		James Ward	14 Nov.	Major 4 June 1814
		Francis Johnston	6 June 1805	
		Charles James Edgell	5 Sept.	
		William Leighton Wood	1 Jan.1807	
		J— W— Fletcher	4 June	
		Richard Henry Shaw	25 Feb.1808	16 July 1807
		Robert Erskine	8 Sept.	
		David S— Craig	16 Mar.1809	
		Euseby Stratford Kirwan	11 Jan.1810	
		Richard Moore	16 Aug.	
		James Jamieson	31 Oct.	
		William Kelly	15 Feb.1811	
		Henry Brereton	1 Aug.	
		Vere Hunt	14 May 1812	
		John Read Vincent	29 July 1813	

Lieutenant	-	{ William Henry Alley	23 Oct.1804	
		Elers Pernell Hopkins	10 Jan.1805	
		Jeffrey Salvin	5 Feb.	
		John Browne	28 do.	
		George Vincent	7 June	
		W— B— C— Edgell	5 Sept.	
		William Brooke	12 do.	25 June 1803
		Benjamin Martin	30 Oct.1806	3 June 1802
		Edward Gichard	28 July 1808	
		John Ken. Mackenzie	15 Dec.	

Lieutenant

| Rank. | Name. | Rank in the | |
		Regiment.	Army.
	John Stavely	9Mar.1809	
	G— Richardson	26May	
	Lewis Moore Bennett	30do.	
	Peter Bowlby	31do.	
	Thomas Moody	1June	
	Edmund Feilde	22Nov.	
	John Clarke	1Feb.1810	
	Hygatt Boyd	16Aug.	
	Robert Mackintosh	20Sept.	
	George Henry Hearne	29Oct.	
	John Warde	31do.	
	Benj. Marshal Collins	1Nov.	
	William Squire	14Feb.1811	
	William Graham	12May1812	
	John Bushell	do.	
	Richard Mulholland	14do.	
	William Lonsdale	15do.	
Lieutenant -	William Ramsden	8Oct.	
	James White	26Nov.	
	John Alexander Copley	25Jan.1813	3Aug.1809
	Edward Boulby	25Feb.	
	William Clarke	28July	
	Charles Hen. Farrington	29do.	
	Frederick Hyde	16Sept.	
	John Sutherland	21do.	
	James Marshall	23do.	
	H— Andrews	7Oct.	
	Edward Rawlings	19do.	
	—— Richardson	20do.	Adjutant
	D— M'Crohan	21do.	
	—— Pickering	16Nov.	Adjutant
	Frederick Feilde	17do.	
	J— C— Crellen	18do.	1Oct. 1807
	George Gabb	16Dec.	
	Edward Town	17Mar.1814	
	—— Buchanan	25Feb.1813	
	William Reddock	8Apr.	
	Arthur Gerard	29do.	
Ensign - -	—— Crowe	10June	
	T— Benwell	21Sept.	
	—— Fernandez	22do.	
	John Joseph Kane	21Oct.	

Ensign

Rank.	Name.	Regiment.	Army.
			Rank in the

Rank.	Name.	Regiment.	Army.
Ensign - -	—— Blagrave	17Nov.1813	22July 1813
	Richard Levinge	18do.	
	William Taylor	9Dec.	
	Nathaniel Scully	16do.	
	Edward Newton	25do.	
	Wm. M'Donald Matthews do.		
	Thomas E— H— Holland do.		
	Isaac Beer	21Apr.1814	
	John Jackson	19May	
Paymaster 1	James Lonsdale	20Dec.1798	
2	Christopher Hancorn	13June1805	
Adjutant -	—— Richardson	15Aug.1811	Lieut. 20Oct.1813
	—— Pickering	30Sept.1813	Lieut. 16Nov.1813
QuarterMaster	Thomas Richards	22Aug.1805	
	John Jenkins	15Aug.1811	
Surgeon -	John Desailly	3Sept.1812	
	Francis Burton	9Sept.1813	
Assistant Surg.	William Morrah	25Jan.1810	
	James French	8Feb.	
	James Smith	25Sept.1812	
	Duncan M'Gregor	5Nov.	

Facings blue.—Lace gold.

Agent, Messrs. Greenwood, Cox and Hammersley.

		Rank in the	
Rank.	Name.	Regiment.	Army.
Colonel - -	William Wynyard	7Nov.1812	Lt.Gen. 4June1814
Lieut. Col. ◎	William Cockell	8Oct.1802	Lt.Gen. 4June1814
	Charles Pratt	25Mar.1808	Col. 4June1814
◎-	Hon. Henry King	16Jan.1809	Col. 4June1814
◎	Edward Copson	21Mar.1805	Col. 4June1814
Major - ◎	Thomas Emes	8May1806	Lt.Col. 4June1814
	John Grey	13June1811	Lt.Col. 6Feb.1812
	Henry Bird	10June1813	Lt.Col. 1Jan.1812
	George Clarke	28Aug.1804	Major 22Nov.1813
	J— Cully	24Jan.1805	Major 3Mar.1814
	Alex. Maxwell Bennett	8May1806	Major 12Apr.1814
	Robert Bateman	5Mar.1807	
	John S— Simcocks	7May	
	John Hamilton	25Feb.1808	
◎-	Richard Bishop	14Apr.	Major 17Aug.1812
	John Spearman	28do.	
	Arthur Dubourdieu	2June	26Nov.1806
Captain -	Geo. Davis M'Kenzie	30Aug.1809	
	John Bent	31do.	
	J— Rivers	26Sept.	
	Charles Louis Ramus	28do.	
	Edward Drury	12Oct.	
	Michael Doyle	1Feb.1810	
	David England Johnson	12Mar.1812	
	John Macpherson	2July	
	John Leech	10June1813	
	John Croasdaile	5Aug.	
	T— A— Girling	13Oct.1814	
	Jonas Welsh	22Sept.1805	
	—— Smith	25do.	
	—— Equino	9July1806	
	John Gunn	1Oct.	14Aug.1805
	Henry Edward O'Dell	25Feb.1808	
	J. Masterson Pennington	31Mar.	
	John Holland M'Kenzie	21Apr.	
	Samuel Belton	19May	
	John Pigot	9Mar.1809	
Lieutenant -	Arthur England Johnson	31Aug.	
	William Bennett	25Sept.	
	Morgan Galbraith	27do.	
	Fred. George Drewry	12Oct.	
	Christopher Hilliard	22Feb.1810	
	Rowland D. Pennington	23May1811	
	Wm. Villiers Fitzgerald	13June	
	John Dennis	21Nov.	25June1796
	Mich. Greatheed Hamer	23Apr.1812	

Y   Lieutenant

Rank.	Name.	Regiment.	Rank in the Army.
Lieutenant -	Starkey Hyde Wilkinson 28 May 1812		
	Robert Wallace 2 July		
	James Banbury Hamilton 23 do.		
	Henry White 8 Oct.	2 Aug. 1810	
	William Pratt 12 May 1813		
	Thomas Canch 13 do.	Adjutant	
	Archibald Campbell 29 July		
	Wm. Randolph Hopkins 5 Oct.		
	Lionel Ford 6 do.		
	Richard Nicholson 7 do.		
	Thomas William Dillon 17 Nov.		
	William Harding 18 do.		
	Samuel Armstrong 13 Oct. 1814		
	William Henderson 17 do.		
	Philip Johnson 18 do.		
	Wm. Lockyer Freestun 19 do.		
	Joseph Foot 20 do.		
Ensign - -	George Fred. Greaves 15 Apr. 1813	14 Jan. 1813	
	Walter Harris 13 May		
	George Proctor 23 June		
	William Orpe 24 do.		
	Wm. Wald. Pelham Clay 1 July		
	O— M— Fry 19 Aug.		
	Henry Bishop 18 Nov.	Adjutant	
	Edward Making 25 Dec.		
	Charles Pickering do.		
	Charles Pratt Wyatt do.		
	Adam Foskett 13 Jan. 1814		
	John Brooke 28 July	25 Dec. 1813	
	Richard J— Collins 19 Oct.		
	Torriano Fra. L'Estrange 20 do.		
	Hon. Robert King 1 Dec.	6 July 1814	
Paymaster 2	James Boyd 2 Dec. 1813		
Adjutant -	Thomas Canch 26 Mar. 1812	Lieut. 13 May 1813	
	Henry Bishop 18 Nov. 1813	Ensign 18 Nov. 1813	
QuarterMaster	John Watson 10 Oct. 1811		
	William Colls 12 Dec.		
Surgeon -	Samuel Scott 25 May 1809	27 Apr. 1809	
	Andrew Blake 28 July 1814		
Assistant Surg.	Godfrey Heathcote 6 July 1809		
	W— B— Lynn 13 do.		
	J— M— Bartley 8 Aug. 1811	27 Dec. 1810.	

Facings gosling green.—Lace silver.

Agent, Messrs. Greenwood, Cox and Hammersley.

Rank.	Name.	Rank in the Regiment.	Army.
Colonel	Sir George Nugent, Bt. K.B.	26 May 1806	Gen. 4 June 1813
Lieut. Col.	◎ { Archibald Campbell Thomas Carnie	17 Sept. 1812 18 Mar. 1813	8 Mar. 1810 4 June 1811
Major	◎ (John Gardiner Henry Gomm James T— Robertson ◎ (Guy Campbell	28 May 1807 18 May 1809 30 Jan. 1812 1 Apr. 1813	Lt.Col. 29 Oct. 1809 Lt.Col. 26 Aug. 1813 Lt.Col. 26 Aug. 1813
Captain	Hugh Maurice Scott Sackville Taylor Edward Fitz Gerald Henry Rogers William Gordon Richard A— Dewgard James Thomson Sam. Delacherois Smith Edward Cox Andrew Crean W— H— Majendie Wm. Philip Jas. Lodder William Clarke Frederick Macbean Libanus Tilsley Robert W— Gordon Duncan Graham Alexander Macpherson Alexander Jones	26 Jan. 1799 23 Nov. 1804 25 Dec. 1806 26 Mar. 1807 8 Oct. 15 do. 22 do. 9 Mar. 1809 18 May 27 Dec. 1810 30 Jan. 1812 20 Feb. 7 Jan. 1813 do. 15 Apr. 16 Sept. 18 Nov. 10 Feb. 1814 8 Dec.	Lt.Col. 26 Aug. 1813 Major 3 Mar. 1814 26 Nov. 1806 12 May 1805 30 Nov. 1806 11 May 1805 29 Jan. 1807
Lieutenant	Thomas Andrews Clement Peat James Burgess Ralph Meredith Sewell Ormsby Henry Bennett Everest George Tarleton Theoph. Ja. Clarkson David Blyth Edwin Sandys Edmund H— Plunkett George Carter Robert Stanford George Renwick Thomas Clarke William Stott Thomas Duke	30 Oct. 1806 20 Nov. 24 Dec. 25 do. 8 Jan. 1807 1 Mar. 16 Apr. 31 Mar. 1808 9 Mar. 1809 18 May 13 July 15 Mar. 1810 19 July 9 Aug. 11 Apr. 1811 19 Dec. 16 Jan. 1812	6 Feb. 1806 Adjutant 26 Sept. 1807 12 July 1810

Y 2

Lieutenant

Rank.	Name.	Rank in the Regiment.	Rank in the Army.
Lieutenant -	James Brock	25Jan.1813	20Sept.1808
	James Gell	do.	29June 180
	Thomas Dutton	14Apr.	
	Alexander Hogg	15do.	
	S— W— Swiney	29do.	
	Mathew Wm. Gilder	26Aug.	
	Stephen Radcliffe	16Sept.	
	—— Crauford	17do.	
	Anthony Tatlow	21Oct.	
	Henry Dechair	8Feb.1814	
	Pierce Gaggin	9do.	
	John Bonamy	10do.	
	William Henry Dobson	14Apr.	
	William Russell	26May	
	John Price	5Sept.	Adjutant
	Richard Brownsmith	6do.	
	George Bailey	7do.	
	William Blood	8do.	
	James Tyner	8Dec.	
Ensign - -	Thomas Carnie	6Jan.1814	
	William H— Eden	31Mar.	
	Charles Huson Bigger	14Apr.	
	Frederick Thornbury	21do.	
	Robert Boyes	26May	
	Thomas Labey	27do.	
	John Henry Heigham	25Aug.	
	John Thomas Griffiths	6Sept.	
	Thomas Dawson Wood	8do.	
	Price C— Edwards	20Oct.	
	James D— Chambers	27do.	18Nov.1813
	George Wyse	1Dec.	
Paymaster	1 John Blakeman	7May1807	
	2 John Butcher	23May1811	
Adjutant -	James Burgess	12Oct.1804	Lieut. 24Dec.1806
	John Price	23July1812	Lieut. 5Sept.1814
Quarter-Mast.	Robert Smart	2Apr.1807	
	James Piggott	31May1810	
Surgeon - -	John Fisher	15Dec.1804	
	John Heriot	24Nov.1814	16Apr. 1812
Assistant Surg.	Charles Collis	17Oct.1811	
	Robert Goodriche	11Mar.1813	
	Thomas Fred. Lacon	27Jan.1814	
	Francis George Wilbran	24Feb.	

Facings yellow.—Lace silver.
Agent, Messrs. Greenwood, Cox and Hammersley.

7th

Rank.	Name.	Rank in the Regiment.	Army.
Colonel - -	*Sir* Alured Clarke, *K.B.*	21 Aug.1801	Gen. 29 Apr.1802
Lieut. Col.	⊠ ⎰ Edward Blakeney ◎ ⎱ John Mervin Nooth	20 June 1811 2 Jan. 1812	Col. 4 June 1814 20 June 1811
Major -	◎ ⎧ John William Beatty ◎ ⎪ George King ⎨ John Crowder ⎩ Sam. Benj. Auchmuty	2 Jan.1812 14 May 9 Sept.1813 28 Oct.	Lt.Col. 12 Apr.1814 17 Aug.1812 Lt.Col. 12 Apr.1814
Captain -	⎧ John Orr ⎪ James Robinson ⎪ Alex. Campbell Wylly ⎪ John Mair ⎪ T.T. Arenburgh Mullins ⎪ W. Meadows Hamerton ⎪ Edward Morgan ⎪ Hamilton English ⎪ William Edward Page ⎨ Mathew Ford ⎪ Digby Mackworth ⎪ Thomas Moses ⎪ Robert Hammill ⎪ Anthony Baldwin ⎪ James Anderson ⎪ George Henry ⎪ Frederick Temple ⎪ James Johnston ⎪ Richard Hackett ⎩ George Loggan	27 Apr.1809 1 June 19 June 1811 17 July 8 Aug. 16 Jan.1812 5 Mar. 14 May 15 do. 2 July 16 do. 20 Aug. 6 May 1813 3 June 1 Sept. 9 do. 18 Nov. 16 Dec. 6 Jan.1814 21 Apr.	 23 Apr. 1812 29 July 1811 27 Sept.1809 10 June 1813
Lieutenant -	⎧ Richard Kirwan ⎪ Patrick J — Burke ⎨ Robert Muter ⎪ Pitt Hannam ⎩ John Healey	27 Oct.1807 28 do. 3 Mar.1808 20 Apr. 8 Sept.	

Lieutenant

| Rank. | Name. | Rank in the | |
		Regiment.	Army.
Lieutenant	Edward Penrice	10Apr.1809	
	Robert Daniell	11do.	
	William Payne	12do.	
	Richard Nantes	19Oct.	
	Hugh R— Wallace	16Nov.	
	Tristram Squires	1Mar.1810	31Jan. 1810
	Joseph Hutchinson	26Apr.	
	James Hay	3May	Adjutant
	Thomas Young Lester	30do.	
	George Seton	31do.	
	Martin Orr	28June	
	Charles Lorentz	2Aug.	8Oct. 1809
	John L— Nunn	17Jan.1811	
	Alured L'Estrange	4Apr.	
	D— Cameron	7May	
	Robert Huggup	11do.	
	Edward Wells Bell	16do.	
	John Duncan King	13June	12Feb. 1808
	Timothy Meagher	17July	Adjutant
	Aug. Frederick D'Este	26Sept.	
	James S— Gage	24Oct.	
	John George	7Nov.	
	Alex. John Wynch	9Apr.1812	
	William P— Keane	23do.	
	Henry Stephen Nooth	14May	
	Kinder Crewe	4June	
	Richard Graves	16July	
	William Trevenen	27Aug.	
	John Hancock Westcott	26Nov.	12Aug.1812
	Matthew Higgins	3Dec.	13Aug.1812
	Henry Arthur Magennis	4Mar.1813	1Oct. 1812
	Richard Creser	3June	
	A— Kirwan	5Aug.	
	John Brownlow	9Sept.	
	Tho. Henry Wingfield	11Nov.	
	John Dolman	23Dec.	
	John Morton Stuart	6Jan.1814	
	Philip Mair	7Apr.	
	Hec. Wm. Bower Monro	3May	
	Peter Backhouse	4do.	
	Thomas Bulkeley	5do.	

Lieutenant

Rank.	Name.	Rank in the	
		Regiment.	Army.
Lieutenant	Rob. Preston Campbell	26May1814	1Nov.1811
	Meyrick Shawe	23June	
	George Sweeting	4Aug.	
	Henry Mervin	13Oct.	
	James Browne Stewart	24Nov.	
Paymaster 2	George Murton	26Mar.1812	
1	Justin Brenan	11Mar.1813	
Adjutant -	James Hay	22Nov.1810	Lieut. 3May1810
	Timothy Meagher	23June1814	Lieut. 17July1811
Quarter-Mast.	John Hogan	25Sept.1806	
	William Greenwood	14July1814	
Surgeon -	Martin Mahony	3June1813	
	Thomas Batt	15July	
Assistant Surg.	Philip Duigan	16Nov.1809	
	Michael Sweeny	26July1810	
	Henry Fisher	3June1813	
	William Henry Hume	26May1814	24Feb. 1814

Facings blue.—Lace gold.

Agent, Messrs. Greenwood, Cox and Hammersley.

176   8th (or the King's) Regiment of Foot.

Permitted to bear a " SPHINX," with the word " EGYPT," on their Colours and Appointments, in commemoration of the Campaign of 1801.

		Rank in the	
Rank.	Name.	Regiment.	Army.
Colonel - -	Edmund Stevens	8Feb.1814	Gen. 25Sept.1803
Lieut. Colonel {	Peter Thomas Roberton	6June1811	4June1811
	James Ogilvie	28July1814	4June1813
Major - - {	Thomas Buck	6June1811	
	Thomas Evans	6Feb.1812	
	James Munday	21Oct.1813	5June1813
	John Blackmore	29Sept.1814	4June1814
Captain - {	James S— Tyeth	21Mar.1805	
	William Cotter	25Apr.	
	William Robinson	5Sept.	Major 19Dec.1813
	Francis Campbell	21Nov.	
	Henry Sadlier	4June1807	
	James Agnew	17Dec.	28Nov.1806
	Peter Moyle	3Feb.1809	
	Edward Connor	20July	
	Walter Sweetman	26July1810	5Apr.1810
	William Walsh	16May1811	
	John Fitz Gerald	6June	
	John Bradbridge	12Sept.	
	James Hardy Eustace	6Feb.1812	
	John Goldrisk	do.	
	Wm. Hanbury Davies	2July	16July 1807
	Henry Brewster	4Aug.1813	
	Thomas Cross	5do.	
	Thomas Miller	12do.	
	Edward Brown	24Feb.1814	
	Austin Neame	10Aug.	
	George Rawlinson	11do.	
	John M'Mahon	29Sept.	
Lieutenant {	William Collis	21Jan.1808	
	J— T— Weyland	1Mar.1809	
	Herbert Raban	2do.	
	Thomas Ivers	30do.	
	Edward Finch	20July	
	Roger M— Swiney	19Oct.	23Mar.1809
	Marshal M'Dermott	19July1810	
	Malcolm Ross	14Mar.1811	
	Jacob Ruddock	16May	

Lieutenant

| Rank. | Name. | Rank in the | |
		Regiment.	Army.
Lieutenant	Michael Flanagan	6June1811	
	Edward Boyd	15Aug.	
	J— Palmer Hill	12Sept.	
	Thomas Price	30Apr.1812	
	Robert Spiers	2Sept.	
	Robert Dunbar Taylor	3do.	
	William Bradford	22Oct.	
	Alexander Bourke	5Nov.	
	John Lowry	24Dec.	
	Frederick William Vieth	3Aug.1813	
	William Kidman	4do.	
	J— G— Powell	5do.	
	Brooke Young	6do.	
	Alexander Greig	7do.	
	Thomas Russell	12do.	
	James O— Flanagan	24Feb.1814	
	Wm. H. Clar. Scarman	22Mar.	
	James Grey	23do.	
	Robert Mac Nair	24do.	
	John Radenhurst	7July	5Aug.1813
	George R— Campsie	14do.	
	Thomas Swayne	9Aug.	
	Samuel Garner	10do.	
	Edward Murray	11do.	
	Charles Millar	29Sept.	
	Thomas Moyle	24Nov.	
Ensign	Luke Vipont	25Feb.1813	
	George Jarvis	3Aug.	
	George Richardson	4do.	
	A— Thompson	5do.	
	H— Francis	6do.	
	Donald Macdonald	7do.	
	John Street	21Oct.	Adjutant
	George Aug. M'Dermott	2Dec.	
	Richard Shaw	24Feb.1814	
	John Mathewson	25do.	
	John Farnam	26do.	Adjutant]
	William Wainwright	22Mar.	
	Charles Barry	23do.	
	Rutherford Thompson	24do.	
	William Calder	14July	

Z

Ensign

Rank.	Name.	Rank in the	
		Regiment.	Army.
Ensign - -	Charles Cotter	9Aug.1814	
	War. Lut. Pur. Moriarty	10do.	
	—— Short	11do.	
	Robert Mawdsley	29Sept.	
	James White	24Nov.	
Paymaster	2 Mark Hodgson	5Jan.1805	
	1 Henry Howe	17Mar.1814	
Adjutant -	John Street	21Oct.1813	Ensign 21Oct.1813
	John Farnam	26Feb.1814	Ensign 26Feb.1814
QuarterMaster	George Shaw	12Feb.1807	
	George Kierman	1Nov.1813	
Surgeon -	John Moore	28Sept.1809	
	Charles Waring	6Jan.1814	
Assistant Surg.	Charles I— Ingham	16Aug.1810	
	William Steele	18May1812	
	John Douglas	17June1813	26Sept.1811

Facings blue.—Lace gold.

Agent, Messrs. Greenwood, Cox and Hammersley.

9th

Permitted to bear on their Colours and Appointments the Figure of " BRITANNIA."

Rank.	Name.	Rank in the Regiment.	Army.
Colonel - -	Robert Brownrigg	3Oct.1805	L.Gen. 25Apr.1808
Lieut. Col. ✠ {	John Cameron	3Sept.1807	Col. 4June1814
	Wm.GordonMac Gregor	3June1813	4Feb.1813
Major - - {	David Campbell	2Aug.1804	Lt.Col. 4June1811
	Peter Warren Lambert	3Sept.1807	Lt.Col. 4June1813
	Thomas B— Aylmer	4do.	Lt.Col. 4June1813
	Samuel Sankey	2Sept.1813	
Captain - {	Thomas Ferrars	3Aug.1804	Major 21Sept.1813
	Adam Peebles	4do.	Major 7Oct.1813
	Hector Cameron	25do.	Major 21Sept.1813
	Daniel Orchard	14Nov.1805	
	Alexander Simpson	5Nov.1807	
	Benjamin Siborn	do.	
	Henry D— Loftus	18Aug.1808	Major 19May1814
	George Sanderson	2Sept.	
	James Boyd	do.	
	Patrick B-- Foley	28June1809	Major 4June1814
	Isaac Jervoise	29do.	
	William Percival	29Mar.1810	
	William F— St. Clair	3Oct.1811	
	Matthew Armstrong	17do.	
	Valentine Fleming	18do.	
	Rob. Gordon Thompson	22Oct.1812	
	John Macnamara	do.	
	James Whitley	17June1813	
	Peter Sutton	do.	
	John Shelton	do.	
	John Ackland	26Aug.	
	Robert William Mills	2Sept.	Major 25July1810
	Robert E— Broughton	20Oct.	2July 1812
	Henry Dumaresque	21do.	4Feb. 1813
	William M'Adam	17Nov.1814	
Lieutenant - {	Richard Dale	30Aug.1807	
	John Taylor	1Oct.	
	John Ogle	12Dec.	
	John Richardson	15do.	
	Thomas Harrison	25Feb.1808	
	Thomes Shepherd	28Mar.	
	John H— Challis	1Sept.	Adjutant
	James Wigton	2do.	
	George Stirling	19Oct.	
	William Seward	26Apr.1809	
	Richard Ruse	29June	
	George Lindsay	7Dec.	18Jan. 1808

Lieutenant

Lieutenant	Alexander Fraser	12Apr.1810	
	William Dallas	13Oct.1811	
	Jame Stephen Mitchell	14do.	
	George Lenox Davies	15do.	
	Wm. Hor. Cockburne	25June1812	
	Edward Watkins	13Aug.	
	James Scargill	21Oct.	
	Charles Carver	22do.	
	Peter R— Brown	24Dec.	
	Robert Brooks	23Aug.1813	
	Henry M'Dermott	24do.	
	William Telford	25do.	
	James Syret	26do.	
	Thomas Jones	21Sept.	
	James Sutton	22do.	
	Thomas L— Butler	23do.	
	David Holmes	20Jan.1814	
	—— Nash	28Apr.	
Ensign - -	Hugh Moises	11Feb.1813	
	Robert Storey	15Apr.	
	Alfred Ricketts	8July	
	William Hoe	23Aug.	
	John Mahon	25do.	
	William Siborn	9Sept.	
	John Martin	21do.	
	William Wade Leslie	22do.	
	Francis Smith	11Nov.	
	Stephen Plympton	16Dec.	
	Fred. Æmilius Hodgson	25do.	
	William Haydon	do.	
	George Green Watkins	do.	
	Richard Telford	20Jan.1814	
	Samuel Hart	3Feb.	
	Hon. Ferdinand Curzon	3Mar.	16Aug.1813
	Thomas Scott	20Oct.	
Paymaster 2	George Fraser	24Jan.1805	
1	Henry William Hall	4Apr.	
Adjutant -	John H— Challis	17June1813	Lieut. 1Sept.1808
QuarterMaster	Joseph Scott	17Dec.1807	
	Samuel Reves	2Oct.1814	
Surgeon -	Andrew Brown	25Sept.1806	28Mar.1801
	Thomas Bulkeley	28Oct.1813	5Nov.1812
Assistant Surg.	William Dent	2Aug.1810	
	John Johnston	26May1814	
	Clement Ekins	24Nov.	9Sept.1813

Facings yellow.—Lace silver.

Agent, Messrs. Greenwood, Cox and Hammersley.

10th

Permitted to bear on their Colours and Appointments a " SPHINX," with the word " EGYPT," in commemoration of the Campaign of 1801.

Colonel		*Hon.* Thomas Maitland	19July1811	Lt.Gen. 4June1811
Lieut. Col.	◎ {	Robert Travers	15Feb.1810	Col. 4June1814
	{	Francis Wm. Cashell	3Jan.1811	
Major	{	John Otto Beyer	20June1805	Lt.Col. 1Jan.1812
	{	Octavius Carey	2Nov.1809	Lt.Col.30Sept.1811
	{	Thomas Trustey Trickey	7Feb.1811	
	{	John Allen	1Dec.1814	
Captain	{	William Waldon Brome	1Aug.1804	Major 4June1814
	{	E— J— R— Green	5Oct.	Major 4Mar.1807
	{	Edward Powell	23Nov.	Major 4June1814
	{	Thomas Dent	26Sept.1805	
	{	Wm. Brewse Kersteman	17Oct.	Major 18Aug.1814
	{	Digby Tho. Carpenter	29Sept.1808	18Aug.1808
	{	Peter Grieve	16Mar.1809	
	{	Felix Brady	22June	
	{	Joseph Rudsdell	12Oct.	
	{	Thomas Fothergill	2Nov.	
	{	Henry Heathcote	23do.	19Oct. 1809
	{	Charles Scott	25Jan.1810	Major 1Jan.1812
	{	William Hoar	29Mar.	
	{	Stephen D'Arcey Kelly	2Aug.	12Nov.1807
	{	William Mainwaring	14Mar.1811	
	{	Joseph Hicks	18June1812	
	{	John Carr	20Aug.	Lt.Col. 4June1814
	{	Francis Innes	14Apr.1813	
	{	E— Blomfield	15do.	
	{	Peter Edwards	1July	17Mar.1811
	{	*Hon.* John Mad. Maitland	15do.	30Aug.1810
Lieutenant	{	Charles J— Tench	22May1806	
	{	Edward Mullenger	28Dec.	
	{	Elias Brooke Thane	30do.	
	{	William Holden	31do.	
	{	John Robinson	8Jan.1807	
	{	Rodney Sims	25Aug.	
	{	Charles Moore Campbell	27do.	
	{	—— Layard	26Nov.	
	{	David Henderson	23Jan.1808	
	{	John Gallie	24do.	
	{	John Shepard Windle	25do.	
	{	William Rannie	29do.	
	{	John Knight Jouncey	10Feb.	
	{	Mathias Rosengrave	11do.	
	{	Francis Upton Tripp	13Oct.	
	{	Frederick Foaker	21Dec.1809	
	{	Hen. Stewart Nixon	15Mar.1810	15Sept.1808
	{	Alex. John Nowell	28do.	

Lieutenant

	Ralph Marshall	12Apr.1810	
	James Ferguson	23Jan.1811	
	E— Allen	24do.	Adjutant
	Edward Supple	11July	
	James A— Anderson	26Feb.1812	
	John Peppard	27do.	
	Robert Travers	28do.	
	Thomas Baylis	9Apr.	
	Rutledge Phibbs	13Aug.	
	George Birch	20do.	
Lieutenant -	James T— Tisdall	14Apr.1813	
	Luke Horner	15do.	
	Nicholas Wrixon	13May	
	William Mayes	19do.	
	Jonas Rudland	20do.	
	William Sayers	15July	
	Robert Gardner Locke	19Jan.1814	
	Henry Salmon	20do.	
	Francis Dickson	27do.	
	John M— Maitland	14Apr.	
	Denis Fairchild	12May	Adjutant
	William Ridsdale Bustin	3Sept.1812	
	Rich. Walter Shinkwin	10do.	
	Richard Lane	2Oct.	
	John Sherriff	14Jan.1813	
	Philip Ryan	28do.	
	Tho. L— L— Galloway	14Apr.	
	Charles Campbell	15do.	
Ensign -	Henry H. Farquharson	20May	
	Robert Birch	4Nov.	
	Cecil Hammond	19Jan.1814	
	Thomas Berwick	26do.	
	John Styles Powell	27do.	
	David Jevers	12May	
	George Crowe Hodges	2June	
	George Henry Brown	16do.	
Paymaster 1	Hugh Dive	31Mar.1808	
2	Robert Bluntish	14Dec.1809	
Adjutant -	E— Allen	29Sept.1814	Lieut. 24Jan.1811
	Denis Fairchild	30do.	Lieut. 12May1814
QuarterMaster	Henry Whalley	5Oct.1804	
	Thomas Lynch	9Jan.1812	
Surgeon -	Charles B— Hill	13May1813	2Aug.1810
	Octavius Pritchard	do.	
	John Baird	21Jan.1813	
Assistant Surg.	Hugh Orr	6Jan.1814	
	Gavino Portelli	26May	

Facings yellow.—Lace silver.
Agent, Mr. Bownas, Whitehall.

		Rank in the	
Rank.	Name.	Regiment.	Army.

Rank.	Name.	Regiment.	Army.
Colonel - -	*Sir* Charles Asgill, *Bt.*	25Feb.1807	Gen. 4June1814
Lieut. Colonel	◎ George Cuyler	16Nov.1809	Col. 4June1814
	Charles Griffiths	13June1811	M.Gen. 4June1813
	◎ Frederick Newman	4June1813	17Aug.1812
Major - -	George Granby Hely	8Aug.1808	Lt.Col. 4June1814
	Wm. Sandys Elrington	4June1813	1Jan. 1812
	Henry Bristow	20Jan.1814	
	Colquhoun Grant	13Oct.	Lt.Col. 19May1814
Captain -	John Campbell	9July1802	Major 4June1813
	George Teale	16Oct.1806	Major 12Apr.1814
	Denis O'Kelly	12Nov.1807	Major 22Nov.1813
	William Owen	7Aug.1808	29May 1806
	Francis Gualey	25Nov.	Major 12Apr.1814
	Archibald Hook	12Oct.1809	
	William Dunlop	30Aug.1810	
	Nicholas Brown	6Dec.	3May 1810
	John George Cox	20Feb.1811	
	Donald M'Arthur	7Mar.	
	John Danger	18July	
	Charles Barker Turner	15Oct.1812	
	Richard Haynes Jones	1Apr.1813	
	Andrew Leith Hay	15do.	
	Edward Vardy	4June	
	James N— Charles	25Aug.	
	James Williams	14Sept.	
	Alexander Jaffray Bell	22Dec.	
	Thomas Stephens	23do.	
	John Arnaud	13Jan.1814	
	John Fry	5May	2May 1811
	Patrick M'Dougall	28July	
Lieutenant -	William Walker	14Sept.1808	
	Walter Daniell	15do.	
	Isaac Richardson	1Oct.	
	Cosmo Cameron	2do.	
	David Read	4do.	
	Patrick O'Connor	6do.	
	Thomas Shervinton	7do.	
	F— Armstrong	1Dec.	
	William Moore	5Jan.1809	
	John Davison	6Apr.	3Sept.1806
	Alexander Sinclair	13July	

Lieutenant

Rank.	Name.	Rank in the Regiment.	Army.
Lieutenant	Thomas B— Lander	4Aug.1809	
	Walter White	7do.	
	John Dolphin	8do.	
	Alexander Boyd	9do.	
	John Walsh	19Oct.	
	Walter Lambert	9Nov.	
	R— Daniel	28Dec.	
	Boyce Smith	13Sept.1810	
	James Christian	19Feb.1811	
	Richard Pilkington	21do.	
	John Mowlds	28do.	
	John Day	21Mar.	
	Patrick Stanton	25Apr.	
	D— D— Gallagher	1May	21Sept.1809
	James Ffennell	2do.	
	James Maclean	8do.	
	James Mason	9do.	
	William Greer	9July1812	
	R— Ferrall	22Oct.	Adjutant
	Richard Long	5Nov.	
	James O'Kelly	16do.	
	Isaac M'Mullen	19do.	
	William Trimble	15Apr.1813	
	William L'Estrange	20May	
	John Conroy	27do.	
	Robert Ross	29July	
	John Khrone	15Sept.	Adjutant
	J— Reilly	16do.	
	—— Armstrong	23Dec.	
Ensign	Charles West	9May1811	
	Henry Lindsay	5Dec.	
	William Berne	19do.	
	Francis Marsh	5Mar.1812	
	Henry Hopkins	15July	
	Matthew Trimble	16do.	
	A— H— Rowan	5Nov.	
	John Henry Kerr	21Jan.1813	
	Richardson Mason	14Apr.	
	Francis Hurst	20May	
	John James Peck	27do.	

Ensign

Rank.	Name.	Rank in the Regiment.	Army.

Ensign -	John M'Dermott	29July1813	
	Alexander Henry	5Aug.	
	——— Conolly	15Sept.	
	George Moore	22do.	
	Alexander Grant	23do.	
	Richard Cross	28Oct.	
	James Waller Sidney	17Feb.1814	
Paymaster	1 Malcolm M'Gregor	6Apr.1803	
Adjutant - -	John Khrone	31Oct.1811	Lieut. 15Sept.1813
	R— Ferrall	4Nov.1813	Lieut. 22Oct.1812
QuarterMaster	Timothy Coghlan	19Oct.1800	
	Valentine Lott	8Sept.1808	
Surgeon -	Thomas Moore	16Jan.1812	
	George Barker	17Apr.	
Assistant Surg.	Alexander Stewart	27Dec.1810	
	Frederick Dix	19Aug.1813	
	Michael X. Considine	5May1814	
	George Richmond	26do.	

Facings deep green.—Lace gold.

Agent, Messrs; Greenwood, Cox and Hammersley.

a

12th

Permitted to inscribe on their Colours and Appointments the words " GIBRALTAR" and " MINDEN."

Rank in the

Rank.	Name.	Regiment.	Army.
Colonel - -	*Sir* Charles Hastings, *Bt.*	15Oct.1811	Gen. 4June1813
	(Julius Stirke	27Dec.1810	Col. 4June1813
Lieut. Colonel	⟨ Henry Frederick Cooke	4June1813	7Nov.1811
	(Nicholas Eustace	16Dec.	
	(Wm. Henry Forssteen	2Jan.1812	18July 1811
Major - ◎	⟨ Richard Bayley	15Oct.	
	) Richard G— Hare	1July1813	Lt.Col. 16Sept.1813
	(Robert Henry Sale	30Dec.	
	(William Frith	16June1807	
		Henry M'Keady	23Aug.1809	
		Mark John Molloy	1Sept.1810	
		Jarvis Turberville	14Mar.1811	
		George Llewellyn	25Sept.	
		John Campbell	31Dec.	25Apr.1811
		Richard England	1Jan.1812	11July 1811
		Ronald Macdonald	2do.	
		Francis Polhill	29do.	Major 1Jan.1812
Captain -	⟨ George Blanchard Grey	2Apr.	
		James Nestor	28May	24Oct.1811
		John Spinks	13Oct.	
		James Keappock	14do.	
		John B— Whannell	20Oct.1813	
		William Reid	21do.	
		Charles Shee	18Nov.	
		Thomas O'Neill	25do.	
		John Chisholm	30Dec.	
		George Humphry	17Nov.1814	Major 4June1814
	(John Garvock	1Dec.	20Sept.1810
	(Rob. Edward Burrowes	23Aug.1809	
		John Baxter	1Jan.1810	
		John N— Read	12July	
		Robert Jenkins	12Sept.	
		George Lawson	28Apr.1811	
		Marshall Thornton	25Aug.	12Sept.1808
		——— Walsh	2Jan.1812	24Jan. 1810 Adjut.
Lieutenant -	⟨ David Durie	15do.	
		Robert Blythe	16do.	
		Robert Bradfute	20Feb.	
		James Powell	26do.	
		Henry R— Shepard	28do.	
		William Donald	12Mar.	
		Thomas Gale	2Apr.	28Dec.1809
		Adam Philip Walsh	14May	
	(Alexander Cruice	24Sept.	

Lieutenant

Lieutenant	James Wadeson	13Oct.1812	
	Morgan James Jenkins	14do.	
	Thomas Dun	29do.	1Sept.1808
	James Barrett	30do.	
	George Money	15July1813	
	John Morgan	11Aug.	
	John Hart	12do.	
	BickertonChamberlayne	20Oct.	
	Charles Benson	21do.	
	John Davey	22do.	
	William Glasscott	23do.	
	Richard Myddleton	18Nov.	
	EdwardRaymond Hicks	15Feb.1814	
	Frederick Clarke	16do.	
	Robert Paget	17do.	
	John Grover	31Mar.	
	John Blackhall	4May	
	Henry Clinton	5do.	
Ensign	Thomas Manby	8Apr.1813	
	John St. John	15July	
	Robert Higgin	11Aug.	
	Thomas Vincent	20Oct.	
	Luke Prior	21do.	
	James Smith	22do,	
	Wm. Gascoyne Shafto	23do.	
	Hugh de Carteret	24do.	
	John Borthwick	2Dec.	
	Jonathan Priestley	30do.	Adjutant
	William Derenzy	13Jan.1814	
	Henry Fosberry	17Feb.	
	Charles Williams	31Mar.	
	Samuel White	14Apr.	
	Thomas Carlton	4May	
	George Thomson	5do.	
	Thomas Earls	12do.	
	Julius Stirke	24Nov.	4Aug.1814
Paymaster	1 James O'Keeffe	16Jan.1812	
	2 Charles Finch	13Feb.	
Adjutant -	—— Walsh	6Feb.1812	Lieut. 24Jan.1810
	Jonathan Priestley	30Dec.1813	Ensign 30Dec.1812
QuarterMaster	George Crabtree	25Oct.1809	
	William Page	13Feb.1812	
Surgeon -	Robert Erskine	25Aug.1805	
	John Washington Price	13Feb.1812	
Assistant Surg.	William Morrison	23May1811	19July 1810
	Edward Burton	21Jan.1813	
	George Martin	10Mar.1814	

Facings yellow.—Lace gold.

Agent, Messrs. Greenwood, Cox and Hammersley.

Permitted to bear on their Colours and Appointments a " SPHINX," with the word " EGYPT," in commemoration of the Campaign of 1801.

| Rank. | Name. | Rank in the | |
		Regiment.	Army.
Colonel - -	Edward Morrison	15Feb.1813	Gen. 4June1814
Lieut. Col.	✕-William Williams	25June1812	15Nov.1809
Major - -	{ Francis Weller	27Nov.1806	Lt.Col. 1Jan.1812
	{ Richard B— Handcock	1Nov.1810	
Captain -	{ Arthur Wilkinson	4Aug.1798	Lt.Col. 4June1814
	John Staunton	3Sept.1801	Major 4June1813
	George Thornhill	12June1805	
	Alex. Baron Moncreiff	26Nov.1806	Major 4June1814
	Soden Davys	31Dec.1807	
	Bennet Holgate	23June1808	
	Robert Preston	1Nov.1810	
	Henry Ellard	·30Jan.1812	
	Anthony Blake	10June1813	
	John Johnson	23June1814	
	Beauchamp Colclough	24Nov.	
Lieutenant	{ James Campbell	31Dec.1807	
	Edward Tronson	26Jan.1808	
	William Dickson	28do.	
	Thomas Eden Kelly	11Feb.	
	Henry Burnside	18do.	
	Henry Waterman	23June	
	Michael Fenton	26Jan.1809	
	Thomas Triphook	30Mar.	13Oct. 1808
	Thomas Fenton	28June	
	John Davis	29do.	
	John Reed	1Jan.1810	
	Alexander Gunning	2do.	
	Knox Barrett	3do.	
	Robert Pattisson	4do.	
	Stephen Major	11July1811	26July 1810
	J— Richardson	11Sept.	
	Neil Campbell	12do.	
	Thomas Gooden Davey	5Mar.1812	
	John Kemple	26do.	Adjutant
	Thomas Isaac Wright	16Apr.	
	William Whitehead	15Apr.1813	
	Boyle Meredith	1July	
	Abraham Gapper	14July1814	

Ensign

Rank.	Name.	Rank in the Regiment.	Army.
Ensign	{ John Whiteford	12Sept.1811	
	Robert Bunney	21Nov.	
	Valentine Brown	16Apr.1812	
	F— W— Stehelin	8Oct.	
	John Hart Rawlins	18Feb.1813	
	Edward Keily	15Apr.	
	William N— Barrett	6May	
	William Pyne	13July1814	
	James M'Coy	14do.	
Paymaster	Charles Grimes	16Apr.1812	
Adjutant	John Kemple	6June1811	Lieut. 26Mar.1812
Quarter-Master	Edward Sheridan	18Feb.1813	
Surgeon	William Gill	26Sept.1811	3Mar.1808
Assistant Surg.	{ James Henderson	22Mar.1810	
	Stratford A— Eyre	1Sept.1814	

Facings yellow.—Lace silver.

Agent, Messrs. Greenwood, Cox and Hammersley.

14th

190   14th (or the Buckinghamshire) Regt. of Foot

Permitted to bear the " WHITE HORSE" and Motto on a red ground, on the front of their Caps.
The 2d Battalion also to inscribe the word " CORUNNA" on their Colours and Appointments in commemoration of the Action of the 16th January, 1809.

Rank.	Name.	Rank in the Regiment.	Rank in the Army.
Colonel - -	Harry Calvert	8Feb.1806	Lt.Gen. 25July1810
Lieut. Col.	◎ { James Watson	15May1806	Col. 4June1814
	Montagu Burrows	14May1807	Col. 4June1814
	◎ { Jasper Nicolls	31Mar.1808	Col. 4June1814
	Nathaniel Burslem	13Oct.1814	1Mar.1811
Major - ◎	Francis Skelly Tidy	10Sept.1807	Lt.Col. 4June1813
	William Fawcett	22Apr.1813	
	Peter Johnston	1Dec.	
	William Percival	12Jan.1814	21June1813
	John Keightley	13do.	
	Eyre Coote	13Oct.	4June1814
Captain - -	Jacob Watson	5Aug.1804	Major 4June1814
	William Moore	29May1806	
	Matthias Everard	21May1807	23Apr. 1807
	Robert Ramsay	30July	30Apr.1807
	John Marshall	21Apr.1808	28Nov.1806
	Henry Nooth	2June	Major 4June1814
	Cecil Bisshopp	23do.	
	Thomas H— Light	18Aug.	
	Octavius Temple	15Sept.	Major 4June1814
	Thomas Dunn	22do.	
	◎ George Marlay	14June1810	Major 21June1813
	George Rawlins	5July	
	Thomas Ramsay	18Oct.	17May 1810
	W— S— Bertrand	7Mar.1811	
	William Turnor	15Aug.	
	John Dyson	28Nov.	
	James Roche	5Nov.1812	
	Thomas Savage	29Apr.1813	
	Thomas Hall	16Sept.	
	Gerald Rochfort	1Dec.	
	Charles Knolles	3do.	
	William Ross	24do.	16Dec. 1813
	Harcourt Morton	12Jan.1814	
	Richard Adams	13do.	
	John Maxwell	7July	
	William Betts	1Nov.	
	Henry Hill	2do.	
	Charles Stanhope	3do.	6Oct. 1814
	Christian Wilson	4do.	
	J— L— White	5do.	

Lieutenant

Lieutenant -	George Bolton	21 May 1807	11 Dec. 1806
	Hercules John Heyland	do.	
	Thomas Hewitt Baylie	25 June	
	John Casimer Harold	16 July	28 May 1807
	William Akenside	6 Aug.	2 Jan. 1807 Adjut.
	Charles Myler Brannan	3 Dec.	29 Jan. 1807
	Jos. Brancr. Ainsworth	18 Aug. 1808	
	Kenneth M'Kenzie	22 Sept.	
	Hen. Bruere Armstrong	27 Oct.	23 Jan. 1806 Adjut.
	Henry Gamble	22 Dec.	
	Thomas Kirkman	9 Mar. 1809	
	Thomas Jenour	25 May	
	Thomas Way	27 do.	
	Henry Johnson	30 do.	
	Dominick C— Lynch	31 do.	
	Henry John Henley	15 June	
	George Mackenzie	29 do.	4 May 1809
	Hugh Lloyd Franklin	19 Oct.	8 May 1805
	Geo. Thurles Finnucane	15 Mar. 1810	
	Edward L'Estrange	19 Apr.	
	D— Hazlewood	13 Dec.	
	Richard Stack	3 Mar. 1811	
	Samuel Park	4 do.	
	William Fowler	6 do.	
	James Gordon	7 do.	
	Simon Kent	28 do.	
	George Fitzherbert	31 July	
	Thomas Powell	1 Aug.	
	Henry Mansell	14 do.	
	Charles Rayner Newman	15 do.	
	Cha. Francis Jennings	27 Nov.	
	Samuel Beachcroft	28 do.	
	Edward Pender	27 Aug. 1812	
	Jacob Meek	22 Oct.	
	James M'Dermott	2 Nov.	
	William Buckle	3 do.	
	Charles Chichester	4 do.	
	Vesey Temple	5 do.	
	William Jappie	29 Apr. 1813	
	John Campbell	1 Dec.	
	Thomas Hemans	2 do.	
	E— H— Cosens	3 do.	
	James E— M'Arthur	4 do.	
	Robert James	5 do.	
	James Sidney	26 Jan. 1814	
	James Hartley Patterson	27 do.	
	Grenville Pigott	26 May	
	Charles Grove	13 Oct.	
	Christ. Francis Holmes	1 Nov.	
	Edward Gyfford	2 do.	

Lieutenant

Lieutenant -	Patrick M'Kie	3 Nov. 1814		
	James Grant	6 do.		
	Ja. Cha. O'Hara Dickens	7 do.		
	J— C— Lambie	8 do.		
	George Baldwin	9 do.		
	Orlando Felix	10 do.		
	Thomas Woodford	7 Dec.		
	William Harrison Hill	8 do.		
Ensign - -	James Heally	1 Nov. 1813		
	George James Bower	2 do.		
	Robert Innes	2 Dec.		
	John Nickelson	25 do.		
	Lyttleton Westwood	do.		
	William Reed	13 Jan. 1814		
	George Mackenzie	22 do.		
	Walt. Nongreate Williams	23 do.		
	James Campbell Hartley	24 do.		
	Francis Richard Tane	25 do.		
	Gilbert Pasley	26 do.		
	Robert Burton Newenham	27 do.		
	C— Fraser	10 Feb.		
	Aug. Fred. Fra. Adamson	3 Mar.		
	William Keowen	21 Apr.		
	John Manley Wood	19 May		
	Arthur Ormsby	2 June		
	James Ramsay Smith	13 Oct.		
	A— Cooper	1 Nov.		
	Joseph Bowlby	2 do.		
	John Powell Mathews	3 do.		
	Richard John Stacpoole	8 do.		
	George Foreman Morden	9 do.		
	Richard Birt Holmes	10 do.		
Paymaster 2	William Wilkinson	3 Mar. 1808		
1	John Henry Matthews	21 Oct. 1813		
3	Robert Mitton	17 Feb. 1814		
Adjutant -	Hen. Bruere Armstrong	21 Mar. 1811	Lieut.	23 Jan. 1806
	William Akenside	27 Jan. 1814	Lieut.	2 Jan. 1807
QuarterMaster	William Harris	25 Jan. 1810		
	Luke Lambert	21 Nov. 1811	29 Jan. 1807	
	Alexander Ross	20 Jan. 1814		
Surgeon - -	Thomas Jackson	17 June 1800	25 Jan. 1800	
	George Adams	3 June 1813		
	William P— O'Reilly	27 Jan. 1814		
Assistant Surg.	W— J— B— Parker	8 Nov. 1804		
	John Smith	30 Jan. 1806		
	James Trigge	29 June 1809		
	Alexander Shannon	27 Jan. 1814		
	Henry Terry	21 Mar.		

Facings buff.—Lace silver.

Agent, Messrs. Greenwood, Cox and Hammersley.

15th

| Rank. | Name. | Rank in the | |
		Regiment.	Army.
Colonel -	⊚Moore Disney	23July1814	Lt.Gen. 4June1814
Lieut. Colonel	Andrew Davidson	4Feb.1813	4June1811
Major - -	⎰ John Romer Meadows	27Dec.1810	
	⎱ John Maxwell	8Oct.1812	
	⎱ *John Moore*	4Feb.1813	
Captain -	⎧ Thomas Conolly	5Aug.1804	Major 4June1814
	⎪ William Grierson	27do.	Major 4June1814
	⎪ George Barrow	28do.	Major 4June1814
	⎪ James Hogg	25Mar.1805	
	⎪ Daniel Wright	26Feb.1807	
	⎪ G— Quill	12Apr.	
	⎨ Sinclair Manson	2Mar.1809	
	⎪ Francis Carpenter	26Apr.1810	30Aug.1805
	⎪ Robert Deane Spread	31May	5Sept.1805
	⎪ Robert C— Harker	22Aug.1811	7Mar.1808
	⎪ Charles H— Smith	8Oct.1812	18Jan. 1806
	⎪ *John Fisher*	24June1813	
	⎪ *Thomas Reeves*	3Mar.1814	
	⎩ *Walter Dillon*	24do.	
Lieutenant -	⎧ G— D— Colman	21May1806	Adjutant
	⎪ J—T— King	16Oct.	
	⎪ J— Carroll	11June1807	26Nov.1806
	⎪ William Forde	12do.	
	⎪ Rowland W. Maxwell	25Aug.	
	⎪ Alexander Barnetson	29Sept.	
	⎪ Philip O'Reilly	30do.	
	⎪ Henry Temple	17Dec.	
	⎪ Robert Lewis	7Apr.1808	
	⎨ John Humphrys	14July	
	⎪ Thomas Colman	26do.	
	⎪ Jon. Pockeridge Seaver	do.	
	⎪ Samuel Grayson	28do.	
	⎪ Robert Richardson	3Aug.	
	⎪ H— Barry Barnham	22June1809	
	⎪ Alexander Wishart	29do.	26May 1808
	⎪ Alan Finey	19Apr.1810	
	⎪ James Garstin	9Aug.	12Nov.1809
	⎪ William Macnamara	13Dec.	4May 1808
	⎪ Robert Rideout	5Mar.1812	
	⎩ William Woods	9Apr.	

b   Lieutenant

		Rank in the	
Rank.	Name.	Regiment.	Army.

Lieutenant	⎧ William Carroll	28May1812	
	⎪ Joseph Armstrong	9July	23Aug.1810
	⎪ *J— T— Quill*	3Sept.	
	⎨ *David Torrance*	8Oct.	
	⎪ John Gun	15do,	
	⎪ George Illingworth	3Feb.1814	
	⎩ *Redmond Byrne*	3Mar.	

Ensign	⎧ Robert Brown	7May1812	
	⎪ James Ryan Smyth	3Sept.	
	⎪ Edward Henry Herrick	8Oct.	
	⎨ George Norton	8Apr.1813	
	⎪ Jos. Thomson	29do.	25June1812
	⎪ Charles Lynam	16Sept.	
	⎪ Thomas Steret	3Nov.	
	⎩ William Galway	4do.	

Paymaster	William Wood	20Feb.1806	
Adjutant	G— D— Colman	29Dec.1804	Lieut. 21May1806
Quarter-Master	George Clare	5Sept.1805	
Surgeon	⎰ William Richards	15Oct.1807	
	⎱ *Christopher Gill*	28Jan.1813	23June 1808
Assistant Surg.	⎧ Francis Jones	27June1811	20Sept.1810
	⎨ John Waterson	28Jan.1813	22Mar.1810
	⎩ *Robert Graham*	3June	26Sept.1811

N. B. *The Officers printed in Italics are to be placed upon Half-pay on arrival from Foreign Service.*

Facings yellow.—Lace silver.

Agent, Mr. Disney, No. 26, Parliament-street, Westminster.

Rank.	Name.	Rank in the Regiment.	Army.
Colonel - -	*Sir* George Prevost, *Bt.* 17Feb.1814		Lt.Gen. 4June1811
Lieut. Colonel	Henry Tolley	23Nov.1809	Col. 4June1814
Major - -	{ Francis Heaton Thomas 26June1808		Lt.Col. 4June1814
	{ William Vandeleur	29Sept.1814	1Jan. 1812
Captain -	John Campbell 5Jan.1804		Major 4June1814
	John W— Audain 24July		Major 4June1814
	Sackville Berkeley 25Dec.		Lt.Col. 20June1811
	John Gallwey 2Jan.1806		
	William Broomfield 8Oct.1807		
	Nicholas Doolan 25Dec.		
	Philip F— Hall 26June1808		
	Thomas Derenzy Turner 8Feb.1810		25Nov.1807
	Richard Ross Nugent 3Jan.1811		5Mar.1807
	James Straker 29Sept.1814		
Lieutenant	S— Carter 27Mar.1805		
	Richard Vareilles Bates 5Dec.		
	Edw. Calvert Timperley 2Jan.1806		
	John Macfarlane 25July		Adjutant
	Edw. Benj. Stehelin 22Aug.		
	John Walton 23do.		
	John Wall 12May1807		
	William Ross 25July		22Mar.1807
	Charles Eyre 1Dec.1808		3Apr. 1806
	Felix O'Hara 12do.		
	John Claude de Loppinot 25May1809		
	Robert Browne 8June		
	H. J. Mitchell Gregory 29Dec.		
	Gilb. Ell. Drummond 31July1810		
	Scott Rigney 1Aug.		
	William Gale Hasleham 23do.		25Aug.1809
	John Smith 21Sept.		16June1808
	John Dalzell 10Sept.1812		
	William Orr 18Mar.1813		18Nov.1807
	John L— Hargrove 8July		28Mar.1812
	Donald Maclean 5Aug.		
	Darby Mahony 6Jan.1814		
	John Busteed 29Sept.		

Ensign

Rank.	Name.	Rank in the Regiment.	Army.
Ensign	Thomas Peter Burke	21May1812	
	Simon Purdon	18June	
	George Rivers Maltby	11Mar.1813	
	William Henry Shafto	5Aug.	
	William M'Carthy	7Oct.	
	William Clarke	18Nov.	
	Purefoy Lum	25Dec.	
	L— Leslie	do.	
	Tho. Grif. Wainwright	14Apr.1814	
	John O'Donnell	5May	
Paymaster	Robert George Bankes	18Nov.1813	
Adjutant	John Macfarlane	25Dec.1804	Lieut. 25July1806
Quarter-Master	William Rowen	25July1806	
Surgeon	Joseph Morrice	26Mar.1812	11Jan. 1810
Assistant Surg.	John Comins Bulkeley	10Feb.1814	17Sept.1812
	James Walsh	10Mar.	30Sept.1813

Facings yellow.—Lace silver.

Agent, Mr. Brett, No. 19, Gerrard Street, Soho.

Rank.	Name.	Rank in the Regiment.	Army.
Colonel - -	George Garth	8Aug.1792	Gen. 1Jan.1801
Lieut. Colonel	{ Richard Stovin Frederick Hardyman Thomas M'Mahon	6Sept.1798 31Oct.1805 20June1811	M.Gen. 4June1811 Col. 4June1813 Col. 4June1814
Major - -	{ Philip Nicoll Garret Fitzsimmons	19July1808 25Mar.1813	Lt.Col. 1Jan.1812 Lt.Col. 1Jan.1812
Captain -	{ Nathaniel Bean Henry Despard William Croker Charles Wilson Thomas Merrick Edward Byne Benjamin Halfhyde Donald Campbell John Nixon George Macauley Henry Woodd	2June1804 19Nov.1806 20do. 18Nov.1807 do. do. 25Aug.1809 1Aug.1811 30Jan.1812 25Mar.1813 5Aug.	Major 4June1814 28Nov.1806
Lieutenant	{ Wm. Milton Thomson Robert Lachlan George James Romney Robinson Gale Richard Saunders Arthur Poyntz Allen Stewart John Stalkart Frederick Hawkins Charles Evans Edward Austen Richard Goodacre George Peevor Dobson Young Richard Swinton James Jeffries Henry Wm. Walbridge James Greenhill Wm. White Crawley Septimus Harrison Matthew Pickering J— Maw Philip Jacob Demoor	26Oct.1805 25Aug.1806 15Jan.1807 26Feb. 18Nov. 20do. 3Dec. 1Apr.1808 3Nov. 16Feb.1809 7Sept. 1Oct. 1Jan.1810 1Aug. 1Nov. 28Mar.1811 2Jan.1812 20Feb. 19Mar. 1May 2do. 2Feb.1813 5Aug.	9Mar.1805 14Feb. 1807 Adjutant

Ensign

Rank.	Name.	Rank in the	
		Regiment.	Army.

Rank.	Name.	Regiment.	Army.
Ensign	James Waller Samo	16May1811	
	John Church	12Dec.	
	Samuel Oliver	26Mar.1812	
	Martin Mulkern	23Apr.	
	William Despard	1May	
	Tho.ShuldhamO'Halloran	2Feb.1813	
	Alured Willam Gray	do.	
	Wm. Martin Yorke	25Mar.	
	Philip Nicolle Anley	2Sept.	
Paymaster	Thomas Bourke	12Oct.1804	
Adjutant	Charles Evans	2Dec.1813	Lieut. 16Feb.1809
Quarter-Master	——— Kitsell	1May1808	
Surgeon	Charles Corfield	13Oct.1806	25Feb. 1799
Assistant Surg.	St. George Ardley	30June1804	3Sept.1803
	James Harrison	20Dec.1810	

Facings white.—Lace silver.

Agent, Messrs. Greenwood, Cox and Hammersley.

Permitted to bear on their Colours and Appointments a " SPHINX," with the word " EGYPT," in commemoration of the Campaign of 1801.

Rank.	Name.	Rank in the Regiment.	Rank in the Army.
Colonel -	John, *Ld.* Hutchinson, *K.B.*	27Apr.1811	Gen. 4June1813
Lieut. Colonel	James Graves	5Mar.1807	Col. 4June1814
Major - -	⎰ Robert Smyth	31Jan.1811	Lt.Col. 1Jan.1812
	John M'Niel	29Oct.1812	
	William Fraser	25Nov.1813	4June1811
	⎱ *Jeffery O'Connell*	8Sept.1814	4June1814
Captain -	⎧ Robert Percival	9July1803	Major 4June1814
	William Conolly	1Sept.1804	Major 4June1814
	Gideon Gorrequer	14do.	Major 4June1814
	Richard Weld	7Jan.1808	
	—— Montgomery	28July	
	Henry Pratt	12Oct.1809	
	⎨ Henry W— Whitfield	25Jan.1810	31Jan. 1805
	Cole Maxwell	19July	
	George Jackman Rogers	6Dec.	Major 4June1814
	George Stuart	21Feb.1811	
	John Warren	13June	28Oct. 1805
	John Doran	26Sept.	
	⎩ *James Forrest*	5Mar.1812	
Lieutenant	⎧ Alexander Clark	1Aug.1806	
	Jeremiah Cooper	25Dec.	
	Francis Wm. Dillon	6Mar.1807	
	Edmund Stacpoole	6Jan.1808	
	James Gruber	17May	
	—— Graves	26Oct.	
	Andrew O'Flyn	27do.	
	Abraham Reed	9Feb.1809	
	Henry Mosse	4Jan.1810	
	T— F— Boyle	3May	
	⎨ William Dempster	11Apr.1811	
	William Anderson	8Aug.	3Nov.1808
	Joseph Hammill	13May1812	Adjutant
	John Gordon	24June	
	Edward Cassan	25do.	
	Constantine Bennison	8Oct.	
	Oliver St. George	5Nov.	
	George Wade	14Jan.1813	
	Henry Vereker	11Feb.	
	⎩ Frederick E— Steele	11Mar.	

Lieutenant

Rank.	Name.	Rank in the Regiment.	Rank in the Army.
Lieutenant	William S— Hall William Roper Little Robert Uniacke Henry Harding Samuel H— Whalley *R— W— Tarleton* *George Manners*	22Apr.1813 17June 9Sept. 16do. 30do. 11Nov. 8Sept.1814	11June1809
Ensign - -	William Farmerie John Grattan Francis Holmes Stephen Hope Cooke John Campbell Thomas Thompson Henry Senior John George Young *John Trevor Hull*	24June1813 8July 21do. 22do. 16Sept. 7Oct. 2Dec. 20Jan.1814 27do.	6May 1813
Paymaster -	William Este	28Oct.1813	
Adjutant - -	Joseph Hammill	5Mar.1812	Lieut. 13May1812
Quarter-Master	Hugh Galley	25Feb.1810	
Surgeon -	Walter Carver *William Seaman*	1June1809 13Jan.1814	6Apr. 1809 22Aug.1811
Assistant Surg.	John Richardson Thomas Lewis	6Aug.1812 9Sept.1813	

N. B. *The Officers printed in Italics are to be placed upon Half-pay on arrival from Foreign Service.*

Facings blue.—Lace gold.

Agent, Messrs. Greenwood, Cox and Hammersley.

[1815]

19th (or the 1st Yorksh. N. Riding) Regt. of Foot. 201

Rank.	Name.	Rank in the	
		Regiment.	Army.
Colonel -	*Sir* Hilgrove Turner, *Kt.*	27Apr.1811	Lt.Gen. 4June1813
Lieut. Colonel	{ *Hon.* Patrick Stewart	25Sept.1806	Col. 4June1814
	{ Wm. Henry Rainsford	24Sept.1812	Col. 4June1814
Major - -	{ James M'Nab	26Nov.1809	Lt.Col. 4June1814
	{ Donald M'Donald	11June1812	
Captain -	{ Alexander Robson	1Jan.1805	
	Tho. Aldersey Jones	28Aug.	
	Edmund Lockyer	29do.	
	Tho. Ajax Anderson	23Mar.1807	
	Ja. Peter Fitz Gerald	24do.	
	Robert Watts	25do.	
	William Wildey	29Sept.1808	
	Henry Hardy	30Jan.1809	Major 4June1814
	Hugo Wemyss	25June1812	
	Thomas Dobbins	10Apr.1813	
	William Nihill	23Dec.	29Oct. 1807
Lieutenant -	{ William Cox	8Aug.1807	
	William D— Robertson	9do.	
	R— B— Duke	10do.	Adjutant
	Charles Drieberg	3July1808	
	Ronald M'Donald	1Dec.	
	Hugh Moore	1Jan.1809	16July 1808
	Philip Casby Lamphier	7Sept.	
	James Bagnett	11Oct.	
	Edmund Tubbs	18do.	
	George L— Hallilay	19do.	
	Victor Raymond	16Nov.	
	John Gore Langton	15Jan.1810	
	Lionel Hobart Hughes	16do.	1July 1808
	Francis Goodhall	18do.	
	Charles Hunt Lorimer	29Mar.	28Apr. 1806
	Harry Beaver	24May	18Feb. 1808
	Crosbie Christian	6Feb.1811	1June1809
	Henry O'Shea	7do.	
	Robert Cormack	29Aug.	
	Donald M'Donald	12Sept.	
	Timothy Raper	19Dec.	
	John Bowyer Edensor	20July1812	
	Donald Campbell	10Apr.1813	
	Robert Gardner	1Nov.	
	James Sullivan	17Mar.1814	20June1811

c   Ensign

[1815]

202 19th (or the 1st Yorksh. N. Riding) Regt. of Foot.

Rank.	Name.	Rank in the Regiment.	Army.

Ensign - -	Charles Macdonald	7Feb.1811	
	Robert Layton	7Mar.	
	Fortescue Hatherley	8May	
	John Rhodes	9do.	
	Thomas Taloe	29Aug.	
	David Burns	17Oct.	
	Henry Frederick Hawker	24do.	
	John William Preston	11June1812	
	George Denison	18do.	
	William Thornton	21Jan.1813	
	Adam Callander	15Apr.	
	Forbes Robinson	30Sept.	
	Thomas Hart Davis	1Nov.	

Paymaster -	Robert Nichols	14Apr.1803	
Adjutant - -	R— B— Duke	30Mar.1810	Lieut. 10Aug.1807
Quarter-Master	T— Blake	12Apr.1804	
Surgeon - -	William Wybrow	15Sept.1808	9Feb. 1804
Assistant Surg.	William M'Donald	20Sept.1810	
	Richard Hooper	do.	

Facings green.—Lace gold.

Agent, Mr. Croasdaile, Silver Street, Golden Square.

20th (or the East Devonshire) Regt. of Foot. 203

Permitted to bear on their Colours and Appointments a " SPHINX," with the word " EGYPT," in commemoration of the Campaign of 1801 ; also the word " MAIDA," in commemoration of the Action of 4th July, 1806.

Rank.	Name.	Regiment.	Army.
			Rank in the
Colonel -	◎ { Sir John Stuart, K. B. & C. Count of Maida	29 Dec. 1809	L. Gen. 25 Apr. 1808
Lieut. Colonel	Charles Steevens	21 Oct. 1813	26 Aug. 1813
Major - - ◎	{ Samuel South John Murray	21 Oct. 1813 30 Mar. 1814	21 Sept. 1813
Captain -	Edward Jackson	20 Aug. 1807	
	William Russell	21 Jan. 1808	Major 3 Mar. 1814
	John Hogg	9 Mar. 1809	
	George Tovey	9 Nov.	Major 12 Apr. 1814
	Robert Telford	17 Oct. 1811	
	Hamlet Obins	19 Dec.	Major 12 Apr. 1814
	—— Lutyens	25 Aug. 1813	
	David Augustus Smith	26 do.	
	Thomas Falls	23 Sept.	Major 29 Sept. 1814
	Forbes Champagné	30 Mar. 1814	
	William Crockatt	31 do.	
Lieutenant -	Roger Lambert Lewis	10 Nov. 1808	16 June 1808
	Frederick Fitz Gerald	9 Feb. 1809	
	Guy Rotton	30 Mar.	
	James Goldfrap	22 June	
	James White	6 July	
	John Gilbert	3 Aug.	
	George Strode	5 Apr. 1810	
	Mark Anthony Stanley	9 May 1811	16 Aug. 1810
	Charles Connor	27 June	
	Alexander Baillie	4 July	
	Edward Cheek	7 Nov.	
	Joseph William Watson	18 June 1812	
	John Smith	7 Oct.	
	Thomas Edwards	8 do.	
	John Porter Shepherd	31 Dec.	
	Edward Lee Godfrey	25 Aug. 1813	
	George Edward Maltby	26 do.	
	Richard Cater Oakley	21 Oct.	
	William O'Donnell	18 Nov.	
	William Kirsopp	25 do.	
	Joseph Tompson	10 Feb. 1814	
	James Battersby	30 Mar.	
	Edward Ffennell	31 do.	
	John Storey	1 Apr.	Adjutant
	Charles Smith	21 do.	

c 2

Ensign

Rank.	Name.	Rank in the Regiment.	Army.

Ensign - -	Alexander Tovey	21Oct.1813	
	James Rae	18Nov.	
	George Horsley Wood	25do.	
	Charles South	9Dec.	
	Donatus O'Brien	10Feb.1814	
	Joseph Margitson	24Mar.	
	Thomas Moore	30do.	
	Henry Dundas Campbell	31do.	
	John Fausset Wallace	21Apr.	
Paymaster -	Rochfort Bloomfield	8June1809	
Adjutant - -	John Storey	26Aug.1813	Lieut. 1Apr.1814
Quarter-Master	Charles Houth	5Nov.1807	
Surgeon - -	Archibald Arnott	17May1803	23Aug.1799
Assistant Surg.	David Gordon	2Mar.1809	
	Robert Renwicke	9Sept.1813	

Facings yellow.—Lace silver.

Agent, Mr. Macdonald, Pall Mall Court.

[1815]

21st Regt. of Foot (or Royal N. Brit. Fuzileers.) 205

Colonel - -	*Hon.* William Gordon	6Aug.1803	Gen.	1Jan.1798
Lieut. Colonel	William Paterson	20June1805	Col.	4June1813
Major - -	{ Robert Henry	20June1805	Lt.Col.	1Jan.1812
	Alexander James Ross	31May1810		
	John A— Whitaker	8Oct.1812		
	Norman Pringle	23June1814		
Captain -	{ Robert Renny	3Aug.1804	Lt.Col.	29Sept.1814
	Valentine Joseph Quin	4do.	Major	4June1814
	Stuart Home Douglas	22do.	Major	4June1814
	James M'Haffie	24do.	Major	4June1814
	Edward Anth. Angelo	14May1807	Major	2June1814
	Archibald Maclean	6Aug.		
	William Conran	14Apr.1808		
	Nich. Lawson Darrah	30June		
	William Henry Meyrick	8Sept.	11Aug.1808	
	Daniel Hewan	21Sept.1809		
	John George Green	31May1810		
	John Carey Champion	19July		
	James M'Nab	21Mar.1811		
	Donald Mackenzie	do.		
	Archibald Kidd	10Sept.1812		
	Robert Gordon	15Oct.		
	Aldcroft Waller	12Nov.		
	Donald Mackay	25Feb.1813		
	George Campbell	9Dec.		
	Roderick M'Donald	2Feb.1814		
	John Hall	3do.		
	Hon. Francis H. Morris	14July		
First Lieut.	{ Duncan Dewar	29Nov.1805	Adjutant	
	James Stewart	1Dec.		
	John M'Pherson	19do.		
	William Orr	14May1806		
	Charles Minter	15do.		
	Thomas Fairweather	6Aug.1807		
	David Anderson	7Jan.1808	26Mar.1807	
	John Sabine	14Apr.		
	Angus Mackay	30June		
	Francis Whitfield	16Feb.1809	21May 1801	
	John William Cole	16Nov.		
	ArchibaldMontgomerie	31Dec.		
	Charles J— Furlong	3Jan.1810		
	John Waters	10do.	17Aug.1809	
	Donald M'Donald	22Mar.		
	Robert Mackay	26July		
	Patrick Clason	3Jan.1811		
	James Brady	2July		
	John Leavock	3do.		
	William Peddie	30Jan.1812		

First

[1815]

206 21st Regt. of Foot (or Royal N. Brit. Fuzileers.)

First Lieut.	J. S. M. Fonblanque	18June1812	
	James Rynd	26Nov.	
	John Spooner	25Jan.1813	27Oct. 1808
	Robert Brown	24Feb.	
	John Doig	25do.	
	Harry Pigou	11Mar.	
	Edmund Nash	8Dec.	Adjutant
	John Sampson	9do.	
	Ralph Carr	27Jan.1814	
	James Egan	2Feb.	
	Andrew Spotiswood	3do.	
	Eardley Hodges	4do.	
	Alexander B. Armstrong	5do.	
	Holland M'Ghee	3May	
	Robert Crawford	4do.	
	John Dunbar Moodie	5do.	
	Wm. James Sutherland	22Sept.	
	David Rankine	17Nov.	
Second Lieut.	Sir William Crosbie	4Mar.1813	
	James Brown	13May	
	William Leavock	8Dec.	
	David Home	9do.	
	Peter Quin	27Jan.1814	
	Hon. James Sinclair	2Feb.	
	Alexander Geddes	3do.	
	Charles Lonsdale	4do.	
	William Armstrong	5do.	
	Alexander Lindsay	7Apr.	
	John Crofton Peddie	4May	
	Charles Waller	5do.	
	Henry Keating Strettell	27Oct.	7Apr. 1814
	Thomas Traill	28do.	
	Richard Hill	17Nov.	
Paymaster 1	Robert Mackay	19June1801	
2	Thomas Armstrong	18Sept.1809	
Adjutant -	Duncan Dewar	25Oct.1804	1st Lt. 29Nov.1805
	Edmund Nash	13Jan.1814	1st Lt. 8Dec.1812
QuarterMaster	William Walsh	16June1808	
	John Wilkie	25Feb.1813	
Surgeon -	W—S—Nice	25Feb.1805	9July 1803
	Thomas Carey	30Apr.1807	
Assistant Surg.	Charles Clarke	26Apr.1810	5Nov.1807
	Robert Berry	25Apr.1811	
	Thomas Pack	7Oct.1813	

Facings blue.—Lace gold.

Agent, Mr. Lawrie, Adelphi.

22d

[1815]

22d (or the Cheshire) Regiment of Foot. 207
(2d BATTALION DISBANDED.)

Rank.	Name.	Rank in the	
		Regiment.	Army.
Colonel - -	*Hon.* Edward Finch	18Sept.1809	Lt.Gen. 25Ap.1808
Lieut. Colonel {	John Dalrymple	2Oct.1806	Col. 4June1813
	Robert Kelso	8June1809	Col. 4June1813
Major - - {	Effingham Lindsay	18July1807	Lt.Col.17Sept.1812
	William Shaw	8June1809	Lt.Col. 4June1814
Captain - {	James Cullen	25May1803	Major 4June1811
	Hector Hall	25Feb.1804	Major 4June1811
	John Boyde	8Apr.1807	
	John Moir	3Mar.1810	2Feb. 1809
	George Hewett	19July	Major 18June1812
	William H— Dennie	4Oct.	
	Thomas Poole	26Dec.1811	
	William Norton	9Apr.1812	
	George William Lay	14Jan.1813	
	James Fleming	10Feb.1814	
	Charles Henry Watson	11do.	
Lieutenant {	James Hervey	19Feb.1807	17Dec. 1806
	Bibye Le Sage	12June	
	H— F— Cane	23Sept.	
	Thomas Keappock	1Oct.1808	
	Heneage Girod	4May1809	10Nov.1808
	John Kendall	25do.	
	Peter Barlow	1June	
	John Stevens	1Aug.	14June1809
	James Craster	20Nov.	
	George Topp Lindsay	23do.	21Sept.1809
	A— F— Dobree	18Dec.	28Sept.1809
	John Byrne	21do.	
	Peter Valentine Wood	3Jan.1811	
	Alexander Clarke	20Feb.1812	
	Robert Kearnander	13May	
	Richard Collins	14do.	
	William Ball	11Mar.1813	
	William Raban	2June	
	—— Bird	3do.	
	Richard Ellis Rowlands	10do.	
	Thomas Edwards	22Dec.	Adjutant
	Robert Welling. Kyffen	23do.	
	Henry Ramus	10Feb.1814	
	William Fred. Ebhart	11do.	
	Edward Remon	5May	
			Ensign

Rank.	Name.	Rank in the	
		Regiment.	Army.

Ensign	{ Francis Tipping Hall	24June1812	
	James Chambers Park	12Apr.1813	
	James Stewart	15do.	
	John Caulfeild	3June	
	Alex.Camp.Macdougall	23Dec.	
	Thomas Brown	25do.	
	James Telfair	11Feb.1814	
	John Poole	24Mar.	
†	Eyre Butler	28July	

Paymaster	Thomas Patterson	29Oct.1807	
Adjutant	Thomas Edwards	15Feb.1811	Lieut. 22Dec.1813
Quarter-Master	William Mansfield	21Apr.1811	
Surgeon	James Hacking	8Aug.1804	
Assistant Surg.	{ Woodhouse Martin	18Oct.1810	27July 1809
	James Black	13May1813	

† *To be placed upon Half-pay on his arrival from Foreign Service.*

Facings buff.—Lace gold.

Agent, Messrs. Greenwood, Cox and Hammersley.

(2d BATTALION DISBANDED.)

Permitted to bear on their Colours and Appointments the word " MINDEN." Also a " SPHINX," with the word " EGYPT," in commemoration of the Campaign of 1801.

Rank.	Name.	Rank in the Regiment.	Rank in the Army.
Colonel - -	Richard Grenville	21Apr.1786	Gen. 1Jan.1801
Lieut. Col. ✠—	Henry Walton Ellis	23Apr.1807	Col. 4June1814
Major - ◎— {	Thomas Dalmer	10Dec.1807	Lt.Col. 17Aug.1812
◎— {	J— Humph. Edw. Hill	12Mar.1812	Lt.Col. 21Sept.1813
Captain -	Peter Brown	28Mar.1805	Major 21June1813
◎	Joseph Hawtyn	11Sept.1806	Major 17Aug.1812
	Francis Dalmer	10Dec.1807	Major 26Aug.1813
	Henry Wynne	29Sept.1808	
	Thomas Strangeways	6Apr.1809	
	William Campbell	15June	Major 12Apr.1814
	Charles Jolliffe	18June1811	
	Thomas Farmer	16Apr.1812	
	Henry Johnson	14May	
	J— C— Harrison	20do.	
First Lieut.	Francis O'Flaherty	6Aug.1807	
	J— Milne	21Oct.	
	William Walley	10Dec.	
	Tho. Edwardes Tucker	22Sept.1808	
	Sir Geo. R. Farmer, Bt.	12Jan.1809	
	Thomas Turner	16Mar.	
	E— M— Brown	20Apr.	
	F— L— G— Cowell	28Dec.	26Nov.1801
	G— Fensham	4Jan.1810	
	Ralph Smith	22Mar.	
	Hon. Thomas Jocelyn	14Feb.1811	
	Harry Palmer	11Apr.	
	Isaac Watkins Harris	20June	
	J— Enoch	15Aug.	Adjutant
	Gismond Phillips	5Sept.	
	John Macdonald	10Oct.	
	George Fielding	7Nov.	
	Robert Pattison Holmes	12Dec.	
	Robert Trotter	16Apr.1812	
	Charles Fryer	7May	
	W— A— Griffiths	13do.	
	John Clyde	14do.	
	Alexander Adair Brice	21do.	

d   Second

| Rank. | Name. | Rank in the | |
		Regiment.	Army.
Second Lieut.	⎧——— Methold ⎪ Thomas Lilly ⎪ Henry John Pemberton ⎨ George Dunn ⎪ George Allan ⎪ George Stainforth ⎪ Gerald Fitz Gibbon ⎩ William Leebody	17 Sept. 1812 1 Oct. 17 Dec. 15 Apr. 1813 29 do. 29 July 26 Aug. 9 Sept.	
Paymaster -	Richard Julian	8 Oct. 1812	
Adjutant - -	J— Enoch	16 Sept. 1813	1st Lt. 15 Aug. 1811
Quarter-Master	——— Sidley	14 Apr. 1808	
Surgeon - -	John Dunn	10 Sept. 1803	9 July 1803
Assistant Surg.	⎰ Thomas Smith ⎱ John Williams	2 July 1812 13 May 1813	

Facings blue.—Lace gold.

Agent, Messrs. Greenwood, Cox and Hammersley.

(2d BATTALION DISBANDED.)

Permitted to bear on their Colours and Appointments a " SPHINX," with the word " EGYPT," in commemoration of the Campaign of 1801.

Rank.	Name.	Rank in the Regiment.	Rank in the Army.
Colonel	⊚*Sir* David Baird, *Bt. K. B. & C.* 19 July 1807		Gen. 4 June 1814
Lieut. Col.	⊚ ⎰ William Kelly 22 Feb. 1810		Col. 4 June 1813
	Charles Hicks 3 Oct. 1811		25 July 1810
	⊚ ⎱ *Thomas Chamberlin* 4 June 1813		4 June 1811
Major	⎧ Samuel Taylor Popham 14 Sept. 1804		Lt. Col. 4 June 1811
	⎨ Tho. Watkin Forster 22 Feb. 1810		
	⎪ *William Robison* 3 Oct. 1811		
	⎩ *Henry White* 4 June 1813		
Captain	⎧ Thomas Charles Green 4 Aug. 1804		Major 4 June 1814
	⎪ Ludovick Stewart 27 do.		Major 4 June 1814
	⎪ Charles Hughes 28 do.		Major 4 June 1814
	⎪ Thomas Craig 26 Oct.		Major 4 June 1814
	⎪ John Cathcart Meacham 28 Mar. 1805		
	⎪ William Hedderwick 12 Sept.		Major 22 Oct. 1812
	⎨ Charles Collis 31 Oct.		
	⎨ Daniel Baby 6 Aug. 1806		
	⎪ Thomas Andrews 7 Apr. 1808		
	⎪ William Tudor 21 June 1809		
	⎪ James Lepper 22 do.		Major 3 Mar. 1814
	⎪ *Thomas Malkin* 31 Aug.		
	⎪ *John Ward* 22 Oct. 1812		
	⎪ *Cornelius Dennehy* 6 May 1813		
	⎩ *John James Grindley* 24 June		
Lieutenant	⎧ Edward George Smith 8 Aug. 1805		
	⎪ John Blake 22 do.		
	⎪ Cromwell Doolan 13 Jan. 1806		
	⎪ Ponsonby Kelly 27 Nov.		
	⎪ John Ewing 28 May 1807		
	⎪ Thomas Maling 23 Aug.		
	⎪ Robert Watson 25 do.		
	⎪ David Warburton 13 Feb. 1808		
	⎨ Alexander N— Findlater 15 do.		
	⎨ Charles Augustus Stuart 18 do.		
	⎪ George Stack 25 do.		4 Dec. 1806
	⎪ Thomas Allen 29 Sept.		
	⎪ Joseph Brooksbank 22 June 1809		
	⎪ George L'Estrange 19 July		
	⎪ John Harris 21 do.		
	⎪ Francis Grant 22 do.		
	⎪ Robert Robison 23 do.		
	⎩ —— Nokes 22 Feb. 1810		

d 2

Lieutenant

Rank.	Name.	Rank in the Regiment.	Rank in the Army.
Lieutenant	Tho. Barker Bainbrigge	3May1810	
	Frederick Barton	30May1811	
	Michael Hunt	8Aug.	
	Alexander Cameron	3Oct.	
	Charles Jago	23Jan.1812	
	George Erratt	2Apr.	
	George Sunbolf	16Oct.	28Feb. 1811
	William D'Acre	25Feb.1813	
	Hugh Fleming	26Mar.	Adjutant
	Robert Jones	2Dec.	
	Arthur O'Leary	25Jan.1814	
	John M'Gregor	24Feb.	
Ensign - -	Alexander Child	16May1811	
	Arthur Gray	11July	
	Ronald Campbell	3Oct.	
	Robert Marsh	31do.	
	George Hewson	2Apr.1812	
	Thomas F— Smith	4June	
	William Mellis	7do.	
	Henry Wigmore	15Oct.	
	Thomas Kennedy	30do.	
	——— *Dore*	8Apr.1813	
	Edward Thomas Smith	9do.	
	Thomas Town	22July	
	John Spooner	25Dec.	
Paymaster -	Richard Morse Payne	2Sept.1799	
Adjutant - -	Hugh Fleming	11Jan.1810	Lieut. 26Mar.1813
Quarter-Master	Robert Belcher	1Aug.1805	
Surgeon - -	Jonathan Featherstone	31Dec 1803	9July 1803
Assistant Surg.	Dennis Kearney	11Mar.1813	
	John Fawcett	do.	

N. B. *The Officers printed in Italics are to be placed upon Half-pay on arrival from Foreign Service.*

Facings green.—Lace silver.

Agent, Mr. Macdonald, Pall Mall Court.

25th

Permitted to bear on their Colours and Appointments the word " MINDEN." Also " SPHINX," with the word " EGYPT," in commemoration of the Campaign of 1801.

Colonel - -	Hon. Charles Fitzroy	25 Mar. 1805	Lt.Gen.	25 July 1810
Lieut. Colonel	George Robert Ainslie	21 May 1807	M.Gen.	4 June 1813
	J— Alex. Farquharson	4 June 1813	25 July 1810	
	Alexander Light	1 July	4 June 1811	
Major - -	V— W— Hompesch	28 Feb. 1805	Lt.Col.	1 Jan. 1812
	Alex. Wolf M'Donell	7 Mar. 1811		
	James Peat	4 June 1813		
	Abraham Freer	1 July		
Captain - -	Robert Terry	8 Oct. 1803	Major	4 June 1814
	William Bailie	31 July 1804	Major	4 June 1814
	John Austin	4 Aug.	Major	4 June 1814
	Garnet Wolseley	5 do.	Major	4 June 1814
	George Juxon	6 Sept.	Major	4 June 1814
	Adolphus Munstal	7 do.	Major	4 June 1814
	Peter Trip	6 Nov. 1805		
	Thomas Murray Crooke	8 Sept. 1808		
	William Lyons	11 May 1809		
	Valentine Grantham	26 July 1810	2 Mar. 1809	
	Edw. Tho. Fitz Gerald	13 Sept.	28 Aug. 1806	
	William Hutcheon	14 Feb. 1811	Major	4 June 1814
	Duncan M'Laren	10 Oct.	18 Dec. 1806	
	Peter Macdougall	13 Feb. 1812	12 Dec. 1805	
	William O'Doherty	28 do.	19 Dec. 1805	
	J— J— Mitchell	14 May	1 Oct. 1807	
	Alexander Graham	10 Sept.	21 Feb. 1811	
	George Herbert	20 May 1813	22 Sept. 1812	
	John Kelly	4 June		
	Francis Cosgrave	1 July		
	Henry Warren	9 Dec.		
	James L— Macdonnell	16 do.	8 June 1809	
Lieutenant	James M— Robertson	7 Nov. 1805		
	James Thornhill	21 do.		
	Thomas Stewart	25 Dec. 1806	30 Oct. 1806	
	Thomas Swyny	1 Jan. 1807		
	S— R— Jarvis	8 do.	19 June 1806	
	R— Benjamin Wolseley	27 May		
	David Hamill	28 do.		
	Richard Pratt	10 Sept.		
	George Jebb	25 do.		
	Robert Williams	28 Jan. 1808		
	Fleetwood Rawstorne	7 July		
	Henry Kane	8 do.		
	Thomas Lynch	9 do.		
	Robert Simpson	10 do.		
	Robert Tracey	11 do.		
	William Lamphire	14 do.		
	Abraham Shuttleworth	22 Sept.		
	Thomas White	8 Dec.		

Lieutenant	Michael Bourke	2Feb.1809	
	Robert Hamilton	23do.	
	Alexander Menzies	11May	
	John Vowell	15Mar.1810	2Nov.1809
	Charles Leslie	25Sept.	
	William Anderson	7Mar.1811	Adjutant
	James Blagg	14do.	
	John Sinclair	4Apr.	10Dec.1807
	Edward Muckleston	27June	
	George Manners	12Sept.	
	Alexander Buchan	3Oct.	
	George Compson	24do.	
	John Keens	14Nov.	Adjutant
	George Needham	9Apr.1812	
	Samuel Brown	28Jan.1813	
	Edmund Burke	21Oct.	
	Alexander Stewart	6Dec.	
	Edward Huie	7do.	
	Christ. John Halse	8do.	
	Thomas Jenkin Robinson	9do.	
Ensign - -	Robert Young	3Oct.1811	
	Robert Small	4do.	
	Richard C— Halahan	12Mar.1812	
	J— W-- C— Reid	23July	
	Rob. Stephenson Amiel	31Dec.	
	Daniel Blackwell	28Jan.1813	
	Mathew Keough	27May	
	David Dickson	9Sept.	
	William Ravenscroft	21Oct.	
	Roger Stewart	6Dec.	
	Thomas Lingard	7do.	
	Francis Moss Smith	8do.	
	William Pigott	14Apr.1814	
	Thomas Gordon	11Aug.	
Paymaster 2	John Loch	29Aug.1805	
1	Philip Smith	17Feb.1814	
Adjutant -	John Keens	2Nov.1809	Lieut. 14Nov.1811
	William Anderson	25Oct.1810	Lieut. 7Mar.1811
QuarterMaster	James Leech	18Nov.1807	
	J— Smith	6June1811	28Apr.1808
Surgeon -	Alexander Melville	25Dec.1812	26Sept.1811
	William Cringan	17Mar.1814	
Assistant Surg.	William Munro	16Feb.1809	
	Francis Kelly	28May1812	26Sept.1811
	Francis Reid	15July1813	

Facings blue.—Lace gold.

Agent, Messrs. Collyer, Park Place, St. James's.

26th

(2d BATTALION DISBANDED.)

Permitted to bear on their Colours and Appointments a " SPHINX," with the word " EGYPT," in commemoration of the Campaign of 1801.

Rank.	Name.	Rank in the Regiment.	Rank in the Army.
Colonel	©–Geo. E. *of* Dalhousie, *K.B.*	21May1813	Lt.Gen. 4June1813
Lieut. Colonel	© Guy G. C. L'Estrange	10Dec.1812	30May 1811
Major - -	{ Edward Shearman	11Jan.1810	
	Frederick Jones	15Feb.	
Captain -	© Charles Stuart Campbell	14May1804	Major 21Sept.1813
	Edward Witty	5Jan.1805	
	Adam G— Campbell	13June	
	Charles Addison	3Apr.1806	
	Joseph Smith	11Jan.1810	
	William Chartres	11July1811	
	William H— Scott	28Nov.	21Mar.1811
	John Farquharson	15Jan.1812	
	William Beetham	16do.	
	James Hogg	30do.	4May 1808
	Simon Hehl	25Jan.1813	7Jan. 1813
	Andrew Lett	2Feb.1814	
	Francis Shearman	3do.	
	George Pipon	28July	
Lieutenant -	Robert Smith	20Feb.1806	
	James Dunn	18Mar.1807	
	Thomas Murray	19do.	
	Hugh M'Latchie	23June1808	
	Fred. Campbell Heatley	14July	
	John Wright	3Aug.	
	Donald M'Calman	6do.	
	Henry Roberts	7do.	
	Edward Jordan	10do.	
	John Marshall	11do.	
	John Alexander Maxwell	2Mar.1809	
	Colin Campbell	9do.	
	William Launie	30do.	
	William Johnston	do.	
	James Fraser Ross	4May	
	Francis R— Masters	11July1811	
	Robert Robson	30ct.	
	Alexander Arnott	28Feb.181	
	Thomas Taylor	5May	
	Thomas William Boyes	6do.	
	Charles Frederick Sweeny	7do.	
	Walter Graham	4June	

Lieutenant

Rank.	Name.	Rank in the Regiment.	Army.
Lieutenant	David Black	18June1812	
	Michael Pointon	2July	Adjutant
	John Kyle	5Nov.	
	William Ross	3Dec.	
	William Ross	27Jan.1814	
	Fleming Smith	19May	
Ensign - -	Nicholas Terrence	4June1812	
	Alexander Fraser	5Nov.	
	Alexander Calder	3Dec.	
	Robert Maxwell	5Aug.1813	
	William Glennie	16Sept.	
	Thomas Simpson Pratt	2Feb.1814	
	Humphrey Babington	3do.	
	John E— Brown	3Mar.	
Paymaster -	Hugh Pollock	23Dec.1813	Lieut. 2July1812
Adjutant - -	Michael Pointon	4Oct.1810	
Quarter-Master	——— Buchanan	6Feb.1812	
Surgeon - -	John Coldstream	25Sept.1809	
Assistant Surg.	James Brady	18Dec.1811	
	Charles Foote	11Aug.1814	

N. B. *The Officers printed in Italics are to be placed upon Half-Pay on
arrival from Foreign Service.*

Facings yellow.—Lace silver.

Agent, Mr. Gordon, No. 10, Woodstock Street, Oxford Street.

27th

27th (or Inniskilling) Regiment of Foot.

Permitted to inscribe on their Colours and Appointments the word "MAIDA," in commemoration of the Action of 4th July, 1806. Also to bear a "SPHINX," with the word "EGYPT," for the Campaign of 1801.

Rank.	Name.	Rank in the Regiment.	Rank in the Army.
Colonel	Francis, *Earl of* Moira, *K.G.*	23May1804	Gen. 25Sept.1803
Lt. Colonel ☒ {	Lemuel Warren	16Aug.1804	Col. 4June1813
	John Maclean	9June1808	Col. 4June1814
	George James Reeves	4June1813	1Jan. 1812
Major - - {	William Brydges Neynoe	7Sept.1804	Lt.Col. 4June1811
	Charles Thompson	25Feb.1808	Lt.Col. 4June1814
	Peter Nicolson	16June	Lt.Col. 4June1814
	Mark Butcher	11July1811	
	Wheeler Sparrow	4June1813	
	Charles Mill	10Nov.	
Captain - {	John Jordan -	5Aug.1804	Major 22Apr.1813
	Thomas Molloy	1Dec.	Major 4June1814
	Thomas Reade	8Sept.1805	Major 3Jan.1811
	John Hare	9do.	Major 17June1813
◎	Henry Thomas	10do.	Major 26Aug.1813
	Henry Balneavis	11do.	Major 30May1811
	Charles Pepper	14May1806	2Jan. 1806
	William Moore	4Dec.	Major 4June1814
	George Holmes	30Apr.1807	
	John Tucker	3Mar.1808	
	John Waldron	15Sept.	
	John Geddes	1Dec.	
	Robert Haggerston	25Mar.1811	5Apr. 1810
	William Winser	9July	
	Lennox Stafford	10do.	
	John A— Amiel	11do.	
	Nicholas Smith Kirkland	6Feb.1812	
	Philip Bass	14May	
	William Butler	25June	
	Thomas Hamilton	24Sept.	
	Martin Lynch	24Dec.	
	Charles Chitty	13Jan.1813	
	Hugh Mackay	1July	
	Arthur Judge	28Sept.	
	Edward Pope	29do.	

e

			Rank in the	
Rank.	Name.	Regiment.	Army.	

Rank	Name	Regiment	Army
Captain -	John Blakiston	30Sept.1813	
	Daniel Hogan	13Jan.1814	
	Alexander Drysdale	10Feb.	
	John Mackay	5July	
	Frederick Crewe	7do.	
	John Espine Batty	14Dec.	
	John Taylor Mackenzie	15do.	7Feb. 1811
Lieutenant	James Steele	11Feb.1806	
	John Clarke	12do.	
	George M'Donnell	25July	
	William Henderson	8Oct.	
	George Acton	30do.	
	Richard Handcock	5Nov.	
	Bartholomew Tho. Duhigg	9do.	
	Duncan M'Pherson	10do.	
	William M'Lean	12do.	
	Wm. Faithful Fortescue	4Dec.	
	Francis Shee	1Jan.1807	
	Thomas Craddock	7May	
	John Harnet	27Oct.	
	William Talbot	7Feb.1808	
	E— W— Drewe	9do.	
	Alexander Fraser	10do.	
	George Lennon	11do.	
	Thomas Furnas	3Mar.	
	William Dobbin	17do.	
	Daniel Arundel	31do.	
	Charles Manley	28July	
	John Peddie	10Sept.	
	John Millar	11do.	
	J— Kane Jameson	12do.	
	George Pratt	9Mar.1809	
	James Maddocks	14Sept.	
	John Betty	7Mar.1810	
	William Armstrong	15Nov.	
	Joseph Smith	14Mar.1811	
	James Graham	11Apr.	
	Xavier Choiseul	2May	
	Feth Hanly	10July	
	Carlisle Pollock	11do.	
	William Weir	17Oct.	
	John Doris	14Nov.	
	William Boyle	6Feb.1812	

Lieutenant

Rank.	Name.	Rank in the Regiment.	Army.
Lieutenant -	James Adair	13Feb.1812	10Oct. 1811
	Joseph Hill	14May	
	William Sampson	8Sept.	
	John Little	9do.	
	John Wright	10do.	
	Robert Jocelyn Phillips	6Oct.	
	John M'Leod	7do.	
	Benjamin Beaufoy	8do.	
	Lewis Maclean	19Nov.	
	William Crawley	31Dec.	
	Robert Edmonds	7Jan.1813	4Jan. 1810
	Charles Crowe	14do.	24Dec. 1812
	Edward Forde	27do.	
	Robert Stewart Ruddach	28do.	
	Wm. Harlow Phibbs	24June	
	Edward Fairfield	24Aug.	
	Arthur Byrne	25do.	Adjutant
	Thomas Radcliffe	26do.	
	George Latham	29Sept.	
	Andrew Gardner	30do.	
	Alexander Nixon	4Nov.	
	Mich. de St. Hippolite	13Jan.1814	
	John Smith	8Feb.	
	D— Donovan	9do.	
	Nicol M'Nicol	10do.	
	John Armit	10Mar.	
	David Scott	14Aug.	
	John Ovens	5July	
	Christ. Stewart Betty	6do.	
	John Waller	7do.	
	Richard Clunes	11Aug.	
	Robert Weir	15Dec.	
Ensign -	Martin Mac Leod	8Oct.1812	
	James O'Connor	22do.	
	John Galbraith	13Apr.1813	
	B— Slattery	14do.	
	——— Mac Andrew	15do.	
	William Kater	22do.	
	John Ditmas	3June	
	Thomas Smith	24do.	
	C— Cailius de Pontcarré	25do.	27Oct. 1812
	Samuel Ireland	25Aug.	
	Lewellin Nelson	4Nov.1813	

		Rank in the	
Rank.	Name.	Regiment.	Army.

Rank	Name	Regiment	Army
Ensign	James Grant	8Feb.1814	
	Joseph Johnstone	9do.	
	Joseph M'Leod Tew	10do.	
	Edw. Beauch. St. John	10Mar.	17June 1813
	James Wallace	14Apr.	
	——— Botham	9June	
	Wm. Bigoe Buchannan	5July	
	Robert Hawthorne	6do.	
	William Carroll	7do.	
	Lawrence Ward	14do.	Adjutant
	Thomas Trotter	27Oct.	Adjutant
	James Graydon	15Dec.	
Paymaster 2	William Mackie	24Jan.1805	
Paymaster 1	George William Crowe	7Mar.1811	
Paymaster 3	Henry Wolseley	10Dec.1812	
Adjutant	Arthur Byrne	21Apr.1814	Lieut. 25Aug.1813
	Lawrence Ward	14July	Ensign 14July1814
	Thomas Trotter	27Oct.	Ensign 27Oct.1814
QuarterMaster	Thomas Taylor	26Sept.1805	
	William Doyle	14Mar.1811	
	——— Lynch	7Nov.	
Surgeon	Henry West	27Nov.1806	
	John M'Roberts	24Oct.1811	
	Henry Franklin	26May1814	
Assistant Surg.	Gerald Fitz Gerald	25Apr.1811	
	Thomas Mostyn	19Dec.	
	James Maxwell	21Jan.1813	
	W— Forrester Bow	28do.	
	Thomas Proudfoot	4Feb.	
	John Harcourt	26May1814	

Facings buff.—Lace gold.

Agent, Mr. Ridge, No. 44, Charing Cross.

28th (or the North Gloucestershire) Regt. of Foot. 221
(2d BATTALION DISBANDED.)

Permitted to bear on their Colours and Appointments a " SPHINX," with the word " EGYPT," in commemoration of the Campaign of 1801; also the word " BARROSA," for the Action of 5th March, 1811.

Rank.	Name.	Rank in the Regiment.	Rank in the Army.
Colonel - -	Robert Prescott	6July1789	Gen. 1Jan.1798
Lieut. Col.	✕◄Charles P— Belson	23Nov.1804	Col. 4June1813
Major -	◎—{ Robert Nixon	15Dec.1804	Lt.Col. 30May1811
	John Ross	16Apr.1807	Lt.Col. 4June1814
	✕{ Frederick Stovin	9July1803	Lt.Col.26Aug.1813
	Wm. Prescott Meacham	do.	Major 4June1814
	William Irving	do.	Major 4June1814
	Richard Llewellyn	28Feb.1805	Major 23Apr.1812
	Thomas Wilson	14Nov.	
Captain -	{ Charles Caddell	9Mar.1809	
	Richard Kelly	13Apr.	
	John Bowles	20July	
	Thomas English	31Jan.1810	
	Charles Teulon	27Sept.	
	{ Henry Moriarty	3Oct.1811	
	{ James Henry Crummer	2July1807	
	John Fred. Wilkinson	8Sept.1808	
	Matthew Semple	6Oct.	
	R— P— Gilbert	27Apr.1809	
	Robert Prescott Eason	17May	
	William Irwin	20July	
	Henry Hilliard	16Nov.	
	Samuel Moore	28Jan.1810	
	John Coen	29do.	
	Charles B— Carrothers	30do.	
	J— P— Clarke	1Mar.	
	I— William Shelton	22do.	
Lieutenant	{ Samuel Sweeny	22Nov.	
	James Deares	25Apr.1811	
	Richard Chadwick	16May	
	George Ingram	6Aug.1812	
	Robert Mitchell	11Feb.1813	
	John Clark	4Mar.	
	—— Bridgeland	15Apr.	Adjutant
	John Small Robertson	5Aug.	
	John Clarke Nelson	25do.	
	Henry Alexander	26do.	
	Edward Embury Hill	9Sept.	
	Thomas Wm. Colleton	25Nov.	
	James Parry	27Jan.1814	
	{ *Tho. Ilderton Ferrier*	19May	

Ensign

Rank.	Name.	Rank in the	
		Regiment.	Army.
Ensign	⎧—— Stewart	5Aug.1813	
	William Serjeantson	26do.	
	Richard Martin	8Sept.	
	James Simkins	9do.	
	William Mountsteven	25Nov.	
	Henry Olivier	27Jan.1814	
	W— Lynam	31Mar.	
	⎩George Shawe	17May	
Paymaster	John Dewes	20June1799	
Adjutant	—— Bridgeland	4Feb.1811	Lieut. 15Apr.1813
Quarter-Master	Richard Reynolds	9Mar.1809	
Surgeon	William Byrtt	9Sept.1813	
Assistant Surg.	⎰Patrick H— Lavens	24Oct.1811	
	⎱Alexander Stewart	9Feb.1815	25Nov.1813

Facings yellow.—Lace silver.

Agent, Mr. Macdonald, Pall Mall Court.

29th

29th (or the Worcestershire) Regiment of Foot. 223

Permitted to inscribe on their Colours and Appointments the Word " ROLEIA," in commemoration of the Action of 17th August, 1808.

Rank.	Name.	Rank in the Regiment.	Army.
Colonel - -	Gordon Forbes	8Aug.1797	Gen. 1Jan.1812
Lieut. Colonel	John Tucker	29Sept.1814	30Sept.1813
Major - -	{ Peter Hodge { George Tod	29Aug.1811 2Dec.1813	20June1811 31Oct. 1811
Captain -	⎧ Andrew Patison ⎪ Henry Birmingham ◎⎪ Thomas Gell ⎪ William Wade ⎪ Thomas Langton ⎨ William Elliot ⎪ Denis Mahon ⎪ Thomas Lewis Coker ⎪ Robert Stannus ⎪ James Brookes ⎩ Adam Gregory	18Dec.1806 30Nov.1807 17Nov.1808 17Aug.1809 18Jan.1810 9Oct.1811 9Apr.1812 28May 1July1813 2Dec. 24Nov.1814	6June1811 13Feb. 1812
Lieutenant -	⎧ ——— Popham ⎪ William Penrose ⎪ Alexander Young ⎪ Henry Pennington ◎⎪ Charles Western ⎪ Benjamin Wild ⎪ Henry Reid ⎪ J— Viney Evans ⎪ Thomas Biggs ⎪ Miles Sandys ⎪ John Vesie ⎪ John Cornelius Sullivan ⎨ ——— Lovelock ⎪ Richard Lucas ⎪ Thomas Hamilton ⎪ Henry Brodrick ⎪ Edward Kearney ⎪ George Ford ⎪ William Clarke ⎪ Arthur Richardson ⎪ Charles Fitz Gerald ⎪ Richard Doyne ⎪ Stephen Gibbons ⎪ William Legh Hilton ⎩ Edward Bovill	17Feb.1808 18do. 2Sept. 3Nov. 25May1809 8June 26July 14Dec. 18Jan.1810 5Apr. 19June1811 20do. 4July 24Oct. 31do. 28Feb.1812 6Aug. 17June1813 1July 2Dec. 16do. 9Nov.1814 10do. 1Dec. 2do.	Adjutant 16Sept.1813

Ensign

| Rank. | Name. | Rank in the | |
		Regiment.	Army.
Ensign	William Johnson	19Aug.1812	
	Henry Dixon	20do.	
	William Parker	8Oct.	
	John Lacon Akers	31Dec.	
	John Fitzgerald	19Aug.1813	
	Charles Wright	25Dec.	
	Henry Wild	10Nov.1814	
Paymaster	Christopher Humfrey	25Apr.1811	
Adjutant	Benjamin Wild	18Jan.1810	Lieut. 8June1809
Quarter-Master	William Gillespie	13June1805	
Surgeon	I— A— Stanford	4Jan.1810	
Assistant Surg.	William Parker	19Mar.1812	
	James Lawder	12Nov.	

Facings yellow.—Lace silver.

Agent, Messrs. Greenwood, Cox and Hammersley.

30th (or the Cambridgeshire) Regt. of Foot.   225

Permitted to bear on their Colours and Appointments a " SPHINX," with the word " EGYPT," in commemoration of the Campaign of 1801.

Rank.	Name.	Rank in the Regiment.	Rank in the Army.
Colonel - -	Robert Manners	7Nov.1799	Gen. 4June1813
Lieut. Colonel	William Wilkinson .	1Sept.1795	Lt.Gen. 4June1814
	William Lockhart	9July1803	M.Gen. 4June1813
	Philip Vaumorel	27Dec.1810	25Oct. 1809
◎	Alexander Hamilton	25July1811	4June1811
	Christopher Maxwell	4June1813	
Major - ◎	Norris William Bailey	26Dec.1808	Lt.Col. 4June1814
	Thomas Roberts	4June1812	
	Charles A— Vigoureux	4June1813	Lt.Col. 21June1813
	Peter Ryves Hawker	23June1814	4June1811
Captain -	Samuel Bircham	9July1803	Major 4June1814
	Robert Murray	19Nov.	Major 4June1814
	Thomas Jackson	17Dec.	Major 4June1814
	B— R— Lynch	23Nov.1804	Major 4June1814
	Samuel Fox	28Mar.1805	
	Tho. Walker Chambers	2Apr.1807	
	Richard Machell	27Oct.1808	2June1808
	Alexander M'Nabb	11May1809	
	James Fullarton	18do.	18Aug.1808
	Henry Craig	16Nov.	11Feb. 1808
	William Stewart	21Feb.1811	
	John Tongue	7Mar.	
	Robert Douglas	25do.	5Oct. 1809
	John Powell	22Apr.1813	
	Robert Howard	1Sept.	
	W— C— Harpur	do.	
	James Skirrow	2do.	
	Henry Cramer	3odo.	
	Arthur Gore	11Feb.1814	14July 1808
	Matthew Ryan	26May	Major 4June1813
	Donald Sinclair	7July	
	Owen Wynne Grey	8Sept.	
Lieutenant -	Hinton Easte	10Apr.1806	
	James Lewen	13do.	
	Benj. Walter Nicholson	15do.	
	Thomas Jones	16do.	
	William Sullivan	7May	
	John Gowan	8do.	
	John Thomas Barlow	19Mar.1807	
	Stephen Masters	16Apr.	15Jan. 1807
	Washington Carden	12June	

f

Lieutenant

Rank.	Name.	Rank in the Regiment.	Army.
Lieutenant	John Perry	15 Sept. 1808	
	John Wade	23 Feb. 1809	
	Richard Mayne	8 June	
	John Winrow	25 do.	25 Feb. 1808
	M— Andrews	19 Sept.	Adjutant
	Richard Heaviside	20 do.	
	Thomas Kettlewell	29 Mar. 1810	
	John Garvey	19 July	
	James Light	7 Mar. 1811	
	William Pennefather	20 June	
	Richard C— Elliott	23 do.	
	A— W— Freear	24 do.	
	John Rumley	25 do.	
	Geo. Wm. Aug. Brisac	26 do.	
	Andrew Baillie	27 do.	
	George Teulon	14 July	
	Robert Daniel	15 do.	
	George Stephenson	16 do.	Adjutant
	Parke Pepper Neville	17 do.	
	John Roe	18 do.	
	Theophilus O'Halloran	8 Aug.	
	Richard Harrison	11 Sept.	
	Walter Ross	12 do.	
	John Roe	26 do.	
	George Thomas Ness	4 June 1812	
	—— Campbell	25 do.	
	—— Hughes	29 Oct.	
	Purefoy Lockwood	22 Apr. 1813	
	John Pratt	6 May	
	Edward Parry	1 Sept.	
	Richard Wedge	2 do.	
	Samuel Robert Poyntz	29 do.	
	William Atkinson	30 do.	
	George Darling	14 Apr. 1814	
	John Wm. Head Brydges	7 July	7 Apr. 1802
	Henry Beere	7 Sept.	
	Francis Tincombe	8 do.	
	Donald Macdonald	22 Nov.	
	Edmund Prendergast	23 do.	
	William Ouseley Warren	24 do.	

Ensign

Rank.	Name.	Rank in the Regiment.	Army.

Ensign	Richard Fraser	18Apr.1813	
	Thomas Moneypenny	22do.	
	David Latouche	20May	
	Robert Nayler Rogers	29July	
	Edward Windus	1Sept.	
	John James	2do.	
	Edward Drake	25Nov.	
	William Moore	30Dec.	
	James Poyntz	14Apr.1814	
	Edward M'Creary	8Sept.	
	William Biston Frizell	22Nov.	
	James Bullen	23do.	
	—— Warren	24do.	
Paymaster 1	Michael Jones	21Apr.1798	
2	Hugh Boyd Wray	9Aug.1806	
Adjutant	George Stephenson	25Jan.1810	Lieut. 16July1811
	M— Andrews	30Dec.1813	Lieut. 19Sept.1809
QuarterMaster	J— F— Kingsley	9July1803	
	—— Williamson	27Oct.1814	
Surgeon	Robert Pearce	10Sept.1803	
	J— G—Elkington	11Mar.1813	
Assistant Surg.	Samuel Piper	27Dec.1806	
	John Evans	22Aug 1811	
	Patrick Clarke	25June1812	

Facings pale yellow.—Lace silver.

Agent, Mr. Croasdaile, Silver Street, Golden Square.

(2d BATTALION DISBANDED.)

Rank.	Name.	Regiment.	Rank in the Army.
Colonel - -	Henry, *Earl of* Mulgrave	8Feb.1793	Gen. 25Oct.1809
Lieut. Colonel ⊚	*Hon.* Robert Meade Henry Bruce Alexander Leith	10Apr.1801 24Mar.1803 7Feb.1811	Lt.Gen. 4June1814 M.Gen. 4June1814
Major - -	George Augustus Tonyn Robert Brice Fearon *Michael Coast*	2Aug.1804 20Dec.1810 31Dec.1812	Lt.Col. 4June1811
Captain -	Henry Cumming Patrick Cruice Alexander Stewart Robert Elder Edward Stafford Thomas Samuel Nicolls Patrick Dowdall Francis Eager Charles Blomer Edward Knox Richard Cust *J— W— Nunn* *Joseph Burton*	2Aug.1804 4do. 5do. 28do. 31Jan.1805 20Mar.1806 4Dec. 15Jan.1807 7Feb. 5Nov. 18Aug.1808 13Dec.1810 21Apr.1814	Major 1Jan.1812 Major 4June1814 Major 4June1814 Major 4June1814 Major 22Nov.1813 Major 26Dec.1813
Lieutenant	Francis John Ryan Samuel Hawkins William Gibson Hugh Lumley George Beamish John Hutton William Shaw Richard Lodge Adderley Beamish James Nangle Richard Kirby George M'Cullock Samuel Shawe Henry Harman Young Samuel Bolton Andrew Wm. Gamble Charles Bailey David Macpherson Francis Knox Charles M'Carthy Howard Paterson James Spence	7Nov.1805 13do. 11Mar.1806 12do. 13do. 20do. 5Nov. 6do. 26Mar.1807 31May 22Mar.1808 24do. 29Sept. 25Nov. 6Apr.1809 24Aug. 25do. 22May1810 23do. 24do. 20Sept. 20Dec.	Adjutant

Lieutenant

Rank.	Name.	Rank in the Regiment.	Rank in the Army.
Lieutenant -	John W— Owens	7 Feb. 1811	
	William Raymond	1 Aug.	
	Loftus Nunn	15 Jan. 1812	
	Ralph Nicholson	31 Dec.	
	William Ryan	21 Apr. 1814	
Ensign - -	William Smith	11 Oct. 1810	
	William Aug. Hardcastle	7 Mar. 1811	
	William Smith	16 May	
	Charles Shaw	15 Jan. 1812	13 May 1811
	Arthur Grueber	25 June	
	John Edwards	23 July	
	Henry Brown	5 Nov.	
	—— Astier	26 do.	
Paymaster	William Bell	12 Dec. 1811	
Adjutant - -	William Shaw	18 Apr. 1805	Lieut. 5 Nov. 1806
QuarterMaster	James Spence	7 Sept. 1804	
Surgeon -	Fletcher Wells	16 Apr. 1807	26 Sept. 1795
Assistant Surg.	Maurice F— G— Quill	19 May 1808	17 Apr. 1806
	Edward Graham	18 Oct. 1810	
	Mathew Farnan	18 July 1811	

N. B. *The Officers printed in Italics are to be placed upon Half-pay on arrival from Foreign Service.*

Facings buff.—Lace silver.

Agent, Messrs. Greenwood, Cox and Hammersley.

(2d BATTALION DISBANDED.)

Rank.	Name.	Rank in the Regiment.	Army.
Colonel - -	Alexander Campbell	15Feb.1813	Gen. 1Jan.1812
Lieut. Colonel	James Maitland	18Aug.1814	30Nov.1809
Major - ◎− {	John Hicks John Bennet	3Aug.1804 12June1806	Lt.Col. 4June1811 Lt. Col. 4June1813
Captain -	Charles Hames Henry Ross Lewen William H— Toole John Crowe Goodwin Purcell Jaques Boyse Thomas Cassan Edward Whitty William Trueman Robert Dillon	25May1803 6Aug.1804 7Sept. 30May1805 3Mar.1808 17do. 14Sept.1809 17May1810 8Nov. 10Oct.1811	Major 1Jan.1812 Major 4June1814 Major 4June1814 Major 4June1813 7Aug.1806 16Apr.1807
Lieutenant	Charles Wallett Wm. Henry Thornton Henry William Brookes David Davies George Barr Michael William Meighan Samuel Hill Lawrence Theobald Butler John Boase Thomas Ross Lewin Henry Butterworth John Shaw M'Culloch James Robert Colthurst Michael Dennie Boyle Hill James Jarvey William Sherlock James Robinson George Brock R — Tresillian Belcher James Fitz Gerald Thomas James Horan Edward Stephens	9Oct.1806 23do. 14May1807 6Nov. 7do. 9do. 10do. 28Apr.1808. 9June 15Dec. 27Apr.1809 10Aug. 13Oct. 15Mar.1810 22do. 26Apr. 3May 17do. 19July 17Jan 1811 11July 11June1812 10Sept.	 18June1807 Adjut. 8May 1806 16Jan. 1806 26Mar.1807 10Apr. 1806 31Dec. 1807

Ensign

Rank.	Name.	Rank in the Regiment.	Army.
Ensign	George Small	31 Dec. 1812	
	Jasper Lucas	6 Jan. 1813	
	James M'Conchy	7 do.	
	Henry Metcalfe	18 Mar.	
	John Birtwhistle	14 Apr.	
	Alexander Stewart	15 do.	
	George Brown	10 June	
	Wm. Richard Tisdall	14 Aug.	
Paymaster	Thomas Hart	26 July 1810	
Adjutant	David Davies	16 Mar. 1809	Lieut. 18 June 1807
Quarter-Master	William Stevens	19 Sept. 1804	
Surgeon	William Buchanan	17 Mar. 1804	9 July 1803
Assistant Surg.	Rynd Lawder	25 May 1809	
	Hugh M'Clintock	5 Nov. 1812	

Facings white.—Lace gold.

Agent, Messrs. Hopkinson and Son, No. 5, St. Alban's Street, Pall Mall.

232 33d (or the 1st Yorkshire W. Riding) Regt of Foot.

Rank.	Name.	Rank in the Regiment.	Rank in the Army.
Colonel -	©*Sir*J.CopeSherbrooke,*K.B.*1Jan.1813		Lt.Gen. 4June1811
Lieut. Colonel	Wm.Keith Elphinstone 30Sept.1813		
Major - -	{ William Lambton	1Mar.1808	Lt.Col. 4June1814
	{ Edward Parkinson	17Mar.1814	27Oct. 1810
	{ John Guthrie	7July	
Captain -	{ Matthew Rob. Freeman 25June1809		
	William M'Intyre	3Dec.1810	
	George Colclough	26Aug.1811	27June1811
	Charles Knight	26Dec.	30Aug.1810
	John Haigh	6Aug.1812	
	{ William Pagan	4Feb.1813	
	J— M— Harty	11Mar.	
	Benjamin Sullivan	6May	Major 4June1814
	Lachlan M'Quarrie	7Apr.1814	
	Ralph Gore	28July	
	{ John Longden	8Sept.	
Lieutenant -	{ John Haigh	16Apr.1806	
	Thomas Reid	20July	
	Robert Kerr	23Dec.	
	Peter Barailler	7Sept.1809	21Mar.1807
	George Barrs	14Nov.	
	Henry Rishton Buck	16do.	
	Arthur Hill Trevor	1Jan.1810	
	Edward J— Priestley	24Aug.	Adjutant
	John Boyce	1Jan.1811	
	William Pode	12do.	
	J— Hart	25Apr.	
	{ James Murkland	1June	1June1810
	Frederick Hope Pattison 24Sept.1812		
	Arthur Gore	11Mar.1813	
	Richard Westmore	1Apr.	
	Thomas D— Haigh	29July	28Jan. 1812
	George Whannell	16Mar.1814	
	James Gordon Ogle	17do.	
	Donald Miller	6Apr.	
	Samuel Alexander Pagan 7do.		
	Edward Clabon	18Aug.	
	Joseph Lynam	8Sept.	
	{ John Archbold	27Oct.	

Ensign

| Rank. | Name. | Rank in the | |
		Regiment.	Army.
Ensign	John Cameron	14May1812	
	Frederick Bannatyne	1Oct.	
	Henry Bain	15do.	
	James Forlong	11Mar.1813	
	Edward Canning	8Apr.	
	John Alderson	21do.	
	William Bain	22do.	
	James Arnot Howard	6May	
	William Thain	13do.	
	Andrew Watson	10June	
	Charles Smith	24do.	
	William Hodson	21Apr.1814	
	Gerald Blackall	12May	
	Wm. Jervis Ricketts	29Sept.	
Paymaster	Edward Stoddart	2Apr.1807	
Adjutant	Edward J— Priestley	2Dec.1813	Lieut. 24Aug.1810
Quarter-Master	James Fazarekerley	25Sept.1808	
Surgeon	Robert Leaver	31Mar.1814	
Assistant Surg.	William D— Fry	12Nov.1812	
	D— Finlayson	31Mar.1814	

Facings red.—Lace silver.

Agent, Messrs. Greenwood, Cox and Hammersley.

Rank.	Name.	Rank in the Regiment.	Army.
Colonel - -	*Sir* Eyre Coote, K. B.	25June1810	Gen. 4June1814
Lieut. Colonel	{ John Maister	20Aug.1807	Col. 4June1814
	John M— Everard	23Jan.1812	
	Henry Roberts	27Jan.1814	
Major - ◎—	{ Henry Charles Dickens	26June1809	Lt.Col. 4June1814
	Henry Worsley	23Jan.1812	Lt.Col. 21June1813
	Geo. Edw. Pratt Barlow	26Mar.	
	Charles Ramus Forrest	2June1814	
Captain - -	{ Jerome Burdett	20May1805	
	Thomas Faunt	9July1806	
	Thomas Hogarth	10do.	
	William Salter Willett	10Nov.1807	2Dec. 1806
	Edward Broderick	11do.	2Dec. 1806
	C— B— Fancourt	12do.	3Dec. 1806
	John Arms Ellard	2Dec.	
	Richard Egerton	14Apr.1808	Major 26Aug.1813
	Mark M'Leod Tew	19Jan.1809	
	Francis Hay	21Sept.	
	Timothy Davies	1Feb.1810	
	William Baker	11Oct.	
	Philip Geo. Wroughton	3Jan.1811	
	Samuel R— Dickens	20June	
	Hector Macalister	29Aug.	
	Richard Daily	17Oct.	
	Moyle Sherer	26Mar.1812	
	D— W— Ross	10June1813	
	George Bristow	13July	Major 4June1814
	Robert Brown	21Oct.	
	Thomas Gerrard Ball	7Apr.1814	
Lieutenant -	{ John Stack	18Dec.1805	25Feb. 1805
	Alexander Davidson	30Oct.1806	3July 1806
	Peter Stone Barron	8Sept.1807	
	Edward Conolly	9do.	
	G— M— Ellis	10do.	
	Charles Pratt	3Dec.	
	George Robert Lascelles	1June1808	17Oct. 1799
	John Norton	22Sept.	2July 1807
	John Hay	9Mar.1809	

Lieutenant

Rank.	Name.	Rank in the	
		Regimen.	Army.

Lieutenant -	Thomas Thompson	7June1809	
	L— D— C— Walsh	8do.	
	Frederick Hovenden	21do.	
	James Sarjeant	22do.	
	Fitzm. Wm. Colthurst	12Oct.	
	John Huddleston	29Nov.	
	Thomas Mann Simkins	30do.	
	Edward Picking	7Dec.	
	David Richardson	13do.	
	Alexander M'Farlane	4Jan.1810	
	Wm. Henry Hamilton	18do.	
	John Elgie	1Feb.	
	John Harden	22do.	
	Nathan Hood	1Mar.	1June1801
	W— B— Stiles	10May	
	Henry Faunt	18do.	
	Thomas Thomson	24do.	
	——— Hearn	27June	
	James Edward Mogridge	28do.	
	John Henry Crawford	2Aug.	
	Edward Franco	23do.	9Nov.1809
	Maude Simmons	14Mar.1811	
	Newcomen Algeo	21do.	15Mar.1810
	James Robinson	2May	
	Godfrey Greene	30do.	15Jan. 1807
	Hector Straith	29Aug.	
	Charles Stewart	17Oct.	
	Joseph Murphy	9Apr.1812	
	John Shaw	2July	
	John Ainsworth	10June1813	
	William Macleod	20Oct.	
	Francis Bellingham Ellis	21do.	
	George Bell	17Feb.1814	
	John Duncan	17Mar.	12Oct. 1809
	A— Orrell	21Apr.	
	William Ewbank	8Dec.	
Ensign - -	George Manning	15May1811	
	Francis Pope	16do.	
	Francis Russell	29Aug.	
	John Harding	5Mar.1812	

Ensign

Rank.	Name.	Rank in the	
		Regiment.	Army.

Rank.	Name.	Regiment.	Army.
Ensign - -	Thomas L— Whitaker	13May1812	
	Thomas Mathison	1July	
	John Norman	2do.	
	—— Higginbottom	1Oct.	
	George Wilson	12Nov.	
	John Ready	31Dec.	Adjutant
	Sampson Pickett	25Feb.1813	Adjutant
	Thomas Eyre	7Apr.	
	Joseph Fletcher	8do.	
	Richard Chambers	13May	
	William Lax	5Aug.	
	Francis Stanford	21Oct.	
	Edward Bulkeley	25Dec.	
	Henry Trewhitt	30do.	
	Richard Hovenden	13Jan.1814	
	John Montgomerie	10Mar.	

Paymaster	2	Cornwall Jolliffe	27June1805	
Adjutant -		John Ready	31Dec.1812	Ensign 31Dec.1812
		Sampson Pickett	14Oct.1813	Ensign 25Feb.1813
Quarter Master		J— Stoddart	1May1805	
		Thomas Howe	23Jan.1812	
Surgeon -		Edw.ThornhillLuscombe	1Aug.1805	
		James Allardyce	17Mar.1814	30Mar.1809
Assistant Surg.		John Graham	7Oct.1805	
		Reginald Orton	30Sept.1810	
		Andrew Thompson	16Apr.1812	
		Robert Shean	28Jan.1813	

Facings yellow.—Lace silver.

Agent, Mr. Macdonald, Pall Mall Court.

Flank Companies of the 1st Battalion, and such other Officers and Men as served with the Army in Calabria under Sir John Stuart, permitted to bear the word " MAIDA" on their Appointments, in commemoration of the Action of 4th July, 1806.

Rank.	Name.	Rank in the Regiment.	Rank in the Army.
Colonel -	Cha.*D.*of Richmond,*K.G.*17Mar.1803		Gen. 4June1814
Lieut. Col. ✕⊂	{ Lorenzo Moore 14Sept.1809		
	{ Geo. Hen. F. Berkeley 13June1811		
Major - -	{ CæsarColclough Armett 26May1808		Lt.Col. 4June1814
	{ Charles Macalister 13June1811		
	{ Joseph Phillott 27May1813		
	{ John Slessor 7Oct.		Lt.Col. 4June1814
Captain -	{ Charles William Wall 19May1805		
	{ Phineas M'Pherson 21do.		
	{ William Johnson 22do.		
	{ Thomas Edgeworth 30do.		
	{ William Green 26July1806		
	{ Andrew Wilder 29July1807		
	{ Alexander Shaw 30do.		
	{ Theophilus Daly 11Feb.1808		
	{ —— May 18Aug.		4Feb. 1808
	{ William Rawson 4May1809		
	{ Henry Rutherford 3Aug.		
	{ Phillips Newton 13Sept.		
	{ Thomas King 14do.		
	{ Thomas Weare 19Apr.1810		Major 21June1813
	{ George Moulson 10Dec.1812		
	{ Thomas M'Niell 11Mar.1813		8Sept.1808
	{ Robert Cameron 10June		
	{ N— F— Dromgoole 29July		
	{ Archibald Macdonald 7Oct.		
	{ Charles Gregory 8Dec.		
	{ William M'Donald 9do.		
	{ Henry G— Macleod 10do.		29Sept.1813
Lieutenant	{ Samuel Scarfe 28Nov.1805		
	{ I— M— Philpot 12June1806		
	{ Thomas Stapley 5Aug.		
	{ William Walker 25Dec.		
	{ Hubert Theballier 26do.		
	{ —— Shadwell 22Jan.1807		
	{ —— Freeman 30July		
	{ Edward Davies 27Aug.		
	{ —— Ellis 21Jan.1808		

Lieutenant

Rank.	Name.	Rank in the Regiment.	Army.

| | | **Rank in the** | |
| **Rank.** | **Name.** | **Regiment.** | **Army.** |

Rank.	Name.	Regiment.	Army.
	Thomas Eustace	18Feb.1808	
	Richard Webb	26May	
	Alexander Sharrock	30June	
	Alfred Denison	25Aug.	
	J— W— Amos	13Apr.1809	
	———-- Emerson	11May	
	Francis Stenton	18do.	
	John Osbourne	3Aug.	
	John Denny	13Sept.	
	Thomas M'Donough	30Oct.	
	Christ. Spencer Breary	2Nov.	Adjutant
	Robert Thoburn	18Oct.1810	12Jan. 1809
	Angus M'Pherson	6June1811	
	William Farrant	29Jan.1812	
	Richard E— Butler	30do.	
Lieutenant -	Aylmer Barnewell	10Dec.	
	Joseph Routledge	24do.	
	Aralander Tennent	10June1813	
	——— Smelt	12Aug.	
	John Hildebrand	23Sept.	
	John Rudge	6Oct.	
	Nicholas Wilson	7do.	
	Thomas Austin	6Dec.	
	Thomas Badham	7do.	Adjutant
	———-- Murdock	8do.	
	James Wilder	9do.	
	Newland Rich. Tomkins	10do.	
	Edward Shewell	22do.	
	William Rainsforth	23do.	
	George Wilkins	1Sept.1814	
	H-- Middleton	1Dec.	7Oct. 1813
	John Murray Bliss	24Dec.1812	
	William Levitt Hedding	7Jan.1813	
	John Hewetson	13May	
	William Macalister	10June	
	John Lyster	12Aug.	
Ensign - -	John Conyers	23Sept.	
	Jeremiah Dawson	7Oct.	
	Hon. Schomberg Kerr	7Dec.	23Sept.1813
	Henry W-- S— Nixon	8do.	
	John Barwis Wyatt	22do.	
	Ant. Joseph Macdonnell	7Apr.1814	

Ensign

Rank.	Name.	Rank in the	
		Regiment.	Army.
Ensign - -	Herbert Potenger	7July1814	
	Robert Lizar	1Sept.	
	Alex. Duke Hamilton	27Oct.	
	—— Thomas	22Dec.	
	Edward Noel Gwinnell	16Feb.1815	
Paymaster - 1	David Home	20June1798	
Adjutant -	Thomas Badham	6Dec.1810	Lieut. 7Dec.1813
	Christ. Spencer Breary	23Dec.1813	Lieut. 2Nov.1809
QuarterMaster	—— Fitton	27June1805	
	—— Foote	2Dec.1813	
Surgeon -	James D— Tully	15Oct.1807	
	Charles Simon Doyle	31Mar.1808	
Assistant Surg.	Ralph Edon	22Sept.1808	
	William Keoghoe	22Feb.1810	
	John H— Ludlow	5Dec.1811	
	John Purcell	28July1814	

Facings Orange.— Lace silver.

Agent, Mr. Macdonald, Pall Mall Court.

(2d BATTALION DISBANDED.)

Rank.	Name.	Regiment.	Rank in the Army.
Colonel - -	Hon. Henry St. John	26Nov.1778	Gen. 26Jan.1797
Lieut. Colonel	Hon. Basil Cochrane	9Oct.1806	Col. 4June1814
Major - ◎ ◎	William Cross Martin Leggatt	8Dec.1808 30Jan.1812	Lt.Col.22Nov.1813
Captain - ◎–	Wm. Wright Swain Henry Vernon William Campbell William Wingfield Joseph Crosse John Fraser Richard Gilbert Charles Bayley Robert Blakeney *Hugh Douglas* Robert Noble Crosse	6Aug.1804 25do. 22Dec. 6Nov.1806 25Sept.1807 23May1811 2Jan.1812 15do. 16do. 1Oct. 16Feb.1815	Major 4June1814 Major 4June1814 Major 26Aug.1813 Major 12Apr.1814 1Dec.1806 Major 4June1811 10Sept.1812
Lieutenant	John Vincent James Thompson James Prendergast Thomas L'Estrange John H— Cruice Charles Moody Thomas Smith William M'Leod N— Cahill George Cairnes John Charles William Turnstall Noble Breton Henry O'Bré William Peacocke Richard Jas. Bourchier Benj. Hayes Holmes Wm. Henry Robertson John Dearman Gilbert Wakefield Edward Lewis Henry Ormsby *Richard Perham* John Colcroft	8Oct.1807 15do. 26Nov. 29Feb.1808 3Mar. 30June 2Mar.1809 27Apr. 30Aug.1810 2Jan.1812 20do. 21do. 22do. 13May 14do. 25June 13Aug. 3Sept. 6do. 8do. 9do. 1Oct. 25Jan.1813 27May	 10Feb. 1808 3Sept.1806 27July 1809 Adjutant

Ensign·

Rank.	Name.	Rank in the Regiment.	Army.
Ensign - -	⎧ Henry Blunt	25 June 1812	26 Mar. 1812
	William Pottinger	13 Aug.	
	Evan Macpherson	6 Sept.	
	Richard Montgomery	7 do.	
	James M'Cabe	8 do.	
	Thomas Gibbons	9 do.	
	George Dowman	8 Oct.	
	⎩ John Skerry	9 Dec.	
Paymaster -	William Fraser	7 Feb. 1804	
Adjutant - -	John Colcroft	28 Feb. 1812	Lieut. 27 May 1813
Quarter-Master	Joseph Kemp	16 June 1808	
Surgeon - -	William Harrison	29 Apr. 1813	
Assistant Surg.	⎰ William Lindsay	2 Nov. 1809	6 Apr. 1809
	⎱ John Simpson	8 Nov. 1810	

Facings gosling green.—Lace gold.

Agent, Mr. Croasdaile, Silver Street, Golden Square.

Permitted to inscribe on their Colours and Appointments the word " MINDEN."

Rank.	Name.	Rank in the Regiment.	Rank in the Army.
Colonel - -	*Sir* Charles Green, *Bt.*	17Feb.1814	Lt.Gen.25Oct.1809
Lieut. Colonel {	Fitzroy Grafton Maclean	30June1804	Lt.Gen. 4June1814
	Reginald James	20Feb.1812	
	Simon Hart	10June1813	1Jan. 1812
Major - - {	Andrew Tilt	20Feb.1812	
	G. Germaine Cochrane	10June1813	
	Gabriel Burer	1July	
Captain - - {	Edward Barwick	27June1805	
	Temple Fenton	14Nov.	
	George Brock	23Oct.1806	Major 4June1814
	Samuel Busby	7Apr.1808	
	William Bruce	4Aug.	
	Richard Walton	2Mar.1809	
	Herbert P— Cox	15June	
	Archibald Taylor	14Feb.1811	20Sept.1810
	George C— Hicks	20Feb.1812	
	Robert Stephens	10June1813	
	Pierce Butler Galway	11do.	
	James Jackson	25do.	
	Henry Hofman	1July	
	Charles Waldron	2do.	
	Henry Owen Wood	22do.	
	Robert Rist	9Dec.	
	Edward Butler	2Feb.1814	
	Edward Druitt	3do.	
	Hon. John Finch	17do.	
	John Armstrong	10Mar.	
	Charles Elias Bird	11do.	
Lieutenant - {	John Costley	25Aug.1806	1Mar.1806
	Richard Graham	25Nov.	
	Cha. Amable Loppinot	5Mar.1807	
	John Daxon	12Apr.	
	John Grant	24June	
	Dillon Massey	7Apr.1808	
	John Spread Fenton	13Oct.	13June1806
	James Chalmers	1Mar.1809	
	John Sheppard	2do.	
	Silvanus Jones	11Apr.1811	27Oct. 1810
	John Alex. Wilkinson	3Oct.	
	Henry Dyer	17do.	
	George Middleton Dale	20Feb.1812	
	Henry Wilson	29Apr.	
	Francis Herrick	30do.	
	Garrett Hugh Fitz Gerald	9June1813	
	Richard Ker	10do.	

Lieutenant

Lieutenant	Henry Sadlier	11June1813	
	Thomas Plunkett	1July	
	Robert Stowards	2do.	
	William Johnson	22do.	
	John Griffin	23Sept.	
	Phillip Sullivan	6Dec.	
	Francis Lane	7do.	
	William Moir	8do.	
	John Ottey	9do.	
	George Garth Robinson	30do.	26Aug.1813
	William Jameson	2Feb.1814	
	John Bevan	3do.	
	Andrew Armstrong	4do.	
	Robert Crisp	5do.	Adjutant
	John Trydell	6do.	
	George Joynt	10Mar.	
	William Morgan	11May	
	William Ralph	12do.	
Ensign	George Milne Stevenson	21Apr.1813	
	John Fleming	22do.	
	George Chapman	29do.	
	William Metge	21July	
	John Lang	22do.	Adjutant
	Thomas L— Butler	5Aug.	
	Mark Rainsford	2Dec.	
	William Pearce	9do.	
	Thomas M'Leod	12Jan.1814	
	Isaac Moses	13do.	
	——— Blake	3Feb.	
	Michael Connolly	4do.	
	Edward Cox	10Mar.	
	William Long	17do.	
	Thomas Walsh	11May	
	Richard Gardiner	12do.	
Paymaster 1	James Halfhide	29June1809	
2	Robert Mackie	14Oct.1813	
Adjutant	John Lang	22July1813	Ensign 22July1813
	Robert Crisp	6Jan.1814	Lieut. 5Feb.1814
QuarterMaster	Samuel Woodford	25June1800	
	John Maitland	22July1813	
Surgeon	Samuel Tilt	9Sept.1813	4Feb. 1808
	William Thomas	28July1814	
Assistant Surg.	William Trumble	16May1811	
	Stephen Burke	10Sept.1812	
	Thomas Stobo	9Sept.1813	
	Robert A— M'Munn	1Sept.1814	

Facings yellow.—Lace silver.

Agent, Messrs. Greenwood, Cox and Hammersley.

244 38th (or the 1st Staffordshire) Regiment of Foot.
(2d BATTALION DISBANDED.)

Rank.	Name.	Rank in the Regiment.	Rank in the Army.
Colonel -	Geo. Ja. *Earl* Ludlow, *K.B.* 10Oct.1805	Gen.	4June1814
Lieut.Colonel ✕←*Hon.* Charles I. Greville 21Mar.1805		Col.	4June1813
Major - ◎- { Edward Miles 21Mar.1805		Lt.Col.	1Jan.1812
{ *Hon.* J— T— F— Deane 8Feb.1807		Col.	4June1814

Captain -			
	Thomas Evans	25June1803	Major 17Aug.1812
	Fletcher Wilkie	2Aug.1804	Major 1Jan.1812
	Thomas Willshire	28do.	Major 21Sept.1813
	William Taylor	7Sept.	Major 4June1814
	John L— Gallie	27do.	Major 4June1814
	John Philip Perry	14Apr.1808	
	Matthew Forster	2Nov.1809	Major 12Apr.1814
	James Baillie	14Feb.1811	
	Archibald Fullarton	2Apr.1812	
	George Hussey	10Sept.	

Lieutenant -			
	Wm. Handfield Wrench	22Oct.1807	
	Richard Cross	4Nov.	
	James Mathews	2June1808	Adjutant
	Duncan M'Gregor	15Sept.	3Jan. 1808
	John Magill	30Mar.1809	
	D— Osborne	11May	
	Geo. Henry Richardson	23Nov.	
	John M— Tittle	1Nov.1810	
	Edward Hopper	21Mar.1811	
	William Campbell	2Apr.1812	
	Adolphus Cooke	16July	
	Robert Dighton	7Sept.	
	Thomas G— Twigg	8do.	
	Thomas M— Oliver	9do.	
	Samuel Green	10do.	
	George Young	24Nov.	
	John Anderson	25do.	
	Alexander Campbell	26do.	
	James Martin	25Jan.1813	21Nov.1811
	Robert Read	23Apr.	
	Jas. Fitz Maurice Magee	12Aug.	
	R— Wilcocks	26do.	
	William Henry Robinson	27do.	

Ensign

Rank.	Name.	Rank in the Regiment.	Army.
Ensign	Robert Campbell	6May1813	
	James Horton Law	22July	
	Thomas Adams	27Aug.	
	Patrick Bain	22Sept.	
	Andrew Oliver	23do.	
	James Dunlop	24do.	
	Robert Matthew	26do.	
	Alexander Campbell	27Dec.	
Paymaster	Alexander Tod	28June1810	
Adjutant	James Mathews	1Sept.1808	Lieut. 2June1808
Quarter-Master	Thomas Biggar	14Sept.1804	
Surgeon	Dillon Jones	3Sept.1812	
Assistant Surg.	William Thompson	18Oct.1810	
	Samuel Cottnam	18Feb.1813	

Facings yellow.—Lace silver.

Agent, Messrs. Greenwood, Cox and Hammersley.

246 39th (or the Dorsetshire) Regiment of Foot.

Permitted to inscribe on their Colours and Appointments the word " GIBRALTAR."

Rank.	Name.	Rank in the Regiment.	Rank in the Army.
Colonel - -	Nisbett Balfour	2July1794	Gen. 25Sept.1803
Lieut. Colonel	Cavendish Sturt	1Apr.1813	25Oct. 1809
Major -	◎- Charles Bruce	21Mar.1805	Lt.Col. 25July1810
	◎ Patrick Lindesay	1Oct.1807	Lt.Col. 20June1811
	Roger Parke	25Feb.1808	Lt. Col. 4June1814
	Henry Standish	1Apr.1813	1Jan. 1812
Captain -	✖ Bryan O'Toole	9July1803	Lt.Col. 21June1813
	William Hart Lapslie	do.	Major 4June1813
	George D'Arcy	do.	Major 22Nov.1813
	◎ Duncan Campbell	31Mar.1804	Major 3Mar.1814
	John Watling	28Sept.	Lt.Col. 1Jan.1812
	Donald Macpherson	5Jan.1805	
	Charles Carthew	12Sept.	
	Stephen Cuppage	15Oct.1807	
	James Brine	3Mar.1808	
	Hardress Saunderson	5May	
	Robert Walton	15June1809	
	James William Wilson	14Feb.1811	Major 4June1814
	Samuel Thorpe	30July1812	16Apr. 1812
	Thomas Crosbie Meech	1Oct.	
	Exham Vincent	1Apr.1813	
	Joseph Allingham Jones	3June	
	John Bown	25Aug.	
	Alfred Barton	9Sept.	
	Francis Crotty	5May1814	
Lieutenant -	John Torner	14Mar.1805	
	John William Pollard	20Feb.1806	5Jan. 1805
	Simon Newport	3July	
	Henry Smith	14Jan.1807	
	Francis H— Hart	15do.	
	Wm. Johnston Hughes	12May1808	
	Coyne Reynolds	26do.	21Apr. 1808
	Stephen C— Bowen	17May1809	25July 1795
	Collet Barker	18do.	
	William Wheatley	19do.	
	George Coleman	21do.	
	Edward M'Arthur	6July	
	Thomas Baynes	20do.	
	Colwell Langton	21Dec.	
	James L— Hudson	19Apr.1810	
	A— G— Speirs	25Oct.	
	C— W— Campbell	2May1811	

Lieutenant

	Henry M'Minn	20June1811	
	Charles Cowley	10Sept.1812	
	Charles Cox	1Oct.	
	Arnold Nesbitt Purefoy	1Apr.1813	
	——— Caldecott	10June	
	Purefoy Poe	1July	
	Wm. Allan Courtenay	23Aug.	
	Robert Rhodes	24do.	
Lieutenant -	Robert Deane Franklin	25do.	
	Henry Erasmus South	26do.	
	Thomas Meyrick	9Sept.	Adjutant
	James Simpson	23do.	
	John Kingsbury	5Oct.	
	Richard Henry Evans	4Nov.	
	Edward Williams	12Dec.	26May 1813
	Daniel Grueber	21Apr.1814	
	George Hennell	24Nov.	22Oct. 1813
	Alfred J— Cathery	25June1812	
	Richard Meredith	1Apr.1813	
	Norman J— Bond	15do.	
	Mathew Fitz Patrick	24Aug.	
	——— Burns	25do.	
	Tho. Cochrane Cameron	26do.	
	Charles Sturt	9Sept.	
	John Leckie	5Oct.	
Ensign - -	John Fitz Gerald	6do.	
	Robert Miller	7do.	
	John Manby	4Nov.	
	W— H— Wilson	25Dec.	
	Sir Orford Gordon, *Bt.*	10Mar.1814	
	William Fenwick	17do.	
	——— Lloyd	21Apr.	
	Thomas Hunter	12May	
	William Nibbs	27Oct.	Adjutant
Paymaster - 2	Benjamin Bunn	26Aug.1806	
1	John Grant	21Sept.1809	
Adjutant -	Thomas Meyrick	26May1814	Lieut. 9Sept.1813
	William Nibbs	27Oct.	Ensign 27Oct.1814
QuarterMaster	John Sutcliffe	12Nov.1802	
	F— F— Wainwright	28Apr.1804	
Surgeon -	Roger Walker	3Dec.1803	
	Edward Johnson	15July1813	
	Arthur Hamilton	17May1810	
Assistant Surg.	Thomas Dillon	19Dec.1811	
	John Parke	26Nov.1812	26Mar.1812
	William Bromet	3Nov.1814	

Facings pea green.—Lace gold.

Agent, Messrs. Greenwood, Cox and Hammersley.

40th

Flank Companies permitted to bear on their Caps a " SPHINX," with the word " EGYPT," in commemoration of the Campaign of 1801.

Rank.	Name.	Rank in the Regiment.	Army.
Colonel - -	*Sir* George Osborn, *Bt.*	11Aug.1786	Gen. 26Jan.1797
Lieut. Col. ◎- ◎-	{ James Kemmis { Henry Thornton	1Aug.1804 13June1811	M.Gen. 4June1811 4June1811
Major - - ◎ ◎	⎧ John Gillies ⎨ John Whetham ⎪ James Moore ⎩ Arthur Rowley Heyland	8Feb.1807 13June1811 6Jan.1814 10Nov.	Lt.Col. 4June1813 M.Gen. 4June1814 26Aug.1813
Captain - ◎ ◎	⎧ Fielding Browne ⎪ Sempronius Stretton ⎪ Charles Downes ⎨ Richard Turton ⎪ Conyngham Ellis ⎪ James Lowrey ⎪ John Henry Barnett ⎪ Robert Phillips ⎪ William Fisher ⎨ Edward Cole Bowen ⎪ Peter Bishop ⎪ George Crompton ⎪ Robert Petty Stewart ⎪ Robert Morow ⎪ George Isaac Call ⎪ James Johnston ⎪ Benjamin M— Ball ⎪ Richard Jebb ⎩ Tho. Decimus Franklyn	22Dec.1804 11Sept.1806 12Feb.1807 10Feb.1808 30Nov.1809 14Mar.1811 13June 25July 19Sept. 7Nov. 12Mar.1812 13Aug. 7Oct. 21do. 22do. 24Feb.1814 21Apr. 12May 10Nov.	Major 4June1814 Major 22Nov.1813 25Apr. 1806 16June1808 21Sept.1809 26Dec. 1811 9May 1811
Lieutenant -	⎧ John Thorau ⎪ —— Kelly ⎪ William Toole ⎪ Theobald O'Dogherty ⎪ Michael Chadwick ⎪ Robert Moore ⎪ Wm. Oliver Sandwith ⎨ William Manning ⎪ James Butler ⎪ Nathan Truman Carter ⎪ Henry Millar ⎪ John Richardson ⎪ James Anthony ⎪ Constantine Gorman ⎩ —— Mill	28May1807 13Aug. 25do. 28do. 25Mar.1808 14Apr. 25May1809 14Sept. 14Dec. 1Mar.1810 5Sept. 6do. 16May1811 12Sept. 18do.	 2Oct. 1805 Adjutant

Lieutenant

Lieutenant	——— Glynne	19Sept.1811	
	William Neilly	26do.	
	Richard Hudson	7Nov.	
	John Armstrong	23Apr.1812	
	Henry Wilkinson	12May	
	John Foulkes	14do.	
	Thomas Campbell	3Sept.	
	H— B— Wray	10do.	
	Richard Jones	8Oct.	
	Hon. Michael Browne	10Dec.	
	Isaac Chetham	17do.	10Dec. 1812 Adjut.
	Charles Shuckburgh	5Aug.1813	
	Hugh M'Dougall	12do.	
	Michael Smith	23do.	
	J— Charles Wallace	24do.	
	Hayes Queade	25do.	
	Illay Robb	23Dec.	
	J— A— Widenham	24Feb.1814	
	John Moloney	20Apr.	
	John Garner	21do.	
	James Glynn	16Feb.1815	
Ensign	Donald M'Donald	22Oct.1812	
	Frederick Ford	10Dec.	
	George Hibbert	25Feb.1813	
	Richard Rudd	22Apr.	
	Henry Hemsley	25do.	
	J— L— Wall	25Aug.	
	P— Harley	26do.	
	Henry Glyn	25Nov.	
	Edw. John H. Brisco	23Dec.	
	William Clerke	6Jan.1814	
	William Browne	21do.	
	George Atkinson	16June	
	Gustavus Lambart	20Oct.	1July 1813
	Henry Sturt Napier	16Feb.1815	
Paymaster 2	George Godfrey	5June1810	
1	Fred. Holland Durand	10Mar.1814	
Adjutant	William Manning	24Oct.1811	Lieut. 14Sept.1809
	Isaac Chetham	17Dec.1812	Lieut. 10Dec.1812
Quarter Master	——— Sanderson	28May1807	
	——— Randall	14Mar.1811	
Surgeon	Thomas Fearon	27Aug.1812	9June1808
	William Jones	3Sept.	
Assistant Surg.	William Barry	4Jan.1810	
	George Scott	9Sept.1813	
	James Ewing	26May1814	

Facings buff.—Lace gold.

Agent, Messrs. Collyer, Park Place, St. James's.

i

41st

Rank.	Name.	Rank in the Regiment.	Rank in the Army.
Colonel - -	Josiah Champagné	22Feb.1810	Lt.Gen. 25July1810
Lieut. Colonel {	Henry Proctor	9Oct.1800	M.Gen. 4June1813
	William Evans	13Aug.1812	
Major - - {	Richard O'Farrell Friend	9Dec.1813	25July 1810
	J. Goulston PriceTucker	27Jan.1814	Col. 4June1814
Captain - {	William Derenzy	25June1803	Major 4June1814
	Adam Muir	9Feb.1804	Major 4June1814
	Joseph Tallon	17Apr.1806	
	Peter L— Chambers	12May1808	
	Richard Bullock	14Sept.1809	
	W. Caulfield Saunders	16May1811	
	Edward M'Coy	1Aug.	
	Hedges Cradock	11Aug.1812	
	Hugh Bowen	12do.	
	James Lewis Hill	13do.	
	Joseph Barry Glew	4Jan.1813	18May1809
Lieutenant {	B— W— Bluett	8Feb.1810	
	Angus M'Intyre	2Apr.	
	Alexander Major	3do.	
	Benoit Bender	4do.	
	Edward Cartwright	5do.	29Jan. 1807
	Harris Hailes	19do.	
	William Watson	26do.	
	Thomas Taylor	13Dec.	
	Benjamin Geale	24Apr.1811	
	Allan Henry Maclean	25do.	
	Charles Lenn	15Aug.	
	George Taylor	10Aug.1812	
	James Clemens	11do.	
	Wm. Gregory Gardiner	12do.	
	Reginald Barnett	10Dec.	
	Samuel Smith	24do.	
	John Smith	3Jan.1813	Adjutant
	John Highmore Jeboult	4do.	
	William Edge	5do.	
	Walter O'Reilly	6do.	
	William Hickey	7do.	
	Francis Wm. Small	22Apr.	14Nov.1811
	James Mompesson	15July	
	George Charles Mence	21Oct.	

Ensign

Rank.	Name.	Rank in the	
		Regiment.	Army.

Rank.	Name.	Regiment.	Army.
Ensign -	Henry Dive Townshend	16July1812	
	Philip Purdon	10Sept.	
	James Cochran	17do.	
	John Dardis	29Oct.	
	Henry Procter	7Jan.1813	
	Robert Edward Carey	28do.	
	Charles Harrison	10Feb.	
	William Jones Hall	11do.	
Paymaster -	James Raye	27Aug.1803	
Adjutant -	John Smith	30May1811	Lieut. 3Jan.1813
Quarter-Master	———— Bent	30May1811	
Surgeon - -	John Harford	8July1813	8Nov.1810
Assistant Surg.	William Faulkner	14June1810	
	William Forsyth	26Jan.1815	

Facings red.—Lace silver.

Agent, Messrs. Greenwood, Cox and Hammersley.

252   42d (or the Royal Highland) Regt. of Foot.

(2d BATTALION DISBANDED.)

Permitted to bear on their Colours and Appointments a " SPHINX," with the word " EGYPT," in commemoration of the Campaign of 1801 ; also the word " CORUNNA," for the Action of 16th Jun. 1809.

Rank.	Name.	Rank in the Regiment.	Rank in the Army.
Colonel - -	Geo. *Marq. of* Huntly	3Jan.1806	Lt.Gen.25Apr.1808
Lieut. Col.	◎–Robert Macara	16Apr.1812	1Jan. 1812
Major -	◎– { Robert Henry Dick	14July1808	Lt.Col. 8Oct.1812
	◎ { William Cowell	30May1811	Lt.Col. 3Mar.1814
	{ James Walker	28Sept.1804	Major 12Apr.1814
	| Archibald Menzies	5June1805	
	| George Davidson	25Sept.1807	Major 4June1813
	| John Campbell	3Dec.	Major 12Apr.1814
	| Murdoch M'Laine	16June1808	Major 4June1814
Captain -	{ Mungo Macpherson	9Feb.1809	
	| Thomas Francis Wade	13July	Major 21June1813
	| Donald Macdonald	25Jan.1810	
	| Daniel M'Intosh	2May1811	
	| Robert Boyle	11July	
	(Alexander Fraser	10Oct.	
	(Donald Chisholm	10Oct.1805	
	| Duncan Stewart	1Jan.1807	
	| Donald M'Kenzie	23July	3Dec. 1806
	| James Stirling	27Aug.	
	| James Young	25May1808	Adjutant
	| Charles M'Laren	2June.	28Apr. 1808
	| Hugh Andrew Fraser	8Feb.1809	
	| Ron. Angus M'Kinnon	16Nov.	
Lieutenant -	{ John Malcolm	14Dec.	
	| Alexander Dunbar	25Jan.1810	
	| Alexander Stewart	27Dec.	
	| James Brander	2May1811	
	| Roger Stewart	11July	
	| Robert Gordon	29Aug.	
	| James Robertson	10Oct.	
	| Alexander Strange	18Dec.	10Oct. 1811
	(Kenneth M'Dougall	12Feb.1812	

Lieutenant

Rank.	Name.	Rank in the Regiment.	Army.
Lieutenant -	Donald M'Kay Alexander Innes John Grant Alexander Wishart John Orr	28May1812 15Oct. 18Feb.1813 25do. 29Apr.	9July 1812
Ensign -	Alexander Mercer George Gerard William Fraser George Gordon A— L— Fraser Alexander Brown John Malcolm Alexander Cumming	15Apr.1813 29do. 10June 5Aug. 23Sept. 25Dec. 6Jan.1814 17Feb.	16Sept.1813
Paymaster -	John Home	21Mar.1800	
Adjutant -	James Young	31Mar.1814	Lieut. 25May1808
Quarter-Master	Donald Macintosh	9July1803	
Surgeon - -	Swinton Macleod	9July1803	
Assistant Surg.	Donald Macpherson John Stewart	1June1809 20July	4May 1809

Facings blue.—Lace gold.

Agent, Messrs. Greenwood, Cox and Hammersley.

(LIGHT INFANTRY.)

Rank.	Name.	Regiment.	Army.

Rank in the

		Regiment.	Army.
Colonel -	*Sir* John Fra. Cradock, *K.B.*	7 Jan. 1809	Gen. 4 June 1814

Lieut. Col.	◎ { C— C— Patrickson { Joseph Wells	17 June 1813 4 Aug. 1814	30 May 1811

Major -	◎—(Wm. Fra. Patr. Napier) Nicolas Alex. Mein ◎) John Duffy (William Haverfield	14 May 1812 25 Jan. 1813 17 June 11 Aug. 1814	Lt.Col. 22 Nov. 1813 Lt.Col. 4 June 1814 6 Feb. 1812

Captain -	(Robert Dalzell | Saumarez Brock | William Sherran | Thomas Champ | Joseph Chapman | John Proctor | Robert Simson | *Sir* J. Max. Tylden, *Kt.* | John Swinburn | George Johnson { William Morrison | John Paul Hopkins | John Pitts | Thomas Rylance | Henry Booth | James Shaw | Samuel Hobkirk | Samuel Pollock | William Freer | Bernard Murphy (Cooke Tylden Pattenson	26 Aug. 1804 6 Aug. 1807 8 Sept. 1808 15 do. 9 Mar. 1809 4 May 17 Aug. 28 Sept. 15 Aug. 1810 16 do. 27 Dec. 29 Aug. 1811 10 Oct. 14 May 1812 25 June 16 July 3 Dec. 18 Feb. 1813 1 Dec. 2 do. 18 Aug. 1814	Major 12 Apr. 1814 28 Mar. 1805 Major 19 Dec. 1811

Lieutenant -	(George Houlton) George Berkeley { Wyndham Madden) J— C— Lunn (Thomas Lalor	6 Oct. 1808 6 Apr. 1809 3 May 17 Aug. 17 Oct.	

Lieutenant

[1815]

43d (or the Monmouthshire) Regt. of Foot.   255
(LIGHT INFANTRY.)

Rank.	Name.	Rank in the Regiment.	Rank in the Army.
Lieutenant -	*Hon.* Charles Gore	4 Jan. 1810	
	John Cooke	19 Apr.	
	John Montgomery Hill	28 June	
	Edward D'Arcey	22 Aug.	
	John Meyricke	23 do.	
	James Considine	27 Dec.	
	John Maclean	27 M. r. 1811	
	Richard Carroll	2 May	
	Philip Macpherson	13 June	
	Duncan Campbell	29 Aug.	
	Henry Banbrick	12 Sept.	
	Alexander Steele	7 Nov.	
	William Havelock	12 May 1812	
	Bartholomew Casey	21 do.	
	George Hood	28 do.	
	Robert Crawford	25 June	
	Benjamin Whichcote	16 July	
	Thomas Hunt Grubbe	15 Oct.	
	John Maclean	10 Dec.	
	James Imlach	25 Jan. 1813	23 July 1812
	Thomas Beckham	23 Feb.	
	Nicholas Cundy	24 do.	
	Hon. Charles Monck	25 do.	
	John Nevill Robinson	18 Mar.	
	Lawrence Steele	21 Apr.	Adjutant
	John Echlin Matthews	22 do.	
	Richard O'Connell	15 July	
	G— C— Campbell	2 Sept.	
	Ben. Hutcheon Edwards	21 Oct.	
	William Carruthers	1 Dec.	
	Massey Hutch. Warren	2 do.	
	Henry Wise Coates	9 do.	
	George Dobson	22 Feb. 1814	
	John Marshal Miles	23 do.	
	Edward Rowley Hill	24 do.	
	William Allan	3 Mar.	
	Ro. Mulcaster Auchmuty	22 Sept.	
	Samuel Curtis	24 Nov.	7 Oct. 1813
	Isaac Herbert	8 Dec.	31 Mar. 1808

Ensign

(LIGHT INFANTRY.)

Rank.	Name.	Rank in the Regiment.	Army.
Ensign - -	Richard James Shaw	25Feb.1813	
	John Maxwell Williams	22Apr.	
	Alex. Browne Baxter	5Aug.	
	John Finley	2Sept.	
	Thomas Thornelly	21Oct.	
	John Pollock	25Nov.	
	—— Harris	16Dec.	Adjutant
	Henry Hatton	23do.	
	Thomas H— Bishop	25do.	
	William Kirshaw	do.	
	Robert Wm. Henry Drury	do.	
	—— Considine	23Feb.1814	
	William Cradock	3Mar.	
	Richard Ponsonby Webb	20Apr.	
	Rich. Wm. Lambrecht	21do.	
	William Powell	28do.	
	William Sharpe	2June	
Paymaster 2	David Fraser	11Oct.1810	
1	Thomas Tierney	23July1812	
Adjutant -	Lawrence Steele	21Nov.1811	Lieut. 21Apr.1813
	—— Harris	16Dec.1813	Ensign 16Dec.1813
Quarter-Mast.	James Elliott	23Nov.1804	
	David Williams	29Nov.1810	
Surgeon - -	James Gilchrist	15Dec.1804	
	William Jones	9Mar.1809	
Assistant Surg.	Henry Edwards	15Oct.1812	
	Archibald Hair	12Nov.	
	Thomas M— Perrott	25Mar.1813	26Apr. 1810

Facings white.—Lace silver.

Agent, Messrs. Greenwood, Cox and Hammersley.

*Permitted to bear on their Colours and Appointments a " SPHINX," with the word " EGYPT,"
in commemoration of the Campaign of 1801.*

Rank.	Name.	Regiment.	Army.
Colonel - -	John, *Earl of* Suffolk	12Jan.1814	Gen. 29Apr.1802
Lieut. Colonel {	Arthur Brooke	15June1804	Col. 4June1813
	John M— Hamerton	31Mar.1814	4June1811
Major - ⊚ {	Charles Phillips	14Jan.1802	M.Gen. 4June1814
	George Harding	16Aug.1805	Lt.Col. 1Jan.1812
	Edward Gregory	27Nov.1806	Lt.Col. 4June1813
	Fountain Elwin	31Mar.1814	4June1813
Captain - {	*Hon.* Thomas Mullens	9July1803	Lt.Col. 1Jan.1812
	Henry Nixon	do.	Lt.Col. 1Jan.1812
	Henry Debbeig	do.	Lt.Col. 29Sept.1814
	John A— Johnson	do.	Lt.Col. 29Sept.1814
	Archibald M'Auley	do.	Major 4June1814
	John Cruice	do.	Major 4June1814
	J— Chilton L— Carter	do.	Major 4June1814
	Ambrose Lane	18Feb.1804	Major 4June1814
	John Jessop	15June	Major 4June1814
	John Cleland Guthrie	21Mar.1805	
	Adam Brugh	11June1807	12Feb. 1807
	David Power	31Dec.	
	T— A— Dudie	1Mar.1810	
	George Henderson	22do.	18May 1809
	Bostock Jacob	20Sept.	
	George Crozier	16Jan.1812	
	Thomas Mackarell	1Oct.	
	George Clarges Hill	19May1814	
	William Burney	2June	
	Wm. Alexander Craig	7July	
Lieutenant - {	John Blakeney	16Aug.1805	
	Andrew Donaldson	22Jan.1807	
	Rowland Davies	5Mar.	
	Thomas Mackrell	25May	
	Richard Cruice	26do.	
	William M'Lean	27do.	
	William Knight	28do.	
	Daniel Caulfield	18June	
	James P— Shaw	13Aug.	8Jan. 1807
	Thomas Ricketts	2Dec.	22Oct. 1807

k

Lieutenant

Rank.	Name.	Rank in the Regiment.	Army.
Lieutenant -	Robert Russell	14July1808	
	Frederick Hemming	23Mar.1809	
	Ralph John Twinberrow	30do.	
	Thomas Palmer	8Feb.1810	
	John Connor	9Aug.	
	Robert Smith	15Aug.1811	
	William Wood	29do.	
	Henry Brush	12Dec.	
	George Clark Beatty	30Jan.1812	
	Temple Fred. Sinclair	20Feb.	
	Robert Grier	13May	
	Dering Carey	14do.	
	Richard Perry	3Sept.	
	George Newberry	1Oct.	
	Richard Phelan	26Nov.	
	Charles Monck	31Dec.	
	John O'Reilly	22Apr.1813	
	William Tomkins	20May	
	William Jones	21do.	
	EdwardStephens Clarke	10June	
	Thomas Horner	9Dec.	
	W— B— Strong	16do.	
	John Campbell	28Mar.1814	
	Nich. Toler Kingsley	29do.	
	James Burke	30do.	
	Henry Martin	31do.	
	William Marcus Hern	7July	
	Robert Peacocke	14do.	
Ensign - -	Alexander Reddock	11June1812	
	Haffez Mence	13Aug.	
	James White	25Nov.	
	James Christie	26do.	
	Benjamin Whitney	25Feb.1813	
	Henry Woodcock	22Apr.	
	Gillespie Dunlevie	20May	
	Philip North	5Aug.	
	Matthew Mac Closkey	1Nov.	
	Peter Cooke	18do.	
	Robert L— Haydon	24Feb.1814	
	Robert Barry	10Mar.	Adjutant
	Richard Mackrell	28do.	
	John Donaldson	29do.	

Ensign

Rank.	Name.	Rank in the	
		Regiment.	Army.
Ensign - -	Thomas M'Cann	31Mar.1814	Adjutant
	Wm. Henry Sperling	14Apr.	
	James Carnegie Webster	21do.	
	Alexander Wilson	19May	
	William Rogers	7July	
Paymaster 1	James Allsop	12Nov.1807	
2	James Williams	4Oct.1810	
Adjutant -	Robert Barry	10Mar.1814	Ensign 10Mar.1814
	Thomas M'Cann	7Apr.	Ensign 31Mar.1814
QuarterMaster	—— Jones	9July1803	
	Richard Berry	10Mar.1814	
Surgeon - -	Griffith Jones	5Nov.1812	28Mar.1811
	Oliver Halpin	29Apr.1813	11Apr.1811
Assistant Surg.	John Collins	1Dec.1808	
	William Newton	27Dec.1810	
	William Vallange	22Aug.1811	7Dec. 1809
	George Barclay	do.	

Facings yellow.—Lace silver.

Agent, Mr. Macdonald, Pall Mall Court, Pall Mall.

(2d BATTALION DISBANDED.)

Rank.	Name.	Rank in the	
		Regiment.	Army.
Colonel - -	Cavendish Lister	22Apr.1802	Gen. 25Sept.1803
Lieut. Colonel	⊚Leonard Greenwell	19May1814	17Aug.1812
Major - -	{ David Leckey	28Feb.1811	Lt.Col. 1Jan.1812
	{ Hugh Stacpoole	18July	
Captain -	⎧ Oliver Mills	21Nov.1805	Major 4June1814
	⎪ James Campbell	29Dec.1808	Major 3Mar.1914
	⎪ Alexander Martin	30Mar.1809	
	⎪ Alexander M'Dougall	28Dec.	
	⎨ William Hardwick	1Mar.1810	
	⎪ J— Massey Stacpoole	31May	Major 4June1811
	⎪ Thomas Hilton	23Aug.	26Jan. 1809
	⎪ Alexander Anderson	25Oct.	
	⎪ John Cole	28Feb.1811	
	⎩ Henry Evelyn	26June	Major 4June1814
Lieutenant -	⎧ Richard Colley	22June1809	
	⎪ Thomas Parr	20July	
	⎪ Richard Kelly	27do.	
	⎪ James M'Pherson	28Feb.1810	
	⎪ Hans Stevenson Marsh	1Apr.	
	⎪ Edmund French Boys	3do.	
	⎪ William Berwick	4do.	
	⎪ John Evans Trevor	18Oct.	
	⎪ Hugh Forbes	20Nov.	
	⎪ Daniel Stewart	21do.	
	⎨ Edward Francis Moore	22do.	
	⎪ William Francis Reynett	28Feb.1811	
	⎪ Joseph Douglas	10Apr.	20Dec. 1810
	⎪ Philip Stopford Cosby	11do.	
	⎪ Richard Hill	2Mar.1812	
	⎪ James Coghlan	3do.	
	⎪ Charles Munro	5do.	
	⎪ James Stewart	1Apr.	
	⎪ John Grant	30do.	
	⎪ R— M'Gibbon	14May	
	⎪ John Forbes	21do.	
	⎩ Tankerville Drew	20Aug.	

Ensign

Rank.	Name.	Rank in the Regiment.	Army.
Ensign	Lamb. Brabaz. Urmston	1 Apr. 1813	
	George Croasdaile	15 do.	
	——— Edmonds	13 May	
	William Carstairs	17 June	
	William Arthur Browne	29 July	
	William Gibson Willes	9 Sept.	
	Edward Smyth	16 do.	
	——— Creswell	7 Oct.	
	John Maples	16 June 1814	Adjutant
Prymaster	Marcus Dalhunty	28 Oct. 1807	
Adjutant	John Maples	16 June 1814	Ensign 16 June 1814
Quarter-Master	Lawrence Walsh	19 Dec. 1811	
Surgeon	William Smyth	22 Aug. 1811	
AssistantSurg.	Henry W— Radford	19 Apr. 1810	
	James Patterson	22 Aug. 1811	

Facings dark green.—Lace silver.

Agent, Messrs. Greenwood, Cox and Hammersley.

Permitted to bear the word " DOMINICA" on their Colours and Appointments, in commemoration of the Defence of that Island, 22d February, 1805.

Rank.	Name.	Rank in the Regiment.	Army.
Colonel - -	John Whyte	5Jan.1804	Gen. 1Jan.1812
Lieut. Colonel	{ George Molle { Archibald Campbell	3June1813 17Feb.1814	Col. 4June1814
Major - -	{ Alexander Ogilvie { John M'Kenzie	4Feb.1813 17Feb.1814	
Captain -	{ John Campbell James Stewart William G— B— Schaw John Mander Gill William Nairn Edward Sanderson James Wallis Alexander Thompson Andrew Clarke Thomas Miller { Henry Taylor Budd	29Aug.1805 12Apr.1807 8Oct. 24Mar.1809 29June 27Sept.1810 19Dec.1811 17Sept.1812 4Feb.1813 17Feb.1814 21Apr.	Major 1Jan.1812 Major 1Jan.1812 4Aug.1813
Lieutenant -	{ Thomas Thompson John Watts Nathaniel Browne Charles Higgins William James Carr Alexander Campbell Hans Morrison John Crabb Hen. K— Hemsworth Charles Dawe James Henry Hamilton Thomas Kenagh Smith Bern. Rich. O. Connor George Grant Tobias Purcell Douglas Leith Cox Thomas Carne William Cox John Henry French H— Tisdall Adamson George Parker { David Vans Machen	27Sept.1804 25Dec. 27Mar.1805 1Sept. 16Jan.1807 16June 15Feb.1808 10Nov. 15June1809 15Feb.1810 1Aug. 11Oct. 22Nov. 2Jan.1811 17Sept.1812 29Oct. 4Feb.1813 27July 26Aug. 10Nov. 11do. 24Nov.1814	 4Mar.1805 2Dec. 1812 27July 1814

Ensign

Rank.	Name.	Rank in the Regiment.	Army.

Ensign	Hamilton Joseph Wilson	7Jan.1813	Adjutant
	James Madigan	29Apr.	
	John Skelton	20May	
	JohnOliver HoweNunn	26Aug.	
	George Stuart	10Nov.	
	G— A— Mahon	13Jan.1814	
	Thomas Stedman	14Apr.	
	William Abbott	15Sept.	

Paymaster	John Campbell	9June1808	
Adjutant	James Madigan	29Apr.1813	Ensign 29Apr.1813
Quarter-Master	Hugh Macdonald	8July1813	
Surgeon	Thomas Forster	19Nov.1812	26July 1810
Assistant Surg.	George Bush	3June1813	
	Samuel Hood	17do.	

Facings pale yellow.—Lace silver.

Agent, Messrs. Greenwood, Cox and Hammersley.

47th

264 47th (or the Lancashire) Regiment of Foot.

(2d BATTALION DISBANDED.)

*Permitted to inscribe on their Colours and Appointments the word " TARIFA" in comme-
moration of the defence of that place, 31st Dec. 1811.*

Rank.	Name.	Regiment.	Rank in the Army.
Colonel -	Hon. Sir Alex. Hope, *K.B.*	26Apr.1813	Lt.Gen. 4June1813
Lieut. Colonel	Humphrey Bland	3May1810	
	James Cuming	13June1811	M.Gen. 4June1814
	R— George Elrington	4June1813	
Major - -	William Cheyne	9Aug.1810	
	Charles Haynes	4June1813	
	Byse Molesworth	29Sept.	
Captain -	John Wm. Hutchinson	11Apr.1805	
	Francis Fetherston	25do.	
	Archibald Campbell	14Nov.	
	John Wm. O'Donoghue	12June1806	Major 31Dec.1811
	P— W— Ramsay	23June1808	
	Thomas Backhouse	7July	
	Fade Heatley	14Sept.1809	
	William Kirk	28Dec.,	
	Ponsonby Mathews	22Mar.1810	
	Henry Parsons	13June1811	
	William Atherton	28Feb.1812	
	James Pickard	14Jan.1813	
	George Forster Sadlier	24June	
	Robert Wood Baggott	30Sept.	
	Patrick Forbes	10Feb.1814	
Lieutenant -	Joshua Deverell	17Apr.1806	
	Edward Templeton	29May	
	Thomas French	16July1807	
	Philip Dundas	25Aug.	
	John Thomas Keays	1Oct.	11Sept.1806
	James Clarke	5Nov.	
	James Hutchinson	14Apr.1808	
	George Nangle	30June	
	John Hill	21July	
	George Mackay	17Aug.1809	20Oct. 1808
	Henry Wainwright	3Sept.	
	William Scott	4do.	
	James R— Cochrane	5do.	
	Christ. Irwin Cochrane	6do.	
	Henry Pierard	28do.	
	Edmund Robinson	5Oct.	
	Thomas Daly	19do.	
	James Davis	28Dec.	19June1808
	John Henry De Burgh	1Mar.1810	

Lieutenant

Rank.	Name.	Rank in the Regiment.	Army.
Lieutenant	Michael Lyne	29Mar.1810	
	William Kendall	12Apr.	
	David Stapleton	3May	
	Addison Lowe	10Apr.1811	6Apr. 1810
	Johnston Burrows	13June	Adjutant
	John Atherton	25do.	
	Thomas Noble Cochrane	13Feb.1812	
	John Liston	29Sept.1813	
Ensign	John Sands	18Mar.1813	
	——— Young	13May	
	——— Murray	28July	
	Thomas Luttrell	29do.	
	William R— Bangs	30do.	
	——— Edwards	27Sept.	
	——— Gordon	28do.	
	Charles Lowry	29do.	
	William Marriott	30do.	
	John Riddell	23Dec.	
Paymaster	William Phillips	19Nov.1803	
Adjutant	Johnston Burrows	13Apr.1809	Lieut. 13June1811
Quarter-Master	James Young	7Jan.1813	12Jan. 1809
Surgeon	John Eason	22Apr.1809	
Assistant Surg.	James Tushell	7Apr.1804	
	Thomas M'Curdy	23July1812	

N. B. *The Officers printed in Italics are to be placed upon Half-pay on arrival from Foreign Service.*

Facings white.—Lace silver.

Agent, Messrs. Greenwood, Cox and Hammersley.

266 48th (or the Northamptonshire) Regt. of Foot.

(2d BATTALION DISBANDED.)

Rank.	Name.	Regiment.	Army.
		Rank in the	

Rank.	Name.	Regiment.	Army.
Colonel - -	*Lord* Charles Fitzroy	1Jan.1805	Gen. 4June1814
Lieut. Colonel	◎James Erskine	20June1811	25July 1810
Major -	◎- { William Grove White	25Nov.1809	Lt.Col.26Aug.1813
	{ Molyneux Marston	3May1810	Lt.Col. 1Jan.1812
Captain -	◎ ⌈ Gilbert Cimitiere	28Aug.1804	Major 20June1811
	⎮ G— S— Thwaites	7Mar.1805	Major 4June1814
	◎⎯ ⎮ Thomas Bell	12Sept.	Major 26Aug.1813
	⎮ James Morissett	26Dec.	
	⎨ James Taylor	4June1807	Major 21Sept.1813
	⎮ Patrick Campbell	10Mar.1808	25Nov.1806
	◎ ⎮ Wm. Parry Jones Parry	17May	
	⎮ Francis Allman	1June1809	
	⎮ Robert Gray	10Aug.	
	⌊ Robert Andrew Wauch	15Feb.1810	
Lieutenant -	⌈ Alexander Macintosh	18June1807	
	⎮ John Brooke	25do.	
	⎮ John Campbell	26Nov.	8Oct. 1805
	⎮ John Cuthbertson	28Jan.1808	
	⎮ George Wilson Leroux	3Feb.	
	⎮ Edward Vincent	4do.	
	⎮ Thomas Wright	5do.	
	⎮ John Grant King	8do.	
	⎮ Henry E— Robinson	9do.	
	⎮ John William Duke	10do.	
	⎨ John Archer	26do.	
	⎮ —— Ellwood	18May	
	⎮ John Marshall	19do.	
	⎮ William R— Steell	4Aug.	16June1808
	⎮ George Sach	31May1809	
	⎮ Thomas Brotheridge	1June	
	⎮ Edward Charles Close	2do.	
	⎮ Cha. J. Vander Meulen	10Aug.	
	⎮ James Black	7Dec.	
	⎮ Francis Armstrong	21June1810	
	⎮ John De Lacey	15June1811	
	⌊ Valentine Bloomfield	17do.	

Ensign

Rank.	Name.	Rank in the Regiment.	Army.

Rank.	Name.	Regiment.	Army.
Ensign	Benjamin Thompson	11 July 1811	
	William Stawell	19 Sept.	
	Edward Gibson	30 Dec. 1812	
	John Croker	31 do.	
	William Veitch	25 Jan. 1813	30 Jan. 1812
	William Kenworthy	17 June	
	Thomas Weston	15 July	
	Henry Donovan	25 Aug.	
	George Skeene	11 Nov.	Adjutant
Paymaster	Hans Fowler Hughes	15 Feb. 1798	
Adjutant	George Skeene	11 Nov. 1813	Ensign 11 Nov. 1813
Quarter-Master	—— Stubbs	5 May 1808	
Surgeon	Alexander Stephenson	28 Oct. 1813	
Assistant Surg.	James Burne	21 Jan. 1808	
	David Wright	17 May 1810	

Facings buff.—Lace gold.

Agent, Messrs. Greenwood, Cox and Hammersley.

(2d BATTALION DISBANDED.)

		Rank in the	
Rank.	Name.	Regiment.	Army.
Colonel - -	Hon. Alex. Maitland	25May1768	Gen. 12Oct.1793
Lieut. Colonel {	John Vincent Jonathan Yates	13June1811 13May1813	M:Gen. 4June1813 19July 1810
Major - - {	Adam Ormsby Alexander Clerk	13June1811 4June1813	Lt. Col. 4June1814 25July 1810
Captain - {	Thomas Manners James Dennis John Baskerville Glegg John Williams Robert Johnston Augustine Fitz Gerald Alexander Lewis Henry Ormond John Day Edward Hackett Timothy Dillon William Jones Norton Wightwick	25June1803 6Aug. 20do. 4Aug.1804 21Aug.1806 22Mar.1810 13June1811 24Sept.1812 10May1813 11do. 12do. 24Feb.1814 23June	Major 4June1814 Major 28Nov.1812 Major 8Oct.1812 Major 28Nov.1812 Major 14July1814 5Mar.1812
Lieutenant {	Robert Bartley Dixie Ellis Thomas Lamont Alexander Garrett Grenville Bradford Samuel Holland William Alex. Danford Edward Danford Edmund Morris John Sewell Sylvester Richmond William Winder J— W— Birmingham Robert Alexander Samuel Blyth John Hollis Rolle Foote Joseph Stean John Otter James King Hector Munro John Thomas Westropp	12Feb.1807 1June1809 8do. 21June1810 11July1811 8Aug. 9July1812 20Apr.1813 21do. 23do. 24do. 25do. 26do. 27do. 28do. 29do. 9May 10do. 13do. 20do. 23Sept.	 6June1811 12Nov.1812 Adjutant

Lieutenant

Rank.	Name.	Rank in the Regiment.	Army.
Lieutenant -	Hender Mountsteven	6Jan.1814	
	Henry Maxwell	13do.	
	Edward Glasgow	24Feb.	
	Donat O'Brien	3Mar.	
	John Hazen	23June	
Ensign - -	Richard Gregory	25Apr.1813	
	Archibald Maclachlan	10May	
	David Morrison Sanders	12do.	
	James Simpson	13do.	
	Robert Innes	14do.	
	George Mathew	24June	
	Philip Stacpoole	22July	
	Kerziel de Lisle	23Sept.	
	Allan M'Nab	3Mar.1814	
Paymaster -	James Brock	7July1803	
Adjutant - -	Joseph Stean	5July1812	Lieut. 9May1813
Quarter-Master	Peter Murta	27Aug.1812	
Surgeon - -	J—W—Korb	21Sept.1809	
Assistant Surg.	Henry W— Develin	20May1813	
	Daniel O'Doherty	15July	
	Alexander D. Anderson	12May1814	

N. B. *The Officers printed in Italics are to be placed upon Half-pay on arrival from Foreign Service.*

Facings green.—Lace gold.

Agent, Mr. Gilpin, No. 33, Villiers Street, Strand.

270   50th (or the West Kent) Regiment of Foot.

(2d BATTALION DISBANDED.)

Permitted to bear on their Colours and Appointments a " SPHINX," with the word " EGYPT," and the words " VIMEIRA" and " CORUNNA," in commemoration of the Campaign of 1801, and the Battles of 21st August, 1808, and 16th January, 1809.

Rank.	Name.	Regiment.	Rank in the Army.
Colonel - -	*Sir* James Duff, *Kt.*	31Aug.1798	Gen. 25Oct.1809
Lieut. Colonel ◎Charles Hill		13June1811	25July 1810
Major - ◎ { John Bacon Harrison		23Feb.1809	Lt.Col. 19June1812
{ Tho. Dundas Campbell		13June1811	
Captain - { William Alex. Gordon		23Oct.1806	Lt.Col. 26Dec.1813
{ Thomas Wemyss		12Nov.1807	Major 21June1813
{ William Mason		19do.	
{ Benjamin Rowe		26Aug.1808	Major 3Mar.1814
{ Henry Montgomery		5Jan.1809	Major 26Dec.1813
{ John W— Henderson		9Mar.	12Mar.1807
{ Charles Grant		8June	
{ James Ballard Gardiner		20July	
{ Andrew Mitchell		27June1811	
{ Nicholas Wodehouse		26Sept.	
Lieutenant { Charles Heatly		27Dec.1807	
{ Wm. John Hemsworth		28do.	
{ Robert Keddle		7Jan.1808	
{ Thomas Ryan		28Apr.	
{ Edward Richardson		5May	
{ Henry Fyge Jauncey		7July	
{ William Turner		26Aug.	
{ John Power		3Nov.	22Oct. 1807
{ John Patterson		22Dec.	
{ William Nowlan		12Jan.1809	
{ George Bartley		13Apr.	
{ James Thomas		4May	
{ Richard Jones		18do.	
{ Rich.Woodward Swayne		19Oct.	
{ Daniel Lyon		31May1810	Adjutant
{ Charles North		12July	
{ Arthur Piggott Browne		13Feb.1812	
{ George John Eady		26Mar.	
{ Patrick Plunkett		25June	
{ John W— Plunket		3Sept.	
{ James Burrell		17do.	20Sept. 1808
{ John Godfree		16Dec.	
{ William Crofton		17do.	

Ensign

| Rank. | Name. | Rank in the | |
		Regiment.	Army.
Ensign - -	Richard Seward	19Nov.1812	
	——— Bateman	16Dec.	
	J— Richards	17do.	
	Samuel Lumsden	21Jan.1813	
	Harry J— Shawe	15July	
	W— R— Greenham	22do.	
	John Dillon	7Oct.	
	John Mahon	8do.	
Paymaster - -	John Montgomery	17Oct.1799	
Adjutant - -	Daniel Lyon	28Nov.1808	Lieut. 31May1810
Quarter-Master	Benjamin Baxter	5Oct.1804	
Surgeon - -	Baillie Ross	11Mar.1813	
Assistant Surg.	Joseph Brown	14Dec.1809	
	John Tobin	19Dec.1811	

Facings black.—Lace silver.

Agent, Messrs. Greenwood, Cox and Hammersley.

[1815]

272 51st (or the 2d Yorksh. West Riding) Regt. of Foot.

(LIGHT INFANTRY.)

Permitted to inscribe on their Colours and Appointments the word " MINDEN."

		Rank in the	
Rank.	Name.	Regiment.	Army.
Colonel - -	William Morshead	9May1800	Gen. 1Jan.1812
Lieut. Colonel ◎Hugh Henry Mitchell		13June1811	Col. 4June1813
Major -	◎ { Samuel Rice	13July1809	Lt.Col.22Nov.1813
	◎- { David Roberts	12Dec.1811	Lt.Col. 21June1813
Captain -	{ John Thomas Keyt	24June1804	Major 4June1814
	James Campbell	1Aug.1805	
	William Thwaites	2Jan.1807	Major 4June1814
	Edward Kelly	21Apr.1808	11Feb. 1808
	Richard Storer	13July1809	
	James Henry Phelps	21Sept.	
	Peter Smellie	21Feb.1811	
	James Ross	12Dec.	
	John Ross	15Apr.1813	
	Samuel Beardsley	16Sept.	
	Edward Frederick	28Apr.1814	
Lieutenant	{ Henry Bayly	6May1809	
	Benjamin Buck Hawley	10do.	
	Thomas Brook	18do.	
	Francis Minchin	12July	
	Walter Mahon	13do.	
	William Henry Hare	20do.	
	Richard Hicks	21Sept.	
	James Varden	25July1810	
	Oliver Ainsworth	26do.	
	Henry Read	20Feb.1811	
	Francis Kennedy	21do.	
	Joseph Dyas	11July	
	John Flamanck	12Dec.	
	William Henry Elliott	13Aug.1812	
	Wm. Davidson Simpson	3Dec.	
	Frederick Mainwaring	15Apr.1813	
	William Jones	16do.	Adjutant
	Charles Wm. Tyndale	3June	
	William Galbreath	22July	
	Henry Martin	21Oct.	
	Charles Tho. Thurston	22Nov.	
	Harry Hervis Roberts	7Jan.1814	
	Egerton Isaacson	14July	
	Edward James Taylor	28Sept.	
	Thomas Troward	29do.	

Ensign

51st (or the 2d Yorksh. West Riding) Regt of Foot. 273
(LIGHT INFANTRY.)

Rank.	Name.	Regiment.	Rank in the Army.
Ensign	G.Fred.Berkeley St. John	3June1813	25Oct. 1813
	Francis Percy	22July	
	William Henry Krause	21Oct.	
	R— B— Walton	25Dec.	
	William Johnstone	6Jan.1814	
	Alexander Frazer	21Apr.	
	John Blair	14July	18May1814
	Henry Lock	13Oct.	
Paymaster	John Gibbs	15Feb.1810	
Adjutant	William Jones	21Feb.1811	Lieut. 16Apr.1813
Quarter-Master	Thomas Askey	18Mar.1813	
Surgeon	Richard Webster	14July1808	26Oct. 1804
Assistant Surg.	John F— Clarke	25June1812	
	Percy Fitz Patrick	11Mar.1813	

Facings grass green.—Lace gold.

Agent, Messrs. Greenwood, Cox and Hammersley.

274   52d (or the Oxfordshire) Regiment of Foot.

(LIGHT INFANTRY.)

| | | | Rank in the | |
Rank.	Name.	Regiment.	Army.
Colonel	- *Sir* Hildebrand Oakes, *Bt.* 25Jan.1809		Lt.Gen. 4June1811

| Lieut. Col. ☒ { | John Colborne | 18July1811 | Col.   4June1814 |
| ⊚ { | Edward Gibbs | 8Apr.1813 | 6Feb. 1812 |

Major - ⊚ {	Charles Rowan	9May1811	Lt.Col. 27Apr.1812
	James Henry Reynett	8Apr.1813	Lt. Col. 1June1814
	William Mein	11Nov.	Lt.Col. 7Oct.1813
	Tho. T. F. E. Drake	26May1814	

Captain - ⊚ {	Patrick Campbell	16Aug.1804	Major 21June1813
⊚	Robert Campbell	24do.	Major 21Sept.1813
	William Chalmers	27Aug.1807	Major 26Aug.1813
	William Rowan	19Oct.1808	Major 3Mar.1814
⊚-	Kenneth Snodgrass	20do	Major 21Sept.1813
	Robert Brownrigg	20July1809	Major 16June1814
	Charles Diggle	24May1810	
	John Shedden	9May1811	
	James Frederick Love	11July	
	George Young	20Jan.1812	
	James M'Nair	11May	
	Edward Langton	12do.	
	William Rentall	13do.	
	John Cross	31Dec.	
	Charles, *Earl of* March	8Apr.1813	9July 1812
	James Ormsby	22June	
	Charles Kinloch	22July	18Mar.1813
	William Henry Temple	9Dec.	
	William Chalmers	24do.	
	Charles Yorke	do.	
	Archibald Douglas	28Apr.1814	
	William Royds	9June	

Lieutenant - {	John Dobbs	14Feb.1809	
	John Winterbottom	28Feb.1810	Adjutant
	Charles Dawson	21June	
	Mathew Anderson	19July	12Oct. 1809

Lieutenant

[1815]

52d (or the Oxfordshire) Regiment of Foot. 275
(LIGHT INFANTRY.)

Rank.	Name.	Rank in the Regiment.	Army.
Lieutenant	Charles Kenny	13 Sept. 1810	
	Sam. Dilman Pritchard	11 Apr. 1811	Adjutant
	G— H— Love	18 do.	
	William Ripley	2 May	
	John C— Barrett	9 do.	
	George Cleghorn	11 July	
	William Henry Clerke	19 Sept.	25 July 1811
	George Hall	9 May 1812	
	W— R— Nixon	11 do.	
	George Gawler	12 do.	
	Nicholas Nepean	13 do.	
	George Whichcote	8 July	
	Matthew Agnew	9 do.	
	William Ogilvy	17 Sept.	
	Edward Richard Northey	10 do.	
	Hon. William Browne	26 Nov.	
	Edward Scoones	24 Dec.	
	George Campbell	25 Feb. 1813	
	William Austin	6 Apr.	
	—— Snodgrass	7 do.	
	J— Stewart Cargill	8 do.	
	William Hunter	28 do.	
	William Crawley Yonge	29 do.	
	Thomas Cottingham	5 Aug.	
	Charles Holman	11 Nov.	
	George Moore	6 Dec.	
	John Leaf	7 do.	
	Edward Michell	8 do.	
	Charles Shaw	9 do.	
	John Hart	20 Jan. 1814	
	George Ewing Scott	10 Feb.	
	Henry Thomas Oakes	11 do.	
	Dahort Macdowall	10 Mar.	
	Sir Hen. John Seton, *Bt.*	21 Apr.	
	Robert Lockwood	28 do.	
	—— Radford	16 June	
	Peter E— Craigie	29 Sept.	
	Martin Maher	15 Dec.	17 Jan. 1811

Ensign

(LIGHT INFANTRY.)

Rank.	Name.	Rank in the Regiment.	Army.
Ensign	John Burnet	27May1813	
	John Rogers Griffiths	24June	
	Ronald Stewart	5Aug.	
	George Robson	23Sept.	
	Frederick Aug. Love	6Dec.	
	Joseph Jackson	7do.	
	Thomas Massie	8do.	
	William Nettles	9do.	
	—— Macnab	16do.	
	John Montague	10Feb.1814	
	Richard Bracken	3Mar.	
	James Frere May	28Apr.	
	Henry P— Smith	16June	
	Eaton Monins	1Dec.	
Paymaster 2	Pierce Butler	28Feb.1805	
1	James Clark	25Aug.1814	
Adjutant -	John Winterbottom	24Nov.1808	Lieut. 28Feb.1810
	Sam. Dilman Pritchard	1July1813	Lieut. 11Apr.1811
QuarterMaster	John Campbell	4Apr.1805	
	Benjamin Sweeten	22Apr.1813	
Surgeon -	J— B— Gibson	20Dec.1810	7Dec.1809
	Robert Todd	18Feb.1813	
Assistant Surg.	Pryce Jones	20Apr.1809	
	William Macartney	3Sept.1812	
	Thomas Brisbane	3June1813	

Facings buff.—Lace silver.

Agent, Messrs. Greenwood, Cox and Hammersley.

Rank.	Name.	Rank in the Regiment.	Rank in the Army.
Colonel - -	*Hon.* John Abercromby	21Mar.1807	Lt.Gen. 1Jan.1812
Lieut. Col. ✠—	{ Sebright Mawby	5Oct.1804	Col. 4June1813
	{ Geo. Ridout Bingham	14Mar.1805	Col. 4June1813
	{ John Buckland	13June1811	Col. 4June1814
Major - -	{ Terence Mac Mahon	28Feb.1805	Col. 4June1814
	{ John Mansel	22Aug.	Lt.Col. 1Jan.1812
	{ Jeffery Piercy	13June1811	
	{ William Ingleby	24Oct.	
	{ O— G— Fehrszen	24Dec.1813	26Aug.1813
Captain -	{ John Giles	9July1803	Major 4June1813
	{ John Wheatstone	do.	Major 4June1814
	{ Wheeler Coultman	7Sept.1804	Major 4June1814
	{ J— Clifton Andrews	26Oct.	Major 4June1814
	{ Henry Parker	28Mar.1805	
	{ John M'Caskill	6Mar.1806	
	{ Thomas Poppleton	13Nov.	
	{ William A— Haly	12Jan.1809	4June1806
	{ William Cuppage	1June	
	{ Henry Yonge	12Oct.	Lt.Col. 1Jan.1812
	{ Robert Younghusband	1Jan.1811	
	{ William Russell	2Oct.	
	{ John Fernandez	3do.	
	{ Charles Chepmell	1Oct.1812	
	{ John Stone	10Dec.	
	{ James Mackay	17do.	22Mar.1810
	{ Robert Christ. Mansel	8July1813	4Feb.1813
	{ Charles Harrison	24Dec.	
	{ Hen.ThomasM'Donald	31Mar.1814	
	{ John Stewart	19May	
Lieutenant	{ Matthew Young	29Mar.1805	26Oct.1804
	{ Fred. Harvey Fuller	4Apr.	
	{ Pierce Hovenden	6do.	
	{ Charles F— Hunter	29Aug.	31Mar.1804
	{ John Montgomery	1Jan.1806	21Jan.1805
	{ Cope Williams	15May	
	{ Thomas Price	2Oct.	
	{ William Portbury	31Mar.1807	23Mar.1806
	{ Richard George Horsley	16Apr.	
	{ Arthur Daly	23July	Adjutant
	{ William Harrington	25Aug.	

Lieutenant

| | | Rank in the | |
Rank.	Name.	Regiment.	Army.
	Thomas Emery	7 Jan. 1808	
	Charles Nice Davies	7 June	8 Apr. 1807
	Robert Thomas Greene	18 Oct.	
	William Booth	25 Mar. 1809	
	A— H— Dillon	27 May	
	Edward Barlow	29 do.	
	Alexander Knox	11 Jan. 1810	
	James Hamilton	14 Mar.	
	Thomas Impett	26 July	
	Joseph Nicholson	9 Aug.	
	Digby H— Anstice	29 Jan. 1812	
	Stephen Fraser Ward	30 do.	
	John Fraser	12 Feb.	
Lieutenant -	Joseph Hutchinson	13 do.	
	David M'Pherson	6 Aug.	
	William Harrison	3 Dec.	
	Josh. Chap. Heathcote	10 do.	
	John C— Brodie	11 Mar. 1813	
	William Baxter	10 June	
	Cathcart Taylor	27 Jan. 1814	
	James Trevenen	17 Feb.	1 July 1813
	George Fitz Gerald	24 do.	
	John Mackay	30 Mar.	
	Peter Bunworth	8 June	
	——— Hilliard	9 do.	
	Andrew Browne	3 Nov.	
	Robert Macalpine	24 do.	16 Dec. 1813
	——— Nagle	9 Apr. 1812	
	George Aufrere	16 July	
	Mars Morphett	10 Oct.	
	Charles Auber	2 do.	
	P— R— Cameron	10 Dec.	
Ensign - -	Charles Smallwood	14 Jan. 1813	
	J— Wilton	10 Mar.	Adjutant
	Edm. Saunderson Prideaux	11 do.	
	Robert George Scott	15 Apr.	
	George Hamilton	29 do.	
	George Stoat Jeffery	8 May	
	D— O— Host	25 do.	

Ensign

Rank.		Name.	Rank in the	
			Regiment.	Army.
Ensign - -		Charles Williams	24June1813	
		Jacob Silver	11Sept.	
		Thomas Adams	10Nov.	
		John Whitfield	2Dec.	
		James Stewart	9June1814	
		George Laye	14July	
Paymaster	1	Henry Sherwood	1May1804	
	2	John Maclean	3May1810	
Adjutant -		Arthur Daly	20May1813	Lieut. 23July1807
		J— Wilton	26Aug.	Ensign 10Mar.1813
QuarterMaster		—— Hanson	12Sept.1800	
		—— Blackie	9July1803	
Surgeon -		Robert M'Intyre	5Oct.1804	1Oct. 1801
		Peter Papps	25Nov.1813	5Nov.1812
Assistant Surg.		William Pollock	24Oct.1803	
		Robert Miller	15Dec.1804	
		James Dunne	25Nov.1806	13Oct. 1808
		Charles M'Lean	27Dec.1810	

Facings red.—Lace gold.

Agent, Messrs. Greenwood, Cox and Hammersley.

54th

Permitted to bear a " SPHINX," with the word " EGYPT," on their Colours and Appointments in commemoration of the Campaign of 1801.

Rank.	Name.	Regiment.	Rank in the Army.
Colonel - ·	James, *Lord* Forbes	18Sept.1809	L.Gen. 25Apr.1808
Lieut. Colonel	{ John Thomas Layard { John, *Earl* Waldegrave	16May1800 26Nov.1812	M.Gen. 4June1811
Major - ◎–	{ *Sir* Neil Campbell, *Kt.* { Allan Kelly	20Feb.1806 31Oct.1811	Col. 4June1814
Captain -	{ Thomas Cox Kirby Thomas Reeves Robert Pigott Richard Blakeman Walter Crofton Duncan Campbell James Leslie Gillow J— Tappenden George Black Archibald Smith Thomas Chartres	25Sept.1806 25June1807 9July 15Mar.1809 16do. 15June 3Jan.1811 12Dec. 9July1812 17Sept. 28Apr.1814	25July 1811
Lieutenant -	{ George Fraser Alexander Burnett Gonville Bromhead Edw. Alleyne Evanson John Pillon Robert Woodgate William Claus Richard Kelly Daniel Keogh Richard O'Meara John Blake John Grey Philip Mandilhon Joseph Henry Potts Robert Leacroft Francis Taylor Edward Marcon Andrew Pattison Carlisle John Reid Richard Stacpoole Francis Burgess William Pilkington William Persse Dixon Denham Francis Hutchinson	11Dec.1806 15Mar.1809 23do. 20Apr. 11May 28Sept. 22Feb.1810 14June 13Dec. 28Mar.1811 18July 19Sept. 7Nov. 12Dec. 21Aug.1812 10Sept. 20May1813 21Oct. 22do. 15Dec. 16do. 12May1814 2June 1Dec. 8do.	20Mar.1807 5Apr. 1810 18Dec. 1806 24Aug.1806 Adjutant 7Sept.1813

Ensign

| | | Rank in the | |
| Rank. | Name. | Regiment. | Army. |

Ensign - -	⎰ M.Stoug.HeyligerLloyd	16Dec.1813	
	Edward Nugent	23do.	
	Alexander Maclachlan	13Jan.1814	
	Thomas Fraser	5May	
	Charles Hill	12do.	
	John Clark	2June	
	C— W— Thomas	17Nov.	15July 1814
	⎱ Alexander Mathewson	8Dec.	
Paymaster -	Henry Irwin	11Feb.1813	18June 1801
Adjutant -	And. Pattison Carlisle	19Dec.1811	Lieut. 21Oct.1812
Quarter-Master	William Coates	1Aug.1811	
Surgeon -	George Redmond	11Sept.1806	
Assistant Surg.	⎰ Moore F— Fynan	28Feb.1811	
	⎱ George Leech	25Nov.1813	

Facings green.—Lace silt.

Agent, Messrs. Greenwood, Cox and Hammersley.

Rank.	Name.	Rank in the	
		Regiment.	Army.

Rank.	Name.	Regiment.	Army.
Colonel - -	William Henry Clinton	25Apr.1814	Lt.Gen. 4June1813
Lieut. Colonel	John Nugent Smyth	14Oct.1813	Col. 4June1813
Major - -	{ Robert Frederick	15Dec.1808	Lt.Col. 4June1814
	Alexander Hog	14Oct.1813	Lt.Col. 17Mar.1814
Captain -	George Evatt	20Apr.1802	Major 4June1813
	Richard Jones	25June1803	Major 4June1814
	Abraham Creighton	25Jan.1804	Major 4June1814
	Allan Macdonald	22Jan.1808	
	John Campbell	19May	Major 4June1814
	Mark H— Dickens	27Sept.1810	28Dec. 1809
	Henry Rainey	10June1813	13Apr.1809
	ThomasWm. Nicholson	14Oct.	
	John Saunders Elligood	9Dec.	
	Thomas Coleman	10Feb.1814	16Aug.1810
	Albert Frend	7Apr.	
Lieutenant -	John Buller	19Mar.1807	
	William Kemp	20Nov.	
	Tho. Goodrick Peacocke	3Mar.1808	
	Alexander Gardner	2May1809	
	William Henry Armstrong	4do.	
	Andrew M'Donnell	30Nov.	6June 1805
	Samuel Bolton	29Mar.1810	
	Wm.M'DonaldMackay	23Aug.	
	Edward Henry Adams	20Dec.	2Sept.1809
	Cunningham Douglas	18July1811	
	Æneas Macd. Nicholson	5Dec.	
	Thomas Major	13Feb.1812	
	Geo. Edward Clements	30Apr.	
	Neil Sinclair	25Feb.1813	13Feb. 1812
	William Delgairnes	8Dec.	5July 1810 Adjut.
	Joseph Dover	9do.	
	George William Reveley	6July1814	
	Robert Irving	7do.	

Ensign

| Rank. | Name. | Rank in the | |
		Regiment.	Army.
Ensign -	Harry Lumsden	22Aug.1811	
	William Gibbens	19Mar.1812	
	John Heard	29Oct.	
	John Montgomery Russell	5Nov.	
	George Goodall	9Sept.1813	
	Edward Ring	28Oct.	
	William Macdonald	5May1814	
	William Nelson	20Oct.	
	George Wyse	3Nov.	
Paymaster -	John Goddard	29Aug.1811	
Adjutant - -	William Delgairnes	8Dec.1813	Lieut. 5July1810
Quarter-Master	Arthur Hutchinson	30Dec.1805	
Surgeon - -	Thomas B— Sharpe	27July1809	
Assistant Surg.	George Martin	28Feb.1811	
	Thomas Lukis	16Dec.1813	9Apr.1812

Facings green.—Lace gold.

Agent, Messrs. Greenwood, Cox and Hammersley.

284 56th (or the West Essex) Regiment of Foot.

(2d BATTALION DISBANDED.)

Permitted to inscribe on their Colours and Appointments the word " GIBRALTAR."

Rank.	Name.	Regiment.	Rank in the Army.
Colonel - -	*Hon.* Chapple Norton	24Jan.1797	Gen. 29Apr.1802
Lieut. Colonel	Philip K— Skinner	11Dec.1799	M.Gen. 1Jan.1812
	Fletcher Barclay	27June1811	4June1811
	Nigel Kingscote	17Oct.	
◎	John Frederick Brown	5Mar.1812	25July 1810
	Henry Sullivan	1July1813	
Major - -	*Sir*C.Wynd.Burdett,*Bt.*29Nov.1810		Lt.Col. 4June1814
	Robert Grant	27June1811	
	Joseph Hanna	2Jan.1812	
	William S— Forbes	6Nov.1813	
Captain -	Henry Capadose	3Aug.1804	Major 4June1814
	John Gualey	19Sept.	Major 4June1814
	Howel H— Pritchard	12Sept.1805	
	Robert Seymour	10Oct.	28Feb. 1805
	James Grant	24June1806	2July 1805
	Alexander M'Donald	15Apr.1807	
	Richard Barrington	20Oct.1808	
	Dawson Gregory	14Sept.1809	14Feb. 1805
	P— Shadwell Norman	8Mar.1810	
	Archibald Campbell	7June	12Oct. 1809
	John M'Auley	29Aug.	
	Isaac George Ogden	13Sept.	
	Lawrence O'Hara	26Aug.1811	23Dec. 1806
	John Warren	26Dec.	3July 1806
	John R— Barry	2Jan.1812	
	John E— Cairnes	1Feb.	
	Charles Forbes	9Apr.	10Oct. 1811
	Philip J— Stanhope	1July1813	7Feb. 1812
	James St. John Rancland	6Nov.	
	Frederick Gibbons	7do.	
	John Newman Wylde	9do.	
	Joseph Perry	7Dec.	
	—— Burgh	30do.	
	Henry Jacob	10Mar.1814	
Lieutenant -	John Campbell	26Jan.1807	Adjutant
	William Mallet	27do.	
	James Crosley Lewis	28do.	
	William Gunn	29do.	
	Thomas Wilson	4Feb.	
	Henry Geale Carpenter	5do.	
	Montgomery Cairnes	12do.	

Lieutenant

Rank.	Name.	Rank in the Regiment.	Army.

Rank.	Name.	Regiment.	Army.
	William Galway	16Apr.1807	
	Robert Warren	13May	
	Loud. Harcourt Gordon	18June	
	William Edwards	26Aug.	
	Amos Thorne	1Jan.1808	
	William Henry Arthur	25Feb.	21Jan. 1808
	O'Connor Higgins	14July	
	Redmond Brough	15do.	
	John Kenny	27Oct.	5Feb. 1808
	Thomas Foreman	12Jan.1809	25Aug.1808
	Leonard Smelt	9Nov.	17Mar.1808
	——— Strangeways	18Dec.	
	James Reid	19do.	
	W— Thomas Ridge	20do.	
	John Drummond	21do.	
	William Woulds	12July1810	
	Robert Robertson	1Mar.1811	
	Benjamin Mason	25do.	
	Thomas Wilson	6Feb.1812	
	C— Wilson	7May	
	James Cowburne	12do.	
Lieutenant	Warburton Grey	13do.	
	Peter Abercromby	16Oct.	14July 1806
	Thomas Van Buerle	23Dec.	11Mar.1812
	——— M'Donnell	24do.	
	James Glover Finn	25Jan.1813	13Aug.1812
	Brickell Alexander	17June	
	Alexander Hanna	7Oct.	
	D— Dundas	23do.	1July 1813 Adjut.
	George Nesbitt	6Nov.	
	Charles Charsley	7do.	
	Edward Nugent	8do.	
	James Fraser	9do.	
	James Begbie	10do.	
	John Laplain	6Dec.	
	Anthony F— Wm. Lynch	7do.	
	——— Dames	8do.	
	George Geary	9do.	
	J. H. John Meikeljohn	10do.	
	Bernard Beale	30do.	
	Henry Edwards Hill	7Apr.1814	
	John Rancland	6July	
	Thomas Pelling Lang	7do.	

Ensign

Rank.	Name.	Rank in the Regiment.	Army.
Ensign	Archibald M'Lean	24Sept.1812	
	Henry Leslie	3Jan.1813	
	J— F— Nelson	1Apr.	
	David Rutledge	5do.	
	John Marklove	8do.	
	Edward Hervey Foster	8Nov.	
	William Burrow	9do.	
	Lister Nason	10do.	
	Nicholas Palmer	11do.	
	Thomas Mitchell	12do.	
	James Edward Taylor	13do.	
	Frederick Richard Lee	6Dec.	
	Edward John Chauvel	7do.	
	James Butt	8do.	
	William Henry Pyne	9do.	
	Robert Shafto Vicars	10do.	
	Forester Owen Leighton	30do.	
Paymaster 1	John Finnis	8Oct.1807	
Paymaster 2	Andrew Moore Dawe	do.	
Adjutant	William Mallet	1Jan.1811	Lieut. 27Jan.1807
	D— Dundas	23Oct.1813	Lieut. 1July1813
QuarterMaster	Richard Mullingan	30Jan.1803	
	—— Johnston	14Mar.1805	
Surgeon	Francis Forster	26Sept.1805	
	AnthonyC— Colclough	14Apr.1813	
Assistant Surg.	James Kennedy	7Jan.1813	
	William Bell	4Mar.	
	Archibald Shanks	17Mar.1814	
	John Jobson	1Sept.	

N. B. *The Officers printed in Italics are to be placed upon Half-pay on arrival from Foreign Service.*

Facings purple.—Lace silver.

Agent, Messrs. Greenwood, Cox and Hammersley.

Rank.	Name.	Rank in the Regiment.	Rank in the Army.
Colonel - -	Sir Hew Dalrymple, Kt.	27Apr.1811	Gen. 1Jan.1812
Lieut. Col.	William Collis Spring	4June1813	30May 1811
	Thomas Arbuthnot	24Mar.1814	Col. 4June1814
Major - -	Robert Shelton	1Mar.1810	
	Thomas Shadforth	20June1811	
	Walter M'Gibbon	4June1813	
	John Burrows	10Nov.	26Aug.1813
Captain -	Joseph Marke	12Feb.1807	Major 26Dec.1813
	John Stainforth	19do.	
	Hugh Montgomerie	7Jan.1808	
	Hector M'Laine	21do.	Major 19May1814
	John Campbell	5May	
	Hugh Mosman	26do.	
	Robert Hunt	11May1809	
	Price Hely	15Feb.1810	
	John Jackson	18June1811	
	George Baxter	20do.	
	Donald M'Lachlan	11July	
	Gregory Paul	30Oct.	20June1811
	Angus M'Donald	21Nov.	
	Daniel Falla	28Feb.1812	Major 4June1814
	William Jervoise	25Mar.1813	Lt.Col.22Sept.1814
	William Mann	29Apr.	
	Tho.H.Shadwell Clarke	10June	22Aug.1811
	Vance Young Donaldson	24do.	
	William Hunt	10Nov.	
	Edward Wilson	6Jan.1814	28June1810
Lieutenant	Robert Ross	27Dec.1805	
	George M'Farlane	6Feb.1806	
	James Tasker	16Oct.	
	Thomas Dix	5Mar.1807	
	Leeson Paterson	4Feb.1808	
	John Hughes	6do.	
	John Connor	9do.	
	William Henry Hollis	5May	
	Rice Price	21July	
	Thomas Charteris	20Oct.	
	Peter Macdougall	15June1809	
	Henry Oulton	15Feb.1810	
	F— G— Keogh	7Mar.1811	29Mar.1810

Lieutenant

Rank.	Name.	Regiment.	Rank in the Army.
	James Jackson	19June1811	
	George Francies	2odo.	
	Adam Murray	18July	
	Andrew Robinson	10Oct.	
	—— Leslie	21Nov.	Adjutant
	Edward Powell	25Jan.1813	30Aug.1805
	Kilmer Waller	25Feb.	
	Patrick Logan	25Mar.	
	Philip Aubin	29Apr.	
	Peter Reid	23June	
Lieutenant -	George Vaughan	15July	
	Humphrey Rob. Hartley 2Sept.		
	Thomas Sheridan	16do.	
	Samuel Brierly	10Nov.	
	Philip Smith	8Feb.1814	
	William Benjamin Bartlett 9do.		
	George Raymond	10do.	
	Hugh M'Kenzie	24do.	
	Alexander Veitch	31Mar.	
	James Ferguson	21Apr.	
	Thomas Hamilton	9June	
	D— Campbell	8Dec.	
	Neil M·Gibbon	23Dec.1813	
	George Comerford	13Jan.1814	
	William Baxter	9Feb.	
	Alexander M'Farlane	10do.	
	Alexander Eagar	31Mar.	
Ensign - -	Alexander M'Glachlan 21Apr.		
	—— Deaman	28do.	Adjutant
	Eglintoune Montgomerie 9June		
	William Bourchier	8Sept.	
	Thos. Daniel Anderson 27Oct.		
	John William Donelan	8Dec.	
Paymaster	1 Thomas Shapter	8Aug.1798	
	2 Bernard Reilly	28June1810	
Adjutant -	—— Leslie	20May1813	Lieut. 21Nov.1811
	—— Deaman	23June1814	Ensign 28Apr.1814
QuarterMaster	George Moore	18Dec.1806	
	R— R— Coomb	12Sept.1811	
Surgeon -	James Evans	10Aug.1809	15June1809
	Thomas Bouchier	22Aug.1811	
Assistant Surg.	Christopher Humphrys	3Jan.1810	
	Duncan Campbell	19Apr.	
	Patrick Pope	24Feb.1814	

Facings yellow.—Lace gold.

Agent, Messrs. Greenwood, Cox and Hammersley.

Permitted to inscribe on their Colours and Appointments the word " MAIDA," in commemo-
ration of the Action of 4th July, 1806 ; to bear a " SPHINX," with the word " EGYPT,"
for the Campaign of 1801; also the word " GIBRALTAR."

Rank.	Name.	Rank in the Regiment.	Rank in the Army.
Colonel - -	Richard, *Earl of* Cavan, K.C.	1July1811	Gen. 4June1814
Lieut. Colonel	David Walker	16Nov.1809	Col. 4June1814
	Richard Buckby	8Nov.1810	Col. 4June1814
Major - -	Francis B— Campbell	29Mar.1810	Lt.Col.26Aug.1813
	Frederick Ashworth	22Nov.	
	Thomas Kenah	5Nov.1812	Lt.Col. 27Dec.1813
	George Druitt	4Apr.1813	
Captain -	Frederick Tompkins	9July1803	Major 4June1811
	James Price	do.	Major 4June1811
	William O'Brien	do.	Major 1Jan.1812
	Samuel Colburg	do.	Major 4June1814
	Charles Baldwin	do.	Major 4June1814
◎	Baynton Stone	1Dec.1804	Major 22Nov.1813
◎	John Gomersall	25do.	Major 26Dec.1813
	John Austin	28Nov.1805	Lt.Col. 25Feb.1813
	Lionel John Westropp	5Mar.1807	
	Peter Dudgeon	19do.	
	Adam Ferguson	4Feb.1808	
	John Ryves	25Mar.	
	J— Charles Wood	15Nov.1809	
	Ponsonby Christ. Willoe	16do.	
	Randolph Crewe	29Mar.1810	
	Henry Pratt	22Nov.	
	E— Kingsley	5Nov.1812	
	Horatio George Broke	18Mar.1813	Major 28July1814
	Rowland Chute	15Apr.	
	Francis Pyner	29July	
	Dansie Carter	4Aug.1814	
Lieutenant	Thomas Rogers	16Jan.1806	
	John Shee	3July	
	Patrick Shea	28Oct.	
	Edward Fitzgerald	29do.	
	Robert Park	26Feb.1807	
	David Morrison	20Mar.	
	John Fowle	2Apr.	
	Thomas Hayton	28May	
	Nathan Tipson	27Oct.	Adjutant
	William Bale	28do.	
	Moses Morton	28Apr.1808	
	Abraham Briggs	29Dec.	
	William Sadler	4May1809	
	John Rolfe	2Nov.	
	William Fitzgerald	10do.	Lieutenant

o

Lieutenant -	Robert Ball	14Nov.1809	
	Richard Waite	15do.	
	George Collins	16do.	
	Richard Hargrave	14Dec.	
	Henry Alcock	22Feb.1810	
	Matthew Powell	5Apr.	
	Cyrus Brohier	5July	
	Edward Fugion	25July1811	
	Richard Burton	5Nov.1812	
	Thomas William James	25do.	
	Charles Wm. Hockley	26do.	
	Charles Campbell	23Dec.	23June 1812
	Henry Stoughton	24do.	
	Edmund Baylee	21Oct.1813	
	Edward Smith	20Jan.1814	
	John Beresford Dunlop	17Feb.	
	John Slater	20Apr.	Adjutant
	R— D— Nicholson	21do.	
Ensign - -	William Grey	25July1811	
	Thomas Long	17Oct.	
	G— Wilson	4June1812	
	Charles Alex. M'Donald	2July	
	James William Young	3Sept.	
	John Pasley	24do.	
	———— Campbell	25Nov.	
	James Travers Burke	26do.	
	John Sage	10Dec.	
	Charles Duckers	24do.	
	Frederick James Ranie	31do.	
	Thomas Richard Davis	26Aug.1813	
	Nesbitt Wood	20Jan.1814	
	W— G— Sheppard	17Feb.	
	William Rheamsbottom	20Apr.	
	———— Dillon	21do.	
Paymaster 1	Hugh Lewis Albert	5Feb.1798	
2	John Briggs	25Apr.1805	
Adjutant -	Nathan Tipson	26Nov.1812	Lieut. 27Oct.1807
	John Slater	17Nov.1814	Lieut. 20Apr.1814
QuarterMaster	John Armstrong	25Apr.1805	
	William Phillips	19May1808	
Surgeon -	Henry Marsh	25Feb.1805	
Assistant Surg.	Charles St. John	3Sept.1812	
	Robert Starke	21Jan.1813	
	David Thomas	10June	11July 1811

Facings black.—Lace gold.

Agent, Messrs. Greenwood, Cox and Hammersley.

*The 2d Bn. permitted to inscribe on their Colours and Appointments the word " CORUNNA,"
in commemoration of the Action of 16th Jan. 1809.*

Rank.		Name.	Regiment.	Army.
				Rank in the
Colonel - -		Alexander Ross	28Mar.1801	Gen. 1Jan.1812
Lieut. Col.	◎	Francis Fuller	30June1794	Lt.Gen. 4June1811
		Alexander M'Leod	13June1811	25July 1810
		George M'Gregor	4June1813	1Jan. 1812
		Henry Austen	23Sept.	25Jan. 1812
Major - -		Matthew Shawe	4June1813	Lt.Col. 27Apr.1812
		Frederick W— Hoysted	17do.	Lt.Col. 26Dec.1813
		Joseph Creighton	23Sept.	
		John T— Horsley	24do.	
Captain -	◎	Charles Douglas	19May1808	
		William Wilkinson	1Sept.	
		George Halford	29do.	Major 21Sept.1813
		Francis Fuller	5Oct.1809	
		David Graham	11Jan.1810	
		George Elde Darby	14Mar.1811	
		John Butler	26Aug.	
		Henry Pittman	27do.	
		RobertCharlesStevenson	12Feb.1812	
		Francis Fuller	13do.	
		Edward Gregory	10June	
		William Ridding	3Aug.	
		Alexander Mancor	3Sept.	
		John Belshes	4do.	
		James Cockburn	do.	
		Abraham Pilkington	17June1813	
		George Forrest	1July	
		JamesArchibaldCrawford	22do.	
		William Mandeville	23Sept.	
		James Chadwick	24do.	
		James Mac Gregor	25do.	
		John Fawson	11Nov.	
Lieutenant		Duncan Gordon	9June1808	
		Robert Preedy	15do.	
		J— Erasmus Spier	23Aug.	
		William F— Mayne	4Sept.	
		John Dillon	21do.	
		John Pine Penefather	22do.	
		Samuel Clutterbuck	17Nov.	

Lieutenant

| Rank. | Name. | Rank in the | |
		Regiment.	Army.
	James Strangeways	1June1809	
	John Bayle Broheir	3do.	
	Abraham Dent	4do.	
	Richard Howard	5do.	
	John Cowper	7do.	
	Marlborough Seymour	29do.	
	Henry Brown	26Oct.	
	Alexander Macpherson	21Dec.	
	Richard Manners	8Feb.1810	
	Samuel Stewart	21do.	31Dec.1807
	Robert Whittle	22do.	
	Edward Duncan	28Feb.1811	
	Archibald Campbell	28Mar.	Adjutant
	James Doran	18Apr.	
	Nicholas Chadwick	5Dec.	
	Nicholas Hovenden	12do.	
	Lewis Carmichael	7Mar.1812	
	William Waters	8do.	
	Edward Bushel	10do.	
	Peter M'Lauchlan	11do.	
	Henry Hartford	12do.	
Lieutenant -	W— C— Holmes	25June	
	John Lukis	6Aug.	
	Edward Mitchell	1Sept.	
	Paterson O'Hara	2do.	
	Richard Wolfe	3Dec.	
	Edward Long	16June1813	
	Edward Scott	1July	
	William Veal	23Sept.	
	Michael H— Hoctor	24do.	
	Æneas M'Pherson	26do.	
	William Pittman	27do.	
	Alexander Howard	28do.	
	Edmund P— Duncan	29do.	
	John W— Gilson	6Oct.	
	Wright Edwards	10Nov.	
	Peter Robertson	11do.	
	George Dixon	5May1814	
	Thomas Crawley	24do.	Adjutant
	William H— Hill	25do.	
	James Ralph	26do.	
	Gilmour Robinson	1Sept.	
	James Geddes	8do.	

Ensign

Rank.	Name.	Rank in the Regiment.	Army.
Ensign	John Burne	1 Oct.1811	11July 1811
	Robert Scott	9Sept.1813	
	Andrew Clark Ross	23do.	
	Fred. Philipse Robinson	24do.	
	John Fra. Gray Maclean	26do.	
	James Gammell	29do.	
	Henry Keane Bloomfield	30do.	
	John Mackintosh	6Oct.	
	Cornelius Hogan	7do.	
	—— Sampson	14do.	
	Tho. L. Stuart Mententh	4Nov.	
	Robert White	10do.	
	Rowley F— Hill	25May1814	
	John M'Nabb	26do.	
	Charles Gardiner	15Dec.	
Paymaster 1	Hickman Rose	25Oct.1804	
2	Charles Marr	7Mar.1805	
Adjutant	Thomas Crawley	24Sept.1812	Lieut. 24May1814
	Archibald Campbell	24Sept.1813	Lieut. 28Mar.1811
Quarter-Mast.	William Moorhead	6July1799	
	William Baird	31May1810	
Surgeon	Michael Reynolds	18Nov.1813	1Dec. 1802
	James Hagan	25do.	9Sept.1813
Assistant Surg.	Robert Bradenach	1May1805	4Apr. 1805
	William Thompson	4May1809	
	Peter K— Lambe	8Feb.1810	
	Andrew Colvin	9Sept.1813	

Facings white.—Lace gold.

Agent, Messrs. Greenwood, Cox and Hammersley.

60th

Rank.	Name.	Rank in the Regiment.	Rank in the Army.
Colonel in Chief	{ His Royal Highness Frederick, *D.of* York, *K.G.*23Aug.1797		F.Mar. 10Feb.1795
Col. Comm.	Thomas Carleton	6Aug.1794	Gen. 25Sept.1803
	Napier Christie Burton	3Jan.1806	Gen. 4June1814
	Hon. Edmund Phipps	25Aug.1807	L.Gen. 25Apr.1808
	John Robinson	2Jan.1813	Lt.Gen. 4June1811
5	*Hon.* Charles Hope	15Feb.	Lt.Gen. 1Jan.1812
⊚–	*Sir* Henry Clinton, *K.B.* 20May		Lt.Gen. 4June1814
✗	*Sir* George Murray, *K.B.* 9Aug.		M.Gen. 1Jan.1812
✗	James Kempt	4Nov.	M.Gen. 1Jan.1812
Lieut. Colonel	George William Ramsay	30Dec.1797	M.Gen. 4June1811
	Edward Codd	26Oct.1804	Col. 4June1813
	Thomas Austen	20June1805	Col. 4June1813
	Paul Anderson	14Jan.1808	Col. 4June1813
5	Fra. Ger. *Visc.* Lake	10May	M.Gen. 4June1811
	George Mackie	22Dec.	Col. 4June1814
	James Lomax	16Nov.1809	
	Henry John	9Aug.1813	
	William Marlton	26May1814	1Jan. 1812
10	Adolphus J. Dalrymple	1June	
⊚	William Woodgate	16do.	30May 1811
Major	James Grant	8Nov.1809	Lt.Col. 4June1814
⊚–	John Forster Fitz Gerald	9do.	Lt.Col. 25July1810
⊚–	John Galiffe	15Mar.1810	Lt.Col. 3Mar.1814
	Anthony Rumpler	16Aug.	25July 1810
5	Alexander Andrews	17Jan.1811	
	Ch.de laHoussayeBouverie	2Oct.	Lt.Col. 14July1814
⊚	Gustavus Brown	3do.	Lt.Col. 17Aug.1812
	Ernest Otto Tripp	10Nov.1813	1Apr. 1813
	Henry Fitz Gerald	11do.	
10	James Stopford	10Feb.1814	
	Henry Tarleton	21Apr.	
	Robert Barton	28do.	Col. 4June1813
	John William Aldred	26May	1Jan. 1812
	William Batteley	11Aug.	Lt.Col. 4June1814
15	Lewis de Mangou	8Dec.	4June1814
Captain	Philip Mauriage	2July1803	Major 4June1814
	John Macmahon	20Aug.	Major 4June1814
	Charles Vigny	1Nov.1804	Major 4June1814
	Michael de Wendt	7Dec.	Major 4June1814
₰	Jacob Jordan	28Mar.1805	Lt.Col. 4June1814

Captain

Rank.	Name.	Regiment.	Army.
		Rank in the	
	Frederick Imthurn	24Apr.1805	
	Lewis Imthurn	25do.	
	Adam Krien	23May	
ⓒ	John Schoedde	19Sept.	Major 21June1813
10	Henry Rennells	2Dec.	Major 4June1814
	Peter Blassiere	4do.	
	John Anthony Wolff	5June1806	
	Galenius Reynaud	11Dec.	
	Charles Hinckleday	7May1807	
15	Edward Purdon	27Aug.	Major 12Apr.1814
	James Erskine Bell	20Jan.1808	
	Alexander Ligertwood	30Mar.1809	Major 25Oct.1810
	Charles Du Sable	29June	
	Anthony Stampa	10Oct.	
20	Henry Petrie	11do.	
	C— W— H— Koch	12do.	
	Philip Mayer	23Nov.	
	Charles Mackenzie	10Jan.1810	Major 4June1811
	William Friess	24May	
25	Robert Kelly	16Aug.	
	John Moore	2Jan.1811	
	Leonard Gibbons	14Feb.	Major 4June1814
Captain	Francis Holmes	19Sept.	
	Daniel Page	16Oct.	
30	George F— Gibson	9Jan.1812	
	Everard Baring	13Feb.	
	Melville Glenie	26Mar.	14July 1808
	John Wm. Harrison	12Aug.	15Oct. 1807
	Hon. Esme Stuart Erskine	13do.	27Dec. 1810
35	Richard Henry Hughes	27do.	
	J— Trumback	28do.	
	Henry Dibley	23Dec.	
	John Franchini	28Jan.1813	
	Aubre Carteret Bowers	11Feb.	
40	Adam Alexander Wood	4Mar.	
	William Henry Sewell	29Apr.	Major 3Mar.1814
	Francis Beritze	1Aug.	
	Valentine Reichard	2do.	
	Charles Deckner	3do.	
45	Ern. A. Baron Eberstein	4do.	
	John Strongitharm	5do.	
	Cuthbert Ward	9do.	
	J— N— Nealson	10do.	
	Adolphus de Damas	12do.	
50	Peregrine Fra. Thorne	13do.	

Captain

Rank.	Name.	Rank in the	
		Regiment.	*Army.*
	⎧ Charles Barrington	14Aug.1813	
	⎪ William Pearce	15do.	
	⎪ A— E— D'Orfeuille	17do.	
	⎪ John Bagwell	18do.	
	55 ⎪ Charles Leslie	5Nov.	
	⎪ Thomas Power	6do.	
	⎪ James Dent Weatherley	7do.	
	⎪ John Carmichael	8do.	
	⎪ Colin Campbell	9do.	
	60 ⎪ Richard Brunton	10do.	
	◎- ⎪ John S— Lilly	11do.	
	⎪ Richard Getbin	12do.	
	⎪ George Phelan	13do.	
Captain -	⎨ William Wilkinson	16Dec.	2Sept.1813
	65 ⎪ George Warde Clarke	6Jan.1814	
	⎪ William Rafter	10Feb.	
	⎪ Roche Meade	17do.	
	⎪ John Hewett	14Apr.	
	⎪ George Germain	19do.	
	70 ⎪ Frederick Duncker	20do.	
	⎪ William Henry Taynton	2June	Major 4June1813
	⎪ John Correvont	27July	
	⎪ Charles Johnson	18Aug.	
	⎪ Thomas Maling	17Nov.	11July 1805
	75 ⎪ Roderick M'Neill	1Dec.	
	⎪ Edward Wildman	7do.	
	⎩ John Hovenden	8do.	
	⎧ Frederick Schroen	6Feb.1806	
	⎪ M. Francis A. Tresson	29Nov.1807	
	⎪ William Simpson	1Dec.	
	⎪ Joseph Von Konig	2do.	
	5 ⎪ Maximilian du Chatelet	3do.	
	⎪ John Panton Passley	5do.	
	⎪ Henry Muller	8do.	
Lieutenant	⎨ William Linstow	9do.	
	⎪ Colin Campbell	18Feb.1808	3Sept.1795
	10 ⎪ Robert Mitchell	22Sept.	
	⎪ R— S— Redman	14June1809	26Feb. 1808
	⎪ Frederick de Gilse	26Sept.	
	⎪ Johan Hein Adair	28do.	
	⎪ John Carloss	29do.	
	15 ⎩ Frederick Strobeck	30do.	

Lieutenant

Rank.		Name.	Rank in the	
			Regiment.	Army.
Lieutenant	⎧ Isaac Raboteau Darcy	2Oct.1809	
		William Wynne	3do.	
		Andrew Lacho	4do.	Adjutant
		John Joyce	5do.	
	20	Julius Von Boeck	9do.	
		Andrew Ellison	12do.	
		R— B— Hislop	29do.	
		Leopold de Froger	30do.	
		J— T— Allinson	2Nov.	
	25	Matthew Furst	4do.	
		James Fontaine	5do.	
		Richard Pasley	6do.	
		George Robinson	7do.	
		Augustine F— Evans	9do.	
	30	Charles Andrews	10do.	
		John Hearn	18Feb.1810	
		Peter Kennedy	19do.	
		Alexander Rule	20do.	Adjutant
		Thomas Jack	23do.	
	35	Thomas Smith	24do.	
		Hector Downie	25do.	
		Mayne de Ravarier	26do.	
Lieutenant	⎨ Henry, *Baron* Altenstein	28do.	
		Robert Ellison	do.	Adjutant
	40	George Frederick Stern	1Mar	
		Andrew Leitch	5do.	
		William Goldsmith	11June	
		Maurice Cottman	12do.	
		Richard Hilliard	13do.	
	45	Sylvester O'Hehir	14do.	
		James Brown Donnelly	16Aug.	
		Peter Eason	8Oct.	
		Thomas Marsh	9do.	
		Stephen Price	10do.	
	50	John James Sargent	13do.	
		Samuel Kerr	14do.	
		James D— Kent	16do.	
		Samuel Serjeant	17do.	
		Michael M'Namara	18do.	
	55	Eugene Downing	24do.	
		Richard Saunders	25do.	
		David Le Count	26do.	
		Terence M'Mahon	28do.	
		Frederick de Lahrbusch	29do.	
	60 ⎩	Fred. P— N— de Kruger	30do.	

Lieutenant

Rank.		Name.	Rank in the	
			Regiment.	Army.
Lieutenant	65	Dawson Carr	1Nov.1810	
		C— B— Alcock	6Dec.	
		Edward Burghaagen	28Mar.1811	
		A— P— de Borgh	18Apr.	
		Samuel Burges	10July	9Feb. 1809
		Arthur Mitchell	11do.	4Dec.1806
		William Coleman	15Aug.	
		Cha. Jos. de Franciosi	10Oct.	
		——— de Schanz	3do.	
	70	James Briscoe Gaff	4do.	
		Lew. Valentine Fleischbut	5do.	
		Christ. Wm. Bretthauer	6do.	
		Rich. Henry Lew. Schoffer	7do.	
		Donald Drummond	19Dec.	
	75	Govert Roepel	28Feb.1812	
		John Humphreys	12Mar.	
		James Fleeson	26do.	
		Henry Hudson	27do.	
		Joseph Crow	29do.	
	80	Donald Urquhart	30do.	
		George Cochrane	31do.	
		Dugald Carmichael	2Apr.	
		William Taaffe	14May	
		Henry Heil	6Aug.	
	85	James Kent	2Sept.	Adjutant
		John W— Patterson	3do.	
		Henry Molloy	29Oct.	
		James Beatty	19Dec.	
		Charles Maclean	20do.	
	90	John Currie	22do.	
		Robert Mackenzie	23do.	
		William Brady	24do.	
		Hugh Sutherland	30do.	
		W— Cuthbert Bagnall	14Jan.1813	
	95	James Lawless	21do.	
		Cuthbert Forneret	6Feb.	
		William Batteley	7do.	
		Frederick Baring	8do.	
		William Lupton	9do.	
	100	Jeremy Jones	10do.	
		Matthew Moore	11Mar.	31May 1810
		A. M. Isaacson Durnford	5May	
		W. F. Anderson Gilfillan	6do.	
		Mark Hayes	8July	15Oct. 1812
	105	John Moore	22do.	

Lieutenant

Rank.	Name.	Rank in the Regiment.	Army.
	John Torbock	1 Aug. 1813	
	Robert Pannell	2 do.	
	Christ. Bernard Martin	3 do.	
	Hugh Dickson	4 do.	
110	Robert Nettles	5 do.	
	William Nixon	9 do.	4 Feb. 1813
	Henry James Russell	10 do.	
	Edward Hunter	11 do.	
	Richard Tighe	12 do.	
115	John Frend	13 do.	
	Adam Mellis	14 do.	
	Gottlieb Lerche	19 do.	
	Peter R. A. Van Dyck	2 Sept.	18 Aug. 1812
	James Wallace	9 do.	
120	Edmond Worsley	14 do.	
	Adolphus Bronckhurst	15 do.	
	Edward Webb	21 Oct.	2 Jan. 1811
	L— A— Van Batenburg	22 do.	
	Charles Ross	4 Nov.	
125	Thomas Acton	5 do.	
	Samuel Tresidder	6 do.	Adjutant
	Hodson Gage	7 do.	
Lieutenant	Stephen Thomas Nason	17 do.	19 Sept. 1811
	Augustus Keily	18 do.	
130	Edward Jones	2 Dec.	
	Harry Thomas Heath	9 do.	
	John Caldow	22 do.	
	Matthew Nixon	23 do.	
	Frederick Pictet	22 Jan. 1814	
135	Jerome Cochrane	23 do.	
	Joseph Stewart	24 do.	
	John Hay Crawford	25 do.	
	Lewis Clare	26 do.	
	Richard Aylmer Coates	27 do.	
140	P— Nugent	3 Mar.	
	Hugh Goldicutt	17 do.	
	Ja. Ed. Moreton Douglas	14 Apr.	
	John Armstrong	19 do.	
	Robert Hall	20 do.	
145	Andrew Weiburg	21 do.	Adjutant
	Thomas Wright	22 do.	
	James Freeth	23 do.	
	Richard Archdall	24 do.	
	Ambrose Spong	26 do.	
150	Ja. Rou. Lewis Nealson	27 do.	6 Jan. 1814

Lieutenant

Rank.		Name.	Rank in the	
			Regiment.	Army.
Lieutenant	155	Frederick Klossius	19May1814	21Mar.1805
		Henry Matson	2June	
		Samuel Ridd	11Aug.	25June1805
		Henry Perry	18do.	
		Thomas Beauclerk	8Sept.	30Nov.1809
		William Williams	9Dec.	
		John Brown	10do.	
		Benjamin Clare	11do.	
		Henry Shewbridge	12do.	
	160	Richard Farrar	13do.	
		William Scott	14do.	
		Philip Vignan	15do.	
Ensign		John Hanley	29Sept.1811	
		Hon. Arch. Macdonald	29Dec.1812	
		Henry Morgan Randall	21Jan.1813	
		Edward John Bruce	6Feb.	
	5	John Thomas Hislop	7do.	
		Thomas Lemmon	8do.	
		Thomas Burton	9do.	
		William Donavan	10do.	
		James Lewis	4May	3Mar.1813
	10	Thomas Abell	15July	
		George Eberstein	2Aug.	
		Alexander Blood	3do.	
		Kerry Supple	4do.	
		Hamilton Reed	9do.	
	15	William Henry Barnes	10do.	
		Charles Harris	11do.	
		Martin Burke	13do.	
		Simon M'Queen	14do.	
		Richard Percy Pack	16do.	
	20	John Curtis	17do.	Adjutant
		Thomas Keal	18do.	
		Peter Moore	19do.	
		Frederick George Bartlet	20do.	
		John Frederick Myers	26do.	Adjutant
	25	Clifton Curtis	6Nov.	
		Arthur Smith	7do.	
		John Kelly	8do.	
		George Campbell	9do.	
		J— Gourville	2Dec.	
	30	George Prittie	3do.	

Ensign

| | | Rank in the | |
| Rank. | Name. | Regiment. | Army. |

Ensign	┌ Alexander Paterson	4Dec.1813	
	│ Carl Wevel Von Krüger	22Jan.1814	
	│ Christian Katzmann	23do.	
	│ Frederick Weiss	24do.	
35	│ William Bruns	25do.	
	│ Charles Wilhelme	26do.	
	│ William Heurman	27do.	
	│ Richard Stapleton	19Apr.	
	│ William Slater	20do.	
40	│ Joseph Robinson	21do.	
	│ Robert Alex. Andrews	18Aug.	
	┤ Daniel O'Brien	1Sept.	3Mar.1814
	│ William M— Collings	28do.	
	│ Wm.Bletterinan Caldwell	29do.	
45	│ Walter Bernard	20Oct.	
	│ Edward Maguire	1Dec.	
	│ Cha. Osborn Bushnan	9do.	
	│ John Day	10do.	
	│ ——— Smith	11do.	
50	│ R— Newman	12do.	
	│ Donald M'Kay	13do.	
	│ Ernest Pollman	14do.	
	│ John Magennis	15do.	
	└ Michael Pack	16do.	
Paymaster	3 ┌ Patrick Heyns	19Jan.1809	
	6 │ George Milner Slade	19Oct.	
	1 │ Richard Barnard Fisher	19July1810	
	5 ┤ Henry Biggs	22Oct.1812	
	2 │ George Read	6May1813	
	4 │ Henry Heartszoak	7do.	
	7 │ Cha.Corn.Sey.Worsley	25Nov.	
	8 └ Richard Jellicoe	24Feb.1814	
Adjutant	┌ Andrew Lacho	23Apr.1807	Lieut. 4Oct.1809
	│ Robert Ellison	28Mar.1811	Lieut. 28Feb.1810
	│ Alexander Rule	17Oct.	Lieut. 20Feb.1810
	┤ Andrew Weiburg	10Dec.1812	Lieut. 21Apr.1814
	│ James Kent	31do.	Lieut. 2Sept.1812
	│ John Frederick Myers	26Aug.1813	Ensign 26Aug.1813
	│ Samuel Tresidder	9June1814	Lieut. 6Nov.1813
	└ John Curtis	1Dec.	Ensign 17Aug.1813

Quarter

Rank.	Name.	Rank in the Regiment.	Army.
QuarterMaster	Joseph Chattoway	3July1800	
	Augustus Hennerhofer	25Nov.1807	
	—— Maxwell	6July1812	
	Alexander Johnston	24Sept.	
	—— Reckney	31Dec.	
	Thomas Burrowes	26Aug.1813	
	George Waldt	20Jan.1814	
	Thomas Adams	27do.	
Surgeon -	John Faries	21Dec.1800	
	William Ireland	29June1809	
	William B— Morle	2Nov.	
	John Arthur	5Sept.1811	
	A— L— Loinsworth	28May1812	26Sept.1811
	Joseph Abell	9Aug.1813	15July 1813
	George Vermeulen	2Dec.	
	John Gray Hibbert	8Dec.1814	26May 1814
Assistant Surg.	John H— Walker	2Nov.1809	
	George M'Dermott	30do.	
	Francis Murray	31Jan.1811	
	Lebrecht Mendorff	14Mar.	
	Alexander Melvin	26Sept.	
	Arthur Johnson	28May1812	
	Charles Dealey	4Mar.1813	
	Peter Smith	11Nov.	
	William Stevenson	25do.	
	Charles Newcome	24Feb.1814	
	William Dawson	9June	
	Alexander Spalding	6Oct.	
	Charles Simpson	8Dec.	

Agent, Messrs. Greenwood, Cox and Hammersley.

[1815]

61st (or the South Gloucestershire) Regt of Foot. 305

(2d BATTALION DISBANDED.)

Permitted to bear on their Colours and Appointments a "SPHINX," with the word "EGYPT," in commemoration of the Campaign of 1801. The Flank Companies, and such other Officers and Men as were serving in Calabria, to bear also the word "MAIDA" on their Appointments, for the Action of 4th July, 1806.

Rank.	Name.	Regiment.	Army.
			Rank in the
Colonel - -	*Sir* George Hewett, *Bt.*	4Apr.1800	Gen.　4June1813
Lieut. Colonel	{ James Campbell	16Jan.1804	Lt.Gen. 4June1813
	{ William Carr Royall	23July1812	
Major - -	{ John Oke	23July1812	Lt.Col.22Nov.1813
	{ John Owen	14Aug.	20July 1812
Captain -	{ William Greene	11June1807	Major　3Mar.1814
⊚	Marcus Annesley	24Dec.	
	Algernon Langton	25do.	25Apr.1805
	David Goodsman	28Nov.1808	
	Edward Charleton	22June1809	
	James Mackrill	15Aug.	
	John Hamilton	16do.	
	John Chancellor	14Sept.	
	Richard Giles	28Dec.	
	Duncan M'Dougall	13June1811	
Lieutenant -	{ Martin Irving	16Jan.1806	
	Samuel Falkiner	11June1807	
	James Chapman	2July	
	Alexander Porteus	23do.	
	Norbury Furnace	16Mar.1808	
	Thomas Gloster	17do.	
	Denis O'Kearney	13Oct.	13July 1808
	Robert Armstrong	20Apr.1809	
	Robert Belton	11May	
	John Wolfe	22June	
	William Brackenbury	16Aug.	
	P— Meredith Irwin	1Mar.1810	
	Edward Gaynor	13June1811	
	William Bace	20Oct.	Adjutant
	Alexander M'Leod	12Dec.	
	Archer Toole	30Jan.1812	
	Thomas Williams	23July	
	William White	24do.	
	John Singleton	25do.	
	John Harris	26do.	
	Thomas Harold Meade	27do.	
	James O'Brien	28do.	
	Charles P— Vandreuil	14Aug	
			Ensign

| Rank. | Name. | Rank in the | |
		Regiment.	Army.
Ensign - -	⎧ ——— Atkins	24Nov.1812	
	Spry Bartlet	25do.	
	Edward Waldron	26do.	
	Robert Magee	5Aug.1813	
	Graves Ackland	18Nov.	
	Robert Norris Verner	9Dec.	
	William Briggs	13Jan.1814	
	⎩ E— Mac Donnell	20do.	
Paymaster -	William Moss	3Mar.1804	
Adjutant - -	William Bace	9Feb.1809	Lieut. 20Oct.1811
Quarter-Master	William Hall	14June1810	
Surgeon - -	Samuel Peacock	15Dec.1808	
Assistant Surg. ⎰	Samuel Burd	21Dec.1809	
⎱	Edward Giddens	19Dec.1811	

Facings buff.—Lace silver.

Agent, Messrs. Greenwood, Cox and Hammersley.

Colonel - -	Samuel Hulse	25 June 1810	Gen.	25 Sept. 1803
Lieut. Colonel	Trevor Hull	6 Sept. 1798	M. Gen.	4 June 1811
	George Gauntlett	2 May 1811		
	Nathaniel Blackwell	13 June	Col.	4 June 1814
Major - -	David Ximines	28 Aug. 1804	Lt. Col.	4 June 1811
	Daniel Francis Blommart	12 Oct.	Col.	4 June 1814
	John F— Goodridge	1 Feb. 1810	Lt. Col.	4 June 1814
	Edward Darley	2 May 1811	Lt. Col.	1 Jan. 1812
	Richard Robarts	31 Jan. 1799	Major	4 June 1811
	Eyre Smyth	27 Nov. 1801	Major	4 June 1813
	William Hull	25 June 1803	Major	4 June 1814
	William Riddell	23 July	Major	4 June 1814
	James Butler	2 Aug. 1804	Major	4 June 1814
	John Pollock	27 do.	Major	4 June 1814
	Paulus Æmilius Irving	19 Sept.	Major	4 June 1814
	Skene Keith	19 Oct.	Major	4 June 1814
	Richard Edwards	1 Dec.	Major	4 June 1814
	James Sweeney	31 Jan. 1805		
Captain -	C— W— Kerr	22 Aug.		
	William Hartley	22 Dec. 1808		
	Andrew Creagh	21 Sept. 1809	1 Mar. 1809	
	William Johnstone	1 Feb. 1810		
	Hen. Lewis E. Gwynne	23 Aug.		
	William Hodgkinson	2 May 1811		
	John Walter	24 Mar. 1813		
	John Reed	25 do.		
	Richard Bates	29 July	21 July 1810	
	Isaac Humphries	21 Oct.		
	James Fielding Sweeney	22 do.		
	John Radford	28 July 1814		
	Robert Martin	28 Mar. 1805		
	Richard Wood	3 Apr.		
	Charles Nangle	18 do.		
	William Lowe Peard	1 Aug.		
	Roger Sweeney	19 Dec.		
	John Mahon	3 Apr. 1806		
	James Twigg	1 May		
	Richard Usher	17 July		
	William Bellingham	27 Aug. 1807		
	John Shearman	1 Nov.	27 Nov. 1806	
Lieutenant -	Sackville H— Eaton	3 do.		
	Christopher Heyland	5 do.		
	Edward Parker	6 do.	Adjutant	
	John Keith	7 do.		
	Alexander Thompson	8 do.		
	James Butler	9 do.		
	Alexander Scott	12 do.		
	Philip Ricketts	25 Mar. 1808		
	A— Stewart	29 Sept.		
	James Dennis	15 June 1809		
	Ferdinand Spiller	1 Feb. 1810		
	William Hodgkinson	26 Dec. 1811		

q

Lieutenant

	Lloyd Henry de Ruvyne	5Mar.1812	
	William Blakeley	15Oct.	
	William Dundee	29Apr.1813	
	John O'Grady	22Sept.	
	Macarty Colclough	23do.	
	Thomas Humfrey	21Oct.	
	William Hewat	22do.	
	James Fraser M'Donell	23do.	
	Walter Strang	24do.	
	George Raye	20Jan.1814	
	Maurice O'Halloran	11Feb.	10June1812
Lieutenant -	T— G— Elrington	12do.	
	David Davies	13do.	
	Alfred Knight	14do.	
	Robert Gumbleton Daunt	15do.	
	Ralph Evans	16do.	
	Richard Barnet	17do.	
	Samuel Henry Coleman	10Mar.	10Dec.1811
	W— R— Towers	30do.	5Apr.1801
	Robert Markham	31do.	
	Francis Thompson	8Sept.	
	John Summers	20Oct.	
	John Hawkins	1Dec.	
	Alexander Reid	14Jan.1813	
	Henry Cuffe	8Apr.	
	Henry Law	29do.	
	Henry Williams	21Oct.	
	John Judge	22do.	
	Francis Leatham	4Nov.	
	Eneas M'Goldrick	11do.	
	John Walker	15Dec.	
Ensign - -	John Higginbotham	16do.	
	Henry Michell	6Jan.1814	
	Thomas Russell	17do.	Adjutant
	Francis Sweeney	20do.	
	John Mansell	16Feb.	
	John Johnston	17do.	
	John H— Whitney	17Mar.	
	Robert Brooke Wilson	21Apr.	
	William Henry Sayer	28do.	
Paymaster 1	Hugh Darley	1July1803	
2	Francis Edward Leech	19Nov.1807	
Adjutant -	Edward Parker	25May1808	Lieut. 6Nov.1807
	Thomas Russell	17Jan.1814	Ensign 17Jan.1814
QuarterMaster	George Robertson	1Nov.1809	
	George Mac Beath	2do.	
Surgeon -	John Mackesey	19Mar.1812	
	George Purdon	30Sept.1813	
Assistant Surg.	John Horne	28Jan.1813	
	John James Fawcett	4Feb.	
	Edward Hollier	7Oct.	

Facings buff.—Lace silver.

Agent, Messrs. Greenwood, Cox and Hammersley.

[1815]

63d (or the West Suffolk) Regiment of Foot. 307
(2d BATTALION DISBANDED.)

		Rank in the	
Rank.	Name.	Regiment.	Army.

Rank.	Name.	Regiment.	Army.
Colonel - -	Alex. *Earl of* Balcarres	27 Aug. 1789	Gen. 25 Sept. 1803
Lieut. Colonel	David Rattray	27 Sept. 1810	25 July 1810
Major - -	{ Robert Macleroth	28 June 1810	
	{ John Stafford	4 Apr. 1811	Lt.Col. 4 June 1811
Captain - -	⎰ John Wynne	3 Aug. 1804	Major 4 June 1814
	James W— Fairtlough	14 Mar. 1805	
	William Boxall	13 June	
	Robert Menzies	19 Dec.	
	John Blake Lynch	30 Apr. 1807	21 Aug. 1805
	William Snape	14 July 1808	
	William Smith	12 Nov. 1809	
	Robert Martin Leake	14 Feb. 1811	
	Thomas Rickets Myers	25 July	
◎	Edward Knight	19 Sept.	21 June 1810
	Basil Fisher	16 Jan. 1812	Major 4 June 1814
	William Groombridge	17 Dec.	19 Apr. 1810
Lieutenant	⎰ John Charles Boyd	19 Dec. 1805	
	William Cosby	8 May 1806	
	Robert Brereton	25 June	Adjutant
	Walter Ward	26 do.	
	William Penefather	20 Aug. 1807	
	David Campbell	5 Feb. 1808	
	Robert Walsh Richardson	5 Apr.	
	George E— M'Connell	6 do.	
	Richard Grant	7 do.	
	Richard Church	1 June 1809	
	William M'Causland	3 Oct.	
	Christopher Plunket	4 do.	
	Edward Walter Dillon	5 do.	
	Thomas Illingworth	16 Nov.	
	John Duport	17 Jan. 1810	
	Edward Brown	18 do.	
	George James Wigley	25 Mar.	
	Robinson Sadlier	5 Apr.	
	Michael Vicary	16 May 1811	
	William Gilbert	20 June	

q 2

Lieutenant

| Rank. | Name. | Rank in the | |
		Regiment.	Army.
Lieutenant -	Philip Bolton	25July1811	21Oct.1795
	Thomas Fairtlough	9Apr.1812	
	Richard Fry	18June	
	Denny F— M'Carthy	19Nov.	
	Foillet Wynne	24Dec.	
	Charles Perceval	4Mar.1813	
	William Davey	12Aug.	
	Edward Cooper Colls	23Dec.	
Ensign - -	Webb Lowman	4July1811	
	Hugh Percy Forster	24do.	
	Henry Nason	19Sept.	
	Tho. William Thornton	28Nov.	
	William Houghton	6Feb.1812	
	—— O'Neill	9Apr.	
	George Palmer	7May	
	Edward Back	4June	
Paymaster -	John Jones	14Mar.1811	
Adjutant - -	Robert Brereton	24Jan.1805	Lieut. 25June1806
Quarter-Master	George Lynn	25July1802	
Surgeon - -	William Macnish	6July1809	
	Jeffery Hateley	28July1814	
Assistant Surg.	Rob.JohnPrylisBurkitt	22Aug.1811	
	William Dudgeon	26Sept.	19July 1810

N. B. *The Officers printed in Italics are to be placed upon Half-pay on arrival from Foreign Service.*

Facings deep green.—Lace silver.

Agent, Mr. Fowlis, No. 3, New Basinghall Street.

Rank.	Name.	Rank in the Regiment.	Army.
Colonel - -	Henry Wynyard	15Sept.1808	Lt.Gen.25Apr.1808
Lieut. Colonel	*Sir* John Wardlaw, *Bt.*	8May1806	Col. 4June1814
Major - - ⊚	{ John Macdonald { William Beatty	19Mar.1807 24May1810	Lt.Col. 4June1813 Lt.Col. 3Mar.1814
Captain -	⎰ John Buckworth John Jameson Henry Bishop Joseph Hill Pears Arthur Dickson Wm. Henry Newton Charles Bennett Redmond Hinton Kelly Cha. Stanhope O'Meara Ralph Johnson James Thomas Galbraith	25May1803 25Nov.1804 1Dec. 20Feb.1806 8May 25June1808 17Aug.1809 4Jan.1810 9Aug. 21Nov.1811 2June1814	Major 1Jan.1812 Major 4June1814 Major 4June1814 21Apr. 1814
Lieutenant	⎰ John Arthur Allen ——— Hunter Samuel S— Parker James H— Weir John G— Hall John Bennett Edward Windsor J— George Blake James Morson John Jervois H— R— Daly John Walsh James Knox John Thomas Walford Thomas Thomas Peter Gapper Antho. Von Som Forbes George Ramsay Rich. Woodward Isbell John Letham Samuel Chambers William C— Oates	29Sept.1805 17Apr.1806 29do. 30do. 1May 23Oct. 12Apr.1807 9July 10Feb.1808 6Mar. 18Apr. 25Aug.1809 26do. 26Oct. 1Feb.1810 3May 14June 9Aug. 11July1811 2Jan.1812 18Feb.1813 17Feb.1814	 12June1805 26Mar.1804 22June1809 25Dec.1806 16Feb. 1809 10Sept.1811 7Oct. 1813

Ensign

		Rank in the	
Rank.	*Name.*	*Regiment.*	*Army.*

	William Pears	24May1810	Cornet 25Oct.1809
	Samuel Hugghue	30Aug.	
	Cornwall Burn	4Oct.	
Ensign -	John Piercy	11July1811	
	William Jackson	3Oct.	
	Edmund Alex. Douglas	9Apr.1812	
	Samuel Moore	27May1813	Adjutant
	James Rolston	25Dec.	

Paymaster -	Israel Moss	3June1813	
Adjutant - -	Samuel Moore	27May1813	Ensign 27May1812
Quarter-Master	William Crymble	27May1813	
Surgeon - -	Alexander M'Lean	11Nov.1813	
Assistant Surg. {	Thomas O'Halloran	3Mar.1813	26Sept.1811
	William Austen	4do.	

Facings black.—Lace gold.

Agent, Messrs. Greenwood, Cox and Hammersley.

[1815]

65th (or the 2d Yorksh. N. Riding) Regt. of Foot. 311

Rank.	Name.	Rank in the Regiment.	Army.
Colonel - -	Thomas Grosvenor	8Feb.1814	Lt.Gen.25Apr.1808
Lieut. Colonel	Lionel Smith	25Nov.1806	Col.　　4June1813
	Colin James Milnes	4June1811	
Major - -	Nathaniel Warren	1Apr.1810	
	J— Henry Fitz Simon	2Jan.1812	Lt.Col.　1Jan.1812
Captain -	Edward Watkin	11Dec.1804	Major　4June1814
	Dunlop Digby	16Sept.1806	
	James Keith	24Sept.1807	3Oct. 1805
	Thomas Hutchings	19May1808	Major　4June1814
	William Hinde	28Sept.1809	
	John Clutterbuck	14Nov.	
	R— James Debnam	1Apr.1810	
	Thomas Strangwayes	2Jan.1812	
	John Goodyer	22do.	
	Alexander Campbell	4Feb.1813	26Sept.1805
Lieutenant	Tho. H. Smeeton Hutton	1Nov.1806	
	James Maclean	21Apr.1808	
	Henry Taylor	18Aug.	
	George Wilson	10Oct.	
	James Place	15Dec.	
	Henry Stracey	22June1809	
	Isaac Hart	1Aug.	
	Sam. Robinson Warren	23Oct.	
	Michael Henley	27Feb.1810	
	Peter M'Laine	25Apr.	
	Peter Farquharson	1May	
	Henry Francis Sharp	31Aug.	
	John Rawson Stepney	1Sept.	
	Thomas White	21Jan.1812	
	George Thomas Parker	22do.	
	William Warde	23do.	Adjutant
	Francis Strangwayes	15May	
	John Hunt	2June	
	Benjamin Robert Ottley	16July	
	William Hall	3Feb.1813	
	Henry Rich	4do.	

Ensign

[1815]

312 65th (or the 2d Yorksh. N. Riding) Regt. of Foot.

Rank.	Name.	Rank in the Regiment.	Army.
Ensign	{ George Latham Blacker	10Sept.1812	
	William Andros	24do.	
	William Booth	3Feb.1813	
	William Barnes	do.	
	Hon. Charles Turnour	do.	
	Adam Cuppage	11Mar.	
	Edward Thomson	26Aug.	
	Henry Tudor	1June1814	
Paymaster	Archibald Colquhoun	11Feb.1813	4May 1809
Adjutant	William Warde	1Sept.1810	Lieut. 23Jan.1812
Quarter-Master	John Ottey	30July1800	
Surgeon	J— Dick	26Sept.1812	
Assistant Surg.	{ Charles O'Reilly	1June1812	
	Patrick Mackenzie	13May1813	

Facings white.— Lace gold.

Agent, Messrs. Greenwood, Cox and Hammersley.

66th

Rank.	Name.	Rank in the Regiment.	Rank in the Army.
Colonel	Oliver Nicolls	3 Aug. 1808	Gen. 4 June 1813
Lieut. Col. ◎	Alex. Cosby Jackson Charles Nicol John Ross John Wardell	27 Dec. 1810 13 June 1811 18 July 4 June 1813	M. Gen. 4 June 1813 Col. 4 June 1814
Major ◎	Edmund Lascelles Daniel Dodgin William Parke Edward Carlyon	23 Feb. 1809 29 June 5 Mar. 1812 4 June 1813	Lt. Col. 4 June 1814 Lt. Col. 21 June 1813 25 July 1810
Captain ◎	J— Innes Henry Pearse Blakeney James Baird W—H— Stephens Samuel Zobell George Leigh Goldie William Baird William Dunbar Anthony Richards George Nicholls Charles White John Jordan John Hitch Ellis Augustus Bulstrode William Ferns Peter Duncan J—D— Dunne Vaun Brice Francis Frome William Barstow Samuel Turton John Deane	14 Aug. 1805 25 Apr. 1806 14 July 26 Feb. 1807 27 Aug. 21 Jan. 1808 11 Feb. 4 Aug. 25 Nov. 23 Feb. 1809 15 June 4 Oct. 5 do. 21 Dec. 4 Jan. 1810 1 Aug. 1811 9 Jan. 1813 16 Sept. 18 Oct. 23 Dec. 13 Jan. 1814 17 Mar.	8 Jan. 1807 Major 20 June 1811 19 Sept. 1805 Major 12 Apr. 1814 15 Sept. 1808
Lieutenant	Henry Thompson Shapland Carew Morris Stepeny St. George Thomas B— Hicken Thomas John Harvey —— L'Estrange	28 Feb. 1806 29 Jan. 1807 6 Aug. 28 Jan. 1808 2 Feb. 3 do.	31 Oct. 1805

r

Lieutenant

Rank.	Name.	Rank in the Regiment.	Army.
Lieutenant -	Apollos Morris	6Feb.1808	
	Henry Blake	8do.	
	James Chambers	25do.	
	Thomas Moffatt	1Oct.	
	George Farr	26do.	31Dec. 1807
	William Davy	27do.	
	Hamilton Edmonds	23Feb.1809	
	——— Lambrecht	30May	
	Herbert Morgan	31do.	
	James P— Rose	1June	
	Robert Carew Wogan	17Aug.	
	John Clarke	3Oct.	
	Charles M'Carthy	4do.	
	John Codd	5do.	
	R— H— Reardon	1Feb.1810	
	Nicholas Whitney	4Apr.	
	John Ellis	21June	
	James Roberts	8Nov.	24May 1809
	John Ussher	31July1811	
	Henry Young	1Aug.	
	J— Ekins Waring	28Feb.1812	
	James Hay	30Apr.	
	Thomas Chatterton	30July	
	William Kingsmill	17Sept.	
	Augustus Nicolls	1Sept.1813	
	John Garstin	2do.	
	Thomas Mack	7Oct.	
	William Chadwick	24do.	13Aug.1812
	Cuthbert Barlow	13Jan.1814	
	Robert Johnstone	20do.	
	John Donelan	9June	
Ensign - -	Anthony Browne	15Feb.1810	
	William Servantes	13July1811	27June 1811
	Bingham Sarsfield	1Aug.	
	Joseph Gun	9Jan.1812	
	Richard Bullen	30do.	
	Bartholomew Mahon	28Feb.	
	George Tolfrey	20Mar.	
	Thomas Swayne	30Apr.	
	William Dunn	16July	
	Walter M'Kenzie	23June1813	Adjutant

Ensign

Rank.	Name.	Rank in the Regiment.	Army.
Ensign - -	Charles Mitchell	1Sept.1813	
	William Rhynd	2do.	
	William Morton	10Nov.	
	William Gilbert	23Dec.	Adjutant
	John Clarke	13Jan.1814	
	Bannastyne Lamont	20do.	
	Henry Duncan Dodgin	24Mar.	
	Charles Mitchell	9June	
Paymaster 1	William Mansell	4Apr.1811	
Paymaster 2	Thomas Lediard	do.	
Adjutant -	Walter M'Kenzie	23June1813	Ensign 23June1813
	William Gilbert	23Dec.	Ensign 23Dec.1813
QuarterMaster	John Macdonald	25Sept.1799	
	William King	9July1803	
Surgeon -	Matthew Heir	1Feb.1811	2Nov.1804
	Francis Leigh	9Sept.1813	
Assistant Surg.	Walter Henry	19Dec.1811	
	Thomas Laidlaw	9Sept.1813	
	Thomas Morse	7July1814	

Facings gosling green.—Lace silver.

Agent, Messrs. Greenwood, Cox and Hammersley.

		Rank in the	
Rank.	Name.	Regiment.	Army.

Colonel - - *Sir* William Keppel, *K.B.* 7Feb.1811 | Gen. | 4June1813

Lieut. Colonel ⊚ { William Aug. Prevost 30May1805 Col. 4June1813
Samuel Huskisson 16June1808 Col. 4June1814
William Kinloch 4June1813

Major - - { Charles Maxwell 27Dec.1810 Lt.Col. 1Jan.1812
Nathaniel Benjafield 4June1813
George Cowell 1July
Martin Corry 13Oct.1814 4June1814

Captain - { Frederick P— Noble 9July1803 Major 4June1814
David Scott 3Dec. Major 4June1814
William Owen 3Mar.1804 Major 4June1814
James Cassidy 18Apr.1805
Michael Tho. Browne 16May
Abraham James 30Sept.1806
David Browne 24Nov.1807
Alexander Beck 26do.
John M'Namara 13Apr.1809
Edw. Despard Palmer 7Sept.
Samuel Patrickson 21do.
Colin Campbell 20Feb.1811
Swift Armstrong 21do.
Charles Moore 25Apr.
William Hoare 1Aug.
Thomas Hall 16Jan.1812
John Algeo 28Feb.
Alex.Wedd.Mackenzie12Aug. 23Jan. 1812
Robert Betteridge 1July1813
Harry Walker 22do.
Robert Johnson 12Oct.1814
Cha. Henry Mainwaring 13do.

Lieutenant

Rank.	Name.	Rank in the Regiment.	Rank in the Army.
Lieutenant -	John Dowland	28Mar.1805	
	George Mathers	1May	
	Donald Cameron	14Aug.	30May 1805
	George Coote	30Nov.	
	George Rea	21May1807	
	Moore Scott	18Oct.	
	Donald Macpherson	14Jan.1808	
	George Mitchell	20do.	19Mar. 1807
	Robert Cockerell	7Apr.	9May 1805
	Edward William Bray	20do.	
	Richard Dickson	16June	
	James Kirby	15Dec.	1Dec. 1808
	George Cosby Harpour	29do.	
	James Ronald	5Apr.1809	
	William Rowan	6do.	
	David Hunter	13June	
	William Ronald	15do.	
	Thomas Fraser	7Sept.	
	Kirkwood Cassidy	2Nov.	
	Alexander Clark	17May1810	
	James Adair	20Feb.1811	
	Emer Baynham	21do.	
	Robert Sutherland	21Mar.	
	William Jones	25do.	
	William Webster	1Aug.	26Sept.1805
	Charles L— Stretch	24Oct.	
	Herbert Vaughan	16Jan.1812	
	Francis Agar	12Mar.	
	William Warburton	2Apr.	
	Wellesley Medlicott	13Aug.	
	Robert Gilly	3Dec.	
	John Manning Mailleue	4Feb.1813	
	Boyce Walker	10June	
	Charles Moore Harrison	8July	
	Edward Smith Delamain	28July1814	
	Foster Fyans	1Sept.	
	John Hanna	17Nov.	
	James M'Pherson	24do.	Adjutant
	John Connell	22Dec.	

Ensign

Rank.	Name.	Rank in the Regiment.	Army:

Rank.	Name.	Regiment.	Army:
Ensign	Wm. Octavius Atkinson	1Aug.1811	
	Job Dickson	do.	
	Robert Davis	2Jan.1812	
	Joseph Everett	16do.	
	William Blair	2Apr.	15May1811 Adjut.
	J— William Sloane	1June	
	Richard Tidmarsh	10do.	
	David Duff	20Aug.	
	Charles Rainsford	2Sept.	
	Lucius French	3do.	
	A— K— Huston	20May1813	
	William Jones	27do.	
	James Thompson	3June	
	Henry Richardson	17do.	
	Thomas J—J—Avarne	12Aug.	
	Thomas Arrow	1Nov.	
	Benjamin Barrie	4do.	
	John Bolton	5do.	
	Daniel M'Daniell	17Nov.1814	
Paymaster 1	Alexander Pilfold	23May1811	
2	James Armstrong	6Jan.1814	
Adjutant	James M'Pherson	25Mar.1811	Lieut. 24Nov.1814
	William Blair	3Dec.1812	Ensign 15May1811
QuarterMaster	Mathias Hennessy	19June1806	
	—— Hales	25Mar.1811	
Surgeon	John Crake	22Dec.1808	
	Edmund Weld	19July1810	
Assistant Surg.	Michael W— Kenny	25Sept.1803	
	James Gelder	4Jan.1810	10Sept.1807
	James Ward Martindale	23Jan.1812	
	Andrew Mackay	6Oct.1814	

Facings yellow.—Lace silver.

Agent, Mr. Ridge, No. 44, Charing Cross.

			Rank in the	
Rank.	Name.	Regiment.	Army.	
Colonel -	◎Henry Warde	1Jan.1813	Lt.Gen. 4June1813	
Lieut. Col. ◎-	{ John Simon Farley { William Johnston	1Mar.1800 13July1809	M.Gen. 4June1811 Col. 4June1814	
Major - ◎	{ John P— Hawkins { James Winnett	17Sept.1812 26Aug.1813	Lt.Col. 21June1813 4June1813	
Captain -	{ William Gough John Reed Nathaniel Gledstanes William North William Mackay Peter le Mesurier Simson Kennedy Robert Melville Henry Archdall George Macdonald { William Abbott	13May1804 12May1808 13July1809 8Nov. 9Jan.1812 27Aug. 8Oct. 19Aug.1813 26do. 6Jan.1814 31Mar.	Major 4June1814 22Mar.1810	
Lieutenant -	{ James Menzies Sholto Sorlie George Archbold William Smyth Honeyman Mackay James Sloan John Hinds Robert Jackson Patrick Grant William Bolton James Thomson Robert Clarke William Mendham James Carson David Dawes William Gibson James Mitchell David J— Skene John Fowke Robert Ball Sev.Wm.Lynam Stretton Thomas Sheddon Joseph Gibson ——— Berkeley { Robert Francis Saunders	1May1806 25Dec. 21Sept.1808 22do. 18May1809 7Sept. 7Nov. 8do. 16do. 8Feb.1810 19Apr. 26Dec.1811 30Jan.1812 4June 7Oct. 8do. 29July1813 30do. 19Aug. 26do. 6Jan.1814 30do. 31do. 14Apr. 22Dec.	 25Apr. 1806 30June 1808 29Jan. 1807 Adjutant 12July 1808	

Ensign

[1815]

320   68th (or the Durham) Regiment of Foot.
(LIGHT INFANTRY.)

Rank.	Name.	Rank in the Regiment.	Army.
Ensign	Thomas Browning	26Aug.1813	
	J— Kearns	5Jan.1814	
	Donald Macdonald	6do.	
	John Blood	3Mar.	
	George Carson	30do.	
	Edward Dillon	31do.	
	John Harvey	14Apr.	
	Thomas Black	1Sept.	24Feb. 1814
Paymaster	John Lewis White	25Feb.1813	
Adjutant	John Hinds	3Dec.1807	Lieut. 7Nov.1809
Quarter-Master	Nicholas Ross	13May1813	
Surgeon	James Reid	5Nov.1812	
Assistant Surg.	Archibald Fraser	25June1812	
	Richard Williams	24Feb.1814	

Facings bottle green.—Lace silver.

Agent, Messrs. Greenwood, Cox and Hammersley.

Rank	Name	Date	Army Rank	Date
Colonel - -	*Sir* Cornelins Cuyler, *Bt.*	20June1794	Gen.	25Sept.1803
Lieut. Col.	Thomas Browne	30May1805	M.Gen.	4June1813
◎	Miles Nightingall	8May1806	Lt.Gen.	4June1814
	Phineas Riall	27Dec.1810	M.Gen.	4June1813
◉	Walter Symes	27Aug.1811		
	Charles Morice	4June1813	Col.	4June1814
	Price Robbins	do.		
Major - -	George Muttlebury	28Nov.1811	Lt.Col.	17Mar.1814
	Henry de la Douespe	10June1812		
	C— J— Barrow	11do.		
	Archibald Maclachlan	4June1813	25July 1810	
Captain -	J— Lewis Watson	9July1803	Major	4June1813
	Henry Lindsay	do.	Major	4June1814
	William Carroll	17Sept.1807	Major	5Nov.1812
	Thomas Magennis	10Feb.1809		
	John Leslie	30Nov.		
	Robert Cary	30Aug.1810		
	James Mellis	4Apr.1811	8Sept.1808	
	Matthew Gunning	26Sept.		
	George Lane	12Dec.		
	William W— Read	8June1812		
	J— H— Holland	9do.	Major	19Dec.1813
	Charles Lowrie	11do.	Lt.Col.	1Jan.1812
	Henry Cox	19Nov.		
	Hon. William Curzon	17Dec.		
	George Sacville Cotter	3June1813		
	Charles Cuyler	10do.		
	Benjamin Hobhouse	12Aug.		
	Isaac Downing	9Dec.		
	George Ulrick Barlow	30do.		
	Francis John Davies	17Feb.1814	12Aug.1813	
	Matthew Jenour	5May		
	WilliamHamiltonWest	10Nov.		
Lieutenant -	Robert Baker	22May1806		
	Duncan M'Pherson	1Feb.1807		
	Charles E— Freeman	20Nov.		
	William Harrison	27Jan.1808		
	John Foulstone	29Sept.		
	Peter Browne	1Feb.1809		
	W.HamiltonBurroughs	15June		
	John Smith	9Nov.		
	L— Webb	22do.		
	A— Wardlock	31Jan.1810		
	Edward Sproule	1Feb.		
	Roger Franklyn	18Apr.		
	Joseph Gillam James	19do.		
	Alexander Mullingan	18July		
	William Tedlie	6Dec.		
	Stephen Parker	11Apr.1811		

Lieutenant

Lieutenant -	Brooke Pigot	9May1811	
	William Grenville	12Dec.	
	William Moorhead	4Mar.1812	
	Joseph Ducker	5do.	
	W— E— Ellis	9June	
	William Har. Shurlock	10do.	
	George Harper	11do.	
	William Ruxton	25do.	
	G— B— Rose	26do.	Adjutant
	Luke Glover Finn	2July	
	Christopher Busteed	25Jan.1813	15Jan. 1813
	Neil Roy	1July	
	John Lamb Harrison	8Dec.	
	Lodge Morris Prior	9do.	
	Charles William Ingle	1Feb.1814	
	Joseph Hill	2do.	
	Henry Oldershaw	3do.	Adjutant
	Charles Lenox Dickson	21Apr.	
	Edm. Martin Wightwick	5May	
	Joseph Deighton	16June	
	Peter Taylor	8Sept.	
	John Stewart	10Nov.	
Ensign - -	Charles Francis Pelly	21July1813	
	Henry Anderson	22do.	
	Edward Hodder	29do.	
	William Bartlett	3Feb.1814	
	Charles Seward	24do.	
	Henry Duncan Keith	21Apr.	
	——— Bailey	5May	
	Joseph Langson	28July	
	Geo.Simon Har. Ainslie	10Nov.	
	George Ronsden	11do.	
	John Weir	1Dec.	
	Roger Duke	22do.	
Paymaster 1	Edward Mundell	28Jan.1813	24Apr. 1809
2	Philip Vyvyan	do.	
Adjutant -	G— B— Rose	25Dec.1810	Lieut. 26June1812
	Henry Oldershaw	19May1814	Lieut. 3Feb.1814
QuarterMaster	William Henry	9July1803	
	Matthew Stevens	6Dec.1810	
Surgeon -	George Rowe	18June1807	
	Alexander M'Kechnie	30July1812	
Assistant Surg.	Edward Tedlie	18Dec.1806	
	James Bartlet	16July1812	
	James Gibson	28Apr.1814	
	William Gracie	15Dec.	

Facings green.—Lace gold.

Agent, Messrs. Greenwood, Cox and Hammersley.

70th

		Rank in the	
Rank.	Name.	Regiment.	Army.

Rank.	Name.	Regiment.	Army.
Colonel	✗ *Hon.Sir* Gal.Low.Cole, *K.B.* 12Jan.1814		Lt.Gen. 4June1813
Lieut. Colonel	Lewis Grant	18Feb.1804	Col. 4June1813
Major -	{ Charles M'Gregor 13Aug.1812		30Apr. 1812
	Thomas Ralph Congreve 4June1813		4June1811
	Hon. Gerard De Courcy do.		
Captain -	Richard Green	17Jan.1806	
	William Bernard	22Oct.1807	Major 4June1814
	Allen Cameron	29Sept.1808	28Nov.1806
	Thomas Huxley	6Dec.1810	15May 1800
	Thomas Howard	21Mar.1811	Major 4June1814
	Babington Nolan	30Jan.1812	
	John Tredennick	12Mar.	
	Donald Mackay	9Apr.	
	AugustusC—Drawwater	2July	15Aug.1811
	Joseph Kelsall	11Nov.1813	
	* Daniell O'Neill	25Dec.	
	* James Patrick	do.	
Lieutenant -	J— De la Haye	26Feb.1805	
	Theobald Hunt	25Mar.	
	William Poole	1Aug.	
	James Mackay	21Nov.	
	John Landon	16Jan.1807	
	Jacob Ogden Creighton	15Dec.1808	
	Felix Kearns	27July1809	
	Robert Kirk	9Nov.	3Nov.1808
	Henry Ross Lewen	22Feb.1810	
	Edward James White	25Mar.1811	5Apr. 1810
	Edward Stevenson	12Sept.	
	George Goldfrap	3Oct.	
	John Austin	29Jan.1812	
	Edward Smith	30do.	2May 1811
	George Collis	12Mar.	
	Donald M'Iver	9Apr.	
	James Samson	22do.	Adjutant
	William Taylor	23do.	
	Richard Armstrong	23Dec.	7Mar. 1810
	John Graham	11Nov.1813	
	John Alexander	12do.	
	* J— M'Laurin	25Dec.	
	* Matthias Castle	do.	

s 2   Ensign

| Rank. | Name. | Rank in the | |
		Regiment.	Army.
Ensign - -	⎧ Robert Bland	29Aug.1811	
	Alexander Forbes	10Mar.1812	
	Peter Collis	11do.	
	Edmund Mahon	12do.	
	James Hunter	23Apr.	
	John Alston	21May	
	William Craufurd	22do.	
	George Clark	4June	
	Frederick Lenox Ingall	8Apr.1813	
	Thomas Trigge	22do.	
	John Savage	20May	
	Samuel White	1July	
	Thomas Henry Martin	2do.	
	William Mercer	16Sept.	13Aug.1813
	James Gaston	25Dec.	
	James Maxwell	do.	
	John Penniger	13Jan.1814	
	⎩ John Brown	28Apr.	
Paymaster -	Thomas Scott	16Jan.1812	
Adjutant - -	James Samson	13Sept.1810	Lieut. 22Apr.1812
Quarter-Master	Thomas Norman	4May1809	
Surgeon - -	George Garrett	18June1812	
Assistant Surg.	⎧ J— F— Swindell	8July1813	
	⎩ J— Farnden	12May1814	

Facings black.—Lace gold.

Agent, Mr. Ridge, No. 44, Charing Cross.

71st

Rank.	Name.	Rank in the Regiment.	Army.
Colonel - -	Francis Dundas	7 Jan. 1809	Gen. 1 Jan. 1812
Lieut. Col. ⓒ	{ Thomas Reynell { Charles Cother	5 Aug. 1813 13 Oct. 1814	Col. 4 June 1813 19 June 1812
Major - -	(Arthur Jones { Leslie Walker { George Spottiswoode (Charles M— Graham	22 June 1809 2 Sept. 1813 31 Mar. 1814 13 Oct.	Lt. Col. 4 June 1814
Captain - -	(Samuel Reed | Joseph Thomas Pidgeon | Archibald Armstrong | Donald Campbell | Edmund L'Estrange | William Alex. Grant | James Henderson | Augustus J— M'Intyre | *Hon.* Edward Cadogan { Geo. Hamilton Gordon | Charles Johnstone | Alexander Grant | James B— Ness | James Aaron Roy | Ralph Dudgeon | Henry Clements | William Lockwood | William Graham (Thomas Parke	29 Sept. 1808 1 Dec. 10 May 1809 22 June 6 July 12 Oct. 19 do. 17 May 1810 23 Aug. 6 Dec. 10 Dec. 1812 15 Apr. 1813 10 June 5 Aug. do. 1 Sept. 2 do. 20 Jan. 1814 31 Mar.	29 Nov. 1806 Major 12 Apr. 1814 4 Jan. 1810 Lt. Col. 4 June 1814 Major 4 June 1814
Lieutenant -	(Samuel C— Grey | Joseph Barrailler | William M'Craw | Loftus Richards | John Raleigh Elwes { Charles Stewart | Robert Baldwin | William Crosbie Hanson | Robert Lind | John Roberts (James Coates	6 Feb. 1808 7 do. 10 do. 21 Apr. 12 May 29 Dec. 11 May 1809 6 July 10 Oct. 12 do. 13 do.	

Lieutenant

Rank.	Name.	Rank in the Regiment.	Army.
	John Fraser	17Oct.1809	
	Edward Gilborne	18do.	
	John Witney	19do.	
	William Long	14June1810	
	Robert Law	27May1811	
	John M'Intyre	28do.	Adjutant
	Charles T— Cox	29do.	
	Carique Lewin	27June	
	William Woolcombe	19Sept.	
	William Torriano	12Dec.	
	George Wm. Horton	23Jan.1812	25July 1811
	William Peacocke	14May	
	John Coote	27do.	
	William Anderson	7Aug.	Adjutant
	Charles Moorhead	3Sept.	
	David Soutar	24do.	
	Hector Munro	25Mar.1813	
Lieutenant -	Norman Campbell	14Apr.	
	Thomas Commeline	15do.	
	Anthony Pack	3June	
	Hon. Charles Napier	24do.	
	Robert Dalgleish	1July	
	Robert Hall	3Aug.	
	William Bristow	4do.	
	John Methold	1Sept.	
	William Elliott	2do.	
	Richard Ashe	18Jan.1814	
	Henry Frederick Lockyer	19do.	
	Abraham Goff	20do.	
	William Moore	30Mar.	
	Richard Greenhalgh	18May	
	William Wilson	19do.	
	Samuel Hardy	1Dec.	9Feb. 1809
	John Fullarton	7do.	
	John Streatfield	8do.	
	Edward Nicholas	4Aug.1813	
	Abraham Moffatt	5do.	
Ensign - -	William Smith	1Sept.	
	HenryWalker Thompson	16do.	
	John Todd	18Nov.	

Rank.	Name.	Rank in the Regiment.	Rank in the Army.
Ensign	John Barnett	25 Nov. 1813	
	Arch. Mont. Henderson	25 Dec.	
	John Spalding	20 Jan. 1814	
	John Impett	14 Apr.	
	John Synge Folliott	18 May	
	Edward James O'Brien	19 do.	
	George Home Lightbody	9 June	
	Robert M'Dougall	7 July	
	Anth. Rob. L'Estrange	7 Dec.	
	——— Montagu	8 do.	
	Alexander M'Leroth	22 do.	
Paymaster 1	Hugh Mackenzie	8 Nov. 1798	
Paymaster 2	Donald Harrow	2 Apr. 1812	
Adjutant	William Anderson	2 Aug. 1810	Lieut. 7 Aug. 1812
Adjutant	John M'Intyre	25 Nov. 1813	Lieut. 28 May 1811
QuarterMaster	John Ross	26 Oct. 1804	
QuarterMaster	William Gavin	2 Apr. 1812	
Surgeon	Arthur Stewart	3 Sept. 1812	
Surgeon	Edward O'Reilly	9 Sept. 1813	
Assistant Surg.	John Winterscale	8 Feb. 1810	
Assistant Surg.	Samuel Hill	22 Mar.	
Assistant Surg.	Henry Walker	7 June	

Facings buff.—Lace silver.

Agent, Messrs. Greenwood, Cox and Hammersley.

Rank.	Name.	Rank in the	
		Regiment.	Army.
Colonel	James Stuart	23Oct.1798	Gen. 1Jan.1812
Lieut. Colonel	Henry Monckton	18June1807	Col. 4June1814
Major	Ronald Campbell	22Nov.1807	Lt.Col. 23Apr.1812
	Walter Nath. Leitch	20July1809	Lt.Col. 4June1813
	Benjamin Graves	24Sept.1812	
	George Raitt	1July1813	
Captain	William R— Lawrence	1Aug.1804	Major 4June1814
	Charles Robinson	2do.	Major 4June1814
	William Burke Nicolls	3do.	Major 4June1814
	Tho. Chaloner Martelli	28do.	Major 4June1814
	John Black	4Apr.1805	
	John S— Jackson	22Jan.1807	Major 4June1814
	Robert Owen	29May	
	Robert K— Abbey	15Oct.	Major 4June1814
	Henry Wilson	22Nov.	
	Charles Gardiner	27July1809	
	Charles Trappes	1Mar.1810	9Mar.1809
	William Ebhart	10May	12Nov.1807
	Howard Drummond	26July	
	Whiteford Bell	20Aug.1812	
	Robert Bland	15Oct.	
	Wm. Basset Saunderson	4Mar.1813	
	Trevor Owen Jones	13May	23June 1808
	Charles C— Webb	1July	
	Dugald Carmichael	10Feb.1814	
Lieutenant	John Grant	28Sept.1804	23June 1796
	Donald M'Lean	14Apr.1805	
	A— M— M'Gachan	15do.	
	J— M'Kenzie Cameron	14Jan.1807	
	Peter Sutherland	15do.	
	Alexander Logie	21May	
	John Sharp	29Oct.	
	William Graham	21Apr.1808	
	Ogilvie Stuart	28do.	
	Donald John Maclean	13Oct.	
	Andrew Chisholm	3Aug.1809	
	William Steele	28Sept.	
	Cha. Maxwell Maclean	21Dec.	
	Walter Henderson	18Oct.1810	
	Moses Campbell	13Feb.1811	
	James Hudson Atkinson	14do.	
	William Mackenzie	15do.	
	Henry William Maxwell	17do.	
	William J— F— Wall	20do.	
	Colin Macdonald	21do.	

Rank.	Name.	Regiment.	Army.
		Rank in the	
Lieutenant	Charles Kerr	7 Mar. 1811	
	James Russell	25 Apr.	
	George Sampson	5 Mar. 1812	
	—— Coventry	20 Aug.	Adjutant
	James Gowan	3 Sept.	
	Barton Tennison	22 Oct.	
	David Manson	20 May 1813	
	Dugald Campbell	8 July	
	Alexander Maclean	14 Oct.	
	Stirling Glover	25 Nov.	
	William Mackenzie	10 Feb. 1814	
	W— H— Pickthorn	28 July	
	John Goudie	1 Dec.	
Ensign	John Mac Gachan	5 Dec. 1811	
	Henry Jarvis	19 do.	
	Hugh Rose	31 Dec. 1812	
	William Fraser	1 Apr. 1813	
	Thomas William Yates	20 May	
	William Fitz Gerald	17 June	
	Thomas Whitaker	24 do.	Adjutant
	Henry Hurst	8 July	
	Robert Aitken	15 Aug.	
	Wm. Robert G— Bell	14 Oct.	
	Robert Norie	25 Nov.	
	Michael Adair	16 Dec.	
	Deane Josias Conroy	10 Feb. 1814	
	John Elmore	24 do.	
	Mathew Stewart	17 Mar.	
	Jeremiah Campion	28 July	
	Thomas Bevan	1 Dec.	
Paymaster	1 J. Chr. Caulfield Irvine	27 Sept. 1810	
	2 John Rae	19 June 1813	
Adjutant -	—— Coventry	11 Jan. 1810	Lieut. 20 Aug. 1812
	Thomas Whitaker	24 June 1813	Ensign 24 June 1813
QuarterMaster	William Benton	1 Nov. 1804	
	Samuel Blay	5 Mar. 1812	
Surgeon -	John Hume	21 Apr. 1803	11 June 1800
	Daniel O'Flaherty	29 Aug. 1811	
Assistant Surg.	Charles Hamilton	20 Apr. 1809	
	Alexander M'Kee	17 Aug.	27 Oct. 1808
	Thomas Clarke	3 June 1813	

Facings yellow.—Lace silver.

Agent, Messrs. Greenwood, Cox and Hammersley.

t   73d

Permitted to inscribe on their Colours and Appointments the word " MANGALORE,"
in commemoration of their distinguished conduct in India.

Colonel - -	George Harris	14Feb.1800	Gen. 1Jan.1812
Lieut. Colonel	Lachlan Macquarie	30May1805	M.Gen. 4June1813
	William George Harris	29Dec.1806	Col. 4June1814
	M— Charles O'Connell	4May1809	
	Andrew Geils	4June1813	
Major - -	George Alex. Gordon	19Jan.1809	Lt.Col. 4June1814
	Dawson Kelly	31Oct.1811	
	Arch. John Maclean	28May1812	
	Hugh Cameron	4June1813	
Captain - -	J— Murray	22Jan.1807	Major 4June1814
	John Ritchie	7July1808	
	Henry Antill	11Jan.1809	
	William Kenny	12do.	
	Henry Glenholme	1Feb.	
	Anthony Coane	9Mar.	
	Loftus Owen	16do.	8Dec.1808
	Haddon Smith	3Mar.1810	30Oct. 1807
	Henry Coane	8do.	8Feb. 1810
	James Vallance	17Jan.1811	Major 4June1814
	Edward Auriol Hay	10Oct.	
	Robert Durie	20Nov.	
	Alexander Robertson	21do.	
	Richard Drewe	28May1812	
	John Pike	10Aug.	
	Morgan Carroll	12do.	
	William Wharton	13do.	
	John M— Kennedy	8Oct.	30Apr. 1812
	John Morrice	18Mar.1813	30Apr. 1812
	John Garland	26Nov.	
	Ernest Frederick Pirch	20Jan.1814	
	Robert Crawford	10Mar.	Lt.Col. 2July1810
Lieutenant	Tankerville Crane	11June1807	
	Thomas Scottowe	4Feb.1808	
	Francis Eagar	5Jan.1809	Adjutant
	David Rose	1Feb.	
	Richard Leyne	2do.	
	William Raymond	3do.	
	George Weston Gunning	9do.	
	Archibald M'Creery	9May1810	
	Jos.Wm.Hen.Streaphan	11Oct.	26Oct. 1809
	John Maclaine	8Nov.	
	James Taylor	10do.	
	Tho. Frederick James	11do.	Adjutant
	James Primrose	12do.	
	Duncan Campbell	13do.	
	Wm. Thomas Lyttleton	15do.	
	Martin Murphy	21Feb.1811	
	Thomas Atkins	21Mar.	30Jan. 1806

Lieutenant

Lieutenant -	John Hepenstal Burbridge 9May1811		
	John R— M'Connell 8 Aug.		
	Andrew Greenshields 12Sept.		
	John Acres 20Nov.		
	Thomas Brereton Watson 21do.		
	Matthew Hollis 12Dec.		
	Hugh Holmes 19Feb.1812		
	James Gregorson 7Aug.		
	—— Wentworth 9do.		
	Joseph Dowling 13do.		
	George Dawson 7Jan.1813		
	CharlesNormanMaclean10June	29Dec. 1812	
	George Anthony Pook 25Nov.		
	Thomas B— Bicknell 26do.		
	Thomas Allen Lascelles 27do.		
	Thomas Reynolds 10Mar.1814		
	C— H— Farren 23do.		
	Donald Browne 24do.		
	John Y— Lloyd 4Aug.		
	William Keys 10do.		
	Robert Stewart 11do.		

Ensign - -	RobertGrevilleHeselrige17Sept.1810	
	William Mac Bean 1Apr.1813	
	Thomas Deacon 5do.	
	Charles Bedford Eastwood 6do.	
	Geo. Dondridge Bridge 7do.	
	George Hughes 29do.	
	William Law Lowe 19Aug.	
	AldworthBlennerhassett23Mar.1814	
	Rich. W. Glode Douglas 21Apr.	
	—— Page 10Aug.	
	Colin Macdonald 11do.	
	Jone Lane 22Dec.	

Paymaster	1	John Birch	21Aug.1806	
	2	John Williams	31May1810	
Adjutant -		Thomas Frederick James	12Jan.1809	Lieut. 11Nov.1810
		Francis Eagar	2Mar.	Lieut. 5Jan,1809
QuarterMaster		John Miniken	7Jan.1813	30June1804
		Jeremiah Campbell	28July1814	
Surgeon - -		John Carter	2Mar.1809	
		Duncan M'Dearmid	5Sept.1811	24Jan. 1811
Assistant Surg.		John M— Dermott	4May1809	
		George Martin	1June	
		John Riach	2July1812	
		PatrickHay	10June1813	

Facings dark green.—Lace gold.

Agent, Messrs. Greenwood, Cox and Hammersley.

t 2

74th

332 74th (Highland) Regiment of Foot.

Permitted to bear the " ELEPHANT," with the word " ASSAYE" superscribed, on their Colours and Appointments, in commemoration of the Battle of 23d Sept. 1803.

Rank.	Name.	Regiment.	Rank in the Army.
Colonel - -	James Montgomerie	26Apr.1813	Lt.Gen. 4June1814
Lieut. Col. ✗	*Hon.R.* Le PoerTrench	21Sept.1809	Col. 4June1814
Major - ☺ {	Russell Manners	11Mar.1808	Lt.Col. 6Feb.1812
	John Alexander Mein	11Nov.1813	
Captain -	William Moore	25Sept.1806	Major 21June1813
✗	James Miller	26do.	Major 21June1813
◎	Alexander Thompson	14May1807	Lt.Col. 21Sept.1813
	Donald Macqueen	25Jan.1810	
	David Stewart	5Apr.	
	John Ovens	8Oct.1812	18July 1811
	William Cargill	31Dec.	
	George Hillier	1July1813	9July 1812
	ThomasSt.GeorgeLister	26Aug.	
	R— Robertson	18May1814	
	Eyre John Crabb	19do.	
Lieutenant	Francis Ansell	17Nov.1808	1Jan. 1806
	AlexanderHopePattison	26Apr.1810	
	Jason Hassard	18Oct.	6Sept.1809
	John Alves	25Dec.	
	Charles King	27do.	
	W— Graham	28do.	
	John Black	30do.	
	Francis Duncombe	1Jan.1811	
	George Edward Ironside	31do.	
	Samuel Heron	30May	
	Thomas Mannin	31Oct.	
	William Percy	23Jan.1812	6June 1811
	Abraham Atkinson	28Apr.	
	Henry White	29do.	Adjutant
	James Fleetwood	30do.	
	James Henry	11June	
	Robert Barker	22Oct.	
	Richard Davis	31Dec.	
	William Black	15Apr.1813	
	Gregory Dolphin	26Aug.	
	Hew Shaw	21Oct.	
	Ross Flood	31Mar.1814	
	Luke Champion	18May	
	Thomas Shore	19do.	
	John Macdonald	20do.	

Ensign

| Rank. | Name. | Rank in the | |
		Regiment.	Army.
Ensign - -	Jonathan Luttrell	26Aug.1813	
	Samuel Spooner	27do.	
	John Ormsby Lloyd	25Nov.	
	Richard Champney	25Dec.	
	John Taylor	do.	
	Loughlan M'Pherson	31Mar.1814	
	John M'Clintock	4Aug.	14June1814
	Colin Campbell	25do.	
Paymaster -	John Hassard	6Sept.1809	
Adjutant - -	Henry White	5Apr.1810	Lieut. 29Apr.1812
Quarter-Master	Donald Fraser	25Dec.1806	
Surgeon - -	Colquhoun Grant	16Apr.1812	
Assistant Surg.	Robert Ranken	16Apr.1812	
	Thomas Napier	11Mar.1813	

Facings white.—Lace gold.

Agent, Mr. Macdonald, Pall Mall Court.

75th

Permitted to bear on their Colours and Appointments the " ROYAL TIGER," with the word " INDIA" superscribed, in commemoration of their distinguished services in India, during a period of 19 years.

Rank.	Name.	Regiment.	Rank in the Army.
Colonel -	*Sir* Robert Abercromby, *K.B.* 12Oct.1787		Gen. 29Apr.1802
Lieut. Colonel	Samuel Swinton	16Jan.1806	Col. 4June1813
Major - -	{ Jonathan Brown	16Feb.1813	
	{ Allan M'Lachlan	26Aug.	
Captain -	⎰ Thomas Grant	22Aug.1805	1Feb. 1805
	John Maclean	5June1806	
	Hugh Stewart	15Dec.	
	William Taylor	30Mar.1809	
	John Williams	13July	
	Thomas Atkins	11Oct.1810	
	John Hely Hutchinson	7Nov.1811	
	Hugh Mole	21do.	Major 4June1811
	J— Craig Dumas	2Jan.1812	
	Donald M'Lachlan	16Feb.1813	
	⎱ James Buchanan Barry	7Oct.	
Lieutenant -	⎰ Joseph Richardson	2Mar.1805	
	John Brutton	1Mar.1806	
	Alexander M'Lean	19Aug.1807	
	Dougald Campbell	20do.	
	Hugh Maclean	26Jan.1809	
	Alexander M'Neill	13July	
	Thomas Hood	19Oct.	
	George Dick	5Apr.1810	
	Humphrey Palmer	11Oct.	
	Mark M'Callum	18do.	
	Archibald Fraser	1Jan.1812	
	Duncan Macpherson	2do.	
	Wm. Moncrief Taylor	27May1813	
	Thomas Fergusson	5Aug.	
	James Hutcheon	6Oct.	Adjutant
	⎱ Thomas Withy Inman	7do.	

Ensign

Rank.	Name.	Rank in the Regiment.	Army.
Ensign - -	Elias Payne	18Oct.1810	
	John Winckworth	14Nov.	
	John Crofton	13Dec.	
	Wm.ConynghamGeorge	14Feb.1811	
	James Cameron	2May	14Dec. 1809
	Richard Lott Knight	16do.	
	Hugh Pattison	12May1814	
	William Orr	6Dec.	21Apr. 1814
	R— R— Hepburn	7do.	
	Arthur Cope	8do.	
Paymaster -	Henry Tiddeman	28May1807	
Adjutant - -	James Hutcheon	10Aug.1809	Lieut. 6Oct.1813
Quarter-Master	Matthew Murray	20Jan.1802	
Surgeon - -	George Treyer	12Oct.1805	22Oct. 1794
Assistant Surg.	David Jameson	15Oct.1807	
	William Goodison	23Aug.1810	

Facings yellow.—Lace silver.

Agent, Messrs. Greenwood, Cox and Hammersley.

Permitted to bear on their Colours and Appointments the " ELEPHANT," (inscribing the word " HINDOOSTAN" around it,) in commemoration of their distinguished Services in India.

Rank.	Name.	Rank in the	
		Regiment.	Army.
Colonel -	◎Christopher Chowne	17Feb.1814	Lt.Gen. 4June1813
Lieut. Colonel	John Wardlaw	10May1810	
Major - -	{ Alexander Fraser	8Sept.1808	Lt.Col. 4June1814
	{ Joseph Skerrett	1June1814	
Captain -	⎧ Alexander M'Donald	4Sept.1803	Major 4June1814
	⎪ John Rankin	16July1807	
	⎪ Thomas Vilett	27Aug.	
	⎪ John Gaff	26Nov.	
	⎪ Harry Powell	31Mar.1808	27Nov.1806
	⎨ Robert Bartlett Coles	8Sept.	
	⎪ William Bampton	6July1809	
	⎪ Richard Armstrong	3Jan.1811	Lt.Col. 4June1814
	⎪ Robert Henry Hamilton	24Feb.1814	
	⎪ Edward Hetherington	9June	
	⎩ Andrew K— Torrens	12Sept.	
Lieutenant -	⎧ John Fraser	5Mar.1805	
	⎪ Christopher Hatchell	7do.	
	⎪ Neil Mackay	30Apr.1807	27Feb. 1806
	⎪ George Hatch	25Sept.	
	⎪ George Ogilvie	5Nov.	
	⎪ Francis Austin	16June1808	
	⎪ John Clarke	3Aug.	27Mar.1808
	⎪ Phileman Coultman	1Sept.	
	⎪ Edward R— Stevenson	16Mar.1809	
	⎪ John Gould	22do.	
	⎪ Rich. Stanton Cleary	23do.	
	⎨ Benjamin Rooth	10May	Adjutant
	⎪ John Faincombe	11do.	
	⎪ Cyrus Daniell	6July	
	⎪ Richard W— Hopkins	21Sept.	
	⎪ Charles H— Sache	17May1810	
	⎪ John Vesey	2Aug.	
	⎪ Nathaniel James Scott	25Mar.1813	
	⎪ Joseph Clarke	10June	
	⎪ John Paxton	24Feb.1814	
	⎪ William Grimshaw	9June	
	⎪ Francis Dermot Daly	23do.	26Nov.1813
	⎩ Alexander Carnaby	24Nov.	

Ensign

| | | Rank in the | |
| Rank. | Name. | Regiment. | Army. |

Ensign	Robert Nicolls Frizell	8 Oct. 1812	
	Henry Wood	25 Mar. 1813	
	Judge Burton	10 June	
	Charles Eliot	14 Oct.	
	J. Mackenzie Kennedy	24 Feb. 1814	
	Luke Scott	7 Apr.	
	Edw. Kendall Champion	7 July	
	Thomas Mott	1+do.	
	Geo. Burgoyne Sutherland	8 Dec.	

Paymaster	William Crossgrove	20 Nov. 1806	Lieut. 10 May 1809
Adjutant	Benjamin Rooth	30 June 1808	
Quarter-Master	Thomas Bamborough	11 Oct. 1810	22 Jan. 1807
Surgeon	Thomas Hogg	6 Dec. 1810	
AssistantSurg.	Archibald Fraser	22 Dec. 1808	
	John Bunny	25 Oct. 1809	

Facings red.—Lace silver.

Agent, Mr. Tilson, Henrietta Street, Covent Garden.

Rank.	Name.	Regiment.	Rank in the Army.
Colonel - -	⚔Sir Thomas Picton, K.B.	15Oct.1811	Lt.Gen. 4June1813
Lieut. Col. ◎ ◎	{ John Bromhead { John H— Dunkin	26June1809 15Nov.	
Major - -	{ John Rudd { MurdockHughMaclaine	25Jan.1810 20May1813	Lt.Col. 27Apr.1812
Captain -	{ George Westcott Henry Fletcher Robert Place P— M'Lachlan Roderick Mackenzie Patrick Baird J— William Rogers William Queade John Aveling Hubert Gould John V— George	5Aug.1807 29June1809 13July 15Feb.1810 24Jan.1811 6June 16Jan.1812 22Oct. 20May1813 21Apr.1814 10Nov.	Major 3Mar.1814 Major 4June1814 23July 1812
Lieutenant -	{ John Jeffrey George Parish Bradshaw N— Orgill Leman Edward Jones John Wilson James Cameron James Algeo Jonathan Howells St. John Augustus Clerke Richard Tattan Hector Graham Richard Burnaby R— H— Farmar Parry Mitchell Charles Cotes Pigott Richard Penefather Archibald Campbell Edward Thorp John Augustus Mathison William Brierly Alexander Campbell J— Fitz Gerald William Place Henry Marq.of Worcester	3Mar.1808 16June 13July1809 15Nov.1810 10Jan.1811 21Mar. 4June 5do. 6do. 7do. 8do. 9do. 13do. 15Aug. 19Sept. 26do. 5Mar.1812 28Jan.1813 12Aug. 2Sept. 3Mar.1814 21Apr. 10Nov. 8Dec.	 Adjutant 4Sept.1806 1Dec.1809 20Sept.1810 21Aug.1811

Ensign

Rank.	Name.	Rank in the	
		Regiment.	Army.
Ensign - -	John Tayloe	12Mar.1812	
	William Thomas	1Apr.1813	
	James Crossgrove	29July	
	Augustus Spry Faulknor	3Feb.1814	9Sept.1813
	William Bowen	3Mar.	
	Jacob Glynn Rogers	6Oct.	
	Edward Jenkins	10Nov.	
	Joseph Delafere Harris	24do.	
Paymaster -	Richard Heavock	28Apr.1814	
Adjutant. - -	Edward Jones	2Feb.1809	Lieut. 15Nov.1810
Quarter-Master	John Powell	21June1810	
Surgeon - -	Frederick Micklam	4May1809	30June1808
Assistant Surg.	John Bridges	13July1809	
	Wynne Fraser	28Apr.1814	

Facings yellow.—Lace silver.

Agent, Mr. Croasdaile, Silver Street, Golden Square.

340 78th (Highland) Regt. of Foot (or the Rossshire Buffs.)

Permitted to bear on their Colours and Appointments, the " ELEPHANT," with the word " ASSAYE" superscribed, in commemoration of the Battle of the 23d Sept. 1803; also the word " MAIDA," for the Action of the 4th July, 1806.

Rank.	Name.	Regiment.	Rank in the Army.
Colonel -	⊚ *Sir* Sam. Auchmuty, K.B.	13Jan.1812	Lt.Gen. 4June1813
Lieut. Col.	⊚ ⎰Alexander Adams	7Apr.1802	M.Gen. 4June1814
	⎱John Macleod	12May1808	Col. 4June1813
	⊚ ⎰Martin Lindsay	25Nov.1813	
	⊚ ⎱David Forbes	28July1814	
Major - -	⎧Duncan Macpherson	7Nov.1811	
	⎪James M'Vean	14Dec.	
	⎨Duncan Mac Gregor	25Nov.1813	
	⎩Colin Campbell Mackay	11Aug.1814	
Captain -	⎧C— Grant Falconer	7Aug.1806	26Dec.1805
	⎪Donald Macleod	17Mar.1807	
	⎪Thomas Cameron	18do.	
	⎪Joseph Bethune	3Mar.1808	
	⎪John Thornton	28July	26Nov.1807
	⎪Arthur Forbes	26Jan.1809	3Oct. 1805
	⎪Robert Sime	15Mar.1810	
	⎪William Mackenzie	24Oct.	
	⎪John Matheson	6Dec.	
	⎪John Grant	18July1811	
	⎨Malcolm M'Gregor	7Aug.	
	⎪William Cameron	6Nov.	
	⎪Alexander Gallie	7do.	
	⎪Charles Robertson	6May1813	
	⎪Henry N— Douglas	3June	
	⎪Henry Hely Hutchinson	22July	
	⎪Roderick Macqueen	27Jan.1814	
	⎪Neil Campbell	3Feb.	
	⎪Stephen Holmes	4do.	28Jan. 1813
	⎪James Fraser	8Sept.	
	⎩Lachlan Grant	9do.	
Lieutenant -	⎧Phineas Ryrie	26Sept.1805	
	⎪Richard Hart	25Apr.1806	
	⎪Alexander Fraser	17Sept.	17July 1805
	⎪Alexander M — Cameron	9Jan.1807	
	⎪Joshua Gregory	19Jan.1808	
	⎪Farquhar M'Rae	21do.	
	⎨John M'Iver	8Dec.	
	⎪Alexander Sutherland	6July1809	
	⎪John Macleod	22Mar.1810	
	⎪Joseph M'Kenzie	25Apr.	
	⎪Alexander Campbell	26do.	
	⎪John Cooper	17May	Adjutant
	⎩John M'Dougall	7Mar.1811	

Lieutenant

Rank.	Name.	Rank in the Regiment.	Army.
Lieutenant	Alexander Brodie	6June1811	
	James Stewart	8Aug.	
	John Marquis	21Nov.	
	William Bath	20Feb.1812	20Dec.1810
	John Pennycuick	11June	
	John Chisholm	2July	
	Alexander Waters	6Aug.	
	Donald Cameron	21Jan.1813	
	John Mitchell	4Mar.	
	Allen Dregborn	6May	
	DonaldE—Mac Queen	25Nov.	
	Roderick Cameron	20Jan.1814	
	John Smith	3Feb.	
	William Smith	4do.	Adjutant
	Ewan Macpherson	5do.	
	Fr.Alex.Mackenzie Fraser	6do.	
	William Hole	7do.	
	Charles M— Macleod	17do.	
	Charles Jack	17Mar.	
Ensign	John M'Crummin	15Jan.1812	
	George Hutton Douglas	1Jan.1813	
	Joseph Martin Huntley	2Sept.	28Mar.1811
	WilliamJ—Cockburne	25Nov.	
	Jonathan Forbes	19Jan.1814	
	George Munro	20do.	
	Edward Twopeny	27do.	
	William Beales	4Feb.	24June1813
	John Drew	5do.	
	William Bain M'Alpin	6do.	
	George Sinclair	17do.	
	MartinG—F—Lindsay	10Mar.	16Dec.1813
	James Reid	17do.	
	John Lee	8Sept.	
Paymaster -			
Adjutant -	John Cooper	19July1807	Lieut. 17May1810
	William Smith	24June1813	Lieut. 4Feb.1814
QuarterMaster	William Gunn	6Aug.1812	
Surgeon -	Neil Currie	1Sept.1808	
	William Munro	3June1813	
Assistant Surg	John Hughes	28Mar.1811	
	William M'Leod	24Feb.1814	
	George G— M'Lean	1Sept.	

Facings buff.—Lace gold.

Agent, Messrs. Greenwood, Cox and Hammersley.

342 79th Regt. of Foot (or Cameron Highlanders.)

Permitted to bear on their Colours and Appointments a " SPHINX," with the word " EGYPT," in commemoration of the Campaign of 1801.

Rank.	Name.	Regiment.	Rank in the Army.
Colonel - ◎	Alan Cameron	1Jan.1805	M.Gen.25July1810
	Lt. Col. Comm.	30Jan.1794	
	Major Comm.	17Aug.1793	
Lieut. Col. ◎– {	Neill Douglas	3Dec.1812	
	Nathaniel Cameron	24June1813	
Major {	Andrew Brown	15Oct.1812	Lt.Col.26Aug.1813
	Duncan Cameron	29do.	Lt.Col. 12Apr.1814
	Evan Macpherson	24June1813	4June1811
	Donald Campbell	13Jan.1814	
Captain - {	Thomas Mylne	24Apr.1805	
	Peter Innes	4Sept.	
	James Campbell	5do.	
	Neil Campbell	8Apr.1806	
	William Marshall	19July1810	
	Malcolm Fraser	29Nov.	
	William Bruce	14Mar.1811	
	J— H— Christie	29May	
	Patrick M'Crummen	30do.	
	John Sinclair	4July	
	John Cameron	1Apr.1812	
	Robert Mackay	2do.	
	James Campbell	2July	31Mar.1808
	Alexander Maclean	15Oct.	
	John M'Neill	29do.	
	Alexander M'Intyre	12Nov.	
	James Barwick	29Apr.1813	
	William Cameron	17June	
	Kenneth Cameron	18May1814	
	John Cameron	26do.	
Lieutenant {	Alexander Cameron	12Mav1807	Adjutant
	Donald Cameron	13do.	
	Thomas Brown	15Dec.	
	William Maddocks	21Apr.1808	25July 1801
	William Leaper	15Dec.	
	James Fraser	16Mar.1809	
	J—WhitefordMorrison	17Aug.	
	Duncan M'Pherson	19July1810	
	Donald M'Phee	29Nov.	
	Fulton Robertson	21Feb.1811	
	Ewen Cameron	29May	
	John Ford	30do.	
	John Kynock	13June	Adjutant
	Alexander Robertson	4July	
	Alexander Forbes	8Aug.	
	Charles M'Arthur	17Oct.	

Lieutenant

Rank.	Name.	Rank in the Regiment.	Army.
Lieutenant	Kewan Izod Leslie	1Apr.1812	11July 1811
	Thomas Walbeoffe	13Oct.	
	James Hall	14do.	
	John Powling	15do.	
	N— Carter	29do.	
	John M'Gibbon	24Dec.	
	James Cameron	25Jan.1813	
	Ewen Kennedy	25Feb.	
	W— A— Riach	17June	
	John Thompson	18Nov.	
	Allen Macdonnell	6Jan.1814	
	Alex. Mich. Macdonell	13do.	
	Robert Christie	18May	
	Jeremiah Balfour	19do.	
	Lachlan M'LeanCameron	20do.	
	Ogle O'Connor	21do.	
	Thomas Cowen	26do.	
	Allan Maclean	28July	
Ensign	George Harrison	10Dec.1812	
	John Mackenzie	24do.	
	John M'Phee	25Feb.1813	
	Charles James M'Lean	17June	
	John Nash	18Nov.	
	James Robertson	6Jan.1814	
	Archibald Cameron	13do.	
	A— S— Crawford	18May	
	James Campbell	19do.	
	T— Tharpe	20do.	
	George Courtenay	21do.	
	John M'Arthur	26do.	
	David Matheson	28July	
Paymaster	2 Richard Brittain	1Feb.1810	
	1 John M'Arthur	21Nov.1811	
Adjutant	Alexander Cameron	13Feb.1812	Lieut. 12May1807
	John Kynock	19May1814	Lieut. 13June1811
Quarter-Mast.	Angus Cameron	13Feb.1812	
	Archibald Sinclair	25Feb.1813	
Surgeon	William Bowen Miller	25Feb.1808	11June 1807
	George Ridesdale	9Sept.1813	
Assistant Surg.	William G— Burrell	14Dec.1809	13July 1809
	David Perston	18Oct.1810	1Feb. 1810
	John Divie	25June1812	

Facings dark green.—Lace gold.

Agent, Mr. Lawrie, Robert Street, Adelphi.

80th

344 80th Regt. of Foot (or Staffordshire Volunteers.)

Permitted to bear on their Colours and Appointments a "SPHINX," with the word "EGYPT," in commemoration of the Campaign of 1801.

Rank.	Name.	Regiment.	Rank in the Army.
Colonel -	⊚*Hon.Sir*EdwardPaget,*K.B.*23Feb.1808		Lt.Gen. 4June1811
Lieut. Colonel {	John White John Ashley Sturt	12May1809 4June1813	1Jan.1812
Major - - {	John Edwards Joseph Cookson	12May1809 4June1813	Lt.Col. 4June1814
Captain - {	John Dalrymple Dennis Kingdon Robert Dashwood Eyre Evans Kenny Henry James Phelps Henry Jones Grove P— W— Harness William Thomé James Maclean Andrew Kelly Stepney RawsonStepney	25June1803 15Apr.1804 30Oct.1806 22Jan.1807 12Nov. 1Nov.1810 28May1812 30June 25Oct. 4June1813 30Mar.1814	Major 4June1814 Major 4June1814 Major 4June1814 27June1805 30Aug.1810 18Oct.1810
Lieutenant - {	James H— Walsh William Musgrave F— Grove Henry Stodart Thomas Bailie Charles Dick Richard John Castell John Bowler S— S— Burns Acheson French Narborough Baker William Trant Joseph Ellis Thomas Langley Colt Francis Brown Henry Nott William Penny John Molony Charles Anderson Peter Mosse Thomas Darke —— Wilson John Donavan Verner James Inkson —— Archer	27Sept.1803 15Sept.1804 17do. 2Nov.1805 29Jan.1807 1Feb. do. 1July 1Dec. 17do. 10Mar.1808 7July 1Dec. 18Jan.1809 1Aug.1810 1Oct. 25do. 26do. 27Aug.1811 3May1812 11June 5Aug.1813 12do. 30Dec. 30Mar.1814	 Adjutant 25May1808 22Sept.1808 1Apr.1810 15June1808 27Nov.1812

Ensign

Rank.	Name.	Rank in the	
		Regiment.	Army.

Ensign - -	⎰ Clement Wolseley	4June1812	
	⎰ Rich. Robertus Halahan	23July	
	J— Southwell Stokes	29Oct.	
	William Burke	10Dec.	
	Robert C— Greaves	8Apr.1813	
	William Harvey	5Aug.	
	William Clarke	30Dec.	
	John M'Queen	30Mar.1814	
	James M'Queen	31do.	
	George Vernon	5May	
Paymaster -	James Cruckshanks	16Sept.1813	
Adjutant - -	S— S— Burns	1Sept.1811	Lieut. 1Dec.1807
Quarter-Master	John Middleton	27Jan.1803	
Surgeon - -	William Browne	25Jan.1808	
Assistant Surg. ⎰	Andrew Nicoll	21Feb.1811	
	Louis Sheppard	17Mar.1814	

Facings yellow.—Lace gold.

Agent, Mr. Watson, No. 1, Poland Street.

Permitted to inscribe on their Colours and Appointments the words " MAIDA," in commemoration of the Action of 4th July, 1806 ; the 2d Bu. also the word " CORUNNA," for the Action of 16th January, 1809.

		Rank in the	
Rank.	Name.	Regiment.	Army.
Colonel - -	Henry Johnson	18June1798	Gen. 25Apr.1808
Lieut. Colonel {	Patrick M'Kenzie	28Aug.1804	Col. 4June1813
	Henry Milling	21Nov.1811	
Major - - {	James Farrer	2July1807	Lt.Col. 4June1813
	Edward Gillman	23Nov.1809	Lt.Col. 4June1814
	Peter Waterhouse	21Nov.1811	
	Robert Charles Lang	25June1812	
Captain - {	Adam Giff Downing	26Dec.1805	
	Josiah Stevenson	25Dec.1806	
	John Murdock Wardrop	4June1807	
	Henry Bowles	31Mar.1808	
	Richard Cole	18Aug.	25Nov.1806
	Philip C — Taylor	26Jan.1809	15Sept.1808
	Richard Pilkington	6Apr.	
	Francis J — Edwards	25Dec.	10Feb. 1807
	George Adams	15Feb.1810	
	J — Duval	18Oct.	
	Joseph Ginger	1May1811	
	Robert Duff	2do.	
	Edward Dudreneuc	15Aug.	Major 4June1814
	Charles French	31Oct.	11July 1811
	Thomas B— Ball	14May1812	
	George Pearson	25June	
	Robert Hipkins	13May1813	
	James Sinclair	10June	
	Henry Thomas Hearn	9Sept.	
	Thomas Collard	3Feb.1814	
Lieutenant - {	Edward Kingsbury	6Feb.1806	
	A— Macalpine	27do.	Adjutant
	Thomas Robert Dundas	26May	
	Francis D— Dundas	27do.	
	James Henderson	30do.	
	William Fenton	31July	
	Samuel Jenkins	4June1807	
	Edward Smith	30July	
	Lawrence M'Cartney	29Oct.	
	David Fair	7Jan.1808	
	Knox Montgomery	17Mar.	
	Edward Brewster	25Aug.	
	Joseph Sisson	26do.	Adjutant
	Edward Lee	2Feb.1809	

Lieutenant

Lieutenant -	Holmes Biggam	6Apr.1809	
	William Hyde	13June	
	—— Manning	14do.	
	Wm. Henry Armstrong	27July	22Sept.1808
	Thomas Clifton Wheat	30Aug.1810	
	Francis Home	13Sept.	10Aug.1808
	Alexander Napper	24Jan.1811	16Mar.1809
	Alexander Gordon	2May	
	George Smyth	4July	
	William Jones	8Aug.	27Aug.1807
	Robert Mostyn	26Sept.	
	Samuel Steele	14May1812	
	William Edyvean	30July	
	John Lutman	13May1813	
	David Duval	3June	14Nov.1811
	Henry Croly	10do.	
	James Pringle	5Aug.	
	James Mollan	3Feb.1814	
	Francis Dempsey	do.	
	James Gibbings	4do.	
	Joseph Jones	5do.	
	Edward Hall	21Apr.	
Ensign - -	John Godwin	30May1811	
	Patrick Chevers	12Sept.	
	Thomas Milnes Smith	28Nov.	
	John Smith O'Donnell	23July1812	
	W— C— Betteridge	7Apr.1813	
	Charles Beale	8do.	
	Robert Beadle	22do.	
	Edw. Thomas Thomson	10June	
	Thomas Whitley	21Oct.	
	Ryan Flattery	25Dec.	
	Charles Oakley	do.	
	Charles Irvine	3Feb.1814	
	John Brown	17Mar.	
	Anthony Donaghue	21Apr.	
	Robert Hamilton	15Dec.	
Paymaster	1 Arnold Thompson	18May1809	
	2 Charles Henry Marshall	do.	
Adjutant -	A— Macalpine	16Feb.1809	Lieut. 27Feb.1806
	Joseph Sisson	26Sept.1811	Lieut. 26Aug.1808
QuarterMaster	—— Harding	31Oct.1803	
	Peter Baker	22Jan.1807	
Surgeon - -	Peter Schooles	17Apr.1806	25Aug.1803
	William Bamfield	13May1813	
Assistant Surg.	Herman S— May	19Mar.1812	
	Joseph Stockdale	7May	
	William R— Gibb	25July	

Facings buff.—Lace silver.

Agent, Messrs. Greenwood, Cox and Hammersley.

Rank.	Name.	Rank in the	
		Regiment.	Army.
Colonel - -	Henry Pigot	23Oct.1798	Gen. 1Jan.1812
Lieut. Col. ©-	William Grant	15Aug.1805	M.Gen. 4June1814
©	Henry King	31Dec.1811	
Major - -	Charles Edward Conyers 16Feb.1809		Lt.Col. 3Mar.1814
	Henry Adolphus Proctor 30Apr.1812		
	William Fitz Gerald 4June1813		
	William Vincent 18Nov.		
Captain -	Robert Carew 5Jan.1805		
	© John B— Walmsley 9May		Major 26Aug.1813
	Brook Firman 23Nov.		
	George Marshall 27Oct.1808		
	Frederick Langley 1Nov.1809		11Mar.1808
	G. Wrough. Montague 28June1810		
	James Stewart 9Aug.		
	George William French 14Mar.1811		
	H— S— Hart 25do.		7Feb. 1811
	Henry Robert Cole 4July		
	Thomas Stirling Begbie 7May1812		
	William Sterne 24June1813		
	John M'Kay 16Aug.		
	William J— Campbell 2Sept.		1July 1813
	John Boyd 2Dec.		
	Richard Le Royd 6Jan.1814		
	George Wood 17Feb.		
	Henry Crofton 1Dec.		
	William E— Buchanan 8do.		
	George Lamfrey 29do.		
Lieutenant -	George V— Derenzy 25Dec.1807		
	Henry Pigott 26do.		
	Gilbert O'Mahee Field 7Feb.1808		
	Edward Stephen Marlay 8do.		
	Charles Mortimer 9do.		
	Edmond Davenport 17Mar.		
	Walter W— Starkie 2June		
	Kingston Cuthbert 13Oct.		
	Edward Phineas Davies 27do.		
	John Ryan 13Apr.1809		Adjutant
	Thom. Ramsden Agnew 12Oct.		
	Samuel Holdsworth 1Nov.		Adjutant
	Hugh S— Donnellan 8Mar.1810		
	Thomas Tollemache 7Mar.1811		
	J.M'GregorDrummond 23May		
	William Mason 19Mar.1812		

Lieutenant

Rank.	Name.	Rank in the Regiment.	Rank in the Army.
Lieutenant	Edward Francis French	10Sept.1812	7Jan. 1813
	Robert Latham	2Dec.	
	John Gordon	3do.	
	Henry Hewetson	10do.	
	Donald Robertson	25Jan.1813	
	Edmund Harding	14Sept.	
	Edward W— Mason	15do.	
	Samuel Walker Lacy	16do.	
	George Goulden	22do.	
	Edward Milton Holgate	23do.	
	George Harman	18Nov.	
	David Fraser	2Dec.	
	John Buchan Sydserff	6Jan.1814	
	Richard Whitaker	17Feb.	
Ensign	William Dickenson	3May1810	16Nov.1809
	William Taylor	3Dec.1812	
	William Tudor	24do.	
	Michael Blood	24Mar.1813	
	John Cundall	25do.	
	William Hawkins	15Sept.	
	James Seddon Garnet	16do.	
	John M'Millan	17do.	
	Maurice O'Connell	22do.	
	George Mackay	23do.	
	W— H— Bourne	6Jan.1814	
	Robert Elliott	7do.	
	Nathaniel Greene	24Feb.	
	T— G— Castieau	3Mar.	
Paymaster 1	Matthew Ottley	15Aug.1798	
Paymaster 2	Edw. Heppell Lonsdale	23May1805	
Adjutant	Samuel Holdsworth	31Dec.1807	Lieut. 1Nov.1809
	John Ryan	14Nov.1810	Lieut. 13Apr.1809
Quarter Master	Robert Walker	19Sept.1804	
	Joseph Goslett	13July1809	
Surgeon	Robert Winning	3Nov.1808	2Aug.1796
	JohnBickertonFlanagan	21Oct.1813	
Assistant Surg.	H— B— Scott	29June1809	
	John M'Keown	21Jan.1813	
	William Milligan	10Feb.1814	

Facings yellow.—Lace silver.

Agent, Mr. Lawrie, Robert Street, Adelphi.

83d

Rank.	Name.	Rank in the Regiment.	Rank in the Army.
Colonel - - -	James Balfour	18Nov.1795	Gen. 25Oct.1809
Lieut. Colonel	Joseph Baird	17Mar.1803	M.Gen. 1Jan.1812
	Jacob Brunt	13June1811	
XC	Henry William Carr	22Sept.1814	27Apr. 1812
Major - -	John Napper	15May1806	Lt.Col. 4June1813
	Abraham Brunt	19Aug.1813	
	James Sullivan	11Aug.1814	4June1814
	Allan Cameron	13Oct.	4June1814
Captain -	Thomas Somerfield	19Sept 1804	Major 4June1814
	Francis Creagh	24Mar.1806	
	William Geddes	19Feb.1807	Lt. Col. 4June1814
◎	Samuel Hext	25Sept.	Major 21June1813
	Robert Fraser	1Jan.1808	
	George Noleken	11Aug.	Major 4June1814
	Alexander Campbell	29Mar.1809	
	Robert Thompson	6July	
	Edward Renwick	14Dec.	
	Gilbert Elliot	14June1810	Major 12Apr.1814
	John Terry	31Jan.1811	
	Donald Campbell	5Mar.1812	
	Edmund Gapper	3June	
	Edwin Cheere Emett	4do.	
	Thomas Fraser	4Feb.1813	2July 1812
	George Buchan	11do.	
	William Macpherson	19Aug.	
	—— Dorrell	28Apr.1814	
	William Holland	21July	
	Daniel Wiley	11Aug.	
	James Hardman	17Nov.	
Lieutenant -	W— Townshend	29Oct.1806	
	—— Trydell	30do.	
	Alexander M'Bean	30Jan.1807	17Dec. 1806
	John Shaw	9Feb.	
	William Phillips	10do.	
	James Cruttwell	11do.	
	Thomas F— Smith	26Mar.	

Rank.	Name.	Rank in the Regiment.	Army.
Lieutenant	George Mee	26Nov.1807	29Sept.1806
	Charles Abell	11Mar.1808	
	Henry Brahan	13do.	
	Connell James Baldwin	16do.	
	RichardFitzGeraldHolmes	30do.	
	James Hingston	21Apr.	22Apr.1807
	Henry Vereker	29Sept.	
	James Smith	23Mar.1809	
	Tho. Bamber Gascoyne	25do.	
	Francis Johnson	27do.	
	Charles Watson	15Aug.	
	Thomas Boggie	16do.	
	Frederick Irwin	17do.	
	J— Emslie	8Nov.	
	Charles Proby Bowles	9do.	
	Charles O'Neill	4Jan.1810	
	John Evans	21June	
	Michael Carey	7Mar.1811	
	Francis M— Barry	29May	
	Henry Letoler	30do.	
	William Macarmick Cox	do.	
	Joseph Mathews	13June	
	———— Broomfield	28Feb.1812	
	———— Swinburne	4June	Adjutant
	R— Woodhouse	5do.	
	John Green	29Dec.	
	William Henry Wiley	30do.	
	Beauford Crowgey	31do.	
	Arthur J— Stephenson	25Jan.1813	23Mar.1807
	Herbert Wyatt	17June	
	Ambrose Lane	28July	
	William Illius	29do.	
	W— Fitz Gibbon	16Sept.	
	John Brahan	21Oct.	
	Thomas Neligan	11Nov.	
	John Vavasour	16Dec.	
	Alex. Gordon Stevens	3Mar.1814	
	Ch. Lodewyk Wykherd	28Apr.	
	Francis Burgess	4Aug.	
	John Summerfield	8Sept.	
	John Parnall	17Nov.	

Ensign

Rank.	Name.	Rank in the	
		Regiment.	Army.
Ensign - -	William O'Neil	12Aug.1812	
	——— Browne	31Dec.	
	William Maxwell	11Feb.1813	
	Thomas Young	15Apr.	
	Charles Irwin	22do.	
	Thomas Peter Grieves	17June	
	Edward Nihell	11Nov.	
	——— Mac Nab	16Dec.	
	Robert Henry Dwyer	2Mar.1814	
	Richard Hely	10do.	
	Florence O'Brien	31do.	
	——— Rawlins	28Apr.	
	George Dewsnap	12May	Adjutant
	Francis Warre	11Aug.	
	James Sullivan	8Sept.	
	——— Carmack	17Nov.	
Paymaster	1 Thomas Boulton	19Apr.1799	
	2 Henry Cross	15Oct. 1808	
Adjutant -	——— Swinburne	25July1811	Lieut. 4June1812
	George Dewsnap	12May1814	Ensign 12May1814
QuarterMaster	Samuel Holt	1Aug.1809	
	William Hall	12May1814	
Surgeon -	Charles Waite	25Feb.1805	31Dec.1803
	Robert Sanford	9Sept.1813	
Assistant Surg.	Walter Ward	16Oct.1806	
	John Glasco	21Apr.1808	
	Andrew Tonnere	28Oct.1813	
	Thomas James Meharey	1Sept.1814	

Facings yellow.—Lace gold.

Agent, Messrs. Greenwood, Cox and Hammersley.

Rank.	Name.	Regiment.	Rank in the Army.
Colonel - -	George Bernard	28Feb.1794	Gen. 4June1813
	Lt. Col. Comm.	2Nov.1793	
Lieut. Colonel {	Archibald Campbell	29Mar.1810	
	Peter Carey	18July1811	Col. 4June1813
	Henry Daubeny	20Jan.1814	
Major - - {	John Locke	25Aug.1808	Col. 4June1813
	Courtland Schuyler	11Feb.1813	
	Robert Cockburne	13May	
	John Carter	20Jan.1814	
Captain - {	Richard Dale	25Mar.1808	26Nov.1806
	Arthur Bernard	20May	
	Mathew Burns	do.	
	James Jenkin	do.	Major 26Dec.1813
	Donald Urquhart	21do.	
	Arthur Bernard	9June	
	Jacob Tonson	14Aug.	Lt.Col. 26Dec.1813
	James Lane	16do.	30Nov.1806
	William Pigott	18do.	5Nov.1807
	Edward Nichol	14Sept.1809	
	John Johnson	26Oct.	
	Stephen Shute Rowe	26Apr.1810	
	George Macdonald	21Nov.1811	
	Henry Hayes	19Dec.	
	Richard Stannard	25Jan.1813	26Oct. 1809
	Stephen Pendergast	11Feb.	
	John Fraser	27May	
	Charles Walker	21Oct.	
	Edward Lane	22do.	
	William P— French	19Jan.1814	
	James Cooke	20do.	
	John Salisbury Jones	16June	
Lieutenant - {	John Dale	10Sept.1807	
	George Charles Smith	1Apr.1808	4Aug.1805
	John Warren Bernard	13do.	
	John Spottswood	do.	
	Edward Croker	14do.	
	William Bindon	19May	
	Robert M'Carthy	20do.	

y

Lieutenant

Rank.	Name.	Rank in the	
		Regiment.	Army.
	Charles Bowsar	21May1808	
	Samuel B— Beamish	23do.	20Aug.1807
	John Cooper	24do.	
	C— B— Munden	26do.	
	Francis St. Clare	2June	
	Richard Cruice	8Sept.	
	Samuel T— Basden	9Oct.	
	Henry Statham	10do.	
	John Bernard Beamish	11do.	
	William Bernard	12do.	
	Henry Rounds	19do.	
	John Peach	20do.	
	F— J— Whiteford	25Nov.	
	James Archdeacon	20Mar.1809	2Oct.1806 Adjut.
	Robert Holt	25June	14July 1808
	Richard Burke Warren	12Sept.	
	Charles Pullman	13do.	Adjutant
	Charles Westley	14do.	
	Philip Bize Entwisle	28do.	
	—— M'Gregor	12Oct.	
Lieutenant -	William Fordyce	18Jan.1810	6Apr. 1809
	Joseph Holmes	26Apr.	
	James Kaye	21June	
	Thomas Tucker	13Dec.	
	Charlton O'Neil	2May1811	
	Francis BernardHingston	5Dec.	
	—— Battersby	19do.	
	Thomas Clubley	30Apr.1812	2Jan. 1812
	Michael Rafter	24Sept.	
	E— J— Mockler	15Oct.	
	Mathew Thackwray	25Feb.1813	
	James Lloyd	27May	
	James B— Hingston	22Oct.	
	William Osburne Gregg	23do.	
	—— Barry	24do.	
	Henry Scott	25Nov.	
	John Campbell Stewart	19Jan.1814	
	Robert Cart	20do.	
	Joseph Haddon Slyfield	30Mar.	
	Michael Crowe	31do.	
	John Crossley	15June	
	Julius Brockman	16do.	
	William Skelton	23do.	16Mar.1808

Ensign

Rank.	Name.	Rank in the	
		Regiment.	Army.
Ensign	Henry Holyoak	22Oct.1813	
	——— Langton	23do.	
	Weston Yonge	24do.	
	George Byne	25do.	
	——— Burns	25Nov.	
	Richard G— Daunt	9Dec.	
	——— Walpole	20Jan.1814	
	Charles Maypother	10Mar.	
	John Brockman	30do.	
	Thomas Andrews	31do.	
	A— Nightingale	2June	
	Ralph Mitf. Prest. Ingilby	16do.	
	·George Wyse	17do.	
	Peter Mansell	20Oct.	
Paymaster 1	Henry Clarke	5Apr.1798	
2	John Griffin	11Aug.1808	
Adjutant	Charles Pullman	25May1808	Lieut. 13Sept.1809
	James Archdeacon	2May1811	Lieut. 2Oct.1806
QuarterMaster	H— Cockburne	29Mar.1810	
	Robert Whetham	10Mar.1813	
Surgeon	James Williamson	12June1804	
	William R— White	24Feb.1814	
Assistant Surg	John M'Laine	6Dec.1806	
	John Bell	18Jan.1810	
	David M'Cullock	24Feb.1814	

Facings yellow.—Lace silver.

Agent, Messrs. Donaldson, Juitt, and Boaden, Whitehall.

[1815]

356 85th Regiment of Foot (or Bucks Volunteers.)
(LIGHT INFANTRY.)

		Rank in the	
Rank.	Name.	Regiment.	Army.

Colonel - -	Tho. Sloughter Stanwix	25Feb.1807	Gen. 25Apr.1808
Lieut. Colonel {	William Thornton William Wood	25Jan.1813 8Apr,	Col. 4June1814
Major - - {	Peter Deshon George Brown	25Jan.1813 26May1814	16Aug.1810 Lt.Col.29Sept.1814
Captain - {	Richard Gubbins William C— Ball D— M'Dougall Charles Schaw W— P— de Bathe James Knox Charles Grey Henry Fairfax * John D— Hickes Thomas Wilkinson Charles Harris William Williams	25Jan.1813 do. do. do. do. do. 28do. 22July 25Dec. 26May1814 23June 13Oct.	Lt.Col.29Sept.1814 Major 29Sept.1814 Major 20Oct.1814 10Jan. 1811 Major 27Oct.1814 8Oct. 1812 10Nov.1813
Lieutenant {	William Walker George Wellings John Burrell R— M— Lord Belhaven Charles Fisher A— R— Charleton John Watts Matthew Forster Frederick Maunsell G— F— G— O'Connor James Watson Boyes B— C— Urquhart Frederick Gascoyne William Hickson Kirk Boott Henry Belstead John Green G— R— Gleig Henry John French	25Jan.1813 do. do. do. do. do. do. do. 18Mar. 15Apr. 29do. 6May 13do. 20do. 26do. 9June 10do. 20July 21do.	13June1811 14Nov.1811 20Feb. 1812 4June1812 18June1812 13Aug.1812 12Nov.1812 24Dec.1812 28Jan. 1813 20Feb. 1812 1Sept.1808

Lieutenant

85th Regiment of Foot (or Bucks Volunteers.) 357
(LIGHT INFANTRY.)

Rank.	Name.	Rank in the Regiment.	Army.
Lieutenant -	⎰ Robert Charlton * ⎪ Thomas Crouchley ⎪ Joseph Blake ⎨ Charles Nayler ⎪ John Duthy ⎪ James M'Gillewie ⎱ Thomas Hunt	23Sept.1813 25Dec. 24Feb.1814 2June 13Oct. 14do. 17Nov.	Adjutant
Ensign -	⎰ Thomas Ormsby ⎪ Sir Frederick Eden, Bt. ⎪ George Ashton, jun. ⎨ William Marsh ⎪ Morris Barlow ⎪ William Hunt ⎪ ——— Boyes ⎱ H— Brooke	21July1813 22do. 25Dec. 13Jan.1814 21July 8Sept. 13Oct. 17Nov.	14Jan. 1814
Paymaster -	Alexander Biggar	1Apr.1813	
Adjutant - -	James M'Gillewie	18Feb.1813	Lieut. 14Oct.1814
Quarter-Master	J— Duxbury	18Mar.1813	
Surgeon - -	Rees Williams	25Feb.1813	2Mar.1809
Assistant Surg.	⎰ Luke Whitney ⎱ Beresford Tedlie	27May1813 8July	25Oct. 1810

Facings yellow.—Lace silver.

Agent, Messrs. Greenwood, Cox and Hammersley.

(2d BATTALION DISBANDED.)

Permitted to bear on their Colours and Appointments a " SPHINX," with the word " EGYPT," in commemoration of the Campaign of 1801, and to bear the Irish Harp and Crown on their Buttons.

Rank.	Name.	Regiment.	Army.
Colonel - -	Hon. Francis Needham	25June1810	Gen. 1Jan.1812
Lieut. Colonel {	Hastings Fraser	18Apr.1805	Col. 4June1813
	John Johnson	18Nov.1813	25Oct. 1812
Major - - {	Daniel Marston	18Nov.1813	
	William Baird	25Dec.	
Captain - {	William Williams	29Aug.1805	Major 4June1814
	Robert Marcus Shearman	2Jan.1806	Major 4June1814
	Thomas Lamphier	2Apr.	
	David Morrice	13Feb.1807	
	Robert Nicholson	23Feb.1809	
	Michael Creagh	25Nov.	
	William Richardson	1Aug.1810	
	Archibald M'Laine	5Mar.1812	
	James Stuart	25Nov.1813	
	Charles Richardson	10Feb.1814	
	John Hamilton Edwards	11do.	16Aug.1813
Lieutenant - {	Lachlan M'Quarie	15Sept.1805	
	Alexander M'Lean	16do.	
	Colin M'Laurin	17do.	
	William Home	7Jan.1806	
	John Webb	6Mar.	18July 1805
	Thomas Mercer	28Mar.1807	
	John Campbell	20Apr.1808	
	Dav.Kennedy Kirkland	17Nov.	28Dec.1807
	Henry Vanspall	1Aug.1809	
	John Kedgel Sandon	12Dec.	
	James Birkett	1Jan.1810	Adjutant
	Thomas E— Cannell	1Feb.1811	
	John Hodson	25do.	
	Robert Porter	3Mar.1812	
	James Creagh	4do.	
	John Grant	5do.	
	Donald Munro	24Nov.1813	
	Francis Perry	30Dec.	18Feb. 1813
	Duncan M'Lachlan	10Feb.1814	
	Duncan Mac Lean	11do.	

Lieutenant

Rank.	Name.	Rank in the Regiment.	Army.
Lieutenant	Hector Mac Quarie	12Feb.1814	
	J— Henry	13do.	
	James Leche	10Mar.	
	Duncan Henry Kennedy	30do.	
	Pierce Purcell Goold	31do.	
	David Bradford	2June	
	William Gillespie	27Oct.	
Ensign	—— Caddell	19Aug.1813	
	Henry Stuart	2Dec.	
	Alexander Read	16do.	
	James Law	25do.	
	Joseph Morton	30do.	
	Andrew Russell	10Mar.1814	
	John Holland	11do.	
	John Lewis	12do.	
Paymaster	Harry Cope	20June1805	
Adjutant	James Birkett	25Dec.1813	Lieut. 1Jan.1810
QuarterMaster	Richard Gill	13Sept.1813	
Surgeon	R— Bellars	12Aug.1806	
Assistant Surg.	Thomas James Wharrie	21Feb.1811	
	Robert Henry Bell	do.	

N. B. *The Officers printed in Italics are to be placed upon Half-pay on arrival from Foreign Service.*

Facings blue.—Lace silver.

Agent, Messrs. Greenwood, Cox and Hammersley.

360 87th (or Prince of Wales's own Irish) Regt. of Foot.

Permitted to bear on their Colours and Appointments " an EAGLE with a wreath of laurel above the Harp," in addition to the Arms of the Prince Regent, in commemoration of their distinguished Services on various occasions, and particularly at the Battle of Barrosa, 5th March, 1811. The 2d Battalion also the word "TARIFA," in commemoration of the Defence of that place, 31st December, 1811.

Rank.	Name.	Rank in the	
		Regiment.	Army.
Colonel -	Sir John Doyle, Bt. K. B. & K. C.	3May1796	Lt.Gen. 25Ap.1808
	Lt. Col. Comm.	18Sept.1793	
Lieut. Colonel	SirEdw.Ger.Butler,Kt.	16Aug.1804	M.Gen. 4June1814
	Charles William Doyle	22Aug.1805	Col. 4June1813
Major -	Francis M— Miller	13June1805	Lt.Col. 1Jan.1812
	Hugh Gough	8Aug.	Lt.Col. 29July1809
	Jos. Fred. Desbarres	11Apr.1811	Lt.Col. 3Mar.1814
	Henry Wm. Davenport	6May1813	13June1811
Captain -	Archibald Cameron	9May1805	
	Henry Hooper	30do.	Major 12Apr.1814
	Henry Browne	13June	
	Henry C— Streatfeild	7Nov.	
	William King	8Feb.1807	
	Charles Conway Costley	1Oct.	
	Anthony Wm. Somarsall	7July1808	7Apr. 1808
	James Jones	17Aug.	
	William Slade Gully	9Mar.1809	
	Charles Lucas Bell	16do.	
	Rodney Bell	28Dec.	
	W— G— Cavanagh	22Nov.1810	
	James King	4July1811	28Feb. 1811
	Edward Goate	19Feb.1812	27June1811
	Malachi Fallon	20do.	
	Edward Hen. Fitz Gerald	2July	
	William Crow	8Oct.	
	Charles Cox	1Apr.1813	
	Robert John Love	5Aug.	
	James Hunt	21Apr.1814	7Aug.1806
	James Stewart	9June	
	James Campbell Barton	8Dec.	
Lieutenant -	Charles Bagot	16Jan.1806	
	John Fenton	13Feb.	
	Joseph Turner	25Sept.	
	William Hutchinson	26do.	Adjutant
	Stephen Maincy	4June1807	

Lieutenant.

Rank.	Name.	Rank in the	
		Regiment.	Army.

Rank.	Name.	Regiment.	Army.
	John Coghlan	17Sept.1807	
	Philip Higginson	23do.	
	Arthur Holmes	24do.	
	John Slade	19Nov.	
	George Beere	29do.	
	Joseph Barry	30do.	
	John Doyle Bagenal	1Dec.	
	James Gubbins Fennell	3do.	
	James Carroll	31Mar.1808	
	—— Clifford	7July	14Apr. 1808
	Peter Benson Husband	13Sept.	
	William Dunlevie	15do.	
	William Mountgarrett	6Oct.	
	James Thompson	20do.	
	Wright Knox	16Aug.1810	
	James Wilkins	23Jan.1811	3Oct. 1805
	John Kelly	10Apr.	
	John Day	11do.	
	W— W— Lamphier	30May	18Oct. 1810
Lieutenant -	James T— Moore	18Feb.1812	Adjutant
	Peter Paterson	19do.	
	—— Grady	25June	
	Stanley Ireland	17Sept.	
	Joseph Leslie	8Oct.	
	Patrick Kelly	25Jan.1813	26Apr. 1810
	—— Waller	25Mar.	
	James Bowes	1Apr.	
	William Maginnis	4Aug.	
	John Gordon	5do.	
	George Maunsell	19do.	28Jan. 1812
	Thomas Lee	7Oct.	
	—— Masterson	17Nov.	
	James Kennelly	18do.	
	Richard Irvine	23Dec.	
	Henry G— Bailey	9June1814	
	William Byrne	11Aug.	
	Alexander Irwin	24Nov.	
	Henry Wind. Desbarres	8Dec.	
	John Carrol	22do.	

Ensign

Rank.	Name.	Rank in the Regiment.	Rank in the Army.
Ensign	Terence O'Brien	22Apr.1813	
	Abraham Forde Royse	20May	
	R-- Ryan	1July	
	———— O'Grady	29do.	
	John G— Baylee	4Aug.	
	Robert Bagenall	18Nov.	
	Anthony Carroll	23Dec.	
	Arthur Stanley	12May1814	
	Edward Cox	7July	
	James Philip Devenish	22Sept.	
	Edward Burford Shorter	24Nov.	
	John Hassard	22Dec.	
Paymaster 2	John Sherlock	29Sept.1808	
1			
Adjutant -	William Hutchinson	27Nov.1811	Lieut. 26Sept.1806
	James T— Moore	11Mar.1813	Lieut. 18Feb.1812
QuarterMaster	Robert Paul	10July1807	
	William Gready	1Oct.	
Surgeon -	Hugh Mackay	9May1805	19Dec.1799
	Alexander Leslie	7Oct.1813	
Assistant Surg.	Henry O'Hara	19Dec.1805	
	Robert Rule	13Oct.1808	
	Samuel Coulthard	9May1811	
	Maurice Owen	9June1814	29Oct. 1812

Facings green.—Lace gold.

Agent, Messrs. Greenwood, Cox and Hammersley.

Permitted to bear on their Colours and Appointments a " SPHINX," with the word " EGYPT," in commemoration of the Campaign of 1801.

Colonel	◆✕᷄ {	Wm. Carr, *Lord* Beresford, *K. B.*	9Feb.1807	Lt.Gen.	1Jan.1812
Lieut. Col.	◎‾ {	Alexander Wallace	6Feb.1805	Col.	4June1813
	◎) }	John Taylor	18May1809	Col.	4June1813
Major - -	(	R. Barclay Macpherson	17Mar.1808	Lt.Col.	4June1814
	)	Robert B— M'Gregor	23Nov.1809	Lt.Col.	4June1814
	)	John Dunn	25Oct.1810		
	◎-(	William Cardon Seton	30Apr.1812		
Captain - -	⎰	James Poole Oates	19Oct.1804	Major	3Mar.1814
	◎	Charles Tryon	4Apr.1805	Lt.Col.	26Aug.1813
		H— G— Buller	17Mar.1808		
		Robert N— Nickle	1June1809		
		George Henry Dansey	3Aug.		
		Robert Christie	2Nov.		
		Duncan Robertson	28Dec.		
		John Bower Lewis	25Oct.1810		
	⎰	Robert O'Hara	4Apr.1811		
		Richard Bunworth	30May		
		John Stewart	5Sept.		
		Hamilton Bagwell	16Jan.1812	Major	4June1814
		Isaac Walker	26Mar.		
		William Flack	30Apr.		
		William Mackie	14May		
		James Flood	21Apr.1814		
	⎱	John Fitzpatrick	8Sept.		
Lieutenant -	⎰	John Armstrong	4June1807	26Sept.1804	
		Timothy Richard Janns	13do.		
		William Nickle	1Oct.		
		John Davern	11Nov.		
		Frederick Meade	30Mar.1809		
		Hercules Ellis	20Apr.		
		George F— Faris	11July		
		Bartholomew Mahon	12do.		
		Peter Pegus	13do.		
	⎰	Thomas J— Lloyd	5Sept.		
		James Stewart	23Nov.		
		George Cresswell	18Oct.1810	1Dec.1808	
		Christopher Hilliard	23do.		
		John Graham	24do.		
		Maurice O'Connor	25do.		
		W— H— Rutherford	22Nov.		
		Simon Fairfield	7Mar.1811		
		Parr Kingsmill	8May		
		William Kingsmill	30do.		
	⎱	George Hill	10Oct.		

Lieutenant -	Maurice Mahon	5Mar.1812	
	Wm. Devereux Jackson	12do.	
	Walter Croker Poole	26do.	
	Joseph Owgan	29Apr.	
	William Grattan	30do.	
	John Christian	11May	
	John Darcy	12do.	
	Henry Peter Delmé	3Sept.	
	John Fairfield	11Nov.1813	
	Richard Holland	12do.	
	James Mitchell	13do.	Adjutant
	* John Wilkinson	25Dec.	
	* Christopher Banco	do.	
	* George Allen	do.	
	* St. Leger John Watkins	do.	
	George Charles Stewart	20Apr.1814	
	D— M'Intosh	21do.	
	—— Gardiner	24Nov.	
Ensign - -	Thomas Taylor	3Oct.1811	
	Charles Crawford Peshall	10do.	
	Samuel S— Fisher	21Nov.	5Sept.1811 Adjut.
	John Atkin	30Jan.1812	
	James M'Clintock	12May	
	George Bunbury	14do.	
	William Smith	11June	
	Edmund Hackett	25Dec.1813	
	John Hickson	do.	
	Charles Ashmore	do.	
	Marshal Clarke	3Feb.1814	
	John Gells	10do.	
	Cha. Blake Morgan	21Apr.	
	William Atkin	12May	
	John Carey	23June	
	Donald Robertson	24Nov.	
Paymaster - 1	John Grosser	27May1813	1Aug.1811
2	Wm. Adair Macdougall	1July	
Adjutant -	James Mitchell	26Sept.1811	Lieut. 13Nov.1813
	Samuel S— Fisher	21Nov.	Ensign 5Sept.1811
QuarterMaster	M— Collins	25Mar.1808	
	Donald Stewart	29Jan.1812	
	—— Clifford	30do.	
Surgeon -	George Johnstone	22Aug.1811	
	William Cumin	15Oct.1812	
Assistant Surg.	Andrew Gregg	3Sept.1812	
	John Wyer	9Sept.1813	
	John Wright	18Mar.1814	

Facings yellow.—Lace silver.

Agent, Mr. Macdonald, Pall Mall Court.

89th

89th Regiment of Foot.

Permitted to bear a " SPHINX," with the word " EGYPT," on their Colours and Appointments in commemoration of the Campaign of 1801.

Rank.	Name.	Rank in the Regiment.	Rank in the Army.
Colonel -	Albemarle, *Earl of* Lindsey	25 Mar. 1808	Gen. 25 Sept. 1803
Lieut. Colonel	Robert Sewell	3 May 1810	Col. 4 June 1813
	Donald M'Bean	1 July	
	Joseph W— Morrison	11 July 1811	30 Nov. 1809
Major - -	◎ Richard Butler	1 May 1809	Lt.Col. 30 Sept. 1811
	Samuel Hall	28 Nov. 1810	8 Mar. 1810
	Miller Clifford	29 do.	
	Richard Trench	13 June 1811	
Captain -	Lawrence Oakes	27 Aug. 1804	Major 4 June 1814
	Lorenzo Nunn	15 Dec.	Major 4 June 1814
	Johnston St. Leger	18 July 1805	
	Robert Ongley Hilden	6 Mar. 1806	
	James Basden	4 Sept.	
	Thomas Browne	25 Dec.	
	Henry Gore	5 Feb. 1807	4 Dec. 1806
	Richard Croker Rose	1 May 1809	
	George West Barnes	17 May 1810	27 May 1806
	Thomas Ramsay	18 Dec.	
	William Lancaster	20 do.	
	J— M— Shand	5 Mar. 1812	
	William Hill	2 Sept.	
	George Jones	8 Oct.	
	Thomas Daniel	16 Dec.	
	Charles Croker	9 June 1813	
	Vesian Pick	10 do.	
	Charles Coates	8 July	
	Abraham Low	24 Feb. 1814	
	William Barney	24 Mar.	22 July 1813
	Francis Savage	11 Aug.	
	John Cunningham	27 Oct.	
Lieutenant	Plomer Young	3 Sept. 1806	
	Roger Sheehy	22 Oct.	
	John Armstrong	23 do.	
	Robert Sanderson	4 June 1807	11 Dec. 1806
	Walter Pearse	6 Aug.	9 Dec. 1806
	Charles Redmond	27 do.	7 May 1807
	Watson A— Steel	5 Nov.	4 Dec. 1806
	Oliver Brush	16 June 1808	
	Charles Cannon	21 July	Adjutant

Lieutenant

| Rank. | Name. | Rank in the | |
		Regiment.	Army.
	Alexander Dalgety	28July1808	
	John Hewson	21Dec.1809	20May 1781
	David Chambers	5Apr.1810	
	James Blagrave	8May1811	
	William Bell	9do.	
	John Crawford	18July	
	Daniel Browne	5Mar.1812	
	Osman Charles Watts	19do.	
	Thomas Taylor	do.	
	Edward Moulson	24June	
	George Hopper	25do.	Adjutant
	William Gray	27Aug.	30Jan. 1805
	Patrick Agnew	1Sept.	
	J— Smith Reynolds	2do.	
	Allen Stuart	3do.	
	Robert Chapman	4do.	
	And. Snape Ham. Aplin	24do.	
Lieutenant -	John Caulfield	23Dec.	
	Abraham B— Taylor	24do.	
	John Orr	25Jan.1813	13Oct. 1808
	James Davidson	do.	26Sept.1811
	John Robert Baker	8July	1Apr. 1812
	Robert Lloyd	3Aug.	
	Mortimer Jones	4do.	
	Emanuel Thomas Poe	5do.	
	Henry Ogle Lewis	3Feb.1814	
	Francis Miles	4do.	
	George Wm. Thompson	5do.	
	John Petry	6do.	
	George Madden	7do.	
	George Bertles	24do.	
	William Nesfield	30Mar.	
	Edward Davenport	31do.	
	James M— Noble	14Apr.	
	William Leader	27Oct.	
	Fra. Hutch. M. Johnson	18July1811	
	J— M— Hewson	2Sept.1812	
Ensign - -	William Saunders	3do.	
	Wm. Windham Philan	4do.	
	Matthew Handcock	24do.	
	John William Leslie	21Jan.1813	

Ensign

Rank.	Name.	Rank in the	
		Regiment.	Army.
Ensign	⎧ James Oughton	15 Apr. 1813	20 Feb. 1812
	⎪ John Coventry	6 May	
	⎪ Aylmer Dowdall	20 do.	
	⎪ John Goodwin	5 Aug.	
	⎪ William Horne Dougan	4 Feb. 1814	
	⎨ William Nesbitt Orange	5 do.	
	⎪ John Macdonald	6 do.	
	⎪ Edward Kenny	3 Mar.	17 June 1813
	⎪ Thomas Lewis	12 May	
	⎪ Felix Smith	11 Aug.	
	⎩ James Imlach	27 Oct.	
Paymaster - 1	⎰ James White	19 Mar. 1803	
2	⎱ Cha. Pakenham Roddy	18 Apr. 1805	
Adjutant - -	⎰ Charles Cannon	8 July 1812	Lieut. 21 July 1808
	⎱ George Hopper	14 July 1814	Lieut. 25 June 1812
QuarterMaster	⎰ T— Sheridan -	20 Mar. 1806	
	⎱ H— Selway	5 Jan. 1809	
Surgeon -	⎰ Henry Reed	1 Jan. 1799	
	⎱ Henry D— Goodsir	28 Mar. 1811	20 Dec. 1810
Assistant Surg.	⎧ Michael Duigan	8 Feb. 1810	
	⎨ Alexander Finlay Gray	8 Oct.	
	⎪ William Dunlop	4 Feb. 1813	
	⎩ John W— Brown	25 Nov.	

Facings black.—Lace gold.

Agent, Messrs. Greenwood, Cox and Hammersley.

368 90th Regt. of Foot (or Perthshire Volunteers.)

Permitted to bear on their Colours and Appointments a " SPHINX," with the word " EGYPT," in commemoration of the Campaign of 1801.

Rank.	Name.	Regiment.	Rank in the Army.
Colonel -	✕-Tho. *Lord* Lynedock, K.B.	25Sept.1803	Lt.Gen. 25July1810
	Lt. Col. Comm.	10Feb.1794	
Lieut. Colonel {	John M'Nair	1Aug.1804	Col. 4June1813
	Mark Napier	29Mar.1810	
	George Burrell	30Apr.1807	Lt.Col. 4June1813
Major - - {	Thomas Wright	10Sept.	Lt.Col. 4June1813
	Alex. Thistlethwaite	17June1813	
	Edward Currie	13Oct.1814	Lt.Col. 19June1812
Captain - {	Benjamin Preedy	20Aug.1803	Lt.Col. 4June1814
	William Holland	2Aug.1804	Major 4June1814
	Andrew Wood	28do.	Major 4June1814
	Dudley Ackland Gilland	11Jan.1805	
	Thomas Ware	7Mar.	Major 4June1814
	Arthur Bowen	13June	
	Albert D'Alton	15Aug.	Major 4June1814
	Manley Dixon	20Oct.	
	William Henry Wilby	21Jan.1806	Major 15Mar.1810
	George Williamson	2Apr.1807	Major 4June1814
	Charles Cranston Dixon	5Aug.	Major 4June1814
	John Dickins	18Feb.1808	3Dec.1806
	John Birch	14May1809	
	Samuel Fairtlough	23Aug.1810	
	Richard Dogherty	21May1812	
	William James	5Nov.	
	Allan Maclean	3Dec.	
	William Read	13Jan.1814	
	James Fraser	13Oct.	
Lieutenant - {	Henry Micajah Williams	26Sept.1805	
	Daniel O'Keefe	28Apr.1806	
	William J— Speed	25Aug.	24Dec.1804
	Robert Conry	2Oct.	
	John Lucas Cox	19Mar.1807	
	Jeremiah Marsh	3May	
	James Crawford	5do.	
	George Darley Cranfield	12do.	Adjutant
	John Fleming	5June	
	Charles Dowson	17Sept.	
	Thomas Nickoll	25do.	29Apr.1806
	Henry Eager	17Mar.1808	
	John Grant	21Apr.	
	William Hind	12Jan.1809	
	Gilbert Conry	14May	
	C— Le Hunte	15do.	
	William Laing	7Sept.	
	Charles M'Anally	12Oct.	31Dec.1807

Lieutenant

Rank.	Name.	Rank in the Regiment.	Army.
Lieutenant -	Patrick Lynch	3May1810	
	William Gibson	13Sept.	
	David Campbell	5Dec.	
	Samuel Bell	3Jan.1811	
	E— S— Davys	16May	
	Robert Bannerman	8Aug.	
	—— Buchanan	28Nov.	
	Walter Gray	13Aug.1812	
	Kenneth T— Ross	8Oct.	
	Charles Boyd	3Dec.	
	Charles M'Cartie	31do.	
	Thomas Fane Uniacke	1Apr.1813	11June1811
	Angus M'Donald	13Jan.1814	
	Henry Terry	19May	
	John Wood	8Sept.	
	Edward Warren	13Oct.	
	John Orde	10Nov.	
Ensign -	James Abbott	9Apr.1812	
	Nathaniel Taylor	21May	
	John Nunn	4June	
	William Macpherson	5Nov.	
	John Kerr	31Dec.	
	Alexander Wilson	11Feb.1813	Adjutant
	John Bayley	3Mar.	
	Alexander Stuart	4do.	
	Francis Newton	27May	
	MonkhouseGra. Taylor	10June	
	Jacob Sankey	27Jan.1814	
	John Duncan Bentham	19May	
	William Furlong	8Sept.	
	Edward Last	13Oct.	
	Noble George White	10Nov.	
Paymaster 1	Harry Allison	31Mar.1802	
2	Charles Jones	3Oct.1808	
Adjutant -	James Crawford	17Apr.1806	Lieut. 5May1807
	Alexander Wilson	11Feb.1813	Ensign 11Feb.1813
QuarterMaster	Peter Maitland	9Feb.1809	
	—— Blood	28Dec.	
Surgeon -	Isaac Silcock	16Feb.1809	
	Henry Hamilton	25Nov.1813	10Aug.1809
Assistant Surg.	John Henley	4Aug.1808	
	Joseph Ewing	7Sept.1809	
	James Cardiff	22Feb.1810	4Aug.1808
	Alexander Hamilton	17Feb.1814	28May1812

Facings buff. — Lace gold.

Agent, Messrs. Greenwood, Cox and Hammersley.

Rank.	Name.	Regiment.	Rank in the Army.
Colonel - -	Duncan Campbell	3May1796	L.Gen. 25Apr.1808
	Lt.Col.Comm.	10Feb.1794	
Lieut. Col. ⊚̱ ⎰	William Douglas	25Nov.1808	Col. 4June1814
⎱	Benjamin Wynne Ottley	2Jan.1812	Col. 4June1814
◎ ⎛	Donald Mac Neill	1Aug.1811	Lt.Col.26Aug.1813
Major - - ⎜	Augustus Meade	28Feb.1812	Lt.Col. 4June1811
⎟	Donald Gregorson	30Apr.	
⎝	Jas. Milford Sutherland	10Sept.	
⎛	James Walsh	28Aug.1804	Major 12Apr.1814
⎜	Thomas Hunter Blair	28Mar.1805	Major 30May1811
⎜	William Steuart	17Apr.1806	
⎜	Archibald Campbell	1Oct.1807	
⎜	Dugald Campbell	23Nov.1809	
⎜	William Gun	7June1810	30Nov.1809
⎜	James C— Murdoch	29Nov.	
◎ ⎜	Archibald Ross	12Sept.1811	Major 21June1813
⎜	Alex. James Callander	10Oct.	Major 4June1814
⎜	Ronald M'Donald	2Jan.1812	
Captain - ⎨	Archibald Campbell	15do.	
⎜	Robert Anderson	30Apr.	
⎜	Hugh M'Gregor	2July	17Aug.1806
⎜	Andrew Macfarlane	10Sept.	
⎜	John Murray	10Dec.	16June1808
⎜	Thomas Hugo	22July1813	
⎜	John Young	6Oct.	
⎜	Archibald Mac Neill	25Nov.	
⎜	David Bowman	16Dec.	
⎜	Duncan Campbell	3Mar.1814	
⎜	S— Nicholas Ormerod	31do.	
⎝	John Campbell	19May	
⎛	Robert Gresley Lavers	31Oct.1805	
⎜	John Campbell	24Aug.1807	
⎜	John Russell	11May1808	
⎜	Alexander Campbell	12do.	
⎜	Robert Stewart	13do.	
⎜	Andrew M'Lachlan	14do.	
⎜	Robert Campbell	16do.	
Lieutenant ⎨	Carberry Egan	19do.	
⎜	Andrew Cathcart	11May1809	
⎜	John Macdougall	15June	
⎜	James Hood	3Aug.	
⎜	John Marshall	23Nov.	
⎜	Alexander Smith	30Aug.1810	22Feb. 1810
⎜	Thomas Lisle Fenwick	13Sept.	3Nov.1808
⎜	Thomas Murray	11June1811	
⎝	Robert Spencer Knox	2Jan.1812	

Lieutenant

Lieutenant	Charles Stuart	16Jan.1812	
	John Campbell	23do.	
	John M'Donald	30Apr.	
	Eugene Brown	9July	
	——— Macdougall	19July1813	
	A— Campbell	20do.	
	George Scott	21do.	Adjutant
	William Smith	do.	
	James Black	22do.	
	Peter Macfarlane	23do.	
	John Andrew Ormiston	29do.	
	John O'Leary	6Oct.	
	John Rutherford	7do.	
	Alexander Roberton	25Nov.	
	Alex. D— M'Laren	31Mar.1814	
	Hugh M'Dougall	14Apr.	
	Richard Butler	9June	
	John Taylor	14July	
	James Briggs	28do.	
	Benjamin Forster	24Nov.	28Mar.1805
Ensign	Robert Power	17Sept.1812	
	Alexander Sword	28Jan.1813	
	Nicholas Horsley	18Mar.	
	John M'Kenna	29Apr.	
	William Henry Barker	29July	
	Norman Lamont	26Aug.	
	William Trimmer	18Nov.	
	James Paton	30Dec.	
	——— Ducat	24Feb.1814	
	——— Cahill	31Mar.	
	Andrew Smith	14Apr.	
	Lawrence Lind	9June	
	——— Henry	do.	Adjutant
	Robert Gamble	14July	
	James Scott	27do.	
	Duncan Livingstone	25Aug.	
Paymaster 1	Dugald Campbell	16May1808	
2	John Fairfowl	16Feb.1809	
Adjutant	George Scott	26Apr.1810	Lieut. 21July1813
	——— Henry	9June1814	Ensign 9June1814
Quarter-Mast.	James Stewart	16Apr.1807	
	Archibald Ferguson	24May1810	
Surgeon	Robert Douglas	6June1805	
	William Young	31Oct.1811	
AssistantSurg.	George M. M'Lachlan	26Mar.1812	
	William H— Young	4Feb.1813	
	Hugh J— O'Donel	27Jan.1814	
	Hugh Caldwell	10Mar.	

Facings yellow.—Lace silver.

Agent, Mr. Campbell, No. 18, Suffolk Street, Charing-cross.

(2d BATTALION DISBANDED.)

Permitted to bear on their Colours and Appointments the words " EGMONT-OP-ZEE," and " MANDORA," for the Actions of 2d October, 1799, and 13th March, 1801 ; also a " SPHINX," with the word " EGYPT," in commemoration of the Campaign of 1801.

Rank.	Name.	Rank in the Regiment.	Army.
Colonel -	⊚John, *Lord* Niddery, *K.B.*	3Jan.1806	L.Gen. 25Apr.1808
Lieut. Colonel	⊚John Cameron	23June1808	Col. 4June1814
Major -	{ James Mitchell	30Mar.1809	Lt.Col. 3Mar.1814
	{ Donald Macdonald	26Nov.1812	
Captain -	{ Samuel Maxwell	26Jan.1804	Major 4June1814
	George W— Holmes	28Mar.1805	
	Ronald Macdonald	23May	
	Dugald Campbell	13June	
	Peter Wilkie	21May1806	
	George Couper	14Apr.1808	Major 21June1813
	William Charles Grant	28July	
	William Little	7Jan.1813	
	Archibald Ferrier	4Mar.	
	{ John Warren	15Apr.	
Lieutenant -	{ Ronald M'Donald	17Sept.1805	
	Claude Alexander	19do.	Adjutant
	James John Chisholm	4Feb.1808	
	Robert Winchester	6do.	
	Thomas Hobbs	7do.	
	Thomas Macintosh	9do.	
	Donald Macdonald	10do.	
	Andrew Will	18do.	
	Alexander Gordon	3Mar.	
	James Ker Ross	4May	
	Ronald Macdonald	5do.	
	Thomas Gordon	28July	
	William M'Eachran	6Apr.1809	
	Hector Innes	13do.	
	George Logan	5Oct.	
	Ewen Campbell	30do.	
	Richard M'Donell	1Nov.	
	John M'Kinlay	2do.	
	Richard Josiah Peat	12Apr.1810	
	George Mackie	8Oct.1812	
	Alexander M'Pherson	22do.	
	Ewan Ross	26Nov.	
	{ James Hope	7Jan.1813	

Ensign

Rank.	Name.	Rank in the	
		Regiment.	Army.
Ensign - - {	John Branwell	29July1813	
	Robert Logan	5Aug.	
	John Clarke	26do.	
	Angus M'Donald	15Sept.	
	Abel Becher	16do.	
	Robert Hewitt	21Oct.	
	John M. Ross M'Pherson	22do.	
	James Campbell	11Nov.	
	——— M'Pherson	23Dec.	
Paymaster -	James Gordon	16Apr.1807	
Adjutant - -	Claude Alexander	2June1808	Lieut. 19Sept.1805
Quarter-Master	Duncan Macfarlane	9July1803	
Surgeon - -	George Hicks	22Aug.1811	
Assistant Surg. {	John Webb	16Dec.1810	
	John Stewart	5Nov.1812	

Facings yellow.—Lace silver.

Agent, Mr. Bruce, No. 47, Parliament Street.

Rank.	Name.	Rank in the Regiment.	Army.
Colonel - -	William Wemyss	25Aug.1800	Gen. 4June1814
Lieut. Colonel {	Robert Dale	10Feb.1814	4June1813
	Andrew Creagh	29Sept.	4June1814
Major - - {	William Wemyss	27May1813	
	Alexander Gordon	10Feb.1814	1Jan. 1812
	Alexander Mackay	29Sept.	1Jan. 1812
Captain - {	Thomas Hickens	21Feb.1805	
	Richard Ryan	1Aug.	
	Donald M'Leod	11Sept.1806	
	Edward Fawconer	5Mar.1807	Major 4June1814
	Persse O'Keefe Boulger	2Apr.	Major 4June1814
	A— Douglas	16June1808	Major 4June1813
	Alexander Mackenzie	22June1809	
	Henry Ellis	25July1811	5June1806
	William Lunt	21Jan.1813	
	Neil M'Kinnon	25May	
	James Gunn	26do.	
	Samuel Robert Cooke	26Aug.	28Apr.1806
	Edward Harte	10Feb.1814	
	John Tyler	11do.	
	Alexander Muirhead	9June	
Lieutenant - {	William Munro	18Sept.1805	
	Alexander M'Donnell	7Nov.	
	Hugh H— M'Lean	10Sept.1806	
	J— Hedderick	11do.	
	Robert Sparks	3Sept.1807	
	Æneas Macpherson	29Oct.	
	Andrew Phaup	3Mar.1808	
	J— Thompson	31do.	
	George Munro	13July	
	William Van Ryneweld	14do.	
	Dugald Mackenzie	9Apr.1810	
	John White	11do.	
	John Brown	6Sept.	21Mar.1805
	James Ewart	6Dec.	
	David Macpherson	9Jan.1812	
	John Macdonald	21May	
	Charles Gordon	15Oct.	
	Alexander Rose	25May1813	
	James Hay	26do.	
	Wemyss Ersk. Sutherland	27do.	
	Charles Head	3June	
	Wm. Valentine Graves	29July	

Lieutenant

Rank.	Name.	Rank in the Regiment.	Army.
Lieutenant -	Charles O'Neil	11Nov.1813	
	Angus Leslie	10Feb.1814	
	William Rose	11do.	
	James Millis Nairne	12do.	
	Donald Cumming	9Mar.	
	Francis Archibald Stuart	10do.	
	Richard Connop	15Sept.	
Ensign -	George Menzies	15Oct.1812	
	James Ireland	25Apr.1813	Adjutant
	Howall Ball	20May	Adjutant
	Archibald Fraser	22do.	
	Peter Grant	23do.	15Apr.1813
	Alexander Douglass	24do.	
	Peter Cheape	25do.	
	Bruce Lamb	17June	
	Lewis Grenier	22July	13Jan. 1813
	James Walker	12Aug.	
	David Cowan	26do.	
	John Arthur	25Dec.	
	Charles Gordon	9Mar.1814	
	Robert Mackay	10do.	
Paymaster 1	Thomas Patullo	23Apr.1807	
2	Alexander Aitken	26Aug.1813	
Adjutant - -	James Ireland	25Apr.1813	Ensign 25Apr.1813
	Howall Ball	20May	Ensign 20May1813
QuarterMaster	George Mackay	3Sept.1801	
	—— Duncan	10Mar.1814	
Surgeon - -	George Mann	13Sept.1810	3July 1806
	Robert Punshon	15July1813	
Assistant Surg.	James Dempster	24Jan.1811	
	George Inglis	29July1813	
	John Regan	1Sept.1814	

Facings yellow.—Lace silver.

Agent, Messrs. Greenwood, Cox and Hammersley.

94th

Permitted to bear the " ELEPHANT " on their Colours and Appointments, in commemoration of their services in India.

Rank.	Name.	Rank in the Regiment.	Army.
Colonel - ✗☐Rowland, *Lord* Hill, *K.B.*		18Sept.1809	Lt.Gen. 1Jan.1812
Lieut. Colonel ☒James Campbell		27Sept.1804	Col. 4June1813
Major - ◎ { James Allan Thomas Laing		20July1809 6Jan.1814	Lt. Col. 4June1814
Captain - -	◎ { James Bogle Charles Campbell Edward Kingdom Alexander Cairncross Alexander Kyle John Napper Jackson Frederick Campbell David Munro John Bogue John Charles Griffiths David Campbell	25Dec.1804 14July1808 19Apr.1810 7June 11Oᴄt. 28Feb.1812 25Jan.1813 10Feb.1814 17do. 7July 20Oᴄt.	Major 26Aug.1813 Major 12Apr.1814 21Dec. 1809
Lieutenant -	{ William Cannon John Thornton John Hutchinson James Tweedie Thomas Scott William Watson John Edward Hunt Archibald Robertson Andrew Robertson David Ogilvy James M'Cormick Francis Murray James Rutherford	7June1810 2Aug. 27Dec. 27Feb.1812 28do. 23Sept.1813 10Nov. 6Jan.1814 10Feb. 17do. 17Mar. 7July 27Oᴄt.	 26Feb. 1806

Ensign

Rank.	Name.	Rank in the Regiment.	Army.
Ensign -	{ John M'Nab	4July1811	
	James Jackson	12May1812	Adjutant
	Robert Lorimer	12June	
	Robert Macnab	15Oct.	
	Robert Mac Intosh	15July1813	
	GeorgeWentworthMalim23Dec.		
	Tho. Richardson Timbrell	7July1814	22Dec.1813
	Shirley Conyers Leslie 29Dec.		
Paymaster -	James Wright	25Mar.1810	
Adjutant -	James Jackson	12May1812	Ensign 12May1812
Quarter-Master	William Chalmers	27July1805	
Surgeon -	George Loane	26May1814	
Assistant Surg.	{ Moses Griffith	24Oct.1811	
	James Cross	11Mar.1813	

Facings green.—Lace gold.

Agent, Messrs. Greenwood, Cox and Hammersley.

Rank.	Name.	Regiment.	Rank in the Army.
Colonel in Chief	Sir David Dundas, K.B. 31 Aug. 1809	Gen. 29 Apr. 1802	
Col. Com. ◎ ☒	Forbes Champagné 31 Aug. 1809	Lt.Gen. 25 July 1810	
	Sir Brent Spencer, K.B. do.	Lt.Gen. 4 June 1811	
	Hon. Sir Wm. Stewart, K.B. do.	Lt.Gen. 4 June 1813	
Lieut. Col. ◎ ◎ ☒ ◎-	Sir T. S. Beckwith, Kt. 20 Jan. 1803	M.Gen. 4 June 1814	
	Hamlet Wade 6 May 1805	Col. 4 June 1813	
	Andrew F— Barnard 29 Mar. 1810	Col. 4 June 1813	
	Dugald Little Gilmour 16 June 1814	30 May 1811	
Major - ◎ ◎ ◎ ◎ ◎- ◎	Amos Godsill Norcott 22 Dec. 1808	Lt.Col. 25 July 1810	
	George Wilkins 10 May 1809	Lt.Col. 4 June 1814	
	John Ross 11 do.	Lt.Col. 6 Mar. 1811	
	Alexander Cameron 14 May 1812	Lt.Col. 27 Apr. 1812	
	Samuel Mitchell 2 Sept. 1813	21 June 1813	
	William Balvaird 21 July 1814	22 Nov. 1813	
Captain - ◎	Jonathan Leach 1 May 1806	Major 21 June 1813	
	Francis Glass 18 Sept.		
	Loftus Gray 16 Apr. 1807	Major 12 Apr. 1814	
	George Miller 21 Jan. 1808	Major 3 Mar. 1814	
	Thomas Drake 25 Mar.	Major 22 Apr. 1813	
	Charles Beckwith 28 July	Major 3 Mar. 1814	
	J— B— Hart 1 Feb. 1809		
	Joseph Logan 2 do.		
	Charles George Gray 6 May		
	James Fullerton 7 do.	Major 7 Apr. 1814	
	James Travers 9 do.		
	John Kent 10 do.		
	William Hallen 11 do.		
	Charles Smyth 4 Oct.	16 June 1808	
	Alexander Andrews 21 Dec.	28 Feb. 1805	
	John M'Dermid 21 Aug. 1810		
	Henry Lee 20 Sept.		
	Boyle Travers 2 May 1811		
	Henry George Smith 28 Feb. 1812	Major 29 Sept. 1814	
	Michael Hewan 13 May		
	Edward Chawner 14 do.		
	Donald Cameron 10 Oct.		
	William Johnston 22 do.		
	Thomas Mac Namara 26 Aug. 1813		
	William Cox 16 Sept.		
	John Garlies M'Cullock 21 Oct.		

Captain

Rank.	Name.	Rank in the Regiment.	Army.
	William Eeles	7 Dec. 1813	
	James Percival	8 do.	
	Andrew Wale Pemberton	9 do.	
Captain	Charles Eaton	21 Apr. 1814	
	Charles Eeles	20 July	
	Nicholas Travers	21 do.	
	Francis Le Blanc	1 Dec.	28 Sept. 1813
	Walter D— Bedell	11 Aug. 1808	
	William Humbley	13 Oct.	
	H— Manners	1 Feb. 1809	
	John Charles Hope	2 do.	
	Thomas Cochrane	22 do.	
	John Robert Budgen	4 May	
	Jonathan Layton	3 June	
	John Molloy	5 do.	
	William Campbell	6 do.	
	Thomas Smith	7 do.	Adjutant
	——— Cox	8 do.	
	Colin Clarke	9 do.	
	Francis Bennett	1 Oct.	
First Lieut.	Archibald Stewart	2 do.	
	John Middleton	4 do.	Adjutant
	John Reynolds	14 Dec.	
	Francis Dixon	4 Jan. 1810	
	Duncan Stuart	22 Feb.	
	William Chapman	26 Apr.	
	Edward Coxon	28 June	
	Richard B— Freer	21 Aug.	
	Joseph Austin	22 do.	
	William Lister	23 do.	
	John Gardiner	30 do.	
	Henry Llewelyn	21 Nov.	
	John Gustavus Foster	30 Apr. 1811	
	Dugald Cameron	1 May	
	John Kincaird	23 do.	Adjutant
	Alexander M‘Gregor	29 do.	
	F— Aldrich	23 July	
	George Simmons	25 do.	
	John Stilwell	26 Sept.	
	Charles Peter Traille	10 Oct.	
	Daniel Forbes	28 Feb. 1812	
	Robert Cochran	8 May	

Rank.	Name.	Rank in the Regiment.	Army.
First Lieut.	John Allen Ridgeway	9May1812	
	John Fry	10do.	
	Henry Scott	11do.	
	James Penman Gairdner	12do.	
	William Haggup	13do.	
	Gentle Vickers	14do.	
	Robert Fernyhough	11June	
	Sir John Ribton, Bt.	25do.	
	Loftus Francis Jones	10Oct.	
	Thomas Taylor Worsley	2do.	
	David Fensham	22do.	
	John G— Fitzmaurice	14Jan.1813	
	William Gammell	25do.	25Jan. 1809
	George Drummond	28do.	
	Thomas H— Kirkley	25Feb.	
	Edward Madden	13May	
	John Gossett	17June	
	John Wm. Backhouse	26Aug.	
	—— Mitchell	16Sept.	
	Thomas Sarsfield	21Oct.	
	Wm. John Geo. Farmer	6Dec.	
	Elliott Dunkin Johnston	7do.	
	Lord Charles Spencer	9do.	9Sept.1813
	Vere Webb	do.	
	Donald Ferguson	10do.	
	James Simmons	23do.	
	Godfrey H— Shenley	17Mar.1814	
	Charles Gordon Urquhart	27Oct.	11Aug.1814
2d Lieutenant	Frederick Mansell	2Apr.1812	
	—— Lynam	25June	
	Samuel Curry	30July	
	Rich. Henry Fitzgerald	10Oct.	
	George Carey	2do.	
	Dugald Macfarlane	22do.	
	Allen Stewart	10Dec.	
	George Drummond	25Feb.1813	
	Charles Rochfort	26do.	
	William Wright	11Mar.	
	William Campbell	25do.	
	William Shaw	25Apr.	
	James Church	26Aug.	30July 1813
	John Peter Boileau	9Sept.	18Mar.1813

2d Lieu.

Rank.	Name.	Regiment.	Army.
		Rank in the	

Rank.	Name.	Regiment.	Army.
2d Lieutenant	R— Barker	16Sept.1813	22Feb. 1813
	Richard Fowler	22Oct.	
	J— Amphlett	23do.	
	Allexander Milligan	25Nov,	
	Henry John Brownrigg	6Dec.	
	Edward Otter	7do.	
	John Bligh	9do.	
	T— Drury	24do.	
	Thomas Bowen Sheean	25do.	
	Charles Probart	do.	
	John Woodford	30do.	
	Peter Nugent Daly	20Jan.1814	
	William Shenley	21Apr.	
	Richard Cocks Eyre	22do.	
	John Prendergal Walsh	5May	
	Alexander Maclachlan	19do.	
	Charles Lostock Boileau	17Nov.	
	John Bruce	8Dec.	
Paymaster - 1	John Mackenzie	27June1805	
2	Angus M'Donald	15Feb.1810	
3	Mathew Cadoux	11Feb.1813	
Adjutant -	Thomas Smith	15Apr.1813	1st Lt. 7June1809
	John Middleton	7Dec.	1st Lt. 4Oct.1809
	John Kincaird	21July1814	1st Lt. 23May1811
QuarterMaster	Donald Ross	3Apr.1806	
	William Surtees	8June1809	
	—— Bagshaw	13Oct.1814	
Surgeon -	Joseph Burke	29June1809	
	Francis Scott	25Jan.1810	
	Thomas H— Ridgway	5Nov.1812	
Assisant Surg.	Philip O'Reilly	27July1809	
	James Robson	21Nov.1811	22Feb. 1810
	Robert H— Hett	3Sept.1812	
	John Armstrong	11Mar.1813	
	Thomas P— M'Cabe	19Aug.	
	Robert Scott	15Sept.1814	5Nov.1812

Regimentals green.—Facings black.

Agent, Mr. Adair, Pall Mall Court.

96th Regiment of Foot.

(2d BATTALION DISBANDED.)

Rank.	Name.	Rank in the	
		Regiment.	Army.
Colonel - -	George Don	10Oct.1805	Gen. 4June1814
Lieut. Colonel	Henry Elliot	25Nov.1808	Col. 4June1813
Major - -	{ Hugh Hamilton 20Sept.1810 { Henry B— B— Adams 4June1813		1Jan. 1812
Captain -	⎧ Donald M'Gregor 8Oct.1805 ⎪ James Dunbar Tovey 9do. ⎪ Anthony Hellermann 22do. ⎪ Philip Berger 23do. ⎪ John Franklin 18Sept.1808 ⎨ Cha. Lionel Fitz Gerald 2Aug.1810 ⎪ Henry Leahy 18Oct. ⎪ Francis Hawker 22Aug.1811 ⎪ John Farmer Gell 6May1813 ⎪ Joseph Le Gay 1July ⎪ Wm. O'Bryen M'Mahon 9Sept. ⎩ *John Cudbertson* 17Mar.1814		23Aug.1806 Major 4June1814
Lieutenant	⎧ John Gordon 9Oct.1806 ⎪ John William Campbell 25do. ⎪ Hugh Smith Spear 25Aug.1807 ⎪ John Snow 12Nov. ⎪ William Carrington 12July1808 ⎪ Godfrey Henry James 20Sept. ⎪ George Forman 22do. ⎪ Henry Rickards 23do. ⎨ Alexander Stewart 16Dec. ⎪ John Wadams 15Feb.1810 ⎪ John Rose 1Aug. ⎪ John Richard Joyes 15Nov. ⎪ Thomas Taylor 10July1811 ⎪ Charles Shawe 11do. ⎪ Arthur White Ford 3Oct. ⎪ Luke Stock 9Apr.1812 ⎪ James Pratt 14May ⎪ Thomas Anderson 25June ⎩ Charles Dutton 15Oct.		25Sept.1807 Adjutant 26Nov.1807

Lieutenant

Rank.	Name.	Rank in the	
		Regiment.	Army.

Rank.	Name.	Regiment.	Army.
Lieutenant	Thomas Eagan	24Dec.1812	
	John Cusine	4Mar.1813	
	Humphrey Nixon	8July	
	George Wood	2Dec.	
	Daniel Ferguson	17Mar.1814	
	Thomas Gifford	5May	
	James O'Connor	26do.	
	William Stritch	4Aug.	
Ensign - -	Henry Leslie Prentice	4Feb.1813	
	Conyng. Foster O'Brien	4Mar.	
	Richard Hawkey	5do.	
	James Brand	11do.	
	Peter Forbes	18do.	
	Wm.Alex.Cuninghame	22Apr.	
	Henry Palling	8July	
	James Sweeney	9Sept.	
Paymaster -	Alexander Anderson	29Nov.1799	
Adjutant -	Henry Rickards	28Nov.1811	Lieut. 23Sept.1808
QuarterMaster	Joseph Ralph	24Oct.1811	
	Cornick Burns	11Mar.1813	
Surgeon -	David Linn	4July1811	
	Henry Wm. Markham	7July1814	28Jan. 1813
AssistantSurg.	Thomas Walker	2Dec.1813	
	David Leahy	9June1814	2Dec.1813

N. B. *The Officers printed in Italics are to be placed upon Half-pay on arrival from Foreign Service.*

Facings buff.—Lace silver.

Agent, Messrs. Greenwood, Cox and Hammersley.

97th

Permitted to bear on their Colours and Appointments a " SPHINX," with the word " EGYPT," in commemoration of the Campaign of 1801.

Colonel - -	Gordon Drummond	8Feb.1814	Lt.Gen. 4June1811
Lieut. Col. ◎- {	James Lyon	13May 1802	M.Gen. 4June1814
{	William M'Carthy	16June1814	4June1814
Major - - {	Peter Warburton	26May1814	
{	John Howard	16June	4June1813
{	James Nash	4June1807	
	Lewis Rumann	31Dec.	Major 26Aug.1813
	Henry Zwickey	2Feb.1809	
	Ernest Olferman	13Dec.1810	
Captain - {	ThomasG— Coppinger	24Sept.1812	
{	Maurice De Courcy	25Jan.1813	
	Francis de Guilhermy	24June	
	Thomas Lloyd	8July	
	Hypolite Mitchell	14Oct.	
	Robert Garrett	7July1814	
{	A— Hypolite de Froger	4June1807	
	George Shaw	20Apr.1808	
	Evans Kettlewell	21do.	
	G— Shipley	11May1809	
	Edward Briscoe	23Nov.	
	Robert W— M'Illree	28Feb.1811	
Lieutenant {	Alexander Walker	26Sept.	Adjutant
	John Flyan Downing	6May1813	
	Standish B— Power	15July	
	James Nash M'Grath	16do.	
	James Grant	14Oct.	
	Charles O'Beirne	19May1814	
	Edward Pratt	20do.	
{	Arthur Duggan	10June1813	
	Alexander Gardiner	15July	
	Charles Boileau	30Sept.	
	James Walker	14Oct.	
Ensign - - {	Richard Hoey	11Nov.	
{	George Roch	11May1814	
	John Foot	12do.	
	William Lindsay	19do.	
	F— Ebhart	20do.	
{	George Gustavus Tuite	23June	
Paymaster -	William Shaw	9Jan.1800	
Adjutant - -	Alexander Walker	25Feb.1813	Lieut. 26Sept.1811
Quarter-Master	Nicholas Belair	26Dec.1798	
Surgeon - -	James Butler Kell	10Feb.1814	
Assistant Surg. {	Samuel Holmes	19Apr.1810	
{	Henry King	22Sept.1814	

Facings blue.—Lace silver.

Agent, Mr. Ridge, No. 44, Charing-cross.

98th

Rank.	Name.	Rank in the	
		Regiment.	Army.

Rank.	Name.	Regiment.	Army.
Colonel - -	*Sir John Burke, Bart.	22May1804	
Lieut. Colonel	William Douglas	22May1804	Col. 4June1813
Major -	{ Arthur Lloyd	22May1804	Lt.Col. 4June1811
	{ John Nicolls	7May1812	
Captain -	{ Thomas Hare	22May1804	Major 4June1814
	Henry Croasdaile	do.	Major 4June1814
	William Milne	do.	Major 4June1814
	Philip Delisle	22June1809	
	John Malone	19Apr.1810	Major 4June1814
	Thomas Laycock	19Sept.1811	
	Gillias M'Pherson	7May1812	
	St. John Wells Lucas	17Sept.	20June1811
	Jas. Norman Creighton	22Apr.1813	
	Nicholas Wrixon	26May1814	
	Macnamara Morgan	22Dec.	
Lieutenant	{ Nicholas D'Arcey	22May1804	
	Josiah Crampton	do.	
	Walter Butler	27Jan.1807	
	John Kelly	28do.	
	Joseph Killikelly	27July1809	
	W— F— Holt	29Aug.1811	13Aug.1807
	John Flinter	16July1812	
	Richard Ellis	17do.	Adjutant
	Walter Teeling	15May1813	
	Henry Wilson	16do.	
	Hyacinth French	17do.	
	B— Brady	18do.	
	John Binning Monck	19do.	
	Matthew Villiers Sankey	20do.	
	Joshua Fothergill	10June	
	Thomas M— Anderson	30do.	
	Edmond Waller	1July	
	William Keen	6Oct.	
	John Burke	16Dec.	
	Richard Bradish	17Feb.1814	2Apr.1812
	Lewis Joseph Brown	24do.	
	Samuel Scott	1Dec.	25June1812
	Thomas Gibson	2do.	
	George Ferguson	3do.	

C c   Ensign

Rank.	Name.	Rank in the Regiment.	Army.
Ensign	George Gahagan	15May1813	
	Jeffery Prendergast	1July	
	James Gibbons	16Dec.	
	Joseph Winniett	24Feb.1814	
	Patrick M'Gawley	21Apr.	
	Charles James Bullivant	2Dec.	
	John Carroll	3do.	
Paymaster	Patrick Brenan	11Nov.1813	
Adjutant	Richard Ellis	2Feb.1809	Lieut. 17July1812
Quarter-Master	William Kenny	10June1813	
Surgeon	William Cogan	7Mar.1805	
Assistant Surg.	Daniel Rossiter	17Feb.1814	22Feb. 1810
	John Fergusson	3Mar.	

Facings buff.

Agent, Messrs. Greenwood, Cox and Hammersley.

99th

Rank.	Name.	Rank in the Regiment.	Army.
Colonel - -	Hon. Montagu Mathew	6June1811	Lt.Gen. 4June1813
Lieut. Colonel	John Daniel	16June1814	1Jan. 1812
Major - -	A— S— King	3May1810	
	George Tryon	27Oct.1814	
Captain -	John Bazalgette	17Oct.1805	
	Peter Dumas	19Mar.1807	26Nov.1806
	Daniel Geale	11June	12June1806
	Jonas Fitzherbert	19Nov.	Col. 4June1814
	Michael H— Campbell	30Mar.1808	18June1807
	John Mann	8June1809	
	William Burton	31Aug.	8May 1806
	Joshua Wilson	7Mar.1811	
	Anthony Suasso	9Apr.1812	3Jan. 1811
	Hon. John Nevill	27Jan.1814	
	John Thomson	27Oct.	
Lieutenant	George Lidwell	23May1805	
	Thomas Armstrong	11Sept.	
	John Atkinson	12do.	
	Richard Ffennell	1Oct.1807	26Oct. 1806
	Edmund W— O'Dell	12May1808	13Aug.1807
	John O'Farrel	8Dec.	17May 1808
	Miles Bourke	6Mar.1811	
	Ambrose Lane	7do.	
	John Gallagher	29Aug.	22May 1804
	O— Sullivan	20Feb.1812	
	John Blackall	8July1813	
	Ballard J— Nembhard	9Dec.	
Ensign - -	William M'Couchy	3May1810	7Mar.1810
	Henry Montgomery	6Mar.1811	
	Benjamin Garrett	9May	
	William Brady	20Feb.1812	
	John Rothwell	23Apr.	
	John Hutchinson	12Nov.	Adjutant
	William M'Vitty	9Dec.1813	
	Thomas Fitzherbert	14July1814	
Paymaster -	Thomas King	5Sept.1811	
Adjutant - -	John Hutchinson	12Nov.1812	Ensign 12Nov.1812
Quarter-Master	George Mathew	25Aug 1808	
Surgeon - -	Samuel Barnard	8Mar.1810	
Assistant Surg.	Thomas Wahab	27June1811	

Facings pale yellow.
Agent, Messrs. Greenwood, Cox and Hammersley.
C c 2 100th

388 100th (or His Royal Highness the Prince Regent's County of Dublin) Regiment of Foot.

| Rank. | Name. | Rank in the | |
		Regiment.	Army.
Colonel - -	*Sir Fred.J.Falkiner, Bt.	28Feb.1805	
Lieut. Colonel	©Geo. Marq. of Tweedale	20Jan.1814	21June1813
Major - -	{ Christopher Myers	4June1813	Col. 4June1814
	Thomas Rynd	10Mar.1814	
Captain -	{ John Martin	28Feb.1805	Major 19Dec.1813
	Thomas Ormsby Sherrard	do.	
	George Thew. Bourke	do.	
	Thomas Dawson	1May	
	F— Tracy Thomas	28Aug.1806	
	David Byron Davies	10Aug.1809	Major 25July1810
	Lewis Ritter	30ct.1811	
	Thomas Fenn Addison	5Mar.1812	Lt.Col. 13Oct.1814
	William Sleigh	19do.	
	Richard Vyse Fawcett	24June1813	Major 19Dec.1813
	Charles Hanley	4Aug.1814	
Lieutenant	{ James Armstrong	28Aug.1806	
	George B— Williams	17Sept.1807	
	Edward Murray	25do.	
	George Lyon	25May1809	10Feb. 1808
	M— G— Olding	4Oct.1810	5Aug.1807
	Francis Rawdon Fortune	18July1811	28Sept.1809
	Irwin Dawson	14May1813	
	Samuel Hingston	15do.	Adjutant
	Allan Ramsay	16do.	
	John Stevenson	18do.	
	Joseph Maxwell	19do.	
	Edward Hobson	24June	
	Valentine Lloyd Hall	29July	
	William Norman	27Aug.	14May1812
	Despard Humphreys	21Oct.	
	John Valentine	22do.	
	Andrew Campbell	17Feb.1814	31May1809
	Henry Driscoll	3Mar.	
	John Clark	25Aug.	
	Charles Campbell	29Sept.	

Ensign

100th (or His Royal Highness the Prince Regent's 389 County of Dublin) Regiment of Foot.

Rank.	Name.	Rank in the	
		Regiment.	Army.
Ensign - -	John N— Fox	15July1813	
	James Johnstone	22Oct.	
	Tho. Lancaster Davies	3Mar.1814	
	George Daly	17do.	
	J— Davidson	18Aug.	
	J—Tayler	25do.	
	Henry Stubinger	28Sept.	
	John M'Intyre M'Colla	29do.	
Paymaster -	Thomas Ferns	28June1810	
Adjutant - -	Samuel Hingston	4Jan.1810	Lieut. 15May1813
Quarter-Master	Edward Pilkington	5Aug.1812	
Surgeon - -	William Thornton	10Sept.1812	6Oct. 1808
Assistant Surg.	David Rees	12May1814	
	David M'Laughlin	10Nov.	3Sept.1812

Facings deep yellow.

Agent, Messrs. Greenwood, Cox and Hammersley.

101st

Rank.	Name.	Regiment.	Army.

Rank in the

Colonel -	*Henry Aug. *Visc.* Dillon	20Aug.1806	
Lieut. Colonel	William Pollock	20Aug.1806	Col. 4June1814
Major - - {	George O'Malley	21Aug.1806	Lt.Col. 4June1813
	John Fogerty	3Feb.1814	

Captain - {	Edward Brown	27Aug.1806	
	Thomas Carter	3Sept.1807	29Nov.1806
	Francis Barailler	6July1809	
	Peter O'Shaugnessy	21Nov.1811	21Mar.1805
	Walter B— Scully	4Dec.	
	Joseph Otway	30Jan.1812	
	Hugh M'Intosh	6May1813	11July 1811
	Edmund Killikelly	4Feb.1814	
	Henry Boone Hall	5do.	Major 4June1814
	William Girod	17do.	
	Thomas Thompson	10Mar.	

Lieutenant - {	Thomas Lynch	20Aug.1806	
	Robert Nolan	31do.	
	Andrew Dillon	2Sept.	
	Thomas Mackglashan	30Dec.1810	8June1809
	George Hinde Edwards	18July1811	16Aug.1810
	George Cozens	5Dec.	
	——— Hemsworth	21Apr.1812	
	Thomas Stack	22do.	
	John E— Hemmings	7May	
	Thomas Dillon	9Sept.	
	David Kinsly	10do.	
	William Buckley Park	24do.	
	Richard Cargill Orgill	19Aug.1813	
	James Tennison	16Sept.	
	William Cary	30do.	
	William Slater	20Jan.1814	
	Cornelius Murray	17Mar.	
	Daniel O'Meara	23May	
	Joseph Fowkes	24do.	
	Frederick Farquharson	25do.	
	William Sutherland	26do.	
	William Fred. Putnam	3Nov.	

Ensign

Rank.	Name.	Rank in the	
		Regiment.	Army.
Ensign	John Montgomery	4 Dec. 1811	
	Richard Cross Brown	20 Jan. 1814	
	Daniel Ralph Addison	17 Mar.	
	Charles King	24 May	
	Harlow Dennis	25 do.	
	Bryan O'Donnel Bennett	26 do.	
	Alexander Ja. Moorhead	3 Nov.	
	Ja. Johnson Rochfort	15 Dec.	
Paymaster	James Patrick Dillon	25 Apr. 1811	
Adjutant			
Quarter-Master	Charles King	11 Aug. 1814	
Surgeon	Arthur M'Cann	13 Jan. 1814	
Assistant Surg.	John Reid	6 Oct. 1814	

Facings white.

Agent, Messrs. Greenwood, Cox and Hammersley.

Rank.	Name.	Regiment.	Army.
			Rank in the
Colonel - -	*Sir* Alb.Gledstanes, *Kt.*	12May1814	Lt.Gen. 4June1814
Lieut. Colonel	John Herries	16Sept.1813	
Major - -	{ Gustavus Rochfort	10July1811	
	{ *Lord* G. William Russell	4Feb.1813	Lt.Col 12Apr.1814
	⌈ Henry Steele	18June1807	
	⎪ Duncan M'Arthur	7Apr.1808	
	⎪ Monson Madden	19Apr.1809	
	⎪ Hugh Piper	13June1811	
	⎪ James Finucane	15Aug.	
Captain -	⎨ Barrington Price	3Oct.	
	⎪ William Minchin	10Sept.1812	
	⎪ Stephen Grier	24do.	
	⎪ John Brown	15July1813	
	⎪ James Price Holford	17Mar.1814	
	⎩ Cadwallader Draffen	28July	
	⌈ James Mason	5Mar.1807	
	⎪ Alex.HarryCha.Villiers	16June1808	
	⎪ William Lyster	26Sept.1811	
	⎪ John D— Lyster	12Mar.1812	
	⎪ Henry Fry	3Dec.	
	⎪ Robert T— Hume	11Feb.1813	
	⎪ Henry Kelly	8Apr.	
Lieutenant -	⎨ Walter St. John	27July	25June 1805
	⎪ Alexander M'Duff	28do.	9July 1812
	⎪ John Williams	29do.	
	⎪ Edward Sutherland	26Aug.	
	⎪ Arthur Grueber	16Dec.	
	⎪ —— Wikeley	5Jan.1814	Adjutant
	⎪ John R— Balderson	28July	27Jan. 1814
	⎩ Thomas Mills	25Aug.	
	⌈ Samuel North	10Feb.1813	
	⎪ Edward Croker	11do.	
	⎪ Westropp Watkins	18do.	
Ensign - -	⎨ Thomas Kerr .	10June	
	⎪ William Henry Minchin	6Jan.1814	
	⎪ Charles Phibbs	28Apr.	
	⎩ John Thomas	25Aug.	
Paymaster -	John Mell	2June1808	
Adjutant - -	—— Wikeley	12Nov.1812	Lieut. 5Jan.1814
Quarter-Master	Hugh Flaherty	1Dec.1814	
Surgeon - -	Henry Daviss	5Sept.1811	
Assistant Surg.	{ James Price	24July1813	
	{ James Johnson	25do.	

Facings yellow.—Lace silver.

Agent, Mr. Macdonald, Pall Mall Court.

Rank.	Name.	Rank in the Regiment.	Army.
Colonel - -	George Porter	12 Jan. 1814	Lt. Gen. 4 June 1813
Lieut. Colonel	William Smelt	24 Nov. 1814	4 June 1814
Major - -	John Harvey	1 Sept. 1814	Lt. Col. 25 June 1812
Captain -	James Browne	27 Nov. 1806	
	James Bowie	25 Mar. 1808	14 Jan. 1808
	James Powell	16 June	Major 4 June 1813
	Hon. S. Martin Gardner	17 Aug.	
	George Augustus Eliot	15 Sept.	Major 19 Dec. 1813
	Thomas Couche	26 July 1810	17 Oct. 1805
	Thomas Vyvyan	5 June 1811	25 Dec. 1807
	William Cochrane	18 Mar. 1813	Major 17 Mar. 1814
	Guy Carleton Colclough	21 Oct.	
Lieutenant	John Magennis	18 Dec. 1806	
	———— Charleton	31 Dec. 1807	
	G— J— Joynt	14 Apr. 1808	13 Aug. 1805
	Matthew Willock	11 Jan. 1809	
	Thomas Griffith	12 do.	
	John Fallon	28 Sept.	
	Alexander Cuppage	1 Mar. 1810	
	J— J— Frederick Haly	15 do.	1 Sept. 1809
	John Grimshaw	7 Mar. 1811	1 Feb. 1810
	Fenton Finlay	5 May 1812	
	Richard Rose	7 do.	
	George Henry Hazen	6 Oct.	25 Dec. 1807
	John Connor	25 Dec.	7 Jan. 1808
	Thomas Kaye	26 do.	
	John Montgomerie	27 do.	
	Alexander Cuppage	29 do.	
	Kildare Burrowes	30 do.	
	Wm. Henry Vinicombe	31 do.	
	Charles Blanckenberg	28 Jan. 1813	25 Jan. 1811
	Rob. Brand. Edyvean	4 Mar.	
	Charles Kelson	do.	
	Timon Meagher	21 Oct.	
	John Kendall	10 Mar. 1814	1 Jan. 1811
	Bernard Crumpe	3 Nov.	10 Mar. 1814

Rank.	Name.	Rank in the Regiment.	Army.
Ensign	Henry Ibbotson	1 Apr. 1812	16 Jan. 1812
	William Weinright Lynar	2 do.	
	Robert Huey	6 May	
	Tho. Curran M'Question	28 do.	
	Charles Nash	9 July	
	James Peyton Gallaher	31 Dec.	
	John Mill Fortescue	19 Aug. 1813	
	John N— Barber	11 Nov.	
	George Walsh	12 May 1814	
Paymaster	-		
Adjutant	- -		
Quarter-Master	James Farrants	9 May 1811	
Surgeon	Colin Young	8 Sept. 1808	15 Oct. 1807
Assistant Surg.	John Rose Palmer	30 May 1811	
	Peter Fraser	10 Dec. 1812	

Facings white.

Agent, Messrs. Greenwood, Cox and Hammersley.

Rank.	Name.	Rank in the	
		Regiment.	Army.
Colonel - -	Martin Hunter	9July1803	Lt.Gen. 1Jan.1812
Lieut. Colonel	Robert Moodie	27Oct.1814	
Major - -	{ Thomas Hunter	4June1813	
	{ Richard Leonard	27Oct.1814	
Captain -	⌠ John Maule	1May1805	Lt.Col. 4June1814
	│ A— G— Armstrong	15Mar.1810	
	│ George Shore	23Aug.	
	│ P— Dennis	1Aug.1811	
	│ William Procter	5Mar.1812	
	⌡ William B— Bradley	16Apr.	
	│ Edward Holland	25June	
	│ Robert Roberts Loring	26do.	
	│ George Jobling	17June1813	
	│ Andrew Rainsford	24Feb.1814	
	⌊ Charles Rainsford	24Nov.	
Lieutenant	⌠ John M'Kinnon	15Mar.1810	
	│ William B— Phair	9Aug.	7Dec.1809
	│ ——— Carmichael	23do.	
	│ L— Basserer	31Oct.1811	
	│ Thomas Leonard	1Nov.	
	│ C— D— Rankin	2do.	
	│ Samuel Rigby	3do.	
	│ Alexander Campbell	5do.	
	│ Andrew William Playfair	7do.	
	│ George Croad	14do.	
	│ John Le Couteur	21do.	
	⌡ Alex. Coll. M'Donnell	5Mar.1812	
	│ Richard Irwin Ireland	16Apr.	
	│ Fowk Moore	17do.	Adjutant
	│ Henry Long	23do.	
	│ James Gray	9July	
	│ E. Wentworth Solomon	29Oct.	
	│ Charles Jobling	26Aug.1813	
	│ J.AugustusM'Lauchlan	24Feb.1814	
	│ James Coyne	2Mar.	
	│ William Martin	3do.	
	│ James Coates	14Apr.	
	│ ——— Considine	23Nov.	
	⌊ Francis Henry Cumming	24do.	

D d 2

Rank.	Name.	Rank in the	
		Regiment.	Army.
Ensign	A— William Tinling	31Dec.1812	
	Waldron Kelly	26Aug.1813	
	Gabriel Tunstall	13Jan.1814	
	G— Home	24Feb.	
	Thomas Pigott	2Mar.	
	Alexander Garden	3do.	
	William Roberts	14Apr.	
	Joseph Simpson	23Nov.	
	Robert Moorhead	24do.	
Paymaster	H— H— Carmichael	24Feb.1814	
Adjutant	Fowk Moore	14Apr.1814	Lieut. 17Apr.1812
Quarter-Master	William Macdonald	14Apr.1814	
Surgeon	William Dyer Thomas	17Dec.1807	
Assistant Surg.	Thomas Emerson	8Nov.1803	

Facings buff.

Agent, Mr. Gilpin, No. 33, Villiers Street, Strand.

Royal

Royal Staff Corps

(Attached to the Quarter-Master General's Department.)

Rank.	Name.	Rank in the Regiment.	Rank in the Army.
Colonel - -	John Brown	25July1810 Lt.Col.Comm. 6May1802	M.Gen. 4June1813
Lieut. Colonel	William Nicolay	4Apr.1805	Col. 4June1813
Major - ✖- {	*Hon.* Rob. Law. Dundas	14July1804	Lt.Col. 11Apr.1811
	Andrew Long	21Apr.1814	
Captain - - {	James Roupell Colleton	25June1806	Major 22Nov.1813
	Henry William Lauzun	26do.	
	Alexander Todd	21Apr.1808	Major 26Aug.1813
	Henry Du Vernet	30May1809	
	Sir Nicholas Trant, *Kt.*	1June	
	Frederick William Mann	17Dec.1812	
	Michael Shannahan	6May1813	
	Thomas Wright	23Dec.	
	William King	17Feb.1814	
	James Freeth	21Apr.	
Lieutenant {	John Westmacott	31May1809	
	Francis Read	1June	
	Edward Thompson	1Mar.1810	
	Nicholas Thomas Hill	13Sept.	Adjutant
	Thomas Harriott	11Oct.1811	
	Henry Piers	12do.	
	William Dumaresq	13do.	
	Francis Du Vernet	14do.	
	Samuel Perry	15do.	
	George Longmore	16do.	
	William Tait	17do.	
	Geo. Mordaunt Dickens	27Nov.	
	George D— Hall	28do.	
	Edward Boyd	1July1812	
	James Horton	2do.	
	John Pardy	17Dec.	
	E— P— White	31do.	24May 1810 Adjut.
	Basil Jackson	6May1813	
	William Hilhouse	10June	
	Thomas Campbell	23Dec.	
	A— C— G— Brauns	17Feb.1814	
	Kingston D— Lloyd	21Apr.	

Ensign

(Attached to the Quarter-Master General's Department.)

Rank.	Name.	Regiment.	Army.
		Rank in the	
Ensign -	Thomas Harris	28Nov.1811	
	Charles R— Scott	2Jan.1812	
	William Dillon	6Aug.	
	Daniel Frazer	28Apr.1813	31Oct. 1811
	Edward Cleather	29do.	15Oct. 1812
	John Sumner Sedley	6May	
	John Milliken	10June	
	Henry Cole	16June1814	
Paymaster -	Robert Shearman	6Nov.1806	
Adjutant -	Nicholas Thomas Hill	14Nov.1811	Lieut. 13Sept.1810
	E— P— White	31Dec.1812	Lieut. 24May1810
QuarterMaster	Daniel Heatley	17May1810	
	G— Gott	30Sept.1813	
Surgeon - -	J— G— Cavenagh	21Feb.1800	
AssistantSurg.	David Jearrad	10Sept.1812	

Facings blue.—Lace silver.

Agent, Messrs. Greenwood, Cox and Hammersley.

Permitted to inscribe on their Colours and Appointments the word " DOMINICA," in commemoration of the Defence of that Island on the 22d February, 1805.

Rank.	Name.	Rank in the Regiment.	Army.
Colonel - -	*Lord* Cha. Hen. Somerset	5 Jan. 1804	Gen. 4 June 1814
Lieut. Colonel {	Clement Wm. Whitby	11 July 1811	
	J— Maillard Clifton	23 Aug. 1814	4 June 1814
Major - - {	Robert Torrens	4 Mar. 1813	Lt.Col. 14 July 1814
	Richard Weston	25 Aug. 1814	4 June 1814
Captain - {	James Cassidy	25 Sept. 1804	Major 4 June 1814
	John Winkler	23 May 1805	
	William Davis	25 Jan. 1808	
	Edward Ellis Isles	12 Sept.	
	George Saville Burdett	13 Oct.	Major 4 June 1813
	Lorenzo Nixon	16 May 1811	
	Conrad Mayers	24 Sept. 1812	2 Apr. 1812
	Francis Collins	2 Dec. 1813	
	Thomas Hay	2 June 1814	
	John Macnamara	25 Aug.	
Lieutenant - {	Henry Hyde	25 July 1808	
	Angus M'Donald	12 Sept.	
	Samuel Gordon	19 Dec.	
	William Webster	1 Feb. 1809	
	Garrett Hemsworth	18 Apr.	
	John Plucket	14 May	Adjutant
	Henry Lodge	9 Aug. 1810	13 Oct. 1808
	G— R— Magee	6 Jan. 1811	
	Harman Jeffares	4 Mar. 1812	
	George Walker	5 do.	
	William Fraser	13 Aug.	11 Sept. 1800
	John Robert Rose	10 Nov.	
	Thomas Phelan	11 do.	
	Richard Story	12 do.	
	Daniel Crotty	4 Mar. 1813	
	John Morgan	21 Oct.	
	John Mackenzie	2 Dec.	
	Thomas Abbott	7 Apr. 1814	
	John Delamel	25 Aug.	
	John Cornell Chads	1 Dec.	

Ensign

Rank.	Name.	Rank in the Regiment.	Army.
Ensign	⌈ George Hubbard	16June1812	
	│ Geo. Wm. Hen. Miller	11Mar.1813	
	│ Bolton Stretch	21Oct.	
	⎨ Philip Voltbat	11Nov.	
	│ Wm. Alex. Caldow	2Dec.	
	│ John Pilkington	17Mar.1814	
	│ S— Lynch	7Apr.	
	⌊ Alexander Turner	29Dec.	
Paymaster	John Francis Burke	10Apr.1806	
Adjutant	John Plucket	10May1810	Lieut. 14May1809
Quarter-Master	George Douglas	14Oct.1808	
Surgeon	Patrick Keane	28Jan.1813	
Assistant Surg.	⎰ Henry M'Creery	3June1813	23Mar.1809
	⎱ Hugh Kelly	27Jan.1814	

Facings white.—Lace silver.

Agent, Messrs. Greenwood, Cox and Hammersley.

Rank.	Name.	Rank in the Regiment.	Army.
Colonel -	*Sir* Geo. Beckwith, *K. B.*	31Aug.1809	Gen. 4June1814
Lieut. Col. ✂ {	Benjamin D'Urban	7Jan.1808	Col. 4June1813
	Alexander Maclean	1Apr.1813	
Major - - {	John Ross	22Nov.1810	
	Edward Fleming	1Apr.1813	
Captain - {	George Evans	19July1804	Lt.Col. 25July1810
	Thomas Bradley	11Sept.1806	
	William Major	12Oct.1807	
	Thomas Daunt Lord	1Jan.1808	
	A— Macpherson	18June	
	Joseph Walton	16Nov.1809	
	George Sloane Conolly	21June1810	
	John Schoedde	22Nov.	
	Abraham Shaw	13May1813	
	Joseph Eysing	30Dec.	
Lieutenant {	Hugh Brenan	12Oct.1807	
	William James Hance	4Apr.1808	Adjutant
	Cornelius Delaboussy	15May	
	John Murray Wegg	18June	
	Henry Fowles	28Apr.1809	
	John Galpine	3Apr.1810	
	Henry Barry	5do.	
	Andrew Philip Cramer	21June	
	John Anderson	24Jan.1811	
	Henry John Ricketts	21Mar.	
	Nicholas Henry Sorell	8Aug.	
	Henry Nosworthy	12Nov.1812	
	William Allen	21Jan.1813	
	Thomas M'Pherson	19May	
	Charles Holland Hailes	20do.	
	—— Gough	12Aug.	
	Julius William Hield	3Feb.1814	
	Edward Barry	27July	
	Alexander Morrow	28do.	

E e   Ensign

Rank.	Name.	Rank in the Regiment.	Army.

Rank.	Name.	Regiment.	Army.
Ensign - -	{ Robert Clarke	20May1813	
	Geo. Forbes Campbell	12Aug.	
	James Wylly Armstrong	9Sept.	
	Pierrepoint M. Downer	3Feb.1814	
	Edward Parson Webb	10do.	
	—— Finlayson	27July	
	William Dunlop	28do.	
	John Mackenzie	29do.	
	James Gilchrist	1Sept.	
Paymaster -	Richard Nosworthy	7May1807	
Adjutant - -	Wm. James Hance	28June1810	Lieut. 4Apr.1808
Quarter-Master	John M'Kenzie	14Apr.1814	
Surgeon - -	Thomas Murray	14Feb.1811	
Assistant Surg. {	William Bohan	25July1813	10July 1806

Facings yellow.—Lace gold.

Agent, Mr. Graves, the King's Printing Office.

3d

Rank.	Name.	Rank in the	
		Regiment.	Army.

Colonel - - Sir John Murray, Bt.   27May1809 | Lt.Gen. 1Jan.1812

Lieut. Col. ⊚ { A— W— Young   25Jan.1813
              { William Marlay   16June1814 | 25July 1810

Major - - { Joshua Gledstanes   11July1811
          { Joseph Maclean   1Sept.1814 | 4June1814

Captain -
{ James Ross   23Aug.1805
  Archibald M'Intyre   17Oct.
  Foster Lech Coore   3Mar.1808 | Major   8Oct.1813
  Samuel Workman   22Mar.1810
  James Crooke   21June
  Charles Tharpson Frith   15Oct.
  George Warren   6Dec.
  John Campbell   11July1811
  George Elrington   19Aug.1813 | Major   4June1813
  John Heazle   1Sept.1814

Lieutenant -
{ William Henry Butler   15Jan.1807
  Paul Steele Hunt   12May
  John M'Gregor   6Feb.1808
  George Cochrane   7do.
  Alexander Anton   25Nov.1809 | 25Dec. 1804
  ——— Le Maitre   16Aug.1810
  Thomas Jameson   15Oct.
  George Palmer Hawkins   6Jan.1811
  Thomas Pilkington   3July
  Richard Hughes   11Sept.
  Augustus Tweed   12do.
  A— Farrington   2Apr.1812
  John Goode   12Nov.
  Andrew Halfhide   18Feb.1813 | 12May 1808
  William Kirkby   4Mar.
  Robert Turnbull   2Dec.
  George Ensor   7Apr.1814
  William Gorge   28July
  Conrad Heel   25Aug.
  Joseph Albert Gillmore   1Sept.

E e 2   Ensign

Rank.	Name.	Rank in the	
		Regiment.	Army.
Ensign -	⎧ William Abingdon	12Aug.1813	
	⎪ Archibald M'Tavish	2Dec.	
	⎪ W— Fraser	24Mar.1814	Adjutant
	⎪ John Gunn Collins	8Apr.	
	⎨ Adam Gordon	28July	
	⎪ Robert Crosby	26Aug.	
	⎪ Thomas Minton	27do.	
	⎪ David Cumming	27Oct.	
	⎩ Tho. Frederick Aldred	8Dec.	
Paymaster -	Thomas Crawford	9Aug.1804	
Adjutant - -	W— Fraser	24Mar.1814	Ensign 24Mar.1814
Quarter-Master	William Brice	16Dec.1810	
Surgeon - -	John B— Dougal	21Jan.1813	
Assistant Surg. ⎰	John Wm. Payne	3June1813	
⎱	Alex. M'Andrew	11Nov.	

Facings yellow.—Lace silver.

Agent, Messrs. Donaldson, Juitt and Boaden, Whitehall.

4th

Colonel -	✠ *Sir* James Leith, *K. B.*	19July1811	Lt.Gen. 4June1813
Lieut. Col. ◎-	{ John Buchan	30Mar.1809	
	John Lyons Nixon	11July1811	
Major - -	{ Francis Eddins	14May1809	Lt.Col. 4June1814
	Matthew Read	2Jan.1812	
Captain -	{ John Reed	25Sept.1804	Major 4June1813
	Samuel Watts	22July1806	
	James Anton	6Dec.1810	6Sept.1806
	Carew Reynell	11Apr.1811	
	Patrick Cruikshanks	24Oct.	
	Andrew Hamilton	19Dec.	Major 3Mar.1814
	B— A— Watson	8July1813	21Sept.1809
	Thomas Reed	26Aug.	27May 1813
	Lewis Des Vignes	21Oct.	
Lieutenant -	{ Daniel Maclean	25Oct.1804	24July 1804
	George Allen	26Feb.1805	
	Felix Thompson	4Mar.1807	
	Richard Spratt	27June1808	
	Denny Ruck	1Mar.1810	
	Thomas Pilkington	3Jan.1811	
	Daniel Delaney	18Apr.	
	Robert Latham	11Sept.	
	John Cavendish	31Oct.	
	Thomas Workman	2Apr.1812	
	James Croke	11Nov.	Adjutant
	George Browne O'Brien	12do.	
	William Sherlock	4Mar.1813	
	Gabriel Lynch Thomas	13Apr.	
	Charles Miller	14do.	
	William Boxall Scott	15do.	
	Robert Ware	25Sept.	
	John Forbes	21Oct.	
	Thomas Jones	17Mar.1814	
Ensign - -	{ John Tod	4Mar.1813	
	Thomas Gordon	13Apr.	
	James Buchanan	15do.	
	John Keir	27May	
	Arthur J— Gonne	9Sept.	
	Charles Bayly	25do.	
	John Macleod	17Mar.1814	
	Ferguson Burrell	21Apr.	
Paymaster -	Edward Tichborne	2Apr.1812	
Adjutant - -	James Croke	15Apr.1813	Lieut. 11Nov.1812
Quarter-Master	William Fair	15Apr.1813	
Surgeon - -	Edward Owen	28May1812	
Assistant Surg.	{ John O'Toole	11Nov.1813	
	James Johnstone	2Dec.	

Facings yellow.—Lace silver.
Agent, Messrs. Donaldson, Juitt and Boaden, Whitehall.

5th

Rank.	Name.	Rank in the	
		Regiment.	Army.
Colonel - -	John Despard	29Dec.1809	Gen. 4June1814
Lieut. Colonel {	Thomas Barrow	8Oct.1802	M.Gen. 4June1811
	Alex.MarkK.Hamilton	11Apr.1805	Col. 4June1813
	Hugh Henry	28Jan.1813	1Jan. 1812
Major - - {	Joseph Twigg	9July1812	1Jan. 1812
	Henry Godwin	26May1814	
Captain - {	Charles Reynolds	3Mar.1804	Major 4June1814
	Charles Vallancey	21Feb.1810	
	David Gordon	10Dec.	
	Joseph Roche	16May1811	
	Randall M'Donald	9July1812	
	A— Frederick Barbauld	6Aug.	
	Daniel Roberts	17Sept.	Major 4June1814
	Philip George Lewis	29Oct.	
	Patrick M'Manus	19Aug.1813	
	John Blossett	7July1814	Major 4June1814
Lieutenant - {	Henry Bersma	22Feb.1810	Adjutant
	James Grant	9Aug.	
	Thomas Fitzgerald	7Feb.1811	
	Archibald Hamilton	15May	
	Thomas Miller	4Dec.	
	John Gordon Pechon	5do.	
	William Leslie	24Sept.1812	
	Alexander Geddes	14Jan.1813	
	Edward Codd	25Feb.	
	William Robertson	3Mar.	
	John Nelson	4do.	
	John Campbell	1Apr.	
	Robert Hughes	27Jan.1814	
	William Clune	1Feb.	
	John Gay	2do.	
	Alexander Russwurn	3do.	
	John Hylton	24do.	
	James Usher	29Mar.	
	Arthur G— Lewis	30do.	
	Hugh Donald Mackay	31do.	

Ensign

Rank.	Name.	Rank in the Regiment.	Army.
Ensign	⎰ Robert Irvine	22July1813	
	——— O'Hara	30Sept.	
	James Crowe	16Dec.	
	Henry Irving	1Feb.1814	
	William Earle Godfrey	2do.	
	Hugh Maclean	3do.	
	Lewis Barrow	31Mar.	
	John Caldwell	28July	
	Anthony Keogh	8Sept.	
	——— Haymard	29do.	
Paymaster	Charles Sheil	4Nov.1813	
Adjutant	Henry Bersma	20Apr.1809	Lieut. 22Feb.1810
Quarter-Master	Robert Bell	25Sept.1812	
Surgeon	Samuel Davies	4May1809	
Assistant Surg.	Tully Daly	6Oct.1814	

Facings dark green.—Lace gold.

Agent, Messrs. Greenwood, Cox and Hammersley.

6th

Rank.	Name.	Rank in the	
		Regiment.	Army.

Rank.	Name.	Regiment.	Army.
Colonel - ✕ {	Hon. Sir E. M. Pakenham, K. B.	21May1813	M.Gen. 1Jan.1812
Lieut. Colonel {	Hen. Benedict Dolphin John Castle	12Apr.1807 10Jan.1811	Col. 4June1814
Major - - {	Francis Frye Brown T— B— Bamford	20Oct.1808 12Aug.1813	Lt.Col. 1Jan.1812
Captain - {	J— C— Eddington William Hill George Ross Richard P— Burnett William Loftie J— L— Verety James Read Joseph Welsh William Killikelly Wm. Erskine Grant	3Mar.1804 23Nov. 29Dec. 13June1805 3Jan.1811 10Sept. 24Dec.1812 15Apr.1813 do. 2Dec.	Major 4June1814 Major 4June1814 Major 4June1814 Major 4June1812
Lieutenant - {	W— H— Glover Charles Grant J— R—S—Longworth John Kennedy William Boardman Patrick Carton Isaac Wood Alexander Campbell Robert Gregg Robert Hutton Alexander Knowles Thomas Stewart William Welstead Broom Penniger John Church John Henderson	13May1807 27Sept.1808 10Mar.1809 13Apr. 17Sept. 10Jan.1811 11Sept. 12do. 28May1812 30July 9Nov. 3Mar.1813 12Aug. 1Dec. 2do. 7Apr.1814	5Feb. 1808 3Aug.1809

Ensign

| Rank. | Name. | Rank in the | |
		Regiment.	Army.
Ensign - - {	S— R— Gordon	10Nov.1812	
	Charles Andrews	11do.	
	Henry Smith	12do.	
	Joseph Jones	20May1813	
	——— Parlour	5Aug.	Adjutant
	John Joseph Romney	12do.	
	John Benjamin Smith	15Sept.	
	George Powell	16do.	
	Adam Beverhoudt	21Oct.	
	J— Johnson	1Dec.	
	Richard Wickham	2do.	
Paymaster -	Philip Budd	10Aug.1809	
Adjutant - -	——— Parlour	5Aug.1813	Ensign 5Aug.1813
Quarter-Master	——— Henderson	2Dec.1813	
Surgeon - -	James Gowen	7July1814	
Assistant Surg. {	Thomas Kettle	28May1812	
	Thomas P— Warren	9June1814	

Facings yellow.—Lace silver.

Agent, Messrs. Greenwood, Cox and Hammersley.

F f

7th

Rank.	Name.	Rank in the	
		Regiment.	Army.
Colonel - -	Isaac Gascoyne	10Oct.1805	L.Gen.25Apr.1808
Lieut. Colonel	Archibald Maclaine	25Jan.1813	
Major - -	* { H— Clermont	15Sept.1808	
	{ George Arthur	5Nov.1812	
Captain -	{ William Massey	15Oct.1803	Major 4June1811
	Charles Poitiers	do.	Major 4June1811
	John M'Neil	28Mar.1805	Major 4June1814
	John Weeks	28Jan.1808	Major 4June1814
	Thomas Iles	28June1810	
	Rowland E— Williams	23Aug.	13Oct. 1808
	Tho. Johnson Williams	5Dec.1811	
	Etienne Noel	19Mar.1812	
	——— Cornalet	23Apr.	
	Joseph Anderson	15Apr.1813	
Lieutenant	{ Alphonso Kirk	24Mar.1805	
	James Carey	26do.	
	Anthony Hardman	15Jan.1807	
	Rich. Krohan Gatehouse	12May	
	Samuel Buchanan	12June	
	Henry Kelly	1Sept.1808	
	——— Eve	18July1809	
	Charles W— Stewart	26Oct.	
	Robert Dobyns	27Mar.1811	
	John Scates	28do.	
	James Killikelly	17Oct.	
	John M'Pherson	23Apr.1812	
	George Clibborn	25June	
	William Nimmo	11Nov.	
	Thomas Chadwick	12do.	
	George Foskey	21July1813	Adjutant
	George Flinter	22do.	
	Joseph Atkinson	29do.	
	Jeffery Prendergast	14Apr.1814	
	Thomas Parker	9June	
	William Hodgkinson	22Dec.	26Dec.1811

Ensign

Rank.	Name.	Regiment.	Army.

Rank in the {Regiment. | Army.}

Ensign - -	Tho. Newenham Blair	23Sept.1812	
	William Large	24do.	
	Joseph Bee Wollams	13Nov.	
	Cornelius Jones Dunn	4Feb.1813	
	John Maclean	21July	
	John Foskey	22do.	
	Charles Leisring	29do.	24Sept.1812
	Unsworth Chaffers	13Apr.1814	
	Joseph Greenwood	14do.	
	Henry Williams	9June	

Paymaster -	Richard Allen	8Aug.1811	
Adjutant - -	George Foskey	12Nov.1812	Lieut. 21July1813
Quarter-Master	Richard Archer Spencer	13Jan.1814	
Surgeon - -	Colin Allen	8May1806	
Assistant.Surg. {	George K— Agnew	12May1814	

Facings yellow.

Agent, Messrs. Greenwood, Cox and Hammersley.

Colonel - -	*Sir* Thomas Hislop, *Bt.*	29Apr.1802	Lt.Gen. 4June1814
	- Lt. Col. Comm.	6Sept.1798	
Lieut. Colonel {	William Stewart	5Sept.1807	Col. 4June1814
{	Luke Alen	11July1811	
Major - - {	Neil Cockburn	6May1813	25Jan. 1813
{	David Jolly	23Sept.	
Captain - {	William M'Intagert	20July1805	
	John Lagoutte	3Mar.1806	
	Thomas Walker	25Dec.	Lt.Col. 4June1814
	Duncan M'Bean	12Apr.1807	
	George A— Delhoste	15Feb.1810	
	John Blood	14May1812	
	George Gordon	5Aug.1813	
	Cayley Johnson	6do.	
	William Hadley	2Dec.	
	William G— Douglas	3Feb.1814	
Lieutenant {	John Dudgeon	6Mar.1806	
	William Lorimer	20Aug.	
	John Donaldson	21do.	
	Thomas Corsbie	27Oct.	
	John Cummings	5Nov.1807	
	Joseph Robert Raines	5Oct.1809	28May 1807
	Simon Fraser	17July1811	
	Henry Buschman	18do.	Adjutant
	James Anderson	25Sept.	
	Benjamin Symons	14Apr.1812	
	Henry Glass	15do.	
	William Brown	16do.	
	John Maxwell	24Dec.	
	Charles Trotman	5Aug.1813	
	Norman M'Iver	12do.	
	John Hudson	30Sept.	
	E— E— Grant	27Jan.1814	
	M'Carthy Geagan	1Dec.	
Ensign - - {	Henry Davis	21Jan.1813	
	Roderick Mackenzie	20May	
	John Robinson	12Aug.	
	James Coates	30Sept.	
	William Stead	2Dec.	
	George Moss	23do.	
	Benj. Miller Jones	27Jan.1814	
	William Taylor	3Feb.	
	James Barkeley	26May	
	James Partington	1Dec.	
Paymaster -	George Christie	25Dec.1806	
Adjutant - -	Henry Buschman	23June1814	Lieut. 18July1811
Quarter-Master	Stewart Maxwell	12May1807	
Surgeon - -	Thomas Nicholls	16Dec.1813	
Assistant Surg. {	J—B— Lenon	9June1814	

Facings green.

Agent, Messrs. Greenwood, Cox and Hammersley.

Royal

Rank.	Name.	Rank in the	
		Regiment.	Army.
Colonel - -	Ja. Willoughby Gordon	25July1810	M.Gen. 4June1813
	Lt. Col. Comm.	13June1808	
Lieut. Colonel	{ Charles Maxwell	29Dec.1809	
	{ Charles M'Carthy	30May1811	
Major - -	{ James Chisholm	16June1808	Lt.Col. 4June1814
	{ John Joseph Maling	11Nov.1813	
Captain -	{ Edward Hare	22Sept.1808	
	Donald Mackenzie	23Feb.1809	
	Alexander Grant	31Aug.	
	Charles Kinsley	13June1811	
	William Appleton	3Oct.	20May 1810
	Michael J— Sparks	21Nov.	
	Adam Fife	15Oct.1812	
	William Staveley	6May1813	Major 15Dec.1814
	William Masters	13do.	
	C— M— Meehan	22July	
	Bradshaw Clarke	17Nov.1814	
Lieutenant -	{ James Chisholm	14Dec.1809	
	Oswald Pilling	31Jan.1810	
	John Dodd	3May	Adjutant
	William Gray	20Dec.	1Jan. 1808
	John Ousely Kearney	4Apr.1811	
	Valentine Al. Chisholm	9June	
	Gabriel Dunn	12do.	
	Alexander Heddle	11Feb.1813	20Mar.1810
	William Pass	21Mar.	
	Charles M'Combie	23do.	
	Christopher M·Rae	25do.	
	William Salter Saunders	15Apr.	
	George Lee	5Aug.	
	Joseph Hilton	20Jan.1814	
	James Walker	16Feb.	
	Archibald Chisholm	17do.	
	Peter Wallace	16June	4May 1809
	John Sutton	25Aug.	
	Abraham Odlum	26do.	
	James Maclean	8Nov.	
	James Kingsley	9do.	
	Jonathan Woods	10do.	

Ensign

Rank.	Name.	Rank in the	
		Regiment.	Army.

Rank.	Name.	Regiment.	Army.
Ensign - - {	Frederick Clements	16Feb.1814	
	George Adamson Stanley	17do.	
	Daniel Alt	31Mar.	
	James Maybury	25May	
	Wm. Francis Cartwright	26do.	
	Daniel O'Meara	25Aug.	
	John Godwin	26do.	
	William Everett	9Nov.	
	Charles Tidmarsh	10do.	
	Richard Bryant	17do.	
	Edward Middleton	22Dec.	
Paymaster -	Thadeus O'Meara	9Sept.1813	
Adjutant - -	William Gray	18Feb.1813	Lieut. 20Dec.1810
Quarter-Master	George Richardson	6May1813	
Surgeon - -	William Wilson	27May1813	
Assistant Surg. {	Francis M'Cann	14July1814	
	Daniel Armstrong	22Dec.	

Facings blue.

Agent, Messrs. Greenwood, Cox and Hammersley.

Royal

Rank.	Name.	Rank in the	
		Regiment.	Army.
Colonel - -	John Fraser	28Aug.1800	Lt.Gen. 4June1813
Lieut. Col. ◎	{ Sir John Wilson, Kt.	22Dec.1808	Col. 4June1814
	Matthew Mahon	2Jan.1812	1Jan. 1812
Major - -	{ Godfrey Starck	2Jan.1812	
	Matthew Stewart	8Dec.1814	
Captain -	{ Matthew Hunt	14Oct.1807	
	Peter Mathewson	15June1808	
	Lewis Bird	6Oct.	
	John E— Ware	22June1809	
	John Fletcher	25Aug.1811	
	Peter Mac Gregor	21Nov.	
	Thomas White	2Jan.1812	
	William Manby	9do.	
	Thomas Enraght	21Oct.1813	
	George M. Fahie Mercer	5May1814	25Jan. 1813
	Charles M'Donald	17Nov.	
	George Blomer	25Dec.	1Apr. 1813
Lieutenant -	{ John Frederick Schultz	23June1808	
	Walter Radford	4Aug.	
	Matthias Hunt	19July1809	
	William Edwards	7Sept.	
	George Cauty	20Mar.1810	
	George Davidson	22do.	
	Arthur Buchanan	15Aug.	
	John Bologne	16do.	
	James Patience	24Oct.1811	
	John Atkinson	6Feb.1812	19July 1794
	Robert Constable	9July	2May 1806
	P. M. La Berthodierre	12Nov.	
	E— Lacey Morley	13Jan.1813	
	Gabriel Marre	14do.	
	William Hunt	11Mar.	
	And. Mackenzie Shaw	5Aug.	3Aug.1809
	Thomas Hogg	13Oct.	
	Alexander M'Lennon	14do.	
	Richard Fare Walton	6Apr.1814	
	Colin Buchanan	7do.	
	William Wright	25May	Adjutant
	Bartholomew Hartley	26do.	
	Humph. Clugston Gray	25July	
	Benj. William Champion	22Sept.	
	Charles West	22Dec.	

Ensign

Rank.	Name.	Rank in the	
		Regiment.	Army.

Ensign	Montgomery Armstrong	10 June 1813	
	George Ormond	23 Sept.	
	Creighton J— Leonard	13 Oct.	
	Edward Wilton	14 do.	
	Richard Ransome	21 do.	
	W— H— Windsor	5 Apr. 1814	
	Thomas Parkinson	6 do.	
	R— Chartres Brew	7 do.	
	Jeffery Eagar	26 May	
	William Firebrace	28 July	
	Henry Lurting	22 Sept.	
	Edward Havers	22 Dec.	

Paymaster	James Culmer	18 July 1811	
Adjutant	William Wright	14 Jan. 1813	Lieut. 25 May 1814
Quarter-Master	Ferdinand Aug. Benhold	7 July 1814	
Surgeon	James Beresford	24 Jan. 1811	
Assistant Surg.	James M'Cabe	28 Jan. 1813	
	James Cochrane	7 July 1814	

Regimentals green.—Facings scarlet.

Agent, Messrs. Greenwood, Cox and Hammersley.

Royal

Rank.	Name.	Rank in the	
		Regiment.	*Army.*

Rank.	Name.	Regiment.	Army.
Colonel - -	◎*Hon.* William Lumley	7Nov.1812	Lt.Gen. 4June1814
Lieut. Colonel {	Charles Turner	18Apr.1807	Col. 4June1814
	Benjamin K. Lavicourt	25Dec.1814	4June1813
Major - - {	Edward O'Rourke	18Apr.1807	Lt.Col. 4June1813
	Thomas Brereton	15Mar.1810	
Captain - {	——— Troya	24Oct.1805	
	George Jack	30Apr.1807	
	William Kennedy	4June	
	Richard Annesley	25Feb.1808	Major 4June1813
	Edward L— Hubbard	21Sept.1809	
	F— B— Lynch	15Mar.1810	
	William Harper	7Feb.1811	
	James Smith	10June1813	
	Mar. Bethel Robinson	16Sept.	
	George Frederick Angelo	20Jan.1814	
Lieutenant {	John Boyton	27Aug.1807	30Oct. 1806
	Thomas Donald	17Sept.	
	John Knox	26Mar.1808	
	Thomas Kennedy	12Jan.1809	
	Robert Robertson	12Oct.	
	Charles Boehmler	15Mar.1810	
	Robert Hanns	20Mar.1811	
	Robert George	21do.	
	Thomas Boys	28do.	2Aug.1810
	John Prendergast	25Oct.	
	Thomas Younger	7May1812	
	Dugald M'Nicoll	23July	
	——— Langley	11Nov.	
	J— H— Edwards	12do.	
	Robert Clark	7June1813	Adjutant
	John Elley	8do.	
	Wm. Frederick Archdall	9do.	
	Wiltshire Austen	10do.	
	Mark Michael Quin	16Sept.	
	James Kennedy	24Feb.1814	

Rank.	Name.	Rank in the Regiment.	Army.
Ensign	{ Clement Archer	11Nov.1812	
	Charles Digges	4Mar.1813	
	C— Gurley	11do.	
	Arthur Walsh	8Apr.	
	Robert Myles	7June	
	Francis Hurst	9do.	
	John Thompson	10do.	
	Neil Stewart	30Sept.	
	John James Lambert	24Feb.1814	
	George Flood	31Mar.	
	Arthur Freer	25Aug.	
Paymaster	Robert Charles Graham	5Aug.1813	
Adjutant	Robert Clark	1Nov.1810	Lieut. 7June1813
Quarter-Master	Richard Welley	25Oct.1806	
Surgeon	Robinson Aytoun	10Sept.1812	
Assistant Surg.	{ William Kennedy	2Dec.1813	
	Joseph Allen	9June1814	27Jan. 1814

Regimentals green.—Facings scarlet.

Agent, Messrs. Greenwood, Cox and Hammersley.

York

Rank.	Name.	Rank in the Regiment.	Rank in the Army.
Colonel - -	Hugh Mackay Gordon	2May1814	M.Gen. 4June1811
Lieut. Colonel {	Andrew Coghlan John Ewart	11Nov.1813 15Sept.1814	
Major - - {	Charles Duke Joseph Paterson	11Nov.1813 29Sept.1814	
Captain - {	Holland Daniel Joseph Anderson Richard Lundin Jonathan Parker Edward Cottingham E— B—Balguy	7Nov.1813 20Jan.1814 do. 31Mar. 23June 25Aug.	 28Jan. 1813 15Dec. 1808
Lieutenant {	James Stewart Hector Mackay William Heath William Hay Joseph Stainton James Richards William Rothwell Simeon Farrar Benjamin Warton William Roxby Humble Bowker Walsham Charles Henry Delamain Adolphus Leighton Gray	5Nov.1813 do. 6do. 7do. 8do. 10do. 25do. 26do. 9Dec. 16do. 6Jan.1814 16June 10Nov.	2Jan.1810 Adjut. 30Apr. 1812
Ensign - {	John Hodges James Macbean Francis M'Murran William Fleming Bell J— Conry James Robert Disney	11Nov.1813 13Jan.1814 14do. 7Apr. 16June 10Nov.	 30Dec. 1813
Paymaster -	Thomas Tompson	3Feb.1814	
Adjutant - -	James Stewart	5Nov.1813	Lieut. 2Jan.1810
Quarter-Master	James Lowry	2Dec.1813	
Surgeon - -	August. Stromeyer	16Dec.1813	
Assistant Surg. {	J— Sproule George Brien	17Mar.1814 22Sept.	

Agent, Mr. Kirkland, No. 8, Bennett Street, St. James's.

Rank.	Name.	Rank in the Regiment.	Rank in the Army.
Colonel - -	Frederick Maitland	22Feb.1810	Lt.Gen. 1Jan.1812
Lieut. Colonel	W.T. *Visc.*Molesworth	28Mar.1805	M.Gen. 4June1814
Major - -	{ Samuel Moffatt { Boyle Octavius Loane	28Jan.1813 1July	
Captain - -	{ Philip Delatre { John Clarke Docwray { Francis Nicholas Rossi { John J— Blackenberg { Ralph Coxon { French Gray { Samuel Allen Wheeler { Samuel L— Jenkins { John Fraser { —— Richter	16June1803 27Mar.1806 12Nov. 20Mar.1809 10Aug. 10Feb.1810 30June1812 26Nov. 28Jan.1813 22July	Major 4June1814 18Mar.1807 12May 1808
1st Lieutenant	{ William Virgo { John West Wilkins { George F— Dick { Alfred Mylius { Paul Secluno { John Page { Thomas Yoon { H. J. Duggan Courtayne { George Stavert { Edward Hughes	26May1803 17June1808 18do. 1June1810 25Oct. 8Aug.1811 24Sept.1812 17Dec. 30Apr.1813 17Mar.1814	16July 1800 16Sept.1804 11Apr.1808 9Sept.1813
2d Lieutenant	{ Peter Crofton { Brindley Hone { —— Moore { George William Crooke { William Malcolm { Richard Pollington { John Mainwaring { H— Fleming { Samuel Braybrooke { —— Conradi { George Johnson { Wm. Richard Henderson	5Apr.1810 6do. 12do. 31May 2May1811 20July 24Sept.1812 29Oct. 17Dec. 30Apr.1813 23Sept. 9June1814	 Adjutant 25Nov.1813
Paymaster -	John Boustead	21June1810	
Adjutant - -	Richard Pollington	20July1811	2d Lt. 20July1811
Quarter-Master	—— Kennedy	2July1813	
Surgeon - -	Abraham White	10Nov.1814	
Assistant Surg. {			
Agent,			

Rank.	Name.	Rank in the	
		Regiment.	Army.
Colonel -	◎– *Sir* John Hamilton, *Bt.*	18Jan.1813	Lt.Gen. 4June1814
Lieut. Colonel	Thomas Wm. Kerr	28Mar.1805	Col. 4June1813
Major - -	{ Alexander Chaplin	13Nov.1806	Lt.Col. 4June1811
	{ Frederick Hankey	13July1809	Lt.Col.15Aug.1811
Captain -	{ Lionel C— Hook	29Apr.1803	Major 4June1813
	John Bradish	2June	Major 4June1814
	J— M— Truter	3Apr.1806	
	John Antill	29Sept.1808	
	John Parker	10Feb.1810	
	John Tupman	19July	
	Edward Smith	19Nov.	
	John Kitson	3Oct.1811	
	William Willermin	22Apr.1813	Major 18Feb.1813
	{ Alex. C— Craufurd	9June1814	
1st Lieutenant	{ Joseph Reed	26Nov.1807	
	——— Hunter	1Jan.1808	
	William Franchell	2June1809	
	M— H— Fagan	26July1810	
	Frederick Ostheyden	26Jan.1811	
	Gerald A— Giesler	1Mar.	
	Charles W— L—Roberts	17do.	
	Alexander Kellett	25May1813	21July 1808
	William Croudace	4Feb.1814	
	{ Samuel Rind	10Nov.	
2d Lieutenant	{ Simon Pierce Davis	25July1810	
	John Burke	27do.	
	William Boyton	1Sept.	
	——— Berkeley	13Dec.	
	Charles Button	3Jan.1811	
	James Holowell	1Feb.	
	John Wardell	17Mar.	
	Isaac Foster	25May	
	William Stewart	13Aug.1812	
	H— W— Smyth	27Mar.1813	Adjutant
	John Whitehead	16Sept.	
	Luke Prior	4Feb.1814	
	{ Alexander Murray Hay	10Nov.	
Paymaster -	William Moir	16Aug.1810	
Adjutant - -	H— W— Smyth	27Mar.1813	2d Lt. 27Mar.1813
Quarter-Master	John Staples	21Jan.1803	
Surgeon - -	George Burleigh	24Aug.1814	
Assistant Surg.	{ Alexander Mac Queen	13May1813	
	{ Henry Tedlie	do.	

Agent,

3d

(ORDERED TO BE DISBANDED.)

Rank.	Name.	Rank in the Regiment.	Army.
Colonel - -	William Thomas	22Feb.1810	Lt.Gen. 4June1814
Lieut. Colonel			
Major - - {	Donald Mackay	16May1811	7Mar.1811
	George Nixon	15July1813	
Captain - {	Edward Lenn	7Apr.1804	Major 4June1814
	Thomas Bayley	2June	Major 4June1814
	Henry de la Harpe	22Nov.1806	Major 4June1813
	Philip Peckham	24Jan.1809	
	Alexander Alexander	30do.	Major 4June1814
	Mark Prager	20Mar.	18Sept.1806
	George Stewart	25Oct.	5Oct. 1809
	William Edward Frye	15Feb.1810	18Apr. 1805
1st Lieutenant {	James Taree	6Mar.1806	
	William Black	25Jan.1807	
	M— Wake	31Aug.	
	John White	2Sept.	
	James Bell	25Jan.1809	
	Charles Hay	16Jan.1810	11Aug.1807
	George A— Franchell	10June	
	Louis de Pons	24Jan.1811	
	Isaac Ligor	25do.	Adjutant
	Hen. Earberry Hendley	29Oct.1812	
	John Crotty	24Oct.1813	1Mar.1806
2d Lieutenant {	John Thistleton	13July1810	
	James Titus Murphy	20Sept.	
	John Tulloh	12Nov.	
	William Atkinson	14Mar.1811	
	Robert Spratt	9May	
	George Minter	14Nov.	
	James Barnes	28do.	
	T— Addison	9Apr.1812	
	F— Driberg	13Aug.	
Paymaster -	John Kerr	26July1810	
Adjutant - -	Isaac Ligor	2July1810	1st Lt. 25Jan.1811
Quarter-Master	Thomas Taylor	15Nov.1804	
Surgeon - -	David Moffatt	1June1805	
Assistant Surg.	Hugh Rose	30Aug.1810	

Agent,

4th

4th Ceylon Regiment.
(ORDERED TO BE DISBANDED.)

Rank.	Name.	Rank in the Regiment.	Army.
Colonel - -	John Wilson	8Mar.1810	M.Gen. 4June1811
Lieut. Colonel	A— M'Gregor Murray	17Sept.1812	Col. 4June1814
Major - -	{ John Huskisson	8Mar.1810	
	{ Richard Kelly	6Dec.	
Captain -	⎰ William Riddle	10Mar.1810	
		Thomas Fletcher	12do.	
		Lawrence Brown	13do.	
		William B— Fairman	2Aug.	
		WilliamHenryCleather	21Nov.	
		George Ingham	19Mar.1812	
		Thomas James	28May	14Jan. 1812
		Anthony Troyer	15July1813	
	⎱ George Stace	5Nov.	
1st Lieutenant	⎰ Henrich Munich	8Mar.1810	
		George Durnford	10do.	
		Charles Forbes	11do.	
		——— De Busche	12do.	
		John Gill	13do.	
		Thomas Wilkinson	14do.	
		R— F— Fellowes	16do.	Adjutant
		Edward Nolan	25Sept.1811	
		William Fraser	26do.	
		Joseph Fraser Wilson	28Feb.1812	10June1811
	⎱ Arthur Cassan	5Nov.1813	
2d Lieutenant	⎰ William Lewis	12Mar.1810	
		Alexander Mackenzie	14do.	
		Walter Boyd	17do.	
		Martin Browne	5July	
		John Moffett	22Nov.	
		——— Robertson	20July1812	
	⎱ Sackville Sackville	6Nov.1813	
Paymaster			
Adjutant - -	R— F— Fellowes	25Mar.1811	1st Lt. 16Mar.1810
Quarter-Master	Thomas Hogg	25June1811	
Surgeon - -	James Adams	15Apr.1813	
Assistant Surg.			

Facings white.

Agent,

A Regi-

| Rank. | Name. | Rank in the | |
		Regiment.	Army.
Colonel - -	George Moncrieffe	27Apr.1811	Lt.Gen.25July1810
Lieut. Colonel	John Graham	26Jan.1806	Col. 4June1814
Major - -	{ Jacob Glyn Cuyler	26Jan.1806	Lt.Col. 4June1813
	{ Geo. Sackville Fraser	21Oct.1812	
Captain -	Patrick Craufurd	28May1806	
	John Thomas Prentice	23Apr.1807	Lt.Col. 4June1814
	Clement Kirby	12Jan.1809	20Mar.1806
	Donald Macniel	28Dec.	Major 4June1814
	Matthew G— Blake	25July1811	Major 12Nov.1812
	Michael Lynch	3Oct.	
	William W— Harding	19Dec.	12Oct. 1809
	Cæsar Andrews	6Feb.1812	9Aug.1810
	Andrew Bogle	21Oct.1813	
	Lewis Ellert	9June1814	
Lieutenant -	James Gair	24Mar.1806	
	John Bell	25do.	
	—— Schonfelt	27June	
	George Ledingham	17July	
	Henry Hanson	2June1808	23Jan. 1797
	Charles J— Devenish	27Apr.1809	9Oct. 1805
	John Baird	9July	
	—— Hart	27Sept.1810	Adjutant
	Matthew M'Innes	5Mar.1812	
	Kenneth Forbes	1June1814	
	George Paton	2do.	
	John Laycock	3do.	
	Donald M'Niel	4do.	
	Francis Rousseau	5do.	
	Hugh Fraser	6do.	
	Andrew Stockenstrom	7do.	
	Peter Rousseau	8do.	
	Adam Gordon	9do.	
	Edward Heard	11Aug.	
	Wm. M'Kenzie Johnson	18do.	23Sept.1812

Ensign

Rank.	Name.	Rank in the	
		Regiment.	Army.
Ensign - - {	William Vander Reit	6June1814	
	Orlof Gonf. Stockenstrom	7do.	
	Robert Henry Dingley	8do.	
	William Mackay	16June	
	Arthur Evans	11July	
	William Hatch	12do.	
	Thomas Sollers Knight	14do.	
	Hugh Huntley	4Aug.	
	Charles Robinson	8Dec.	1Sept.1814
Paymaster -			
Adjutant - -	——— Hart	26June1806	Lieut. 27Sept.1810
Quarter-Master	John M'Pherson	9Sept.1813	
Surgeon - -	William Milton	13Sept.1810	
Assistant Surg. {	G— Glaeser	11Sept.1806	
	John Dempster	1Sept.1814	

Agent,

(ORDERED TO BE DISBANDED.)

Rank.	Name.	Regiment.	Army.
		Rank in the	
Colonel - -	Hen. Sheehy Keating	4June1813	
	Lt. Col. Comm.	25Jan.1812	
Lieut. Colonel	Wilbrah. Tol. Edwards	25Jan.1812	
Major - -	Geo. Fr. Waldo Fluker	20Feb.1812	
Captain -	Francis Maclean	25Jan.1812	
	Gustavus Munro	26do.	
	A— Duperon Baby	27do.	
	William H— Ashe	28do.	
	John Frith	29do.	
	Edward Hill	30do.	
	Martin Hillhouse	2Apr.	
	Peter Willatts	22Dec.1814	
1st Lieutenant	Adam Twigg	26Jan.1812	1Apr. 1809
	Francis Stubb Grogan	27do.	
	Donald M'Donald	25June	1Sept.1808
	Johnstone Martin	29Oct.	
	Thomas Patton	18Feb.1813	28Nov.1809
	Henry Watson	19Aug.	16Sept.1807
	J— Cauty	23Dec.	
	Wm. Henry Douglas	29Sept.1814	9Nov.1813
2d Lieutenant	J— F— S— L'Ecoliere	27Jan.1812	
	Andrew Fere	28do.	
	——— Gunn	30do.	Adjutant
	Thomas Rice	31do.	
	Patrick Rice	1Feb.	
	——— Crofton	2do.	
	——— Quin	29Oct.	
	Cha. Mack. Campbell	22Dec.1813	
	Theodore Mylius	23do.	
Paymaster -	John Lawton	10June1813	
Adjutant - -	——— Gunn	30Jan.1812	2d Lt. 30Jan.1812
Quarter-Master	Robert Edwards	25Dec.1813	
Surgeon - -	John Hodson	29Oct.1812	
Assistant Surg.	John Armstrong	1Sept.1814	

Regimentals green.—Facings black.

Agent,

Royal

Rank.	Name.	Rank in the Regiment.	Army.
Col. Comm.	*Digby Hamilton	5Nov.1803	*M.Gen.12Au.1813
Major - -	George Darley	2June1814	
Captain -	Felix Blœme	9Feb.1809	
	Robert Murray	15Aug.1811	15Mar.1810
	Samuel Johnson	3Oct.	
	Thomas Pardoe	1Oct.1812	
	John Sidaway	15do.	
Lieutenant	Valentine Ravenscroft	26Oct.1808	
	Samuel Beattie	27do.	
	John M'Vicar	28do.	Adjutant
	Charles Morrison	15Nov.	
	William Mellish	17do.	
	William Aitkin	9Feb.1809	
Cornet - -	Edward Smith	26Nov.1812	
	Henry O'Neil	18Mar.1813	
	Samuel Walby	19do.	
	Robert Parkinson	22Apr.	
	Robert Kerr	1Sept.1814	11Feb.1811
Paymaster -	William Pettigrew	25May1802	
Adjutant - -	John M'Vicar	27Apr.1809	Lieut. 28Oct.1808
Quarter-Master	John Tennant	25Aug.1809	
Surgeon - -	Thomas Wynne	6Oct.1808	20June1799
Veterinary Surg.	Frederick Cherry	16July1807	

Blue.—Facings red.—Lace silver.

Agent, Messrs. Greenwood, Cox and Hammersley.

Rank.	Name.	Rank in the Regiment.	Army.
Colonel - -	Baldwin Leighton	18Sept.1809	Lt.Gen.25Oct.1809
Lieut. Colonel	William Nedham	16May1805	Col. 4June1813
Major - -	{ George Stracey Smyth { Charles Bayley { Archibald Macdonald	9May1805 2Jan.1812 21Jan.1813	M.Gen. 1Jan.1812 Lt.Col.25Nov.1813
Captain -	{ H— Fred. Courtney { Charles M'Gregor { Hamilton Newton { Richard Young { George L— Spinluff { William Thorne { John Renny { Thomas Richardson { Alexander Livingstone { H— Welman	18July1805 30Apr.1807 26May1808 14Feb.1811 12Mar.1812 10ct. 21Jan.1813 29Apr. 20May 21Oct.	 Major 4June1814 Major 4June1814 Major 4June1814 14May 1807 25Jan. 1810 8Aug.1805 2Nov.1809
Lieutenant	{ Tears Rankin { George Levick { Sampson Cox { John Haire { George Ball { Richard Allen { Henry Daunt { Charles Busteed { George Jennings { George Evans { John Crause { Joseph Saunders . { William Williams { William Wilkins { Henry Le Mesurier { Walter Samuel Griffiths { John Densly Hoopwood { Kenneth Mackintosh { William Tapp	4Apr.1805 6Mar.1806 17July 18Feb.1808 15June 29June1809 20Sept.1810 20Dec. 9Apr.1811 2July1812 26Dec. 28do. 29do. 30do. 31do. 21Jan.1813 13May 30Dec. 13Jan.1814	 5Nov.1805 4July 1805 6June1805 8June1809 22Sept.1808 19Mar.1807 19Nov.1807 25Apr.1811 18Dec.1806 1Jan. 1811 Adjutant

Ensign

Rank.	Name.	Rank in the Regiment.	Army.
Ensign	John Levicke	8Oct.1812	
	J— Adolph. Kemmeter	31Dec.	
	Henry Bromfield	14Jan.1813	
	Timothy Carroll	22do.	
	Robert Dutton	25do.	21Nov.1811
	George Mackay	1July	
	Peter Karr	29do.	
	Jonathan Levick	2Dec.1814	
Paymaster	James Duff	7Oct.1807	
Adjutant	William Tapp	12Mar.1812	Lieut. 13Jan.1814
Quarter-Master	Alexander Harrison	22Jan.1813	
Surgeon	William Stafford	30Nov.1809	9June1804
Assistant Surg.	Oliver Dease	17Aug.1809	

Facings yellow.

Agent, Messrs. Greenwood, Cox and Hammersley.

2d

2d Garrison Battalion.

(Late 4th.)

Rank.	Name.	Regiment.	Rank in the Army.
Colonel -	ⓢWilliam Houstoun	1July1811	L.Gen. 4June1814
Lieut. Colonel	Alexander Lawrence	28May1812	
Major - -	{ Carlo Joseph Doyle	23Jan.1812	
	{ Hon. Henry E—Butler	19Mar.	30May 1811
	⌠ John Hardy	13May1807	Major 4June1811
	⎮ Richard Hart	19May1808	Major 4June1814
	⎮ Arthur Morris	22Mar.1810	Major 4June1814
	⎮ George Snow	11Oct.	31Oct. 1805
	⎮ J— A— Gibson	4Apr.1811	Major 4June1814
	⎮ James Johnston	15July1813	
Captain - -	⎨ John Field Oldham	29do.	Major 4June1814
	⎮ Charles Douglas	27Sept.	
	⎮ Thomas Fonblanque	30do.	
	⎮ James Kirkman	18Nov.	
	⎮ Henry Crause	16Dec.	
	⎮ John Ringrove Drew	3Nov.1814	
	⌊ John Ward	1Dec.	5Oct. 1809
	⌠ Thomas Jackson	21Jan.1808	
	⎮ Thomas Walsh	25Feb.	4May 1807
	⎮ William Bell	14Apr.	25Feb. 1808
	⎮ John Cameron	26May	13Aug.1807
	⎮ Cha.NewhamHinchley	17Aug.	13Feb. 1806
	⎮ John Kirk	2Feb.1809	9Apr.1807
	⎮ William Tyler	23do.	
	⎮ John Dixon	19July	3Oct. 1805
	⎮ John Miles	19June1810	5Feb. 1801
	⎮ John Anderson	20do.	
Lieutenant -	⎨ Valentine Lawford	11July1811	23Sept.1806
	⎮ John M'Kellar	23Jan.1812	11Oct. 1809
	⎮ John Fortescue Cockburn	30do.	17Oct. 1811
	⎮ Joseph Crawford	23July	
	⎮ John Tice	3Dec.	9May 1811
	⎮ Tristram Carey	28Jan.1813	26July 1800
	⎮ John Watson	20May	
	⎮ Thomas Griffiths	3June	28Feb. 1812
	⎮ Edward Bayntun	10do.	28Mar.1805
	⎮ Edward Guest	28July	10Sept.1812
	⌊ Thomas Money	21Oct.	

Lieutenant

Rank.	Name.	Rank in the Regiment.	Army.
Lieutenant	William Harden	22Oct.1813	
	Anthony Moran	do.	
	James Wemyss Disney	23do.	
	John Stalliard	20Jan.1814	
	Wm. Stewart Griffith	21do.	Adjutant
	Arthur Boyd	16Feb.	
	George Knox	17do.	
	P— W— Burke	5May	25Dec.1807
Ensign	Rich.Geth.CreaghCoote	25Sept.1813	
	Edward Moore	21Oct.	
	Edward Daniell	22do.	
	——– Fortune	23do.	
	—— Rooney	4Nov.	Adjutant
	George Armstrong	2Dec.	
	John Walker	6do.	
	—— Molloy	7do.	
	Wm. Horwood Freame	8do.	
	Joseph Reade	9do.	
	Robert Vincent	20Jan.1814	
	James Knox	17Feb.	
	Thomas Tuckett	10Mar.	
Paymaster	William Bromley	19Nov.1807	
Adjutant	William Stewart Griffith	8Oct.1812	Lieut. 21Jan.1814
	—— Rooney	4Nov.1813	Ensign 4Nov.1813
QuarterMaster	William Simpson	8Oct.1812	
	—— M'Clenahan	4Nov.1813	
Surgeon	Edward Smith	6Aug.1812	9July 1789
Assistant Surg.	John Crapp Spry	30Dec.1813	29Aug.1811
	Joseph Hunter	17Feb.1814	6Sept.1810

Facings yellow.

Agent, Messrs. Greenwood, Cox and Hammersley.

2d

6th (or Royal North British) Veteran Battalion.

Rank.	Name.	Regiment.	Rank in the Army.
Colonel - -	*Sir* Paulus Æmilius Irving, *Bt.* 25 Dec. 1802	Gen.	1 Jan. 1812
Lieut. Colonel	Alexander Mair	1 Aug. 1811	Col. 21 Aug. 1795
Major - -	Thomas Fortye	9 Apr. 1807	24 Oct. 1804
Captain -	John Mac Donnell	13 June 1805	9 July 1803
	John M'Dermid	2 Apr. 1807	28 Aug. 1804
Lieutenant -	James M'Intosh	5 June 1806	1 May 1805
	Alexander Robertson	3 Feb. 1813	4 July 1781
Ensign - -	James Patterson	13 Aug. 1807	12 Mar. 1807
	David Crooks	1 Feb. 1810	Adjutant
	Alexander Mackenzie	23 July 1812	
Paymaster - -	James Wright	12 Apr. 1803	
Adjutant - -	David Crooks	4 Oct. 1810	Ensign 1 Feb. 1810
Quarter-Master	Charles West	9 July 1812	6 Apr. 1797
Surgeon - -	Peter Macarthur	7 Mar. 1811	5 Sept. 1805
Assistant Surg.	Andrew Ligertwood	10 June 1813	11 July 1805

Facings blue.—Lace gold.

Agent, Messrs. Brooksbank and Morland, No. 19, Craven Street, Strand.

8th Royal Veteran Battalion.

Rank.	Name.	Rank in the Regiment.	Army.
Colonel - -	John Watson T. Watson 29Dec.1804	Gen.	25Apr.1808
Lieut. Colonel	Wm. Osborn Hamilton 25Oct.1805	29Apr.1802	
Major - -	Clark Caldwell	10Sept.1812	4June1811
Captain - -	James Young	14May1807	15Aug.1805
	William Dawson	26Jan.1809	22Apr.1808
	John Smith	30Mar.	9July1803
	Frederick Killenbach	28Aug.1811	5Dec.1805
Lieutenant -	James Stewart	23Dec.1804	22Aug.1796 Adjut.
	Edward Bremner	26do.	27Oct.1803
	James Sloan	17Mar.1808	1July1806
	Philip Dowling	10Apr.	
	William Hughes	12do.	
	John Marsh	2Mar.1809	9Nov.1807
	Francis L'Estrange	2Apr.1812	13Jan.1805
	Thomas Furse	16July	
	William Russell	10Dec.	
	Thomas Hunt	3June1813	
Ensign - -	James Booth	17May1810	
Paymaster - -	John Wright	20Jan.1814	
Adjutant - -	James Stewart	16Oct.1806	Lieut. 22Aug.1796
Quarter-Master	John Morrison	6Feb.1805	
Surgeon - -	Michael Balfour	24Jan.1811	30Aug.1799
Assistant Surg.	George Griffin	28Apr.1814	

Facings blue.—Lace gold.

Agent, Messrs. Brooksbank and Morland, No. 19, Craven Street, Strand.

Rank.	Name.	Rank in the Regiment.	Rank in the Army.
Colonel - -	Colin Mackenzie	21Mar.1805	Gen. 4June1814
Major - -	Alexander Rose	4Oct.1810	10Dec.1807
Captain - -	{ Sam. Barker Edmeston { Archibald M'Neill	25June1807 16June1808	1Jan. 1794 13Aug.1805
Lieutenant	{ Joseph Heamer { Kenneth Murchison	23Mar.1805 20Jan.1814	21June1810
Ensign - -	{ Walter Thompson { George Gunn { Hugh Macpherson	2Apr.1805 18do. 8Aug.1811	Adjutant
Paymaster -	John Mackenzie	19Sept.1805	
Adjutant - -	George Gunn	18Apr.1805	Ensign 18Apr.1805
Quarter-Master	Thomas Sneath	15Aug.1811	
Surgeon - -	James Scott	7Mar.1811	24Aug.1807
Assistant Surg.	Henry Mostyn	19Aug.1813	4Jan. 1810

Facings blue.—Lace gold,

Agent, Messrs. Brooksbank and Morland, No. 19, Craven Street, Strand.

Rank.	Name.	Rank in the Regiment.	Rank in the Army.
Colonel -	Lowther, *Lord* Muncaster	25Dec.1806	Gen. 25Apr.1808
Lieut. Colonel	Donald Macpherson	18Nov.1813	
Major - -	◎George Miles Milne	18Nov.1813	6Feb. 1812
Captain -	Hector M'Lean	25Dec.1806	10Jan. 1805
	Charles Roberts	29Jan.1807	17Sept.1801
	Forbes J — M'Donnell	25Dec.	17Apr. 1805
	Neal O'Donell	28Jan.1808	21Aug.1806
	John Flack	28Apr.	5Dec.1805
	David Rome	26Jan.1809	16June 1804
	John Prime	16Nov.	14June1808
	John Gardiner Herbert	23Aug.1810	16Sept.1806
*	G— V— Gerau	31Dec.1812	20Aug.1803
	Alexander Skene	10Nov.1814	11Nov.1813
Lieutenant	Daniel Mylrea	25Dec.1806	6Sept.1795
	Joseph Lambeth	do.	
	John Jameson	do.	
	Alexander Murray	do.	
	William Taylor	do.	
	William Bailley	9Apr.1807	27June1805
	Donald M'Crummen	6Apr.1808	
	Thomas O'Regan	10do.	2Oct. 1806
	John Wilson	12do.	
	Patrick Corbett	19Jan.1809	19Nov.1807
	Charles M'Carthy	17Aug.	19July 1809
	Peter M'Gregor	29Nov.1810	
	Alexander M'Millan	28Mar.1811	
	James Hinckes	13Feb.1812	
	John Everett	20Aug.	29Sept.1808
	Robert Hobson	17June1813	25Dec.1805
	Thomas Chettle	29July	
	John Bruce	28Apr.1814	Adjutant
	F— M'Innes	25Sept.	12June1805
	Peter Wilson	10Nov.	

Rank.	Name.	Rank in the	
		Regiment.	Army.
Ensign - - {	Matthew Gould	25Dec.1806	
	John Lambton	do.	
	James Thompson	do.	
	John Nicholls	22Jan.1807	
	John Hall	29Oct.	
	Ralph Ross Lewen	16Nov.1809	
	Henry Smith	14June1810	28Apr. 1807
	William M'Cance	2Jan.1812	
	John M'Lauchlan	5Nov.	
	John Hartley	29July1813	
Paymaster -	Thomas Stott	25Apr.1811	
Adjutant - -	John Bruce	5Apr.1810	Lieut. 28Apr.1814
Quarter-Master	William Rogers	2July1807	
Surgeon - -	Richard Armstrong	23Apr.1807	12Nov.1803
Assistant Surg. {			

Facings blue.—Lace gold.

Agent, Messrs. Brooksbank and Morland, No. 19, Craven Street, Strand.

Rank.	Name.	Rank in the Regiment.	Rank in the Army.
Colonel - -	And. John Drummond	25 Apr. 1807	Gen. 1 Jan. 1812
Lieut. Colonel	Henry Powlett	5 Sept. 1811	25 Nov. 1806
Major - -	Tho. Berkeley Campbell	25 Sept. 1807	13 May 1804
Captain -	Wm. Thomas Tayler	14 Mar. 1805	29 May 1796
	Thomas Fellowes	25 Apr. 1806	12 Jan. 1800
	Thomas Snowe	13 Sept. 1810	14 Apr. 1803
Lieutenant -	Henry Heely	12 Dec. 1805	3 Dec. 1803
	George Donaldson	27 June 1811	6 Feb. 1811
	Whiteside Godfrey	3 Feb. 1812	3 July 1808
	John Buchanan	5 do.	9 Mar. 1810
	Charles Hart	26 do.	
	William Pettigrew	27 do.	
	John Crampton	28 do.	Adjutant
Ensign - -	William Halliday	9 May 1811	
	Charles Alexander	27 Feb. 1812	
	Angus M'Taggart	25 Nov.	
Paymaster -	David Wainwright	10 Sept. 1812	7 Sept. 1808
Adjutant - -	John Crampton	31 May 1810	Lieut. 28 Feb. 1812
Quarter-Master	William Fuller	28 May 1807	
Surgeon - -	William Turner	21 Nov. 1811	9 Aug. 1810
Assistant Surg.	William Jones	2 Feb. 1809	
	James Curtis	25 May	19 Oct. 1804

Facings blue.—Lace gold.

Agent, Messrs. Brooksbank and Morland, No. 19, Craven Street, Strand

13th Royal Veteran Battalion.

| | | | Rank in the | |
| | | | Regiment. | Army. |
Rank.	Name.			
Colonel - -	William Raymond		19Nov.1812	M.Gen. 1Jan.1812
Lieut. Colonel	Robert H— Burton		21Oct.1813	26Aug.1813
Major -	◎–George Langlands		25Jan.1813	27Apr.1812

Captain -			
	William Gibson	25Jan.1813	19Sept.1804
	John Hitchen	do.	13June1805
	William M'Leod	do.	11Sept.1806
	James Porter	do.	10Aug.1808
	William Baird	do.	24Apr.1809
	Brinsey Purefoy	do.	20July 1809
	Alexander Gourlay	do.	9Oct. 1811
	Bartholomew Hickey	do.	31Dec.1812
	A— Sutherland	23Sept.	13May 1813
	James Theodore Bryett	31Mar.1814	11Feb. 1808

Lieutenant -			
	Fra. *Baron* Eberstein	25Jan.1813	10Dec.1807
	Donald Ross	do.	26May 1808
	John Munton	do.	16Mar.1809
	Henry Richardson	do.	30Mar.1809
	Thomas Brown	do.	19July 1809
	Hill Phillips	do.	21July 1809
	James Eagar	do.	21June1811
	Peter Broetz	do.	9Oct. 1811
	J— Mackie	do.	
	John Hagger	do.	
	Thomas Clark	do.	
	John Scott	do.	
	James Yates	do.	
	A— Veitch	do.	
	William Harris	do.	
	John Harford	do.	
	D— Wood	do.	
	—— Little	do.	
	—— Williams	do.	
	James Mason	15Apr.	

Ensign

Rank.	Name.	Rank in the Regiment.	Army.
Ensign	—— Wood	25 Jan.1813	
	—— Fawcett	do.	
	—— Gordon	do.	
	J— Barnes	do.	Adjutant
	—— Knight	do.	
	—— Garret	do.	
	—— Coxson	do.	
	G— Boreham	do.	
	T— Thomas	do.	
	William Perry	do.	

Rank.	Name.	Rank in the Regiment.	Army.
Paymaster -	Charles Rowan	27 Jan.1814	8 Oct. 1798
Adjutant - -	J— Barnes	25 Jan.1813	Ensign 25 Jan.1813
Quarter-Master	George Woods	15 Apr.1813	23 Dec.1808
Surgeon - -	John Lear	11 Mar.1813	15 Aug.1801
Assistant Surg. {	Thomas Watkins	11 Mar.1813	19 Dec.1799
{	E— Tongue	28 Oct.	

Agent, Messrs. Brooksbank and Morland, No. 19, Craven Street, Strand.

GARRISON

GARRISON COMPANIES.

European Garrison Companies for Service in the West Indies.

First.

Captain - -	John Smith	25Nov.1804	
Lieutenant	{ James Paul	5June1805	
	{ Silvester Connor	15Dec.1808	
Ensign - -			

Seeond.

Captain - -	Benedict Simon	8June1805	30Dec. 1797
Lieutenant	{ Henry Boone	25Apr.1804	17Sept. 1801
	{ Frederick Passow	15Dec.1808	
Ensign - -	William Young	12Aug.1813	

Third.

Captain - -	John Blair	31Mar.1814	21Jan. 1813
Lieutenant -			
Ensign - -	Charles Baker	31Mar.1814	

Agent, Messrs. Brooksbank and Morland, No. 19, Craven Street, Strand.

For Service at the Cape of Good Hope.

Captain - -	Francis Evatt	25Mar.1813	
Lieutenant	{ William Slater	25Mar.1813	
	{ Martin Fleischer	do.	
	{ William Gardner	10Mar.1814	
Ensign - -	—— de la Pole	10Mar.1814	

Agent, Messrs. Brooksbank and Morland, No. 19, Craven Street, Strand.

Garrison

Captain -	{ Augustus C— Mercer	27Oct.1814	12Sept.1805
	{ Alexander Sutherland	do.	
Lieutenant	(James Kennedy	27Oct.1814	18Dec. 1803
	) David Sutherland	do.	11Feb. 1807
	) John O'Brien	do.	24Nov.1809
	(Daniel Gardner	do.	1Feb. 1811
Ensign -	{ James Kirkwood	27Oct.1814	
	{ John Worlledge	do.	

Agent, Messrs. Brooksbank and Morland, No. 19, Craven Street, Strand.

A Veteran Company attached to such Corps as may be stationed in New South Wales.

Captain - -	John Brabyn	5Feb.1811	11Feb. 1808
Lieutenant	{ William Lawson	6Feb.1811	14Nov.1806
	{ Archibald Bell	7do.	15Oct. 1807
Ensign - -	Charles M'Intosh	28July1814	

Agent, Messrs. Greenwood, Cox and Hammersley.

K k   Royal

Rank,	Name.	Regiment.	Rank in the Army.	
Colonel -	◎ William Henry Pringle	12May1814	M.Gen. 1Jan.1812	
Lieut. Colonel	Rowland Heathcote	16June1814	4June 1814	
Major - -	Elias Pipon	28July1814	4June 1814	
Captain -	William Morris	6Aug.1803	Major	4June1814
	* John Hierliegh	13do.		
	Tito Lelievre	20do.		
	John Thomas Whelan	24Nov.	Major	4June1814
	John Evans	21Nov.1805		
	R— P— Skinner	2Nov.1809		
	Robert Mockler	31May1810		
	William Walsh Winter	4Oct.		
	* Charles Blaskowitz	4June1812	16May 1800	
	Thomas Stewart	5Aug.1813		
Lieutenant	Robert Cooke	19Nov.1805	Adjutant	
	A— Bulger	30July1806		
	Alfred Armstrong	4Mar.1807		
	John Le Breton	5do.		
	Philip Ingouville	12Nov.		
	Patrick Walsh	2Nov.1809		
	Edward Enwright	31May1810		
	——— De Koven	23Aug.		
	James Garden	21Feb.1811		
	Daniel Rieley	3Aug.1813		
	Edward Gouvreau	4do.		
	Charles Davis	24Feb.1814		
	John George Hierlihy	7July		
Ensign ⸱	Alexander Maclean	24June1813		
	Joseph H— O'Brien	5Aug.		
	Cha.Wm.MacarmickDodd	6do.		
	Charlton Dennis	3Feb. 1814		
	Duncan Campbell Napier	24do.		
	George Macauley	7July		
	John Macdonnell	25Aug.		
	Edward Walker Carter	26do.		
Adjutant - -	Robert Cooke	2Dec.1803	Lieut. 19Nov.1805	
Quarter-Master	Bryant Finan	5Mar.1812		
Surgeon - -	Thomas R— Harris	8July1813		
Assistant Surg.	James Sampson	26Mar.1812	27June1811	

Facings blue.

Agent, Messrs. Greenwood, Cox and Hammersley.

Nova

Rank.	Name.	Regiment.	Rank in the Army.
Colonel - -	◎Fred. Aug. Wetherall	9July1803	Lt.Gen. 4June1814
Lieut. Colonel	Henry C— Darling	10Sept.1812	Col. 4June1814
Major - -	William Haly	20Aug.1812	Lt.Col. 1Jan.1812
Captain - -	{ John Edward Courtenay 11Feb.1807 George Lowen 30July1811 Anthony Gilbert Douglas 31do. William Armstrong 19Sept. R— E— Armstrong 22Oct.1812 Joshua W— Weeks 6May1813 John M'Nab 12Aug. Timothy Ruggles 30Dec. Richard Despard 25Aug.1814 James Moore Young 8Sept.		Major 4June1814 Lt.Col. 25July1810 15May1812
Lieutenant	{ Isaac Glenie 17July1806 Otto Schwartz 18Sept. Charles Stewart 8Oct.1807 Thomas C— Hammill 5Apr.1810 Samuel Nichols 19do. Gustavus A— Thomas 1Aug.1811 Charles Augustus Hayes 22do. Colin M'Nabb 25June1812 Joseph Marchington 22Oct. Roderick Matheson 12Aug.1813 Frederick Skinner 25Aug.1814 William Blanchard 13Oct.		28Nov.1811 7May1812
Ensign - -	{ Philip Van Courtland 4Apr.1810 Edward Davidson 3Sept.1812 Thomas Nowlan 12Aug.1813 Richard Green 30Dec. Richard Uniacke Howe 18Aug.1814 Ronald Macdonnell 25do. Francis Wilson Lewis 6Oct. Edward Sands Bradley 13do. James M'Donnell 14do.		Adjutant
Adjutant - -	Thomas Nowlan	13Oct.1814	Ensign 12Aug.1813
Quarter-Master	Francis Gillman	8Oct.1803	
Surgeon - -	John Fraser	24Sept.1803	
Assistant Surg.	George Tremble	3Apr.1806	

Facings yellow.

Agent, Mr. Kirkland, No. 8, Bennett Street, St. James's.

| | | Rank in the | |
Rank.	Name.	Regiment.	Army.
Colonel - -	Thomas Peter	16July1803	Lt.Gen. 4June1813
Lieut. Colonel	David Shank George Robertson	3Sept.1803 27June1811	M.Gen. 4June1811 25July 1810
Major - -	Peter William de Haren James F— Fulton	20Feb.1812 27Oct.1814	28Nov.1812
Captain - -	Edward Cartwright George Ferguson Alexander Mac Queen James Pentz John Hall John S— Peach Harris William Hailes William Marshall Josias Taylor William Radenhurst	3Feb.1804 19Sept.1805 28Sept.1809 24May1810 27Feb.1812 9Apr. 25June 13Aug. 13May1813 8Sept.1814	Lt.Col. 1Jan.1812 25Feb. 1813
Lieutenant	Henry Weatherstone John Johnstone Alexander Grant Patrick Nowlan Benjamin de Lisle Ulysses Fitzmaurice John de Hertel Barth. Con. Aug. Gugy Edmund W— Antrobus John Carrol Peach John M'Kenzie Samuel Brampton	19Oct.1809 8Aug.1810 24Dec. 25Aug.1812 2Sept. 3do. 12Nov.1813 13do. 14do. 25Aug.1814 8Sept. 13Oct.	22Oct. 1807 13Aug.1812 Adjut.
Ensign - -	Alexander Wilkinson Walter Davidson —— Dufresne Robert T— Scott William Taylor Oliver Faribault Jas.Doug.HamiltonHay Benjamin Holmes	25Mar.1813 12Nov. 13do. 14do. 15do. 16do. 25Aug.1814 8Sept.	
Adjutant -	Patrick Nowlan	25Aug.1812	Lieut. 13Aug.1812
Quarter-Master	Alexander Fraser	28Sept.1809	
Surgeon -	William Daunt	12May1814	
Assistant Surg.			

Facings yellow.

Agent, Messrs. Greenwood, Cox and Hammersley.

Glengarry

Rank.	Name.	Rank in the Regiment.	Army.
Colonel - -	Edward Baynes	6Feb.1812	M.Gen. 4June1814
Lieut. Colonel	Francis Battersby	6Feb.1812	
Major - -	{ Robert M'Douall	24June1813	Lt.Col. 29July1813
	{ Thomas Bunbury	14Apr.1814	
Captain -	(Foster J— Weeks	6Feb.1812	
	Daniel M·Pherson	do.	
	John Jenkins	do.	
	Thomas Fitz Gerald	do.	
	Robert M— Cochrane	do.	
	Alexander Roxborough	do.	
*	Thomas Powell	11Mar.1813	
	Alexander M'Millan	5Aug.	
	James Fitz Gibbon	14Oct.	
	William Campbell	25Aug.1814	
Lieutenant	(James Stewart	6Feb.1812	
	Anthony Leslie	do.	
	Henry F— Hughes	do.	
	James Macaulay	do.	
	William Kemble	do.	
	Walter Ker	do.	
	Æneas Shaw	do.	
	Roderick Matheson	5Aug.1813	
	Angus Macdonnell	24Feb.1814	
	Robert Kerr	25do.	
Ensign - -	(James Robins	6Feb.1812	
	John Mackay	do.	
	Joseph Frobisher	do.	
	Alexander Macdonnell	do.	
	William Blair	5Aug.1813	Adjutant
	Alexander Macdonald	24Feb.1814	
	Thomas Gugy	25do.	
	Simon Fraser	26do.	
	John Fraser	25Aug.	
	John Moorhead	24Nov.	
Adjutant -	William Blair	5Aug.1813	Ensign 5Aug.1813
Quarter-Master	John Watson	6Feb.1812	
Surgeon -	Alexander Cunningham	6Feb.1812	
Assistant Surg.	{ Robert C— Horne	29Oct.1812	

Agent, Messrs. Greenwood, Cox and Hammersley.

New

| | | Rank in the ||
Rank.	Name.	Regiment.	Army.
Colonel - -	John Coffin	25Mar.1813	Lt.Gen.25Oct.1809
Lieut. Colonel	Francis Cockburn	27Oct.1814	
Major - -	Tobias Kirkwood	10Mar.1814	

| Captain - | ⎧ Henry Cooper ⎪ Richard Gibbons * ⎪ John Allen * ⎨ John Delancey ⎪ Noah Freer ⎪ Edward F— Davis ⎪ Warnford Ridge * ⎩ Anthony Barker | 25Mar.1813 do. do. do. 25Oct. do. do. do. | |

| Lieutenant | * ⎧ Joseph Kenah * ⎪ Abraham Baxter ⎨ Alexander Lindsay ⎪ Travers Hart. Vaughan ⎩ | 25Mar.1813 do. 25Oct. 25Mar.1814 | |

| Ensign - - | ⎧ Alexander Fraser ⎪ Charles Hatheway ⎪ Thomas Dely ⎪ William Hatch ⎨ George Kimball ⎪ —— Minchin ⎪ Alexander Mackenzie ⎪ George Moorhouse ⎩ F— Bruguier | 25Mar.1813 do. do. do. do. do. 25Oct. do. 25Mar.1814 | Adjutant |

Adjutant - -	Alexander Fraser	25Mar.1813	Ensign 25Mar.1813
Quarter-Master	—— Barclay	24Feb.1814	
Surgeon - -	William O'Donnell	12May1814	
Assistant Surg. {	William Woodforde	12May1814	16Jan. 1812

Agent, Mr. Gilpin, No. 33, Villiers Street, Strand.

FOREIGN

FOREIGN CORPS.

THE KING'S GERMAN LEGION.

Colonel in { *His Royal Highness*
Chief   { A. *Duke of* Cambridge, *K.G.* 17Nov.1803 |F.Mar.26Nov.1813

1st Regiment of Light Dragoons.

Col. Comm.   ———, *Count* Walmoden 17Mar.1814

Lieut.Colonel◎–John, *Baron* Bulow   1Aug.1810

Major - - { Frederick, *Bar.* Gruben 12Jan.1813 | 25Feb. 1812
              { Aug. *Baron* Reitzenstein 13June

               { Philip de Seighard   18Jan.1806
        ◎ | Hans de Hattorf   8June1807
          | Fred. *Baron* Uslar   24Nov.1809 | 3Jan. 1809
          | Bernard, *Baron* Bothmer 28Aug.1810
Captain -   { Geo. Hen. de Hattorff 25Feb.1812
             { George de Ramdohr   8Mar.
          | Frederick Peters   13do.
          | Charles Elderhost   10Mar.1813
          | Hartwig de Witzendorff 13June
          { Benedix, *Baron* Decken 5Apr.1814 | 18Sept.1813

Lieutenant

Rank.	Name.	Regiment.	Rank in the Army.

1st Regiment of Light Dragoons.

Rank.	Name.	Regiment.	Army.
Lieutenant	(Henry Leftrew	10Mar.1812	
	——— Fischer	13do.	
	Frederick Natermann	do.	
	Cha. F. *Baron* Lovetzow	do.	
	Charles Tappe	24Sept.	
	{ Charles Lindes	11Mar.1813	
	William Mackenzie	13June	
	Offa Kuhlmann	15do.	
	William Fricke	6Oct.	Adjutant
	Henry Bosse	7do.	
	(Charles Spreebach	27May1814	
Cornet -	(Jacob Hoenes	4Dec.1812	
	Otto,*Baron*Hannerstein	27Aug.1813	
	Conrad Poten	28do.	
	Staats Henry Nanne	22Sept.	
	{ Lewis Kirchner	27Oct.	
	William Jones	25Nov.	
	Frederick Breymann	15Mar.1814	
	Charles, *Baron* Decken	18Apr.	
	Lewis de Muller	22do.	
	(Honosch Leschen	27May	
Paymaster -	William Halpin	6Jan.1807	
Adjutant - -	William Fricke	22Sept.1812	Lieut. 6Oct.1812
Quarter-Master	Henry Kranz	25Aug.1809	
Surgeon - -	Frederick Groskopff	27Dec.1813	30June1804
Assistant Surg. {	N— D— Meyer	31Mar.1810	
	J— H— C— Friderici	2Mar.1812	
Veterinary Surg.	Ludolph Heuer	25May1805	

Scarlet.—Facings blue.—Lace gold.

The

Rank.	Name.	Regiment.	Army.
Col. Comm.	Aug. *Baron* Veltheim	24Jan.1814	M.Gen.25July1810
Lieut. Col. ◎ {	Charles de Jonquieres	7May1810	
	Charles, *Baron* Maydell	26Apr.1813	
Major ◎ {	Frederick de Ziegesar	28May1812	
	Augustus Friedericks	14Oct.	
Captain {	Lewis Wilmerding	17May1806	
	George de Weyhe	16Feb.1809	
	George Auhagen	9May1810	
	Lewis Thiele	do.	
	Cha. de Leschen	10do.	
	Cha. *Baron* Marschalk	2July	24Nov.1809
	Lewis Luderitz	15Feb.1812	
	Ernest, *Baron* Lenthe	4Mar.	4Dec.1809
	William Quentin	28May	
	William Seger	27Aug.	
	Theodore Harling	10Oct.	
Lieutenant {	Fred. *Baron* Bulow	10May1810	
	—— Braun	25Feb.1811	
	Augustus Poten	15Feb.	
	Frederick Bergmann	24Mar.	
	Ludolph de Hugo	do.	
	Augustus Fernetti	do.	
	Augustus Kuhls	28May	
	Charles Schaeffer	2Oct.	
	Herman He. Con. Ritter	18Sept.	
	E— Meyer	15Mar.1813	
Cornet {	Valentin Von Massow	6May1814	
	John Uesseler	21July1812	
	CharlesMontaguePocock	8Aug.	
	William Kalckreuth	28do.	
	F— Kuster	5Sept.	
	Herman Voss	1Oct.	
	H— Drankmeister	2do.	
	Frederick Rumann	21May1813	
	Otto, *Baron* Bulow	8Oct.	
	Augustus Niess	26Nov.	Adjutant
	Frederick de Wissell	16Mar.1814	
	Ferdinand Lorenz	11July	
Paymaster	William Armstrong	1May1806	
Adjutant	Augustus Niess	11July1814	Cornet 26Nov.1813
Quarter-Master	Henry Gropp	25Aug.1809	
Surgeon	Frederick Dettmer	27Dec.1813	13July 1813
Assistant Surg. {	John D— Lange	16Mar.1813	6Oct. 1812
	Charles Thalacker	28Oct.	
Veterinary Surg.	Henry Hogreve	12July1806	

Scarlet.—Facings black.—Lace gold.

L l

The

Rank.	Name.	Regiment.	Rank in the Army.

1st Regiment of Hussars.

Rank.	Name.	Regiment.	Army.
Col. Comm.	Cha. *Baron* Linsingen	18Aug.1804	Lt.Gen. 4June1811
Lieut. Colonel	Augustus de Wissell	26Jan.1814	
Major - ⓐ	{ Philip, *Baron* Gruben { Meriz de Muller	13Jan.1813 10Oct.	30May1811
Captain -	⎧ William Linsingen ⎜ George, *Baron* Decken ⎜ Ernest Poten ⎜ Frederick, *Bar.* Decken ⎨ Lewis Krauchenberg ⎜ Ernest Cordemann ⎜ Gustavus Schaumann ⎜ Gottlieb Baertling ⎜ Hieronimus, *Bar.* Wisch ⎩ —— Teuto	16Mar.1810 11July1811 12do. 18Nov. 13Jan.1813 20June 10Oct. 27Jan.1814 11Sept. 12do.	Major 11Nov.1813 6Apr.1814
Lieutenant	⎧ George Baring ⎜ Conrad Poten ⎜ Adolphus de Ilten ⎜ Leopold Schulze ⎜ Siegesm. Freudenthal ⎨ Frederick Holzermann ⎜ Henry Behrens ⎜ Ad.*Count*Wall.Gimborn ⎜ Frederick Wm. Trittau ⎜ FrederickBlumenhagen ⎩ George Leonhardt	13July1811 14do. 15do. 18Nov. 27Mar.1813 20June 19Nov. 27Jan.1814 6Apr. 12Sept. 31do.	Adjutant
Cornet - -	⎧ Lewis Versturme ⎜ Otto Heise ⎜ George Leopold Conze ⎜ ——*Count* Kielmansegge ⎨ Fra. *Baron* Olderhausen ⎜ Wm. Theodore Gibser ⎜ FrederickJacobRahlwes ⎜ Frederick de Quiter ⎩ William, *Baron* Hassel	4June1813 23July 11Nov. 4Jan.1814 27do. 14Feb. 26Apr. 12Sept. 13do.	27Oct. 1812 22July 1814
Paymaster -	James Wm. Longman	27Sept.1810	
Adjutant - -	Siegesm. Freudenthal	27Mar.1813	Lieut. 27Mar.1813
Quarter-Master	Henry Cohrs	20Dec.1811	
Surgeon - -	Frederick Fiorillo	28Oct.1813	9Sept.1813
Assistant Surg.	{ Frederick Deppe { G— C— Meyer	11Apr.1811 15Dec.1813	6Dec. 1805
Veterinary Surg.	—— Power	20July1811.	

The

2d Regiment of Hussars.		Rank in the	
Rank.	*Name.*	*Regiment.*	*Army.*
Col. Comm.	◉–Victor, *Baron* Alten	19Dec.1804	M.Gen.25July1810
Lieut. Colonel	Aug. *Baron* Linsingen	20June1813	4June 1813
Major - -	{ Werner, *Baron* Bussche	1Mar.1813	
	{ William Aly	26Jan.1814	
Captain -	⎧ George, *Baron* Donop	19Nov.1807	
	⎪ John Jansen	9July1811	2Aug.1810
	⎪ Urban Cleve	10do.	
	⎪ Diederick, *Bar.* During	23Aug.	
	⎨ George Meister	10Jan.1812	
	⎪ William *Baron* Issendorff	17Oct.	
	⎪ —— Stolzenberg	14Nov.	
	⎪ Anthony deStreeruwitz	22Mar.1814	11Nov.1813
	⎪ Lewis Koch	23do.	
	⎩ Augustus Krauckenberg	8Oct.	
Lieutenant	⎧ Hennan, *Baron* Estorff	11July1811	
	⎪ Daniel Borchers	23Aug.	
	⎪ Christopher Fahrenkohl	10Jan.1812	
	⎪ Frederick Grahn	28Mar.	
	⎪ Henry Gotz	do.	Adjutant
	⎨ Charles Wiebold	29Aug.	
	⎪ Frederick Roeders	17Oct.	
	⎪ Michael Löning	16Nov.	
	⎪ Moritz, *Baron* Thummel	10Mar.1813	
	⎪ —— Trefurt	23Mar.1814	
	⎩ —— de Witte	8Oct.	
Cornet - -	⎧ Charles Holmstrom	28Feb.1812	
	⎪ James Parodi	5June	
	⎪ James Hay	12Nov.	
	⎪ Herrmann Meyer	16Dec.	
	⎨ Maurice Prendergast	22Feb.1813	
	⎪ Henry Fricke	3Mar.	
	⎪ Ernest Soest	27Nov.	
	⎪ H— Westfeld	23Mar.1814	
	⎪ —— *Baron* Alton	27Apr.	
	⎩ —— Bothmer	20Oct.	
Paymaster -	William Mitchell	13Aug.1812	
Adjutant - -	Henry Gotz	22Nov.1811	Lieut. 28Mar.1812
Quarter-Master	—— Muller	16July1814	
Surgeon - -	Fred. Wm. Woolring	19Apr.1806	
Assistant Surg.	{ William Holscher	19Apr.1806	
	{ Joseph Ader	31Jan.1811	8June 1809
Veterinary Surg.	Frederick Eicke	2Jan.1807	

3d Regiment of Hussars.

Col. Comm.	✗Fred. Bar. deArentsschildt26Jan.1814	4June 1813
Lieut. Colonel	Lewis Meyer 10Oct.1813	
Major - -	George Krauchenberg 20June1813	30May 1811
	Ernest, Baron Linsingen 8Sept.1814	4June 1814
Captain -	Ulrich Hoyer 21Dec.1805	
	Arch. BaronKerssenbruch9June1807	
	Charles Bremer 29May1810	
	Frederick Poten 1Aug.	16Mar.1810
	George Jansen 25Oct.	
	Quintus, Baron Goeben 2May1811	
	Christian Heise 13Nov.1812	
	William Schnehen 15Sept.1813	20Sept.1811
	Ivan, Baron Hodenberg 16do.	
	Augustus Harling 8Oct.	
	George Meyer 27Dec.	
	William von der Hellen 17Feb.1814	
Lieutenant -	Gustavus Meyer 2May1811	
	Henry Brüggeman 16Feb.1812	Adjutant
	Francis Power 14Oct.	
	Eberhard Friedericks 12Nov.	
	Frederick Nanne 13do.	
	Henry de Humboldt 14do.	
	Augustus Reinecke 15do.	
	Joachim Thumann 15Sept.1813	
	Herman True 17do.	
	Christian Oelkers 9Oct.	
	Lewis Krause 10do.	
	Frederick Zimmermann 27Dec.	
	Eberhard Gerstlacher 17Feb.1814	
Cornet - -	—— Floyer 22Mar.1813	
	Frederick du Fresnoy 15Apr.	
	Philip Volbroth 6Aug.	
	Alex. Bar. Hammerstein 9Oct.	
	Rodolphus Friederichs 10do.	
	Conrad Dassell 22do.	
	Charles de Hellen 28Nov.	
	Aug. Baron Hodenberg 30do.	
	Hans, Baron Hodenberg 1Dec.	
	—— Baron Decken 27do.	
	William Deichmann 18Feb.1814	
	Julius Meyer 5May	
Paymaster -	John William Wieler 10Oct.1811	
Adjutant - -	Henry Brüggeman 4Jan.1810	Lieut. 16Feb.1812
Quarter Master	William Hoppe 4Jan.1810	
Surgeon - -	George Ripking 4Feb.1813	
Assistant Surg.	Lewis Wahl 16Dec.1805	
	Lewis Bauermeister 7Sept.1813	
Veterinary Surg.	Frederick Eickmann 12July1806	

The

Rank.	Name.	Regiment.	Army.
Light Infantry—(1st Battalion.)		Rank in the	
Col. Comm.	✗Charles, *Baron* Alten	22Dec.1804	M.Gen.25July1810
Lieut. Colonel	◉Lewis, *Baron* Bussche	8Sept.1813	29Mar.1809
Major - -	◉ { Frederick de Hartwig	4Apr.1809	Lt.Col.21June1813
	◉ { Hans, *Baron* Bussche	26Jan.1811	
Captain -	Ernest, *Baron* During	14Nov.1803	Major 30Sept.1813
	Henry Fred. Halseman	5Feb.1810	17July 1809
	George Lewis Rudorff	22do.	
	Frederick de Gilsa	16Apr.1811	
	Christian Wyneke	17Dec.	
	George Rautenberg	17Mar.1812	
	Gottlieb Thilo Holzerman	20do.	
	Wm. *Bar.* Heimbruch	20July1813	
	Gust. *Baron* Marschalk	26Jan.1814	
	Henry Marschalk	4Apr.	
Lieutenant -	A. A. *Baron* Goeben	25Nov.1809	
	Frederick, *Baron* Both	22Feb.1810	
	Ferdinand Schaedtler	19Jan.1811	
	Anton Albert	27do.	
	Augustus Wahrendorff	16Apr.	
	Frederick de Hartwig	17do.	
	William Fahle	14Mar.1812	Adjutant
	Christopher Heise	20do.	
	Frederick de Fincke	do.	
	George Breyman	do.	
	Herman Wolrabe	do.	
	Augustus von Quistorp	do.	
	William de Heugel	do.	
	John Baumgarten	20Nov.	
	Charles Kessler	20July1813	
	Ernest Fr. Adol. Koester	22Oct.	
	Nicholas de Minuisser	29Jan.1814	
	Harry Leonhart	25Mar.	
	Edgar Gibson	26do.	
	Stephen Macdonald	5Apr.	
	John Frederick Kuntze	28do.	

Ensign

| Light Infantry—(1st Battalion.) | | Rank in the | |
| Rank. | Name. | Regiment. | Army. |

Ensign -	John Henderson	29June1813	3Feb. 1813
	William Rube	7Aug.	
	Gustavus Best	25Nov.	
	Lewis, *Baron* Reben	26do.	
	Adol. Aug. de Gentzkow	27do.	
	Frederick Heise	29Jan.1814	
	H— Welling	16Apr.	
	Charles Behne	6May	
	Otto de Marschalk	16do.	
	Adolphus Heise	28do.	

Paymaster -	Adolphus Nagel	28Apr.1804	
Adjutant - -	William Fahle	5Apr.1810	Lieut. 14Mar.1812
Quarter-Master	Rudolph Hupeden	19June1810	
Surgeon - -	—— Grupe	25Dec.1805	
Assistant Surg.	—— Fehland	9Dec.1805	
	G— H— Duvel	12Dec.1807	

Facings black.

The

Rank.	Name.	Regiment.	Army.
Light Infantry—(2d Battalion.)		Rank in the	
Colonel -	◎— Colin Halkett	1Jan.1812	M.Gen. 4June1814
	Lt. Col. Comm.	9Feb.1805	
Lieut. Colonel	David Martin	26Jan.1811	
Major - -	* { Henry, *Prince* Reuss	23Oct.1812	
	{ George Baring	4Apr.1814	21June1812
	{ Adolphus Bosewell	5May1804	Major 4June1814
	◎— { Augustus Heise	17July1809	Major 21June1813
	{ George Haasman	18do.	
	{ Rudolph Pringle	25Sept.1810	
Captain -	{ William Stolte	24Apr.1811	
	{ Frederick Wyneken	8July	
	{ George Wackerhagen	24Dec.	
	{ Ernest Au.Holzermann	22Mar.1812	
	{ William Schaumann	26May	
	{ George Denecke -	7Feb.1814	
	{ Alexander Home	18July1809	
	{ G— T— Kessler	12Dec.	
	{ George Meyer	29Mar.1810	
	{ Charles Meyer	25Sept.	
	{ James M'Glashan	24Apr.1811	
	{ Lewis Behne	1July	
	{ William Atkin	2do.	
	{ Ohle Lindham	8do.	
	{ Bernhard Riefkugel	18Nov.	Adjutant
	{ M— T— H— Jobin	24Dec.	
Lieutenant	{ J. C. *Baron* Merveden	25Mar.1812	
	{ Thomas Carey	do.	
	{ Emanuel Bierdemann	do.	
	{ John Fred. de Meuron	19Aug.	
	{ G. Drummond Grœme	30do.	
	{ F— L— Ingersleben	2Sept.1813	31Oct. 1810
	{ Solomon Earl	11Oct.	
	{ Alexander Macbean	27Nov.	
	{ Rudolphus Hurtzig	7Feb.1814	
	{ Thomas William Doring	10Apr.	
	{ Frederick Schaumann	2May	

Ensign

Light Infantry—(2d Battalion.)		Rank in the	
Rank.	Name.	Regiment.	Army.

Ensign -	William Trinman	25Sept.1813	
	——— Bolomey	26do.	
	Frederick de Robertson	28Nov.	
	Augustus Friedricks	29do.	
	George Franck	5Jan.1814	
	Augustus Knop	14do.	
	William Smith	8Feb.	
	Charles de Goedke	17Mar.	
	Lewis Baring	11Apr.	
	Charles Meyer	12July	
Paymaster -	John Knight	20Jan.1814	
Adjutant - -	Bernhard Riefkugel	18Nov.1811	Lieut. 18Nov.1811
Quarter-Master	James Palmer	10Nov.1809	
Surgeon -	Ernest Nieter	22July1809	
	George Heisse	5Oct.1812	
Assistant Surg.	H— F— A— Muller	9Dec.1805	
	Henry Geske	3Mar.1812	

Facings black.

The

Infantry of the Line—(1st Battalion.)   Rank in the

Rank.	Name.	Regiment.	Army.
Col. Comm.	{ *His Royal Highness* A.D. *of* Cambridge,KG. 17 Nov. 1803		F. Mar. 26 Nov. 1813
Lieut. Col.	☜ Rudolphus Bodecker	22 Oct. 1810	
Major - -	{ Frederick de Robertson { George Coulon	27 Jan. 1811 17 Feb. 1813	
Captain -	⎰ Lewis de Borstell Charles, *Baron* During Andreas Schlutter Augustus de Saffe Frederick, *Baron* Goeben George, *Baron* Goeben Gerlach Schlutter Charles, *Baron* Holle Leopold de Rettberg Ernest,*Bar.* Hodenberg	17 Aug. 1809 8 Aug. 1810 27 Jan. 1811 11 Mar. 1812 17 do. 18 do. 15 Dec. 19 Feb. 1813 18 Aug. 22 Sept.	Major 21 June 1813
Lieutenant -	⎰ Lied. Lewis, *Baron* Holle Ferd. Christ. de Rössing Christ. H. *Baron* During Ludolph Kumme Thomas Allen Ernest Wilding Charles Lewis Best William Schroeder Diederich de Einem Frederick Schnath George Wickmann Charles Weyhe William Meyer Benjamin Fellowes William Wolff Adolphus Arentsschildt William Drysdale August Muller William Best —— Wilding Alexander Carmichael	3 Jan. 1809 29 May 17 Aug. 18 do. 8 Sept. 18 Mar. 1812 do. do. do. do. 30 Oct. 24 Nov. 25 do. 21 Feb. 1813 21 May 18 Aug. 19 do. 22 Sept. 26 Nov. 28 do. 6 May 1814	22 May 1811 Adjutant

Rank.	Name.	Regiment.	Army.

Infantry of the Line—(1st Battalion.)   Rank in the

Rank.	Name.	Regiment.	Army.
Ensign	Francis Leslie	31 May 1813	
	August, *Baron* Le Fort	9 Sept.	
	August von Brandis	6 Jan. 1814	
	—— Heisse	7 do.	
	Hartwich von Lücken	1 Feb.	
	Augustus Fred. Kersting	19 do.	
	George Lodemann	18 Mar.	
	Adolphus Beaulieu	21 do.	
	Augustus Reiche	12 Apr.	
	Cha. Aug. von der Hellin	7 May	
Paymaster	Thomas Teighe	8 Sept. 1804	
Adjutant	Frederick Schnath	20 Sept. 1810	Lieut. 18 Mar. 1812
Quarter-Master	John Carolin	6 June 1811	
Surgeon	Gottlieb Wetsig	12 Feb. 1813	
Assistant Surg.	—— Hartzig	7 Dec 1805	
	Philip Langeheineken	31 Jan. 1811	

Facings blue.

The

Rank.	Name.	Regiment.	Army.
Infantry of the Line—(2d Battalion.)		Rank in the	

Col. Comm.	Adol. *Baron* Barsse	21 Dec. 1804	M.Gen. 25 July 1810
Lieut. Colonel	⊚Adolphus, *Baron* Beck	8 Sept. 1813	1 Jan. 1812
Major - -	{ George Muller	18 Feb. 1813	
	{ Gebhardus Timæus	26 Apr. 1814	20 Oct. 1812
Captain - -	{ Frederick Breymann	11 Nov. 1803	Major 4 June 1814
	Wm. *Baron* Decken	13 Dec. 1806	
	Augustus Hartman	3 Jan. 1809	
	Frederick Purgold	4 Sept.	
	George Tilee	5 Mar. 1812	
	Charles Beurmann	18 Feb. 1813	
	Claus Wynecke	4 June	
	Fred. *Baron* Wenckstern	17 Aug.	
	Frederick Elderhorst	26 Apr. 1814	
	George Wolkenharr	27 do.	
Lieutenant - -	{ Adolphus Holle	16 Nov. 1807	
	Claus *Baron* Decken	17 do.	
	William Kuhlman	7 Sept. 1809	
	——— Teensch	17 Mar. 1812	
	——— Fleisch	do.	
	Adolphus Heise	do.	Adjutant
	Augustus Schmidt	do.	
	Charles Billeb	do.	
	——— Meyer	1 Oct.	
	Augustus Kathman	15 do.	
	George Frederick Pascal	19 do.	
	Adolphus Kessler	19 Feb. 1813	
	William Dawson	6 May	
	Alexander Patterson	4 June	
	James Hamilton	17 Aug.	
	Patrick Gairdner	30 Jan. 1814	
	C— Fischer	17 Mar.	
	Francis La Roche	27 do.	
	George Fabricius	29 Apr.	
	George Lowson	30 do.	
	Augustus Ferd. Ziel	17 June	

M m 2

Ensign

Rank.	Name.	Regiment.	Army.

Infantry of the Line—(2d Battalion.)   Rank in the

Rank.	Name.	Regiment.	Army.
Ensign - -	Lewis Henry de Sichart	15Feb.1814	
	Charles Lewis de Sichart	16do.	
	Adolphus Lynch	1Apr.	
	——— Distlehorst	14do.	
	Edward Cropp	28do.	
	Gustavus Hartman	8May	
	Henry Bergmann	17do.	
	Henry Garvens	24do.	
	Tils von Uslar	29do.	
	August Luhning	17June	
Paymaster -	Thomas Small	8Sept.1814	
Adjutant - -	Adolphus Heise	17June1814	Lieut. 17Mar.1812
Quarter-Master	John Silvester	21Mar.1804	
Surgeon - -	Charles Thompson	3Sept.1805	
Assistant Surg.	——— Von Bremen	25May1805	
	——— Rathje	7Dec.	

Facings blue.

The

Rank.	Name.	Regiment.	Army.

Infantry of the Line—(3d Battalion.) Rank in the

Rank.	Name.	Regiment.	Army.
Col. Comm. -	Henry de Hinüber	9July1805	M.Gen. 4June1811
Lieut. Colonel	Frederick de Wissell	8Sept.1814	4June1813
Major - -	{ Frederick de Lutterman 25Jan.1811 { Anthony Boden 3Apr.1814		
Captain -	{ William Dammers 14Sept.1804 —— Kuckuck 15do. Geo. *Baron* Honhorst 30Oct.1807 —— de Dreves 18Jan.1808 Augustus Curren 13Dec. Eberhard Lüeder 14Sept.1810 Charles Leschen 6Mar.1812 William de Schleicher 9do. Frederick Diedel 28Aug.1813 Albertus Cordemann 8Sept.1814		Major 4June1814 Major 4June1814
Lieutenant -	{ Justus Tormin 12Jan.1806 Frederick Erdman 25do. Hans, *Baron* Uslar 26do. George Appuhn 27do. Lewis Pauly 28do. Cha. *Baron* Heimburg 22Aug. George, *Baron* Weyhe 30Oct.1807 William Appuhn 14Nov.1809 Charles Brauns 14Sept.1810 —— de Ieinsen 16Apr.1811 Christian de Soden 18Mar.1812 Lorentz Heise do. Fred. Bernhard Schneider do. Weypart de Laffert do. Augustus Kuckuck do. Julius Brinckmann 11May Henry Dehnel 20May1813 Louis Bachellé 20Sept. Frederick Leschen 22Nov. Edward Harry Kuckuck 8Dec. Thomas Lutting 13Sept.1814		Adjutant

Ensign

Infantry of the Line—(3d Battalion.)   Rank in the

Rank.	Name.	Regiment.	Army.

	Frederick de Storren	18Feb.1813	
	Frederick Schlutter	6May	
	William Brandis	25July	
	Cha.Aug.von derSoden	30Nov.	
Ensign - -	August Wm. Kuckuck	8Jan.1814	
	Richard Hupeden	9do.	
	Ernest Rodewald	17Feb.	
	Adolphus Breyman	20Mar.	
	Frederick de Rönne	21do.	
	Ernest John Beurmann	13Sept.	

Paymaster - -	William Anderson	13May1813	
Adjutant - -	Fred. Bern. Schneider	1Apr.1814	Lieut. 18Mar.1812
Quarter-Master	—— Levin	24Aug.1810	
Surgeon - -	Haman Deppe	1Dec.1804	
Assistant Surg.	—— Suntermann	25Oct.1805	
	Francis Dagenhart	7Oct.1813	

Facings blue.

Rank.	Name.	Regiment.	Army.

Infantry of the Line—(4th Battalion.)   Rank in the

Rank.	Name.	Regiment.	Army.
Col. Comm.	◉–Siegesmund, *Baron* Low	17Aug.1809	M.Gen.25July1810
Lieut. Colonel	Charles du Plat	30June1805	Col. 4June1813
Major - -	{ Frederick Reh	26Oct.1810	
	{ George Chuden	8Sept.1814	4June1814
Captain -	{ Henry Meyer	22Sept.1804	Major 4June1814
	George Lene	15Nov.	Major 4June1814
	William Heinreich	31Mar.1807	
	George Ludewig	13Dec.1808	
	Augustus Rumann	2Feb.1809	
	Augustus de Brandis	7Mar.1812	
	—— Heise	10do.	
	Frederick Ludewig	29Oct.	
	Frederick Hotzen	4Mar.1813	
	Conrad Schlichthorst	31Jan.1814	
Lieutenant	{ Frederick Otto	25Jan.1806	
	Frederick Kessler	28do.	
	Christian Bacmeister	10Aug.1807	
	William Pape	13Oct.	
	Gaspar, *Baron* Both	13Dec.1808	
	William, *Baron* Rantzau	3Feb.1809	Adjutant
	Augustus Freudenthal	2May1810	
	Frederick Wm. Krietsch	11Feb.1811	
	Christ. Lichtenberger	1Jan.1812	
	Adolphus de Hartwig	10Mar.	
	Charles de Lasperg	19do.	
	Charles de Jeinsen	do.	
	—— Rumann	do.	
	Adolphus,*Baron* Langwerth	do.	
	Adolphus Ludewig	do.	
	Henry Witte	31Oct.	
	George Siebold	4Jan.1813	
	Wm. Lewis de la Farque	20Feb.	
	Ernestus Brinckmann	4Mar.	
	Frederick Lesperg	8Oct.	
	William Shea	21Apr.1814	

Ensign

Infantry of the Line—(4th Battalion.)   Rank in the

Rank.	Name.	Regiment.	Army.
Ensign - -	Frederick Heitmuller	14Feb.1813	
	William Luning	7May	
	D— Tamm	14do.	
	Fred. Augustus Schulze	15June	
	Frederick Brandis	26July	
	James Mannsback	21Sept.	
	William Schaefer	8Dec.	
	Ferdinand von Uslar	30May1814	
	Arnold Appuhn	6June	
	Theodore Kronhelm	10do.	
Paymaster -	Thomas Jones	8Dec.1804	
Adjutant - -	William, *Baron* Rantzau	15Apr.1811	Lieut. 3Feb.1809
Quarter-Master	Augustus Becker	25Sept.1804	
Surgeon - -	George Gunther	24May1805	
Assistant Surg.	John D— Mathaei	12Dec.1805	
	J— H— Wicke	28Feb.1812	

Facings blue.

| *Infantry of the Line—(5th Battalion.)* | | Rank in the | |
| Rank. | Name. | Regiment. | Army. |

Col. Comm.	ⓒChrist. *Baron* Ompteda	17Aug.1813	4June1813
Lieut. Colonel	Wm. *Baron* Linsingen	8Sept.1814	4June1813
Major - - ⓒ ⓒ	Charles Aly	9Oct.1810	
	Arnold Gerber	10Apr.1811	Lt.Col.21Sept.1813
Captain - -	Lucas Bacmeister	7Nov.1803	Major 4June1814
	Christian de Wurmb	7Dec.1809	
	Lewis Lodders	8do.	
	Frederick Sander	15Mar.1812	
	William Meyer	19do.	
	Frederick Heinemann	22Sept.	
	William Rautenberg	15Oct.	
	George Notting	16do.	
	George Hagemann	16Dec.	
	Char. *Baron* Linsingen	16Apr.1813	
Lieutenant -	Christian, *Baron* Goeben	19July1808	
	Ernest, *Baron* Düring	14Feb.1809	
	Charles de Bothmer	1Aug.	
	Eberhard de Brandis	18Oct.	
	Charles Berger	18July1810	
	Augustus Meyer	1Dec.	
	George Buhse	27Sept.1811	
	Adolphus Rothhard	20Mar.1812	
	George Schauroth	do.	
	Charles de Witte	do.	
	Augustus Winckler	do.	
	Charles Schlaeger	do.	
	Joseph Korschann	25Sept.	
	Henry Llewellyn	20Oct.	
	George Klingsohr	16Dec.	
	Theo. Gallenberg	17Feb.1813	26Sept.1811
	Louis Giesmann	16Apr.	
	Lewis Taenicke	16Mar.1814	
	Lewis Schuck	25Apr.	Adjutant
	Edmund Wheatley	26do.	
	Henry Vassmer	27do.	

N n   Ensign

Rank.	Name.	Regiment.	Army.
	Infantry of the Line—(5th Battalion.)		Rank in the

Ensign - -	George Wischmann	26Jan.1813	
	Bernard Croon	10Feb.	
	Charles Weiss	11do.	
	Ferdinand Scharnhorst	27Mar.	
	Julius de Reinbold	11Oct.	
	William Walther	22Nov.	
	Cha. Christian Winckler	10Jan.1814	
	William Lewis Klingsohr	22Mar.	
	Ernest Baring	25May	
	Adolphus Scharnhorst	7June	
Paymaster	Henry Knight	2July1805	
Adjutant -	Lewis Schuck	15Oct.1812	Lieut. 25Apr.1814
Quarter-Master	Frederick Armbrecht	19Dec.1810	
Surgeon -	Lewis Stuntz	14Aug.1805	
Assistant Surg.	—— Kohrs	6Dec.1805	
	G— H— Gerson	9Aug.1811	

Facings blue.

The

Rank.	Name.	Regiment.	Army.

Infantry of the Line—(6th Battalion.)   Rank in the

Rank.	Name.	Regiment.	Army.
Col. Comm. -	Augustus Honstedt	15Dec.1804	M.Gen. 25July1810
Lieut. Colonel	Wm. de Ulmenstein	25Jan.1811	23Oct. 1810
Major - -	{ Ferd. *Baron* Ompteda 17Feb.1809 { Melchior, *Baron* Decken 9Sept.1814		Lt.Col. 4June1814 4June1814
Captain - -	⎧ Lewin de Harling 20July1804 ⎪ George Wolkenhaar 18Feb.1809 ⎪ Cha. *Baron* Kronenfeldt 20Sept.1810 ⎨ Frederick de Rougemont 11Feb.1812 ⎪ Charles de Brandis 14Mar. ⎪ Christian Kettler 16do. ⎪ Christian Anthony 11May ⎪ Ernest, *Baron* Magius 25Jan.1814 ⎪ Christ. Struver 3Apr. ⎩ Eberhard Kunze 9Sept.		Major 4June1814 23Apr. 1805
Lieutenant -	⎧ George, *Baron* During 2June1806 ⎪ Barth. *Baron* Honstedt 19Nov.1807 ⎪ Joseph Kersting 16Jan.1808 ⎪ John Anton Schaedtler 18Feb.1809 ⎪ Ernest,*Baron*Heimburg 16Mar. ⎪ Otto Schaumann 20Sept.1810 ⎪ Arnold Volger 27Jan.1811 ⎪ Christian Fedden 15Apr. ⎪ William Baring 11Feb.1812 ⎨ Mathias Depps 25do. ⎪ Frederick Hurtzig 21Mar. ⎪ William Benthein do. ⎪ Henry Kirch do. ⎪ Ernest Mensing do. ⎪ Ludewig Klauer do. ⎪ Lewis Benne 13May ⎪ Ferdinand Schaefer,*jun.* 28Jan.1814 ⎪ Francis, *Baron* Acton 4Apr. ⎪ C. Lud. *Baron* Ompteda 26May ⎪ Charles Frederick Apfel 11Sept. ⎩ Edward Martin Muller 19Nov.		Adjutant

Infantry of the Line—(6th Battalion.)	Rank in the

Rank.	Name.	Regiment.	Army.

	⎧ Christian Seelhorst	16Oct.1812	
	⎪ Augustus Fleischmann	29Apr.1813	
	⎪ Adolphus W. Stieglitz	22Mar.1814	
	⎪ Alexander Antran	2Apr.	
Ensign -	⎨ L.Albrecht,*Bar.*Ompteda	15do.	
	⎪ Adolphus von Uslar	31May	
	⎪ William von Linsingen	1June	
	⎪ Herman Fred. Schwenke	8do.	
	⎪ Ferdinand de Wurmb	11Sept.	
	⎩ George de Ulmenstein	19Nov.	

Paymaster -	Henry James Amey	1Mar.1806	
Adjutant - -	Otto Schaumann	10July1813	Lieut. 20Sept.1810
Quarter-Master	John Charles Kruger	4Jan.1813	
Surgeon -	Henry Newman	14Aug.1811	
Assistant Surg. ⎧	——— Rohstradt	30Dec.1805	
⎩	S— J— Einthoven	29Feb.1812	

Facings blue.

Infantry of the Line—(7th Battalion.)		Rank in the	
Rank.	*Name.*	*Regiment.*	*Army.*
Col. Comm. -	Fred. Baron Drechsel	21Jan.1806	Lt.Gen. 4June1811
Lieut. Col.	◎-Hugh Halkett	22Sept.1812	1Jan. 1812
Major - -	George Soest	20Sept.1810	
	William Chuden	28Aug.1813	
Captain - -	—— Ruperti	15Jan.1808	
	William Isenbart	10Sept.1809	
	Frederick de Loesecke	9Oct.1810	
	William Delius	24do.	5Apr. 1806
	William Volger	12Mar.1811	
	Frederick de Siechhart	23July	
	Arnold Backmeister	21Mar.1812	
	Charles Pringle	17Feb.1813	Major 4June1814
	Frederick de Sebisch	1Nov.	
	Frederick Munter	8Dec.	21Sept.1810
Lieutenant -	Ferdinand de Hugo	9Nov.1807	
	Gottlieb de Hartwieg	17Jan.1808	
	George Balk	18do.	
	Charles de Windheim	4Dec.	
	—— De Mutio	21Jan.1809	4Jan. 1809
	John Stutzer	28Oct.	Adjutant
	—— Luttermann	18Jan.1810	
	John Bohn	9July	
	Frederick Conring	9Oct.	
	Augustus de Offen	12Mar.1811	
	Frederick Diebitsch	23July	
	Geo. Wm. de Bachellé	23Mar.1812	
	Charles Poten	do.	
	William Corlien	do.	
	Theodore von Sebisch	do.	
	Frederick Ebell	do.	
	Anthony Ruden	15July	
	Charles Helmrich	20Aug.1813	
	William Leopold	1Nov.	
	Charles Blottnitz	2Apr.1814	
	Christian Eicchorn	3do.	

Ensign

Rank.	Name.	Regiment.	Rank in the Army.

Infantry of the Line—(7th Battalion.)   Rank in the Army.

Rank.	Name.	Regiment.	Army.
Ensign - -	—— Hunt	11Dec.1812	
	August Steffens	15Feb.1813	
	William Losecke	8May	
	Erich Backhaus	18July	
	Gottlieb Siickow	23Mar.1814	
	Adolphus Grahn	6Apr.	
	Ernest F. C. Neuschafer	19do.	
	—— Backhaus	29do.	
	Augustus vonHodenburg	2June	
	——— Martin	9do.	
Paymaster -	Henry Cowper	1Mar.1806	
Adjutant - -	John Stutzer	21Apr.1814	Lieut. 28Oct.1809
Quarter-Master	Gustavus Hagenberg	18June1810	
Surgeon - -	Francis Herring	11Apr.1811	
Assistant Surg. {	Henry Schuchardt	16Jan.1814	

Facings blue

The

Rank.	Name.	Rank in the Regiment.	Rank in the Army.
Infantry of the Line—(8th Battalion.)			
Col. Comm. -	Peter Du Plat	18Sept.1804	M.Gen. 25July1810
Lieut. Colonel	Charles Best	11May1812	1Jan. 1812
Major -	John de Schroeder	1July1806	Lt.Col. 4June1813
	Charles de Petersdorff	6May1814	
Captain -	Julius Brinkmann	30June1806	
	Siegmund Brauns	18Aug.1809	
	William de Voigt	10Apr.1811	
	Frederick de Becker	20Aug.	
	Henry Oehme	26Mar.1812	
	Frederick Marburg	27do.	
	Augustus, *Baron* Wense	18Feb.1813	26Oct. 1810
	Cha.William Rougemont	5June	
	T.*Baron* Westernhagen	10Sept.1814	
	George Delius	11do.	
Lieutenant	George Hotzen	1July1806	
	Frederick Luderitz	5Aug.	
	Charles Poten	9Sept.	
	Lewis,*Baron*Hodenberg	31Mar.1807	
	Wm. *Baron* Marenholz	15Jan.1808	
	Ernest de Weyhe	18Aug.1809	
	William Wilkins	19Dec.1810	
	Frederick Brinckmann	10Apr.1811	Adjutant
	Dav. Fred. de Bachellé	3June	
	George de Witte	20Aug.	
	Christian Sadler	3Mar.1812	
	FrederickWm.Ziermann	27do.	
	Ernest Grahn	do.	
	Otto Brüel	do.	
	Franz Schmits	do.	
	Bernhard Bertram	do.	
	Valentine Buchler	do.	
	Henry Schlichting	5June1813	
	Frederick Muller	1Apr.1814	
	Franz Schultz	10Sept.	
	Augustus Helmrich	12do.	

Ensign

Infantry of the Line—(8th Battalion.)   Rank in the

Rank.	Name.	Regiment.	Army.
Ensign - -	Frederick Dorendorff	12July1812	
	Gottlieb Künott	13do.	
	William de Murreau	11Oct.	
	Edward Stanley	12do.	
	A— Spiel	23Mar.1814	
	FrederickHenry Muller	13Apr.	
	Henry Seffers	3June	
	Ernest Bornemann	10Sept.	
	George Lunde	12do.	
	Frederick Sander	25Nov.	
Paymaster -	James Harrison	12July1806	
Adjutant - -	Frederick Brinckmann	27Dec.1813	Lieut. 10Apr.1811
Quarter-Master	——— Tobing	14Dec.1807	
Surgeon - -	Augustus Ziermann	17June1806	
Assistant Surg.	Ernest Sander	4July1806	
	Lewis Ziermann	5do.	

Facings blue.

The

Rank.	Name.	Regiment.	Rank in the Army.
Artillery.			
Col. Comm. -	Frederick,*Baron*Decken	28July1803	Lt.Gen. 4June1814
Lieut. Colonel	Augustus Röttiger	25Nov.1808	Col. 4June1814
Major - ✖←	⎰ Julius Hartmann	12Apr.1806	Lt.Col.17Aug.1812
	⎱ Henry Brückmann	26Nov.1808	Lt.Col. 4June1814
1st Captain ◎	⎧ Henry Kuhlmann	10Aug.1804	Major 4June1814
	⎪ Augustus Sympher	17Nov.	Major 4June1814
	⎪ George Gesenius	20Mar.1805	
	⎨ Victor de Arentsschildt	26Nov.1808	Major 25Nov.1813
	⎪ Bernard Busman	23Nov.1809	2July 1805
	⎪ Cha. *Baron* Witzleben	11Dec.1812	23Dec.1805
	⎪ Charles de Rettberg	25Nov.1813	12Apr.1806
	⎩ Andrew Cleves	26Mar.1814	5June1807
2d Captain	⎧ Lewis Daniel	26Nov.1808	
	⎪ George Wiering	23Nov.1809	
	⎪ Charles Meyer	24do.	
	⎨ William Braun	11Dec.1812	
	⎪ Augustus Bindseil	12do.	
	⎪ Lewis Jasper	25Nov.1813	
	⎩ William de Schade	26do.	
	Ernest Luckow	26Mar.1814	
1st Lieutenant	⎧ Frederick Erythropel	23May1806	
	⎪ Victor Preussner	5June1807	
	⎪ Ferdinand de Brandis	28Sept.	
	⎪ Henry Mielmann	26Nov.1808	
	⎪ Theodore Speckmann	24Nov.1809	
	⎪ Lewis Stockmann	19Sept.1810	
	⎪ Ernest Thielen	16Apr.1811	Adjutant
	⎨ Charles de Schulzen	11Dec.1812	
	⎪ Anthony Hugo	12do.	
	⎪ Henry Stockman	13do.	
	⎪ William Rummel	14do.	
	⎪ William de Goeben	25Nov.1813	
	⎪ William de Scharnhorst	26do.	
	⎪ Frederick Dreschler	27do.	
	⎪ Augustus Pfannkuche	28do.	
	⎪ Henry Hartmann	26Mar.1814	
	⎩ George Meyer	29Apr.	

Rank.	Name.	Rank in the Regiment.	Army.
2d Lieutenant	Henry Bostelmann	31Jan.1812	
	Henry Heisse	30June	
	Frederick Lucke	11Dec.	
	Frederick Seinecke	12do.	
	Henry Wohler	13do.	
	Lewis Haardt	14do.	
	——— Heisse	15do.	
	Lewis Scharnhorst	15Nov.1813	
	Lewis de Wissell	30do.	
	Cha. Hermann Ludowieg	16Feb.1814	
	Edward Hartmann	23Mar.	
	Augustus Capell	19May	
	John Fred. Schlichthorst	20do.	
	Edward Michaelis	20Oct.	
	Charles du Plat	25Nov.	
	Franz Röttiger	26do.	
Captain Commissary	Frederick Rehwinckell	28Sept.1807	
Paymaster -	John Blundstone	9Apr.1805	
Adjutant -	Ernest Thielen	15Apr.1813	1st Lt, 16Apr.1811
Quarter-Master	Henry Hoyns	5Feb.1807	
Surgeon - -	Henry Kels	18Dec.1805	
Assistant Surg. of Horse	Christopher Schmersahl	15Nov.1809	
	George Crone	10Feb.1810	
Assistant Surg. of Foot	C— Rentzhausen	15Apr.1813	
	William Beyer	16Jan.1814	
Veterinary Surg.	John Fred. Hilmer	22Aug.1806	

Engineers.

Rank.	Name.	Rank in the Regiment.	Army.
1st Captain	Augustus Berensbach	7Apr.1807	Major 4June1814
	Victor Prott	11Feb.1809	23Mar.1805
	Charles Ernest Appuhn	1Apr.1814	25Nov.1808
2d Captain	Charles Wedekind	12Oct.1809	
	George Fred. Meineke	22Feb.1811	
	Augustus Schweitzer	15July1812	
	William Müller	13Dec.	
	Frederick de Gaugreben	5Mar.1814	
1st Lieutenant	William Unger	14Aug.1811	
	John Lattermann	21Nov.1812	
2d Lieutenant			

Rank.	Name.	Regiment.	Rank in the Army.	

Staff.

Brigade Major	Henry Wiegmann	24Oct.1811	Capt.	24Oct.1811
	Ernest, *Bar*.Kronenfeldt	20Feb.1813	Capt.	20Feb.1813
	Mauritz Claud	17Sept.	Capt.	17Sept.1813
	John, *Bar*.Dachenhausen	8Dec.	Capt.	8Dec.1813
	Gottfried de Einem	28Apr.1814	Capt.	28Apr.1814
	Charles de Bobers	13Sept.	Capt.	13Sept.1814

Chaplain	George Henry Gundell	17Mar.1804		
	Frederick Rambke	do.		
	Frederick Buchholz	20June1806		
	——— Pohse	20July		
	Henry Andrew Meyer	25Dec.1807		

Agent, Messrs. Greenwood, Cox and Hammersley.

Rank.	Name.	Regiment.	Rank in the Army.
Colonel - -	{ *His Serene Highness* { W.D.*of* BrunswickOels 25Sept.1809		*Lt.Gen. 1July1809
Cavalry.	*(Hussars.)*		
Col. Comm.	*Wilhelm de Dörnberg 25Sept.1809		*M.Gen. 1Jan.1812
Lieut. Colonel	*Ernst de Schrader	26Sept.1809	
Major -	* { Wilhelm von Wessein 27Sept.1809 * { Carl von Tempsky 28do.		*Lt.Col. 4June1814 *Lt.Col. 4June1814
Captain -	* { Carl Pott 26Sept.1809 * { Wilhelm von Wulfen 28do. * { Alexander Errickson 7Mar.1811 *{ ——— Foster do. { Carle von Gaffron 11June1812 * { ——— Girsewald 4Nov.1813		
Lieutenant	* { Ludwig von Trauwitz 26Sept.1809 * { Wilhelm Diebell do. * { Henry Schaeffer do. * { Wilhelm Butze do. *{ Leopold Marsch de Wedel do. *{ William von Holy do. { Ernst Heisinger 19June1811 { George Scholtz 13Jan.1813 { Charles Platz 14do. { William de Lubeck 4Nov. { David Leibing 5May1814		Adjutant
Cornet - -	{ ——— Missoblett 22July1813 { ——— Loader 1Dec. { ——— Meckells 2do. { ——— Muller 10Mar.1814 { Frederick Pott 5May		
Paymaster -	John Gold	9Aug.1810	
Adjutant - -	Wilhelm Butze	6Dec.1810	*Lieut.26Sept.1809
Quarter-Master	Ferdenand de Bothmer	21June1810	
Surgeon - -	Henry Waiblinger	15Mar.1810	
AssistantSurg.	{ Adrian Gelpke 25Mar.1810 { Frederick Flade do.		
Veterinary Surg.	Frederick von Ohlen	7Feb.1811	

Regimentals green.—Facings black.

Agent, Messrs. Greenwood, Cox and Hammersley.

The

Infantry.		Rank in the	
Rank.	Name.	Regiment.	Army.

Colonel - { His Serene Highness W.D.of BrunswickOels25Sept.1809 } — *Lt.Gen.1July1809

Lieut. Col. ⊛* { J. H. C. de Bernewitz 14Feb.1811 / Fred.Aug. de Hertsberg 28May1812 } — *M.Gen.1Jan.1812

Major - *{ Franz de Fragstein 26Sept.1809 / Frederick de Dornberg 28May1812 } — *Lt.Col.4June1814

Captain -
* { —— Doebel 27Sept.1809
* Frideric Aug. de Proestler 29do.
* Frideric Ludwig Wacholtz do.
* Charles, *Count* Schönfeld do.
* Frideric Henry Wolfradt16Aug.1810
* Hen. von Branderstein 20Feb.1811
*{ Frederic von Steinwher 21do.
* W— de Gillern 4June1812
* William Kock 10Sept.
* William Unruh 26Nov.
* Ernst Henry Foerster 10Dec.
* Julius Lysnewsky 29July1813
* { G— Norman 31Mar.1814

Lieutenant
* { Ernst Palzensky 27Sept.1809
* Frideric Carl Thiele do.
* Wilhelm von Heyde do.
* Carl Wihelm vou Berner do.
Frederick Mosqua 16Aug.1810
Gustavus von Hülsen do.
Franz von Thieschwitz 20Feb.1811
Lud.von Schwartzenberg 21do.
F— S— Hausler 27June
{ Albert von Griersheim 27Aug.
Carl Gruttemann 17Oct.
Augustus Mohner 5Feb.1812
William Ritterholm 22July
William Meyer 23do.
—— Zweifel 27Aug.
Frederick Ritterholm 10Sept.
Charles Muller 17do.
—— Schneider 15Oct.
{ Augustus Gruttemann 10Dec.

Lieutenant

Rank.	Name.	Rank in the Regiment.	Army.
Lieutenant	Henry Schulze	18Mar.1813	
	Otto Broemsen	6May	
	—— Bosse	29July	
	W— Rauch	16Sept.	
	Lewis Wirth	10Nov.	
	—— Biermon	11do.	
	W— de Bredow	6Jan.1814	
	Julius Gerger	31Mar.	
	Carl Haberland	1Apr.	
Ensign - -	John Cornelius Schot	1Apr.1813	
	Wilhelm Brandenstein	8July	
	Augustus Leuterding	5Aug.	
	—— Melihon	7Oct.	
	Michael Charles Edwards	28do.	
	William von Bernewitz	1Dec.	
	Caspar von Bodenstoff	2do.	
Paymaster -	Griffin Jones	21Oct.1813	
Adjutant - -			
Quarter-Master	—— Randle	23May1811	
Surgeon - -	Charles Websarg	12Aug.1813	
Assistant Surg.	Augustus Nave	26Mar.1812	
	Lewis Heimburg	28Oct.1813	

Regimentals green.—Facings black.

Agent, Messrs. Greenwood, Cox and Hammersley.

Permitted to bear on their Colours and Appointments a " SPHINX," with the word " EGYPT," in commemoration of the Campaign of 1801.

Rank.	Name.	Regiment.	Rank in the Army.
Colonel - -	Fra. *Baron* Rottenburgh	2Sept.1813	M.Gen.25July1810
Lieut. Colonel	{ J. *Baron* de Sonnenberg 25Sept.1802		M.Gen. 4June1814
	Frederick, *Baron* Eben 7Mar.1811		Col. 4June1814
Major - -	{ Charles de Vogelsang 25Sept.1802		Lt.Col. 25July1810
	Phelepp, *Baron* de Capol 30Oct.1806		Lt.Col. 1Jan.1812
	Charles Philip de Bossett 15Oct.1808		Lt.Col. 4June1814
Captain -	Anthony Mohr	9Dec.1794	Lt.Col. 1Jan.1812
	Albert Steiger	27Aug. 99	Major 4June1811
	Henry Ryhiner	25Dec.1802	Major 4June1813
	Nicholas Muller	5Jan.1804	Major 4June1814
	Joseph Berbié	10Oct.	Major 4June1814
	Joseph Glutz	4Apr.1805	
	Benoit Ryhiner	3Sept.1807	
	Amantz de Sury	6Oct.1808	
	Lewis Muller	25Jan.1810	
	Antoine Courant	21Mar.1811	5Apr. 1810
	Francis Glutz	29Oct.1812	
	Frederick de Ronsillion	21Apr.1814	
Lieutenant -	Ulisse Gouquelberg	20Oct.1804	
	Jacob Frey	22Dec.	
	Joseph Tugginer	30Oct.1806	
	Conrad Müller	4Nov.1807	Adjutant
	Fost. de Müller	5do.	
	Stephen de Planta	3Dec.	
	Amantz Glutz	23May1808	
	Auguste de Courten	15Dec.	
	Michael Crumm	17do.	
	J— P— Sorgenfrey	21do.	
	Hector de Salis	22do.	
	Charles Dutheil	13Apr.1809	
	Peter Maul	24Jan.1810	
	Charles Pannack	25do.	
	—— de Hertenstein	16May	
	Gabriel de May	17do.	
	Edmund Tugginer	26Feb.1811	
	Otto Henry Salinger	28do.	
	Maurice d'Erlach	29Aug.	
	Cha. Fred. Graumann	20Aug.1812	
	Joseph Gürtler	9Dec.	

Lieutenant

		Rank in the	
Rank.	Name.	Regiment.	Army.

Lieutenant -	⎧ Alexander Gingins	10Dec.1812
	⎪ E— Tugginer	29Sept.1813
	⎨ Nicholas Stutzer	30do.
	⎪ Charles Troit	28Apr.1814
	⎪ William Davis	26Oct.
	⎩ J— Baptiste Phil. Stutzer 27do.

Ensign - -	⎧ —— Meyer	11Apr.1811
	⎪ Xavier Schmid	9Dec.1812
	⎪ Charles Gingins	10do.
	⎨ Patricio Schmid	11do.
	⎪ John O'Gorman	29Apr.1813
	⎪ Alexander Lewis Routh 30Sept.
	⎪ John Henniker	9Dec.
	⎩ George Geronei	28Apr.1814

Chaplain - -	William M'Donald	1July1812		
Paymaster -	Charles Cox	29Jan.1806		
Adjutant - -	Conrad Müller	21Oct.1804	Lieut.	4Nov.1807
Quarter-Master	Enoch Guignard	25Nov.1801		
Surgeon - -	J— A— Romheld	22Dec.1804		
Assistant Surg. ⎰	Wilhelm Heyn	22Dec.1804		
⎱	Frederick Herring	3July1806		

Facings light blue.—Lace silver.

Agent, Mr. Disney, No. 26, Parliament-street.

Meuron's

Rank.	Name.	Regiment.	Rank in the Army.
Colonel -	◎-Geo. Townsend Walker	24Oct.1812	M.Gen. 4June1811
Lieut. Colonel	Meuron Bayard	17June1813	4June1813
Major - -	{ C. E. de May Duzisdorff	17June1813	
	{ Thomas Fane	8Dec.1814	
Captain - -	{ Abraham Lewis Peters	19Feb.1808	
	Frederick Matthey	25Apr.	
	Jean Pierre Sam. Fauche	26do.	
	Rudolph Amédée de May	28Feb.1810	
	Charles de Rham	1Mar.	
	Nicholas Fuchs	21Mar.1811	Major 4June1814
	P. D'Ordet Dorsonnens	14May1812	
	Francis Louis Bourgeois	17June1813	
	William Bock	2Sept.	
	{ George, *Viscount* Forbes	6Oct.1814	Lt.Col. 1Jan.1812
Lieutenant	{ John Peter Lardy	25Apr.1808	
	Frederick Henry Perret	26do.	
	Cha. J— Zehnfenning	9Mar.1809	
	Francis de Graffenried	1Mar.1810	
	John Witmer	5Apr.	
	C— Frederick Lardy	27Sept.	
	Frederick de Bibra	25Apr.1811	1Sept.1806
	Johan Theo. de Mesany	26do.	10Sept.1806
	Nich. Theo. de Gumoens	27do.	
	Charles de Gumoens	28do.	
	Ant. Fred. de Graffenried	30do.	
	A. N. J. D. de Montenach	2May	
	William Robins	19May1812	
	Stanislaus Schoultz	20do.	Adjutant
	Jean Dombré	21do.	
	Jaspard Adolphe Fauche	29Oct.	
	August. de Loriol	28Sept.1814	
	Charles Cæsar de Meuron	do.	
	St. Andrew St. John	29do.	
	{ Louis Simoneau	27Oct.	1June1812
Ensign -	{ —— Bauty	19May1811	
	Carl Von Kap-herr	11Aug.1814	
	{ Gaetana D'Angelo	6Oct.	
	Julius Cæsar Saum	7Dec.	
	{ Wm. Herschel Griesback	8do.	
Chaplain - -			
Paymaster -	Lawrence Castle	26Jan.1807	
Adjutant - -	Stanislaus Schoultz	27Aug.1812	Lieut. 20May1812
Quarter-Master	Jaques Louis Vaucher	2May1811	
Surgeon - -	James Shoreland	14July1814	
Assistant Surg.	L— A— Winter	1Sept.1803	

Facings light blue.—Lace silver.

Agent, Mr. Disney, No. 26, Parliament Street.

P p

Watteville's

Permitted to inscribe on their Colours and Appointments the word " MAIDA" in commemoration of the Action of 4th July, 1806.

Rank.	Name.	Regiment.	Army.
		\multicolumn{2}{c}{Rank in the}	

Rank.	Name.	Regiment.	Army.
Colonel - - ⊚Lewis de Watteville		7May1812	M.Gen. 4June1813
Lieut. Colonel { Victor Fischer		7Mar.1811	Col. 4June1814
Rodolphe de May		21May1812	
Major ~ - { Valentine Winter		7Mar.1811	
Charles de Villatte		21May1812	
Captain - - { Amand de Courten		1May1801	Major 4June1813
Rodolphe de Bersey		23July1803	Major 4June1814
Panorace Legenderw		9July1806	
Frederick Zehender		10do.	
Ferdinand Hecken		13Nov.	
Frederic Kirchberger		22Mar.1810	
Charles Zehender		25Mar.1811	
Louis Ployard		29Aug.	
Rodolphe Steiger		21May1812	
Charles Sturler		31Dec.	
Ulrich Mittelholzer		21Oct.1813	
J— Christian Weiss		25Aug.1814	
Lieutenant - { Louis Rendt		19Feb.1807	
Lewis Pillichody		4Mar.	
Louis de Gingins		5May	
Albert de Steiguer		6do.	
Cæsar Augus. Chambeaux		7do.	
Joseph Mermet		27Jan.1808	Adjutant
Ludewig Hausdorff		18May1809	23Jan. 1804
Albrecht Manuel		5Sept.1810	
Charles Louis Sturler		6do.	
Charles Thorman		25Mar.1811	
Frederick Fischer		26do.	
Rodolphe Steiguer		28do.	
Francis Dicenta		28Aug.	
R— de Bersi		29do.	
Samuel de la Pierre		21May1812	

Lieutenant

Rank.	Name.	Rank in the	
		Regiment.	Army.

Lieutenant -	Francis Rigaud 30Dec.1812 Joseph Pelican 31do. Rodolphe de Watteville 22Feb.1814 Charles May 23do. Ferdinand Hicken 24do. Frederick de Watteville 4Aug.	
Ensign - -	Augustus de Loriol 8Oct.1812 Albert Bondeli 5Aug.1813 Joshua Harman 5Oct. Constantine Fischer 25Jan.1814 Paul Fischer 26do. Albert Fischer 27do. Charles Tscharner 24Feb. Charles de Moulin 28Apr. Albert de Bonstetten 3Aug. Frederick Zehender 20Oct.	
Chaplain - -	P. Jacques de la Mothe 23Apr.1812	
Paymaster - -	Charles Tho. Smeathman 1May1801	
Adjutant - -	Joseph Mermet 22Jan.1807	Lieut. 27Jan.1808
Quarter-Master	Ernest Bellman 29Sept.1814	
Surgeon -	Christophe Millett 1May1801	
Assistant Surg.	John Baptiste Boidin 1May1801	

Facings black.— Lace silver.

Agent, Mr. Ridge, No. 44, Charing Cross.

P p 2

Rank.	Name.	Regiment.	Rank in the Army.
Colonel - -	⊚*Sir* Alex. Campbell, *Bt.*	27Dec.1809	Lt.Gen. 4June1814
Lieut. Colonel	{ Francis Streicher	16Jan.1804	M.Gen. 4June1814
	{ Alexander Mackenzie	20Dec.1810	
Major - -	{ Edward O'Hara	12Apr.1807	Lt.Col. 4June1813
	{ Samuel Browne	25Sept.	Col. 4June1814
Captain - -	⎧ Frederick Crofton	17Jan.1804	Major 4June1814
	⎪ Frederick Franchessin	21do.	Major 4June1814
	⎪ Edmund Moore Bray	18Aug.1808	
	⎪ Frederick W— Kysh	15Dec.	
	⎪ Frederick Welch	8Feb.1810	8June 1809
	⎨ William Maxwell Mills	18Apr.1811	
	⎪ Francis J— Cox	5June	
	⎪ Richard Crompton	6do.	
	⎪ Alexander Mackenzie	31Oct.	27Apr. 1809
	⎪ John Webb	23Sept.1813	
	⎪ Edward Rainsford	17Feb.1814	
	⎩ Abraham Louis Hebert	25Aug.	
Lieutenant	⎧ Arthur de Tinceau	20Oct.1806	
	⎪ A— S— Dolivier	5Mar.1807	
	⎪ James Fulcher	28July1808	
	⎪ James Mennell	15Nov.1809	
	⎪ Jonathan Warner	16do.	
	⎪ John Crofton	11Sept.1810	
	⎪ Menas O'Keefe	12do.	
	⎪ William Newman	7Jan.1811	
	⎪ —— de Menibus	8July	
	⎪ Peter Brown	9do.	
	⎪ —— Ordon	10do.	
	⎨ William Lemonius	11do.	
	⎪ Duncan M'Dearmid	24Oct.	
	⎪ Mark Clancey	24May1812	
	⎪ R— J— Hanley	25do.	
	⎪ William Chambré	27do.	
	⎪ Patrick Thomas	19Nov.	
	⎪ Thomas Stopford	11Mar.1813	
	⎪ Casimer Quesnay	12Sept.	
	⎪ Alexander Schmitt	13do.	
	⎪ —— Symkath	14do.	
	⎪ John Walker	15do.	
	⎪ William Gordon	16do.	
	⎩ Wm. Alex. Anderson	26May1814	

Ensign

Rank.	Name.	Rank in the	
		Regiment.	Army.
Ensign - -	Phillippo Grassi	2Sept.1812	
	—— De Gannes	19Nov.	
	A— G— Laing	11Mar.1813	
	Ernest Jehring	13May	
	Frederick Rosenthall	20do.	Adjutant
	Mathew Handcock	15Sept.	
	James John Grant	16do.	
	Wm. Wilson Hornsby	22do.	22Mar.1810
	John Thomas Guinan	23do.	
	John Rumler	21Apr.1814	
	Thomas Henry	12May	
	W— Campert	26do.	
Paymaster -	John Glass, jun.	30Jan.1812	
Adjutant -	Frederick Rosenthall	20May1813	Ensign 20May1813
Quarter-Master	—— Tetsow	6Jan.1814	
Surgeon - -	Peter H— Lawless	7July1814	
Assistant Surg. {	Martin Cathcart	23Mar.1809	
	Thomas Connolly	26Sept.1811	8June1809

Regimentals green.—Facings black.

Agent, Messrs. Greenwood, Cox and Hammersley.

Royal

486 Royal Corsican Rangers.

The Five Companies which composed part of the Army in Calabria under Sir John Stuart permitted to bear on their Appointments the word " MAIDA," in commemoration of the Action of 4th July, 1806.

			Rank in the	
Rank.	*Name.*	*Regiment.*		*Army.*
Colonel - -	Sir Hudson Lowe, *Kt.*	1Jan.1812	M.Gen. 4June1814	
Lieut. Colonel	John M'Combe	16Nov.1809		
Major - -	{ Abr. Schummelketel	11June1807	Lt.Col. 4June1813	
	{ Arthur Johnston	16May1811	Lt.Col. 4June1814	
Captain -	{ Dominique Rossi	30Sept.1804	Major 4June1814	
	Anthony Guitieria	13Apr.1805		
	* P— A— Girolami	24Nov.		
	Joseph Panattieri	6Jan.1807		
	John Susini	8do.		
	Vincenzo Bernardi	18Oct.1810		
	Pearce Lowen	13June1811		
	William Garland	20do.		
	John de St. Laurent	26Sept.	23Aug.1810	
	Vincent Odiardi	13Feb.1812		
	James Guanter	1June1813	27May 1813	
	{ Adrian Manfredi	19May1814		
Lieutenant	{ Paul Zerbi	26Nov.1805		
	P— F— Ciavaldini	6Jan.1807		
	* Antoni Gaffori	8do.		
	Giovanni Ordioni	16Apr.		
	Philip Fuhrer	11June	6Nov.1806	
	Antonio Astuto	2June1808		
	Michale Scippioni	16Nov.1809		
	Giacomo S— Pancrazio	18Oct.1810		
	Redmondo Corbara	30May1811		
	—— de Kamptz	31do.		
	Antonio Agostini	1June		
	Christian Many	3do.		
	Ludwig von Bibra	4do.		
	Nathaniel R— Guitton	5do.		
	J— B— Zerbi	6do.	13Sept.1810	
	Tottenham Alley	20do.		
	Antonio Odiardi	10Feb.1812		
	John B— Carabelli	11do.		
	Raphael Pagano	12do.		
	{ Cosmo Gugliani	13do.		

Rank.	Name.	Regiment.	Rank in the Army.

Lieutenant	Percy Simpson Jerome Carabelli Dominico Peretté Philip Athy Fallon Francis Salvatelli G— A— Vincenté	18June1812 24do. 25do. 24Dec. 21Jan.1813 19May1814	27Oct. 1806
Ensign - -	Felice Tamajo Casuni Reynach George Black Henry Schummelketel Simcoe Baynes Lewis Orocicchia John Harvey Francisco Minardi ——— Bruno Joseph Susini	10Feb.1812 11do. 12do. 13do. 24June 25do. 24Dec. 15July1813 7Apr.1814 19May	 Adjutant
Paymaster - Adjutant - - Quarter-Master Surgeon - - Assistant Surg.	 ——— Bruno William Hill Morrice Alexander Lorenzo Sammut Alfeo Ferrara	 7Apr.1814 11Feb.1813 13May1813 22Aug.1811 8Oct.1812	 Ensign 7Apr.1814

Regimentals green.—Facings scarlet.

Agent, Mr. Disney, No. 26, Parliament Street.

Sicilian

Rank.	Name.	Rank in the Regiment.	Army.
Colonel -	⊚Ronald Crau. Ferguson	25Jan.1809	Lt.Gen. 4June1813
Lieut. Colonel	{ George D— Robertson Francisco Rivarola	5Feb.1807 7Mar.1811	Col. 4June1814
Major - -	{ Robert Mowbray Henry F— Mellish	12Jan.1809 7Mar.1811	Lt.Col. 4June1813 Lt.Col. 20Feb.1812
Captain -	{ Robert Carter William Fairtlough John Ciravegnac Nicholas Andora Charles Glau —— Count de Clermont Ninian Craig Melchior de Polignac B. J. Muller Friedberg John Charles Smith Thomas Peacocke George King	6Feb.1807 7do. 8do. 20Jan.1808 3Mar. 31do. 16Nov.1809 1Nov.1810 26Sept 1811 24Sept.1812 26Aug.1813 17Nov.1814	Major 27Oct.1814 Major 4June1814 12Mar.1806 Major 4June1814
Lieutenant	ˣ { Charles Stuart Francis Stuart Charles F— Cavallace James Macleod Vincenzo Tedeschi Allan M'Pherson John Stobie Aimar Roquefeuille Henry Stuart Thomas da Fossi T— Bartoli Balthaza Osorio Mariano Zugianni —— de Coulommé Gilbert Stewart GustavusdeRoquefeuille Alexander Robertson Andrew Vieusseux Young Turner Charles Mill Francis Rivarola Nathaniel Strode Charles Williams Charles Thom Alexander Roquefeuil J— Whimster	10Feb.1807 17Apr. 10June1808 11do. do. 12do. 14do. 15do. 3Nov. 6Apr.1809 8Nov. 9do. 8Feb.1810 21do. 22do. 23Aug. 28Nov. 18Apr.1811 1May 11July 6Feb.1812 28do. 16July 15Apr.1813 10June 5Aug.	 20July 1809

Ensign

Rank.	Name.	Rank in the Regiment.	Army.
Ensign	{ Charles Henry	28 Nov. 1810	
	Joseph Massardo	29 do.	
	Malcolm Smith	1 May 1811	
	John Charles Crawford	11 July	
	William Turner	6 Feb. 1812	
	——— Higler	28 do.	
	James Gillbee	15 Apr. 1813	
	Joseph Tullier	10 June	
	{ George D'Heillimer	5 Aug.	
Chaplain	Francis Pulejo	7 Sept. 1809	
Paymaster	Richard White	26 Mar. 1807	
Adjutant			
Quarter-Master	John Nurg	3 Nov. 1808	
Surgeon	Alexander Broadfoot	5 Nov. 1812	
Assistant Surg.	{ Joseph Taberna	16 Sept. 1807	
	{ Michael Fogarty	11 Mar. 1813	

Facings green.

Agent, Mr. Disney, No. 26, Parliament Street.

Rank.	Name.	Regiment.	Rank in the Army.

Colonel - ⊚⎯ John Oswald 25Feb.1811 M.Gen. 4June1811

Lieut. Colonel { *Sir* John'Brown, *Kt.* 25Jan.1813 14Mar.1811
{ Robert Oswald 18May

Major - - { Charles Ashe A'Court 26Feb.1811 Lt.Col. 19May1813
{ Charles Geo. D'Aguilar 1Apr.1813 Lt.Col. 20May1813

Captain -
{ Geo. A. Hatzembuhler 25Feb.1811
| Charles Tuffin do.
* | Giuseppe Laguidara do.
* | Anagnosti Papageorgio do.
* | Costandi Petinresa do.
* | Giovanni Cavadia do.
*{ Caralambi Vilaeti do.
* | Alexi Vlacopulo do.
* | Costandi Stratti do.
* | Belisario Calogero do.
* | Elia Crisospatti do.
* | Cristo Palasca do.
* { Micagli Gusti 1July1813

Lieutenant
* { Janasi Machera 25Feb.1811
* | Costandi Caracugilia do.
* | Giorgio Vasilachi do.
* | Stamatello Thodoropolo do.
* | Giorgio Liva do.
* | Anagnosti di Giorgio do.
* | Costandi Liberopulo do.
* | Panajotti Zanni do.
* | Costandi Vlacopulo do.
* { Pano Dara do.
* { Gica Caluzzi do.
* | Nicolo Vincenzo do.
* | Vasili Politaco do.
* | Gica Lambro do.
* | Nicolachi Petimesa do.
* | ——— Turcoleco do.
* | B— Cormova do.
| Matuo Ordioni 22Oct.1812
* | Anagnosti Zaccoropulo 28Apr.1814
* { Janni Giocadari 27Oct.

Ensign

Rank.	Name.	Rank in the	
		Regiment.	Army.

Ensign - -	* ⎰ Micaghli Gusti	25 Feb. 1811	
	* ⎱ Janni Adami	do.	
	Guiseppe Maria Guasco	5 Mar. 1812	
	——— Sansonetti	25 Feb. 1813	
	George Newsom	26 do.	
	———. Jegle	30 Sept.	Adjutant
	Panajotti Liberopulo	28 Apr. 1814	
	Pasquale Ordisni	do.	
	Demetri Milizzi	26 Oct.	
	Pietro Vurgopulo	28 do.	

Paymaster -	John Bews	28 Nov. 1811	
Adjutant - -	——— Jegle	30 Sept. 1813	Ensign 30 Sept. 1813
Quarter-Master	Elkanah Eccles	25 Feb. 1811	
Surgeon - -	James N— Shelly	25 Feb. 1811	
Assistant Surg.	John Williams	25 Feb. 1811	

Facings yellow.

Agent, Mr. Disney, No. 26, Parliament Street.

Foreign

Rank.	Name.	Regiment.	Rank in the Army.
Colonel - -	Claus, *Baron* Decken	24Jan.1814	4June1813
Lieut. Colonel	ⓢCharles Belleville	11Feb.1813	7Dec.1809
Major - -	ⓢCharles Thalman	28Aug.1813	18Jan. 1808
Captain -	⎧ Ferd. *Baron* Marschalk ⎪ Frederick Bothe ⎨ Charles Ebell ⎪ Frederick Dolge ⎪ Augustus Maimburgh ⎩ George Schrader	11Feb.1813 12do. 13do. 5Mar. 23Jan.1814 24do.	19Dec. 1803 4Apr.1809 23Mar.1812 19Jan. 1806 5Apr.1810 12May 1812
Lieutenant -	⎧ Frederick Schneiring ⎪ Theodore Thalmann ⎨ John Tatter ⎪ Lewis Weyhe ⎪ Henry Schaefer ⎩ Frederick Queade	11Feb.1813 12do. 13do. 14do. 15do. 26Jan.1814	20Oct. 1808 22July 1806 19Aug.1809 8Dec.1809 Adjutant 17Mar.1812
Ensign - -	⎧ George Rumann ⎪ Frederick Kuster ⎨ Charles Dedecke ⎪ ——— Kobetzky ⎪ William Riddle ⎩ Henry Brockmeyer	11Feb.1813 17do. 5Mar. 13Aug. 30Jan.1814 31do.	25June1812 22Sept.1812
Paymaster -	Thomas Finlayson	22July1813	
Adjutant - -	Henry Schaefer	15Feb.1813	Lieut. 15Feb.1813
Quarter-Master	Henry Behnson	16Feb.1813	
Surgeon - -	George Kessler	11Feb.1813	25Dec.1805
Assistant Surg. ⎰⎱	J— C— F— Fischer	17Feb.1814	

Agent, Mr. Disney, No. 26, Parliament Street.

RETIRED

RETIRED

AND

REDUCED OFFICERS

RECEIVING FULL PAY.

Late Horse Grenadier Guards.

1st Troop (Lord Howard de Walden's.)

Sub-Lieut. -	⎰ Richard Weeks	4May1798
	⎱ John Houlditch	29Aug.
	⎱ Robert Halliday	10Oct. 99
Surgeon - -	John Heaviside	29Nov.1771

2d Troop (Duke of Northumberland's.)

Lieut. and Capt.	Vincent Edward Eyre	15Mar.1799	Major	4June1811
Sub-Lieut. -	⎰ Charles Blois	4May1791	14July 1790
	⎱ Thomas Thompson	25Sept. 94	

Foot

Foot Guards.

First.

Surgeon Major	John Charleton	21July1799

Second, or Coldstream.

QuarterMaster	{ John Holmes	25Mar.1798
	{ Henry Harman	18July1805
Surgeon - -	J— A— Gillham	11Mar.1802
Assistant Surg.	Henry Fearon	23Oct.1800

Third.

Quarter-Master	James Lees	6Feb.1779

Regiments of Foot.

5th.

Surgeon - -	William Griffin	15Apr.1813		

12th.

| Major - - | Richard Ashton | 3Dec.1810 | | |

28th.

| Captain - - | Isaac Bean | 7Nov.1805 | | |

35th.

| Captain - - | Duncan Stewart | 18May1805 | | |

42d.

| Captain - - | Murdock M'Laine | 16June1808 | Major | 4June1814 |

61st.

| Lieutenant - | John Collis | 16June1803 | | |

63d.

| Quarter-Master | George Lynn | 25July1802 | | |

79th.

| Lieutenant - | Charles Brown | 9May1811 | | |

87th.

| Paymaster - | William Wetherall | 16Aug.1799 | | |

92d.

| Major - - | Peter Grant | 23June1808 | |
| Surgeon - - | Archibald Hamilton | 21Nov.1811 | 23Aug.1799 |

94th Regiment of Foot.

| Captain - - | James Cooke | 27Feb.1812 |

95th.

| 1st Lieutenant | William Hamilton | 22Oct.1813 |

3d West India Regiment.

| Lieutenant - | Thomas Harrison | 1June1808 |

Late 4th Garrison Battalion.

| Captain - - | Robert Hawthorne | 1Dec.1808 | Major | 4June1814 |

Late Scotch Brigade.

Captain -	David Douglas	5July1793	Major 29Apr.1802
	Colin Dundas Graham	do.	Lt.Col. 25Oct.1809
	Alexander Scott	6do.	Major 29Apr.1802
	John Cameron	do.	Major 29Apr.1802
Captain Lieut.	James Urquhart	10July1793	Major 29Apr.1802
Quarter-Master	Thomas Mason	5July1793	

INVALIDS.

INVALIDS.

Late Royal Garrison Battalion.

Captain -	⎧ William Irvine ⎪ James Mitchell ⎨ John Evatt ⎪ Richard Thompson ⎩ Robert Abraham	1Sept.1795 do. do. 19July 98 22Dec.1804	27Apr. 1792 13Feb. 95 1July 95 20Aug. 94 14Feb. 94
Lieutenant	⎧ James Nunn ⎪ Joseph Tait ⎪ Charles Green ⎪ Thomas Ducksell ⎪ Wm. M'Kenzie Stuart ⎨ Paul Jones ⎪ Philip Bailey ⎪ Wm. Olderston Garrard ⎪ Isaac Sargent Wilmot ⎪ John Munro ⎩ James Wetherherd	1Sept.1795 do. do. do. 22Mar. 98 9Aug. 99 21Mar.1801 22do. 17Apr. 17Sept. 18do.	9Oct.1794 Adjut. 9July 82 22June 99 28Oct. 1800
Ensign - -	Alexander Leishman	14May1801	
Adjutant - -	James Nunn	1Sept.1795	Lieut. 9Oct.1794

Late 41st Regiment of Foot (or Invalids.)

Ensign - - William Silk

Late

Late Independent Companies of Invalids.

Captain -	Thomas Cochrane	12May1779	2Nov.1777
	Edward Barron	3July 82	16Dec. 75
	William Pemble	22June 85	6May 82
	Robert Lumsdaine	25June 90	10Jan. 78
	Benjamin Craven	23Mar. 91	15June 90
	Charles Martin	28Dec.	Lt.Col. 1Mar. 94
	Leonard Browne	20Nov. 93	
	Arthur Pyne	12Mar. 94	5June 81
	Henry Bowen	16Apr.	Major 25Dec.1802
	Robert Bourne	3Sept.	9Apr. 1780
	John Grant	12Nov.	25Sept. 78
	Hugh Munro	28Jan. 95	15May 94
	Anthony Gordon	8July	8Oct. 93
	John Grant	16Sept.	Major 9Sept.1795
	Harry Ditmas	11Jan. 97	Lt.Col. 1Mar. 94
	James Peddie	18Jan. 98	20Oct. 93
	William Archer	15Jan.1801	20May 95
	Hugh Lord	19Mar.	Major 30May 78
	George Vaughan	25do.	Lt.Col. 1Mar. 94
	David Gordon	do.	Lt.Col. 1Jan.1800
	James Rose	do.	Major 25Dec.1802
	Charles Leigh	do.	Major 20May1795
	Michael John Grace	do.	31May 97
	Robert Sutherland	do.	5Oct. 97
	Samuel Mansfield	do.	4Sept. 95
	James Stevenson	do.	3May 1800
	Sir William Wynn, Kt.	3Apr.	11Jan. 1800
	William West	17Sept.	Major 3May1796
	LawrenceRob.Campbell	25Dec.1802	6Dec. 1775
	Charles Murray	do.	29June 80
	Arthur Blackhall	do.	18Mar. 82
	John Rynd	do.	17Dec. 94
	William Stewart	21Feb.1805	4July 81

Lieutenant -	William Brown	6Apr.1785	
	Thomas Field	24Oct. 88	2Apr. 1781
	David Carnie	12Mar. 89	8Mar. 80
	Robert Thomas	7Oct.	10Oct. 88
	Hon. James De Courcy	25June 90	14Jan. 75
	William Monsell	do.	21May 88
	Donald M'Donald	1Sept.	7Jan. 78
	Anthony Pasqueda	17July 93	25June 81
	Paul Doughty	16Apr. 94	
	James Miller	3Sept.	

Lieutenant

	Robert Lear	2Mar.1797	2Apr.	1784
	Alexander Taylor	1June		
	John Gordon	13July	1July	82
	George Munro	do.	25June	96
	James Mackay	18Oct.		
	Dugald Stuart	27Dec.	1June	83
	Jeremiah Martin	14Apr. 98	30Sept.	95
	James Colquhoun	15Aug.		
	Walter Sansbury	22Mar. 99	8June	96
	Felix M'Cullough	do.		
	John Abraham	do.		
	Sir W. C. Edgworth, Bt.	29do.	6July	81
	Henry Heatley	do.	13Dec.	83
	John Magee	do.		
	John Openshaw	do.		
	Hugh Munro	do.		
	Robert Griffiths	8Apr.	19Apr.	61
	Leonard Gibbons	4Apr.1800		
	John Edie	17do.	4Nov.	95
Lieutenant	James Hudson	23do.		
	John Hepburn	19June	1Sept.	95
	Edward Ricard	11Sept.	4Feb.	95
	George Bird	25Mar.1801	27June	98
	Arthur Fleming	do.	29Mar.	99
	John Reay	do.		
	George Leslie	do.		
	James Douglass	do.		
	Daniel Green	31do.	19Mar.	96
	Andrew Wambey	3Apr.	25Mar.	82
	William Moorhead	do.	11Oct.	97
	Richard Rushton	do.	18Sept.	94
	Richard Mallet	25Dec.1802	10Sept.	80
	John Johns	do.	12Oct.	87
	Angus Fraser	do.	3Sept.	94
	John Brown	do.	16Apr.	95
	Anthony George Kysh	do.	27Sept.	98
	James Bell	do.	25Mar.1801	
	John Roy	do.	17Apr.	
	John Bladen Moodie	24Feb.1803	4Feb. 1795	

	Lewis Nathan Brohier	17Oct.1789	9May 1782	
	John Turnbull	4May 91	29Oct. 83	
Ensign - -	Michael Blake	4Feb. 95	Lieut. 19July1804	
	John Beckett	24June		
	Alexander M'Donald	21Sept. 96	30Sept.1795	
	Jonathan Lawson	7Feb. 98		

Ensign

	⎧ J— E— Hemmings	14Apr.1798	1June 1797	
	⎪ William Beech	26do.		
	⎪ Peter Cadwell	1Aug.	20Feb.	96
	⎪ Angus Macdonell	do.	1June	97
	⎪ Benjamin Garnett	15Mar.	99	
	⎪ Daniel Earles	29do.		
	⎪ Henry Chipps	do.		
	⎪ Jeremiah Ellis	19July	25Dec.	96
Ensign - -	⎨ Peter King	25Mar.1801	8Aug.	99
	⎪ Ronald Macdonald	do.		
	⎪ Thomas Wallis	do.		
	⎪ John Heslop	3Apr.	18Feb.	83
	⎪ James Drummond	do.		
	⎪ John Bloxham	10do.	25Mar.1801	
	⎪ Joseph L— Lynn	do.		
	⎪ Francis White	1Jan.1802	8Oct. 1801	
	⎩ Cornelius O'Leary	17Mar.1808	27Mar.1801	

In North Britain.

Blackness Castle - Lieut. Thomas M'Leroth
Dumbarton do. - —— *M. Gen.* Hay Ferrier
Edinburgh do. - —— *Sir* James Foulis, *Bt.*
Stirling do. ⎰ —— Gabriel Forrester
⎱ —— Alexander Grant

Of the late 7th Royal Veteran Battalion.

Lieut. Colonel	John Wilbar Cooke	17May1803	25Dec. 1802
Major - -	Martin E— Alves	25Apr.1807	8Dec.1804
Captain -	⎰ John Ryan	4Sept.1806	7Sept.1805
	⎱ Charles Robert Fead	17Dec.1807	16Oct. 1800
Lieutenant -	Charles Atkinson	20Mar.1806	22Dec.1803

Agent, Messrs. Brooksbank and Morland, No. 19, Craven Street, Strand.

Of

Of the Royal Veteran Battalions.

First.

Captain	{ Daniel Gavey	14July1804	5June1803
	George Sheldon	4Aug.1808	23June1805
	John Jacques	4Jan.1810	27Aug.1803
Lieutenant	{ Philip Pery Carnell	5Apr.1808	16Aug.1799
	William Miller	13do.	
Ensign - -	John Neil	11Apr.1808	

Second.

Captain -	{ John Lucas	21Apr.1804	24June1783
	Henry Blackmore	30Mar.1809	29Apr.1803
Lieutenant	{ Thomas Anderson	25Nov.1808	18June1805
	John M'Phail	17June1810	23Feb.1805
	Francis Lamont	6Nov.1811	23Sept.1801
	William Morgenthall	30Dec.1812	1Nov.1809
Ensign - -	{ C— Francis Thompson	25Dec.1802	5Jan.1780
	Joseph Allen	10Feb.1803	
	John M'Lean	17July1806	

Third.

Lieutenant -	Joseph Barningham	5May1804	11Mar.1795

Fourth.

Captain -	{ George Stephens	10Oct.1805	Major 25Sept.1803
	Richard Humphreys	7June1810	26Sept.1805
Lieutenant	{ Alexander Fraser	18Dec.1805	
	William M'Intosh	26Oct.1809	
	James Robeson	4Jan.1810	
	Samuel Abbott	2Aug.	
	Charles Wright	6Nov.1811	7Nov.1805

Fifth.

Captain -	{ Geo.Hanbury Williams	19Nov.1807	3May1780
	John Allott	10Mar.1808	9July1803
Lieutenant	{ John Hope	3Mar.1803	20Oct.1799
	Joseph Neynoe	1Nov.1804	25June1803
	John Bennett	22Mar.1810	8Mar.1810
	Robert Miller	2Dec.1813	25June1803
Ensign - -	Patrick Ferguson	14Apr.1808	
Quarter-Master	Andrew Morton	20Oct.1808	

Sixth.

Captain -	{ Malcolm M'Neil	25Dec.1802	Lt.Col. 1Jan.1798
	William Fraser	27Mar.1806	9July1803
Lieutenant	{ James Grant	24Feb.1803	4Aug.1783
	Alexander M'Leod	27Sept.1810	27Apr.1762
Ensign - -	{ John Scolley	5Nov.1805	3Mar.1804
	Peter Grant	7do.	

Seventh

Seventh.

Captain -	{ John Phillips	19Sept.1805	
	{ Cæsar Colclough	16Apr.1811	14Nov.1804
	(Thomas Shiels	25July1806	
	) Alien Walker	5Mar.1807	8Jan. 1804
Lieutenant	{ George Palmer	19Nov.	28Apr.1804
	) James Macfarlane	2Feb.1811	
	(William Curby	3do.	

Eighth.

Major - -	William Morris	15Aug.1805	Lt.Col. 1Jan.1798
	(Samuel Montague Sears	20June1805	12June1800
Captain -	) John Hitchcock	27do.	5Aug.1804
	) James Jarvey	14Nov.	28June1801
	(William Pickering	3Jan.1811	23Nov.1804
Lieutenant	{ Zacchariah Wilton	9Apr.1808	
	(Thomas Gaynor	11do.	
Assistant Surg.	John Caldwell	16May1805	

Ninth.

Lieut. Colonel	Robert Walker	25Oct.1805	25Sept.1803
Captain -	{ William Keith	26Feb.1807	19Feb. 1807
	{ John Crooks	5Dec.1811	30Mar.1809
Lieutenant -	John Forbes	11Oct.1810	19Oct. 1781
Ensign - -	{ Alexander Macdougall	22Mar.1805	
	{ William Hamilton	11Apr.1811	26May 1808

Tenth.

Lieut. Colonel	Henry Zouch	8Jan.1807	1Jan. 1800
Captain - -	{ James Enright	25Dec.1806	6Sept.1805
	{ James Turner	25Feb.1808	8Nov.1804
Lieutenant	{ William Patton	25Dec.1806	10June1804
	{ Thomas Stanton	8Apr.1808	5Oct. 1804
Ensign - -	David John	25Dec.1806	

Eleventh.

Captain - -	John Hayes	25Apr.1807	22Aug.1805
	(Daniel Hore	9May1805	
	) William Fitcham Kirke	27Oct.1808	12Feb. 1807
Lieutenant	{ James Haverkam	31Jan.1812	19Mar.1796
	) Peter Kemble	1Feb.	1Jan. 97
	(Henry H— Becher	2do.	25June1803
Paymaster -	William Scott	5Nov.1807	

Agent, Messrs. Brooksbank and Morland, No. 19, Craven Street, Strand.

Of

Of the Royal Veteran Battalions
disbanded in 1814.

First.

Lieut. Colonel	Charles Augustus West	1Aug.1811	5May 1804
Major - -	Simon Fraser	9Apr.1807	14Sept.1804
Captain - -	George Hasleham	11Sept.1806	2May 1805
	William Adams	19Mar.1807	21May 1805
	Chidley Coote	19Nov.	9July 1803
	David Bruce	1Feb.1810	19July 1809
	John Campbell	27Sept.	25June1803
	Bernard M'Namara	14Mar.1811	28Aug.1800
	James Pratt	31Oct.	12Feb. 1807
	Duncan J— Cameron	16Jan.1812	Lt.Col. 25Oct.1809
	Robert Brenan	9Apr.	9July 1803
	Thomas Lambe	9Sept.1813	3Oct. 1811
Lieutenant	James Stevenson	25Dec.1802	25Mar.1795
	John Burke	do.	1July 95
	John Godley	do.	3Apr.1801
	Joseph Turner	do.	10Apr. 1801
	George Sacville Fraser	do.	18Sept.1801
	Hugh Baron	28Feb.1805	
	Alexander Birnie	4Apr.1808	
	George Henry Drewry	6do.	3May 1800
	John Tayler	8do.	5Jan. 1805
	Tho. Herbert O'Sullivan	10do.	
	J— S— Colepeper	29Mar.1810	7Apr.1794
	Francis Walker	28June	24Dec. 1806
	Kenneth Sutherland	2Aug.	25Mar.1801
	William Webster	8Aug.1811	31Aug.1807
	Thomas Martin	12Sept.	16Jan. 1793
	Robert M'Leland	24Mar.1814	27Aug.1807
Ensign - -	Daniel Clark	4Mar.1804	
	John Sinclair	14Aug.1806	Adjutant
	John Nixon	12Apr.1808	
	—— Granger	13do.	
	Marcus Rainsford	3May1810	
	James Burrows	21June	
	John Down Pepperell	22Nov.	
	William Abbott	21Mar.1811	20Sept.1810
	John Martin	23July1812	11Sept.1806
	Frederick Blake	5Nov.	
	Alexander Sutherland	12do.	
Paymaster -	Thomas Trick	14Sept.1809	
Adjutant - -	John Sinclair	19Apr.1810	Ensign 14Aug.1806
Quarter-Master	George Patton	4July1805	
Surgeon - -	William Edwards	10Sept.1807	25Aug.1803
Assistant Surg.	John Jones	4Nov.1813	6July 1804

Second.

Retired and Reduced Officers receiving Full Pay. 503

Second.

Rank	Name		
Lieut. Colonel	George Vigoureux	25Dec.1802	1Jan. 1800
Major - -	William White	22May1806	1Jan. 1805
Captain -	John Mansfield	3Apr.1806	16Jan. 1804
	Francis Higginson	19Nov.1807	29Apr. 1795
	Charles Bentley	12July1809	4Aug.1804
	William Colton	5Dec.1811	30Nov.1807
	Thomas Christian	5June1812	25June1801
	Richard Woods	15Oct.	13Aug.1812
	Thomas Joseph Baines	22do.	10Sept.1807
*	James Eccles	11Feb.1813	6Aug.1803
	T— E— A— Griffiths	10June	7Nov.1811
	Gilbert M‘Donald	11Nov.	4Aug.1804
Lieutenant -	Denis Lahiffe	27Apr.1803	1July 1795
	Archibald Waldie	14Jan.1808	26Nov.1807
	N— F— Nixon	26Nov.	31Oct. 1805
	James D— M‘Arthur	18June1810	18Feb. 1804
	William Travers	22do.	
	Allan Cameron	5July	25Dec.1806
	George Jeffreyson	14Mar.1811	12Jan. 1796
	William Spinks	25Apr.	
	J— Abbott	24July	Adjutant
	William Hartshorn	25do.	
	Edmund Thresher	26Sept.	
	John Mansell	24Oct.	
	John Davis	7Nov.	19Nov.1807
	Charles Elliott	6Feb.1812	
	Thomas Medley	22Oct.	
	B— Jameson	5Nov.	
	George Parker	17Dec.	14Nov.1805
	Charles Moss	10June1813	
	William Jones	5Aug.	27June1805
	William Green	16Sept.	9Sept.1813
	Samuel Bateman	26May1814	
Ensign - -	Jonas Buckley	22Sept.1808	
	——— Hamilton	9Nov.1809	
	Robert Deans	25Apr.1811	
	Samuel Jackson Poe	17Oct.	30Aug.1810
	Ronald Mac Donald	19Dec.	
	Abraham W— Norman	8Oct.1812	29Oct. 1807
	John Niess	5Nov.	
	William Reid	3Dec.	
	Peter Fraser	10June1813	
	Thomas Bush	26May1814	
Paymaster -	James Drury	25Dec.1802	
Adjutant - -	J— Abbott	22June1809	Lieut. 24July1811
Quarter-Master	Thomas Randall	7May1812	
Surgeon - -	Michael Carmac	23Apr.1807	
Assistant Surg.	David Baxter	27Apr.1809	28Feb. 1805

Third.

Third.

Lieut. Colonel	John West	25Dec.1802	
Major - -	Robert Brown	17Mar.1814	25Dec.1802

Captain -	{ P— D— Fellowes	25Dec.1802	Major 26Jan.1797
	Robert Smith	do.	21Jan. 1778
	James Lowe	do.	26Sept. 87
	Touchett B— Campbell	do.	26Mar. 94
	John Morrison	19Nov.1803	25Sept.1803
	Nathaniel Highmore	26Dec.1805	22Dec. 1804
	Robert Turner	2Aug.1810	16Aug.1804
	William Porter	23July1812	9July 1803
	George Coleman	22Apr.1813	25Feb. 1808

Lieutenant -	{ Peter Bonamy Anley	25Dec.1802	5Dec.1781
	James Hanson	do.	13Mar. 93
	John Cox	do.	3May 99
	John Campbell	do.	19Mar.1801
	John Buffett	14Apr.1803	23Mar.1796
	Adam Wilson	9June1804	8Apr. 1801
	John Gilbert	21Mar.1805	31Oct. 1799
	George Watt	29June1809	
	John Stevenson	7Dec.	
	H— Stanford	5Dec.1811	
	Samuel Wall	7Jan.1813	27Feb. 1812 Adjut.

Ensign -	{ Thomas Bradley	28Apr.1804	4Oct. 1797
	M— Connolly	26Dec.1805	
	Frank Hay	2Apr.1807	30Dec. 1797
	Alexander Ross	9Nov.1809	
	John Willis	11Jan.1810	
	James Picken	5July	27Apr. 1807
	William Mac Math	4Apr.1811	
	Joseph Atkinson	5Dec.	
	William Boulton	11June1812	
	William Fowles	21Jan.1813	

Adjutant - -	Samuel Wall	7Jan.1813	Lieut. 27Feb.1812
Quarter-Master	Andrew Hay	30May1805	
Surgeon - -	Samuel Francis	25Feb.1805	26Oct. 1804
Assistant Surg. {	Thomas Le Cloche	25Dec.1802	
	John Hanmer Sprague	24Dec.1812	14June 1810

Fourth.

Fourth.			
Lieut. Colonel	Peter Daly	25Dec.1802	1Mar.1794
Major - -	Edw.Cornw.Moncrieffe	17Mar.1814	Lt.Col. 1Jan.1812
Captain -	Andrew M'Niven	25Dec.1802	8Sept.1790
	George Newell	30Jan.1806	15Aug.1800
	Fra. Graham Fairtlough	5Feb.	24July 1800
	Judge Thomas D'Arcy	5Apr.1810	11May 1808
	George Hicks	18Apr.1811	4Apr.1808
	William Moore	3Oct.	20Apr.1809
	John Dane	22Apr.1813	26Mar.1807
	John Lutman	13May	2Feb. 1809
	Benjamin Jarmy	16Dec.	3Dec. 1803
Lieutenant -	Alexander Murray	25Dec.1802	
	Patrick Tytler	5May1804	
	William Gilland	12Dec.1805	7Dec. 1804
	William M'Laughlin	1Oct.1806	23Aug.1799
	Francis Horton	2do.	5Dec. 99
	Robert Thompson	16Nov.1809	25July 1805
	James Mercer	15Mar.1810	
	John Humber	5Apr.	
	Raymond Hicks	21June	
	Thomas Normington	28do.	12Apr.1808
	Barak Kirk	25Sept.1811	
	Devenish Taggart	26do.	
	James Wilson	28Nov.	
	―― Davidson	18Mar.1813	
	Thomas Parry Price	8Apr.	
	Thomas Mann	29July	
	―― Dalrymple	9Sept.	18Oct. 1810
	John Donaldson	10Mar.1814	
Ensign - -	Henry Danvers	25Dec.1802	
	Frederick King	19Apr.1810	
	―― Davidson	25do.	Adjutant
	David Glass	2Aug.	
	John Chittern	14Nov.1811	
	William Taylor	9Apr.1812	
	John Bartram	27Aug.	
	Henry Kenyon	29Oct.	
	William Sumner	29July1813	
	James Lawson	9Sept.	
	Silvester Fraser	14Apr.1814	
Paymaster -	John Nestor	25June1803	30Mar.1802
Adjutant - -	―― Davidson	25Apr.1810	Ensign 25Apr.1810
Quarter-Master	Thomas Davis	10Dec.1812	
Surgeon - -	William Thomas	18Nov.1813	
Assistant Surg.	Thomas Price Lea	15Nov.1810	4May 1809
	Joseph Poett	10Oct.1811	14Dec.1809

S s

Fifth.

Fifth.

Lieut. Colonel	Henry Le Blanc	5Feb.1807	

Major - -	Robert M'Crea	25Dec.1802	

Captain -	Thomas Power	6July1804	8Aug.1793
	William Murray	18July1805	4Oct. 1804
	William Cartwright	21Aug.1806	15Dec.1800
	Marcus Louis	18Sept.	23May 1800
	Daniel Nixon	9Oct.	25Nov.1798
	James Reynolds	16Nov.1809	6Sept.1804
	Ware Adamson	8Oct.1812	3Sept 1812
	Henry Odlum	29Apr.1813	15Oct. 1807
	William Richardson	5Aug.	Major 4June1811
	John Nicholson	6Jan.1814	6Nov.1813

Lieutenant	William Ross	25Dec.1802	29Mar.1799
	John Jenkinson Roberts	do.	29Mar. 99
	Robert Warren	15Oct.1807	
	David Coghill	28July1808	
	Robert Cash	29Nov.1810	25Aug.1808
	James Cochrane	29Aug.1811	
	James Watson	26Sept.	Adjutant
	William Drew	2Apr.1812	14Apr. 1808
	William Fraser	13Aug.	24Sept.1799
	William Bryson	21Jan.1813	
	John M'Pherson	14Apr.1814	

Ensign - -	James M'Intyre	26May1808	26Apr. 1807
	John Sutcliff	29June1809	
	James Malony	28Feb.1811	
	Anthony Gordon	26Dec.	
	James Lock	29Oct.1812	
	Thomas Evanson	21Jan.1813	5July 1810
	Daniel Fraser	8Apr.	
	James Bourke	22do.	
	James Burke	20May	
	Thomas Holder	15July	

Paymaster -	George De Carteret	27Apr.1809	
Adjutant -	James Watson	10Mar.1804	Lieut. 26Sept.1811
Quarter-Master	Miles Kewin	2July1812	
Surgeon - -	James Curtis	25Dec.1802	23Aug.1799
Assistant Surg.	James Sharpe England	18Feb.1804	21Dec.1800
	Robert Gazeley	14Oct.1813	18Dec.1806

Sixth

Sixth.

	Æneas Macdonell	25Dec.1802	9Mar.1794
	Vaughan Foster	do.	5Sept. 99
	John Grant	do.	15Sept. 99
Captain -	James Scobie	5Oct.1809	26Mar.1807
	Andrew Fraser	15Feb.1810	10Apr.1807
	John Macleod	8Aug.1811	15Dec 1800
	Thomas Levett Metcalfe	22Apr.1813	25Apr.1805
	John Cooke	20Jan.1814	1July 1813
	John Maclean	25Dec.1802	31May 1780
	Nicholas Paterson	do.	17Apr.1801
	John Cameron	16Feb.1803	
Lieutenant	Alexander M'Lachlan	2Aug.1810	14Sept.1804
	Warner Spalding	12Sept.1811	13Nov.1810
	Peter Perry	23July 1812	7Feb. 1810
	Donald Cameron	25Feb.1813	
	Thomas M'Donald	25Dec.1802	
	Peter Wright	16June1803	
	James Stuart	6Nov.1805	
Ensign - -	John Smyth	22Aug.1811	1Jan. 1798
	George M'Culloch	14Nov.	
	——— Shockledge	4Mar.1813	
	Peter Bremner	23June	
	Alexander M'Comb	24do.	

Seventh.

Lieut. Colonel	Hon. William Grey	1Aug.1811	31Mar.1803
Major - -	James Jonathan Fraser	27Dec.1810	4Jan. 1810
	James Douglas	5May1804	Major 29Apr.1802
	Henry Losack	25Apr.1807	7Sept.1804
	Daniel Gordon	27Sept.1810	30May 1805
	Christopher Williamson	6Dec.	1Dec. 1804
Captain -	John Douglas	28Feb.1811	28Feb. 1805
	Peter Keogh	17Apr.	14Nov.1805
	Roger Frederick	9July1812	2July 1812
	Malcolm Maclean	24Dec.	7Nov.1805
	Jervoise Tinley	15Apr.1813	12July 1808
	Charles Martyn	17Feb.1803	25Dec. 1802
	Joseph Balderson	23May1805	1July 1795
	Nathaniel Keen	2Oct.1806	
	Daniel Robinson	25Jan.1810	
	John Tulloch	31Jan.1811	
Lieutenant	John Lamb	5Feb.	
	Robert M'Lennon	11Apr.	
	William Theobald	17Oct.	
	William Hewett	23Jan.1812	
	Samuel Ragg	5Mar.	
	Roland Macdonald	8Oct.	16Feb. 1809
	Richard Gilchrist	29do.	

Lieutenant

Lieutenant -	John Pelt	31Dec.1812	3Nov.1809
	Hugh Mackfield	4Nov.1813	
	Richard Wall	10do.	1May 1809
	James Dudley	11do.	
	Samuel Powell	17Feb.1814	
	John Leavock	7Apr.	
Ensign	Peter Handasyde	26July1810	
	George Tassie	13Dec.	Adjutant
	Patrick Courtney	7Feb.1811	
	Daniel Brooke	18Apr.	
	William Gibbs	1Aug.	
	William Haywood	6Aug.1812	
	Anthony Komareck	29Oct.	
	John M'Koy	4Mar.1813	
	Henry M'Clinchey	11Nov.	
	William Sewell	20Jan.1814	
	Thomas Rivers	17Feb.	
Adjutant -	George Tassie	13Dec.1810	Ensign 13Dec.1810
Quarter-Master	Edward Sawyer	30Apr.1812	
Surgeon -	Matthew Lamert	4July1811	25June 1801
Assistant Surg.	William Parrott	9Apr.1807	10Mar.1804

Eighth.

Captain -	Charles Wm. Hockaday	8Aug.1805	24July 1804
	Henry Dixon	21Jan.1808	24July 1797
	George Pickard	8Mar.1810	15Oct. 1803
	George O'Flaherty	29Aug.1811	3Dec.1807
	William Cresswell	8Apr.1813	5Feb. 1806
	John Hadfield	17Mar.1814	27Apr.1809
Lieutenant	John Egan	24Dec.1804	8Dec.1796
	Alexander Moorhead	27do.	16Jan. 1804
	John P— R— Goodwin	24Jan.1805	3Nov.1799
	Bartholomew Uniacke	6Apr.1808	11Apr. 1805
	Charles King Oakley	7do.	16May 1805
	William Davis	8do.	
	John O'Brien	13do.	
	John Johnson	14do.	
	Robert Wilson	17May1810	
	Richard Kelly	5Aug.1812	29Jan. 1807
	Charles Dixon Green	13do.	14Aug.1800
Ensign - -	P— Burbridge	11Apr.1808	
	William Tansley	12do.	
	Edward Grinter	13do.	
	—— Harrison	14do.	
	Andrew Graham	23Feb.1809	
	Daniel M'Keown	23Aug.1810	
	William Parker	10Dec.1812	
	Dugald M'Illireach	3June1813	
	Ralph Campbell	9Sept.	

Ninth

Ninth.

Captain			
	Robert Peddie	28 Nov. 1805	25 June 1803
	Philip Stewart	25 Feb. 1807	Major 1 Jan. 1805
	Hugh Chisholm	23 Feb. 1811	5 Aug. 1804
	James Bisset	8 Apr. 1813	11 Feb. 1809
	Alexander Munro	22 do.	9 Aug. 1799
	William Mackay	27 May	22 May 1806
	Robert Mackay	13 Jan. 1814	10 July 1807
	John Royal	12 May	10 Nov. 1813

Lieutenant			
	Allan Cameron	21 Mar. 1805	9 July 1803
	John Geddes	22 do.	
	Edward B— Wollams	10 Apr.	
	Alexander M‘Kenzie	11 do.	
	Duncan Macdonald	9 May	19 Oct. 1804
	Adam Glendenning	26 June 1806	
	Donald Cameron	27 Nov.	1 Mar. 1802
	Thomas Bell	9 Apr. 1807	25 Dec. 1806

Ensign			
	Duncan Kennedy	3 Apr. 1805	
	James Cumming	4 do.	
	John Lindsay	1 May	23 Nov. 1804
	Charles Robertson	2 do.	12 Jan. 1805
	William Cartwright	10 Sept. 1807	
	Robert Forsyth	23 July 1812	
	Robert Beavan	24 do.	
	John Birch	14 Apr. 1814	

Assistant Surg.	John Edgar	11 July 1805	13 Apr. 1803

Eleventh.

Captain			
	Leonard K—Willard	13 June 1805	1 Dec. 1804
	John Rutherford	25 Apr. 1807	27 Aug. 1804
	John Clarke	21 May	Major 1 Jan. 1805
	John Charles Mackay	20 Aug.	5 Jan. 1805
	George St. John Gifford	9 Mar. 1809	3 Sept. 1804
	George F— Harrison	18 Apr. 1811	30 Jan. 1804
	George H— Skipton	10 Dec. 1812	16 June 1806

Lieutenant			
	James Findlay	10 Apr. 1806	
	Thomas Phillips	8 May	
	Gavin Stewart	8 Oct. 1807	25 Sept. 1803
	William Groves	4 Feb. 1812	11 Nov. 1809
	Hamilton Finney	6 do.	25 July 1811
	Creighton Irwin	12 do.	7 Nov. 1811
	Thomas Granger	10 Sept.	21 Mar. 1807

Lieutenant

Lieutenant -	Robert Hay	25Nov.1812	
	Henry Peach	26do.	
	Alexander Wright	10Dec.	27Mar.1796
	William Webb	22Apr.1813	25Oct. 1803
	T— Campbell	19Aug.	22Mar.1804
	Donald Robertson	26do.	7July 1783

Ensign -	Joseph Brokenshire	7May1807	
	Thomas Read	5Apr.1810	27Mar.1806
	Peter Mackay	3May	
	John Moon	31do.	
	David Black	10Oct.1811	
	——— Bond	28Feb.1812	
	William Austin	26Nov.	

Agent, Messrs. Brooksbank and Morland, No. 19, Craven Street, Strand.

Medical Department.

| Inspector of Hospitals | James Franck, *M. D.* | 28Apr.1808 |

Retired

Late Independent Companies of Invalids.

Captain - -	{ Thomas Bullen { Daniel Hull	14Feb.1793 25June1808	18Jan. 1782 25May 1803
Lieutenant -	{ Dennis Coleman { Orange Stirling { Mathew O'Hea	25Dec.1802 14Feb.1803 12Nov.1810	13May 1802 12Oct. 1761
Ensign - -	{ Philip Godfrey { John M'Cann	31Oct.1795 21Feb.1801	

Agent, Messrs. Armit and Borough, Dublin.

Of the late Twelfth Royal Veteran Battalion disbanded in 1814.

Lieut. Colonel	Archibald Christie	5Sept.1811	*Col. 4June1814
Major - -	William Collis	14July1808	25Apr. 1808
Captain - -	{ John Armstrong { William Beard { Hon. Charles Southwell { N— B— Dwyer { Francis Zehender { Jonathan Short { Josiah G— Hort { David Lee { John Vicary { Albert Zehender	28July1808 4Aug. 18do. 4Jan.1810 13Dec. 20do. 21Feb.1811 14Mar. 22Oct.1812 24June1813	15Dec. 1804 14Nov.1805 17Sept.1802 7Jan. 1805 24Nov.1803 5Aug.1804 23Aug.1810 27Aug.1804 26Sept.1811
Lieutenant -	{ O'Kane Cameron { George Westphall { Michael Taylor { William Barber { John Adolphus Burton { Hector Maclean { Peter Whannell { Patrick O'Brien { John Armstrong { Peter Squair { Robert Bowsar { Thomas Robert Parker { Richard Lowe { John Maclean { John Paterson	25June1808 do. do. 14July 3Jan.1810 4do. 22Feb. 2Nov. 3do. 4do. 6do. 7do. 8do. 9do. 10do.	1Nov.1799 7May 1807 23Feb. 1805 Adjutant 25Feb. 1802 27Mar.1806 18Apr. 1806 27May 1796 22Dec. 1803 7Aug.1806 13Apr. 1808 23Sept.1808 29June1809 26Apr. 1810

Lieutenant

512 Retired and Reduced Officers receiving full Pay in Ireland.

Lieutenant -	John Buchanan	11Nov.1810	
	William Heron	14do.	
	Norman John Moore	15do.	
	James Newman	21Mar.1811	
	John Thom	27June	15Apr. 1807
	Robert M'Alpin	9Apr.1812	
	John Juxon	12Aug.1813	30Dec. 1807
	Simon Davies	9Sept.	25Dec. 1806
Ensign - -	Isaac Wood	4Jan.1810	
	James Henderson	28June	
	Duncan Maclean	9Nov.	7Aug.1806
	Edward Wright	12do.	
	James Toy	13do.	
	Noble Latimore	14do.	
	James Light	15Jan.1812	
	Thomas Clarke	16do.	
	Alexander Hodgins	24Sept.	
	Alexander Barclay	21Jan.1813	
	John Marston	24June	10Nov.1808
Paymaster -	Charles Abrams	10Sept.1812	
Adjutant - -	William Barber	14July1808	Lieut. 14July1808
Quarter-Master	Alexander Graham	28July1808	
Surgeon -	John Sharpe	27Oct.1808	15June1802
Assistant Surg.	William Gardiner	7Feb.1811	
	Richard Fitzpatrick	10Feb.1814	

Agent,

GARRISONS.

GARRISONS.

IN GREAT BRITAIN.

			l.	*s.*	*d.*
Berwick	Governor	Gen. Banastre Tarleton	568	15	10
	Lt. Governor	Gen.G. J. Earl Ludlow, K.B.	173	7	6
	Town Major	Capt. Vaughan Forster	69	19	2
	Adjutant	Thomas Martin	69	19	2
	Surgeon	James Wood	44	2	1

Blackness Castle	Governor	Gen.Albemarle, E. of Lindsey	284	7	11

Calshot	Governor	Gen.R. Earl of Cavan, K. C.	44	2	1

Carlisle	Governor	◎-M. Gen. Robert Burne	173	7	6
	Lieut. Governor	Lt.Col. JohnFarquharson	173	7	6
	Town Major	Lieut. Duncan Macdonald	69	19	2

Chester	Governor	Gen. Edward Morrison	173	7	6
	Lieut. Governor	Lt. Col. Hon. Wm. Grey	173	7	6

Cinque Ports	LordWarden	Rob.Banks,E.of Liverpool,K.G.	474	10	0
	Lieut of Dover Castle	Thomas Best	173	7	6
	Dep. Lieut. of Ditto	Thomas Bateman Lane	104	18	9
	Captain of Sandgate	William Evelyn	40	0	0
	——— Deal	Lt.Col.Fra.E.of Guildford	20	0	0
	——— Sandown	John Robinson	20	0	0
	——— Walmer	George Leith, jun.	20	0	0

Dartmouth	Governor	Arthur H— Holdsworth	173	7	6
	Fort Major	Lieut. Marshall Wright	69	19	2

Dunbarton	Governor	Gen. A. J. Drummand	284	7	11
	Lieut. Governor	M. Gen. Hay Ferrier	104	18	9

Edinburgh

			l.	*s.*	*d.*
Edinburgh -	*Governor*	*Gen.Sir* R. Abercromby, *K. B.*	284	7	11
	Lieut.Governor	✖*M.Gen.Sir*G.Murray,*K.B.*	173	7	6
	Fort Major	*Lt.Col.* C.Dundas Graham	86	13	9
	Chaplain		100	7	6
	Surgeon	Thomas Hay	44	2	1

| Fishguard - | *Governor* | *Lt. Col.* George Vaughan |

Gravesend and Tilbury Fort	*Governor*	*Gen.* John Floyd	284	7	11
	Lieut. Governor	*Lt.Hon.* James de Courcy	173	7	6
	Fort Major	*Capt.* Thomas Kelly	69	19	2
	Surgeon	Henry Jones	44	2	1

Guernsey -	*Governor*	*Gen.*Geo.*E.of* Pembroke,*K.G.*			
	*Lt.Gov. Lt.Gen.Sir*J.Doyle,*Bt. K.B. & K.C.*	173	7	6
	Fort Major & Adj.	*Lieut.* James Cochrane	82	2	6

Hull - -	*Governor Lt.Gen.*✖Rowland,*Lord*Hill,*K.B.*	568	15	10
	Lieut. Governor	*Lt. Col.* Fra. Cuninghame	173	7	6
	Town Major	*Ensign* John Turnbull	69	19	2
	Surgeon	John Kirkman	44	2	1

| Hurst Castle | *Governor* | *Lt.Col.Hon.* J. Creighton | 173 | 7 | 6 |

Fort George

Inverness -	*Governor, and of Fort Augustus*	*Gen.* Alexander Ross	474	10	0
	Deputy Governor	*Col.* Alexander Mair	284	7	11
	Fort Major	*Capt.* Andrew Fraser	86	13	9
	Chaplain	Robert Milne	115	11	8
	Surgeon				

Fort Augustus

	Deputy Governor	*Lt. Gen.* Arch. Campbell	284	7	11
	Fort Adjutant	*Capt.* Hugh Chisholm	69	19	2

Jersey - - -	*Governor*	*Gen.*J.*E.of* Chatham,*K.G.*			
	*Lieut. Governor Lt.Gen.Sir*Hilg.Turner,*Kt.*	173	7	6
	Fort Major and Adj. Lieut. James Millar	82	2	6

Land-

			l.	*s.*	*d.*
Land-Guard	Governor	Gen. Cavendish Lister	346	15	0
	Lieut. Governor	Lt.Col.Ch.AugustusWest	173	7	6
St. Maws -	Captain or Keeper	Gn.SirG.Nugent,Bt.KB.	104	18	9
	Deputy Governor	Major Martin E— Alves	44	2	1
Pendennis Castle	Governor	Gen. Felix Buckley	284	7	11
	Lieut.Governor ◎-Lt. Col. William Fenwick		86	13	9
Plymouth -	Governor Gen.Cha.Duke of Richmond,K.G.		1221	4	7
	Lieut. Governor	Maj. Gen. Gore Browne	173	7	6
	Fort Major	Lieut. Angus Fraser	69	19	2
Portland Castle	Governor	John Penn	86	13	9
Portsmouth	Governor	Gen. Wm. Earl Harcourt	663	1	8
	Lieut. Governor	◎M.Gn.KennethA.Howard	173	7	6
	Town Major	Lieut. Nathan Ashhurst	69	19	2
	Town Adjutant	Lieut. Robert Wilson	86	13	9
	Physician	James M'Gregor, M. D.	173	7	6
	Surgeon	Isaac Chaldecott	44	2	1
Scarb. Castle	Governor	Gen. Hen. Earl of Mulgrave	15	4	2
Scilly Island	Governor	G. W. Fred. Duke of Leeds			
	Lieut. Governor	Lt. Col. Geo. Vigoureux	173	7	6
	Surgeon	Abraham Legatt	44	2	1
Sheerness -	Governor	Gen. Francis Edw. Gwyn	284	7	11
	Lieut. Governor	Lt. Col. Robert Walker	173	7	6
	Fort Major	Lieut. M— W— Rudd	69	19	2
	Surgeon	Joseph Bassan	44	2	1
South Sea Castle	Dep. Governor	Lt.Col. Alexander Loraine	86	13	9
Stirling Castle	Governor	Gen.J.Lord Hutchinson, K.B.	284	7	11
	Deputy Governor	L.Gen. Samuel Graham	173	7	6
	Major	Patrick Tytler	86	13	9
	Chaplain		76	0	10

			l.	*s.*	*d.*
Tynmouth and { *Governor*	*L.G.*Dav.DouglasWemyss	284	7	11
Cliff Fort { *Lieut. Governor*	*Lt.Gen.* Charles Craufurd	173	7	6

Tower of London	*Constable*	*Gen.*Fra.*E.of*Moira,*K.G.*	947	9	7
	Lieutenant	*Gen.* William Loftus	663	1	8
	Deputy Lieutenant	*Col.* John Yorke	346	15	0
	Major	Lachlan Maclean	173	7	6
	Chaplain		115	11	8
	Physician	Burgoyne Tomkyns	173	7	6
	Surgeon	John Rose	44	2	1
	Apothecary	William Prowton	10	12	11

Upnor Castle	*Governor*	*M. Gen.* Jeffrey Amherst	173	7	6

Wight *Island*	*Governor*	Ja.Edw. *Visc.* Fitz. Harris	474	10	0
	Lieut. Governor	*Gen.* Charles Leigh	346	15	0
	Capt.of Sandown Fort*Capt.Sir*Wm.Wynn,*Kt.*	173	7	6
	——Yarm. Castle John Delgarno		173	7	6
	——Carrisbr.Castle *Lt. Col.* Henry Powlett	173	7	6
	——Cowes Castle *Col.* John Drouly		173	7	6

Fort William	{ *Governor*	*Gen.* Edmund Stevens	284	7	11
	{ *Lieut. Governor* ☒*M. Gen.* James Kempt	173	7	6

Windsor -	{ *Governor and Capt.Gen. Earl of* Harrington	1120	17	1
	{ *Lieut. Governor*		173	7	6

Yarmouth North }	*Governor*	*M.Gen.*W.M.Richardson	173	7	6

EXTRA GARRISON APPOINTMENT.

Alderney - - *Town Major*	*Lieut.* Edward Martin	69	19	2

IN IRELAND.

Belfast - - *Town Major*	—— Fox	73	0	0

Carrickfergus - *Governor*	*Gen.* Francis Dundas	182	10	0

Charlemont

			l.	*s.*	*d.*
Charlemont -	*Governor*	Gen.Hon.Chapple Norton	365	0	0

Cork - -	*Governor*✉*Lt.Gen.*W.Carr*Lord*Beresford,*K.B.*		365	0	0
	Lieut. Governor	*Col.* William Dickson	182	10	0
	Town Major	James Comerford	73	0	0

Dublin -	*Town Major*	Henry Charles Sirr			
	Assistant	William Bellingham Swan			
	Major of Brigade	*Lt. Col.* George Grogan	182	10	0

Duncannon Fort	*Governor* ⊛*Lt.Gen.Sir*JohnHamilton,*Bt.*		365	0	0
	Fort Major	George Quin	73	0	0

Galway -	*Governor*	*Lieut. Col.* Peter Daly	400	0	0
	Town Major	Henry Pilot	73	0	0

Kinsale. -	*Governor*	Gen.*Sir*CorneliusCuyler,*Bt.*	365	0	0
	Lieut. Governor	*Lt. Col.* Arthur Browne	273	15	0
	Fort Major	John Jemmett Denis	73	0	0

Limerick -	*Governor*	*M.Gen.* William Fawcett	365	0	0
	Town Major	Edward Fitz Gerald	73	0	0

Londonderry and Culmore	*Governor*	Gen. John, E. *of* Suffolk	365	0	0

Londonderry -	*Town Major*	John Nicholson	73	0	0

New Geneva	*Fort Major*	Henry Rochfort	182	10	0

Ross Castle -	*Governor*	Gen. Henry Johnson	182	10	0

NORTH

NORTH AMERICA.

QUEBEC.

		l.	*s.*	*d.*
Governor	*M.Gen.*W. Gooddy Strutt	346	15	0
Lieut. Governor	*Lt. Col.* Daniel Paterson	173	7	6
Surgeon		260	1	3
Town Major	*Ensign* Ralph Ross Lewin	86	13	9
Barrack Master	Lewis Foy	69	19	2

MONTREAL.

Town Major	Thomas Hughes	86	13	9
Barrack Master		69	19	2

UPPER CANADA.

Surgeon	James Macaulay	260	1	3
Fort Major		86	13	9
Barrack Master	Thomas Newman	69	19	2

ANNAPOLIS ROYAL.

Governor		947	9	7
Secretary	*Lt.Col.*Tho.FennAddison	173	7	6

NEW BRUNSWICK.

Surgeon		260	1	3
Fort Major	*Capt.* Richard Leonard	86	13	9
Barrack Master		69	19	2

HALIFAX.

Surgeon	James Boggs	260	1	3
Town Major	**Capt.*PhilipVanCourtland	86	13	9
Barrack Master	Stephen Hall Binney	69	19	2

CAPE BRETON.

Surgeon		260	1	3
Town Adjutant	*Lieut.* Otto Schwartz	86	13	9
Barrack Master	*Capt.* William Coxe	69	19	2

PRINCE

PRINCE EDWARD'S ISLAND.

Town Major	*Ensign* Ronald Macdonnell	86	13	9
Barrack Master	*Lieut.* John Holland	69	19	2

St. JOHN'S, NEWFOUNDLAND.

Lieut. Governor	*Colonel* John Elford	173	7	6
Surgeon		260	1	3
Surgeon's Mate		60	16	8
Fort Major	*Ensign* Richard Green	86	13	9

PLACENTIA.

Lieut. Governor	*Gen.* George Garth	173	7	6

WEST INDIES.

JAMAICA.

Major of Brigade		173	7	6
Surgeon	J— L— Bolton	260	1	3

GRENADA.

Surgeon		260	1	3
Fort Adjut. and Barrack Master	John Carleton	69	19	2

St. VINCENT.

Surgeon		260	1	3
Fort Adjut. and Barrack Master		69	19	2

DOMINICA.

Surgeon	John Foreman	260	1	3
Fort Adjut. and Barrack Master	*Lt. Col.* Maine S. Walrond	69	19	2

TOBAGO.

Surgeon		260	1	3
Fort Adjut. and Barrack Master		69	19	2

GIBRALTAR.

GIBRALTAR.

		l.	*s.*	*d.*
Governor	{ F. M. His Royal Highness Edw. D. of Kent, K. G.	691	19	7
Lieut. Governor	Gen. George Don	346	15	0
Secretary to the Governor		173	7	6
Deputy Judge Advocate	Richard Jephson	173	7	6
Commissary of Musters	Richard Jephson			
Town Adjutant		53	4	7
Town Major	Major Ja. Jonath. Fraser	86	13	9
Surgeon Major		260	1	3
Extra Surgeon	Henry Glass	260	1	3
Assistant Surgeon	{ William Williams	91	5	0
		91	5	0
Provost Marshal		69	19	2

EXTRA GARRISON APPOINTMENTS.

NEW BRUNSWICK.

Lieut. Governor		500	0	0

HELIGOLAND.

Quarter-Master	Lieut. Philip Dowling	86	13	9

ANHOLT.

Quarter-Master	Ensign Peter Mackay	86	13	9

ROYAL

ROYAL REGIMENT

OF

ARTILLERY.

| Colonel - - | General Henry, *Earl of* Mulgrave | { MasterGeneral of the Ordnance. |
| Colonel en Second | } Lt. Gen. *Sir* Hildebrand Oakes, *Bt.* | { Lieut. General of the Ordnance. |

		Anthony Farrington	25Apr.1796	Gen.	1Jan.1812
		Ellis Walker	25Sept.	——	do.
		Philip Martin	2Oct. 99	——	4June1814
		Vaughan Lloyd	14Oct.1801	——	do.
Colonel Commandant	5	George Fead	28June1805	Lt.Gen.25July1810
		Sir Tho. Blomefield, *Bt.*	1June1806	——	do.
		Robert Lawson	1Feb.1808	——	4June1813
		Edward Stephens	16Dec.	——	do.
		Robert Douglas	4Sept.1809	——	4June1814
	10	John Ramsey	17Mar.1812	——	do.
		Thomas Trotter	14Feb.1814	M.Gen.25July1810
		John Macleod	1May	Lt.Gen. 4June1814
		John Smith	20July1804	M.Gen.25July1810
		William Cuppage	do.	——	do.
		Thomas Seward	do.	——	do.
		Francis Laye	do.	——	do.
Colonel -	5	Bayley Willington	do.	——	do.
	⊙	Thomas R— Charleton	28June1805	——	4June1811
		Edward Howorth	29Dec.	——	do.
		Thomas Desbrisay	1June1806	——	do.
		James M— Hadden	do.	——	do.
	10	Charles Terrot	do.	——	do.

U u

Colonel

Colonel - ◎	{ George Glasgow	24July1806	M.Gen.	4June1811
	William Bentham	13Jan.1807	————	do.
	Edward Stehelin	1Feb.1808	————	do.
	John Augustus Schalch	do.	————	do.
15	Henry Hutton	do.	————	do.
	{ Flower M— Sproule	16Dec.	————	1Jan.1812
	{ William Borthwick	30Apr.1809	————	do.
	Charles N— Cookson	20June.	————	do.
	John Burton	4Sept.	————	do.
20	George Cookson	17Mar.1812	————	4June1814
	Philip Riou	14Feb.1814	4June1813	
	{ John F— S— Smith	1May	do.	

Lieut. Colonel	{ William Mudge	20July1804	Col.	4June1813
	Henry Shrapnell	do.	———	do.
	George Wulff	28Jan.1805	———	do.
	George William Dixon	2Mar.	———	do.
5	Wiltshire Wilson	10do.	———	do.
	Richard Hamilton	28June	———	do.
	Brooke Young	28Dec.	———	do.
✕–	Haylett Framingham	29do.	———	do.
	John Sheldrake	1June1806	———	4June1814
10	George Ramsay	do.	———	do.
◎	John Lemoine	do.	———	do.
	Spencer C— Parry	do.	———	do.
	Robert Evans	24July	———	do.
	William Miller	24Oct.	———	do.
15	Benjamin Bloomfield	3Dec.	M.Gen.	4June1814
✕	William Robe	13Jan.1807	Col.	4June1814
	George Salmon	18June	———	do.
	Robert Wright	1Feb.1808	———	do.
	Joseph Maclean	do.	———	do.
20	John Harris	do.	———	do.
	Sir George Adam Wood, Kt.	do.	———	do.
	Richard Dickinson	do.	———	do.
	George B— Fisher	28June	———	do.
	Paulette W. Colebrooke	16Dec.	———	do:
25	Edward W— Pritchard	30Apr.1809		
	Thomas Francklin	1May		
	James Viney	20June		
	Charles Waller	17Nov.		
	Robert Beevor	22Jan.1810		
30	Frederick Griffiths	27Sept.		
	William Dixon	17Mar.1812		
	Francis Rey	23Jan.1813		
	Charles Gold	17Dec.		
✕	Joseph Carncross	14Feb.1814		
35	{ Alexander Watson	1May	4June1814	

Major

		Name	Date	Rank	Date
		Edward Worsley	4Sept.1809	Lt.Col.	4June1814
	◎	Thomas Downman	22Jan.1810	—–	17Dec.1812
	◎	Richard Buckner	27Sept.	——	22Nov.1813
		Henry Evelegh	8May1811	25July 1810	
	5	Charles C— Bingham	16Mar.1812	do.	
Major -	◎	John Dyer	17do.	Lt.Col.	12Apr.1814
		Stephen G— Adye	1Oct.	25July 1810	
		Nathaniel Foy	23Jan.1813	4June1811	
		Henry Phillott	17Dec.	do.	
	10	Peter Fyers	14Feb.1814	do.	
		Robert Thornhill	1May	Lt.Col.	1Jan.1812

◎		Augustus Fraser	12Sept.1803	Lt.Col.	21June1813
		Hon. William Gardner	do.	Major	4June1811
		William Scott	do.	——	do.
		Charles Baynes	do.	——	do.
5 ◎		James Hawker	do.	——	do.
		Frederick Walker	do.	——	do.
		Humphrey Owen	do.	——	do.
		George Desbrisay	do.	——	do.
		Turtliffe Boger	do.	——	do.
10		John S— Williamson	do.	Lt.Col.	13Oct.1814
		Alexander Macdonald	13do.	——	2Jan.1814
		Abraham I— Clason	do.	Major	4June1811
		William M— Leake	14do.	——	do.
		Percy Drummond	22do.	——	do.
15		Joseph W— Tobin	1Nov.	——	1Jan.1812
		Hugh Fraser	6Dec.	——	do.
		James Vivion	do.	——	do.
Captain - -		Robert Pym	do.	——	do.
		William R— Carey	1May1804	——	do.
20		Henry Marsh	20July	——	do.
		William Payne	do.	——	4June1813
		George Forster	do.	——	do.
		John Caddy	do.	——	do.
		Alexander Campbell	do.	——	do.
25		Henry M— Farrington	do.	——	do.
		George Skyring	do.	——	do.
		Charles H— Fitzmayer	27do.	——	do.
		Joseph Brome	13Aug.	——	do.
		Richard S— Brough	11Oct.	—–	25July1810
30		Andrew Bredon	23do.	——	do.
		James Power	5Dec.	——	4June1811
		Francis Power	20do.	——	1Jan.1812
		Charles Youngbusband	28Jan.1805	——	4June1813
		George Crawford	1Mar.	——	do.
35—		Alexander J— Dickson	10Apr.	Lt.Col.	27Apr.1812

U u 2

Captain

		Name	Date	Rank	Date
	◎	Robert Bull	28June1805	Major	31Dec.1811
		Francis Smyth	7July	——	4June1813
		Charles Egan	20Sept.	——	do.
		Henry Hickman	29Dec.	——	do.
40	◎	Robert Macdonald	1June1806	——	17Aug.1812
		Thomas I— Forbes	do.	——	4June1813
	◎-	James Webber Smith	do.	Lt.Col.21Sept.1813
		John M— Close	do.	Major 4June1813
		Patrick Campbell	do.	—— 14Oct.
45	✕-	John May	do.	Lt.Col. 27Apr.1812
		Thomas Rogers	do.	Major 4June1814
		Thomas Gamble	do.	—— do.
		Alexander Munro	do.	—— do.
		James P— Cockburn	do.	—— do.
50	◎	Hew D— Ross	24July	Lt.Col. 21June1813
		Philip Durnford	22Oct.	Major 4June1814
		Joseph D'Arcy	24do.	—— 25Nov.1813
		Harcourt Holcombe	3Dec.	Lt.Col. 27Apr.1812
		John S— Sinclair	2Feb.1807	Major 4June1814
55		William Lloyd	13June	—— do.
		Blaney Walsh	18do.	—— do.
		Robert H— Birch	27do.	—— do.
		James Armstrong	15Oct.	—— do.
		Richard Dyas	1Feb.1808	—— do.
60		Edward Wilmot	do.	—— do.
		George W— Unett	do.	—— do.
	◎	George Beane	do.	—— 12Apr.
		Philip I— Hughes	do.	—— 4June
		James M'Lachlane	do.	—— do.
65		William I— Lloyd	do.	—— do.
		James Adams	do.	—— do.
		William Roberts	do.	—— do.
		John Fead	do.	—— do.
		Thomas Paterson	do.	—— do.
70		Adam Wall	do.	—— do.
		William Morrison	do.	—— 21Sept.1813
		William Cleeve	22May	—— 4June1814
		William Holcroft	4June	—— 28Nov.1812
	◎-	Robert Lawson	29do.	—— 17Aug.1812
75		Nathaniel W— Oliver	15July	—— 4June1814
		James T— Cowper	1Aug.	—— do.
		Charles H— Godby	16Dec.	—— do.
		James St. Clair	23Jan.1809	—— do.
		Richard J— I— Lacy	24Mar.	—— do.
80		John A— Clement	30Apr.	—— do.
	◎-	Robert Douglas	1May	—— do.
		Edward P— Wilgress	20do.	—— do.
	◎	Stewart Maxwell	22Jan.1810	—— do.
		Dugald Campbell	3Aug.	—— do.
85		William G— Elliott	27Sept.	—— do.

Captain

Captain

Captain		⊙̄	Frederick Campbell	29Dec.1810	Major 4June1814
			Alexander Tulloh	8May1811	Lt.Col. 27Apr.1812
			George Turner	do.	Major 4June1814
			Richard F— Cleaveland	11July	—— do.
	90		William F— Skinner	11Aug	—— do.
		⊙-	Robert Gardiner	18Nov.	Lt.Col. 3Mar.1814
			Peter Wallace	16Mar.1812	Major 4June1814
			Richard Jones	17do.	—— do.
			John E— Jones	16Apr.	—— do.
	95		William H. C. Benezet	18do.	—— do.
		⊙-	Thomas A— Brandreth	20June	—— do.
			David Storey	21do.	1Mar.1805
			Courtenay Ilbert	1Oct.	2do.
			Thomas Hutchesson	24do.	10Apr.
	100		Edward C— Whinyates	24Jan.1813	8July
			John Michell	25do.	Major 29Sept.1814
			Lewis Carmichael	22July	—— 27Oct.
			Hamelin Trelawney	23do.	28Dec.1805
			John Chester	7Oct.	29do.
	105		*Hon.* Herbert Gardner	17Dec.	13Feb. 1806
			Charles Tyler	do.	27Mar.
		⊙	William N— Ramsay	do.	Major 22Nov.1813
			Christopher Wilkinson	10Feb.1814	24Apr. 1806
			Charles F— Sandham	14do.	1June
	110		Arthur Hunt	17do.	do.
			Henry Onslow	20do.	do.
			Charles Gilmour	1May	do.
			Francis Knox	4Oct.	do.
			John Briscoe	27Nov.	do.
2d Captain			James West	19July1804	Lt.Col. 4June1814
			John Taylor	1June1806	
			George Jenkinson	do.	Lt.Col. 12Apr.1814
			Henry Pierce	do.	
	5		William D— Nicholls	do.	
			Charles G— Alms	do.	
			Stephen J— Rawlinson	do.	
			Thomas Harrison	do.	Adjutant
			Stephen Kirby	do.	Adjutant
	10		James Adye	do.	
			Henry Light	do.	
			Henry Bates	do.	
			Charles Rooke	do.	
			George Cobb	2do.	
	15		Frederick Gordon	15Sept.	
			Samuel Bolton	22Oct.	
			Henry B— Lane	do.	
			John W— Kettlewell	24do.	
			Alexander Mercer	3Dec.	
	20		James Lloyd	19do.	

2d

		William Clibborne	14Jan.1807	
		James Grant	2Feb.	
		William Power	13June	Major 21Sept.1818
		Guy Carleton Coffin	18do.	
	25	John Orlebar	27do.	
		Ernest C— Wilford	29Dec.	Adjutant
		Thomas Greatly	1Feb.1808	
		James Bastard	do.	
		Thomas Van Straubenzie	do.	
	30	John Bettesworth	do.	
		Thomas Cubitt	do.	
		Francis Bedingfield	do.	
		Cyprian Bridge	do.	
		William Twyning	do.	
	35	Henry Baynes	do.	
		Thomas G— Brown	do.	
		Duncan Grant	do.	
		James Gomm	do.	
		Thomas Terrell	do.	
	40	Charles Mosse	do.	
		Matthew Lord	do.	
		William Butts	do.	
		Henry Scott	do.	
	⊚	William Greene	do.	Major 12Apr.1814
2d Capt.	45⊚	Robert M— Cairnes	do.	—— do.
		Archibald M— Maxwell	do.	
		John Marlow	do.	
		Robert S— Douglas	do.	
		John Cade Petley	do.	
	50	William Miller	do.	
		Thomas Dyneley	22May	
		William A— Dingley	4June	
	⊚	John Parker	5do.	Major 21Sept.1818
		Charles Maitland	28do.	
	55	Daniel I— Skelton	29do.	
		Henry C— Russell	15July	
		James Mackonochie	27Aug.	
		Charles P— Deacon	16Dec.	
		Joseph Darby	22Mar.1809	
	60	Edmund Walcott	23do.	Adjutant
		Alexander Dury	do.	Adjutant
		Samuel Rudyerd	24do.	
		William Bentham	30Apr.	
		William Cator	1May	Major 12Apr.1814
	65	John S— Byers	20June	
		Walter C— Smith	10Sept.	
		Charles C— Dansey	1Oct.	
		Samuel Scriven	17Nov.	
		Daniel Bissett	22Jan.1810	
	70	Alfred Thompson	23do.	

	Adam F— Crawford	3 Aug. 1810	
	Henry W— Gordon	do.	Adjutant
	Wm. M. G. Colebrooke	27 Sept.	
	Robert A— Rollo	29 Dec.	
75	John Conroy	13 Mar. 1811	
	Bernard Wills	8 May	
	Richard King	do.	
	William D— Jones	do.	
	William Dundas	11 July	
80	Frederick Arabin	do.	
	Edward Michell	11 Aug.	Major 17 Mar. 1814
	Richard B— Hunt	do.	Adjutant
	Courtenay Cruttenden	do.	
	Peter Faddy	5 Sept.	
85	Christopher Clarke	18 Nov.	
	Charles Napier	16 Mar. 1812	
	William Wylde	do.	Adjutant
	Charles Gordon	17 do.	
	William Eyles Maling	9 Apr.	
90	Mark Somerville	16 do.	
	William Webber	17 do.	
	Daniel Bouchier	30 May	
	Philip Warren Walker	1 June	
	Alexander Maclachlan	17 do.	
2d Captain 95	Thomas Scott	20 do.	
	Charles Blachley	21 do.	
	Marriott C. W. Aytoun	22 July	
	Alexander Macdonald	1 Oct.	
	John Longley	24 do.	
100	Hassel R— Moore	1 Dec.	
	Henry G— Jackson	31 do.	
	Edward Barlow	23 Jan. 1813	
	Edward Sabine	24 do.	
	Henry Curtis	25 do.	
105	W— F— Lindsay	1 July	
	William Dunn	22 do.	
	Frederick Robertson	23 do.	
	Zachary C— Bayly	28 Aug.	
	William A— Davies	29 do.	
110	Henry Festing	7 Oct.	
	James W— Johnston	20 do.	
	Edwin Cruttenden	25 do.	
	Thomas Dewell	17 Dec.	
	John M— Stratton	do.	
115	Charles Close	do.	
	John W— Spellin	do.	
	William C— Lempriere	do.	
	Allen Cameron	10 Feb. 1814	
	James Sinclair	14 do.	
120	Thomas Achison	17 do.	

	Robert Duport	20Feb.1814	
	James A— Macleod	do.	Adjutant
2d Captain	James Gray	1May	
	James Fogo	4Oct.	
125	John Crawley	27Nov.	
	O'Hara Baynes	28do.	Adjutant

	Thomas Trotter	20July1804	
	Hon. Wm. Arbuthnot	21Dec.	
	James Evans	28Jan.1805	
	Thomas Carter	16Feb.	
5	Henry Blachley	18do.	
	James A— Chalmer	1Mar.	
	John E— G— Parker	2do.	
	Falkner Hope	26do.	
	William Pakenham	10Apr.	
10	Charles Wilson	2May	
	Forbes Macbean	20do.	
	Robert Newland	2July	
	William H— Stopford	do.	
	William Oldham	3do.	
15	Elliott Seward	do.	
	Lloyd Dowse	do.	
	George I— Belson	6do.	
	Peter Stewart	7do.	Adjutant
	Robert F— Romer	16do.	
1st Lieut. 20	Richard C— Molesworth	17do.	
	Francis R— Chesney	20Sept.	
	Donald Crauford	2Nov.	
	John Walsh	1Dec.	
	William Bell	2do.	
25	George Frazer	3do.	
	Matthew Louis	28do.	
	Thomas Grantham	29do.	
	Samuel Charters	13Feb.1806	
	Francis Haultain	23do.	
30	Thomas D— Jones	4Mar.	
	Robert H— Ord	7Apr.	
	Josiah Grant	24do.	
	John Gordon	1June	
	William Brereton	do.	
35	Beverly Robinson	do.	
	William Duncan	do.	
	Poole V— England	do.	
	William B— Patten	do.	
	John E— Maunsell	do.	
40	William K— Rains	do.	

1st Lieut.		Henry M— Leathes	1 June 1806
		Irwine Whitty	do.
		William Munro	do.
		Henry L— Sweeting	do.
	45	George Coles	do.
		Archibald M— Campbell	do.
		George Jones	do.
		George A— Witts	do.
		John J— Chapman	do.
	50	Frederick Wright	do.
		James H— Wood	do.
		William R— Ernst Jackson	do.
		John Kane	do.
		Basil R— Heron	do.
	55	William Saunders	do.
		George F— Steele	do.
		Charles J— Downman	do,
		Edmund B— Gapper	do.
		George Durnford	do.
	60	William R— Grant	do.
		George Pringle	do.
		David J— Edwards	do.
		Edward Coxwell	do.
		Charles Dalton	do.
	65	James R— Bruce	do.
		James R— Colebrooke	3do.
		Alexander C— Willock	24 July
		Henry F— Cubitt	15 Sept.
		Richard B— Rawnsley	22 Oct.
	70	William A— Raynes	do.
		Charles S— Torriano	do.
		George H— Mainwaring	24 do.
		Thomas Bowlby	3 Dec.
		George Couse	16 do.
	75	Richard Hardinge	19 do.
		Joseph Hanwell	14 Jan. 1807
		Thomas F— Simmons	1 Feb.
		Robert Harding	6 Apr.
		Gerrard R— Moore	7 do.
	80	Robert Woolcombe	18 June
		William Swabey	13 Aug.
		Robert Andrews	15 Oct.
		Henry Forster	16 do.
		John T— Fuller	1 Feb. 1808
	85	Edmund Sheppard	do.
		Provo W— Lawlor	do.
		George W— Baker	do.
		Edward A— Cotton	do.
		Lewis S— Robertson	do.
	90	Arthur L— Collins	do.

X x

		Walter E— Locke	1 Feb. 1808
		William Smith	do.
		George F— Roberts	do.
		Charles Ford	do.
	95	Philip Sandilands	do.
		Thomas N— King	do.
		Browne Willis	do.
		Benjamin H— Vaughan	do.
		Fortescue Wells	do.
	100	Robert F— Phillips	do.
		Thomas G— Higgins	do.
		George Foot	do.
		John Hincks	do.
		Amherst Wright	do.
	105	George M— Graham	do.
		George Thompson	do.
		Gabriel Mathias	do.
		Joseph T— Ellison	do.
		Thomas Strangways	do.
	110	Samuel Wyatt	do.
		Edward C— Vinicombe	do.
		William H— Hill	do.
		John H— Freer	do.
		Archibald W— Hope	do.
1st Lieut.	115	George M— Baynes	do.
		David Pattullo	do.
		John C— Burton	do.
		John L— Smith	do.
		James Day	do.
	120	John Eyre	11do.
		Charles Otway	5Mar.
		Robert A— Speer	8do.
		William Elgee	20May
		Charles H— Lewis	21do.
	125	Robert 6— Aitchison	22do.
		Charles Shaw	4June
		John M— Stephens	5do.
		William Lemoine	do.
		William L— Robe	28do.
	130	James S— Law	16July
		William C— Anderson	1Aug.
		George Browne	26do.
		John Tucker	27do.
		Charles Manners	24Sept.
	135	Reynolds Palmer	10Œt.
		Douglas Lawson	28do.
		Phipps V— Onslow	16Dec.
		John R— Hornsby	15Jan.1809
		Felix Troughton	20do.
	140	Michael T— Cromie	25do.

1st Lieut.

	J — W— Smith	1 Feb.1809
	Andrew O— Schalch	10 Mar.
	Richard S— Armstrong	22 do.
	Thomas R— Cookson	23 do.
145	John S— Rich	30 do.
	Mark Evans	1 May
	John Davies	20 June
	John Pascoe	29 July
	George T— Rowland	10 Sept.
150	Samuel Phelps	18 do.
	George Birch	1 Oct.
	John Spiller	7 Nov.
	George B— Willis	do.
	Thomas Wynn	do.
155	Arthur Carter	22 Jan.1810
	John Day	25 do.
	James N— Colquhoun	8 Sept.
	Adam Ward	9 do.
	Anthony R— Harrison	27 Oct.
160	Wentworth Cavanagh	28 do.
	George Charleton	29 do.
	Richard Kendall	30 do.
	Henry R— Wright	29 Dec.
	George J— Hunter	13 Mar.1811
165	Robert Manners	do.
	Edward J— Bridges	14 do.
	John F— Breton	15 do.
	John Grant	8 May
	Edward D— Baynes	do.
170	John Street	do.
	Francis Weston	6 June
	Hillebrant M— Parrat	11 July
	William Dennis	do.
	Kenelan C— Wulff	12 do.
175	Robert J— Saunders	11 Aug.
	William H— Bent	do.
	Willoughby Montagu	do.
	Robert Clarke	12 do.
	Richard Litchfield	5 Sept.
180	John Trotter	1 Nov.
	William Furneaux	18 do.
	John Townsend	1 Dec.
	Thomas Trench	2 do.
	Charles Drawbridge	3 do.
185	Hugh Morgan	7 Feb.1812
	William Wood	8 do.
	Francis Warde	8 Mar.
	Robert Grimes	16 do.
	Benson E— Hill	17 do.
190	William B— Ingleby	9 Apr.

1st Lieut.

X x 2

1st Lieut.

		Thomas O'Cator	16Apr.1812
		C— A— Oldham	17do.
		Thomas Lovett	do.
		Claudius Shaw	30May
	195	Alexander Ramsay	15June
		Henry Pester	16do.
		Michael Tweedie	17do.
		Frederick Bayley	21do.
		Francis Stanway	21July
	200	Donald N— Martin	28Aug.
		Charles Spearman	30do.
		Joseph C— Acherley	24Oct.
		John M— Weatherall	23Jan.1813
		Justly Hill	1Feb.
	205	Henry Forster	2do.
	◎	Charles C— Michell	16Mar.
		Lynch Talbot	17do.
		Robert D— Storey	18do.
		James Love	19do.
	210	Francis Dawson	25June
		James Prescott	26do.
		Harry Bisshopp	1July
		Charles Douglas	22do.
1st Lieut.		Henry Slade	23do.
	215	Alexander H— Earle	28Aug.
		Anthony Manley	1Sept.
		Henry Hough	2do.
		Frederick Monro	3do.
		Geo. G— Palmer	1Oct.
	220	Henry Hutchins	7do.
		Peter Thompson	20do.
		Const. Yeoman	21do.
		George James	25do.
		James Christie	1Dec.
	225	G— K— Pemberton	17do.
		Charles H— Nevett	do.
		James Howell	do.
		C— R— Baldock	do.
		John Apreece	do.
	230	Edward W— Wood	do.
		Charles Andrew	do.
		William H— Lawrence	do.
		John Bloomfield	do.
		James H— Castleman	do.
	235	Edward Trevor	do.
		Francis J— Templer	18do.
		Richard R— Drew	10Feb.1814
		George S— Maule	14do.
		Edward Boghurst	17do.
	240	Henry Palliser	18do.

1st Lieut.

1st Lieut.	245	Edward D— Hawkins	19Feb.1814
		Henry N— Daniel	20do.
		Robert Lugger	22Apr.
		Thomas G— Williams	1May
		Archibald Macbean	23July
		Rickard N— King	8Aug.
		Henry Stobart	29do.
		Harry G— Kersteman	20Sept.
		William H— Weaver	4Oct.
	250	Alexander Duncan	27Nov.

2d Lieut.	-	Harry G— Ord	12Dec.1811
		Benjamin L— Poynter	do.
		William Sharpin	do.
		George W— Charleton	do.
	5	Henry Dunnicliffe	do.
		Edward Selwyn	do.
		Hugh Gillespie	do.
		Robert L— Garstin	do.
		John A— Wilson	11Sept.1812
	10	Richard B— Blakiston	do.
		Charles R— Dickens	do.
		George F— Dawson	do.
		Charles E— Wraxall	do.
		William C— Lindsey	do.
	15	William H— Bland	do.
		George Ford	do.
		Richard Tomkyns	do.
		William H— Poole	do.
		Barrington Tristram	do.
	20	Charles Darby	do.
		Henry Williams	17Dec.
		Henry W — Picard	do.
		William Greenwood	do.
		Evan Morgan	do.
	25	Richard G— Wilson	do.
		Anthony O— Molesworth	do.
		Burke Cuppage	do.
		Malcolm Clark	do.
		Robert Burn	do.
	30	George Doyle	do.
		Richard B— Burnaby	do.
		Robert G— Smith	do.
		James Lys	5July1813
		John Blake	do.
	35	Thomas Watkis	do.

2d Lieut.

		Rowland E— Cotton	5July1813	
		Darell Jago	do.	
		John Palmer	do.	
		John H— Griffin	do.	
	40	Thomas A— Lethbridge	do.	
		John Somerville	do.	
		James F— Simmons	do.	
		Alfred L— Milnes	do.	
		Benjamin Lyster	. do.	
	45	Richard L— Cornelius	do.	
		Lewis B— Walsh	do.	
2d Lieut. -	{	William Harvey	13Dec.	
		William H— Hennis	do.	
		Fenton Robinson	do.	
	50	Edward Greene	do.	
		John Johnson	do.	
		Charles G— Kett	do.	
		George Hare	do.	
		Frederick A— Griffiths	do.	
	55	Gustavus T— Hume	do.	
		Harry W— Scott	11July1814	
		Philip L— Foote	do.	
		William E— Richardes	do. ·	

Deputy Adjutant General	} John Macleod	27Mar.1795	Lt.Gen. 4June1814

		Ernest C— Wilford	9Nov.1799	2dCapt.29Dec.1807
		Alexander Dury	1June1806	—— 23Mar.1809
		Henry W— Gordon	do.	—— 3Aug.1810
		James A— Macleod	do.	—— 20Feb.1814
	5	Stephen Kirby	13June1807	—— 1June1806
Adjutant -	{	William Wylde	1Feb.1808	—— 16Mar.1812
		O'Hara Baynes	do.	——28Nov.1814
		Peter Stewart	20Jan.1809	1stLieut. 7July1805
		Thomas Harrison	24Mar.	2dCapt. 1June1806
	10	Edmund Walcott	11July1811	——23Mar.1809
		Richard B— Hunt	16Apr.1812	——11Aug.1811

		George M'Gleazy	10Aug.1795	
		James Reid	1May1803	Lieut. 1Apr.1806
		John Wigton	1Aug.1804	
		Thomas Betts	do.	
	5	John M'Coy	do.	
QuarterMaster {		Charles Hill	4Mar.1805	
		James Ranie	1June1806	
		Samuel Trench	do.	
		Walter Stewart	25Aug.	
	10	Joseph Elliott	19Dec.	
		Samuel Barnes	1Feb.1808	
		Alexander Calder	· 26Oct.1810	

Ordnance

Ordnance Medical Department.

Director General	} John Webb	1 Aug.1813	
Surg. General and Inspector	} Gustavus Irwin	27 Dec.1809	
Assist. Surgeon Gen. and Dep. Inspector	} Macmillan Jameson	27 Dec.1809	
	William Wittman, MD.	26 Sept.1814	
Resident Surg.	{ Richard W— Roberts	16 Feb.1814	1 Jan. 1804
	William Durie	26 Sept.	18 Nov.1805
Surgeon -	Samuel Kenning	1 Aug.1806	
	Michael Parker	1 Oct.	
	Stephen Gaisford	1 Feb.1808	
	John William Lloyd	23 Sept.	
5	Thomas Lloyd	27 Dec.1809	
	William Kebby	11 Nov.1811	
	Nicholas Fitzpatrick	do.	
	Thomas Young	do.	
	James Scratchley	do.	
10	Morgan Thomas	do.	
	Nicholas Phinæas Bradley	do.	
	Edward Beck	do.	
	James Bennett	2 Dec.1812	
	Henry Sproull	do.	
15	Edward Simpson	5 Aug.1813	
	Francis Pery Hutchesson.	20 Nov.	
	Thomas Morgan Jones	do.	
	Munro Blackwell	29 do.	
	John Ridley	do.	
20	John Morgan	16 Feb.1814	
	James Powell	28 May	
	Thomas Macmillan Fogo	26 Sept.	
	John Sandiman	12 Oct.	
	Stephen Cuddy	1 Nov.	
Apothecary -	William Harris	1 Oct.1806	
Assist. Surg.	Dugald Campbell	23 Sept.1808	1 Aug.1806
	William Attree	6 Jan.1809	do.
	John M'Gregor	11 Nov.1811	do.
	Richard Hichins	do.	1 Sept.
5	James Ambrose	do.	4 do.
	George D— Hicks	do.	12 Oct.
	Robert Cooke	do.	do.
	George Nappier	do.	18 Feb.1807
	George Maurice	do.	do.
10	Peter Venables	do.	7 Mar.

Assist.

		John Miller	11Nov.1811	7Mar.1807
		William Oliver Locke	2Dec.1812	29do.
		John S— Gregory	do.	26July
		Alex. Macdonald, *M.D.*	5Aug.1813	2Sept.
	15	James Stewart	20Nov.	1Dec.
		John Mackintosh	29do.	14June1808
Assist. Surg.		John Wooldridge	do.	do.
		Wm. Fletcher Staniland	16Feb.1814	do.
		Alexander Anderson	28May	do.
	20	John Wallen Hallahon	29Aug.	5Dec.
		Samuel H— Hallahon	26Sept.	5Jan. 1809
		John D— Frazer	12Oct.	26June
		Mark Anthony Raneland	1Nov.	do.

		John Thompson	1Dec.1809
		John J— Furnival	do.
		James Verling	25Jan.1810
		Charles Inglis	4Apr.
	5	Thomas Apreece	21June
		James Eddowes	25Aug.
		James O'Beirne	11Oct.
		Mathias Kenny	1Dec.
		John W— Frazer	28do.
	10	Robert Nixon	23Feb.1811
		Alexander Ogilvie	9July
		William Donnelly	10do.
		Æneas Cannon	23do.
		EdwardDowling, *M.D.*	28Aug.
	15	John Humphreys	do.
		Robert Venables	do.
2d Assist.Surg.		Richard Kirby, *M. D.*	15Aug.1812
		Thomas Murray	2Dec.
		Charles T— Whitfield	do.
	20	Bransby Cooper	do.
		Edward Rudge	3do.
		Charles Cupples	4do.
		Samuel M'Cullock	1Jan.1813
		Thomas Seaton	8Feb.
	25	Joseph Priest	26Apr.
		ThomasHaswellQuigley	11June
		James Parratt	do.
		Thomas Beard	5Aug.
		Morgan Nugent	20Nov.
	30	Thomas Whitelaw	do.
		John Wales	do.
		Charles Jaggard	do.
		Wm. Frederick Nelson	do.
		Henry Gatty	do.
	35	James Barlow	29do.

2d

		Edward Donovan Verner	29 Nov. 1813
		William Sproull	10 Dec.
		John Gibbons	2 Feb. 1814
		Henry Peter Locdel	16 do.
	40	William Barker Daniell	16 Apr.
		James Lynch O'Connor	28 May
2d Assist. Surg.		Kilner Baker	30 do.
		Richard Bloxam	15 Aug.
		T— V— Curtis	29 do.
	45	John Bingham	26 Sept.
		Walter Raleigh	12 Oct.
		Stewart Chisholm	20 do.
		John Frederick Davies	1 Nov.

Chaplain -	John Messiter	1 Mar. 1801
	Henry M'Lane	1 Feb. 1812
	Samuel Watson	1 July

Officers of the Company of Gentlemen Cadets.

Captain - -   The Master Gen. of the Ordnance

2d Captain	James West	19 July 1804	Lt. Col. 4 June 1814
	James Gomm	1 Feb. 1808	

1st Lieutenant	James Evans	28 Jan. 1805
	John Walsh	1 Dec.
	George Durnford	1 June 1806
	W— E— Locke	1 Feb. 1808

2d Lieutenant { * *

Paymaster, Messrs. Greenwood and Cox.

Colonel Comm.	Robert Douglas	4Sept.1809	M.Gen.25Oct.1809

Colonel	-	{ *		
		{ *		

Lieut. Colonel	{ George Wilson	1Aug.1800	M.Gen. 4June1811
	{ Samuel Rimmington	12Nov.	—— do.
	{ James Butler	11Feb.1802	Col. 25July1810
	{ Richard W— Unett	4Sept.1809	
	5 { *		

Major	- -	George Rochfort	21Nov.1783	Lt.Gen. 4June1811

Captain	-	{ Francis Downman	11Nov.1779	Lt.Col. 1Mar.1794
		{ F— M— Keith	1Dec. 82	7July 1779
		{ Matthew Young	6Oct. 83	10Aug. 81
		{ M— W— Burslem	10Nov. 90	1Dec. 82
	5	{ Ashton Shuttleworth	14Mar. 92	Major 1Mar.1794
		{ John Wilks	1Nov. 93	—— 6May 95
		{ Edward Wood	6Mar. 95	—— 1Jan.1800
		{ Samuel Reynell	20July1804	Major 4June1849
		{ Oliver Fry	10Mar.1805	14Oct. 1801
	10	{ John Mathews	1June1806	11Feb. 1802
		{ Frederick Glubb	1Feb.1808	14Sept.1803
		{ *		

1st Lieutenant	{ Frederick Chapman	5Aug.1761	Capt. 25May1772
	{ Daniel Grose	7Dec. 63	—— do.
	{ James R— Larive	14Sept. 80	
	{ Henry Ibbott	1Dec. 82	
	5 { George A— Davies	7Mar. 84	
	{ W— H— Brisac	20Apr. 87	
	{ William Moore	30July 96	1Oct. 1783
	{ James G— Burslem	1June 98	
	{ Albert W— Davids	27Oct. 99	Capt. 4Mar.1806
	10 { John W— Tapp	9Feb.1800	
	{ Edward Martin	3Dec.	
	{ William Cozens	25Feb.1813	

2d Lieutenant	{ Thomas Pritchard	29Sept.1790	
	{ John Drew	1May 95	
	{ John Thompson	1Mar. 96	
	{ James Wilson	1July 99	
	5 { John Kane	do.	Adjutant

2d Lieut.

2d Lieut.	10·	{ David Johnstone	1 Aug. 1799
		John Douglas	20 Dec.
		William Walker	3 Mar. 1801
		James Stevenson	14 Sept. 1805
		James Clark	1 Nov.
		Robert Taylor	22 Jan. 1808
		Alexander Reid	1 Sept.
		William Willocks	12 Sept. 1813

Adjutant - - John Kane	12 Sept. 1813	2d Lieut. 1 July 1799
Quarter-Master John Crawford	1 Nov. 1808	

Paymaster, Messrs. Greenwood and Cox.

Officers seconded upon the Invalid Battalion of Royal Artillery.

Major - -	{ George Lewis	14 Oct. 1801	M. Gen. 4 June 1813
	James Miller	11 Feb. 1802	———— 4 June 1814
	Charles Neville	1 Sept. 1803	———— 4 June 1813
	Charles Newhouse	1 Feb. 1808	Lt. Col. 4 June 1814

2d Lieutenant	{ Christopher Funstone	19 Nov. 1766
	George Reynolds	12 May 69

Paymaster, Messrs. Greenwood and Cox.

Major - -	Le *Chev.* De Nacquard	July 1796	Col.	4 June 1814

Captain - -	Lewis Prevost	24 Aug. 1795	Lt.Col.	4 June 1814
	Charles de Menard	12 Mar. 96	———	do.
	——— De Villicy	12 Mar. 97	—·—	do.
	Chev. D'Artez	Mar. 1806		

2d Captain -	J— Coutquelvin	19 July 1804	Major	4 June 1814
	Joseph Beausire	do.	———	do.
	Francis Clark	do.	—·—	do.
	John Gravenbroeck	12 Mar. 1806		

1st Lieutenant	Felix V— De Menard	Sept. 1797
	William Floyd	20 July 1803
	Victor D'Autume	1 Oct. 1804
	Welhelm Ehrhardt	12 Mar. 1806
	Francis J— P— Biffare	do.
	E. Camus de Pontcarré	26 July 1810
	Alexander Le Quin	3 Apr. 1812
	Felix de Real	26 Jan. 1814

2d Lieutenant	A— de la Tour	26 July 1810
	Charles Leneuf Lenox	29 July 1812
	Charles de Jolivette	26 Jan. 1814

Surgeon - -	Petit Jean

Paymaster, Messrs. Greenwood and Cox.

	Horace Churchill	30July1794	M.Gen.	4June1811	
	George Massey	1Sept.1801			
	Charles A— Quist	do.	*Lt.Col.	4June1814	
	Nicholas Turner	11July1804	Major	4June1814	
Captain 5	Gilbert Robinson	12Apr.1805			
Commissary	John Charleton	1Dec.			
	Henry Lane	1Jan.1806			
	W— H— Humphreys	21May			
	George H— Grimes	1Apr.1808			
10	John Crawley	11July1809	Adjutant		
	Hugh Crooke	10Mar.1803			
	James Evans	2Aug.			
	Thomas Richardson	10Sept.			
	John Hay	20do.			
5	John W— Blyth	24Oct.			
	George Smith	25do.			
	Peter H— Short	1Feb.1804			
	Peter Smith	30Apr.			
	George A— Thwing	1May			
10	William Blyth	4June			
	George Fiske	5do.			
	William Harris	6do.			
	Moore Jordan	7do.	Adjutant		
	John Stewart	8do.			
15	William Thomas	19Nov.			
	John Bruce	12Apr.1805			
1st Lieut.	William Goble	1Dec.			
Commissary	Thomas Gibbons	do.			
	John Allen	do.			
20	Edward Stanley	1Jan.1806			
	William Smith	do.			
	Maurice Tanswell	do.			
	John Priest	do.			
	Thomas Jorden	23Aug.			
25	John Wilford	1Sept.			
	William L— Roberts	2Dec.	Adjutant		
	George Weaver	do.			
	Matthew Evans	1Jan.1807			
	William Carthew	14do.			
30	Thomas Rice	1Apr.1808			
	Benjamin D— Nicoll	1Sept.			
	George Wilkinson	do.			
	Edward Philpot	do.			
	J— C— Armstrong	17Dec.			
35	William Smith	3Mar.1809			

1st Lieut·

1st Lieut. 40 Commissary 45	T— W— Muskett	11Mar.1809
	Thomas Read	1May
	John Roberts	1Dec.
	John Dicker	7Aug.1810
	William Payne	1Feb.1811
	John Blair	3Oct.
	George Aynge	6Jan.1813
	David Kennear	19May
	Wm. Howard Gillman	16July
	Edwin Griffiths	12Nov.

2d Lieut. Commissary 5	Thomas Jack	20Feb.1813
	Charles Meade	1May
	Henry Tracy	28do.
	Robert Madden	16July
	T— Boyce	do.
	Joseph Jagger	do.
	John Vaux	23Sept.

Adjutant -	John Crawley	2June1804	Capt. 11July1809
	William L— Roberts	5Dec.1805	1stLieut.2Dec.1806
	Moore Jordan	1Jan.1813	—— 7June1804

QuarterMaster	Alexander Clarke	16Jan.1807
	Joseph Shearer	1Sept.1808
	William Gates	15Nov.1809
	William Pilton	1Jan.1813

Vet. Surg. 5 10	John Percivall	24Apr.1805
	William Stockley	do.
	Richard Cordeaux	do.
	Henry Coward	do.
	Thomas Peall	1Nov.1806
	James Burtt	1June1807
	Charles O'Connor	7Mar.1808
	John Lythe	1June1809
	William Percivall	30Nov.1812
	Henry Smith	26Nov.1813

Paymaster, Messrs. Hopkinsons, No. 5, St. Alban's Street.

Director General	Anthony Farrington		Gen.	1Jan.1812
Chief Commissary	William Stace	8Nov.1810		
Commissary	Thomas W— Vaughan	20Aug.1806		
	John Pickering	17June1807		
	Edward Weaver	1July1809		
	Joseph G— Ellis	22June1811		
	Edward Edwards	do.		
	George Sherlock	25Sept.1812		
	Larratt Smith	1Aug.1813		
	Thomas Pink	19do.		
	Richard D— Henegan	1June1814		
Assistant Commissary	Joseph Lunn	1June1807		
	William Ashton	17do.		
	David Davidson	25Aug.		
	James Gordon	5Feb.1808		
	William Ware	11Aug.		
	Thomas Gibson	12May1809		
	George Pink	1July		
	William Sawyer	1Jan.1811		
	Erasmus Weld	do.		
	William Hoys	21do.		
	James Percival	9Apr.		
	Joseph Jarvis	do.		
	James Barclay	18June		
	Joseph Bullen	do.		
	George Wear	do.		
	John Williams	do.		
	James Walker	do.		
	William B— Coward	22Nov.		
	Edward T— Curry	15Feb.1812		
	Benjamin Fendall	1Jan.1813		
	John Walker	do.		
	George Kearton	do.		
	Leonard Marler	do.		
	Anthony Craswell	19Mar.		
	Thomas Benton	do.		
	John Wilson	1June		
	Anthony Snell	do.		

Assistant

Assistant Commissary	⎧ John Smyth	1June1813
	⎪ George Fergusson	do.
	⎪ Arthur R— Wigton	25Sept.
	⎪ Thomas A— Davis	do.
	⎪ Thomas James	do.
	⎪ Edward M— Sparkes	22Oct.
	⎨ Alexander Rothney	10Jan.1814
	⎪ Robert Hutchesson	5Feb.
	⎪ John Ross	do.
	⎪ James Rickcord	do.
	⎪ Thomas H— Sparkes	1June
	⎪ Samuel J— Tibbs	do.
	⎩ John Robinson	21Oct.

Paymaster, Mr. Wray, No. 11, Park Place, St. James's.

Do.
on Foreign Service ⎱ Mr. Butcher.

[1815]

Officers of the Corps of Royal Artillery Drivers 545
upon Half Pay.

Captain Commissary	⎧ John Bateman ⎨ Frederick Read ⎩ Thomas Berringdon Henry Willis	13June1812 1Nov. 20Feb.1813 15July
1st Lieut. Commissary	William Weir Francis M— Spong John Dalton Charles Park Charles Bennett John G - Griffiths John Beveridge Alexander Matheson James Wills Patrick R— Boyle John Daniel Frederick Bates Peter Smith John Kirsopp	23May1810 5June1811 13June1812 1Nov. do. do. do. do. 17Apr.1813 do. 15July do. do. 23Jan.1814
2d Lieut. Commissary	⎧ John Shore ⎨ J— Huthnance ⎩ Charles Cordeaux	19May1813 12Nov. 23Jan.1814

Paymaster, Messrs. Hopkinsons, No. 5, St. Alban's Street, Pall Mall.

Officers

[1815]

546   Officers of the late Royal Irish Artillery
upon Full Pay.

Colonel - -	John Pratt	31 May 1800	Lt.Gen. 25 July 1810
Lieut. Colonel	William Wright	20 May 1795	Lt.Gen. 4 June 1814
	John Daniel Arabin	do.	——— do.
	William Buchanan	do.	——— do.
	John Bouchier	1 Oct. 97	M.Gen. 4 June 1811
	Joseph Walker	13 Mar. 1800	——— 4 June 1813
	Hugh Swayne	1 Sept.	——— do.
Major - -	Robert Stewart	31 May 1800	Col. 4 June 1814
	Alexander Armstrong	24 July	——— do.
Captain - -	Charles, *Earl* Moore	16 Dec. 1793	
	James Shortall	16 June 94	Lt.Col. 25 July 1810
	Richard Legge	do.	——— do.
	Robert Crawford	17 do.	——— do.
	George Lindsay	do.	
	Peter Kettlewell	1 July	Lt.Col. 1 Jan. 1812
	Forster Coulson	do.	——— do.
	Richard Uniacke	do.	——— do.
	G— J— Hamilton	do.	
	George Irving	do.	Lt.Col. 1 Jan. 1812
Captain-Lieut. and Captain.	Gerv. Rainsford Hall	1 Jan. 1794	
	John Slessor	25 July 95	
	Hans Allen	do.	Lt.Col. 4 June 1814
	J— J— Dunkin	do.	do.
	Thomas Hearn	do.	
	James Irving	do.	Lt.Col. 4 June 1814
	John Carr	do.	——— do.
	John Campbell	1 Jan. 97	——— do.
	William J— Tucker	1 June	——— do.
1st Lieutenant	Richard Hassard	20 Oct. 1794	
	John Semple	do.	
	Charles Sharman	12 Dec.	
	William Kelly	17 do.	
	George Ellison	do.	
	Matthew Hemmings	20 do.	
	S— C— Bowen	do.	
	Ignatius Purcell	21 do.	
	Robert C— Sturrock	22 do.	
	Thomas Tisdall	do.	
	Henry Irving Stewart	10 Mar. 95	
	John Armstrong	do.	

Paymaster, Messrs. Greenwood and Cox.

Officers

[1815]

Officers of the late Royal Irish Artillery   547
upon Half Pay.

Captain - -	William Galbraith	1 July 1794
	Walter Blake	20 Dec.
	Henry Cavendish	do.
	O — C — Jackson	do.

Captain-Lieut. and Captain	James Hamilton	1 Feb. 1800
	John Hillas	31 May

First Lieut.	George R— Perdriau	1 Oct. 1797
	George Armstrong	15 Mar. 1800
	Henry A— Lyster	24 July
	Frederick Stock	5 Nov. 1807
	George Charleton	do.

Second Lieut.	Edward Cullen	20 Feb. 1799
	Richard Griffith	15 Aug. 1800
	Barry Yelverton Shettick	

Chaplain - -	Thomas Goff	28 July 1798
Quarter-Master	Joseph Hanna	28 Apr. 1799
Bridge Master	Michael Shanley	9 Apr. 1789
Surgeon -	Alexander Lindsay	9 Apr. 1789
Assistant Surg.	Joseph Barclay	20 Nov. 1797

Paymaster, Messrs. Greenwood and Cox.

Z z 2

CORPS

[1815]

C O R P S

OF

ROYAL ENGINEERS.

Colonel in Chief General Henry, *Earl of* Mulgrave } Master General of the Ordnance.

Colonel en Second Lt. Gen. *Sir* Hildebrand Oakes, *Bt.* } Lieut. General of the Ordnance.

Col. Comm.	Robert Morse	1 May 1802	Gen. 25 Apr. 1808
	Alexander Mercer	1 Mar. 1805	—— 4 June 1813
	Gother Mann	13 July	{ Lt.G.25 July 1810 Inspector Gen. of Fortifications, &c.
	William Twiss	24 June 1809	Lt.Gen. 1 Jan. 1812
	John Evelegh	21 July 1813	—— 4 June 1813
Colonel -	Thomas Nepean	1 Mar. 1805	M.Gen. 4 June 1811
	Sir Charles Shipley, *Kt.*	13 July	—— do.
	William Fyers	1 July 1806	—— do.
	William Johnston	24 June 1809	—— 1 Jan. 1812
	Sir Cha. Holloway, *Kt.*	1 May 1811	—— 4 June 1814
	John Humphrey	do.	—— do.
	Robert D'Arcy	21 July 1813	4 June 1813
	George Bridges	do.	do.
	Samuel T— Dickens	30 Sept. 1814	do.
Lieut. Colonel	John Mackelcan	13 July 1805	M.Gen. 4 June 1811
	John Rowley	1 July 1806	{ Col. 4 June 1814 Deputy Inspector General of Fortifications, &c.
	Augustus de Butts	do.	Col. 4 June 1814
	William Fenwick	1 July 1807	—— do.
	Alexander Bryce	24 June 1809	—— do.
	Robert Pilkington	do.	
	Henry Evatt	do.	
	William Henry Ford	1 May 1811	
	Frederick Wm. Mulcaster	do.	

Lieut.

	ⓞ	Philip Hughes	14May1812	
		Howard Elphinstone	21July1813	
		Elias Durnford	do.	
		George Whitmore	do.	
		Frederick Thackeray	do.	
		Hen. Anderson Morshead	do.	
Lieut. Colonel	{	John F— Birch	do.	
		Stephen R— Chapman	do.	26Apr. 1812
		John Handfield	do.	
		Gustavus Nicholls	1Sept.	
		James Carmichael Smyth	20Oct.	
		George Landman	16May1814	
		Cornelius Mann	30Sept.	

		George Wright	1July1807	Major 4June1814
		John Hassard	18Nov.	—— do.
		Charles Wm. Pasley	do.	Lt.Col. 27May1813
		Henry Goldfinch	do.	—— 21Sept. 1813
		James R— Arnold	3Jan.1808	1Mar.1805
	ⓒ	John F— Burgoyne	24June1809	Lt.Col.27Apr.1812
		Benjamin Marlow	do.	1Mar.1805
	ⓞ	John T— Jones	do.	Lt.Col. 27Apr.1812
		George Cardew	do.	1Mar.1805
		William Gosset	do.	Major 2Feb.1814
		William Bennett	do.	1Mar.1805
		John By	do.	Major 23June1814
	ⓞ	George H— Henderson	2Dec.	—— 21Sept.1813
		Thomas Fyers	23Apr.1810	21Sept.1805
		Henry Vigoureux	28May	1July 1806
		Henry M— Kilvington	1May1811	do.
		Gilbert Buchanan	do.	do.
Captain	- ⓞ {	Charles Ellicombe	do.	Lt.Col.21Sept.1813
		Edward Fanshaw	do.	1July 1806
		George Macleod	do.	Major 6Feb.1812
		William Douglas	do.	1July 1806
		Thomas Cunningham	18July	24do.
		Edward Figg	3Mar.1812	26Aug.1806
		Thomas Colby	5do.	1July 1807
		Sir Cha. F— Smith, Kt.	15Apr.	Lt.Col.21Sept.1813
		George J— Harding	20May	18Nov.1807
		Sir George Hoste, Kt.	21do.	Major 17Mar.1814
		John Ross Wright	21July1813	18Nov.1807
		Griffith G— Lewis	do.	do.
		Thomas M— Dickens	do.	3Jan. 1808
		Henry Smart	do.	24June1809
		James M'Lauchlan	do.	do.
		Henry Hobbs	do.	do.
		John Hobbs	do.	do.
		Charles Boothby	do.	do.

Captain

	Name		
Captain	William C— Holloway	21July1813	24June1809
	Richard Boteler	do.	do.
	Henry Vavasour	do.	do.
	Samuel Romilly	do.	do.
	William Payne	1Sept.	do.
	George Graydon	do.	2Dec.
	Cavelin Mercer	20Oct.	23Apr. 1810
	Alexander Frazer	28Feb.1814	28May
	Robert Thomson	16May	10July
	Thomas Roberts	30Sept.	1May 1811
2d Captain	Frederick A— York	1May1811	
	John M— F— Smith	do.	
	Rice Jones	do.	
	Robert Hustler	do.	
	Thomas Moody	do.	
	John Henryson	do.	
	John Oldfield	do.	
	Matthew Dixon	do.	
	Alexander Cheyne	do.	
	Patrick D— Calder	13do.	
	Charles Dixon	22July	
	John B— Harris	10Jan.1812	
	William Slade	4Mar.	
	John Harper	26do.	
	William B— Tylden	15Apr.	Major 23June1814
	John N— Wells	20May	
	John Grant	21do.	
	William F— Dawson	25Sept.	
	Richard Zachary Mudge	21July1813	
	Frank Stanway	do.	
	James Vetch	do.	
	Archibald Walker	do.	
	Sherbourne Williams	do.	
	William D— Smith	do.	
	Frederick English	do.	
	Thomas Blanshard	do.	Major 29Sept.1814
	Th. K. Hutchinson Staveley	do.	
	Alexander Brown	do.	
	Loyalty Peake	do.	
	Anthony Emmett	do.	
	Alexander Thomson	do.	
	Edward Fyers	do.	
	William C— Ward	do.	
	William P— Haigh	1Sept.	
	James A— Gordon	do.	
	George Barney	do.	
	Henry A— Colby	2do.	
	Donald M'Donald	20Oct.	

2d Captain	Harry D— Jones	12Nov.1813
	Richard H. Bonnycastle	11Feb.1814
	Henry Cardew	24do.
	Anthony Marshall	28do.
	George F— Thomson	1Mar.
	Robert S — Piper	16May
	George Gipps	30Sept.
	Philip Barry	10ct.

First Lieut.	Hammond A— Tapp	1Mar.1810
	William Reid	23Apr.
	Samuel C— Melhuish	28May
	William R— Ord	29do.
	John L— Hulme	10July
	Peter Wright	25Mar.1811
	James Birch	1May
	John S— Macauley	do.
	Roger Kelsall	do.
	John William Pringle	do.
	Henry F— Savage	do.
	Marcus A— Waters	do.
	Charles E— Prince	do.
	Pennel Cole	do.
	William H— Duvernet	do.
	John S— Kitson	do.
	Henry N— Smith	do.
	Theodore Elliot	do.
	Edward Matson	do.
	James C— Victor	do.
	Crighton Grierson	do.
	Richard J— Baron	do.
	Thomas H— Fenwick	do.
	Lewis A— Hall	do.
	Richard Evans Scott	do.
	Patrick Yule	11do.
	Francis B— Head	13do.
	George Phillpotts	7June
	Francis Y— Gilbert	10do.
	Charles J— Selwyn	18July
	Isaac M— Elton	1July1812
	William M— Gosset	do.
	Philip O— Skene	do.
	Thomas F— Lancey	do.
	John Sperling	do.
	Richard S— Young	do.
	Daniel Bolton	do.
	Frederick W— Whinyates	do.
	Alexander Watt Robe	do.
	Thomas B— Hayter	do.

First

	Ralph C— Alderson	1 July 1812
	Ives Stocker	do.
	George J— West	1 Mar. 1813
	Charles Wright	do.
	Charles Rivers	do.
	Robert Hunt	do.
	Francis R— Thomson	21 July
	Hale Young Wortham	do.
	James P— Catty	do.
	James R— Worsley	do.
	George V— Tinling	do.
	Andrew D— White	do.
	James W— Eyre	do.
	Joshua Jebb	do.
	John Smith	do.
	Henry Hill Willson	do.
	Alexander Henderson	do.
	Thomas Battersbee	do.
	Robert H— S— Cooper	do.
	Arthur Walpole	do.
	William N— Cox	do.
	Richard J— Vicars	do.
	George Tait	do.
	Henry R— Brandreth	do.
First Lieut.	Thomas Locke Lewis	do.
	Charles O— Streatfeild	do.
	John Mudge	do.
	Henry L— Renny	15 Dec.
	Joseph E— Portlock	do.
	John Kerr	do.
	Edward Covey	do.
	Henry Briscoe	do.
	William Gregory	do.
	Charles C— Alexander	do.
	James H— Rutherford	do.
	Arthur Kay	do.
	George C— Page	do.
	Henry Sandham	do.
	Colin Mackenzie	do.
	Christopher K— Sanders	1 Aug. 1814
	Thomas Luxmoore	do.
	Henry M— Buckeridge	do.
	Charles H— Minchin	do.
	William Faris	do.
	William S— Salkeld	do.
	Edward B— Patten	do.
	Frederick H— Baddeley	do.
	William Rogers	do.
	George Dalton	do.

Second

Second Lieut. {
Charles Burt	1 Aug. 1814
George C— Lewis	do.
Thomas H— Blackiston	do.
Charles H— Beague	do.
Gustavus C— Duplat	do.
Henry G— Boldero	do.
Thomas Budgen	do.
Macclesfield W— Heath	do.
Vincent J— Biscoe	do.
Rawdon F— Clavering	do.
Henry P— Wulff	do.
Francis E— Elliott	do.
James T— Tweed	do.

Agent, Messrs. Greenwood, Cox and Hammersley.

Corps of Royal Sappers and Miners.

	James Smith	1Dec.1806
	William Browne	do.
	Anthony Haigh	do.
	John Eaves	2do.
	David Falconer	1June1807
	Robert Davie	12Nov.
	George Robinson	do.
	Charles Millar	22May1809
	Thomas Longshaw	1June1811
	Alexander Munro	do.
	Alexander Ross	do.
	John Smith	do.
	Patrick Whelan	do.
Sub Lieut. -	Robert Gibb	do.
	Deskford Charles	1July
	Alexander Wallace	do.
	Stewart Calder	do.
	Richard Turner	16Mar.1812
	John Sparks	8Apr.
	William Robertson	1July
	Charles Grattan	1Dec.
	Hugh Bailey Mackenzie	1Feb.1813
	James Allen Stephenson	1Mar.
	William Stratton	1Apr.
	W— Knapp	1July
	Edward Sanders	14Jan.1814
	Patrick Johnson	21Mar.
	James Adam	do.

Adjutant and Quarter-Mast. }	Rice Jones	1Feb.1812	2d Capt. 1May1811
Adjutant - -	John M— F— Smith	1Dec.1812	2d Capt. 1May1811
Quarter-Master	James Galloway	1Feb.1814	

Agent, Messrs. Greenwood, Cox and Hammersley.

Corps of Royal Invalid Engineers.

Colonel - -	William Kersteman		28May1810	M.Gen. 4June1813
Lieut. Colonel {	Thomas Hartcup		27Nov.1793	Lt.Gen.25Oct.1809
	Henry Rudyerd		3Mar. 97	M.Gen. 4June1811
Captain - {	Sir Tho. Hyde Page, Kt.		1Oct.1784	
	Henry Haldane		15Nov. 86	Lt.Col. 13Apr.1795
	William Booth		20Dec.	——— 1Jan.1800
	Thomas Smart		18Aug. 97	27Nov.1793

Agent, Messrs. Greenwood, Cox and Hammersley.

Seconded

Seconded upon the Corps of Royal Invalid Engineers.

Lieut. Colonel   William Gravatt   1May1811|

Agent, Messrs. Greenwood, Cox and Hammersley.

Officers of the late Corps of Royal Engineers in Ireland receiving Full Pay.

Colonel - -	Charles Tarrant	1Apr.1796	L.Gen.25Sept.1803	
Captain - -	Alexander Taylor	14Nov.1790	Major 29Apr.1802	
Captain-Lieut. and Captain }	Henry Eustace	14Nov.1796	M.Gen. 4June1814	
First Lieut. -	Daniel Corneille	1Apr.1796	Capt. 2Sept.1795	

Agent, Messrs. Greenwood, Cox and Hammersley.

OFFICERS

OF THE

ROYAL MARINES.

GENERAL.

John, *Earl of* St. Vincent, *K. B.*   7May1814

LIEUTENANT-GENERAL.

Sir Richard Onslow, *Bt.*   7May1814

MAJOR-GENERAL.

Sir Richard Bickerton, *Bt.*   20Apr.1810

COLONELS.

Willoughby Thomas Lake	4June1814
William Charles Fahie	do.
Sir George Eyre, *Kt.*	do.
John Talbot	do.

COLONEL COMMANDANT.
(*Resident in Town.*)

Henry Bell	29Apr.1814	M.Gen. 4June1814

Col. Comm.	Thomas Strickland	29Apr.1814	M.Gen. 4June1811
	Robert Winter	do.	——— do.
	Theophilus Lewis	do.	——— do.
	Richard Williams	do.	——— do.

Col. Comm. en Second.	Laurence Desborough	15Feb.1809	M.Gen. 4June1811
	James Meredith	do.	——— do.
	Robert Hill Farmar	do.	——— do.
	Watkin Tench	25July	——— do.
	David Ballingall	4Aug.1814	——— do.
	George Dyer	do.	——— do.

Lieut.

Rank		Name	Date		
Lieut. Colonel	{	John Miller	15Aug.1805	Col.	4June1813
		Martin Campbell Cole	7July1806	——	4June1814
		Richard Harry Foley	24Sept.	——	do.
		William Binks	23Mar.1807	——	do.
		James Campbell	10Nov.1808	——	do.
		Robert Moncrieff	15Feb.1809		
		John Macintosh	do.		
		Lewis Charles Meares	do.		
Major	{	George Edward Roby	7July1806	Lt.Col.	4June1813
		Richard Lee	24Sept.	——	do.
		Henry Lee	23Mar.1807	——	do.
		Robert M'Cleverty	6Apr.	——	do.
		William Henry Boys	27July1808	——	4June1814
		Richard Williams	15Feb.1809	——	21Jan.1813
		Thomas Abernethie	25July	——	4June1814
		Thomas Timins	1June1810	——	1Jan.1812
Captain	{	Harry Percival Lewis	1June1802	Lt.Col.	4June1814
		John Clark	do.	——	do.
		Charles Stanser	do.	——	do.
		George Dunsmure	do.	——	do.
	5	William Minto	do.	——	do.
		John Long	do.	——	do.
		James Malcolm	do.	——	4June1813
		Palms Westropp	1Jan.1803	——	4June1814
		Benjamin Dickinson	1July	Major	25July1810
	10	William Barry	do.	——	do.
		Wm. Markham Coombe	do.	——	do.
		Paul Crebbin	do.	——	4June1811
		Thomas Mitchell	do.	——	do.
		Francis Williams	do.	——	do.
	15	Anthony Stransham	do.	——	do.
		Martin Horlock	do.	——	do.
		Sam. Madden Middleton	do.	——	do.
		Michael Arnett	do.	——	do.
		William Morrison	do.	——	do.
	20	George Mortimer	do.	——	do.
		Samuel Williams	do.	——	do.
		Joseph Vallack	do.	——	1Jan.1812
		George Lewis	do.	——	4June1813
		Geo. Prescott Wingrove	do.	——	do.
	25	Thomas Shepherd	do.	——	do.
		Elias Lawrence	do.	——	do.
		John Bartleman	do.	——	do.
		Joseph Mignan May	do.	——	do.
		Robert P—— Boys	19do.	——	do.
	30	William Collins	20Sept.	——	4June1814

Captain

	Wm.Hen.MilsonBayley	18Oct.1803	Major	4June1814
	Samuel Claperton	do.	—— do.
	Alexander Watson	17Nov.	—— do.
	Thomas John Sterling	1Dec.	—— do.
35	Arthur H— Ball	21do.	—— do.
	Mark Robinson Glaze	do.	—— do.
	Henry Cox	do.	—— do.
	Edward Carter Hornby	1Feb.1804	—— do.
	Francis Wemyss	12Mar.	—— do.
40	George Jones	8May	—— do.
	Andrew Kinsman	18Aug.	—— do.
	Nathan. Hamilton English	do.	—— do.
	John Hore Graham	do.	—— do.
	William Sladden	do.	—— do.
45◎	Richard Bunce	do.	—— do.
	James Butler Fletcher	do.	—— do.
	Thomas Adair	do.	—— do.
	George Baile	do.	—— do.
	John Jackson	do.	—— do.
50	Charles Meredith	do.	—— do.
	John Ridley	do.	—— do.
	John Parry	do.	—— do.
	Robert Hart	do.	—— do.
	James Thompson	7Sept.	—— do.
Captain - 55	Thomas Henry Morice	do.	—— do.
	Heneage William Creswell	do.	—— do.
	Rob.BartholomewLynch	1Dec.	—— do.
	Alexander Gillespie	21do.	—— do.
	Gilbert Elliot	9Apr.1805		
60	Edward Nicolls	25July	Major 28Aug.1810
	Thomas Clarke	1Aug.	
	James Montagu Bevians	do.	
	Marmaduke Wybourn	do.	
	James Michael Johnson	do.	
65	Thomas Sherman	15do.	
	Alexander Brown	do.	
	John Campbell	do.	
	William Connolly	do.	
	Henry Augustus Durre	do.	
70	William Macdonald	do.	
	Gideon Nicolson	do.	
	James Nicholson	do.	
	George Beatty	do.	
	William Haviland Snowe	do.	
75	Henry Rea	do.	Major 27Oct.1814
	Robert Clarke	do.	
	Edward Coxe	do.	
	Thomas Adams Parke	do.	
	Francis Hole	do.	
80	William Rowe	do.	

Captain

	Edward Jones	15Aug.1805	
	Archibald M'Lachlan	do.	
	Edm. Netterville Lowder	23do.	
	Alexander Shairp	9Nov.	
85	William Thomson	20do.	
	Thomas Carter	26do.	
	John Wolrige	do.	
	James Short	24Dec.	
	George Marshall	1Jan.1806	
90	Christopher Epworth	2Apr.	
	George Gray	26do.	
	Robert Torrens	26July	Major 12Apr.1811
	Nathaniel Cole	24Sept.	
	Dougal Stuart	1Dec.	
95	Edward Michael Ennis	24Mar.1807	
	Isaac I'Anson	24Apr.	
	John Owen	4May	
	John Robyns	19June	Major 27Oct.1814
	Edward Baillie	31Oct.	13Jan. 1807
100	Peter Jones	18Nov.	
	Arthur Hull	16Jan.1808	
	Mortimore Timpson	13Feb.	
	William Ramsay	29do.	
	Thomas Inches	16Apr.	13Jan. 1807
Captain - 105	James Wilson	27July	
	John Wright	do.	
	Robert Commins	do.	
	George M'Gie	do.	
	Hugh Ross	10Nov.	27July 1808
110	Robert Phillips	15do.	do.
	Duncan Campbell	23do.	do.
	Philip Luscombe Perry	20Jan.1809	do.
	Thompson Aslett	15Feb.	do.
	Ed. Hancock Garthwaite	do.	do.
115	Frederick Delmont	20do.	do.
	W.Tho.Joll.Matthews	13Mar.	do.
	Henry Priddle	26Apr.	do.
	Francis Lambert	9June	do.
	Robert Grace	22July	do.
120	Jaspar Farmar	22Nov.	10Nov.
	Robert Stevens	15Jan.1810	23do.
	John Sandford	do.	30Dec.
	Richard Parry	2Feb.	20Jan. 1809
	Robert White	do.	do.
125	Robert Pinkerton	7Mar.	19June1807
	Richard Owen	1June	15Feb. 1809
	Theophilus Paterson	5do.	20do.
	Henry Waring	26do.	5Apr.
	John Brittain	28do.	26do.
130	John Spurin	30do.	22July

Captain

		Charles Fred. Burton	19July1810	9Aug.1809
		Thomas Lake Wills	do.	do.
		Aug. Keppel Colley	22Sept.	2Nov.
		William Robinson	24do.	22do.
	135	Robert Foy	13Aug.	Major 4June1811
Captain -		John Sargent Smith	19do.	2Feb. 1810
		John Turner	26do.	23Mar.
		Richard Roe Bignell	27do.	1June
		George Peebles	3Sept.	1Jan. 1807
	140	Thomas Lewis Lawrence	8Jan.1812	19July 1810
		William Judson	2Jan.1815	22Nov.1809

2d Captain - James Hull Harrison   23Feb.1814

		Gilbert Langdon	1July1804	27Jan. 1796
		Thomas Dymock	12do.	
		James Murray M'Cullock	17do.	
		Rd.JohnFred.Crowther	18Aug.	
	5	Thomas Steele Perkins	do.	
		Joseph Walker	do.	
		George Kendall	do.	
		John Cockell	do.	
		Thomas Appleton	do.	
	10	Charles Cupples	do.	
		Edward Naylor	do.	
		Richard Dexter Hicks	do.	
		Michael Burton	do.	
		Denzil Ede	do.	
	15	Thomas Peebles	do.	Adjutant
		William Pridham	do.	
		Richard Harvey Marcer	do.	
1st Lieutenant		George Cull	1Sept.	
		Thomas Seward	do.	
	20	Lewis Pryse Madden	do.	
		Joshua Saffery Sayer	do.	
		William Murray	7do.	
		Walter Powell	21do.	
		Wm. Moulden Burton	21Dec.	
	25	Tho.BeckfordHornbrook	1Sept.	
		Tho. H. Wm. Desbrisay	19Jan.1805	
		Edward Hancock	23do.	
		John Hayes	1Mar.	
		Geo. Devereux Harrison	14do.	
	30	William Derrington	23do.	
		James Henry Patton	9Apr.	Adjutant
		Cha. Robinson Miller	10May	
		George Augustus Bell	1July	
		Abraham Henry Gordon	18do.	
	35	Henry Spry	25do.	

	Samuel Mallock	4 Aug. 1805	Adjutant	
	Patrick Robertson	do.		
	David Marlay	do.		
	Peter Connolly	15 do.		
40	Thomas Moore	do.	Capt. 21 Nov. 1810	
	Athelstan Stephens	do.		
	William Baker	do.		
	John M— Pilcher	do.		
	Thomas Stevens	do.		
45	William Spittle Bond	do.		
	Wm. Henry Robinson	do.		
	Edmund Affleck Chartres	do.		
	Richard Edwards	do.		
	David Anderson	do.		
50	Samuel Crowe	do.		
	John Fred. Low Crofton	do.		
	David James Ballingall	do.		
	Richard Farmar	do.		
	John Campbell	do.	Adjutant	
55	Henry Timpson	do.		
	Acheson Crozier	do.		
	Charles Griffith	do.		
	Benjamin Bunce	do.		
	Richard Blakeney	do.		
60	Cornelius James Stevens	do.		
	John Campbell	do.		
	William Clarke	do.		
	Robert John Little	do.		
	John Hewes	do.		
65	Alexander Campbell	do.		
	Ambrose A— R— Wolrige	do.		
	Edward Pengelly	do.		
	Thomas Carr Steward	do.		
	John Macintosh	do.		
70	Donald Campbell	do.		
	Wm. Henry Strangeways	do.		
	Robert Kellow	do.		
	John Rawlins Coryton	do.	Adjutant	
	Thomas Pollock	do.		
75	John Lawrence	do.	Adjutant	
	William Bate	do.		
	Richard Turnbull	do.		
	Walter James Stewart	do.		
	John Weaver	do.		
80	William Moore Morgan	do.		
	John Peter Pleydell	do.		
	Robert Beaumont Galloway	do.		
	Joshua John Wylde	do.		
	John Hay	do.		
85	Patrick Toole	do.		

1st Lieut. (bracket spanning rows 60–69)

3 B

		Edward Rees	15Aug.1805
		Hugh Mitchell	do.
		Edward Morgan	do.
		George Grieve	do.
	90	Giles Meech	do.
		Charles Wales	do.
		John James	do.
		Robert Steele	do.
		Samuel John Payne	do.
	95	George O'Neill	23do.
		William Young	12Sept.
		John Wilson	13do.
		William Burton	27do.
		George J— Bristow	28do.
	100	Robert Mercer	18Oct.
		George Wright	25do.
		Henry Elliot	5Nov.
1st Lieut.		Charles Forbes	9do.
		Philip Kinneer Jessop	11do.
	105	Nathaniel Batt Grigg	20do.
		Wm.StephensKnapman	17Jan.1806
		John Cooke	15Feb.
		Henry Lay Hannam	do.
		Wm. Predux Gilborn	18do.
	110	Joseph Cinnamond	22do.
		William Laurie	1Mar.
		Archibald Dunlop	1Apr.
		John Couche	26do.
		Samuel Burdon Ellis	29do.
	115	John Morgan	11May
		Robert Gordon	13do.
		Alfred Burton	7July
		Wm. Summersett Dadd	16Aug.
		James Laurie	24Sept.
	120	George Elliot Vinicombe	1Oct.
		William Nicol	1Dec.

		William Calamy	18June1807
		Edward Hooper Howes	1July
		John Yate	18do.
		James Tho. Cracknell	17Aug.
2d Lieut. -	5	James Thomson	18do.
		John Browne	31do.
		Francis Agar	19Sept.
		Henry James	7Dec.
		John Hicks Mallard	8do.
	10	William Remfry	14do.

2d

	Benjamin Shillito	4Jan.1808
	William Cupples	do.
	Richard Hickman	7do.
	James Flexman	27Feb.
15	John Barker	2Mar.
	John Brutton	15do.
	Joseph Luddington	31do.
	James Hallum	do.
	Richard Couche	28Apr.
20	David John Watts	20May
	John Henry Davies	21do.
	James Patrick Furzer	25do.
	Dover Farrant	1June
	John M'Lauchlan	20do.
25	Henry Arnold	16July
	James Fynmore	1Sept.
	John Baker	6do.
	George Spurin	do.
	John Bloomfield	do.
30	Wm. Burrough Cosens	do.
	John Richard Mascall	7do.
	Walter Biddulph	do.
	Ja. Hungerford Morgan	8do.
	Henry Gritton	do.
35	John Arscott Tickell	do.
	Richard Wm. Pascoe	12do.
	William White	13do.
	Roger Sawry Tinklar	14do.
	Richard Bunce	do.
40	Thomas Sullock	16do.
	James Clarke	19do.
	Henry Hood Hamilton	do.
	John Buckley Castieau	22do.
	Edward Capel	29do.
45	Richard Searle	30do.
	Rob. Gordon Atkinson	5Oct.
	Thomas Blakeney	do.
	John Tothill	8do.
	George John Holton	10do.
50	John Connell	do.
	Fred. Daniel M'Quarrie	11do.
	John Curtayne	29do.
	Robert Henry	1Nov.
	George And. Campbell	5do.
55	Harry Tyrrel Watkins	12do.
	Fortescue Graham	17do.
	Munro Fenton	24do.
	Robert Ogden	26do.
	Fred. Jermyn Casborne	29do.
60	Thomas Wade	5Dec.

2d Lieut.

		John Meadon Croad	8 Dec. 1808
		George Hugh Palliser	2 Jan. 1809
		John Furzer Elliot	4 do.
		Charles Coote Barry	12 do.
	65	Campbell Robertson	10 Feb.
		John Lewis	15 do.
		Henry Smith	18 do.
		John Jackson	22 do.
		Samuel Lloyd	24 do.
	70	Thomas Marshall	25 do.
		Rich. Maurice Morgan	do.
		James Baker	28 do.
		George Baxter	3 Mar.
		Frederick Parker	4 do.
	75	William Allen	10 do.
		Henry Bryant Skinner	do.
		William Roy Pearson	11 do.
		James Whitcomb	13 do.
		William M‘Kinnon	do.
	80	Peter John Jas. Dusautoy	14 do.
		Charles Williamson	16 do.
		John Mears	20 do.
		John Parslow Jones	22 do.
		Rawlins Wm. Walter	1 Apr.
2d Lieut.	85	Thomas Drinkwater	4 do.
		Edmund Herle	do.
		John Stroud Field	7 do.
		Peter Mears	11 do.
		John M‘Arthur	14 do.
	90	George Victor	18 do.
		Joseph Childs	21 do.
		William Ford	29 do.
		Maiden Gray	4 May
		Patrick M‘Veagh	9 do.
	95	Guy Parsons	16 do.
		Charles Rusher	25 do.
		H. Martin Blennerhasset	29 do.
		Charles Wm. Moore	31 do.
		William Oliver Aichison	do.
	100	William Hagerty	5 June
		Hugh Evans	14 do.
		Samuel Robert Wesley	26 do.
		Wm. Grier Williamson	8 July
		Andrew Hendry	do.
	105	William Anderson	12 do.
		George Richard Child	24 do.
		Johnson How	26 do.
		Robert Williamson	10 Aug.
		William Davis	12 do.
	110	Lewis Agassiz	31 do.

2d

		Lewis Dunkerley Woore	21 Aug. 1809
		Thomas Park	30 do.
		James M'Farlane	8 Sept.
		George Griffin	18 do.
	115	John Willcocks	6 Oct.
		Thomas Hicks Cater	12 do.
		Joseph Jameson	15 Nov.
		Samuel Campbell	6 Dec.
		Samuel Cox	22 do.
	120	John Hackett	12 Jan. 1810
		John Jenkins	19 do.
		John Rice Williams	24 do.
		Edward Reeves	25 do.
		William Tod	2 Feb.
	125	John Wood	5 do.
		Charles Clarke	8 do.
		Alexander Jervis	19 do.
		John Scanlan	26 do.
		Richard Knowles Barnes	6 Mar.
	130	Francis Macnamara	7 do.
		Robert Davies	do.
		John Law	14 do.
		Isaac Toby	3 Apr.
2d Lieut.		George James	4 do.
	135	Charles Webb Bridge	9 do.
		Caldwell Glassen	4 May
		Henry Fraser	16 do.
		Thomas Bond	25 do.
		David Jones	6 July
	140	John Ware	14 do.
		James Scott	18 do.
		George Bowden	30 do.
		John W— Simpson	2 Aug.
		Wilson Nicolls	7 do.
	145	Hamilton J— Johnston	25 do.
		John Chidell	do.
		William Richard Flint	3 Sept.
		Philip James Sturgeon	13 do.
		Arnold Beeston	20 do.
	150	Robert Smithwick	3 Oct.
		Robert Moses	16 do.
		Charles Hall	17 do.
		Edmund Nepean	27 Nov.
		Edward Hockley	15 Jan. 1811
	155	George Walter	17 do.
		James Read	21 do.
		Paul R— Carden	22 do.
		John George Hill	28 do.
		Edward Manico	2 Feb.
	160	John Hall Porter	4 do.

		Valentine Beadon	14Feb.1811
		Thomas Armstrong	19do.
		James Barry	21do.
		Robert Hassall Owen	22do.
	165	Edward Bathurst	26do.
		Charles Mathew Purdy	11Mar.
		Charles Vyvyan Hoare	12do.
		Thomas Fynmore	6Apr.
		John Rogers	10do.
	170	William Cookson	16do.
		John Alexander	27do.
		John Fitzgerald	29do.
		Francis Smith Hamilton	2May
		James Henry Meredith	do.
	175	John Missing	10do.
		Herbert Vaughan	14do.
		John T— Brown	21do.
		C.CartwrightWilliamson	23do.
		Charles Roe	1June
	180	Richard Standish	28do.
		Augustus Hailes	do.
		Thomas Mitchell	4July
		Frederick Thompson	6do.
2d Lieut.		James Walter	12do.
	185	James Barry	30do.
		Thomas Stockwell	2Aug.
		John Brown Williams	10do.
		Thomas Mitchell	29do.
		Lansdale Brown	21Sept.
	190	Edward Augustus Parker	23do.
		William Topham	26do.
		Samuel Hugoe	1Oct.
		Henry Forbes Guernsey	9do.
		Edward Basson	5Nov.
	195	Henry Parker	18do.
		David Young	do.
		Joshua Edleston	19do.
		Henry Savage	2Dec.
		George Baker	16do.
	200	Thomas Hawkins	18do.
		Joseph Mullins Dowling	24do.
		John Denman	28do.
		John Stone	20Jan.1812
		Robert Thacke	6Feb.
	205	George Dawkins Lane	15do.
		Charles Sampson	20do.
		Henry Bennett	26do.
		Thomas Thomson	29do.
		Henry Arden	5Mar.
	210	James M'Conechy	10do.

2d

2d Lieut.		Edward John Blake	26Mar.1812
		Charles William Pearce	do.
		William Henry Taylor	30do.
		Thomas William Trollope	1Apr.
	215	Ralph Carr	9do.
		George Serjeant	11do.
		John Wheadon	do.
		George Philipps	15do.
		Alexander M'Dougall	20do.
	220	David Davies	do.
		Thomas Borrett Reed	24do.
		Thomas Hurdle	do.
		James Wood	25do.
		Edw. William Churchill	1May
	225	Edward Mallard	4do.
		Robert Wright	6do.
		Henry Noble Shipton	12do.
		Samuel Brook	13do.
		Thomas Hugo	15do.
	230	John Thomas Hinton	25do.
		Henry Clayton	11June
		Douglass Petteward Brisac	12do.
		Edward Chillcott Gundry	18do.
		Thomas Parson Anderton	19do.
	235	William H— Sturgeon	24do.
		John Colquhoun	29do.
		William Gordon	13July
		Charles Staart	22do.
		Benjamin Yarnold	23do.
	240	John Morgan	25do.
		William Dunston Skinner	do.
		Samuel Walker	30do.
		Frederick Woodcock	3Aug.
		James Coultrey	18do.
	245	Edward Appleton	26do.
		John Morice	28do.
		David Tweedie	do.
		Henry Pitt	2Sept.
		Frederick Hewett	9do.
	250	James Johnston	18do.
		James Watson	21do.

Adjutant		James Henry Patton	15Aug.1805	1st Lt.	9Apr.1805
		Samuel Mallock	do.	————	4Aug.1805
		Thomas Peebles	28Feb.1809	————	18Aug.1804
		John Rawlins Coryton	5Sept.1811	————	15Aug.1805
	5	William Bate	19July1814	————	15Aug.1805
		John Campbell	27Sept.	————	15Aug.1805

Quarter-

QuarterMaster
- Samuel John Payne 18Nov.1808
- Robert John Little 30Aug.1811
- Thomas Moore 3Feb.1812 Capt. 21Nov.1810
- James Faden 23June1813

Paymaster of Division
- *Lt. Col.* Fred. H. Flight 29July1802
- *Capt.* Edward Parke 8May1804
- *Capt.* George Varlo 23Aug.1805
- *Capt.* Thomas Mould 16Sept.1813

BarrackMaster
- *Capt.* George Belson 1Apr.1791
- *Capt.* N— A— Hunt 14Apr. 92
- *Capt.* T— H— Letham 26June 99
- *Capt.* John H— Bright 29Aug.1805

Surgeon -
- James Rickman 30Aug.1791
- Robert Tainsh, *M. D.* 17Nov.1810
- Thomas Kein, *M. D.* 12Feb.1812
- Richard Dobson 17Dec.1814

Assistant Surg.
- John Henry Bridgman 2Dec.1806
- William Billings 29Oct.1810
- Arthur *Fry* 5Dec.1812
- Peter de Porre 9Nov.1814

ARTILLERY

ARTILLERY COMPANIES.

Captain -	William Minto	1Sept.1804	Lt.Col. 4June1814
	Thomas Adams Parke	15Aug.1805	
	Richard Parry	25July1809	20Jan. 1809 '
	William Robinson	22Nov.	
	Tho. Lewis Lawrence	19July1810	
	Charles Fred. Burton	26Oct.1813	9Aug.1809
	James Hull Harrison	23Feb.1814	
First Lieut.	Ambrose R— Wolrige	24Dec.1805	15Aug.1805
	John Lawrence	24Nov.1806	do.
	David Anderson	24Nov.1807	do.
	George Elliot Vinicombe	1Oct.1806	
	George Elliot Balchild	12Mar.1807	
	John Wilson	10June	
	John Ja. Patrick Bissett	13Oct.	
	James Walker	27July1808	
	John Maule	19May1809	
	John Harvey Stevens	2Sept.	
	Richard Charles Steele	11Jan.1810	
	James Adolphus Moore	14May	
	Henry A— Napier	5June	
	Theo.SamuelBeauchant	22Sept.	
	Robert Gilbert	19Dec.	Adjutant
	John Bezant	5Sept.1811	3Feb. 1806
	William Henry Devon	15Jan.1812	11do.
First Lieut. en Second	Jervis Cooke	28Oct.1812	26May 1806
Second Lieut.	Henry James'	14Mar.1809	7Dec. 1807
	Robert Henry	17Jan.1811	1Nov.1808
	Francis Agar	16Feb.	19Sept.1807
	Dover Farrant	17July	1June1808
	Wm. Oliver Aitchison	18Mar.1812	31May 1809
	George John Holton	21May	10Oct. 1808
	John Barker	28July1813	2Mar.1808
	John Lewis	1Oct.	15Feb. 1809
	Robert Wright	4Nov.	6May 1812
	James Barry	20Dec.	30July 1811
	Charles M— Purdy	17Oct.1814	11Mar.1811
Adjutant - -	Robert Gilbert	25June1813	1st Lt. 19Dec.1810

OFFICERS of the ROYAL MARINES

Who have been allowed to retire

ON THEIR FULL PAY.

Colonel	Wm. Souter Johnstone	30Dec.1791	Lt.Gen. 1Jan.1801
	John Barclay	21Dec.1803	Gen. 4June1813
	George Elliot	do.	Lt.Gen.25Oct.1809
	Richard Bright	do.	——— 4June1811
	Henry Anderson	25July1809	21Dec.1803
Lieut. Colonel	Edward Hill	1May1798	16Sept.1795
	Richard Bidlake	6Apr.1807	Col. 4June1814
	James Home	27July1808	——— do.
	James Cassell	15Feb.1809	
	John James	24Mar.1812	1Jan. 1812
	Waldegrave Tane	do.	do.
Major	Samuel Biggs	1Oct.1797	1Mar.1794
	Robert Anderson	1May1800	Lt.Col. 1Jan.1798
	George Ball	1Aug.1805	29Apr.1802
	Henry Reddish Furzer	10Nov.1808	Lt.Col. 4June1814
	James Errol Gordon	23Mar.1810	25Apr.1808
	Hugh Holland	do.	Lt.Col. 1Jan.1812
	Richard Graham	30June	——— 4June1814
	Francis Lynn	24Mar.1812	——— do.
	James Wemyss	16Sept.	——— do.
	Richard Timpson	5July1813	——— do.
Captain	William Sharp	17Jan.1772	Major 12June1782
	Francis Lindsay	20May	——— do.
	Benjamin Weir	14Nov. 76	———18Nov.1790
	Charles Stewart	10May 79	——— 1Mar.1794
	Hugh Dawes	15July 80	Lt.Col. 1Jan. 98
	Peter Desbrisay	1July 81	Major 1Mar.1794
	Cha. Berkeley Money	8Sept. 82	——— do.
	Arthur Ball	28Apr. 93	———29Apr.1802
	James Weir	4May 95	Major 6Dec.1799
	Thomas Young	29Oct.	
	Thomas Guildford	15Mar. 96	Major 25Apr.1808
			Captain

Captain	William Buchan	13June1796		
	John Mich. M'Namara	15do.		
	John Victor	18July		
	David Wilson	28Oct.	Major	25Apr.1808
	Thomas Hopper	29do.		
	Abraham Ja. Tregent	18Nov.		
	John Simpson	23do.		
	James Knox	19Jan. 97		
	George Wolfe	18Apr. 98	Major	25July1810
	Alexander M'Kenzie	1May		
	Benj. W— M'Gibbon	19Aug. 99	Major	4June1811
	Charles Griffith	10July1800		
	Henry Hodge	14Jan.1801		
	William Clements	15do.		
	Robert M'Leod	2July1803		
	John Burn	7do.	Major	4June1814
	James Atcherly	18Aug.1804		
	William Dymock	15Aug.1805		
	Samuel Perrot	27July1808		
	William Bowden	do.		
	Wm.Bennett M'Millan	15Nov.		
	Richard Tucker	26June1810		
First Lieut.	Alexander Thompson	14Apr.1778		
	James Dusautoy	21Jan. 79		
	William Wightman	21Dec.		
	John Campbell	13Aug. 94		
	Thomas Halls	24Apr. 95		
	John Ede	1Jan. 99		
	George Gra. Chambers	30May		
	Charles Rea	4Oct.1800		
	George Meredith	1Oct.1801		
	Zaccheus Miller	19July1803		
	Octavius Scott	15Aug.1805		
	Thomas Snelgrove	7Aug.1806		
	Lewis Rosely	27July1808		
Second Lieut.	Henry Rogers	4Apr.1780		
	Vesey Bishop	11July		
	William Collins	25Nov.		
	Walter Tait	16Mar. 97		
	Ross Morgan	11Sept. 98		
	John Green	1May1801		
	John Henry Mortimer	7May1807		
	James Henry Tregent	13Sept.1808		

Paymaster and Inspector } Francis Hastings Doyle, *Esq.* 29, Parliament Street, Westm.

Assistant to the Resident Commandant, Captain George Kempster, Half Moon Street, Piccadilly.

Agent, Charles Cox, Esq. Bartlett's Buildings, Holborn.

A LIST

[1815]

A LIST

OF THE

REDUCED OFFICERS

OF THE

LAND FORCES AND ROYAL MARINES,

ON HALF-PAY, &c.

Disbanded and Reduced at various times in and since the Year 1745,
and previous to the Year 1814.

600   601

	Rank in the Army.
Colonel Fraser's *Marines*	
2d Lt. John Fleming	
Adjut. Thomas Bennett	
Maj. Gen. Gually's *Dragoons*	
Capt. Rt. Brown (*as Cap. of F.*)	
Earl of Crauford's *Dragoons*	
Cornet Sir Jas. Campbell, Bt. (*en Sec.*)	
Royal Regiment of Horse Guards	
Q. Mrs. Samuel Howlett	
Richard Morton	
George Heap	
1st Regiment of Dragoon Guards	
Cornets John Wright	
Robert Gibson	29Dec.1762
John Lodge Wilcoks	3May1800
Q. Mrs. Benjamin Holmes	
George Newell	
John Reid	
Thomas Holder	
2d Regiment of Dragoon Guards	
Lieut. Henry Legard	31Dec.1761
Cornet William Watts	8Oct.1803
Q. Mrs. John Bowles	
Samuel Wilton	
John Morris	
William Hewitt	
Thomas M'Cann	

	Rank in the Army.
Q. Mrs. Joseph Daum	
Robert Brooks	
Vet. Sur. Thomas Smith	22Apr.1799
3d Regiment of Dragoon Guards	
Capt. H.H.St.Paul (*Infan.*)	25Dec.1802
Cornet Henry Holah	4May1800
Q. Mrs. Edward Bolton	
James Woodehouse	
Percival Spoons	
4th Regiment of Dragoon Guards	
Cornet Samuel Wm. Harrison	16July1800
Q. Mrs. Ham. Hewetson	
Matthew Dunn	
James Henry	
F. H. Bankes	
Darby Coleman	
Surg. John Paddock	2Oct.1806
5th Regiment of Dragoon Guards	
Lieut. John Creagh	8Apr.1799
Q. Mrs. Thomas Bunton	
William Bradbury	
George Dunlop	
Thomas Colts	
James Gill	
John Colts	
James Connor	
Richard Haslam	25Aug.1799
As. Surg. John Richard Elmore	16May1811
	6th

3 G

Rank in the Army.

6th Regiment of Dragoon Guards
Q. Mrs. William Henery
Thomas Thompson
Patrick Fitzsimons
Miles Sweeney
James M'Lean
Vet. Sur. Caleb Blinman — 4Jan.1802
7th Regiment of Dragoon Guards
Cornet J— M— Hamilton — 24June1802
Q. Mrs. John Ingham
Daniel Leeson
Edward Follenus
1st Regiment of Dragoons
Q. Mrs. James Bent
William Braybrook
2d Regiment of Dragoons
Capt. Martin Tho. Cocksedge — 8Apr.1802
Lieut. Henry Moore — 25Dec.1755
Cornets J— W— Barton — 25Sept.1801
George Falconar
Q. Mrs. Richard Oliver
John Livingstone
William Mervie
John Pearton
James Thompson
Gavin Peden
John Richmond
William Hamilton
John Cowan
3d Regiment of Dragoons
Capt. William Bolton — 4Apr 1805
Cornet William Elves — 15July1761
Q. Mrs. William Simpson
John Jackson
Jacob Bean
As. Sur. William Jones
4th Regiment of Dragoons
Cornets Daniel Brown — 8Dec.1759
Joseph Tyndale — 19Aug.1799
Joseph Bidwell — 24June1802
Q. Mrs. Thomas Smith
Hugh Sutherland
Thomas Parkes
John Seymour
John Thompson
James Anderson
Surg. James Mack — 31May1789
Vet. Sur. Thomas Burrowes
6th Regiment of Dragoons
Q. Mrs. Edward Rogers
James Emack
William Bishop
7th Regiment of Light Dragoons
Lieuts. James Macdonald — 23Mar.1797
John Allen Cooper — 27Apr.
Cornet Hen. Hankey Dobree — 24June1802
Q. Mrs. Jacob Pope
James Thompson
William Atkins
George Bright

Q. Mr. John Rudd
8th Regiment of Light Dragoons
Q. Mrs. Edward Reardon
James Davis
Joseph Everitt
9th Regiment of Light Dragoons
Q. Mrs. Bernard M'Guire
John Chartres
John Rutledge
Thomas Wood
Vet. Sur. Joseph Gain — 24Mar.1808
10th Regiment of Light Dragoons
Capt. Martin Williams — 16Mar.1809
Lieut. Jas. Luckett (Infantry) 19June1801
Cornets V— Jones — 24June1802
Henry Carter — do.
Q. Mrs. Peter Edwards
John Masterman
David Lloyd
F— Rumann
Richard Hadden
Joseph Barrow
11th Regiment of Light Dragoons
Lieuts. John Grantham — 27Aug.1801
Stephen Pitt — 29do.
Robert Foot — 30Oct.
George H. Walters — 24June1802
Cornets Robert Boyes — 27Aug.1801
Thomas Napier — 23do.
Q. Mrs. Thomas Watson
James Brokman
Edward Rilley
Thomas Roadley
Surg. Morgan Bullock
12th Regiment of Light Dragoons
Q. Mrs. Douglas Morrison
Pattison Cowen
Peter Hallion
13th Regiment of Light Dragoons
Cornets William Scully — 24June1802
George Sutton — do.
Q. Mrs. John King
William Mitchell
14th Regiment of Light Dragoons
Lieut. Walter Ritchie — 22Apr.1807
Cornet Matthew Kemble — 24June1802
Q. Mr. Joseph Wright
15th Regiment of Light Dragoons
Capt. Rd.W.H.HowardVyse 24June1802
Lieuts. Henry Spooner — 12June1801
Francis Hurt — 16do.
John Every — 17Mar.1802
G— A— Ld. Rancliff 24June
John Newton
Paym. Edw. P. Onslow — 18Aug.1808
Q. Mrs. Richard Collington
John Henry
George Dickson
John Timson
Isaac Wardley

Q. Mrs.

Rank in the Army.

Q. Mrs. Thomas Ledger
James Cock
George Elliott
Vet. Sur. John Feron   1Aug.1805
16th Regiment of Light Dragoons
Capt. John Thurston   7Apr.1802
Lieut. Charles Coles   7Apr.1802
Cornet John Cooper   1Jan.1763
Q. Mrs. Thomas Tranter
Frederick Wm. Murray
Richard Turpin
Edward Caelmed
James Smith
17th Regiment of Light Dragoons
Lieut. Thomas Cockerill   9Aug.1801
Cornets William Woodley   31Dec.1781
Cornelius Low Wallace 8Jan.1783
Robert Knight
Lucius Concannon
C— E— J— Nugent 24June1802
Q. Mr. John Sweeney
18th Regiment of Light Dragoons
Capt. John Priestly (Infan.) 31May1795
Lieut. Duncan Campbell
Cornets John Colinge   10Apr.1762
John Heavyside
Q. Mrs. Joseph Carlisle
Henry Smith
James Grady
As. Sur. W— M— Pitt   23July1803
Vet. Sur. John Nesbitt   21Aug.1800
19th Regiment of Light Dragoons
Capts. John Hare   23Mar.1781
Wm. T. Harwood Col.25Apr.1808
Lieut. William Cave Brown 26June1782
Cornets John Monk   2July1782
Philip Gresley   7Feb.1783
Chaplain William Barrow   6May1783
Q. Mrs. William Cross
Robert Tennent
20th Regiment of Light Dragoons
Cornets John Leche   28Sept.1781
William Cowden 10Apr.1783
Alexander Luders   15May
Surgeon Owen Owen   25Dec.1780
Q. Mrs. James Lambe
John Lawrie
21st Regiment of Light Dragoons
Capt. John Tho. Amherst   12July1788
Lieuts. Frederick Caldwell
Sir Chas. Halket, Bt. 11Oct.1802
Cornets William Stephenson   17May1762
William Hoste   15May1776
Christoph. Codrington 14Aug.1782
John Pidcock   19May1783
Adjutants Philip Perrey   24Oct.1760
George E— Eastaff   1Apr.1783
Surgeon William Thomas   26Jan.1780
Q. Mrs. William Melland
William Hope

Rank in the Army.

Q. Mrs. Francis Scott
George Thorne
William Hunter
William Simms
22d Regiment of Light Dragoons
Capts. Edw. Letherland   Maj.29Apr.1802
John Braddeley   15Mar.1799
John Varlo Petre   3May1800
Lieuts. Timothy Shelley 20June1781
Aaron Lawson   31Aug.1795
Humphrey Bowles   20July1802
W.H.Wynter (Inf.)   12Dec.1805
Cornets Jas. Drake Brockman 28Mar.1783
Benjamin Terry   25Jan.1785
John Cole Cooper   23Dec.1795
Nicholas Fitz Gerald   9Dec.1799
Thomas Reid   3May1800
Robert Colman   17July1801
R— J— Dobree   24July1802
Chaplain Samuel Oliver 27Nov.1781
Q. Mrs. Robert Jamieson
Richard Anderson
James Webster
John Bourke
Richard Minor
Thomas Padget
John M'Laughlin
John Ellis
Henry Delhunty
Thomas Raby
Thomas Hubbard
William Paterson
Surgeon Alexander Barr   8Apr.1782
23d Regiment of Light Dragoons
Q. Mrs. Samuel Smith
John Glynn
25th Regiment of Light Dragoons
Q. Mr. James Finegau
26th Regiment of Light Dragoons
Capts. David Balfour Hay   7Dec.1797
George Bussche   13Sept.1798
29th Regiment of Light Dragoons
Major Edw. Dawes Payne 1Sept.1795
30th Regiment of Light Dragoons
Q. Mrs. Archibald Read
James Roche
Henry Heacock
James Garden
Thomas Hickin Shaw
31st Regiment of Light Dragoons
Major John Pringle Lt.Col.4June1811
Q. Mrs. James Kelly
Henry Johnston
Jasper Brett
James Matthews
William Daw
32d Regiment of Light Dragoons
Chaplain Lewis Henry Young   9Oct.1794
Q. Mrs. Hugh Hall
William Hurst   Q. Mrs.

3 G 2

Rank in the Army.

Q. Mrs. Pierce Byrne
Pierce Costello
John Kenny

33d Regiment of Light Dragoons
Chaplain Arch. Hamilton Trail   31May1795
Adjutant Joseph Ramsay   21Oct.1795
Q. Mrs. Isa.c Horner
William Jackson
Charles M'Cord
Joseph Beazley
Surgeon Edward Campbell   2Oct.1794

Tarleton's Regiment of Light Dragoons
Capts. Francis Gildart   28Dec.1782
George Dawson   31do.
Lieut. Benjamin Hunt   25Dec.1782
Cornet William Wells
Adjutant John Price   6Sept.1783
Q. Mrs. Thomas Embree
John Hagan
Abel Sands

Lister's Regiment of Light Dragoons
Q. Mr. Lawrence Norman

York Hussars
Major Thomas Foster   Lt.Col.25July1810
Capts. Charles Stone   22Nov.1797
Algernon Disney
Lieut. A— Henry Kelsey   24Dec.1802
Cornets Richard Dixon   27June1800
John George Tricke   20Feb.1801
Vet. Sur. Edward Harrison   17Sept.1802

Hompesch's Mounted Riflemen
Major Richard Payne   Lt.Col.4Jan.1811
Capt. Rd. Toulmin North   8Sept.1802
Lieuts. Anthony Berkonhault   30Dec.1797
G— Frederick Vogelly   1June1801
Augustus Grovesteins   4July
Augustus Quintin
Cornets Joseph Kauffman   24Feb.1800
Augustus Bergman   1Sept.1801
E— L— Wilson   24Oct.1802
Paym. Nicholas Malassey   30Dec.1797
Q. Mr. Henry Beil
Vet. Sur. Charles Sheill   1Oct.1797

1st Regiment of Foot Guards
Lt.&Cap. Tho. Marlay   Lt.Col.25Oct.1809
P. Everard Buckworth   4June1798
Sam. J-— Townsend   28Aug.1799
Charles Monday   23Oct.
George Bryan   25Nov.
Q. Mr. Matthew Thomas   1790
As. Sur. Charles Edward Clarke 4June1801

Coldstream Regiment of Foot Guards
Lt.&Cap. Richard Bolton   13July1797
John Allen Lloyd   13Dec.
Hon. Alex. Murray   25Nov.1799
D. Mackenzie (as Cap. Lt. of Inf.)   4Apr.1801
Surgeon Charles Combe   14Nov.1805

3d Regiment of Foot Guards
Lt.&Cap. J. Murray Grant   Major1Mar.1794

Rank in the Army.

Lt.&Cap. Philip Ray   Major1Jan.1812
J.Cha.TuckerSteward   11Nov.1795
Charles Jenkinson   26Feb.1798
Thomas Penruddock   25Nov.1799
Q. Mr. Stewart Kermack   1790

Brigade of Foot Guards, Lt. Inf. Bat.
Surgeon Henry Gore Clough

Earl of Loudoun's Regiment of Foot
Adjutant Ludovick Grant

1st Regiment of Foot
Capts. John Fraser
Jas. Vincent Mathias   5Sept.1782
Lieuts. Dugald Stewart   29May1782
Henry Eaton   9Sept.1799
Ensigns George Turner
John Hamilton

2d Regiment of Foot
Capts. James Ackland   18Nov.1782
Joseph Kirkman   17June1783
Thomas Fairburn   30Sept.1795
Tho. Dean Pearce   17June1800
Lieuts. George Dawson   2Feb.1784
M— K— Young   13Nov.1804
Ensign Robert Farquhar   19June1783

3d Regiment of Foot
Capt. George, Earl of Westmeath   24Sept.1803
Lieuts. James Henry Oswald   30Mar.1789
John, M. of Tullibardine.
Charles Hilditch   15Sept.1808
M— P— Berry   21Oct.1802
Ensign St. George Conyers

4th Regiment of Foot
Majors Alex. Stewart   Lt.Col.25July1810
Capts. Anthony Tho. Lefroy   22May1794
Thomas Winckley   5Sept.1795
William Robins   27Feb.1796
Veddo Glumer   30Dec.1797
George Wilbraham   2Oct.1801
George Cooper Ridge   4Dec.1806
Francis G— Goodwin   5Dec.1811
Lieuts. John Warner   19Feb.1781
William De Stinton   2Jan.1797
L.— de Bosse   30Dec.
SirJohn Gordon, Bt.   24Apr.1798
William Fuller   20Feb.1799
Robert Ludgate   26Oct.
C— Whyte   31do.
David Seton   3Nov.
James Nash   11Dec.
John Robertson
John Smith   19June1800
William Sharpe   31Jan.1801
Alexander Bassett   12Feb.
J. Baron de Souville
William Lang   26Sept.1801
Julius Dalmage   28Aug.
Ensigns Alexander Forbes   23Nov.1781
Benjamin Andrews   24June1783
William Wooton   28Nov.1799

Ensigns

[1815]

Rank in the Army.

Ensigns Joseph Henry Palmer　3Sept.1801
　　　David Plenderleath　6May1802
　　　F— W— Desailly　24Oct.
　　　Henry Edw. M'Niel　15June1804
　　　John Nicolls
　　　James Hook　19May1808
Paym. John Cowell　3Apr.1801
　　　Gustavus Nicolls　29Mar.1798
Q. Mr. Hector Hutchinson　25Dec.1802
Surgeon William Hepburn
5th Regiment of Foot
Majors Dri. J. Morgan Lt.Col.25July1810
　　　Horace St. Paul Lt.Col.25July1810
Capts. Thomas Souter Major4June1814
　　　Richard Croker　29Nov.1780
　　　Hugh Hughes　9July1803
　　　Hon. Richard Murray 18Apr.1805
Lieuts. Charles Morgan　17May1772
　　　John Caldwell　27Nov.
　　　William Meredith　10Apr.1783
　　　John Mackenzie　10Aug.1799
　　　George Ley　23Sept.
　　　Henry Mathey
　　　Edw. V— Fitz-Gerald 14Dec.1796
　　　M— Hare　15Aug.1805
　　　John Kier　4Mar.1806
Ensigns Edward Harling　26Apr.1780
　　　Robert Forster　26Nov.1799
　　　John Taylor　23Apr.1800
　　　William Wheatley　5Apr.1801
　　　Francis Wilkinson　do.
Surgeon Andrew Johnstone　1Dec.1796
As. Sur. Alexander Dawson 19Dec.1799
　　　Lambert Tate　1Aug.1805
6th Regiment of Foot
Lieuts. John Wall　22Nov.1775
　　　William Haynes　24June1783
　　　Michael Silvaugh　24Sept.1787
　　　Alexander Greer　8Jan.1801
　　　Charles Black　6Nov.1802
Ensigns Samuel Dobree　24June1783
　　　James Macpherson　24Sept.1804
7th Regiment of Foot
Capts. Thomas Bilby　18Sept.1781
　　　Humphrey Graham　17Jan.1782
　　　Richard Magennis　15Aug.1811
Lieuts. Sir Wm. Twisden, Bt. 14Oct.1778
　　　Alexander Walker　3May1796
　　　Edward Scott　10Dec.1799
Paym. John Armstrong　23Nov.1804
8th Regiment of Foot
Capt. William Payne　1Apr.1795
Lieuts. Roger Twigge　18Mar.1760
　　　William Marler　20Dec.
　　　Robert M'Dougall　12Dec.1781
　　　John Browne
　　　John Bannatine　6Apr.1801
Ensigns Philip R— Fry　11May1778
　　　George G— Robinson 24July1802

Rank in the Army.

9th Regiment of Foot
Lt. Col. Hon. Wm. J. Gore Col.25July1810
Majors Thomas Brown　29Jan.1802
　　　J. A. Castleman Lt.Col.29Apr.
Capts. Sir Rob. Crauford, Bt. 14Aug.1783
　　　Dick Vandepant　22May1802
Lieuts. Edward Biddulph　1May1772
　　　Henry Waring Knox 31Mar.1787
　　　John Warrington　1Dec.1796
　　　Andrew du Moulin　16Mar.1797
　　　Edward West　9July1798
　　　John Lidderdale　21Feb.1799
　　　Alexander Sutherland　4Nov.
　　　William Crowe　18do.
　　　Charles Evans　21Mar.1800
　　　J— D— Parsons　24Mar.
　　　Thomas Rose　2Oct.1801
　　　William Tomlyn　25Aug.1804
　　　Henry William Lovatt 18June1807
　　　John Harvey Ollney
Ensigns John Skene　3June1795
　　　Robert Macpherson　25Jan.1799
　　　Marmad.Rt.Longdale 17June1802
　　　William Sam. Colket 23June1804
　　　Fred. Le Mesurier
Paym. John Wright　31Oct.1799
Sur. Thomas Wilson　5Sept.1799
　　　Thomas Fitz-Gerald　10Aug.1801
As. Sur. P. Mulheran　11Sept.1797
10th Regiment of Foot
Capts. Robert Adair　8Feb.1781
　　　Hugh Alex.Sutherland 10July1801
Lieuts. Murray Babington　6June1780
　　　George Green　1Oct.1796
　　　Henry Goode　24June1802
Ensign William Ross　20June1783
11th Regiment of Foot
As. Sur. Walter D— Irwin　21Dec.1797
12th Regiment of Foot
Capt. Ligonier Chapman　18Oct.1778
13th Regiment of Foot
Capt. Hay Livingstone　30Sept.1795
Lieut. William French　6Apr.1801
Ensigns John Marson　3Mar.1782
　　　Edward Sheridan　15Mar.1800
15th Regiment of Foot
Capts. Theobald Bourke　9July1803
　　　Henry Kirwan　22May1804
　　　C. Townshend Wilson 1June1809
　　　William Hay　2May1811
Ensigns Nathaniel Coffin　21Mar.1783
　　　Joseph Carter　4Dec.1799
　　　John Humphreys　26Mar.1806
16th Regiment of Foot
Capt. Edward Stirling　27Sept.1799
Lieuts. James Greenough　27Sept.1799
　　　Richard Blakeney　1June1808
Ensign Francis Gordon　6Oct.1784
17th

	Rank in the Army.
17th Regiment of Foot	
Capt. Sir John Scott, Bt.	2May1783
Ensign Duke Gifford	24June1783
18th Regiment of Foot	
Capt. James Sheldon	
Lieuts. Richard Baillie	3Mar.1780
John Marsh	22June1785
Lucius Talbot	20July1809
—— Gooday	25Sept.1811
—— Corry	16Apr.1812
Ensign E. Wentworth Pearce	11June1794
Sur. Bonnell Cory	17Oct.1805
As. Sur. Henry Douglas	28Feb.1811
19th Regiment of Foot	
Capt. J. Car. Smith	Lt.Col.4June1814
Lieuts. Archibald Bogle	12Oct.1760
Evan Baillie	
Surgeon Thomas Clarke	16Sept.1795
20th Regiment of Foot	
Capts. William Culliford	2Mar.1776
Richard Norman	21June1783
Hon. James Stopford	11Aug.1794
Francis Raleigh	1July1795
Thomas Sheridan	19Sept.1805
Lieuts. William Laybourne	24Feb.1762
Robert Lenox Colville	24Dec.1794
Tique Macmahon	18Dec.1797
Francis M— Turner	7Aug.1801
John Probyn	14Apr.1804
Edward John Watton	9June
Ensigns Benjamin Babbage	24June1783
Robert Reid	24Nov.1802
Paym. James Harrison	21Feb.1798
Q. Mr. Peter Robertson	30Aug.1799
21st Regiment of Foot	
Capt. John Jones	2Mar.1776
1stLieut. John Murray	11Mar.1782
22d Regiment of Foot	
Capt. Brereton PoyntonMaj.12June1782	
Lieut. William Bellet	8Dec.1784
Ensigns Matthew Blood	
Edward Darley	13Jan.1800
Thomas Hodson	8June1803
23d Regiment of Foot	
1stLieuts. James Sheviz	12June1801
J— Moss	24July1802
Edmund S— Long	8Aug.1805
Paym. Walter Bromley	14Feb.1805
24th Regiment of Foot	
Capt. William Ferguson	3Feb.1776
Lieuts. Richard Nash	13Feb.1765
Richard Widmore Knight	
William Tho. Lacon	29July1796
Thomas Minster	6Oct.1801
Samuel Harding	27Aug.1803
Bernard Ward	29Jan.1805
25th Regiment of Foot	
Capt. William Adair	1June1780

	Rank in the Army.
Capts. William Henry Short	30July1789
Jas.SholtoDouglas Maj.1Mar.1794	
Hon. H. F. Cavendish	6June1811
Lieuts. William Duncanson	18Sept.1780
Wm. Marq. of Lothian 23Dec.1785	
Edward Collis	3Mar.1799
Ensigns Francis Craig	19Apr.1780
A— D— O'Kelley	20June1783
Chaplain William Parker	
Surgeon Charles Stewart	26Nov.1807
26th Regiment of Foot	
Lt. Col. J. M. Mainwaring	Col.4June1813
Major L— W— Otway	Col.4June1813
Capts. Walter Scott	Major19Mar.1783
Francis B. Eliot	Major4June1814
Hugh Crawford	9Dec.1793
G. Hamilton Dundas	22Apr.1802
Percival Pym	15June1804
Henry Langley	21Mar.1805
Lieuts. Archibald Macdonnell	25Apr.1797
George Ross	29Apr.1806
Walter Nugent	9Nov.1809
Ensign James Scrimger	24June1783
27th Regiment of Foot	
Capts. John Pringle	21Feb.1784
John Pring	27Apr.1809
Lieuts. David Crowe	5Apr.1796
Richard Moore	16May1800
Donald Campbell	
JamesDukeColeridge	21Mar.1805
Arthur Sayers	9Oct.1806
John Edwards	16Dec.1807
Thomas Moore	8Mar.1810
Stephen Hastings	13May1812
Ensigns J— Killingley	20June1799
T— W— Broadbent	30Oct.1800
Richard Graves	26Feb.1801
James Graham	24Nov.1802
John Swabey	29do.
James White	26Oct.1804
Q. Mr. John Mounts	7Mar.1796
28th Regiment of Foot	
Lieut. Richard Leslie Parker 14May1804	
Ensigns Robert Smith	22June1780
Joseph Hammont	30Jan.1806
29th Regiment of Foot	
Capts. DouglasHamiltonCraik24June1783	
James Coleridge	28Feb.1785
Lieuts. W— P— Seymour	21Apr.1795
Samuel Holden	13Mar.1796
James Brown	25July1800
William Short Tyeth	13Nov.
Spoteswood Bowles	26July1801
Ensign Francis Enys	19June1783
30th Regiment of Foot	
Lieuts. Charles Abbott	26May1759
David Maxwell	10Nov.1762
Hugh Kennedy	11do.
Archibald Bertram	2July1796
Rd. Francis Freeman	7Aug.1800
	Lieuts.

Rank in the Army.

Lieuts. Alexander Young   8Oct.1802
      Thomas Pennington   19Nov.1803

31st Regiment of Foot
Capt. Theodore Morrison   30Oct.1777
Lieuts. John Darcus   11Aug.1759
      Vernon Nooke   6Apr.1761
      Hamilton Maxwell   12Nov.1773
      Robert Trotter   30Oct.1801
      James Bond   21Apr.1804
Ensigns Alexander Simpson   5Jan.1782
      Alexander Campbell   24June1802

32d Regiment of Foot
Capt. George Mauritz   12Oct.1809
Lieut. David,*Earl of* Buchan 27Sept.1762

33d Regiment of Foot
Capt. Charles Blackmore   28Mar.1805
Lieuts. Humphry Clarke   27Aug.1759
      Jeremiah Palmer   1June1778
      John Matthew   30May1792
      Robert P— Bell   8May1796
Ensign Darcy Molyneux   12Dec.1787

34th Regiment of Foot
Capts. George Churchill   6Jan.1776
      Archibald Cumine   8Aug.1783
Lieuts. William Watson   13Sept.1760
      James Grant
      Maurice Atkin   20Oct.1781
As. Surg. John Gamble

35th Regiment of Foot
Capts. Nutall Green   Lt.Col.25July1810
      Stewart Henry Drury   3Dec.1794
      John Carden Strong   22Jan.1795
      John Imthurn   30Dec.1797
Lieuts. Ralph Adderley   7Nov.1759
      Charles Skene   2Jan.1794
      Thomas Martin   16Jan.1793
      R. Campbell Hamilton 13Feb.1794
      Thomas Holmes   4Sept.1795
      Alexander Mackenzie 10July1799
      Alexander Campbell   28Apr.1802
      Lewis Gordon   27May
      Edward Wright   13Aug.
      James Skene   25Feb.1804
      ———— Manners   12Mar.1807
      Charles Theo. Hall   16Apr.
Ensigns William Montgomery   4Feb.1800
      Thomas Tyrrell   31Mar.
      John Ella   11Aug.1799
      Roger Vaughton Burnell 21do.
      Saumarez Brock
Q. Mr. P— Steel   16Nov.1799
As. Surg. Evan Morgan   1Nov.1799

36th Regiment of Foot
Major George R. P. Jarvis   20Dec.1810
Capts. John Boland   Lt.Col.1Jan.1812
      Edward Ridgeway   26Nov.1799
      Henry ReynoldsHinde 29Nov.1805
      Maurice Blake   21Aug.1806
      George Burrowes   6Nov.
      J. Percival Beaumont 13Oct.1808

Rank in the Army.

Lieuts. John Fowell   29May1761
      John A— Bradell   25May1809
      James Yearman   28June
Ensign William Blackiston   4Apr.1809
Surgeon John Little   10Aug.1796

37th Regiment of Foot
Capts. Sam. Tuffnell Barrett 19Mar.1783
      William Ogden   24Aug.1802
Lieut. Rd. Tyrrell Barnes   13Oct.1780
Ensigns Augustus Browne   24June1783
      Thomas Andros   do.

38th Regiment of Foot
Capt. Henry Croker   4Dec.1779
Lieut. Shapland Swiney   4Mar.1776
Ensign Christopher Somers   24June1783

39th Regiment of Foot
Lieuts. Emanuel Walton
      George Worseley   21Mar.1805

40th Regiment of Foot
Capts. John Ogilvy   3Sept.1781
      George Chambers   18Sept.1794
      William Williams   23Sept.1799
Lieuts. John Hall   25Aug.1794
      Gilbert Gardiner   22do.
      James Geddes   15Aug.1795
      John Jones   18Aug.1796
      Andrew Batwell   9Feb.1801
      H— John Macquarie   1July1802
Ensigns Thomas Fernybough 21May1783
      John Basset Campbell 24June
      Thomas Rogers   17Oct.1799
      J— Introina   8Oct.1801
      Donald Cameron   8July1800

41st Regiment of Foot
Capt. Fra. William Schuyler   6Feb.1801
Lieuts. Ormsby Claud. Smith 2Sept.1802
      James Saunderson   18Jan.1810
Ensign John Berenger   23Nov.1804
Surg. Thomas Douglass   24Dec.1812

42d Regiment of Foot
Lieuts. Adam Stewart   24July1758
      Christopher Davis   28Dec.1778
      Wastell Cliffe   3Aug.1785
      Simon Fraser   1July1795
      Donald Cameron   7Aug.1805
      Thomas Swanson   25Oct.1810
Q. Mr. Donald Mackay   17Oct.1805
Surgeon Thomas Farquharson

43d Regiment of Foot
Lieuts. Humphrey Lloyd   11May1781
      John Morland   21Mar.1783
Ensign William Coulson   20June

44th Regiment of Foot
Capts. Clifton Wheat   7May1782
      D.W.*Earl of* Mansfield24July1802
Lieuts. John Robins
      Thomas Boles   14May1807
Paym. Thomas Havelock   24Jan.1799

45th Regiment of Foot
Capts. John Bower   6Aug.1793
                       Capts.

	Rank in the Army.
Capts. Peter Cotes	26Aug.1794
Edward Scott	3Dec.1796
Lieuts. Thomas Squire	19July1787
James Miles Milne	31Mar.1810
Ensigns John Eason	27Nov.1802
Thomas Worthington	24June1783

46th Regiment of Foot

Capts. George Price	25Nov.1799
George Young	16May1805
Lieut. John Beckwith	25Oct.1782

47th Regiment of Foot

Capts. Gerrard Irvine	1Apr.1780
William Honywood	12Apr.1782
J. Penniston Milbanke	11Mar.1795
Lieut. William Robinson	28Oct.1795
Ensign Samuel T— Foote	1Aug.1805

48th Regiment of Foot

Capt. William Thomas	11Feb.1794
Lieut. Robert Skerrett	18Mar.1795
Ensign John Dalyell	19June1785

49th Regiment of Foot

Capts. John Biddulph	17Dec.1780
Edward Cheshire	15Dec.1804
Lieut. Ballantine Sewell	18June1801
Ensigns Edward Langford	24June1802
Alex. Brodie Campbell	do.

50th Regiment of Foot

Lt. Col. William Chabot	*Col.* 4June1814
Capts. Samuel Fitzherbert	22Dec.1777
Christopher Sweedland	12Nov.1794
Ivory B— King	12July1810
Lieuts. Isaac Allibone	28Feb.1761
Robert Newman	
Edwin Horsburgh	3Dec.1762
Robert Fraser	29July1784

51st Regiment of Foot

Lieuts. Humphrey Nixon	30July1762
Willis Croft	14Mar.1772
John Handcock	8Oct.1779
Ensign George Sanderson	9May1783

52d Regiment of Foot

Lt. Col. ⊙*Hon.* H. Arbuthnot	9May1811
Lieuts. John Amherst Long	16June1795
John Joseph	6June1800
Lachlan Macpherson	20Mar.1802
Joseph Allen	24Dec.
Ensign Thomas Randall	24June1783

53d Regiment of Foot

Capt. Martin Sayer	31May1809
Lieuts. John Smith	16Apr.1796
Francis Campbell	6Dec.1798
GerardFred.FinchByng	26Jan.1801
Edward Snowden	21Apr.1804

54th Regiment of Foot

Capts. Francis H. Doyle	*Lt.Col.* 1Jan.1812
Alexander Robertson	6Feb.1777
Cha. D. Shekelton	*Maj.* 4June1814
Lieut. Richard Townshend	22Feb.1796
Charles Aylmer	31Mar.1804
George Napper	

	Rank in the Army.
Lieuts. George Connellan	14Mar.1805
William Brooke	4Apr.
Charles Kirby	30Jan.1806
John Sharpe	19Apr.1809
Ensigns Richard Greensword	9Aug.1799
Richard King	16Apr.1800
John Good Murphy	23Oct.
Robert Barrett	20Mar.1806
Paym. William Brereton	

55th Regiment of Foot

Capt. Lewis Fenton	2Apr.1807
Ensigns William Brook	24June1783
Henry O'Hara	do.

56th Regiment of Foot

Lieuts. John Chapman	26June1779
George Johnstone	27Sept.1781
Donald M'Leod	26Aug.1794

57th Regiment of Foot

Capt. James Fenwick	19Apr.1781
Lieuts. Clement Debbieg	12Aug.1785
C. Dom. J. O. Doyer	26Sept.1794
Feltham Watson	8Feb.1808
Michael Busteed	8Aug.1811
Ensign Vaughan Waldron	24June1783

58th Regiment of Foot

Lieut. Alexander M'Adam	20Oct.1782
Ensign James Mead	24June1783

59th Regiment of Foot

⊙ **Capt.** John Taylor	
Ensigns John Robinson Tydd	7Feb.1783
Charles Gouthey	7June

60th Regiment of Foot

Capts. Maines Walrond	*Lt.Col.* 4June1814
Arthur Young	25July1778
Henry J— Kearnay	26Dec.
Fred. de Montrond	24May1779
H. Thurlow Shadwell	2Dec.
Thos. Gunter Browne	20Sept.1781
John Rotton	1July1782
William Gossip	24June1783
Edward Fuller	12Nov.1794
Charles de Hurdt	30Dec.1797
Henry Moissac	do.
Ladis. de Villers Masbourg	do.
James Raymond	do.
Balthazar, *Baron* D'Erp	do.
Charles D'Estienne	do.
Christian de Moutmarin	do.
Lewis Weise	do.
John Campbell	25June1805
James Marsden	14May1807
Thomas Smith	23Mar.1809
Lieuts. Abraham Lowe	1July1765
Conway Blizard	
Robert Holland	29June1780
Barclay Scriven	18Sept.
Charles Brown	23Sept.
John Young	27Apr.1781
Wm. James Stevenson.	5July1782
	Lieuts.

		Rank in the Army.
Lieuts.	Thomas Booker	3Mar.1776
	Lord Charles B. Kerr	1July1795
	Peter King	3Mar.1797
	Louis Desprez	22May
	John Hatz	30Dec.
	Charles Joseph Bellot	do.
	Charles Kraftt	do.
	David M'Andrew	29Jan.1801
	John Morris	26May1805
Ensigns	Robert Simpson	25Feb.1783
	Wm. Bradshaw Clinton	4July
	George Slack	17Feb.1794
	J— Hobday Lade	14Feb.1781
Adjuts.	Colin Mackenzie	
	William Kell	10Dec.1794
Q. Mr.	C— Lewis Sudon	1Sept.1796
Surgeon	Richard Stewart	13Aug.1802
As. Surg.	Joseph Holman	30Dec.1797

61st Regiment of Foot

Capt.	Gilbert Stewart	26July1812
Lieuts.	Hill Christy	24May1762
	Andrew Rock	31June1778
	George Townshend	19Sept.1782

62d Regiment of Foot

Lieuts.	Charles James	
	John Parker	25June1775
Ensigns	Thomas Graham	30Oct.1782
	Thos. Francis Billam	24June1785
Surg.	John Carnegie	5Sept.1811

63d Regiment of Foot

Capt.	Benjamin Barker	25June1775
Lieuts.	Mungo Fleming	14Jan.1762
	James Lindsay	22Aug.1794
	George Browne	19Dec.1799
Ensign	John Milliken	

64th Regiment of Foot

Capt.	Edward Galway	6Mar.1800
Lieut.	John Wilson	4Mar.1806
Ensigns	John M'Kinnon	24June1783
	Joseph Brandon	24Dec.1802
	Neil M'Lachlan	7Sept.1804

65th Regiment of Foot

Capt.	George Duke *Lt.Col.*	30Dec.1795
Lieut.	John Bardsley	26Oct.1761
Ensign	Hersel de Lisle	16June1784
Q. Mr.	John Ferguson	28May1762
As. Surg.	James Jarvis	3Oct.1800

67th Regiment of Foot

Capt.	Richard Mullens	21Aug.1800
Lieut.	Hugh Wm. Smith	29Oct.1811

68th Regiment of Foot

Major	John Campbell *Lt.Col.*	4June1811
Lieuts.	R. Roger Aldworth	1Sept.1781
	Richard Hall Lewis	27Feb.1783
	Samuel Chambers	26June
	John Thomas Brown	26Oct.1799
	John M'Carthy	
	John Scott	3Mar.1800
	George Symes	21Aug.1801
	Thomas Woore	3Feb.1805
Ensign	Thomas Jones	19June1798

		Rank in the Army.
Ensign	Charles Creighton	24July1802
Payn.	Charles Kerr	

69th Regiment of Foot

Capt.	Charles M'Vicar	12Feb.1794
	Thomas P— Mitchell	11Apr.1811
Ensigns	William Paterson	25June1761
	Humphrey Jefferies	2Aug.1783
Chaplain	Norris Forsyth	18Mar.1795

70th Regiment of Foot

Lieut.	John Finlay	11Aug.1781
Ensign	Richard Brackenbury	24June1783
Payn.	William Hutchinson	19Apr.1799

71st Regiment of Foot

Capts.	Æneas M'Intosh	3Dec.1775
	Alexander Sutherland	29Dec.1778
	William Barker	9Jan.1784
	Francis Symes	9June1803
Lieuts.	Thomas Hawkins	
	William Preston	
	William Richardson	27Mar.1776
	Thos. H— Swymmer	16May1778
	Angus M'Donald	18Sept.1779
	John Read	26June1780
	Thomas Watt	2Aug.
	John Stuart	18Sept.
	Patrick M'Dougal	do.
	Robert Campbell	3Nov.
	William M'Leod	10Jan.1782
	Walter Ruddiman	7July1793
	Benjamin Burge	31May1794
	George Wm. Greene	30June1795
	H— M— Ormsby	31Jan.1805
	William Mollison	9Oct.1809
	Robert Roe	
Ensigns	Edward George	
	Dougald M'Donald	5Nov.1780
	William Hammond	26Sept.1787
Chaplains	Claudius Crigan	
	John Rose	11July1785
	William Shaw	12Oct.1787
Surgeons	William Horseman	
	Thomas Macredie	24Jan.1811

72d Regiment of Foot

Capts.	William Brownlow	12Apr.1780
	Charles Wright	4Apr.1782
	George Groeme	
Lieuts.	Thomas Fowler	13Sept.1762
	Christopher Goulton	
	Henry Upton	
	Thomas Ranicar	
	John Upton	
	William Gyde Adey	15July1781
	John Dunlop	14May1782
	William Gunn	20June1805
Ensign	Jonathan Ashe	
Chaplain	Thomas Bedford	30May1794
Q. Mr.	Henry Andrews	
Surgeon	Joseph Sutton	

73d Regiment of Foot

Maj.	Sir A.Cathcart,*Bt.Lt.Col.*	15Aug.1781
Capt.	Nathaniel Cooper	20Aug.1783
		Lieuts.

3 H

Rank in the Army.

Lieuts. John Mackenzie   11Oct.1778
Thomas Orchard   19Sept.1781
John G— White   17Sept.1788
Hugh Campbell   4Aug.1805
Thomas Hyde
Ensigns John Innes   4Oct.1757
Alexander Mackenzie   4Oct.1780
William Bond   9Sept.1783
Allan M'Lean
John Lepine
Chaplain James Duncan   6Sept.1783
Q. Mr. James Fraser
74th Regiment of Foot
Capt. John Forbes   31Aug.1756
Lieuts. Edward Bullingbroke
Lachlan Macquarie
John Cameron
Colin Campbell
Cofin Campbell
Kenneth Campbell
Donald M'Lean
Robert Wallace   1Sept.1781
John Comerford   9do.
Ensigns Francis D'Arcey   23July1762
Neil M'Alpine
Frederick Croker
Surgeon James Wood
75th Regiment of Foot
Capts. SirCuthbertShafto,Bt. 20Aug.1759
Thomas Freer   7Apr.1804
Lieuts. John Shadwell Connell 4Mar.1763
William Evans   23Jan.1778
Edward Lawford Cole   1Feb.
John Chalmers   *Capt.*10Apr.1782
Joseph Bassett
John Galway   6Feb.1783
Ensigns Ewen Baillie
David Gall   1Sept.1762
Michael Allen   30Apr.1763
William Burr   25June1790
Lawrence Daly   3Jan.1811
Chaplain Vere Essex Quaile   28Feb.1788
Adjutant Launcelot Reed   24Jan.1783
76th Regiment of Foot
Major Hon.S.D.StrangwaysLt.Col.22Aug.
1783
Capts. John Vignoles   *Maj.*17Nov.1780
Carr Tho. Brackenbury 1Apr.1781
John Shaw   31Dec.
Capt. Lt. Alexander M'Donald   2Feb.1784
1stLieuts. Hubert Burke   18Dec.1759
Joseph Archer   1May1760
Donald M'Queen   9Jan.1778
Patrick M'Lachlan   13do.
Hugh Rose   14do.
Thomas Kinlock   26Dec.
James Macdonald   9Sept.1780
John Murray
Benjamin Ecuyer   31Dec.1784
Tho. Rich. Hamilton   18Oct.1786
2d Lieut. William Anderson

Rank in the Army.

2d Lieut. John Campbell
Ensigns Robert Styles   28Aug.1782
Thomas Eland   11May1785
Chaplain James Macdonald   25Dec.1778
Adjutant Adam Stewart   25Jan.1783
Q. Mr. Thomas Stewart   6Sept.1780
77th Regiment of Foot
Capts. George Cartwright
James Menzies Clayhill
Thomas Prickett   26Jan.1778
William Johnstone   12Jan.1785
Richard Vachell   18Apr.1788
Lieuts. John Villiers Jacob
William Scott   8Jan.1778
Cornelius Cayley   29Mar.1781
James Mahony   19Oct.1787
Ensigns Matthew Macnamara   22Jan.1783
Robert Ainslie   14Mar.
Chaplain Alexander Mackenzie 25Dec.1777
Adjutants Alexander Campbell   1Feb.1763
Thomas Mackenzie   19Feb.1783
Q. Mr. William Haggart   16Aug.1762
78th Regiment of Foot
Capt. John Macnamara   6Sept.1794
Lieuts. John Fraser   2Oct.1794
Donald Cameron   3June1795
Hugh Fraser
Ensigns Charles Burnett   8May1760
Charles M'Pherson
Chaplain Alexander Niven
Adjutant Donald Fraser
79th Regiment of Foot
Capts. William Purefoy   13Nov.1799
Charles Campbell   25Aug.1809
Lieuts. William Lane   27Jan.1778
Thos. Mitchell Browne 7Mar.1782 ,
Edward Watson   7Aug.1794
William Hamilton
Robert Barnwall   10Oct.1795
Hon. Fran. Arbuthnot 22Apr.1802
Ensigns Nathaniel Stent
George Smith
John Minshull   25Oct.1782
Charles P— Milloway 14Apr.1804
Chaplain Philip Kitchen   8Jan.1778
Surgeon Robert Young Armstrong
80th Regiment of Foot
Lieuts. William Cornish
Robert Anderson   8Mar.1761
William Logan   25Jan.1778
James R— Dickson   1Feb.
John Grant   18Oct.
Will. John Mawhood 21Nov.
C. Maitland Barclay   9Jan.1784
Ensigns Hon.A.R.B.Danvers
John Boyd   5Dec.1782
Chaplain George Marshall   31Oct.1782
81st Regiment of Foot
Capts. Pierce Dalton
Benjamin Bloomfield 27Dec.1778
George Skene   30Apr.1781
Capts.

Rank in the Army.	
Capts. William Geekie	19Feb.1795
Nicholas Brown	29Nov.1806
Lieuts. William Roberts	21July1775
Nicholl Ewing	29Dec.1777
Charles Grant	5Jan.1778
Thomas Smith	2Mar.1785
William Wright	3Aug.
Charles M'Allister	27do.
Charles Hall	21June1794
Luke Haggarty	
Hamilton Ross	15July1795
Ensigns George Skene	25Mar.1783
John Baird	2Apr.
Thomas Francis	23do.
Benjamin Dudley	
Q. Mr. Joseph Kelsall	
Surgeon William Braid	19Dec.1777
As.Surg. Henry Chislette	15Dec.1804

82d Regiment of Foot

Lt. Col. David Cunynghame	Col.26Jan.1797
Major Robert Clayton	27July1785
Capts. Sir N. Duckenfield,Bt.	7May1779
John Houston Akers	6July1784
James Brown	12Sept.1795
Capt.Lt. John Stapleton	16June1800
Lieuts. John Reeves	6Jan.1778
Robert Wellwood	7do.
Roderick M'Neil	9do.
James Farie	16do.
Alexander M'Donnell	21do.
Robert Kennevie	22do.
Wm. F. M. Williams	10Sept.1778
Alexander Leslie	20Sept.1779
Peter Dumas	18Sept.1780
William M'Lachlan	14June1782
Archibald Campbell	18Feb.1783
Charles Coquett	1Apr.1798
John Brown	26June1808
Ensigns Wm.Fred.Mackenzie	14Apr.1784
Thomas Weignll	31Mar.1792
Chaplain Nicholas Carey	
Surgeon William Cleland	5Nov.1778

83d Regiment of Foot

Capts. Robert Davidson	29Jan.1783
Ld.W.SeymourConway	20Mar.
Alexander Prole	
James M'Dermott	25Oct.1798
William Harris	19Sept.1805
Lieuts. William Nevian	20Jan.1778
James Loudoun	22do.
William Miller	25do.
Charles Roberts	26Dec.
Thomas Markham	30Sept.1782
William Fraser	
Chaplain John Playfair	13Dec.1782
Adjutant John Butler	2Apr.1783
Q. Mr. George Innes	8Dec.1780
Surgeon Andrew Marshall	17Jan.1778

84th Regiment of Foot

Major W.Earl of Lonsdale, K.G.	Lt.Col.1Jan.1800

Rank in the Army.	
Capts. Tho. Frederick	Lt.Col.1Jan.1798
George Farquharson	
William Gordon	13Sept.1794
Bright Nodder	
John Campbell	
Lieuts. John Forster	
Robert Coote	
George Fred. Aug. Eiser	
Archibald M'Donnell	
Neil M'Lean	
Luke Crohan	
James M'Donald	14June1775
Laughlin M'Lean	do.
Kenneth M'Donald	
John M'Donald	20Sept.1779
Joseph Hawkins	11Dec.
Ensigns Henry Grant	
James Rivington	28Feb.1782
James M'Dougall	25June
Alexander Stephens	21June1785
Milbourne West	do.
Patrick Brett	24July
John Dupuy	27Sept.1787
Chaplain John Bethune	14June1775
Surgeon Robert Wildgose	

85th Regiment of Foot

Major Evelyn Anderson	Lt.Col.1Mar.1794
Capt. Lt. Joseph Adams	2June1762
Lieuts. Bodychan Sparrow	Capt28June1806
Richard Hughes	21Oct.1761
Edward Dalton	14May1782
William Crane	23Apr.1783
John Spencer Smith	18Jan.1792
Martin Dowlin	17May1796
Rob. Hen. Boughton	3May1800
John Preston Walker	5June
W— H— Garnham	15July
William Connor	20do.
William Garraway	25June1801
Robert Hovenden	11Dec.1805
Henry Prettie Baillie	28June1806
Francis Waldron	8Oct.
2d Lieuts. Needham Chiselden	
John Ruxton	29Oct.1761
John Mitford	
Edward Tudor	
Richard Rudyerd	
Ensigns Arthur Hill Brice	26Feb.1783
Otho Hamilton	
William Pitts	
John Scott	24Dec.1802
Adjutant William Muller	30Mar.1783
Q. Mr. J. Wilson	26Mar.1783
Surgeon Richard Ireland	22Oct.1803

86th Regiment of Foot

Capts. John Smith	7Aug.1780
George Torriano	12Feb.1783
Lieuts. Whitewell Butler	18Aug.1759
William Laird	29Oct.1761
Charles Durie	9Dec.1762
William Isles	5June1781

Lieuts.

	Rank in the Army.	
Lieuts.	John Green	6Dec.1781
	William Johnstone	25Mar.1783
Eusigns	Russell Arden	22Mar.1762
	James Woodward	
	Robert Burn	12Oct.1780
	John Augustus Tulk	7July1784
	Robert Paton	2Nov.1800
	Martin Wilkins	7Jan.1806
Adjutants	Tho. F. Davidson	Lt.24Sept.1787
	John M'Kinnon	

87th Regiment of Foot

Capts.	Gordon Clunes	25Apr.1762
	William Evans	4Oct.1779
	Rich. Temple	Lt.Col.19Feb.1783
	Francis Seymour	Lt.Col.1Jan.1798
	James Bird	3May1800
Lieuts.	James Cameron	3Sept.1761
	John Blaydon Taylor	6Oct.1779
	Edward Roberts	16Feb.1785
	Francis Markett	25Dec.1787
	John James Corry	9July1803
	John Johnston	
	James Garrioch	
Ensigns	William Manson	5Dec.1782
	George Samuel Collyer	24Jan.1783
	William Green	8Feb.
	Robert Young	10do.
Chaplain	James Milnes	27Jan.1761
Q. Mrs.	Robert Waugh	7Aug.1800
	Peter Dickens	

88th Regiment of Foot

Capt.	William Townsend	13Oct.1779
Capt. Lt.	Perkins Magra	Maj.19Feb.1783
Lieuts.	Nicholas Peters	
	John Campbell	7Aug.1761
	James Boyd	9Apr.1783
	William Sneyd	14do.
	John Clement	21June
	Edward P— Pilcher	14Nov.1788
	Robert Miller	
	Alured Clarke	22Feb.1800
	John Peck	3Aug.1804
	John William Armstrong	
2d Lieut.	George Campbell	30July1762
Ensigns	Robert Clowes Potts	14Feb.1783
	Francis Kerby	7June1789
	John Cosmard	11May1791
Chaplain	Edward Gardiner	12Oct.1779
Paym.	Duncan Campbell	
Adjutant	—— Peacocke	31Mar.1783
Q. Mr.	Thomas Bramby	1Nov.1782
Surgeons	John Kestell	
	Robert Bloxham	9Apr.1778

89th Regiment of Foot

Capts.	Rob. Harvey Mallory	20Oct.1779
	Charles Philips	23Feb.1781
	Samuel Evans	7May1782
	Charles Gardiner	10Mar.1783
	Nicholas H. Nicholas	10Sept.
	Edward Sankey	
Lieut.	Alexander Stewart	

	Rank in the Army.	
Lieuts.	John Forbes	
	James Fife	11July1781
	Reuben Joyneur	8Feb.1783
	Henry Deering	10Mar.
	Hugh Josiah Hansard	30Sept.1788
	Andrew Macpherson	9Feb.1804
	William Finlayson	
Ensigns	John Crozier	27Dec.1775
	Thomas Duke	25Mar.1782
	Charles Cooke	27May
	Joseph Hazlewood	24Apr.1783
	Richard Shaw	18do.
	George Gill	16May
Adjutant	Stephen Smith	18Feb.1783

90th Regiment of Foot

Capts.	John Bellairs	
	Edward Naish	28Aug.1804
Lieuts.	John Franklin	
	Alexander Graham	5Dec.1779
	Thomas Fairtlough	28Sept.1781
	H— John Baines	2Oct.
	Dugald Cameron	18Oct.1800
	T. North, Ld. Graves	24June1802
	Richard Jones	25Oct.1804
	Thomas M— Perryn	29Oct.1805
	Bryan Swyuy	
	John Bissett	23Apr.1807
	Sir Brooke Boothby, Bt.	
Ensign	William Elrington	28Feb.1783
Chaplains	Claudius Crigan	
	John Trusler	24Apr.1783
Q. Mr.	Robert Mann	
Surgeon	William Read	3Nov.1773

91st Regiment of Foot .

Major	Thomas Wooldridge	20June1811
Capts.	John Probyn	
	Anthony Kinnersley	25Jan.1780
	George Byng	24Aug.1782
	John Charles Stracie	
	Henry Ravenhill	26Sept.1802
	John Campbell	23Aug.1804
	George Wm. Stamer	
	James Maclean	9Mar.1809
Capt. Lt.	A. E. Cyrus Gordon	6July1781
Lieuts.	Phineas M'Intosh	
	John Jorden	
Ensigns	Atherton Watson	
	Robert Massey	29Sept.1777
	Joseph Pitt Toulmin	2Sept.1794
Adjutant	Thomas Walker	
Surgeon	Samuel Winnall	1Dec.1779

92d Regiment of Foot

Capts.	N— Kirkman	5Mar.1783
	William Peers	18June
	Samuel Orr	2Nov.1785
	Thomas Holmes	25Apr.1795
	Richard Beadon	25Nov.1799
	George Lawson	
	Lewis Mackenzie	25Sept.1807
	Alexander Campbell	15May1808

Rank in the Army.	
Capt. Lt. Alexander M'Donnell	
Lieuts. William Berry	7May1782
David Rae	1May1783
William Macpherson	19Feb.1799
Ensign Gregory Boraston	23May1783
Chaplains David Jones	20Dec.1779
John Webster	
Q. Mr. John Mingay	
93d Regiment of Foot	
Capts. Alexander Forbes	9Oct.1794
John Duff	
Gordon Clunes	29Aug.1800
Lieuts. Henry Overing	7Sept.1781
Francis Clapp	18Apr.1782
Thomas Clarke	18Feb.1783
Nicholas Hue	1Sept.1794
Anthony Gale	23June1804
James Dunbar	28Mar.1805
Ensigns Matthew Howell	4Nov.1782
James Howell	1Apr.1783
John Godin Bigott	14do.
Samuel Corbett	15Dec.1794
John Currie	7Aug.1795
Chaplains Thomas Bateman	7Feb.1780
William Allen	
Adjutant James Carscallion	7Feb.1780
Surgeon Thomas Thomas	7Feb.1780
94th Regiment of Foot	
Capts. Nicholas Parker	1Sept.1775
Charles Semple	21Oct.1779
Rob. Nutter Campbell	5Dec.1781
James Murray	31Mar.1787
Edmund Lombard	
Lieuts. Thomas Bridges	20July1760
Robert Scott	16Feb.1763
Hugh Hawkshaw	10Mar.1777
Richard Landreth	3Mar.1780
Thomas Foy	24Sept.1782
William Wharam	21Feb.1783
James Ferguson	6June1784
Ensigns Stokeham Huthwaite	27Apr.1780
Robert James Talbot	27June1783
John Cameron	29Oct.
C— Grant	
Joseph George Brett	7Mar.1794
Chaplain Carew Gauntlett	
Paym. James Donald	
Adjutant James Dunlop	30July1783
Q. Mr. James Cooke	26Nov.1781
Surgeons St. John Neale	22Oct.1780
J— T— O'Brien	
95th Regiment of Foot	
Major R.Earl of Athlone Lt.Col.4June1814	
Capts. John Jones	1Sept.1779
John Cheap	14Apr.1780
Patrick Jacob	Maj.19Mar.1783
John Baugh	
Alexander Cameron	
Grainger Stewart Murray	
Capt. Lt. William Rowley	15Apr.1780
Lieut. Charles Durand	7Mar.1760

Rank in the Army.	
Lieuts. Symeon Drysdale	19July1780
James Gibbons	13Mar.1783
Matthew Pearson	
Ensigns William Sutherland	28June1762
John Smith	13Apr.1780
John Langton	
William Marsh	13Mar.1783
Tho. Cresswell	Lieut.10July1796
Surgeon John Carstairs	7Apr.1780
96th Regiment of Foot	
Capts. Charles Browne	Col.4June1811
Patrick Burke	Maj.4June1811
Tho. Kennedy	Maj.3Dec.1812
William Anderson	17Apr.1804
Cha. Juste de Corci	6Sept.1806
Lieuts. Uniack Prendergast	
Stuart Adams	
Thomas Kerwan	
Robert Robinson	4Nov.1779
William Smith	23Jan.1800
Thomas Hillas	13June1805
William Ashley	25Aug.
James Pickering	17Dec.1807
John H— Clough	17Feb.1808
Ensigns George Preston	26May1782
Thomas Deane	26Mar.1783
Chaplains D— Francis Durand	8Apr.1780
Barry M'Gusty	
Adjutant James Brownе	
97th Regiment of Foot	
Major George Lind	5July1793
Capts. William Wilson	16July1778
Robert Farmer	12June1782
James Colquhoun	
William Rose	
Thomas Paterson	31Oct.1794
Capt. Lt. Robert Wallace	15Apr.1780
Lieuts. Henry Shewbridge	8Nov.1780
Thomas Thompson	8Dec.
John Edwards	24Apr.1782
Robert Grant	25June1784
Watson P— Berry	30Sept.1787
Joseph Swayne	
Ensigns James Downes	31Jan.1781
William Corbett	31July1783
Robert Phaire	7Dec.1792
John Kirby	31Aug.1794
James Moore	7Sept.1809
Peter S— Barclay	
Chaplains John Grant	
Thomas Maurice	28Aug.1781
Q. Mr. Matthew Grant	
98th Regiment of Foot	
Major H. Mord.Clavering Col.29Apr.1802	
Capt. Fran. Pink, Drummond	
Lieuts. J. Clerk Kilby M'Adam	5Jan.1781
William Wilson	1Sept.
James Nankiville	
Arthur Edwards	
William Bullock	
Ensign Thomas Browne	19Jan.1785
	Ensign

Rank in the Army.

Ensign John Gordon   3Mar.1804
Chaplain John Prichett   25Dec.1797
Q. Mr. Duncan Campbell   29May1780
Surgeon David Ogilvie   6Feb.1761
99th Regiment of Foot
Lt. Col. Francis Erskine   2Jan.1796
Majors William Say   Col.25July1810
    Christopher Bird Lt.Col.1Jan.1812
Capts. Alexander Duffe Maj.19Mar.1783
    Thomas Lane   14Oct.1761
    John Bonjour
    Thomas Christie   3Apr.1801
Lieuts. Joshua Jebb Kent   30Sept.1789
    Thomas Price   5Apr.1795
Ensigns Wm. Campbell Heatly 26May1781
    H. Carrington Bowles 19Aug.1793
    Thomas Martin   24Oct.1799
Chaplain Bryant Broughton
Surgeon James Anderson   7Nov.1794
100th Regiment of Foot
Capts. Hon. Henry Tufton
    Wm. Lord Alvanley   22Dec.1808
Lieuts. John Grant   28Oct.1760
    George Gordon   26Jan.1778
    George Baillie   25July
    Alexander M'Donald   6Oct.1781
    Donald M'Kenzie   8Nov.
    Sir Hector M'Lean, Bt. 30Apr.1784
    James Colthurst   19Mar.1785
    Alexander Forbes   7Dec.
    Edward Heard   15Feb.1786
    Andrew Pallas
Ensigns Joseph Macdonald   22July1784
    J— Fletcher   11Feb.1785
    David Le Boutillier   1June
Chaplain William Kirkbank   9June1784
Q. Mr. Thomas Dale   4Oct.1783
101st Regiment of Foot
Capts. Ludovick Grant   28Oct.1760
    John Ferrier   28Aug.1794
    James Irwin
Lieuts. Benjamin Ashe
    Duncan M'Pherson   28Oct.1760
    John Riky   3May1780
    Samuel Robert Wilson 12July1782
    John George Bell   23Dec.1785
    Adam Callander
    J— Hay   31Oct.1792
    Isaac Riches
    Humphrey Donaldson
    Sir W. Aug. Brown, Bt.
    John Ford   24Aug.1794
Ensigns Evan M'Pherson   31Oct.1760
    Thomas Barber   1Nov.1804
    Thomas Nash
    William Carter
Chaplain William Tennant
Surgeon Thomas Girdlestone
102d Regiment of Foot
Majors G. H. Mason   Lt.Col.1Jan.1801
    Alex. Colsten   Lt.Col. do.

Rank in the Army.

Capts. Lewis Majendie   5Feb.1781
    Charles Beruff   30Dec.1797
    Michael Redmond   18July1811
Lieuts. Robert Holloway   17Aug.1761
    William Harling   18Aug.1778
    Steukeley Shuckburgh 10Aug.1782
    John Murray   19June1783
    Nathaniel Forbes
    Cornelius M'Gillicuddy 1Oct.1794
Ensigns Johnson Butler
    William Sladden   27Sept.1783
Adjutant Roger Remmer
103d Regiment of Foot
Capts. John Bonner   12Feb.1762
    William J— Bethell
Lieuts. Patrick Moncrieffe   8Jan.1761
    Joseph Walsh   17Feb.1765
    Arthur Owen
    William Baugh
    Hector M'Lean   4Nov.1795
    John Reade   28Apr.1806
    James Turner
Ensigns Richard Grattan   1Dec.1779
    Roger Tomlin
Chaplain Charles Whatley
104th Regiment of Foot
Capts. Robert Uniacke   Col.1Jan.1805
    John Paxton   26Dec.1778
    William Bury   27Oct.1779
    William Shillinglaw   19May1781
    Miles Sandys   6Mar.1783
Capt. Lt. John Kortwright   25Feb.1783
Lieuts. Thomas Pembroke
    Robert Ross Rowan   18Aug.1761
    Tho. Dawson Lawrence
    James Jones   10May1781
    James Church   do.
    George Bradshaw   13Mar.1786
    Alexander Lindsay   25Feb.1795
    John Allen Bell   18June1807
    George Tyner
Ensigns William Brown
    Wheeler Barrington   17May1781
Chaplains Philip Fletcher
    William Remmington 10Apr.1782
Q. Mr. Andrew Lawrie   1Apr.1783
As. Sur. Charles Earls   21Jan.1808
105th Regiment of Foot
Capt. Sir Edw. Smith, Bt.   27Feb.1793
Lieut. Luke Dillon   24Nov.1805
Chaplain Wilfred Carter
Q. Mr. James Donald
106th Regiment of Foot
Major Wentw. Serle Lt.Col.19May1794
Capt. James Sutherland
Ensigns John M'Ghee   19Oct.1761
    Edward Barlow   2May1776
    Nicholas Metcalfe
Chaplain Gilbert Barrington
107th Regiment of Foot
Major J. Francis Bland Lt.Col.1Jan.1800

Lieut.

Rank in the Army.

Lieuts. Martin Gilpin   22Oct.1761
    Roger Parke
Ensigns Richard Storey   21Oct.1761
    Joseph Dickenson   24do.
    · John Forbes
Chaplain H— A— Hole
Q. Mr. John O'Neil
Surgeon James Steele   26May1791
108th Regiment of Foot
Lt. Col. Mungo Paumier   1Sept.1795
Q. Mr. Hugh Robertson   15Oct.1761
109th Regiment of Foot
   Major F. de Chambault Lt.Col.1Jan.1800
   Capt. Hugh Robert Duff   26Oct.1793
   Lieut. Lewis Vaslet
   Chaplain Robert Shepherd   2Apr.1794
   Q. Mr. William Skene   2Apr.1794
   Surgeon James Bannerman   2Apr.1794
110th Regiment of Foot
Lt. Col. John Taubman   Col.1Jan.1801
Majors Hon. Rob. Clive Lt.Col.1Jan.1800
    Hon.G.Carnegie Lt.Col. do.
   Capts. Charles Lenn
    William Bainbridge
    William Lloyd
   Lieut. William Tredennick
   Ensign Robert Birmingham   18Nov.1795
   Chaplain Alexander Arbuthnot   6June1794
   Q. Mr. Guy Carleton Cravey   3Nov.1794
111th Regiment of Foot
   Major Edward Charlton   1Mar.1794
   Capt. Hardress Lloyd   28Oct.1761
   Lieut. Sir Robert Grierson   16Oct.1761
   Ensign William Walter
   Adjutant Samuel Boote   17Oct.1761
   Surgeon Baldwin Wake
112th Regiment of Foot
   Majors Hon. L. H. Hutchinson
      Lt.Col.1Jan.1801
    Edward Blewitt   30Oct.1794
   Capts. Adolphus F. Duncker 29Mar.1798
    John Dick   19Sept.1804
   Lieuts. Henry Hunt   17Oct.1761
    James Price
    Thomas Archer   11Feb.1808
   Ensigns Nicholas Geo. Gaynor 30July1762
    · Anthony Gordon   11Oct.1794
   Surgeon Alexander Dunlop
113th Regiment of Foot
   Capts. John Morrison   18Oct.1761
    William Piers
   Lieut. William Rudge Horne
   Ensign William Dawson
   Chaplain John Timbrell   30June1795
114th Regiment of Foot
   Major John Shedden   Lt.Col.1Jan.1812
   Lieut. Ludovick Innes   20Oct.1761
   Ensign Peter M'Arthur   18Oct.1761
   Chaplain Joseph Preston   19July1794
115th Regiment of Foot
   Lieut. John Dalrymple   21Oct.1761

Rank in the Army.

Lieuts. Robert Bruce   24Oct.1761
    Robert Pollock   17Nov.
116th Regiment of Foot
   Capt. Patrick Campbell   10Feb.1794
117th Regiment of Foot
   Capt. Lt. Nathaniel Brown   30Mar.1795
   Chaplain Corbett Hue   9Sept.1795
   Q. Mr. Lazarus V. Morgan   22Aug.1794
118th Regiment of Foot
   Capt. William Stanton   20Nov.1801
   Ensign George Strange Nares 1July1795
119th Regiment of Foot
   Lieut. Edward Mainwaring   7Mar.1760
   Ensign William Love   26June1762
   Chaplain Roger Atcherly   12Nov.1794
   Adjutant Thomas Clarke   25June1762
   Q. Mr. Richard Clifford   29May1794
   Surgeon Thomas Webb   22Sept.1762
120th Regiment of Foot
   Chaplain Joseph Fortune   4Nov.1795
   Q. Mr. John Dupuis   27Aug.1794
121st Regiment of Foot
   Major John R. Broadhead Col.25July1810
    John French   Lt.Col.4June1811
   Capt. William Henry Digby 28Mar.1793
   Adjutant Francis Sweeney   6Sept.1794
122d Regiment of Foot
   Capt. Ninian Imrie   Lt.Col.1Jan.1798
   Chaplain John Dobbs   24Sept.1794
   Surgeon Peter Grant   25July1794
123d Regiment of Foot
   Capt. Walter Raleigh Gilbert 25Aug.1794
124th Regiment of Foot
   Major Hon. J. Creighton Lt.Col.1Jan.1801
125th Regiment of Foot
   Adjutant James Hicks
126th Regiment of Foot
   Chaplain William Jones   12Oct.1794
127th Regiment of Foot
   Capts. William Skerrett   3Nov.1794
    James Tobin
   Chaplain Jonathan Ashe   1Sept.1794
128th Regiment of Foot
   Major Henry King   8Oct.1803
   Capt. Walker Ferrand   14Apr.1804
   Ensign Stephen Bell
   Chaplain Augustus Cane   4Oct 1794
   Surgeon David M'Annaly   1Oct.1794
129th Regiment of Foot
   Capts. William Lambe Palmer 19Dec.1795
    Benjamin Williamson 1Sept.1794
   Q. Mr. Matthew Smith   10June1795
130th Regiment of Foot
   Capts. George James Riddell 14June1794
    Robert Holden   18Feb.1795
   Q. Mr. J. F. Kingsley
   Chaplain Richard Paul   12June1794
131st Regiment of Foot
   Chaplain Richard Fisher   25Mar.1794
   Surgeon Miles Egan   3Dec.1793

132d

Rank in the Army.	
132d Regiment of Foot	
Capts. Charles St. Ours	Maj.1Mar.1794
Philip Codd	12Sept.
David Erskine	29do.
Richard Davies	1July1795
Ensign Hugh Sutherland	
Chaplain Thomas Raddish	15July1795
133d Regiment of Foot	
Capt. James Sinclair	22Aug.1794
Q. Mr. George Burke	29May1806
134th Regiment of Foot	
Majors Launcelot Holland	Col.4June1814
Tho. P₁ Tharpe	Lt.Col.1Jan.1800
Capts. Charles Newton	Lt.Col.1Jan.1800
Richard Henry Stovin	
Lieuts. Richard Barry	
William Craven	24Dec.1794
Chaplain John Isaac Harrison	19Sept.1795
Surgeon Godfrey M'Garry	7Nov.1794
135th Regiment of Foot	
Major Charles Turner	Lt.Col.4June1813
Chaplain Weldon J. Malony	6Sept.1794
Officers of the late Scotch Brigade	
Capts. William Atwood Oliver	
Edward Saunderson	25June1803
Lieuts. Francis Simpson	5July1793
Robert Kennedy	7do.
John Turnbull	8do.
Lewis H— Ferrier	10Feb.1796
John Bamford	17May1803
Ensigns Alexander Campbell	27July1794
Chaplain Charles Ochiltree	5July1793
Adjutant Robert Kennedy	5July1793
Q. Mr. James Johnstone	4Jan.1794
Surgeon Charles Anderson	5July1789
Cheshire Regiment of Foot	
Capt. James Stewart	
Lieut. William Greaves	
Q. Mr. Charles Clarke	
Dublin Regiment of Foot	
Lieut. Alexander Johnstone	
Chaplain Hosea Guinness	3Dec.1794
Surgeon Thomas Smith	3Dec.1794
Glasgow Regiment of Foot	
Capts. John Urquhart	2Sept.1795
James Apthorpe	
Q. Mr. William Finlay	28Aug.1794
Kelso Regiment of Foot	
Lt. Col. John Tho. Maddison	Col.1Jan.1800
Capts. George Mackay	Maj.4June1814
James Poyntz	28Aug.1794
John B— Coulthurst	4Jan.1805
Liverpool Regiment of Foot	
Capts. William Liddiard	6Sept.1795
Arthur Chichester	12Dec.1805
Londonderry Regiment of Foot	
Capt. William Nairn	
Sheffield Regiment of Foot	
Lt. Col. Hon. John Vaughan	Col.1Jan.1800
Capts. Alexander Stewart	27Aug.1794
James M'Killigen	do.

Rank in the Army.	
Capt. Kenneth M'Kay	
Lieuts. Jeremiah Radcliffe	27Aug.1794
Nathaniel Forster	4Nov.1795
Ensigns John Blakeley	25Mar.1795
Thomas Atkins	24Jan.1805
Chaplain John Downes	27Aug.1794
Adjutant Allan Cameron	27Aug.1794
Q. Mr. George Munro	27Aug.1794
York Fusileers	
Major Ralph Gore	Lt.Col.25July1810
Capt. John Midgley	Lt.Col.7Apr.1814
Lieuts. Benjamin Hill	1July1790
Allen Campbell	12Apr.1796
Surgeon James Walker	
The King's American Foot	
Capts. Thomas Cornwall	25Dec.1782
John Wm. Levingstone	do.
Peter Clements	do.
Robert Gray	do.
Lieuts. George Cox	25Dec.1782
Barclay Fanning	do.
Leonard Reid	do.
David Purdie	do.
Thomas Barker	4Apr.1783
Ensigns Henry Nase	4Apr.1783
Serino Dwight	11July
Adjutant Alexander Cumming	25Dec.1782
Q. Mr. Donald M'Intosh	11Sept.1783
Queen's American Rangers (Cavalry)	
Capt. Morris Robinson	25Apr.1783
Lieut. Allan M'Nab	25Dec.1782
Cornets Thomas Morritt	25Dec.1782
Benjamin M. Woolsey	do.
Samuel Clayton	do.
Q. Mrs. William M'Glaughlin	
Edward Wright	
Daniel Morhouse	
Queen's American Rangers (Infantry)	
Capts. John Mackay	25Dec.1782
Francis Stevenson	do.
James Kerr	do.
Stair Agnew	do.
John Whitlock	do.
H.BennetWallop(en sec.)	do.
Lieuts. J. L. Brown	25Dec.1779
Hugh Mackay	25Dec.1782
Adam Allan	do.
Richard Holland	do.
Caleb Howe	do.
Edward Potts	26Apr.1783
Ensigns Edward Murray	25Dec.1782
Arthur Wolseley	30June1783
Surgeon Alexander Kellock	25Dec.1782
North American Rangers	
1stLieut. Thomas Dixon	25Sept.1761
The Queen's German Regiment	
Lieuts. John Grant	1Apr.1795
—— Gualy	2Apr.1800
Rene de Bouch	
John, Baron Tschudy	
Ensign Ruggero Laufranchi	3Sept.1801
	Queen's

	Rank in the Army.
Queen's Rangers	
Major Henry Shadforth Lt.Col.4June1811	
Capt. Charles Bayntum	1Feb.1798
Ensign Tho. Birds Peters	21Apr.1796
Paym. Alexander Burns	17May1799
New South Wales Corps	
Lieut. William Patullo	3Mar.1797
The Cape Regiment	
Capts. Henry Grove	Maj.1Jan.1812
John Campbell	30June1801
William N. Hopkins	26Oct.1804
Lieuts. Angus Campbell	26Sept.1794
Angus Macleod	30Aug.1798
Ensigns Henry Beavis	
A. G. Davidson	10June1802
Q. Mr. Jones Wilkie	25June1801
2d Ceylon Regiment (Ramsay's)	
Major Andrew Pilkington L.Col.2Nov.1809	
Corsican Regiment	
Lieuts. Vincenzo Bartolacci	
Jean Bigou de Cherry	
Archibald Hamilton	
Richard Richardson	5Dec.1799
James Thomas	
Thomas Bonnor	
Ensigns Henry Shawe	
John Saunders	
John Quayle	25Nov.1795
Adjutant Thomas Mortimer	4Apr.1795
Q. Mr. Peter Martin Carey	
Corsican Rangers	
Major Hon. D. G. Hallyburton	Lt.Col.
	25July1810
Capt. Philip Masseria	25June1799
Lieut. Thomas Russell	
As. Surg, William Robins	25June1802
York Rangers	
Majors Sir H. Douglas, Bt.	Col.4June1814
Robert Lucas	Lt.Col.4June1811
Capts. H. Blois Lynch	Major1Jan.1814
Duncan Macrae	
George Billinghurst	
Donald Campbell	
Thomas Webster	
G. H. Finch	29Dec.1804
Lieuts. John Macmahon	
Ulick Burke	
James A. Dennis	19Oct.1809
Ensigns Isaac Germain	
Louis Feriet	
Paym. Peter Cockburn	
As. Surg. George Norman	
Rifle Corps	
Lieut. Thomas Brereton	25Mar.1802
Royal Staff Corps	
Lt.Col.Com. John Rutherford	25Dec.1800
Capt. Henry H. Wall	8June1809
Lieut. Louis Vanzulicom	25July1799
Ensign Donald M'Arthur	18June1800

	Rank in the Army.
Ensign Nathaniel A. Jagger	28Aug.1807
Q. Mr. Robert Laughlen	28Feb.1800
As. Surg. William Stone	21Feb.1800
Dunlop's Corps	
Capt. John Christie	
Lieuts. Robert Harrison	22May1778
James M'Leod	21Aug.1779
Martin Dalrymple	19Dec.1782
David Johnston	26Mar.1783
A. Gilbert Douglas	4Oct.1805
Ensign James Bruce	
Adjutant William Tustin	2Apr.1783
Elford's Corps	
Capt. William Whiston	3May1780
Lieuts. Buckworth H. Soame	
David Gumly	28Jan.1782
Robert Howell	6Mar.
Henry Barnes	20do.
Duncan M'Donell	15July1795
Ensigns Samuel Stevens	23Feb.1781
Samuel Durnsford	
James Dodson	26Feb.1783
Isaac Hunter	4Apr.
Durell Stables	3Sept.1794
Fish's Corps	
Capts. Henry Wills	
Joseph Wilmott	6Jan.1780
Lieuts. Jonathan Arrowsmith	27Sept.1781
Robert Mecan	13Oct.
John Burke	9May1782
Ensigns Thomas Jenkins	29July1779
Wm. B. Cocker	5Apr.1783
Richard Savage	17Oct.1787
Fuller's Corps	
Lieut. Henry Percy	16Sept.1786
M'Donnell's Corps	
Lieut. Henry Rochford	
Chaplain John Webb	30Apr.1795
Pringle's Corps	
Lieuts. John Dunn	20Sept.1780
William Lilly	14May1781
Lord Strathaven's Corps	
Maj.Com. William Chester	17Nov.1780
Lieuts. Alexander Bissett	
John Dinely	
Sir John M. Oldmixon	
Thomas Wollaston	
Robert Johnston	29Jan.1780
Ensigns George Tredenick	
Peter French	
Francis French	
Waller's Corps	
Capts. Patrick Campbell	22Jan.1783
Thomas Askew	26Feb.1794
James A— Chaundy	29Mar.1795
Lieuts. Richard Goakman	17Mar.1780
William Rattray	16May1781
James Cordner	21Mar.1782
Martin Robertson	
Ensign John Sabine	8Mar.1782

3 I   *Wall's*

	Rank in the Army.
Wall's Corps	
Capt. Tho.ParryJonesParry	4Jan.1783
Ensigns George Lucas Studwick	
Humphrey Bellamy	31May1790
Ward's Corps	
Q. Mr. David Keith	20Sept.1798
2d West India Regiment	
Ensign Charles Henry F. Edgar	
Q.Mrs.of C. Henry Sloane	
George Greville	
3d West India Regiment	
Lieut.Col. Charles,*Visc.*Petersham	*Col.*4June 1814
Lieut. Lachlan M'Lachlan	11Dec.1797
4th West India Regiment	
Q.Mr.of Ca. Thomas Hiscock	
5th West India Regiment	
Capt. Cassimer de Briou	
Lieuts. William Mitchell	
Aug. de Spillebant	3May1806
6th West India Regiment	
Capts. C. L. L. Foster	*Major*19Dec.1813
Charles Straubenzie	14Dec.1804
Lieut. Robert S. Cammack	
Ensign Thomas R.Lidderdale	14Aug.1800
Q.Mr.of Ca. William Serle	
7th West India Regiment	
Capts. William Bray	*Lt.Col.*29Apr.1802
Mark William Carr	5Mar.1794
Lieut. Pierce Cotter	10Feb.1797
Ensign John Chawner	10July1801
Q. Mr. Thomas Mason	12Sept.1793
8th West India Regiment	
Major John Gordon	15Aug.1798
Capts. Thomas Huxley	*Major*29Apr.1802
Henry S— Amiel	
Edward Piers	1Sept.1795
Samuel Hayes	8June1796
Nicholas Burnell	
Gerald O'Farrell	26Aug.1806
Ensigns George Forster	25July1801
J. Lewis Butcher	18Oct.1809
Paym. Richard Seward	20Nov.1799
9th West India Regiment	
Lieut. Stephen Savarin	23Dec.1799
10th West India Regiment	
Major Alleyne H. Pye	*Col.*4June1814
Paym. Colin Ritchie	23Jan.1800
Adjutant William Skipton	7Apr.1802
11th West India Regiment	
Capt. James Johnston	
Ensign Edward Stapleton	23June1802
12th West India Regiment	
Capt. John Hay	5Aug.1799
Lieut. Joseph Champion	1Sept.1795
Royal African Corps	
Capt. James Megaw	12Sept.1811
Skerret's Regiment	
Capt. Francis Maule	*Major*4June1811

	Rank in the Army.
Donkin's Royal Garrison Battalion	
Lieuts. Alexander Chisholme	2Oct.1778
Nich. Purdie Olding	25June1781
Joseph Dunn	14Feb.1782
James Sutherland	15Apr.
William Chew	15Aug.
Thomas St. John	15Sept.
Allen Cameron	30Jan.1806
1st Garrison Battalion	
Lt. Col. John M'Donald	*Col.*4June1814
2d Garrison Battalion	
Capt. Richard Timms	14Apr.1804
Ensign Richard Clague	9July1803
3d Garrison Battalion	
Surgeon Michael O'Farrell	9July1803
4th Garrison Battalion	
Capt. John Monk Spence	16May1805
Lieut. Thomas Jones	11May1809
Q. Mr. John King	9July1803
Surgeon Thomas Manson	25Apr.1799
5th Garrison Battalion	
Major Robert Owen	*Lt.Col.*25July1810
Capt. John Cheap	9July1803
Lieut. Thomas Gartside	16Oct.1806
Ensign James Dalton	26Aug.1807
7th Garrison Battalion	
Surgeon Peter Nicoll	
10th Garrison Battalion	
Major JamesDunsmore	*Lt.Col.*25July1810
Lieut. P. Barron	14Sept.1804
Q. Mr. William Berwick	
11th Garrison Battalion	
Major Randall Gossip	*Lt.Col.*4June1814
Capts. WilliamHenryHamilton	9July1803
Barry Drew	5Aug.1804
Henry Hopkins	21Aug.1806
12th Garrison Battalion	
Lt. Col. ©George Middlemore	2Nov.1809
Capt. John Gillam	9July1803
14th Garrison Battalion	
Major Thomas Weston	*Lt.Col.*4June1811
15th Garrison Battalion	
Major John Shaw	*Col.*4June1814
Surgeon Isaac Telford	9July1803
11th Royal Veteran Battalion	
Lieut. Jeremiah Donovan	25Dec.1802
Corps of Waggoners late on the Continent	
Capts. John Dubois	30Apr.1794
Luke Cossens	5Apr.1795
Lieuts. William Johnston	27Feb.1794
John Pritchard	19Oct.
Surgeon George John	29Oct.1794
Corps of Waggoners late serving under the Earl of Moira.	
Lieut. George Thomson	
Ensign John King	
Royal Waggon Train	
Major Hamp. P. Thomas	*Col.*25July1810
Capts. Francis Wright	3Sept.1803
Richard Haviland	28Nov.1805
	Capt.

	Rank in the Army.
Capt. George Lennon	17 Nov.1808
Lieuts. James Bigsby	23Sept.1799
Edw. L. Walford	Adj.16Jan.1800
John Rait Hall	5Nov.1803
Jeremiah Crowther	27Aug.1804
Henry James Reynett	
William Rind	26Oct.
James Dowd	15May1806
John Moore	5Nov.1807
Martin Demay	22Sept.1808
Robert Bell	12Nov.
Francis Richardson	13do.
Philip A. Grobecker	11Feb.1809
William Chas. Sharp	27Apr.
John Phillips (*as Cornet*)	
Francis O'Connor	
Cornets John Bullock	23Sept.1799
William Seymour	26Aug.1804
Ernest Hoffhout	3Dec.1805
John Erasmus Spier	28Sept.1809
James Thompson	
Q. Mrs. Pierre de Calurre	
Abner Wheeler	
John King	
Thomas Patten	
Thomas Williamson	
John Page	
Loft's Recruiting Corps	
Q. Mrs. Thomas Marsh	
William King	
French's Recruiting Corps	
Capt. Charles Abraham Elton	
Lieut. William Morton	21Feb.1800
Ensigns John Thompson	
John Wood	
John Robinson	25Nov.1797
Henry James Rippe	4May1800
Adjutant James Dickson	4Aug.1804
Q. Mrs. Munro Ross	
Owen Fawcett	4Aug.1804
Sir V. Hunt's Recruiting Corps	
Ensign Daniel Overend	26Nov.1799
Bradshaw's Recruiting Corps	
Majors Wm.H.K.Erskine	Lt.Col.1Jan.1812
Alexander Barry	25Jan.1812
Thos. S. Sorell	Lt.Col.4June1814
Capts. Burgess Camac	Major11June1811
Geo. Wm. Tighe	8July1794
William Short	18Apr.1805
Lieut. Samuel Price Howell	
Ensigns John Grant	
William Edward Powell	
Thomas Payler	
Adjutant John Maxwell	19May1808
Q. Mrs. Hugh Mackay	25Aug.1800
Wm. H. Maxwell	19May1808
Jas. Campbell's Recruiting Corps	
Capt. Geo. Clarke Symonds	3Feb.1804
Lieut. W. M'Farlane	
Ensign Edward Whiteford	2Dec.1799

	Rank in the Army.
Adjutant Duncan Kennedy	
Murray's Recruiting Corps	
Lieut. George Pawlay	
Q. Mr. Jonathan Rogers	
O'Connor's Recruiting Corps	
Lieut. Archibald Campbell	
Ensign John Russell	24Oct.1794
Adjutant J. M'Lachlan	
Q. Mr. John Gough Wilson	
M'Donald's Recruiting Corps	
Major Samuel Dales	Lt.Col.25July1810
Capt. Rob. S. Newton	Lt.Col.1Jan.1800
Lieut. James Cornfute	
Ensign James Macdonald	
Adjutant David Morris	
Q. Mr. David Stewart	
Sterle's Recruiting Corps	
Major John Handasyde	Lt.Col.4June1814
Capt. John Tuck	
Lieut. Thomas Ormsby Wood	
Ensign Benjamin Pratt	28Aug.1807
Hon. Geo. Hanger's Recruiting Corps	
Capt. John Crichton	
Ensigns Humphrey Graham	
George Smith	
Ogle's Recruiting Corps	
Major George Crump	Col.4June1813
Capt. John Bonnor	18July1809
Ensign George Payne	
Adjutant Thomas Dixon	
Q.Mr. Samuel Harrison	
Kingston's Recruiting Corps	
Capt. Edward Fitzgerald	16July1800
Lieut. Rod. Robertson	
Ensigns John Wiles	23May1800
William Ashe	
Nugent's Recruiting Corps	
Major David Reid Parker	21June1800
Capt. Harry Green	4Apr.1805
Ensigns G. Dardis	9Aug.1799
William Twiss	25Mar.1800
Adjutants Henry Haven	4Sept.1800
Q. Mr. William Innes	22Dec.1809
Armstrong's Recruiting Corps	
Major Jas.K. Money	Lt.Col.4June1811
Ensigns Thomas Barrow	11Mar.1802
Edw. Omaney Wrench	do.
Adjutant Archibald Armstrong	
Bisset's Recruiting Corps	
Ensign George Durant	25Dec.1800
M'Lean's Recruiting Corps	
Lieuts. C. Gethin Kendrick	
John George Fitzgerald	
Barrack Artificers	
Capt. James Sandys	24Mar.1803
1st Lieuts. William Brew	29Jan.1801
Marcus D. Kennedy	23Nov.1804
2d Lieut. Alexander Campbell	
Invalids	
As. Sur. Henry Robert Ince	

INDEPENDENT COMPANIES.

		Rank in the Army.			Rank in the Army.
Capts.	W. C. Madan	Col.1Jan.1805	Capts.	Hon. J. Tho. Capel	
	J. Buckeridge	Lt.Col.19Dec.1786		William Davies	
	R. Hamilton	Major19Mar.1783		Francis, Earl of Moray	
	Netteville Blake			J. Marina. Grafton	
	Benjamin B. Tathwell			George J. Hamilton	
	Arch. Earl of Cassillis			George Darby	
	William Becher			John Hathorn	
	Arthur Beevor			Thomas Heneage	
	Francis Gregory	1Nov.1780		John Hext	
	Thomas Slater	11Sept.1781		Sir Robert Lawley, Bt.	
	Richard Gardiner	6Nov.		Hon. W. Ramsay Maule	
	Charles Mitchell	28Aug.1782		George Spry	
	Patrick Crichton	10Feb.1784		George Strickland	
	Bryan D. Cooke	13June1789		Robert Wilson	
	Wm. Ogle Wallis	26Feb.1790		Angus Cameron	
	Thomas B. Bower	24Jan.1791	Lieuts.	Jas.Bartlett(Pioneers)	22Oct.1762
	John Lewis Prevost	26do.		Thomas Napper	
	Francis Drouly	23Mar.1792		Charles Farquharson	31Dec.1777
	William Lin. Gardner	2Jan.1794		Thomas Davell	29July1780
	Edward Walsh	16Nov.		Marcus Lynch	8Dec.1781
	Neil Campbell	1Nov.1796		William Pringle	30Sept.1787
	William Shairp	23Feb.1797		James Molyneux	26Dec.
	George Wyke	9Aug.1799		Hon. Wm. Leeson	25June1789
	Richard Folkes	28Nov.1801		Thomas Salisbury	
	Robert Hall	4Oct.1804	Ensigns	Merwin Perry	
	John Grant	21Mar.1805		Philip Durell	14July1784
	John Chaloner	11Feb.1808		George Symmers	
	John Rist	1Jan.1810		John Cranage	26Aug.1794
	John Beynton			D. de Quetteville	
	Robert Campbell			John Geffard	

LATE INDEPENDENT AND UNATTACHED OFFICERS.

Majors	John Magrath	Col.25Apr.1808	Capts.	Walter Prosser	
	W. C. Visc. Clermont	Lt.Col.1Jan.1800		Neil M'Leod	
	G.R.Matthews	Lt.Col.29Apr.1802		George W. Rindsdal	
	J. Grant	Lt.Col.do.		Gilbert Affleck	
Capts.	Thomas Nesbitt	Col 1Mar.1794		Robert Hall	
	Hon.H.A.B.Craven	Col.4June1814	Lieuts.	William Rainsforth	24Sept.1787
	T.Wollocombe	Lt.Col.19Feb.1783		John Creighton	25Jan.1792
	J. Wemyss	Lt.Col.1Jan.1798		Frederick Bowes	30Aug.1793
	J. C. Tuffnell	Lt.Col.1Jan.1800		H. Marsh	8July1795
	Ed.VincentEyre	Lt.Col.4June1814		Walter Ferrier	23Mar.1796
	G. Aubrey	Major1Mar.1794		Dougald M'Vicar	9Nov.
	John Spilsbury	22Mar.1777		Robert Guthrie	6Mar.1797
	William Sneyd	20Aug.1782		W. Lewis de Virna	30Dec.
	Hon. J. Kennedy	8Oct.1793		Robert James Dunn	7Nov.1799
	Robert Brooke	4June1794		William Goodair	9July1803
	George Dickson	6Aug.	Ensigns	J. Neal Baldcock	27June1793
	Henry Morritt	5Oct.		Edward Smith	10July1794
	Abel Rous Dottin	5Dec.1795		Edmund Hammond	do.
	Mur. Farquharson	12Mar.1796		Montague Sadlier	15Oct.
	William Blair	25Mar.1802		John Choyce	
	Colin Campbell			Wm. Andrew Despard	2May1800
	David Gillespie			James Douglas	

FENCIBLE

FENCIBLE CAVALRY.

	Rank in the Army.		Rank in the Army
First Regiment		*Hants*	
Q. Mrs. John Hodder		Q. Mrs. John Godwin	
Matthew Thompson		William Clarkso	
John Nicholson		John Chapman	
Henry Griffith		Thomas Clayton	
Ayrshire		Alexander Reid	
Adjutant John Burrows	24May1798	*Lanark and Dumbarton*	
Q. Mrs. John Brierley		*Adjutant* Thomas Greenwood	2May1795
George Ashton		Q. Mrs. William Hamilton	
John Brown		John Nicol	
Duncan Roberston		John Milner	
Ancient British		James Boag	
Q. Mrs. Moses Levingstone		John Johnston	
John Holt		*Lancashire*	
William Golborne		Q. Mrs. Richard Plant	
William Harrison		Nathaniel Birch	
John Fowler		James Glover	
Berwick		Archibald Davis	
Adjutant John M'Laren	17Sept.1796	John Nevatt	
Q. Mrs. William Lowrey		*Lothian East and West*	
Henry Wilson		*Adjutant* John Hennings	17Apr.1795
Joseph Lowrey		Q. Mrs. John Landless	
Cambridge		John Virtue	
Adjutant William Duxbury	25Apr.1795	John Wingate	
Q. Mrs. William Winkworth		James Hill	
William Furnsworth		William Wright	
Henry Browning		*Lothian Mid*	
William Carpenter		Q. Mrs. Joseph Hopkins	
Thomas Wood		James Orr	
Cinque Ports		William Bachelor	
Q. Mrs. Thomas Stones		Robert Walker	
Thomas Rice		*Norfolk*	
Samuel Palmer		*Adjutant* Robert Alexander	10Apr.1794
Cornwall		Q. Mrs. James Gage	
Adjutant Henry Dupont	3Oct.1798	Nathan Newstead	
Q. Mrs. Stephen Caskick		Dan. Moss Pattle	
T— Kittow		John Durand	
Henry Taylor		*Oxford*	
John Hilliard		*Adjutant* George Burnell	
Thomas Julyan		Q. Mrs. Edward Hughes	
John Jackson		William English	
John Tait		John Clements	
Robert Hair		Thomas Pittard	
John Ryal		*Pembroke*	
George Pagan		Q. Mrs. Richard Bradbury	
Royal Essex		Thomas Chater	
Q. Mrs. James Canham		Charles Guest	
Francis Hayden		Thomas Dunn	
Thomas Payne		Samuel Price	
John Jennings		*Perth*	
Fife		*Adjutant* James Hay	7Feb.1798
Adjutant James Thompson	8May1795	Q. Mrs. William Jackson	
Q. Mrs. Thomas Wrench		Ebenezer M'Harg	
George M'Kelvey		William Proudfoot	
Alexander Dempster		James Duncan	
			Princess

	Rank in the Army.		Rank in the Army.
Princess of Wales's		*Somerset*	
Adjutant William Hopkins	15June1796	*Adjutant* Henry Dowell	12June1799
Q. Mrs. Robert Nich. Sanders		*Q. Mrs.* Thomas Stuart	
George Stuart		Thomas Rodd	
James Murray		Edward Talbot	
John Montfort		Robert Foot	
William Maillew		George Page	
Princess Royal's Own		William Clarke	
Q. Mrs. Charles Paterson		*Surrey*	
John Reid		*Q. Mrs.* John Pulsford	
William Congreve		Daniel M'Kenzie	
Romney		William Smith	
Q. Mrs. William Perry		James Grubb	
John Rodber		*Sussex*	
Samuel Burt		*Q. Mrs.* William Oman	
Thomas Patterson		John Robinson	
Roxburgh		*Warwick*	
Adjutant John Williamson	2July1796	*Adjutant* George M'Dowell	20June1798
Q. Mrs. William Hope		*Q. Mrs.* Thomas Guest	
William Ormston		George Womble	
Robert Helm		James Fell	
John Bruce		*Windsor Foresters*	
Rutland		*Adjutant* Thomas Bruce	18July1799
Q. Mrs. Thomas Kell		*Q. Mrs.* Richard Hayes	
William Carter		Isaac Shakespeare	
Thomas Harris		Thomas Lethgow	
R— Henry Lowe		James Storr	

FENCIBLE INFANTRY.

Aberdeen		*Cinque Port Corps*	
Q. Mr. Charles Lamont	31July1800	*Adjutant* Humphrey Owen	
Angus		*Q. Mr.* George Douglas	
Adjutants James Hunter	22Sept.1794	*Clanalpine*	
George Fairweather	20Oct.	*Majors* James O'Hara *Lt.Col.*3May1796	
1st Argyll		Hon. J. Ramsay *Lt.Col.*25July1810	
Major @ Jas. Bathurst *Col.*4June1813	*Adjutant* William Duffe	21Dec.1799	
Q. Mrs. John Campbell	1Mar.1793	*Devonshire and Cornwall*	
James Mason	22June1799	*Adjutant* Wm. Hen. Carrington 19Oct.1799	
2d Argyll		*Durham*	
Lt. Col. Francis W. Grant *Col.*25Oct.1809	*Adjutant* John Holmes	11May1797	
Q. Mr. Peter M'Dougall	16July1800	*Lord Elgin's*	
Banff, (or Duke of York's Own)		*Q. Mr.* Thomas Harrison	28Nov.1794
Q. Mr. James Hewerdine	23Aug.1801	*Essex*	
Breadalbane		*Q. Mr.* Richard Adkins	5Jan.1799
Adjutant James Ingram *Cornet*10Mar.1797	*Fife*		
Q. Mr. David Williamson	25Apr.1796	*Q. Mr.* Robert Salter	20Oct.1794
Loyal British		*Fraser's*	
Adjutant Alexander Campbell	30Oct.1794	*Adjutant* Simon Simson	29Nov.1794
Q. Mr. William Pitchford	30Oct.1794	*Q. Mr.* David Brown	1Jan.1797
Caithness Highlanders		*Glengarry*	
Adjutant Kenneth Mackenzie	28Oct.1800	*Q. Mr.* Allen M'Lellan	31July1800
Q. Mr. John Henderson	19Dec.1794	*Regiment of the Isles*	
Cambrian Rangers		*Q. Mr.* John M'Donald	4Mar.1799
Major Thomas Mellor	*Col.*1Jan.1812	*Royal Lancashire Volunteers*	
Q. Mr. Duncan Forbes	13Nov.1800	*Q. Mrs.* John Shaw	
		Edward Holme	16Oct.1794
		Limerick	

	Rank in the Army.			*Rank in the Army.*
Limerick			*Ross and Cromarty*	
Major RalphHamilton	Lt.Col.25Oct.1809		*Adjutant* Thomas Thompson	6June1799
West Lowland			*Q. Mr.* Joseph M'Intyre	7Apr.1801
Q. Mr. John Munro	1Mar.1793		*Rothsay and Caithness*	
North Lowland			*Adjutant* David Campbell	7Mar.1794
Adjutant Robert Christie	25Feb.1802		*Q. Mr.* George Sutherland	7Mar.1794
Q. Mr. John Campbell	16Nov.1794		*Scilly*	
1st Manx			*Lieut.* Henry Gudgeon	Capt.19Apr.1796
Adjutant Richard Atkins			*Southern*	
Q. Mr. Joseph Webster			*Q. Mr.* John Johnstone	1Mar.1793
2d Manx			*Surry Rangers*	
Adjutant William Kewley	11Jan.1802		*Major* Hugh Baillie	Col.25July1810
Manx			*Tay*	
Lt.Col.Com. Lord J. Murray	Col.4June1813		*Q. Mr.* Andrew Mitchell	1Apr.1798
Adjutant James Mansfield	25July1808		*The Prince of Wales's Own*	
Q. Mr. Robert Murray	25Feb.1804		*Major* Rob. Campbell	Col.25July1810
Northampton			*Q. Mr.* Thomas Barry	
Q. Mr. Roderick M'Farquhar	25Oct.1794		*The Prince of Wales's* (or Leicester)	
Northern			*Q. Mr.* W. H. Brabazon	31Aug.1796
Adjutants George Reynolds			*Princess Charlotte of Wales's*	
James Brown	10Feb.1794		*Major* E. Jas. O'Brien	Lt.Col.25July1810
Nottingham			*York*	
Q. Mr. John Baker	16Feb.1797		*Major* John Grey	Lt.Col.1Jan.1801
Orkney and Shetland			*Adjutant* Thomas Taylor	18Dec.1799
Q. Mr. George Omand	10Feb.1796		*Q. Mr.* Joseph Fowler	30Oct.1794
Reay			*Duke of York's* (or Inverness)	
Adjutant Aaron Blanche	25Oct.1794		*Q. Mr.* Alexander Cobban	21Nov.1794

OFFICERS who volunteered from the Militia to serve in Regiments of the Line, in the Year 1799.

4th Foot			*Capts.* Francis R. Holdsworth	9Dec.1799
Capts. Philip Henry Roper	25Sept.1799		John Colville	10do.
John Davies	27do.		*Lieuts.* James Bottomley	4Dec.1799
John Jones	28do.		Edward Wimboult	7do.
Richard Gardiner	29do.		*16th Foot*	
Lieuts. John B. Carruthers	25Oct.1799		*Capts.* Philip Stable	25Nov.1799
Joseph Fessey	28Nov.		William Eyre	25Dec.
John Laval	30do.		*17th Foot*	
Vincent Beatty	1Dec.		*Capt.* Robert Johnston	25Nov.1799
Robert Perrott	2do.		*Lieut.* Thomas Stanroyd	25Nov.1799
Thomas Browne	2May1800		*35th Foot*	
5th Foot			*Capt.* Samuel Wright	25Nov.1799
Lieut. Edward Lely	26Nov.1799		*Lieuts.* Stephen Else	25Nov.1799
8th Foot			Anthony Walker	do.
Capt. Stephen Terry	5Dec.1799		*36th Foot*	
9th Foot			*Capts.* Edward Dymock	28Nov.1799
Capts. William Morrall	26Nov.1799		Francis Chambre	2Dec.
Richard Frederick	27do.		John G. Smythe	3do.
15th Foot			Francis Quarme	27Nov.
Capts. Thomas B. Grantham	3Dec.1799		R. Williams	29do.
William Coffin	4do.		Jos. Jones Durbin	30do.
George Noble	5do.		*Lieuts.* Joseph Hughes	26Nov.1799
John B. Pocock	6do.		Thomas Pritchard	28do.
Edward Bayly	8do.		John Gatlive	30do.
				Lieut.

	Rank in the Army.
Lieut. Thomas Crewe	1Dec.1799
46th Foot	
Capts. Francis Huddlestone	26Nov.1799
John Vaughan	23Mar.1801
Lieuts. Humphrey Grant	26Nov.1799
George Little	27do.
32d Foot	
Capts. James South	4Dec.1799
Joseph Creed	6do.
Robert T. Symonds	7do.
Lieut. J. C. Candler	4Dec.1799
56th Foot	
Capt. Thomas H. Cooper	25Nov.1799
60th Foot	
Capt. John Ridge	27Nov.1799

	Rank in the Army.
62d Foot	
Capts. T. Thistlethwayte	4Dec.1799
John Dutton	6do.
Lieut. Archibald Munro	5Dec.1799
82d Foot	
Capt. George Stanier	3Dec.1799
104th Foot	
Lieut. Edmund Byrne	25Nov.1799
Warde's Regiment	
Capts. William Elwin	28Nov.1799
Independent Companies	
Capts. Thomas Honeyborne	25Nov.1799
Walter Hill Coney	26do.
Lieut. John Phillips	25Nov.1799
Ensign Charles Wilkinson	26Nov.1799

STAFF.

Late Permanent Ass. Qr. Mrs. Gen. { Lt.Cols. A. Nisbett 21Dec.1809
J.P.Coffin Col.4June1814

Recruitg. District { Major Fred. W. Trench Lt. Col. 25Nov.1813
Adj. J. Keane Lt.25Feb.1804

Paym. William St. Clair 25Dec.1797
Geo. Aaron Nutt 8Sept.1800
Charles Gordon 23July1803

Chaplains Robert Newburgh
Thomas Tringham 29Apr.1796
Frederick Neve 13Nov.1799

Secretary to the Gov. of Bellisle { Nath. Collyer

ChiefInsp. andComm. Gen. of Musters & Acc. to the French Corps } E. J. A. Woodford 1Aug.1794

Dep. Barr. Mus. Gen. in America } James Putman 30July1798

Deputy Judge Advocate } Stephen Kemble 20Nov.1793

Captain of the Port of Mahon } Narcis.Arguimbeau 29Apr.1802

Provost Marshals } John Thompson
Edmund Dowlin 30Nov.1793
James Mitchell 19Oct.1792

COMMISSARIAT DEPARTMENT.

Commissaries Gen. { John Jaffray 1Nov.1793
Alexander Davidson 21do.

Deputy do. Samuel Drewry 19Nov.1793
Allan Dalzell 10Oct.1795
H. L. Hunter 31May1798
Roger Metcalfe 4Aug.1801
William Booth 17May1804
William Whitmore 22Oct.1806

Dep. { William Bagster 22Feb.1810

Com. Gen. { J. B. de Bels 11Sept.1811

Assistant do. G. Duncan 21June1793
Edward Buckley 6Oct.1803
G. T. Courtenay 26Sept.1806
Theod. Mandeville 12Sept.1808
Sir J. Downie, Kt. 7Nov.1809

MEDICAL

MEDICAL DEPARTMENT.

Super-intendent General }	J. Merv. Nooth
Inspectors	Andrew M. Grieves
	George Hazleton
	William G. Straghan
	Robert Keate
	Wm. Randle Shapter
Field In-spectors }	Alexander Grant
	John White
	Joseph Cope
Dep. Direc.	Thomas Hopkins
Dep. In-spectors }	George Pinckard
	Alexander Robertson
	Charles Lind
	John Phillips
	William Tudor
	John Joberns
	James Whitelocke
	Alexander Thompson
Assistant do.	Law. S. Wilson
Assistant Inspectors }	Robert Walters
	William Greaves
	Patrick Lindsay
Physicians	Robert Gordon
	Richard Fletcher
	F. M'Veagh Macdonnell
	Stewart Crawford
	John Rogerson
	William Domier
	Sir Charles Blagden, Kt.
	William Payne
	William Wright
	Gregory West
	Samuel Cave
	Edward Nathaniel Bancroft
	Joseph Philan
	J. Watson Roberts
	Benj. Hayward Browne
	Charles Larchin
Surgeons	Daniel Jarvis
	Henry Gibbs
	John Califf
	Jonathan Ogden
	Thompson Foster
	G. Frederick Lockley
	John Bolger
	Richard Cobbe
	William Holmes
	William North
	Joseph Goldie
	John Hicks
	George Paterson
	Thomas Watkins
	Matthew Wilcox
	Thomas Davye
	John Marshall

Surgeons	Pennel Cole
	Richard Hope
	John Harris
	Robert Anderson
	Charles Blake
	John Tucker
	Thomas Forster
	Benjamin Radford
	Thomas Ross
	Andrew Bond
	Frederick Thompson
Apothecaries	Robert Constable
	Robert Wightman
	William Philips
	John Clarke
	John Harcourt
	Robert Bishop
	Robert Glasgow
	Thomas Morrison
	Thomas Reeves
	James Bell
	Wm. Hinde Fox
	John Harper Newton
	Wm. Williams
Purveyors	John Fielder
	William Fellowes
	Adam Turnbull
	Adam Murray
	William Robertson
	Thomas Byrdall Hugo
	Dennis Considen
Dep. Purvs.	Charles James Fisher
	Thomas Ogle
	Samuel Gibbons
	George Mont. Seares
	George Charles Jones
	H. Brown
	Charles Morris
	Joseph Patterson
Superann. Surgeons }	H. Portsmouth
	Edward Bishop
	John Harvey
	Archibald Mearns
	James Hall
	Matthew Harbinson
Retir. Surg.	St. Leger Hinchley
	Charles Williamson
	William Grieve
	Joseph Dowse
	James Boggs
	John Perkins Hill
	Charles Pickett Handy
	William Rose
	William Maiben
Chief Vet. Sur.	James Harrison
Vet. Surg.	James Grellier
Hosp. Corps Ensign	Charles Cotterell

PAYMASTER GENERAL's DEPARTMENT.

Ass. Dep. Paym. Gen. Alexander Green

3 K   Disbanded

Disbanded and Reduced in 1814.

Rank in the Army.

2d Regiment of Dragoon Guards
Capt. William Bush   22July1813
Lieuts. Henry Peers   22July1813
    W. Walter Stephenson 19Aug.
3d Regiment of Dragoon Guards
Capts. Hon. P. F. Cust   17Oct.1811
    William Shum   27May1813
Lieuts. James Hadden   4Dec.1806
    James Ormsby   14Mar.1808
    Edward Quilliman   26July1810
    Theobald Pepper   27June1811
    J. J. C. Harrison   21May1812
    Edward Inglis   17June1813
4th Regiment of Dragoon Guards
Capts. Henry Trafford   1Aug.1811
    Theophilus Butler   19May1814
Lieuts. Richard Crookshank   4Feb.1813
    Augustus Amyatt   22Dec.
    Tanfield B. Beridge   3Mar.1814
5th Regiment of Dragoon Guards
Capts. William Spooner   5Dec.1811
    Hon. Edward Cust   9Dec.1813
Lieuts. George Bray   16Nov.1809
    Joseph Pattison   2Jan.1812
    Henry Brooke   5Mar.
    George Spence   12do.
    Frederick Hammersley 9Apr.
    John Clarke   20Aug.
    Aug. Fitzh. Berkeley   28Jan.1813
    W— A— Dobbyn   13May
1st Regiment of Dragoons
Capts. Cha. Lucas Methuen   8July1813
    Samuel Webb   31Mar.1814
Lieuts. Osborne Barwell   2Apr.1812
    Wm. Henry Watson   7May
    Cornthw. Ommaney   13Aug.
    John Henry Slade   25Feb.1813
    John Micklethwaite   19Aug.
    Charles Blois   2Sept.
    Maur. Ceely Trevillian 30do.
    Stephen Goodenough   6Jan.1814
    And. Child. Saunders 31Mar.
    Arthur Ingleby   20Oct.
2d Regiment of Dragoons
Capt. John Pitt Bontein   26May1814
Lieuts. James Wemyss   19Nov.1812
    James Chadwick   15July1813
    —— Lawson   21Apr.1814
Surgeon Richard J. Jones   1July1795
3d Regiment of Dragoons
Capts. William Bragge   24June1813
    Champion E. Branfill 21Oct.
Lieuts. John Morshead   21May1812
    Thomas Trotter   17Dec.
    R. Twis. Fawcett   7Apr.1813
    Jeffries Kingsley   25Nov.
    John Goff   26Jan.1814
    Thomas Leach   24Feb.

Rank in the Army.

4th Regiment of Dragoons
Capts. T. C. Fenton   2Jan.1812
    Malcolm M'Neil   28Feb.
Lieuts. George Hamilton   23Apr.1807
    W. B. H. Rowley   4Oct.1809
    John Luard   30May1811
    George Goodman   28Oct.
    Benjamin Watkins   30do.
    John Waldron   31do.
    Edward G— Cubitt   23Jan.1812
    Arch. J. Hamilton   11June
    Charles Wyndham   5Nov.
    John Rolfe Gordon   15Oct.
    H. Stafford Northcote 18Mar.1813
    Thomas Ellis Hodson 16Sept.
6th Regiment of Dragoons
Capts. Thomas Kersteman   31Mar.1814
    Fielding S. Jones   23June
7th Regiment of Dragoons
Capts. Ernest Schmiedern   15Sept.1813
    Charles Moray   11Aug.1814
Lieut. John Harcourt Powell 30Mar.1813
9th Regiment of Dragoons
Major   G.J. Robarts Lt.Col.2June1813
Capts. Edward Om. Wrench   7July1808
    Alexander Campbell   13Aug.1812
Lieuts. John Wm. Bacon   28June1810
    John Wm. Dunn   3July1811
    John Grattan   4do.
    James Bogle French   21May1812
    Richard Beasley   18Feb.1813
    Philip Tuite Dalton   1Apr.
    Wm. Bloss Armstrong 29do.
    Charles Bacon   20May
10th Regiment of Dragoons
Capts. A. de Grammont Duc de Guiche
        9Mar.1809
    Edward Fitz Gerald   19May1814
11th Regiment of Dragoons
Capts. Thomas Crawford   5Aug.1813
    James Duberly   21Oct.
Lieuts. Thomas B— Wall   15Mar.1810
    Edward Greaves   2July1811
    Charles Eversfield   22Aug.
    Archibald Paxton   19Dec.
    William Leach   9Dec.1812
    William H— Stewart   10do.
    Wm. Knevett   2Sept.1813
    B— Des Voeux   23Dec.
    Samuel Dudley   17Nov.1814
Cornet William Williams 10Sept.1812
12th Regiment of Dragoons
Capts. Stephen White   21Jan.1808
    William Patton   10Dec.1812
Lieuts. Alexis Pellichody   27Jan.1808
    Edward Arnold   25July1811
    Edward Penfold   25Mar.1812
               Lieuts.

Disbanded and Reduced in 1814.

	Rank in the Army.
Lieuts. Edwin Stacey	26Mar.1812
Lindsey James Bertie	7May
Abraham Lane	15Oct.
William Hawksley	31Dec.
Hon. Aug. Stanhope	18Mar.1813
Jos. Healey Newsome	17Mar.1814
13th Regiment of Dragoons	
Capts. Frederick Goulburn	12July1810
R. Bidwell Edwards	28July1814
Lieuts. Geo. L. Hodges	7Jan.1808
James Mill	7Nov.1811
William Turner	6Feb.1812
John Pym	23July
Josias Jackson	31Mar.1813
Richard Adams	15July
Wm. Theo. Buchanan	28Sept.
George Hussey Packe	6Jan.1814
14th Regiment of Dragoons	
Capt. Hon. Evelyn P. Dormer	6June1811
Vet. Sur. Robert Thompson	17Apr.1801
15th Regiment of Dragoons	
Capts. J. Maxwell Wallace	22Oct.1807
Charles Jones	7Oct.1813
Philip de Francke	16Dec.
16th Regiment of Dragoons	
Capts. Hon. Thomas Browne	12Aug.1812
Thomas Penrice	18Feb.1813
Lieuts. John Burke	22May1804
D. Pratt	29Oct.1812
Fred. Chamberlayne	3Dec.
William Harris	21Jan.1813
Anthony Bacon	11Mar.
Hon. C. T. Monckton	8July
Edmund Burke	21Oct.
Alex. Macdougall	30Dec.
Q. Mr. John Peers	
18th Regiment of Dragoons	
Capts. Robert Giveen	18Oct.1812
Robert Russell	26Jan.1814
Staff Corps of Cavalry	
Maj.Com. ⊙ George Scovell *Lt.Col.*	17Aug.1812
Capts. Lewis Daring	15Apr.1813
John Gitterick	do.
James Dryden	22do.
Thomas Jarmy	6May
Lieuts. Thomas M'Dermott	25Feb.1805
James Dowd	15May1806
William Butler Hook	2Oct.
James Rooke	5Aug.1813
Cornets Henry Blakeley	28Apr.1813
John Forsey	29do.
John Tipping	17June
S. C. Hinchcliffe	14July1814
Paym. Thomas Fentiman	25Nov.1813
Adj. Felix Le Neve	*Cornet* 27Jan.1814
Q. Mr. —— Sewell	20Jan.1814
Surgeon Joseph Browne	28Oct.1813

	Rank in the Army.
As. Sur. Henry Fisher	28Nov.1811
Vet. Sur. —— Barrington	16Dec.1813
3d Regiment of Foot	
Capts. William Stephens	30Nov.1806
Walter Snow	29Apr.1813
Lieuts. John Cowcher	23May1809
Frederick Goldfrap	26Dec.1811
4th Regiment of Foot	
Lieut. Patrick Conroy	26July1804
5th Regiment of Foot	
Paym. John Hamilton	9Jan.1799
6th Regiment of Foot	
Capt. William Horton	21Nov.1811
7th Regiment of Foot	
Capt. Henry Fryer Devey	8Sept.1813
9th Regiment of Foot	
Capts. Daniel Orchard	14Nov.1805
Edward Newenham	22Oct.1812
Lieuts. J. B. Ford	31Aug.1808
Hiram Cutler	29Oct.1812
As. Surg. Wm. B. Clements	11Mar.1813
10th Regiment of Foot	
Lieut. J. P. Berry	26Jan.1808
11th Regiment of Foot	
Ensign Matthew Trimble	16July1812
12th Regiment of Foot	
Lieut. A. M. Ayshford	15Apr.1812
15th Regiment of Foot	
Lt. Col. Alexander Milne	4June1813
Major Mark Anth. Bozon	4June1813
Capts. William Slade	27Dec.1810
A.WilliamsonCradock	7Oct.1812
John Cosby	15do.
Peter Powell	4Feb.1813
Lieuts. Philip O'Reilly	30Sept.1807
William Upton	20Oct.1808
Donald Macpherson	24June1813
Ensigns Tho. A. Drought	11Nov.1813
Thomas Allen	25Dec.
John Lawr. Macdonnell	do.
Thomas Bannister	do.
Thomas Hardwicke	do.
John Ogle Gage	do.
Thomas Maunsell	3Mar.1814
John P. Drury	20June
Paym. Sam. Box Drayton	25Nov.1813
Q. Mr. George Norton	8Dec.1808
As. Surg. Francis Jones	20Sept.1810
16th Regiment of Foot	
Ensign John O'Donnell	5May1814
Paym. Edward Byrne	27June1798
18th Regiment of Foot	
Lt. Col. Edward Walker	1Oct.1812
Capts. John Warren	28Oct.1805
John Doran	26Sept.1811
Tho. Ryder Graves	14Jan.1813
H.ManningtonMorgan	21Apr.1814

     Lieuts.

Disbanded and Reduced in 1814.

	Rank in the Army.			Rank in the Army.
Lieuts.	James Wood	25Oct.1808	1st Lieuts. ——— Griffiths	5Aug.1813
	Samuel H. Whalley	11June1809	——— Swayne	26do.
	John Baker Graves	13May1812	James M'Dougall	8Sept.
	Rob.WildonTarleton	11Nov.1813	Neville Custance	9do.
	Samuel M'Caul	2Dec.	Benj. Backhouse	25Nov.
	Charles Lennon	27Jan.1814	W. T. Graham	31Mar.1814
	Edward Inge	10Mar.	Cuthbert French	1Apr.
	Joseph Crips	15June	Thomas Hasker	12May
	William Roper	16do.	2d Lieuts. William Richardson	5Aug.1813
Ensigns	Wm. Isaac Hancorne	27Jan.1814	David Satchwell	21Oct.
	John Butler	2Feb.	Dan. John Murphy	4Nov.
	William Burnett	3do.	William Coningham	24do.
	Dominic French	10Mar.	Thomas Towers	25do.
	John Dalgety	16June	John Dalmage	25Dec.
Paym.	William Iveson	25Aug.1808	William Seton	31Mar.1814
Q. Mr.	Andrew Mulholland	28May1812	Plunket Bourchier	12May
21st Regiment of Foot			Paym. Thomas Felton	8Aug.1811
Capt.	John Montgomery	16June1808	Q. Mr. Edward Hudson	28Sept.1809
22d Regiment of Foot			Surgeon Samuel Roe	26May1814
Lt. Col.	SirGreg.H.B.Way,Kt.30May1811		As.Surg. John Monro	26May1814
Major	PatrickM'NeightLt.Col.4June1814		**24th Regiment of Foot**	
Capts.	Hugh Bowen Mends	12Feb.1814	Capts. Wm. Langworthy Maj.4June1814	
	Arthur Sanders Taylor	13do.	James Brickell	28Sept.1804
Lieuts.	John Maclean	17Dec.1807	James Soden	20Mar.1808
	Richard Burbridge	12Feb.1814	T. G. Coote	22Feb.1810
	John Butler	25Aug.	Wm.Abr.LeMesurier	15Mar.
Ensigns	Thomas Brown	25Dec.1813	John A. Ingram	3Oct.1811
	John Hodges	14Feb.1814	John Parsonage	2Apr.1812
	Henderson Crozier	12May	Lieuts. Wm. Snodgrass	10Mar.1808
Paym.	AdamGordonGeddes	31Mar.1814	Geo.AndrewBowdler	22Sept.
Adj.	Wm.Aug.Bury Ensign10Mar.1814		John Rope	20July1809
Q..Mr.	James Thomson	17Mar.1814	Thomas Dowling	21Feb.1810
Surgeon	Chas. H. Cotton	31Mar.1813	Duncan Rose	17Dec.1812
23d Regiment of Foot			Edwin Pell	25Mar.1813
Lt. Col.	SirCha.Sutton,Kt.	30May1811	James Millerd	6May
Majors	W.LewinHerfordLt.Col.3Mar.1814		Charles Hodge	20Jan.1814
	John Tho. Leahy	27Apr.1812	Ensigns George Hewson	2Apr.1812
Capts.	Lord J.T.H.Somerset	15Apr.1808	——— Fry	14Oct.
	John Vernon	20July1809	Aug. Backhausen	10Dec.
	James Cane	16June1811	Benjamin Everard	25Feb.1813
	Alex. Montgomery	17Sept.1812	W. I. Gregory	25Dec.
	Richard Treeve	1Oct.	James Galbraith	23June1814
	Tho. H. Browne	15Apr.1813	Carysfort Proby	1Sept.
	GordonW.F.Booker	17June	Paym. Isaac Buxton	6Feb.1805
	A. E. D'Orfeuille	17Aug.	Q. Mr. Charles Daelsing	24Oct.1811
	Wm. Henry Jones	25do.	As. Surg. James O'Beirne	1Sept.1814
	George Browne	26do.	**25th Regiment of Foot**	
	Wm.HenryBrownson	13Jan.1814	Surgeon Alexander Cahill	25Aug.1809
1stLieuts.	Thomas Roskelly	21Sept.1808	**26th Regiment of Foot**	
	Sir George R. Farmer, Bt.		Majors James Conolly	2Jan.1812
		12Jan.1809	Edward Warner	30do.
	Humphry Black	16Mar.	Capts. Wm. H. Scott	21Mar.1811
	Thomas Turner	do.	James Nash	2Jan.1812
	Wm. Prich. Lloyd	1Oct.1812	John Westlake	8July1813
	John Wingate	15Apr.1813	Francis Shearman	3Feb.1814
	Albert Gledstanes	17June	James Steadman	16June
	Chas. Wm. Hill	29July	George Pipon	23July
			Lieuts. William Launie	30Mar.1809
				Lieuts,

Disbanded and Reduced in 1814.

		Rank in the Army.
Lieuts.	Montague M'Donagh	8July1813
	William Clark	9Dec.
	Charles Barr	6Jan.1814
	James Mahon	2Feb.
	Adam Gordon Boyes	5Oct.
	Alexander Cummings	6do.
Ensigns	Richard Carruthers	19May1814
	John Philpot	16June
	Robert Allatt	20Oct.
Paym.	Thomas Boyes	3Aug.1809
Q. Mr.	—— M'Gregor	11Mar.1813
Surgeon	Arch. N. Armstrong	21July1814

27th Regiment of Foot

Capt.	Edw. Hughes Griffin	13Feb.1812
Lieut.	Richard Shaw	27Aug.1807

28th Regiment of Foot

Majors	Hon. Edw. Mullens	4June1813
	J— F— Briggs	8Dec.1814
Capts.	Henry Wallace Farr	1Feb.1810
	Henry Moriarty	3Oct.1811
	Sam. J. Macartney	10do.
	Wm. Vere Taylor	29Oct.1812
	Wm. Hen. Hartman	30do.
	Edward Wolfe	9Sept.1813
	Samuel Morris	25Nov.
	Richard Tomlinson	31Mar.1814
	John Green	19May
	John Anderson	8Dec.
Lieuts.	William Bagnett	21Nov.1811
	John Evans	13Apr.1813
	Edw. Embury Hill	9Sept.
	Tho. Wm. Colleton	25Nov.
	James Parry	27Jan.1814
	J. Thur. Scott Waring	31Mar.
	William Campbell	18May
	Tho. Ilderton Ferrier	19do.
	Duncan Slocock	1Sept.
	—— Suter	15Dec.
Ensigns	Maurice Mahon	19Aug.1813
	George Shawe	17May1814
	Thomas Porter	18do.
	Thomas Lewis	19do.
	Thomas Wheeler	26do.
	Brian Shaw Hilditch	8Dec.
Paym.	Richard Moore	22Dec.1807
Q. Mr.	—— Cornish	26May1814
Surgeon	John Lightbody	15Oct.1812
As. Sur.	John N. Ashwood	26Dec.1814

31st Regiment of Foot

Major	J. S. Hawkshaw	7Feb.1811
Capts.	Wm. Beresford	*Maj.*17Aug.1812
	Tho. R. Hemsworth	15Sept.1808
	James Maxwell	20Sept.1810
	James Girdlestone	20Dec.
	Richard Birch	1Aug.1811
	Henry Simmonds	31Mar.1813
	Richard Gethin	29Apr.

		Rank in the Army.
Capts.	Charles Paget	28Oct.1813
	Joseph Burton	21Apr.1814
	Henry Gore Edwards	6July
Lieuts.	Francis Kearney	12Oct.1809
	Edward Thompson	31May1810
	Joseph Newman	19Oct.
	John R. Eagar	3Sept.1812
	James Elwyn	22Oct.
	E. Malb. Fitzgerald	11Mar.1813
	Cornelius O'Connor	27May
	Walter Forster Kerr	14Oct.
	James Thompson	21do.
Ensigns	G. H. Marsac	13June1811
	Gooday Strutt Gilland	31Dec.1812
	Benjamin Sayer	15Apr.1813
	Geo. M'Leod Tew	19Aug.
	Richard Wood	2Dec.
	Samuel O. Goodwin	25do.
	William Seward	24Feb.1814
	T. Nowell Twopeny	14Apr.
	William Simmonds	18Aug.

33d Regiment of Foot

Surgeon	Andrew Trevor	9May1794

34th Regiment of Foot

Capt.	William Chadwick	20Feb.1812
Lieuts.	William Collis	14Dec.1809
	Thomas Smyth	28Aug.1811
Paym.	William Sarjeant	31Mar.1803

35th Regiment of Foot

Paym.	William Bury	7Jan.1808

36th Regiment of Foot

Lt. Col.	⊙Lewis Davies	*Col.*4June1814
Majors	⊙John R. Ward	*Lt.Col.*1Jan.1812
	John Fox	4June1811
Capts.	Rd. Hen. Tolson	*Maj.*1Jan.1812
	Chas. Harvey Smith	26May1808
	Roderick Murchison	13Aug.1812
	Orlando Jones	9Sept.
	Robert Noble Crosse	10do.
	Hugh Douglas	1Oct.
	David Price	8do.
	George Pinckney	19Nov.
	Wm. Hicks Milles	22Apr.1813
Lieuts.	Richard Perham	27July1809
	Lewis Bowen	10May1811
	Craven Copley	7Sept.1812
	Charles Hopkins	9Dec.
	George White	13May1813
	Tho. M— Taylor	7Sept.1814
	Roger Jones	8do.
Ensigns	George Sleeman	12May1813
	J— Weir	13do.
	—— Davenport	27Jan.1814
	John Lawlor	3Feb.
	H. Holmes	19May
	Edward Ingram	15Sept.
	Peter Lawless	8Dec.

Paym.

Disbanded and Reduced in 1814.

		Rank in the Army.
Paym.	Redmond Barry	18Apr.1805
Adjutant	Wm. Wainwright	Lt.10Dec.1812
Q. Mr.	John Manley	22Oct.1812
As. Sur.	Thomas Wm. Jeston	9Sept.1813

38th Regiment of Foot

Lt.Col.	⊙ John Nugent	Col.4June1814
Majors	W.F.W.B.Loftus	Lt.Col.4June1813
	⊚A.C.W. Crookshank	Lt. Col.
		4June1814
Capts.	John J. Seelinger	Maj.4June1814
	Samuel Dowbiggen	11July1811
	John Clerke	7May1812
	Wm. Willshire	25Nov.
	John P— Minchin	26do.
	William Ince	22Sept.1813
	John Peddie	23do.
	F. B. Sandwith	31Mar.1814
Lieuts.	Thomas Dowker	15Mar.1810
	Robert Dighton	7Sept.1812
	Edward Gardiner	23Sept.1813
	Allen Macdougall	24do.
	Charles Roddy	25do.
	James Allen	26do.
	E. Tighe Gregory	17Dec.
	Thomas Evans	19Jan.1814
	George Michell	20do.
	Thomas Walsh	14July
	J— Curran	15do.
	James Briscoe	6Oct.
Ensigns	James Pellett	28Jan.1813
	Alexander Campbell	17Dec.
	William Crosseley	25do.
	George Smith	do.
	John Wood	12Jan.1814
	Cuthbert Daly	13do.
	Rich. Andrew Scott	28Feb.
	George Parke	3Mar.
	Daniel Mackenzie	14July
Paym.	Warren H. White	17Sept.1812
Q. Mr.	Thomas Southall	25Apr.1806
Surgeon	Thomas Fiddes	26May1814
As. Surgs.	John E. Stewart	25June1812
	John W. Watson	4Mar.1813

39th Regiment of Foot

Capts.	Robert Maunsell	Maj.4June1814
	Thomas Landers	25Dec.1806

40th Regiment of Foot

Lt. Col.	⊚Cha. Amedee Harcourt	
		Col.4June1813

41st Regiment of Foot

Capt.	R. T. Fuller	Lt.Col.4June1814

42d Regiment of Foot

Lt. Col.	SirGeorgeLeith,Bt.	Col.4June1813
Majors	⊙ Maxw. Grant	Lt.Col.
		26Aug.1813
	Robert Anstruther	16Apr.1812

		Rank in the Army.
Capts.	William Middleton	13May1812
	Hamilton Maxwell	14do.
	Duncan M'Innes	22Oct.
	David Barclay	29July1813
	Alexander Mackenzie	6Jan.1814
	John Hamilton	17Feb.
	Thomas Munro	19May
	Colin Macdougall	4Aug.
Licuts.	William Lorimer	18June1807
	Huntly Nicolson	5Aug.1813
	Lachlan M'Kay	23Sept.
	William Urquhart	5Jan.1814
	George Gordon	6do.
	Thomas M'Niven	31Mar.
	John Lane	28Apr.
	Mungo Macpherson	19May
	Colin Walker	20do.
	William Milne	21do.
	James Geddes	9June
	Alex. C. Robertson	10Aug.
Ensigns	George M'Iver	31Mar.1814
	P. Campbell	28Apr.
	James Mickleham	19May
	John Cliffe	20do.
	James Clarke	21do.
	Anthony Donald	9June
	George Macintosh	10Aug.
	Norman M'Leod	11do.
Paym.	Robert Carmichael	8Aug.1806
Adjutant	Alpin Grant	Lt.19Dec.1811
Q. Mr.	Hugh Mair	18Mar.1813
Surgeon	Alexander M'Lachlan	22Aug.1811
As. Surg.	Thomas Young	9Sept.1813

43d Regiment of Foot

Lieut.	John Buchanan	5May1808

44th Regiment of Foot

Capt.	John Ponsonby	20Aug.1812

45th Regiment of Foot

Majors	⊙—Tho. Lightfoot	Lt.Col.
		19May1814
	⊚John O'Flaherty	19May1814
Capts.	Hon.G.A.C.Stapylton	Col.
		4June1814
	Robert Hilliard	Maj.4June1814
	James Bishop	27June1811
	Francis Powell	14May1812
	James Henry Reynett	23July
	Francis Andrews	28Jan.1813
	John Harris	22Apr.
	Theo. Byers Costley	7Oct.
	Benj. Geale Humfrey	31Mar.1814
	Charles Barnwell	19May
Lieuts.	John Dedwith Gibbs	1Nov.1809
	James Dale	4Mar.1812
	John Stewart	30Dec.
	James John Rowe	31do.
	George Morgan	28Jan.1813
		Lieuts.

Disbanded and Reduced in 1814.

		Rank in the Army.
Lieuts.	Ralph Smyth Stewart	1Apr.1813
	William Hunt	13May
	Averell Leckey	17June
	Robert Mackenzie	29July
	Geo. Sutherland	21Oct.
	Colin Macdonald	24Mar.1814
	J. T. Ray	30do.
	James Reid	31do.
	Arman Lowry	28July
Ensigns	T. Heppon Vavasour	3Mar.1814
	John Leslie	24do.
	William Turner Ryan	30do.
	Boice M'Kenzie	31do.
	George Welsh	14Apr.
	Elias R. Handcock	28July
Paym.	George Hounsom	29Oct.1807
Q. Mr.	John Harpur	12Aug.1813
Surgeon	Charles Cooke	9Sept.1813
As. Surg.	Richard Lloyd	9Sept.1813

47th Regiment of Foot

Major	Richard Chetham	1Jan.1812
Capts.	William Sall	Maj.4June1814
	William Rutledge	18Mar.1813
	John Doyle	29Sept.
	Michael Hearne	21Oct.
	William Hay	11Nov.
	John Craigie	2Dec.
	Walter O'Hara	24Nov.1814
Lieuts.	John Edw. Hunt	26Feb.1806
	Robert Briscoe	19Jan.1809
	Michael Lyne	29Mar.1810
	Campbell Buchanan	10Apr.
	Robert Butler	9Oct.1811
	Anthony Mahon	27June
	William H. Green	28Feb.1812
	J. Robert Nason	17Mar.1813
	R. W. Macdonnell	28July
	Edward Agar	29do.
	Edward Fred. Austin	30Sept.
	R. Keddy Thompson	21Oct.
	George Sutherland	do.
	Duncan Calder	2Dec.
	John Uniacke	3Mar.1814
	Stephen Burke	26May
	James Ewing	9June
	Percy Pratt	8Sept.
Ensigns	Griffith Ridsdale	3June1813
	Francis Wyse	22Oct.
	Thomas Carmichael	23do.
	Edward Austen	24do.
	Robert Ridge	8Sept.1814
Paym.	John Harley	11July1805
Q. Mr.	James Jackson	15Apr.1813
Surgeon	James Scott	26May1814
As. Sur.	James Hurst	28Oct.1813

48th Regiment of Foot

Lt. Col.	William Wauchope	8Dec.1814

		Rank in the Army.
Majors	✖JamesWilson	Lt.Col.7Apr.1812
	Step.Goodman	Lt.Col.26Dec.1813
Capts.	W. Newell Watkins	8Mar.1810
	Jas. W. Reid	26Apr.
	Barth. E. Drought	21June
	Wm. Gill	20June1811
	Hen. Irwin	15Aug.
	George Mackay	13May1812
	John Allman	do.
	Wm. W. Cheslyn	14do.
	Lawrence Crawley	4June
	Robert Herring	26Aug.1813
	George Wightman	17Mar.1814
Lieuts.	Henry Burke	30Mar.1808
	John Kendall	1Jan.1811
	Hen. James Pountney	16June
	Joseph Clarke	18do.
	John Murray Brown	19do.
	Stephen Collins	20do.
	J— W— Dixon	14Aug.
	William Gilbert	15do.
	Patrick M'Dougall	13May1812
	Edward Johnston	4June
	F— H— Hall	24Dec.
	Charles Bourke	20May1813
	F— M— Scott	12Aug.
	John Pollen	25do.
	Samuel Johnson	6Jan.1814
Ensigns	Henry Costerton	20May1813
	Peter Plunkett	26Aug.
	Henry Wootton	7Oct.
	John Carr	25Dec.
	Henry Spaight	3Mar.1814
	W— Foster	19May
Paym.	Henry Humphreys	20Sept.1810
Adjutant	John Wild	Ens.7July1814
Q. Mr.	James Freer	7July1814
Surgeon	Alex. Coulson	31Jan.1811
As.Surgs.	William Moffatt	4Jan.1810
	Richard N. Starr	11Mar.1813

49th Regiment of Foot

Lt. Col.	Charles Plenderleath	4June1813
Capts.	Wm. B. Hobart	13May1813
	William Jones	24Feb.1814
	Norman Wightwick	23June
Lieut.	J. L. Black	10Mar.1814
Ensigns	Edw. Grant Stokes	23June1814
	James Swabey	1Dec.
Paym.	William Haldane	8July1813
Adjutant	Alex. Downie	Ens.10June1813
Surgeon	William Kettle	26Aug.1813

50th Regiment of Foot

Lt. Col.	◎Charles Napier	27June1811
Majors	Hamilton Archdall	29Aug.1811
	Herman Stapleton	19June1812
Capts.	◎Wm. Smith	Lt.Col.1Jan.1812
	Wm. Roycraft	25Mar.1808

Capts.

Disbanded and Reduced in 1814.

	Rank in the Army.			Rank in the Army.
Capts. John M'Donald	25June1812		*Ensigns* Richard Watts	25Dec.1813
Verney Rt. Lovett	3Sept.		Orlando Cha. Tipton	7Apr.1814
Roger North	17Dec.		W. F. Schaak	5July
Mark Rudkin	21Jan.1813		—— Prichard	7do.
J. E. Con. M'Carthy	4Feb.		Richard Elliott	28do.
William Bower	7Oct.		*Paym.* Thomas Harvey	8Sept.1814
Robert Ray	6Jan.1814		*Q. Mr.* Thomas Grimwood	25Nov.1811
Holman Custance	26May		*57th Regiment of Foot*	
Lieuts. Sam. Dicken Grinsell	30May1811		*Lieut.* George Cocke	30June1808
Geo. Anth. Goddard	21Jan.1813		*60th Regiment of Foot*	
Sholto Douglas	15July		*Capt.* John Knipe	30Jan.1812
Charles Brown	7Oct.		*62d Regiment of Foot*	
Charles Collins	8do.		*Capt.* Henry Kater	13Oct.1808
George Clarke	21do.		*As. Surg.* Giles M'Bain	19Mar.1812
James Campbell	22do.		*63d Regiment of Foot*	
John Williams	23do.		*Lt. Col.* John Ld. Burghersh	Col.4June1814
William Sawkins	6Jan.1814		*Majors* Philip Le Geyte	11July1811
William Freebairn	18May		John Chapman	9July1812
Hugh Johnstone	19do.		*Capts.* James Ormsby	Lt.Col.4June1814
William Jull	11Aug.		John Bridge	Major4June1814
Ensigns James Sweeney	23Oct.1813		Alexander Daniel	Majordo.
Joseph Wynn	18Nov.		Richard Gorham	14Feb.1805
Rob. Clandinen	25Dec.		Robert Menzies	19Dec.
Dennis M'Carthy	do.		Robert Denny	30Nov.1809
Alexander Campbell	6Jan.1814		Edward Lucas	14Jan.1813
Tho. Coombe Vyvyan	21Apr.		Geo. Wm. Savage	2Dec.
Joseph Rawlins	17May		*Lieuts.* James Kerr	18Feb.1804
Stephen Lewis	19do.		John Nott	6Apr.1808
R—— M'Carthy	13July		William Hunter	3Aug.1809
Paym. J. Duff Mackay	26Nov.1812		Thomas Freer	18Dec.1811
Adjutant James Edgelow	Ensign14July1814		George Judge	6Feb.1812
Surgeon John Carter	31May1809		Patrick M'Grath	14Jan.1813
As. Surg. Colin Sievwright	11Mar.1813		George Mackay	15Aug.
51st Regiment of Foot			Henry Nicholls	15Sept.1814
Lieut. Alexander Brown	28Mar.1811		*Ensigns* William Bennett	14Jan.1813
53d Regiment of Foot			Thomas Meldrum	22July
Capts. John Robinson	25Oct.1810		Henry Hickman	18Nov.
Charles Rees	3Feb.1812		Rich. G. Robinson	25Dec.
54th Regiment of Foot			Wm. M'Intosh	27Jan.1814
Lieut. John Robert Irwin	28Dec.1809		J— W— Evans	10Feb.
55th Regiment of Foot			Brian Gaynor	2June
Lieut. Richard Nantes	19Oct.1809		*Paym.* Robert Edie	14Mar.1805
56th Regiment of Foot			*66th Regiment of Foot*	
Lt. Col. John Wm. Mallet	6Nov.1813		*Capt.* Charles Mills	7Aug.1805
Capts. Alexander M'Donald	15Apr.1807		*68th Regiment of Foot*	
Henry Drake	9Dec.1813		*Capt.* James Hunter	28Jan.1812
John Watts Mends	12May1814		*72d Regiment of Foot*	
Edward Irvine	7July		*Lieut.* James Burn	19Feb.1811
Lieuts. —— Denney	27Jan.1807		*78th Regiment of Foot*	
James Crosley Lewis	28do.		*Lieut.* Adam Kennedy	7Jan.1813
Andrew Darling	28Dec.1812		*79th Regiment of Foot*	
John Rancland	6July1814		*Lieut.* Rob. Innes Ackland	11Oct.1810
Ensigns Thomas Sparks	7Apr.1813		*81st Regiment of Foot*	
—— Rose	17Nov.		*Lieut.* Ralph Crofton	15June1809
Rob. Shafto Vicars	10Dec.		*82d Regiment of Foot*	
Thomas Ker	25do.		*Capt.* Charles Huxley	2Nov.1809
			Lieut. David Thompson	3Mar.1808
				Lieut.

Disbanded and Reduced in 1814.

	Rank in the Army.
Lieut. James Hall	1 Dec.1812
As. Sur. John Prendergast	16 Apr.1812
85th Regiment of Foot	
Capt. Tho. Williamson *Lt.Col.*1 Jan.1812	
86th Regiment of Foot	
Major H. Bulteel Harris	27 Oct.1814
Capt. Robert Blackwood	8 Nov.1813
Ensigns Patrick Home	30 Mar.1814
John Robinson	31 do.
—— Rose	28 July.
Paym. Edw. M'Grath	17 Mar.1814
Q. Mr. —— Cross	10 Mar.1814
Surgeon Nicholas Cloak	28 July1814
88th Regiment of Foot	
Capt. Walter Wm. Adair	30 June1808
90th Regiment of Foot	
Capt. James Gauntlett	18 Dec.1806
92d Regiment of Foot	
Lt. Col. John Lamont	*Col.*4 June1813
Majors William Phipps	7 Jan.1813
James Lee	12 Apr.1814
Capts. William Logie	5 May1808
Donald M'Barnet	30 Mar.1809
Angus Fraser	10 June1813
William Baillie	2 July
William Fyfe	16 Sept.
Donald M'Pherson	21 Oct.
John Cattanach	10 Feb.1814
John A. Durie	28 Apr.
William Hewett	24 Nov.
Lieuts. George Gordon	25 Feb.1813
John Grant	15 Apr.
George Mitchell	29 July
Ewen C. M'Pherson	15 Sept.
Ewen Cameron	16 do.
James Patullo	21 Oct.
Samuel Turner	23 Dec.
James Rob. Hart	18 Jan.1814
William Fraser	19 do.
William Grant	20 do.
John James	10 Feb.
John Latham	14 July
Ensigns John Cameron	25 Dec.1813
John Cameron	19 Jan.1814
John Horan	20 do.
John M'Duff	10 Feb.
James M'Lachlan	28 Apr.
Paym. John Philip	28 July1808
Q. Mr. George Wallace	4 Aug.1808
As. Surgs. Thomas Cash	11 July1811
J— F— Symes	9 Sept.1813
94th Regiment of Foot	
Capt. Arch. M'Arthur	6 Jan.1814
95th Regiment of Foot	
2d Lieut. Peter Campbell	23 Dec.1813

	Rank in the Army.
96th Regiment of Foot	
Lt. Cols. David Stewart	*Col.*4 June1814
Mich. White Lee	4 June 1811
Majors James Spawforth *Lt.Col.*4 June1814	
Charles Pratt	24 Mar.
96th Regiment of Foot	
Capts. James Boyd	31 July1806
Cha. L. Fitzgerald	23 Aug.
Samuel Busby	7 Apr.1808
John D. de Carteret	5 May1814
Lieuts. Edw. Chi. Bolton	1 Apr.1805
Eyre Lynch	20 Sept.1808
Rawlins Hartman	17 Dec.
Ralph Blayney	5 Apr.1809
Cha. Davers Allen	20 May1813
Ensigns Robert Montgomery	2 Dec.1813
Thomas Thompson	9 do.
Philip Aubin	17 Mar.1814
Peter Porteus	18 do.
Geo. Gordon Philan	26 May
Daniel Le Geyt	9 June
Richard Downham	4 Aug.
Paym. Philip Jean	1 Oct.2
102d Regiment of Foot	
Capt. David Carnegie	25 July1811
104th Regiment of Foot	
Lieut. —— Shaffalisky	15 June1809
Royal Staff Corps	
Capt. William B. Hulme	31 May1809
5th West India Regiment	
Capt. Thomas Prater	8 June1808
6th West India Regiment	
Q. Mr. John Anderson	11 Oct.1805
2d Ceylon Regiment	
Capt. Champagne Reynolds	8 Oct.1812
3d Ceylon Regiment	
Lt. Col. Wm. Aug. Johnson	17 May1810
Royal Waggon Train	
Lt. Cols. Charles Tudor	25 July1810
Thomas Aird	2 June1814
Major Charles Turner	6 Jan.1814
Capts. Patrick Ewing	3 Dec.1803
Charles Ravenscroft	do.
Barth. Horsell	26 Nov.1812
Basil Jackson	3 Dec.
John de Beaker	6 Jan.1814
William Baylaam	17 Feb.
Lieuts. Matthew Drew	25 May1808
Joseph M'Dowall	4 July1811
William Dean	14 Aug.
Thomas Baldock	2 Oct.
Robert L'Estrange	3 do.
Meredith Jones	2 Oct.1812
Adrian Eyma	15 do.
	Lieuts.

3 L

Disbanded and Reduced in 1814.

Rank in the Army.

Lieuts. George Hakewill   24Nov.1812
Charles Carter   25do.
Henry Green   26do.
John Watton   3Dec.
Charles Price Rose   18Mar.1813
Charles Bott   22Apr.
William Kingsley   21Oct.
James Tracie   18Nov.
Henry Winkelman   9Dec.
George Rd. Langley   7Jan.1814
William Atkinson   8do.
Cornets William Young   3Dec.1812
Thomas Newton   23Apr.1813
John Bickerton   29do.
William Hopwood   13May
Chas. Ern. Turner   17do.
John Mahon   18do.
Jonathan Allen   25do.
George Hayter   10June
• Thomas Cood   12Aug.
—— Molyneux   21Oct.
Wm. Shepherd   18Nov.
—— Glendinning   9Dec.
Charles Brien   25do.
C— J— Beck   6Jan.1814
John Lushington   7do.
Bonnival Church   20do.
—— Fenn   10Feb.
Fred. Æ. Hodson   do.
As. Surgs. Wm. Fasken   26May1814
William Sankey   2June
3d Garrison Battalion
Lieuts. James Westwater   18Apr.1811
William Strangeways   3June1812
4th Garrison Battalion
Lieut. W. K. Burton ·   1June1806

Chasseurs Britanniques
Lt. Col. ⊚ Wm. C. Eustace   23Aug.1810
Capt. Thomas Napier   Maj.26Dec.1813
Lieuts. Frederick de Sunhary   19Feb.1811
E— R— D'Alton   7Sept.1813
Aylmer Dalton   18May1814
John Geo. Rawstorne 18Aug.
Ensigns Alexander M'Crea   9Sept.1813
G. Aug. O'Farrell   16do.
Balthazard Poussin   23Dec.
Paym. James Rawstorne   10June1813
Late Royal Regiment of Malta
Capt. Charles de Haviland   21Mar.1805
Q. Mr. ——— M'Kay   27Apr.1809
Surgeon George Rowe   18June1807

Late serving with the Portuguese Army
Majors John Austen   Lt Col.25Feb.1813
✕ E— K— Williams
Lt.Col.21June1813

Rank in the Army.

Majors ✕ Br. O'Toole   Lt.Col.21June1813
✕ Dudley St. Leger Hill
Lt.Col.21June1813
⊚ Edward Hawkshaw
Lt.Col.4June1814
✕← Alex. Anderson   21June1813
⊚— John M'Donald   26Aug.
⊚→ Ken. Snodgrass   21Sept.
Peter Adamson   26Dec.
Benjamin Sullivan   4June1814
Capts. Thomas Smyth   25Oct.1814
Hugh Hay Rose   do.
Samuel Hawkins   do.
Hugh Lumley   do.
Wm. Henry Thornton   do.
G. H. E. Murphy   do.
Rodolph Steiger   do.
Robert Haddock   do.
John Newman   do.
John Maher   do.
William de Linston   do.
C— J— Fitz Gerald   do.
George Lennon   do.
William Dobbin   do.
Thomas Cox   do.
Graham Henry   do.
William Cotter   do.
B— V— Derenzy   do.
N— Colthurst   do.
John M'Phail   do.
Thomas Shervinton   do.
F— Armstrong   do.
Thomas Potter   do.
John Pigott   do.
G— E— Quinton   do.
Charles Western   do.
William Gordon   do.
John Fowley   do.
James Dodwell   do.
Thomas Bunbury   do.
John Sutherland   do.
William Gordon   do.
David Skeill   do.
Robert Mackintosh   do.

1st Provisional Battalion of Militia
Lt.Col.Com. Rich. *Marq. of* Buckingham
Lt. Col. William L. Young
Majors George Dean   13Jan.1814
Michael Chamberlain 17Mar.
Capts. Thomas M'Dermott
Francis Pettingall
William Jones
Benjamin Vasser
W. Henry Bacchus

Capts.

Disbanded and Reduced in 1814.

	Rank in the Army.
Capts.	Vincent Beatty
	John Fellowes
	J. P. Allen
	Robert M. Bates
	Edward Temple
Lieuts.	George Dardis
	William H. Brown
	Charles Rudge
	Robert Glover
	James Atcherly
	William Whitby
	Walter W. Carrington
	John Harland
	James Grove
	Francis Beale
	Thomas Shillingford
	Francis Martin
	Michael Macnamara
	Henry Bowles
	John Gillman
	W. H. Sadlier 30Mar.1814
	John Ames
	Robert I. Mason
	William Usher 30Mar.1814
	Daniel White do.
	Malachy Donelan do.
	John Bridger do.
Ensigns	John Moore
	Edward Hobro
Adjutant	John Thomas Brown
Q. Mr.	James Masters
Surgeon	Tobias Ledbrooke

2d Provisional Battalion of Militia

Lt.Col.Com.	Edward Bayley
Lt. Col.	Wm. Fisher Hulse
Majors	Robert M. Browne 13Jan.1814
	Charles M. St. Paul do.
Capts.	Roger Banks
	William Davis Jarvis
	Henry Evans
	Mortimer Hicks Lewis
	Joseph Hall Kenneir
	Robert Henry Cooper
	John Evans
	Edward Tufton Phelp
	Michael Edwin Fell
	J. Chambers
Lieuts.	Francis Austin
	George Francis Holt
	John Bass
	Milward Rogers
	John Smith
	Richard Weir
	Jon. Felicitus Singleton (*As. Sur.*)
	John Langdon
	Samuel George Eastaugh
	William Myers

	Rank in the Army
Lieuts.	Thomas Freer
	Joseph Salkeld
	Thomas Hester
	Frederick Burchell
	Thomas Luby (*As. Surg.*)
	William Bolton
	Patrick Henry Kennedy
	E. Heath
	John A. Forster
	James Pritchett
	George Johnston
	George Wilton
Ensigns	John Crotty
	Robert Fosbroke
	Frederick Dimond
	George Byne
	W. J. Bailey
	B. H. Burchell
	C. Brew
Adjutant	William Brew (*Ensign*)
Q. Mr.	John Radford Austin
Surgeon	Robert Wright

3d Provisional Battalion of Militia

Lt.Col.Com.	Sir Watkin Williams Wynne, Bt.
Lt. Col.	John Berington
Majors	James Payler 13Jan.1814
	N. E. Yarburgh
Capts.	Edward Evans
	James Bell
	Thomas Lees
	David Lloyd
	Capel Lechmere
	John Rowland
	Benjamin Dodsworth
	Robert Richardson
	John Yeats
	Charles Latham 29Mar.1814
Lieuts.	Eliezer Watson
	Thomas Luckhurst
	William Nash
	John Emery
	Thomas Sharp
	Jos. Venables Lovett
	James Richardson
	Michael Parker
	Francis Allen
	John Lambert
	James Webster 25Dec.1813
	G. Fortescue
	John Sowden
	Joseph Singlehurst 9Mar.1814
	Joseph Mawbey do.
	Charles Eales do.
	George Taylor 23do.
	—— Massie
	J. Nicholls

3 L 2   *Lieuts.*

Disbanded and Reduced in 1814.

	Rank in the Army.		*Rank in the Army.*

Lieuts. P. Jones
——— Thompson
C. A. Gamlen
John J. Suberkrub
Ensigns James Dirom
James Cameron
John Gray
Benjamin Carey

Ensigns Nathaniel Bliss
J. Bell
Adjutant Stephen Nicholls
Q. *Mr.* Richard Miles Wynne
Surgeon James Hughes
As.Surgs. Thomas Parry
S. G. Lawrence

OFFICERS who volunteered from the Militia to serve in Regiments of the Line, placed on Half-Pay 25th August, 1814.

1st Regiment of Foot
Capt. Charles Gould — 25 Dec. 1813
Lieut. Tenisen Little — 25 Dec. 1813
2d Regiment of Foot
Capt. William Davison — 25 Dec. 1813
3d Regiment of Foot
Capts. Charles Haselfoot — 25 Dec. 1813
W. H. Haselfoot — do.
Lieuts. Thomas Sebborne — 25 Dec. 1813
Henry Dennis — do.
John Wallis — do.
4th Regiment of Foot
Capts. J. D. Horndon — 25 Dec. 1813
S. P. Newell — do.
Henry Wall — do.
Hon. R. Plunkett — do.
H. Bettesworth — do.
R. Riddlesden — do.
Lieuts. Matthew Thackeray — 25 Dec. 1813
J. Bourillion — do.
Spencer Daniel — do.
William Arden — do.
5th Regiment of Foot
Capts. N. T. Still — 25 Dec. 1813
Richard Warner — do.
Thomas Fyler — do.
Robert Allen — do.
Lieuts. Edward Curling — 25 Dec. 1813
David Miller — do.
John Mackintosh — do.
Evan M'Gregor — do.
H. John Knott — do.
7th Regiment of Foot
Capts. Raynor Dixon — 25 Dec. 1813
John Laxon — do.
9th Regiment of Foot
Capts. Robert Page — 25 Dec. 1813
Joseph Giles — do.
Lieut. Zachary Bailey — 25 Dec. 1813
12th Regiment of Foot
Capt. Francis Dobbs — 25 Dec. 1813
Lieut. Henry Smith — 25 Dec. 1813
13th Regiment of Foot
Lieut. J. Cruckshanks — 25 Dec. 1813

14th Regiment of Foot
Capts. John Robertson — 25 Dec. 1813
Henry Nicolls — do.
Henry Coxwell — do.
Grey Edward Boulton — do.
James G. Doran — do.
Thomas Gould — do.
Lieuts. Charles Pycroft — 25 Dec. 1813
R. P. Condonne — do.
Cham. Hill — do.
William Booth — do.
Henry Stephens — do.
Charles Atkinson — do.
Francis Beardsley — do.
Joseph John Moore — do.
15th Regiment of Foot
Capt. Fred. John Meard — 25 Dec. 1813
Lieuts. Jesse Hilder — 25 Dec. 1813
John Ward — do.
16th Regiment of Foot
Capts. John Barnes — 25 Dec. 1813
Joseph Bygrave — do.
Lieut. John O'Brien — 25 Dec. 1813
19th Regiment of Foot
Lieut. Gavin Miller — 25 Dec. 1813
22d Regiment of Foot
Capts. William Carter — 25 Dec. 1813
Griffith Jeffery Morris — do.
Lieut. William Boates — 25 Dec. 1813
23d Regiment of Foot
Lieut. Richard Mathews — 25 Dec. 1813
26th Regiment of Foot
Capts. George Jeffery — 25 Dec. 1813
William Williams — do.
29th Regiment of Foot
Capts. Edward Jones — 25 Dec. 1813
P. F. Parke — do.
Percival Lewis — do.
Lieuts. William Compton — 25 Dec. 1813
Samuel Heelis — do
32d Regiment of Foot
Capt. H. L. Thomson — 25 Dec. 1813
Lieut. William Cochran — 25 Dec. 1813

33d

Disbanded and Reduced in 1814.

	Rank in the Army.
33d Regiment of Foot	
Lieuts. John Oliver	25Dec.1813
E. W. Oddie	do.
34th Regiment of Foot	
Lieut. Frederick Somers	25Dec.1813
35th Regiment of Foot	
Capt. —— Price	25Dec.1813
Lieut. William Spurrell	25Dec.1813
38th Regiment of Foot	
Capt. Harry Low	25Dec.1813
Lieuts. Samuel Moore	25Dec.1813
Thomas Heath	do.
39th Regiment of Foot	
Capt. Henry Winnington	25Dec.1813
Lieut. Henry B. Beales	25Dec.1813
40th Regiment of Foot	
Capts. J. G. Amos	25Dec.1813
Conway Welsh	do.
B. Farwell	do.
41st Regiment of Foot	
Lieut. John James Herbert	25Dec.1813
43d Regiment of Foot	
Capts. Frederick Lawrence	25Dec.1813
John Davie	do.
Horatio Beckham	do.
Lieuts. Thomas Briggs	25Dec.1813
William Henry Bucke	do.
William C. Steggall	do.
49th Regiment of Foot	
Lieuts. John Sullivan	25Dec.1813
Thomas Gee	do.
51st Regiment of Foot	
Capts. William P. Stapleton	25Dec.1813
Frederick Rice	do.
James Kittleby	do.
Lieuts. Nicholas Tyacke	25Dec.1813
Joseph Thackeray	do.
52d Regiment of Foot	
Capts. Henry Hamer	25Dec.1813
J. A. Long	do.
R. G L. Macdonald	do.
Lieut. Charles Kelly Cooper	25Dec.1813
53d Regiment of Foot	
Capts. Cockshutt Heathcote	25Dec.1813
Joseph May	do.
Richard Jefferys	do.
Lieuts. John B. Baxter	25Dec 1813
Robert Prior	do.
56th Regiment of Foot	
Capts. John Cooke	25Dec.1813
J. B. Gregory	do.
Lieut. T. D. Bayley	25Dec.1813
57th Regiment of Foot	
Lieut. C. Mahoney	25Dec.1813
63d Regiment of Foot	
Capt. Walter W. Coyney	25Dec.1813

	Rank in the Army.
Lieut. JohnJonathanWynter	25Dec.1813
64th Regiment of Foot	
Capts. William Rickards	25Dec.1813
John Norris	do.
69th Regiment of Foot	
Lieut. W. C. H. Buchanan	25Dec.1813
70th Regiment of Foot	
Capt. John Long	25Dec.1813
74th Regiment of Foot	
Capt. John Terry	25Dec.1813
Lieut. James Corrigan	25Dec.1813
76th Regiment of Foot	
Capt. Saxe Bannister	25Dec.1813
77th Regiment of Foot	
. Capt. John Cox	25Dec.1813
80th Regiment of Foot	
Capt. John Fitzherbert	25Dec.1813
Lieut. W. H. Dutton	25Dec.1813
81st Regiment of Foot	
Capt. Tho. David Ellis	25Dec.1813
82d Regiment of Foot	
Capt. Thomas Smith	25Dec.1812
85th Regiment of Foot	
Capt. Samuel Ridgway	25Dec.1813
88th Regiment of Foot	
Capts. John Gabbett	25Dec.1813
John Armstrong	do.
Robert Mansergh	do.
John Waller	do.
89th Regiment of Foot	
Lieut. James Watson	25Dec.1813
93d Regiment of Foot	
Lieut. Alexander Campbell	25Dec.1813
95th Regiment of Foot	
Capt. Gamaliel Brattle	25Dec.1813
1st Lieuts. Henry Ketchley	25Dec.1813
Edward Hinde	do.
Charles Denford	do.
98th Regiment of Foot	
Capt. Daniel Cuolahan	25Dec.1813
99th Regiment of Foot	
Lieut. Richard Brough	25Dec.1813
100th Regiment of Foot	
Lieut. John Rochfort	25Dec.1813
103d Regiment of Foot	
Lieut. John Laugharne	25Dec.1813
Royal Waggon Train	
Capts. William Pritchett	25Dec.1813
Edw. Bedwell Law	do.
Lieuts. James Grant	25Dec.1813
Edward Dundee	do.
Tho. Salisbury Price	do.
Fra. N. Newbolt	do.
James Grant	do.
Thomas Plowman	do.
Edward Mount	do.
	Lieuts.

Disbanded and Reduced in 1814.

		Rank in the Army.			Rank in the Army.
Lieuts.	James Coveney	25Dec.1813	Cornets	George Griffith	25Dec.1813
	C— D— Grace	do.		Timothy Egan	do.
	William Bubb	do.		James Smith	do.
	Richard Kendall	do.		Martin Richard	do.
	Charles Steade	do.		William Carter	do.
	Charles Irwin	do.		J— T— Coward	do.
	Francis H. Brown	do.		—— Williams	do.
	Richard Gem	do.			

STAFF.

Spain and Portugal			Paym.	G— F— Harvey	3Nov.1813
Dep. Judge Advocate	Fra. Sey. Larpent	24Aug.1812		Daniel Mitchell	25Dec.
				Barth. Naugle	28Jan.1814
Recruiting District			Adjutants	Rob. Nicholson	Lt.24May1796
Paym.	John Hayman	11Feb.1801		George Lay	1Oct.1803
	Richard Askew	9Aug.1809		Jacob Hopper	19Jan.1808
	Ralph Boteler Johnson	17Oct.1810		W— Shaw	25June1809
	James Shortt	2July1813		Patricius Curwen	23Jan.1812
				John Allen	28May

COMMISSARIAT DEPARTMENT.

Dep. Com. Gen.	George Spiller	2Aug.1801	Dep. As. Com. Gen.	R. Penfold Horne	21Nov.1811
	John Sweetland	16Nov.1802		James Patterson	11Jan.1812
	Tho. Hamlyn Bent	19Mar.1807		Joseph Gillespie	24do.
	Daniel Ord	20do.		Arthur Lovelidge	9Mar.
	Philip Rawlings	27June1809		William O'Meara	do.
	Robert Boyes	7Nov.		Hugh Hill	29Apr.
	Matthew D. O'Meara	10Aug.1811		Richard Green	23May
	R. J. Routh	9Mar.1812		John E. Daniell	23Aug.
	James Ogilvie	22do.		Hon. M. Rodney	27do.
	Gregory Haines	25Dec.1814		Stewart Ryrie	24Nov.
As. Comm. Gen.	Law Gillespie	5Apr.1795		Alex. Schaumann	26Dec.
	Wm. Harris	20Apr.1797		J— H— Edwards	3Feb.1813
	George Grellier	3Feb.1807		Duncan M'Nab	do.
	Thomas Kearney	10Aug.1811		Wm. Cundell	do.
	Samuel Belson	do.		Archibald Riddell	22Apr.
	L. E. Ermatinger	25May1812		Thomas Rayner	do.
	J. J. Moore	3Feb.1813		Thomas Marsden	13July
	Francis Vidau	31Mar.1814		William Coates	1Oct.
	A. R. C. Dallas	1July		John Flanner	15Jan.1814
	Andrew Melville	25Sept.		Charles W. Beverley	do.
	Ignacius Weckinger	do.		William Cordeaux	do.
	Harold France	1Nov.		James Wickens	5Feb.
	James Sams	do.		Jonathan Pate	31Mar.
	Warner Garnham	17do.		J. Henry Allsup	2May
	Denzil Ibbetson	25Dec.		George Elliott	do.
Dep. As. Com. Gen.	P. A. Fountain	23May1810		Robert J— Wyllie	4do.
	Edw. A. F. Cowan	5Aug.1811		James D— Watt	do.
	D— Kearney	10do.		Edward Case	do.
	Thomas Bayley	do.		George Maddox	do.
					Dep.

Disbanded and Reduced in 1814.

	Rank in the Army.			Rank in the Army.
Dep. As. ⟩	Richard Kirton	25Dec.1814	*Dep. As.* ⟩	Peter Roberts 25Dec.1814
Com. Gen. ⟨	John Reid	do.	*Com.Gen.* ⟨	W.Bousselet Whitefoord do.
	James Hodson	do.		H. L. Whitehead do.
	Robert Chartres	do.		Martin Stokes do.
	John Radford	do.		Geo. Moore Dillon do.
	Rowland B— Marshall	do.		William Condamine do.
	John Spencer	do.		Thomas Walker do.
	Samuel Tubby	do.		John Savery Brock do.
	William Hume	do.		Robert Deeker do.

MEDICAL DEPARTMENT.

Inspectors William Moore, M.D. 15Mar.1799
Sir Jas. M'Gregor, Kt. M. D. 25Aug.1809
Gabriel R. Redmond 3Sept.1812
SirJas. Fellowes,M.D. 29Apr.1813
Ralph Green 26Aug.
James Robert Grant 14July1814
Dep. ⟩ Robert Patrick, M.D. 4Apr.1800
Inspecs. ⟨ John Bapt. Weber 14Oct.1805
William Taylor 25July1811
Chas.Fer.Forbes,M.D. 18Feb.1813
John Meade 29Apr.
Charles Tice, M. D. 20May
G. I. Guthrie 16Sept.
Physicians James Buchan, M.D. 3Dec.1800
A. L. Emerson, M. D. 24Jan.1805
G. A. Morewood, M.D. 7Sept.1807
Adam Neale, M. D. 14July1808
Arth.B.Faulkner,M.D. 28do.
John Eyre, M. D. 6July1809
John Vetch, M. D. 16July1812
Henry Irwin, M. D. 15Oct.
James Forbes, M. D. 5Nov.
Edward Walsh, M.D. 12Aug.1813
Lewis Evans, M. D. 26May1814
David M'Lagan, M. D. do.
Wm. G. Wray, M. D. do.
Surgeons Lewis Krazeisen 26May1803
William Lynn 21Nov.1805
Henry Heine 25Dec.
Titus Berry 2Jan.1806
Henry Glasse do.
J. Van Malson 2July1807
J. L. Brandes do.
Charles Quartley 2Mar.1809
James Hosack 25May
Richard Young Vance 1June
G. B. Volmar 15do.

Surgeons Victor Sergel 6July1809
Daniel M'Lean 21Sept.
M. A. Burmeister 4Jan.1810
James Taylor 4July1811
Robert Woulfe do.
William Powell 8Aug.
Robert Grant 22do.
David Wood do.
John Hennon 24do.
John Alex. Campbell 19Mar.1812
Hugh Bone 26do.
Richard Humfrey 16Apr.
Charles Collier 4June
Thomas Donahoe 3Sept.
Charles Boatflower do.
James Arthur 15Oct.
John Boggie do.
Owen Lindsay 5Nov.
Richard Jebb Browne do.
J. Williamson 3June1813
Robert Swallow do.
James Mathews 9Sept.
Thomas Sandell do.
George Beattie do.
James du Moulin do.
John Griffith do.
Richard O'Connell do.
Robert Stratton 30do.
Stephen M'Mullen 18Nov.
John Taberger 27Dec.
John Goodsman 6Jan.1814
William Spence 13do.
JohnG.VanMillangan 26May
Ferdinand Seiler do.
Const. John Laisne 25Oct.
Patrick Hughes do.
A. Kendall do.
Joseph Taylor do.

Surgeons

Disbanded and Reduced in 1814.

		Rank in the Army.			*Rank in the Army.*
Surgeons	John Barr	25Oct.1814	*Dep.*	Christoph.Winnicke	24June1802
	Alexander Schetky	do.	*Purveyors*	Wm. Hen. O'Reilly	5Jan.1809
	Philip Walter	do.		Alexander Copeland	31Aug.
	David Barry	do.		John Saunders	do.
	Alexander Le Sassier	do.		Harry Bacon	21Dec.
	Patrick M'Glashan	do.		John Winter	do.
	Cortes Wm. Clarance	do.		William Vacher	3Oct.1811
	Augustus West	do.		David Roche	do.
	Frederick Jebb	do.		Thomas Hardy	do.
	John Callendar	do.		Francis Bishop	3Sept.1812
Late Sur-	John Short	5Feb 1811		Thomas Smyth	do.
geons with	Edw. F. Coates	10Oct.		William Clapp	15Oct.
Local	W. C. Callow	21Jan.1813		Charles Surtees	15Apr.1813
Rank.	Charles Annesley	do.		George Pratt	3June
	Ebenezer Black	do.		John Dunn	9Sept.
	Gavin Hilson	26May1814		James Wallington	do.
				J. Harrington	do.
Surgeons	Geo. A. Mackenzie	14Apr.1805		Thomas Vaughan	2Dec.
of Re-	John Grant	15Oct.1807		James Findley	10Mar.1814
cruiting	J. H. Fenoulhet	25Feb.1808		William Ivey	26May
District.	Henry Travis	1June		George Mucklow	do.
	Thomas Wilson	8Sept.		Joseph Weaver	do.
	Thomas Woods	27Aug.1812		James H. Harris	13Oct.
Purveyors	George Dickson	4Apr.1800	*Apothe-*	John Maxwell	11July1805
	Joseph Gunson	16Feb.1809	*caries*	Samuel Jones	31Aug.1809
	William James	29June		Thomas Morton	28May1812
	Tho. Hume Bowles	10Nov.1810		William Price	3Sept.
	Edward Hodges	9Sept.1813		Richard Heurtley	3July1813
				William Lyons	9Sept.
				Nilus Hilditch	do.
				James Taylor	do.

OFFICERS.

ON THE

IRISH HALF-PAY,

Previous to the Year 1814.

	Rank in the Army.
Colonel Lucas's	
Major George Duff	30Sept.1789
Additional Officers	
Major Joseph Greene	
Capt. Thomas Lechmere	30Sept.1789
Sir J. Bruce's	
2d Lieut. James Harper	
6th Dragoon Guards	
Capt. James Caulfield	1Mar.1800
Lieuts. Thomas Stracey	1Mar.1800
Richard Thornhill	17Sept.1803
Paym. Owen Wynne Gray	
Q. Mrs. Robert Reilly	
Lawrence Power	
2d Dragoons	
Paym. Richard Cowan	8Mar.1798
5th Dragoons	
Major Redm. Browne	Lt.Col.3May1796
Capts. Ralph James	Lt.Col.1Jan.1812
A. B. Dennistoun	7Sept.1804
Paym. Isaac M'Taggart	
Q. Mrs. Daniel Leslie	
Michael Nowlan	
Arthur Proctor	
William Garvey	
9th Dragoons	
Lieuts. Ponsonby Hore	29Apr.1795
Henry Dawson	1Oct.1801
Thomas Cosby	3Apr.1802
Q. Mrs. Patrick Knowd	
John Nelson	
Robert Martin	
William Hay	

	Rank in the Army.
12th Dragoons	
Cornet Thomas Tarleton	
21st Dragoons	
Capt. Dugald Campbell	12Jan.1805
Lieut. William Wentworth	3May1800
Q. Mrs. Robert Cambridge	
William Sharpley	
23d Dragoons	
Capt. Lt. Thomas Eminson	
Lieut. Robert Salmon	22Aug.1802
Cornets Robert Bushe	1Feb.1798
John Bray	
Hugh Doherty	1May1801
Paym. Nugent Kirkland	1Nov.1798
Q. Mrs. Elias Burt	
Thomas Byrne	
George Spier	
John Gibbons	
William Gough	
C— Ameron	
John Mackie	
William Tipson	
24th Dragoons	
Capts. John O'Neil Bailey	30Mar.1797
John A— Gifford	23Jan.1801
Lieut. Richard Money	1Mar.1800
Cornets William Pilsworth	
William Bonner	5Nov.1800
Edward Lucas	18Apr.1801
Paym. Anthony Cross	6Nov.1801
Q. Mrs. Charles Deacon	
J— Goad	
J— Perry	

3 M   Q. Mrs.

Rank in the Army.

Q. Mrs. A— Baldcock
Anthony Baker
J— Ives
John M'Mullen
Thomas Hirst

28th Dragoons
Majors Hon.W.Collyear   *Lt.Col.*1Jan.1805
    John Cooke   *Lt.Col.*25July1810
Capts. Benjamin Bromhead   6Aug.1799
    J—Hen. Elrington   12June1800
Lieuts. Charles Charteris   12Apr.1796
    George Card
    John Heacock   11Apr.1800
Cornets John Matchett   5Dec.1799
    William Maule   3May1800
    John Veitch   11Mar.1801
    Robert Millett   22Oct.
    William Pegge   17June1802
Q. Mrs. George Spawforth
    John M'Vey
    Michael Ryan
    Robert Belmor
    Robert Wheatley
    Cornelius Card
    Thomas Smith
Vet. Sur. James White   12Apr.1797

1st Fencible Dragoons
Q. Mrs. William Brunskill
    John Gethings
    Henry Neill
    George Young

2d Fencible Dragoons
Q. Mrs. Edward Hayes
    Thomas Johnstone
    John Cruise

Hompesch's Chasseurs
Cornet Roch Billot   12Apr.1798

4th Foot
Lieuts. John Gray
    John Kelly
    Henry Leslie

6th Foot
Ensign Alexander Nightingale

11th Foot
Lieuts. Peter Skerrett
    Wm. Eden Lees   13Aug.1793

15th Foot
Major Sampson Freeth   *Col.*4June1814
Lieuts. Christoph. Atkin   21Aug.1800
    Capel Lechmere   9Feb.1801
    Richard Lucas   23Mar.
    Anthony Williams
    John Otter   5Feb.1806
    John Balaguiere
    Charles Ince   17Jan.1808
Ensigns M. M'Gleazy
    Alex. John Bigger   26Dec.1799
    John Horne
    William Blair
    E. J. Fitzsimons

Rank in the Army.

Q. Mr. Robert Craig   20Feb.1806
Adjutant Thomas Warrington   16Jan.1800

16th Foot
Lieuts. Robert W. Cooke   29July1796
    William Han. Davies   5Feb.1801

17th Foot
Major John Le Mesurier   *Lt.Col.*25July 1810
Lieuts. William White   11Aug.1799
    Robert Cooch   21Oct.
    Jeremiah Thompson   25do.
    George Burridge   26do.
    James Winton   27do.
    Gusta. Hippesley
    John Wisdom
    Thos. B. Bedward   8May1801
    A. Gethin Creagh   10Apr.1806
    Thomas White   29Dec.1807
Ensigns George Whaley
    John Wilkinson   1Jan.1807
Paym. William Raymond

21st Foot
1st Lieuts. Thomas Gill Marsham
    George Scott   19Apr.1796

32d Foot
Lieuts. Ant. Francis Tisdall
    Barry Yelverton
Ensigns Robert Mockler   20Mar.1801
    Edward Mayne   24July1802
    George Luton
    R. W. Alexander

36th Foot
Lieuts. Robert Hughes   28Feb.1796
    T. Dunscombe   25Nov.1799
    Richard Farmer   11Aug.1811
As. Surg. T. E. Arundell

38th Foot
Ensigns Philip Oates   23Mar.1801
    Samuel Porter

44th Foot
Lieuts. Daniel M'Donald   24Mar.1804
    Geo. Henry Elliott   8Feb.1810

46th Foot
Capt. H. R. Featherstonhaugh   *Lt.Col.* 1Jan.1812
Lieuts. F. Bryan Holland   29July1796
    Alexander Dalrymple   1Sept.
    Randell Chetham   19Apr.1799
    Philip Bramer   19Dec.
    Jackman Wilkins   6July1802
    James Burkett
    George Hagar
    Charles Adams
    James Stirling
Paym. Robert Winter   1Aug.1798
Surgeon Gavin Hamilton   30Aug.1799

50th Foot
Lieut. Henry Lewis   4Aug.1800

53d Foot
Surgeon Thomas Carter

56th

Rank in the Army.   *Rank in the Army.*

56th Foot
Lieuts.	John Fitzmaurice	21Dec.1796
	Nathaniel Wright	13June1801
Ensign	William Maxwell	4July1805

58th Foot
Lieut.	Francis G. Despard	
Ensign	John Thompson	

62d Foot
Lieuts.	William Nadould	30Nov.1799
	William Jones	15Nov.1800
	John E. Despard	do.
	Leonard Crooks	
	Charles Leigh	7Aug.1801
	Henry Macnamara	27Nov.
	Victor Lozen	
	James O'Brien	1Dec.
	John Legard	
Ensigns	Mat. Yelverton	26June1802
	William Long	
Paym.	John William Kerr	21Feb.1800
As. Surg.	Thomas Watters	

66th Foot
Lieuts.	Alexander Hewey	31Jan.1780
	John M. Uniacke	8Sept.
	Richard C. Langford	13Oct.1781
	John Buller Elliott	19Nov.
	Godfrey Massey	20Feb.1788

67th Foot
Lieuts.	James M'Gregor	14Dec.1778
	William Cowan	12Aug.1779
	Arthur Fleming	29June1780
	George Davies	5Feb.1781
	Russell Wood	13Oct.
	John Stokes	2Jan.1798

71st Foot
Lieut.	Henry Marder	1June1799

72d Foot
Ensigns	Colin M'Lachlan	9July1800
	James Blair	24July1802
	John Smith	22Oct.1803
	James Christie	28Mar.1805

73d Foot
Lieut.	Charles Higgins	17Sept.1759

83d Foot
Lieuts.	Averell Daniel	
	Robert Lyon	
	John Hasler	8Sept.1790
Ensigns	Henry Palmer	
	Nicholas Betson	

89th Foot
Capt.	Walter Synot	
Lieut.	George Douglas	

90th Foot
Capt.	James Ferguson	15Jan.1807

91st Foot
Lieuts.	Thomas D'Arcy	
	J — Wainwright	

92d Foot
Lieut.	William Spear	

93d Foot
Ensigns	Benson Lawton	
	Mathias Smith	
Adjutant	Henry Clem. Ellis	

103d Foot
Capts.	Walter Hore	15Feb.1782
	Arthur Law	1Mar.
	Robert Bligh	
Lieuts.	Ralph W— Read	27Sept.1783
	Samuel Goodwin	1Jan.1797
	Sir J— Caldwell, Bt.	
Ensigns	John Way	5July1780
	Daniel Jones	27Apr.1781
	John Sandys	22Mar.1782
	James Roach	31Dec.
	St. John Skottowe	25Apr.1783
Chaplain	Brinsley Nixon	3Nov.1781

105th Foot
Capts.	John Steele	28Sept.1799
	Anthony Lister	24Feb.1804
Lieut.	John Fred. Parker	29May1783
Ensigns	Joseph Hudson	21Mar.1782
	William Wright	
	Walter Graham	
	Andrew Macpherson	
Chaplain	James Morgan	21Mar.1782
Q. Mr.	William Campbell	21Mar.1782

108th Foot
Capt.	John Warren	
Lieut.	Gilbert Toler	
Ensigns	Forster H— Forster	
	Allan Grant	

121st Foot
Capt.	Thomas Hill	
Lieut.	Robert Cox	
Chaplain	Francis Gisborne	
Adjutant	Charles Watts	

122d Foot
Lieut.	John Sutherland	
Ensign	Edward Croker	

123d Foot
Capt.	Henry Lumsden	
Ensigns	Richard Rogers	
	Robert Suckling	
Adjutant	Caleb Mason	

124th Foot
Lieuts.	Paget Halpen	
	John Maxwell	
Ensigns	Richard Meredith	
	Thomas Martyn	

5th Garrison Battalion
Lieut.	Richard Edwards	

7th Garrison Battalion
Lieut.Col.	©Wm. Gabriel Davy	28Dec.1809
Majors	Dan. Colquhoun	Lt.Col.4June1811
	Peter D'Arcy	Lt.Col.4June1813
Capts.	John Lev. Campbell	9Mar.1800
	William Balf	3Aug.1804
	Lucas Hunt Jackson	4do.
	William Boothby	28Sept.

                     Capts.

3 M 2

	Rank in the Army.
Capts. Wm. John Chetwynd	9May1805
Wm. Johnson Brazier	8Sept.
William Burke	25Aug.1806
William Ongley	18May1809
Lieuts. John Fitchet	8Oct.1802
William Grant	17Apr.1805
R— O'Neil Singer	8May
John Ross	21Sept.
Michael Creaghe	21Nov.
Stephen Edwards	3Apr.1806
John Harris Arnold	18Dec.
Alexander Rogers	11June1807
———— M'Mahon	5Nov.
Edward Newton	30Jan.1808
Abraham Nowles	22Feb.1809
William Grant	19Apr.1810
Ensigns Morogh O'Brien	31Mar.1808
Francis Atkinson	7Apr.
Thomas Chadwick	3Nov.
William Ogle Sallery	19Feb.1807
John Brown	14Apr.1809
Richard Lloyd	20do.
Bradshaw Rainsford	7Dec.
Paym. Edward Edmonds	
As. Surgs. J— Bomford	4Aug.1808
———— Lloyd	
8th Garrison Battalion	
Lieut.Col.◎Rob.Ld.BlantyreCol.4June1813	
Major Henry Darling	Col.4June1814
Q. Mr. Peter Stewart	3Jan.1804
8th Garrison Battalion	
Lt. Col. Patrick Ross	Col.4June1814
Major Tho.G.Fitzgerald Lt.Col.4June1813	
Capts. Ernest Missett Lt.Col.25July1810	
John Cunningham	23Jan.1801
Tho. Bromley Shairpe 17Mar.1803	
John Hammond	21Feb.1805
William Fagel	25July1806
Roger Finch	25Nov.
William Le Grand	26do.
William W— Algeo	27do.
Lieuts. Medlycott Cane	26Sept.1781
William Gibbs	5Aug.1804
Francis Chamley	26Aug.1805
Stackhouse Thompson 21Nov.	
Francis Mason	9Oct.1806
Alexander M'Donald	26Nov.
James Booth	27do.
James Willington	6Feb.1808
William Roberts	25Oct.
Vaughan Jones	12Jan.1809
William John Lyster	
Ensigns James Bowles Johnson 28Oct.1807	
Peter Meggett	10Mar.1808
W. C. H. Buchanan	30Nov.1809
Adjutant ———— Ellam	25Dec.1806
Q. Mr. ———— Macdonald	19Nov.1807
Surgeon Merrick Gallaher	28Oct.1801
9th Garrison Battalion	
Lt. Col. Hon. F. G. Howard Col.4June1813	

	Rank in the Army.
13th Garrison Battalion	
Ensign Pryce L— Gordon	
16th Garrison Battalion	
Lt. Col. Cosmo Gordon	20July1809
Major Alex. Sharpe	Lt.Col.25Oct.1809
Lieut. John Russell	1Feb.1805
Loyal Irish Fencibles	
Ensign Henry Booth	16Aug.1804
Ancient Irish Fencibles	
Lt. Col. James Foster	Col.4June1814
Adjutant H— H— Beecher	5June1799
LATE IRISH BRIGADE.	
1st Regiment	
Capts. John Geoghegan	1Oct.1794
John Mulhall	do.
Thomas Jones	
Lieuts. William Bulkeley	
James Eustace	
Ensigns Michael Devereux	1Oct.1794
Maurice T— Pierce	do.
Richard Hilliard	do.
Robert Plunkett	do.
Chaplain John Fallon	1Oct.1794
Q. Mr. Francis Sutton	1Oct.1794
2d Regiment	
Lt. Col. John O'Toole	Col.1Jan.1805
Major Ph. Walsh	Lt.Col.1Jan.1800
Capts. John Walsh	1Oct.1794
William Donop	
John Spedding	9July1803
Lieut. William Ricketts	2Nov.1796
Ensign K— M'Dermot	25Sept.1800
3d Regiment	
Capts. JohnScottLindesay Maj.4June1814	
Dennis Mahony	
Lieuts. Alexander Warde	
Donald M'Craw	5Nov.1796
Joseph Bullen	4Jan.1797
4th Regiment	
Major D— Barry	Lt.Col.1Jan.1800
Capts. R— Sutton Clonnard	1Oct.1794
Richard Barry	do.
Marcus O'Sullivan	do.
John, Visc. Arbuthnot	
Thomas D'Arcy	29Nov.1799
Lieut. P— Burton Carter	11Oct.1794
Ensigns Richard Murphy	31Dec.1795
John M'Carthy	29May1796
Richard M'Cartie	do.
Adjutant Thomas Conway	
5th Regiment	
Capt. C— Power	1Oct.1794
Lieut. Neptune Blood	
Ensigns John Evans	31Aug.1795
Thomas Kerr	14Dec.1797
As. Surg. Daniel O'Leary	
6th Regiment	
Capt. George Willis	
Lieuts. John Rose	
John Holland	24June1795
	Lieuts.

	Rank in the Army.			*Rank in the Army.*
Lieuts. Charles W— Davis	2Dec.1799		*Mount Kennedy Yeomanry*	
John Fraser	10July1800		*Capt.* Robert Gore	
Ensigns Giles Rea			*Invalids*	
John Calder			*Capts.* N— L—Tottenham	14May1769
Richard Williams	28Nov.1801		Essex Edgeworth	12May1777
As. Surg. John O'Neal			*Lieut.* Thomas Philips	25Feb.1757
Provincial Regiments			*Unattached Independent Comp.*	
Adjutant Thomas Kirkman			*Capt.* Ponsonby Watts	

Commissariat Department.

Dep.Com.Gen. James Singer	*Commissary of the Corps of Waggoners*
As. Comm. George Cotter	Patrick H— Cannon

Medical Department.

Physician John Haig
Surgeon R— Salmond   16July1803

Disbanded and Reduced in 1814.

1st Regiment of Dragoon Guards
Capts. Hon.G.L.Dawson *Maj.*10Mar.1814
     Charles Lev. Barnard   20Dec.1806
6th Regiment of Dragoon Guards
Capts. John Kennedy   19May1814
     Hon. Arthur Southwell 16June
Lieut. David Waugh   19May1814
7th Regiment of Dragoon Guards
Capt. Tho. William Giffard   24July1814
23d Regiment of Dragoons
Lt. Col. Charles Palmer   *Col.*4June1814
Capts. James Allen   *Major*4June1811
     George Battersby   2Sept.1813
Lieuts. Jeremiah Easter   26July1809
     Hon. St. George Cuff   10Oct.1811
32d Regiment of Foot
Majors Robert Coote   *Lt.Col.*4June1814
     H— Richardson   17May1810
Capts. M.S.O'C. Caulfield *Maj.*4June1814
     Stopford Cane   14Feb.1805
     Thomas Jones   27July1809
     William Trueman   8Nov.1810
     Anthony Graves   14Apr.1813
     John C— Dennis   15do.
     George Eason   10June
     Michael Kilkelly   8July
     William Hinde   27Aug.
     Thomas Rose   15Sept.1814
Lieuts. Hibbert Newton   13Apr.1813
     James Peyton   14do.
     Wm. Henry Lawder   15do.
     Jonathan Jagoe   10June

Lieuts. James Rollo   5Aug.1813
     George Sayer   27do.
     William Blood   1Sept.
     Frederick O'Flaherty   2do.
     E— Taylor   27Jan.1814
     James Henry   10Feb.
Ensigns John Smith   27Aug.1813
     Frederick Lloyd   1Sept.
     Edward Harwood   21Oct.
     Charles Dallas   18Nov.
     John Buchannon   9Dec.
     Stuart Mackay   6Jan.1814
     John Mortished   27do.
     ——— M'Nabb   10Feb.
     James Butler   1Sept.
Paym. Jacob Dudden   26July1810
Q. Mr. Edward Charles   6June1811
Surgeon James Barlow   29July1813
As. Surg. Richard Verling   23June1814
34th Regiment of Foot
Lieut. Thomas Smyth   28Aug.1811
40th Regiment of Foot
As. Surg. Edward M'Iver   3June1813
45th Regiment of Foot
Lt. Col. ⊚*Hon.* JohnMeade*Col.*4June1813
61st Regiment of Foot
Lt. Col. John Chetham   19May1814
Majors Edward Pare Sparrow 12Apr.1814
     James Horton   18May
     Andrew Hartley   19do.
     James Laing   do.
               Capts.

Disbanded and Reduced in 1814.

	Rank in the Army.
Capts. Edward Brackenbury	23July1812
Graves Collins	24do.
Henry Tench	do.
John White	do.
George Allan Maclean	25do.
Lewis Mordaunt	26do.
James Given	14Aug.
Hugh Eccles	15Apr.1813
George Porter	10Aug.
John Chipchase	2June1814
Lieuts. James Chapman	2July1807
John Bain	11Apr.1811
Francis Begg	5Aug.1813
Thomas Ratcliffe	30Sept.
Anthony Bubb	16Dec.
John Ellison	19Jan.1814
George Evans Stuart	20do.
John Spier	10Feb.
James Wright	21Apr.
Thomas Belton	19May
Cuthbert Eccles	20do.
John Kennedy Strong	29Sept.
Ensigns Stopford Tho. Jones	15Nov.1810
John Bell	10Feb.1814
James Wilson	19May
John Slater	20do.
—— Laidlow	9June
William Scott	16do.
Adjutant AndrewConnell *Lieut.*	29Sept.1813
Q. Mr. George Tyrrell	25Feb.1813
Surgeon Andrew Anderson	25June1812

105th Foot

Capt. Charles Hastings	7Mar.1811

1st Garrison Battalion

Lt. Col. John Ready	10June1813
Majors Robert Johns	*Lt.Col.*4June1814
Henry Oglander	14Oct.1813
Capts. Hector Munro	*Lt.Col.*4June1814
DanielO'Donaghue	*Maj.*4June1813
Maxwell Close	*Major*4June1813
James Moultrie	*Major*4June1814
Baptist J. Barton	*Major* do.
David Gregory	*Major* do.
Sampson Carter	*Major* do.
Thomas Wm. Warre	2Dec.1806
Alexander Adams	15Oct.1812
David Brown	24May1810
Lieuts. John Boyton	28Jan.1778
Henry Mahew	23May1804
W. H. Pick	29Mar.1805
W. Prosser Symmonds	2July1807
William Ratcliffe	13Apr.1809
John Gibson Jones	31Aug.
Lachlan M'Queen	30Nov.
William Crean	22Dec.1806
John Boyd	2May1811
Horatio F. Nelson	25Nov.1813

	Rank in the Army.
Lieuts. James Boyton	25Aug.1814
John Enzinger	20Oct.
Ensigns Humphrey Babington	15Mar.1810
John Evans	9May1811
James Fisher	18June1812
Thomas Alley	16Apr.
John Byrne	12Aug.1813
Henry Wm. Hassard	27Jan.1814
Norman Douglas	25Aug.
James Henderson	20Oct.
Paym. James Hamblyn	2Aug.1813
Adjutant John Barrett	*Lieut.*19May1808
Q. Mr. Thomas Allen	21Oct.1813
Surgeon Robert Hill	12Sept.1794
As. Surgs. Thomas Burke	4Aug.1808
George Rutledge	1Mar.1810

2d Garrison Battalion

Lt. Col. Adol. J. Dalrymple	1June1814
Majors Wm. Armstrong	*Col.*4June1813
Wm. Lindsay Darling	14Apr.1814
Capts. Henry Williams	*Lt.Col.*1Jan.1812
John Cameron	*Major*4June1814
Jos. Dacre Lacey	*Maj.* do.
David Ogilvie Stewart	7Mar.1805
Arthur Newport	1May
David King Fawcett	14May1807
Paget Bayly	23Feb.1809
Richard Millard	17do.
Hon. Francis Russell	28Apr.1814
Lieuts. James Stewart	14Apr.1804
Francis B. Pyne	31Aug.1781
Joseph Lamphier	1Sept.1807
William J. Dillon	2Feb.1809
John Wade West	4Jan.1797
Arthur Fraser	12Jan.1805
Arthur Gardiner	11July1811
William Gunn	30Jan.1806
Joshua Gledstanes	27June1809
Roger Finnan	10Oct.1807
James Kershaw	1Oct.1795
Henry Wallis	31Dec.1812
John Minty	27Oct.1814
Ensigns James Horton	19Mar.1807
William Rennick	24May1810
Francis Jack Needham	4Feb.1813
Harry Williams	12Aug.
Wm. Geo. Turnbull	do.
John Hanfield Taggart	17Feb.1814
W. Duncan	2June
William Harly	27Oct.
Paym. Edward Acton	9Mar.1812
Adjutant George Guy	*Ensign*30July1812
Q. Mr. Edward Loggan	20July1813
Surgeon Benjamin Johnston	8Nov.1794
As.Surgs. Basil Johnston	9July1807
John Swift	4Aug.1808

5th

Disbanded and Reduced in 1814.

	Rank in the Army.
5th Garrison Battalion	
Lt. Col. James P. Murray	25May1809
Majors Wm. Belford	Lt.Col. 1Jan.1812
Nich. Ramsay	Lt.Col. 4June1813
Capts. Thomas Reid	Major 4June1814
Wm. Richardson	Maj. do.
Thomas Amory	Maj. do.
Paschal Paoli Hobart	13Mar.1806
Thomas Gregory	25Feb.1808
William Bennett	14Feb.1805
William Pilkington	1Dec.1806
Henry Calthrop	26Apr.1810
James Johnston	7Mar.1811
George Elliot	1Dec.1806
Lieuts. Anthony Robinson	17Dec.1806
Henry M'Cullock	29Jan.1807
James Barrow	20Mar.
Wm. Thomas Pope	12Jan.1809
Richard Edwards	25Oct.1806
George Pope	7Dec.1809
William Sankey	4June1807
William Goddard	28Dec.1809
Joshua Gillespie	7Mar.1811
John Mee	16Feb.1808
Coakley Lewis	28Oct.1807
James Mitchell	13Sept.1810
Ensigns Stephen M. Burrowes	31Jan.1811
William Belford	18Mar.1813
——— Rich	22July
John Manley	19Aug.
J. D. Kane	23Dec.
George Hamilton	2Feb.1814
Spencer Wm. Walsh	3do.
William Roberts	31Mar.
Paym. Richard D. O'Connor	19July1813
Adjutant James Clarke	Lieut.4Jan.1810
Q. Mr. William Buchanan	12Dec.1811
As. Surgs. Richard Swift	19Aug.1813
Henry Hart	31Jan.1811
6th Garrison Battalion	
Majors ParryJonesParry	Lt.Col.4June1811
George Warburton	2Sept.1814
Capts. Thomas Shaw	Major4June1814
Wade Rothwell	Major do.
Lord Robt. Kerr	Major do.
Richard Maxwell	Major do.

	Rank in the Army.
Capt. Joseph Jerrard	Major4June1814
William Henry Newton	4Dec.1806
Christopher Foss	23July1807
George Bury	30Aug.1810
Henry Blake	25Apr.1805
Henry Robert Digby	2Dec.1813
Lieuts. William Ross	2Apr.1807
Francis Moffitt	3Aug.1810
Henry M'Manus	23June1804
Charles Veitch	22July1808
Thomas White	28Aug.1807
W. T. M. Ryan	1May1806
Adam Rogers	15Mar.1809
Thomas Howard	31Oct.
William Bruce Hill	7Apr.1810
John Pike	25June1812
Lewis C. Appelius	7Oct.1813
Mat. Tho. O'Reilly	27Jan.1814
Robert Cashel	23Aug.1809
Ensigns John Ross	20Oct.1810
Robert Wm. Gybon	27Apr.1809
Oliver St. John	9Sept.1813
John O'Mara	7Oct.
Henry Cust	11Nov.
Benjamin Bayley	2Dec.
Ezekiel Tydd Abbott	27Jan.1814
Hon.Wm.St.Lawrence	24Feb.
Paym. Wm. Pulteney Dana	25Apr.1807
Adjutant William Green	Ensign31Mar.1814
Q. Mr. ——— Yates	9Apr.1812
Surgeon Robert Coombs	9July1803
As.Surgs. Copeland Grattan	14June1810
Alexander Stewart	25Nov.1813
7th Garrison Battalion	
Capts. B. W. P. Wallop	26Nov.1806
Hon. Joshua Allen	31May1810
8th Garrison Battalion	
Major R. C. St. John, *Lord* Clinton	
	Lt.Col.20Aug.1812
Capt. Thomas Aubin	1Sept.1814
12th Royal Veteran Battalion	
Paym. Charles Abrams	10Sept.1812
Surgeon John Sharpe	15June1802
As.Surgs. William Gardiner	7Feb.1811
Richard Fitzpatrick	10Feb.1814

Disbanded and Reduced in 1814.

COMMISSARIAT DEPARTMENT.

Dep.Com.Gen. William Finny	*As. Com. Gen.* John Baker 28Apr.1814
As. Com. Gen. William Hughes	William Ledwith do.
John Jones	Henry Rochfort do.
George Birney	H. L. Gordon do.
Robert Colvill	Lendrum Clarke

MEDICAL DEPARTMENT.

Surgeon Matthew Poole, M. D.	*Surgeon* John Brown 9June1808
James O'Connor, M. D.	*Dep.Pur.* James Mould
Simon Rawling	*Apoth.* John Cowan
James Dalzell	Henry White

RECRUITING DISTRICT.

Paym. F. R. Smyth 12Sept.1804	*Adjutants* John Prentice *Lieut.*5Apr.1803
Nicholas Mansell 21Aug.1813	Hugh Lynch ——10Oct.1805
Adjutant Const. Maguire *Lieut.*12Apr.1799	Peter Stewart ——14Oct.1806

OFFICERS

OFFICERS

OF THE

ROYAL MARINES

ON HALF-PAY.

Colonel John Fletcher
Lieut. Colonel George Elliot Vinicombe
     Col. Joseph Lambrecht
     John Boscawen Savage
Majors Lt. Col. Francis O'Dogherty
     John Williams
     Lt. Col. Thomas Davey
     Lt. Col. Walter Tremenhiere

Capts. Hector Macneal
    Jonathan Gunthorpe
    William Seward
    Philip Howe
    Robert Moore
    Major William Bowater
    Major William Adlam
    William Walsh
    William John Madden
    Rog. Mostyn Edwards
    Thomas Pearce
    Lt. Col. Moles. Phillips
    John Smith Halliday
    Major William Ramsay
    John Hale
    Thomas Gilbert
    George Collins
    Lt. Col. James Nicholson
    Samuel H— Baumgarten
    Lt. Col. F. H. Flight
    John Thomas Hobbs
    Neh. Aug. Hunt

Capts. Samuel Ball
    John Agnew Connell
    George Winter
    Richard Higginson
    Matthew Mundy
    Charles Allen Phillip
    George Belson
    Alexander Robertson
    Samuel Forshall
    James Matthew
    George Kempster
    Henry Elliot
    James Maxwell
    Trevor Hull Lethem
    Philip Sturgeon
    Edward Parke
    Robert Torkington
    John Wardlaw
    John Kellet
    George Varlo
    John Henry Bright
    Walter Holland

3 N   *Capts.*

Capts. John Abbs
Peter T— Wilson
J— N— N— D'Esterre
H— B— Downing
Thomas Young
William Reding
Bryan O'Reilly
John Bell. Graham
Thomas Anderson
George Browne
Buller Rolle Langford
Zaccheus Fayerman
Thomas Max. Baguold
Hen. Holmes Haviland
Thomas Willson
Charles O'Bryen
Michael Percival
William Jackson
Richard Lawson
Jacob Harrison
Demetrious Grevis
William Morrice
William Henry Craig
John Shepherd
Stephen Miles Sandys
Richard Welchman
James Crosse
George Richards
Major Paul Hunt
Peter Lely
Thomas Mould
John Witts
Walter Taylor Mitchell
Major John Lodington
—— James Fynmore
—— William Johnstone
—— Christopher Noble
—— John Phillips
—— Roger P— Symons
Christopher Abbott
Philip Patriarche
Robert Alexander
Robert Stewart
John Scriven
Robert Hayes
John M'Leod
John Naughan
Patrick Fottrell
Edw. Alex. Toomer
James Jones
James Stephen Pilcher
James Rives Hore
William Jordan
William Steele
Edw. Smith Mercer
Thomas Hussey
Richard Steele Wilkinson
Joseph Triscott
Thomas Mitchell
John Moore
Malcolm G. M'Arthur

Capts. Alexander Eckford
James Defferd
Joseph Williams
Joseph Williams
William Walker
John Mascall
Frederick Waters
William Taylor
Thomas Moore
George Wright
William Thomas Chartres
John M'Callum
Thomas Lemon
Henry Hole
Edward W. Brown
George Keith
Richard Turner
Thomas Hurdle
Charles Menzies
Robert Hall
Richard Boger
David Holt
Cha. Hamilton Ballinghall
Andrew Herriot
Henry John Murton
William T— Clements
William Fergusson
James Cottell
Samuel Ashmore
Julius Fleming
Richard Swaile
Capt. Lt. Christie Ewart
Henry B— Hillcoat
John Davis Maillard
Alexander Campbell
William Sims
Mark Oates
1st Lieuts. Christopher Abbott
James Urquhart
Alpin Grant
James Bower
Haddock Chudleigh
Neil Wauchope
John Kneebone
James Scott
Aaron Young
John Coulthurst
Alexander Clark
Thomas Thomas
Robert Kellow
John Evelyn
Thomas Fortye
St. George Armstrong
Samuel Jenkin
Robert Beevin
William Ackroyd
H— Norton Gamble
Henry West
Gerald Cotton
George Gibson
J— N— Martin

1st Lieuts.

1st Lieuts. Levinge Ivie
Charles Bourne
James Justice
George Franklin
Robert Dell
John Drummond
John Belson
Edward Wood
Thomas Forwood
John Shuttleworth
William Jerrard
John King
William Carter
Mathew Cadoux
James Baird
William Thompson
Hugh Stewart
John Smith
Robert Martin
William Bourne
John K— Fletcher
G— Ebbery Thomas
William Taylor
Chil. Twentyman
Thomas Elliott
Horatio Gregory
John Henry Beuzelin
Henry Painter
Richard Murphy
George Finlay
James Metcalfe
George Byne
John Lurting
David Logan
John Patten
Edward Kentish
J— Kidgell Sandon
Thomas Winter
John Oakley
Thomas Carthew
Richard Brown
T— Ward Blagrave
J — Venables Hinde
Thomas Crump
Edward Wightman
William Dawes
Daniel Osborn
John Edward Blakeney
Thomas Keane
William Aird
Thomas Wood
Samuel Prother
Mitchell Graham
W— H— Carrington
Thomas Clark
Henry Thompson
T— B— Edgeworth
Duncan Campbell
Richard Barford
W— Lewis Coryton

1st Lieuts. F— B— O'Dogherty
Thomas Avery
James Holmes
John Manners
George Henry Guyon
Alexander Wilson
William Corham
James Marrie
Charles Burdon
Edward Davis Hanmer
Philip L— Powell
William Arnott
William Fowler
James Wheeler
William Lasinby French
John Scobell
John Woodmeston
Alexander Murray
Hector F— M'Neill
Kenneth Scobie
John Smale
John Sandys
Alexander F— D'Asti
Angus Campbell
Robert Irwin
Joseph Coombe
Richard Rouse
John Humphreys
William Swyer
Bertrand Cahuac
William Jeffries
Alexander Smith
James Fichat
T— Wardner Speare
Thomas Marshall
Francis Hodson
S— Graves Averell
John Hawkins
H— Barnet Gascoyne
R— Tapper Parsons
Thomas Piper
Alexander Curry
William Nichols Roe
William Graves
John Yeats
William Magin
Benjamin Beales
James Henry Baker
Theo. Hen. Donne
George Clarke
Joseph Martin
George Fortescue
James Jackson
Geo. Richardson Lapdell
Richard Buchan
Henry Wall
Thomas O'Neill
John Bennett
John Stepney Haswell
Alexander Day

1st Lieuts. Rich. Garret Amyat
Charles Crause
Thomas Morgan
Henry Gape
Charles Higginson
John Mackay
Tho. James Wald. Tane
George Nagle
James Cassell
John Nicholas Fischer
Henry Porter
Thomas Brattle
Edward Morgan
John Simpson
Walter K. Alder
Charles Holmes
Nicholas Millett
Henry Miller
Robert Turtliff Dyer
John Haddy Williams
John Jeffreys
George Nelson
John Shillibeer
Cha. Almond Whiting
George Elliot Balchild
Lewis Buckle Reeves
William Stuart
James Whylock
Edward Bayley
Vans Walker
Thomas Wearing
Armiger Watts Hubbard
Nicholas Phillipps
Thomas Bassan
John Wilson
John Humby
Alexander Grieve
Edward Hobbs Stewart
James Uniacke
John Ja. Patrick Bissett
Duncan Campbell
Andrew Charles Rea
Henry Loveday Vine
Edw. Bamfield Eagles
Valentine Griffith
Harry Hunt
Stephen Giles
Lewis Rooke
William Burrow
Jonathan Baron
Charles Gray
Duncan M'Nicol
George Drew Hawkins
George Tompkins
George Huskisson
Richard Thomas Dixie
Herbert Bowen Mends
William Starke
William Sampson

1st Lieuts. Lau. Boul. Jos. Halloran
Thomas Reeves
Robert Ford
Humphrey Moore
George Butt Bury
James Irwin Willes
William Liddon
James Orr
Thomas Waters
John Sawers
Henry Blacker Fairtlough
James Faden
Frederick Layton
Henry James Gillespie
Francis Owen Enreght
John Neame
John Mitten
Stephen Bridgman
William Hockly
Arthur Molesworth
James Campbell
Philip Laffer
John Lister
David M'Adams
David Miller
Henry Foord
James Walker
Edmund Morrish Wills
Thomas Robert Pye
James Morrish
John Trevanion Cardew
Charles Stuart
Paul Harris Nicholas
George Tho. Welchman
John Godfrey Ruel
John Fennell
Alexander Campbell
John Husband
William Fynmore
James Robert Moriarty
Charles Morgan
John Hanlon
John Norris
Richard Francis Wilkins
William Blucke
Henry Doswell
John George Richardson
Joseph Henderson
William Perham
Peter M'Intyre
John Evans Jones
James Nicholas
William Duguid
John Maule
Robert Webb
John Thomas Williams
Robert Saxby
Tho. Kingsford Morris
Rupert Charles Holland

1st Lieuts.

1st Lieuts. Samuel Garmston
Thomas Salmon
William Taylor
Wm. Townley Pinhey
Sam. Y. Hend. Harding
William Ford
William James Paxton
Wm. Chambres Chambers
Samuel Wall
Benjamin Griffiths Beynon
John Balhatchet
Richard Greenwood
Thomas Quested
George Lander
C. H. J. D. Claperton
Henry Loveridge
Walter Griffith Lloyd
John Serjeant
William Luggatt
John Twyford
John Aslett
John Williams Mehoux
John Drury
Charles Compton Pratt
Charles Butler Greatrex
Wm. Catherwood Chads
Thomas Howe
E. Cha. Murray Carrington
Henry Ivatt Delacombe
Thomas Crebbin
Duncan Campbell
John Macfarlane
James Hubbard
John Lind
George Hunt Coryton
John Hewett
William Douglas
Samuel Waring
John Benson
John Ashmore
Patrick Savage
George Lloyd
Kenyon Stevens Parker
Charles Fagan
James Johns
John Pearce
John Logie
James Adamson
George B. Puddicombe
James Scott
G. A. F. Sandwith
Jeremiah Gibbons
Ingram Pank Taylor
George Hookey
Robert Hotchkin
George Gill
William Beddeck Cock
George Bonnel Pepyat
John Whit. Bennett
Patrick Bryson

1st Lieuts. John Baily
Robert Stewart Blucke
Richard Lyde Hornbock
Thomas Scott
Hugh Brown
Charles Scott
Robert Leonard
George Pattoun
William Ryrie
David Robertson
David Galloway
George Gunn
William Rob. Caldwell
Alexander Cameron
James John C. Rivers
Henry Howard
John Fitzgibbon Scanlan
James Townly
Joseph Mountford
Robert Wilson
William Wilbert Darling
Charles John King
Thomas Rees Thomas
William Collis
George Hely H. Sayer
John Thomas
Charles Stevenson
Arthur Morrison
Christopher Fottrell
William Haig
Henry Harington
Richard Edwards
Charles Lloyd
Benjamin Griffiths
John Coulter
Charles Edward Atkins
Johnston Edwards
James Shute
John Perham
Henry Bell
Robert Barry
John Tudor Tucker
Robert Cooke
Charles Robinson
George Augustus Woods
James Greer
Samuel Barton
William Lewis Dawes
John Alexander Philips
Henry Lewis
Henry T. O'Brien
George Magill
David Davies
Bartholomew Sullivan
Alfred Octavius Carrington
John Edw. Hen. Missing
Bewley Chaproniere
Henry Ward
John Fraser
W. T. Harries

1st Lieuts.

1st Lieuts. Wm. Davis
Wm. Laurence
Fred. Spry
Christ. Roberts
Wm. Jolliffe
Daniel Robinson
Rob. U. D. James
George Clark

2d Lieuts. James Stuart
George Hoggan
G. James Carleton
Thomas Hogg
William Stokoe
Walter Scott
George Shaw
James Fivey
Aulay M'Aulay
Theophilus Lane
Thomas Molison
Henry Lyte
Charles Singleton
Stennous Wood
George Phipps Ellinett
Bernard Mercer
Robert Smith
John Cole
Joseph Boultbee
Thomas Dyne
Edward Wynn
Samuel Peshall
Thomas Lyte
Thomas Rolfe
Jona. Hammond
John Gwinnell
Peter Ilbert
Alexander Gordon
Francis J. Jones
George Cornish
Joseph Hall
Arthur Mackie
Samuel Oliver
Charles Pasheller
J. Tunna. Vincent
Richard Holmes
Hollis Bull Way
Thomas Hollier
T. William Hearne
Andrew Lindsay
Valentine Hoile
John Williams
George Caunter
N. Bacon Harrison
Thomas M. Young
Alexander Clark
David Lee
William Evans
Ganet Lee
Robert Williamson
Joshua J. Wilde
Thomas Francis

2d Lieuts. George Pawsey
Samuel Swallow
Richard Rooke
Joseph Calder
John Mackay
Dun. Sutherland
Dougal Campbell
William P. Desterre
John Hill
John Bulkeley
G. Augustus King
James Beckwith
Charles Martindale
Benjamin Garlike
Robert Bulkeley
John Watt
James Hannay
William Langley
John Thomas
William O'Bierne
George Ward
Benjamin Sayer
Abel Dagge
Edward Bon Prosser
Hector John Weir
J. Row. Gunthorpe
William Colley
William Cecil
James Collins
James Ensor
Joseph Haydon
John French
John Mooney
Arthur Dewell
John Bailey
John Rose Brooke
G. H. Leg. Crespin
John O'Neill
Ralph Lomas
Charles Coleman
Bedingfield Pogson
John Johnstone
John Higgins
Alexander Clements
Arthur Macartney
George Loftin
John James
Thomas Read
John Walton Bullock
Robert James Mason
James Collier
James Reece Lane
Gust. Han. Temple
George Roch
James Campbell
William Trail Douglass
Christopher Savage
John Ward
George King
Alfred Thwaites

2d Lieuts.

2d Lieuts. William Richard Clark
Thomas Winter
Samuel Prytherch
Thomas Walker
John Gunn
Edward Cooper Pulliblank
Thomas Radcliffe
George Alfred Devereux
Colin Campbell
Charles Moone
Peter H. W. Locke
Richard Clark
Mervin West
J. C. Cozens
Francis Baker Billingham
Thomas Dawling Eyre
Charles Atkinson
John Monk
Thomas Bailey
Thomas Crause
Thomas Peard Dwyer
James Getty
Anthony Munton Lyons
William Clendon
Caleb Barnes
James Menzies
James Baugh
James Dowman
Henry Robert Raye
Stephen Collis
Daniel Evans
James Robertson
George Fred. Crown
William Ker Thomson
Michael Bevan
Roger North
George Poe
Richard Stacey
John Colliss
Thomas Patterson
Richard Sargent
Walter Folliott
Joseph Smith
Peter Martin M'Kellar
Simon Murchison
Denis Browne
William Wood

2d Lieuts. David William James
John Wyllie
Thomas M'Leroth
William Dick
John Reed Butter
Cornelius Murray
Wm. Faithful Fortescue
William Horton
William Hyde Abington
George Home
Frederick Fanning
Pyddocke Whately
Edward Boucher Hodges
Andrew Corstorphin
Henry Moss
Edward Wilson
George Mainwaring
William Wyllie
Thomas Stephens
Arthur Madryll Mackie
John Collie
George Skues
James Henry Davidson
John Mac William
Henry George Morrish
Henry Walters
Henry Paget Bayly Ross
George Watson
George Land
George Wm. Harris
John Harvey
Charles Maurice Stack
Clement Fall Le Fevre
Thomas Martin
George Aug. Hopkins
Henry Owen
Louis de Thierry
Henry Weir
John Frett
James Buchanan
Henry George Mitford
Samuel Hawkins
James Kerr
Charles Jackman Long
As. Sur. John Wilkinson
A. Campbell

INDEX.

1815.

3 O   Agar

[1815]

INDEX.

3 O 2

Armstrong

3 P

Bussche

Carmichael

Chadwick

I N D E X.

3 R 2

3 S 2

3 T

INDEX.

3 U

Hervey

Hunt

INDEX.

INDEX.

INDEX.

INDEX.

INDEX.

3 Z.

INDEX.

INDEX.

[1815]

INDEX.

Pigott

Robinson

Ryau

INDEX.

INDEX.

INDEX.

4 E

VACHELL

4 E 2

Wellwood

*4 E

Woods